MODERN
BUSINESS LANGUAGE
AND USAGE
IN DICTIONARY FORM

MODERN
BUSINESS LANGUAGE
AND USAGE
IN DICTIONARY FORM

J. Harold Janis

Doubleday & Company, Inc., Garden City, New York

1984

Thanks are due the following sources for permission to reproduce the illustrations accompanying the entries named.

Appeal. Guerlain, Inc.
Comparative claims. New York Air
Indicia. U.S. Postal Service
Logotype. Raytheon Company
News release. Hoffman-La Roche Inc.
Proof of purchase. Scott Paper Company
Q and A. Mobil Oil Corporation
Tabular summaries. Lee Pitre [Exxon USA] and Larry Smeltzer [Louisiana State University], ''Graphic Reinforcement for an Oral Presentation,'' *ABCA Bulletin,* December 1982 [publication of the American Business Communication Association, Urbana, Ill.].

Library of Congress Cataloging in Publication Data

Janis, J. Harold (Jack Harold), 1910–
  Modern business language and usage in dictionary form.

  Bibliography: p.
  1. English language—Business English—Handbooks, manuals, etc.   2. Business—Terminology.   I. Title.
PE1115.J34   1984   428'.02465

ISBN: 0-385-14489-X
Library of Congress Catalog Card Number   80-1656

PE
1115
J34
1984

Contents

The main entries—contained in a single alphabetical listing—are of two kinds: (1) words and phrases, and (2) topics. Sample entries in both categories are shown below in italics.

• WORDS AND PHRASES, their meaning and usage, as

abeyance, bottom line, due to, exploding bonus, flextime, in lieu of, logotype, (the) undersigned, wish to advise

• TOPICS relating to business language and usage. A list of these is indexed in the Classified Guide to Topics, immediately preceding the Dictionary. The covered topics fall under the following categories:

–Usage and Style, as *ambiguity, euphemism, jargon, readability, wordiness*

–Grammar and Sentence Structure, as *collective nouns, double negative, split infinitive*

–Punctuation and Mechanics, as *abbreviations, capitals, comma, titles, word division*

–Form and Composition, as *forms of address, letter writing, reports, résumés*

–Communication and Persuasion, as *credibility, feedback, listening, motivation, "you" viewpoint*

Preface

usage   Pronounced _yoo_-sij. Customary practice; a manner of doing or treating something. The term is especially applied to the way in which words and phrases are customarily used in a language community. See also USAGES in the main vocabulary.

This is a book about words and their customary use in business. It is not, in the strict sense, a technical dictionary, but it does treat many technical business terms, including especially those that have found their way into the general vocabulary. It is also a record of business expression in its many moods: sometimes conforming to current standards of ''correctness''; sometimes not. Sometimes stale, wordy, vague, affected, tactless; at other times fresh, concise, specific, natural, considerate.

Such variable qualities mark the use of language by any group, but they are viewed with special concern in business. For, more than most people realize, business has become the premier employer of language skills. It has an insatiable appetite for words and a need for people who can use English effectively—use it to record, report, inquire, inform, instruct, command, and persuade. And, allowing for occasional exceptions, business subscribes to the premise that effective English and good English are the same.

A similarly practical view of language has shaped this volume. In its single alphabetical arrangement, it treats some three thousand words and phrases common to business expression. It explains distinctions and peculiarities in meaning, suggestion, and application. It calls attention to words that are overused, misused, and confused with like-sounding words. It lists new words, fashionable words, and ''loaded'' words, and offers advice (and cautions) on their use. Other entries treat topics relating to persuasiveness, style and tone, message form and phrasing, punctuation and mechanics, and grammatical consistency.

Throughout the work, a common perspective on usage prevails. English, especially the English of business, allows great flexibility. So-called standard English—''good English''—stretches from the stiffly formal to the informal and colloquial. Business expression employs the whole range of standard English, but it seems to thrive at the informal end of the scale.

One reason is that so much business is conducted face-to-face. Even when distance intervenes, though, personal relationships are important to success. These relationships and the language used to advance them are almost invariably informal.

Further, the language of business is, to a large degree, an oral language. In addition to the increasing quantity of direct voice communication, a large part of written communication begins as speech or, more precisely, dictation. But whatever the medium, the modern ideal of ordinary business expression is to achieve at least the semblance of one individual talking to another, simply and directly.

In written English, that kind of informality does not come easily. Writing is by its nature deliberate, requiring a set of word patterns—a kind of standardization—that goes far beyond the needs of speech. But the standardization of "business English" is often carried to extremes. A lot of the writing is repetitive, dealing with like situations many times over. That and the pressures of time—prompting the use of archaic models—leads to rigidity of expression and an accompanying relaxation of attention to meaning. The result is a loss of precision and force.

This volume treats the problem of rigidity by providing an infusion of fresh words and alternative modes of expression. For every cliché, pompous word, and grammatical goof, it provides acceptable and effective substitutes. And because those substitutes are part of the natural, literate vocabulary, they stand up to a great deal of use without getting stale themselves.

But a dictionary of usage is not meant to be a catalog of errors. It is better viewed as a positive guide to language and the culture in which it exists. If the faults of business language and usage are well advertised, it may be because business messages are such a prominent—perhaps too prominent—part of our times. But the virtues are also deserving of notice. Just a casual examination of the vocabulary entries in these pages will reveal the current vitality of business expression: its search for freshness, its invention of new words, its way of adapting words in general use to business needs. With the adoption—even if only temporarily—of words like **GOLDEN HANDCUFFS, EXPLODING BONUS, KNOCKOFF, HEADHUNTER, UNBUNDLING, OUTPLACEMENT, BRACKET CREEP,** and **STICKER SHOCK,** the language of business is alive and well.

Here, then, is *Modern Business Language and Usage in Dictionary Form.* The work springs from my early interest in business communication and my active role in it, first as a writer for business, then as a teacher at New York University and a business consultant. In the last capacity, I designed and conducted writing improvement programs for banks, insurance companies, industrial firms, and government bureaus. Many of the examples of business usage I cite come from those sources. Others were extracted from a mountain of all sorts of business documents I have had the chance to study.

Newspapers, magazines, and professional journals have also provided insights into current business usage. These and other printed sources that have been helpful to me in preparing this volume are listed in the Bibliography. I am grateful to all of them.

J.H.J.

Explanatory Notes

The dictionary arrangement and the many cross-references make this book easy to use. Still, it will be worth the time it takes to learn here how the various types of information are treated.

1. Order of entries. 2. Capitalized entries. 3. Run-on entries. 4. Spelling. 5. Pronunciation. 6. Varieties of usage. 7. Grammatical terms. 8. Definitions. 9. Examples of use. 10. Cross-references. 11. Exhibits.

1. Order of entries. All main-entry words and phrases are listed alphabetically letter by letter to the end of the entry or to the break formed by a comma or parenthesis. The entry **job, position,** for instance, follows **job action.** A numeral forming part of a term is treated as if it were spelled out; thus **10-K** is positioned as if it were written **ten-K.**

2. Capitalized entries. Main-entry terms to be treated for meaning and usage are lowercased, except when a term is normally capitalized; thus **lifestyle** (a common noun), but **Murphy's Law** (a proper noun) and **C.P.A.** (an abbreviation).

3. Run-on entries. A term incorporating the main-entry word, or taking a somewhat different form, may be tacked onto the main entry. The "run-on" entry is identified by **boldface** type and the dash preceding it, as **—sellout,** following the main entry **sell out,** and **—in the process of,** following the main entry **process.**

4. Spelling. Some words are listed only to call attention to the spelling, as **incidentally** and **exhilarate.** Attention is called to the spelling of other words only where some difficulty or question is anticipated. Where alternative spellings are given, the first is preferred unless otherwise indicated.

5. Pronunciation. As with spelling, pronunciation is indicated only for words that present some special difficulty. The pronunciation is shown by respelling in ordinary alphabetic symbols, as *af*-loo-

uns. The stress is on the italicized syllable. Where more than one pronunciation is given, the order is that of decreasing preference as determined by dictionary consensus.

6. VARIETIES OF USAGE. The terms used in describing the various usages—as *general, informal, formal, nonstandard, slang, archaic,* and *dialect*—are treated in the entry USAGES. When no usage label is given for a word, it may be assumed that the word is accepted in *general usage*—suitable for all ordinary speech and writing. All words except those labeled *nonstandard* are to be considered *standard.*

7. GRAMMATICAL TERMS. The vocabulary entries are defined and examples of use are phrased to avoid as far as possible the need for grammatical terms. The definitions of words and examples of use are also intended to be self-sufficient even when simple grammatical terms like *noun* and *verb* are used to make distinctions in usage. Less common terms, like *gerund* and *nonrestrictive modifier,* are usually explained at the point where they are introduced into the discussion.

8. DEFINITIONS. Most main-entry terms are defined. Some of the terms, however, are common enough not to need defining and are listed only because of some peculiarity of spelling (as SALABLE) or usage (as ABOVE). In a few instances (KNOW-HOW, for example), the definition is incorporated into the illustration of use.

9. EXAMPLES OF USE. Examples that are run into the text are set in italics or enclosed in quotation marks. Other examples are listed separately, and italics are used only to emphasize those words that relate to the point being made. Newspapers and periodicals from which examples have been abstracted are listed in the Bibliography, following the dictionary entries. Other examples come from private sources. A source credit shown in brackets immediately following an example is given for a verbatim quotation calling for specific attribution.

10. CROSS-REFERENCES. A term referring the reader to another entry in the main vocabulary is set in boldface small capitals. Most cross-references are made explicitly as in "See also PRONOUNS 3." Other cross-references, however, are run into the text, as in the phrase "marketing JARGON" following the entry **upscale.** For conve-

nience, a run-in cross-reference will sometimes add or drop a plural ending; for instance, **clichés** is plural in the main-entry vocabulary, but a run-in reference may read CLICHÉ.

11. EXHIBITS.   Where an entry is accompanied by a chart or other exhibit, the exhibit will be found on the same page or an adjacent one and will carry a caption using the same name as the entry, and a number if there is one, as **ROUTING SLIP** or **LETTER FORM** 3.

Classified Guide to Topics

Listed here are the principal *topics* on business language and usage treated in the Dictionary. This listing does not include vocabulary entries concerned with the meaning and usage of *particular words and phrases* or with their spelling, pronunciation, or other peculiarity. Those terms (e.g., *affect, effect; benchmark; parameter; shan't*) will be found by direct reference to the Dictionary.

I. USAGE AND STYLE

absolute adjectives
abstract and concrete words
active voice, passive voice
ambiguity
circumlocutions (*at* WORDINESS)
clichés
clipped forms
codewords
colloquial English (*at* USAGES 2)
compound connectives (*at* WORDINESS 4)
compulsive words
conciseness (*at* WORDINESS)
connotation
consistency (*at* SENTENCES 4)
contractions
courtesy and tact
deadwood (*at* WORDINESS 2)
elegant variation
enumeration
euphemism
excessive feeling
figurative language
formal English (*at* USAGES 3)
general English (*at* USAGES 1)
gobbledygook
hyperbole

I, we
informal English (*at* USAGES 2)
-ize, -ization
jargon
Latin words
long variants
long words and short
metaphor
nonstandard English (*at* USAGES 4)
passive voice (*at* ACTIVE VOICE, PASSIVE VOICE)
pejoratives
plain English
positive and negative words
prefixed words (*at* HYPHEN 2)
prepossessive words
puffery
readability
redundancy (*at* WORDINESS 3)
sexual bias
stereotyped letter phrases
technical terms
"telegraphic" style
usages
vogue words
wordiness
"you" viewpoint

II. GRAMMAR AND SENTENCE STRUCTURE

absolute adjectives

absolute participles

agreement in number (*at* PRONOUNS 3 *and* SUBJECT AND VERB)

case of pronouns (*at* PRONOUNS 2)

collective nouns

comparisons

compound subjects (*at* SUBJECT AND VERB 2)

correlatives

dangling modifiers

double negative

inverted sentence (*at* SENTENCES 3)

length of sentences (*at* SENTENCES 1 *and* READABILITY)

parallel structure

position of modifiers

possession (*at* APOSTROPHE)

possessive with gerund

prepositions

pronouns

reference of pronouns (*at* PRONOUNS 1)

sentence completeness (*at* SENTENCES 2)

sentences

split infinitive

subject and verb

variety (*at* SENTENCES 3)

III. PUNCTUATION AND MECHANICS

abbreviations

acronyms

addresses

asterisk

brackets

capitals

clock time

colon

comma

compound numbers (*at* HYPHEN 3)

compound words (*at* HYPHEN 1)

dagger

days of the week

ellipsis

exclamation point

headings

italics

names

numerals

parentheses

period

question mark

quotation marks

semicolon

spelling

state postal abbreviations

titles of courtesy (*at* FORMS OF ADDRESS)

titles of office

titles of written material

word division

IV. FORM AND COMPOSITION

bibliography

cover letter

enumeration

footnotes (*at* REFERENCE NOTES)

forms of address

letter form

letter of transmittal

letter writing

V. COMMUNICATION AND PERSUASION

MODERN
BUSINESS LANGUAGE
AND USAGE
IN DICTIONARY FORM

A

a, an   The *a* goes before a consonant sound, the *an* before a vowel sound: *a strong appeal, a hotel, a yard of sand, a unified effort;* but: *an asset, an IBM machine, an heir* (silent *h*), *asked for an Yquem* (pronounced *ee*-kem, a type of sauterne wine). Also, with figures: *a $5 admission charge, a $100 bill;* but: *an 18 percent markup, an $1100 purchase.*

ABA   Abbreviation of both American Bankers Association and American Bar Association.

abbreviations   Abbreviations are common in statistics, tabulations, and other reference data; in technical papers; and in very informal or hurried notes. They are used sparingly in general writing and in business letters, invitations, and announcements. Unsurprisingly, the use of abbreviations increases as the names of business and government entities become longer and as scientific and technical terms become harder to pronounce and spell. In such instances, abbreviations provide a convenient currency for communication, even when the terms they stand for must at some point be defined.

The tendency to overuse abbreviations, however, should be a matter of concern. Unusual or long abbreviations, or the inclusion of several different abbreviations within a short space, are better avoided. A common alternative is the use of a shortened name as a substitute for an abbreviation, as "the Commission" (for the SEC) and "the Board" (for the FRB).

Abbreviations vary widely in such characteristics as capitalization and punctuation; and many terms are abbreviated in more than one way. Organizations that value consistency adopt a uniform style for abbreviations they use frequently.

1. First use.   2. Capitals.   3. Punctuation.   4. Spacing.
5. Plurals.

For abbreviation of personal names and company names, see **NAMES** 1 and 2(a).

1. First use.   All but the most familiar abbreviations are intro-

duced in context only after the term has been spelled out. Several techniques are illustrated below.

For a set annual fee, the typical health maintenance organization, or HMO, permits unlimited visits to a doctor, diagnostic tests, and hospitalization. Many subscribers, however, are not aware of the financial health of their HMO or the risks they would incur if the HMO were to go under.

Mr. Givens had raised almost $66,000, mostly from corporate and conservative-oriented political action committees (PACs). By contrast, all PACs had given Mr. Vollney, the supposedly serious challenger, only $900.

A quality that undoubtedly recommended the new president to the American Petroleum Institute is his analytical skills. Before coming to the API, he sharpened those skills in the Navy and a Washington think tank.

2. CAPITALS.   (a) Ordinarily, abbreviations are not capitalized if the words they stand for are not capitalized (in., gal., vol., bbl.), but the exceptions are many; for example, A (acre), UHF (ultrahigh frequency), C.P.A. (certified public accountant), SW (southwest). Of course, an abbreviation at the beginning of a sentence is always capitalized, as "Vol. 3, p. 244" in a footnote.

(b) Some abbreviations have both a capitalized and a lowercase form: p.m., P.M.; c., C. (capacity); a.w.o.l., AWOL. In other instances, the use of capitals varies with the form of the abbreviation, solid capitals being favored for abbreviations consisting only of initial letters: AMA, CBS, USAF, AT&T (but Am.Tel.&Tel., D.S. (but D.Sc.), N.D. (but N. Dak.).

3. PUNCTUATION.   (a) An abbreviated word is usually followed by a period: Inc., Ave., etc., mfr. A period may also follow each part of an abbreviated compound consisting of lowercase letters or of capitals and lowercase letters: N. Car., Sec.-Treas., sq. ft., e.g.; the periods are often omitted, however, when clarity is not endangered, thus rpm and COD, but *not* am or ie.

(b) Periods with abbreviations are often optional. They are commonly omitted in directory listings and other closely set material. Where optional periods are supplied, they add some formality to the abbreviation. In a letter address, for example, compare *Mr. Robert Tomes, V.P.* with *Mr. Robert Tomes, VP.*

(c) The initials forming ACRONYMS are rarely followed by periods: ASCAP, UNESCO, radar. Periods are usually omitted after the initials standing for the name of a government agency, company, or other organized body: FCC, IMF, UCLA, IBM (but also F.C.C., I.M.F., U.C.L.A., I.B.M.); also ITT or I.T.T. (for International Telephone and Telegraph Company), but ITT (*not* I.T.T.) World Communications, a subsidiary.

(d) Periods usually follow the initials of persons: T. S. Brown, Mr. B., T.S.B. or (especially when used as **IDENTIFICATION INITIALS**) TSB. Abbreviated titles like Mrs., Hon., Sen., and Dr., and designations like Esq. and Jr. are customarily followed by a period. Periods are also preferred and often obligatory after the letters representing **DEGREES AND PROFESSIONAL RATINGS**: M.B.A., C.P.A. (also MBA and CPA) but Ph.D. and LL.D. (*not* PhD or LL D).

(e) **CLIPPED FORMS** and names, as opposed to their abbreviations, are not followed by periods: ad (but advt.), Rob (but Robt.). Apostrophized contractions, as opposed to abbreviations of the same words, are not followed by periods, but the abbreviations are usually preferred: Ass'n (*but* Assn.), sec'y (*but* secy.), cont'd (*but* contd.).

(f) Periods should be omitted in the abbreviations of all metric measures (cm, kl, mg, dkl). No periods are used after the two-letter post-office abbreviations of state names (ME, NY, CA); chemical symbols (CO_2, H_2SO_4); the call letters of broadcasting stations (KDKA, WNEW-FM); stock exchange symbols for listed companies (UK, ANR, SCM); and letters standing for letters, words, or the names of unspecified individuals: from A to Z, Class B stock, grade A eggs, IOU, EZ Cleaner, Dealer A, Dealer B.

(g) The parts of some abbreviations are separated by a **SLANT** to show the omission of one or more words, to take the place of a period, to signify an alternative, or to prevent confusion: n/o (in the name of); a/c (account *or* account current; *compare with* a.c., for alternating current); L/C (letter of credit); Mr./Mrs. (Mr. and/or Mrs.); s/h (shareholder; *compare with* sh., for share); s/t (short ton; *compare with* st., for street).

4. SPACING. Spacing is not customary between the parts of an abbreviation punctuated by periods, except to separate parts containing more than one letter: M.D., R.C.A., M.O., n.d. (no date). But: S. Res. (Senate resolution), H. Doc. (House document), Fin. Secy., fl. oz., cap. stk. (capital stock), So. Amer. No space separates the parts of any academic degrees: B.A., M.B.A., Ph.D., Litt.D. A space is used between two initials preceding a name, but three initials are better set solid: L. B. Smith; but J.B.S. Haldane.

5. PLURALS. (a) With the exceptions noted below, the plural of

an abbreviation is usually formed by the addition of an *s* to the singular: hrs., apts., assts., figs., lbs., M.D.s., IOUs.

(b) To prevent confusion, uncapitalized abbreviations without a final period form their plurals by the addition of an apostrophe and *s* to the singular: btu's, aa's (author's alterations). See also **APOSTROPHE** 2.

(c) The plurals of abbreviated terms of measurement are often the same as the singular: 12 in., 4 oz., 25 mi. Metric plurals are invariably the same as the singular forms: 2 g (grams), 5 m (meters), 12 cc (cubic centimeters), 10 kg (kilograms).

abeyance　Stilted in ordinary use: *The order was held in abeyance (was held up, was suspended, was temporarily set aside) pending a confirmation from the buyer.* The objection does not apply to the legal use of the word, as in ''an estate in abeyance,'' that is, an estate awaiting the determination of ownership.

able to be　Better avoided before a passive verb (see **ACTIVE VOICE**, **PASSIVE VOICE**): *is now able to be told (can now be told)/was unable to be seen (could not be seen).*

about　Unnecessary when the idea of approximation is otherwise indicated: *guessed that there were about 30 dozen left/not more than about 10 or 12 applicants/needed about $20,000 to $25,000.* [Omit *about* in all examples.] See also **AT ABOUT, AT AROUND**.

above　Overworked, often symptomatic of stilted writing.

1. *Above* is well used as a preposition (*above the floor, above reproach*) and as a simple modifier of a preceding noun or adjective (*on the floor above, the policy numbers listed above*).

2. Although *above* is acceptably used in expressions like ''the above conditions'' and ''the above-named applicant,'' many writers prefer less formal substitutes: *these conditions; the applicant named; this applicant; Mr. Conway.* Compare with **AFOREMENTIONED, AFORESAID**, and **SAID**.

3. As a noun following ''the,'' *above* is less favored, but still common. It is best replaced by a specific reference to the thing in question: *The above (This behavior, This incident) should not be treated as exceptional/Please note the above (this provision, the due date, the correct procedure).*

A phrase like *''the above chart''* requires that the material referred to precede and be reasonably close to the statement, but not necessarily on the same page.

above-captioned See CAPTIONED.

absolute adjectives Words like *perfect, complete, fatal, dead, impossible*, and *unique* are not logically subject to comparison *(less perfect, most fatal, least impossible)* because their meaning is unconditional. Still liberties are taken, sometimes with surprisingly good results: *"to form a more perfect union"/"the most complete . . . dictionary in the English language"/He's the most impossible person we ever dealt with/Liberalizing sick-leave pay is a deader issue than I thought.*

No problem is presented when the modifier of an absolute adjective does not involve a comparison: *nearly perfect, not complete, almost impossible.*

absolute(ly), positive(ly) *Absolute* and *positive* are informal when used as intensives: *He's an absolute wizard/The new minicomputer is a positive wonder.*

In general usage, *absolutely* and *positively* are acceptable as unconditional terms meaning "unquestionably" or "completely": *We are absolutely committed to the plan/The work will positively be completed on Friday.* The words are used only informally, however, as substitutes for "very," "indeed," and similar expressions: *The terms are positively (very) lenient/She is positively (indeed) radiant/Your pots and pans will absolutely shine (will shine brilliantly).*

absolute participle Sanctioned, but better avoided. See DANGLING MODIFIER 2(a).

abstract A short, terse summary of a particular text, as a report or an article in a technical journal. An abstract prefacing the text may be required as a condition of publication. In some instances, aides prepare abstracts of incoming reports for the convenience of executives or researchers, who are then spared the time of going through the complete documents for the information they need.

Also a verb: *abstracted the report.*

abstract and concrete words Where a choice is permitted, concrete words are usually preferable to abstract words.

1. Abstract words are general; they stand for qualities, concepts, classes, and relationships that have been distilled and separated from the things they stand for: *environment, transportation, labor, management.* Concrete words, on the other hand, have a direct relation to things; they point to objects, people, and phenomena, those that can be seen, touched, or experienced in some way: *smog, truck, welder, boss.*

Also compare the following:*

ABSTRACT: Based on the additional expenditure of research and development dollars, the B-1 will be a viable weapon system in the 1980s.

CONCRETE: The B-1 will be an effective weapon system only if the fuel leak problems and onboard computers are fixed.

2. Because concrete words are down-to-earth, they have a good reputation and deservedly so. They are clear, alive, and picture-forming. The value placed on concrete words, however, does not diminish the worth of abstract words when they are aptly used. Expressions like "environmental protection," "labor contracts," and "transportation policy" encompass, all in their own way, a great deal more meaning than can be transmitted in as many, or ten times as many, concrete words. Abstract words are especially useful in introducing or summarizing a point and in drawing inferences from specific examples.

Still, they cannot take the place of concrete words when specific details are needed; and in other respects, too, they are easily abused. A hospital becomes a "health-care delivery system"; the study of simple arithmetic, a "program area"; a five-ounce tube of toothpaste, the "family size"; taxis and buses, "ground transportation."

In other instances, the bank speaks of the "account relationship," the educator of a "learning experience," and the snack bar manager of "operational difficulties" when what they are really talking about are the limit on a customer's line of credit, a field trip, and a balky slot machine.

abutting Touching on one side of, adjoining: *an abutting building*. Compare ADJACENT.

academe Also *Academe*. A handy but sometimes pretentious or facetious reference to the academic world and higher learning: *a representative of academe; has long dipped into academe's brain pool; members chosen from both business and academe/Over the years the Eastern Air Shuttle has become a part of life that is not confined to the routine daily commuting between capitol dome, corporate aerie, and the groves of Academe.*

academic Formal, scholarly, classical as opposed to technical: *an academic economist*. Also a noun: *Among academics, talk about the im-*

---

*Both examples are part of a writing exercise by an Air Force training group. Cited by William E. McCarron in *College English*, March 1980.

portance of expectations has proliferated since the late seventies when inflation rendered traditional economic models obsolete.

academic degrees See FORMS OF ADDRESS 1.

academician An ACADEMIC: *Balancing [any conflict of interest] are the contributions academicians can make as directors and the positive impact that board service can have on their teaching and research.*

accede To agree. So spelled (not *acceed*); takes the preposition *to: We will accede to the request.*

access To obtain, to get at, as by tapping a computer's memory or by drawing on available funds: *Even the library is discovering that information is accessed in other ways than by reading/After the holidays, you can use your bonus to pay back the money you accessed from your savings certificate.*

accessorize To select accessories appropriate to one's costume: *Our fashion coordinators will help you accessorize your clothing.* See also -IZE, -IZATION.

accidentally So spelled, and pronounced *-dent*-uh-lee (not *-dent*-lee).

accommodate So spelled (two *c*'s and two *m*'s): *We can accommodate any size order.*

accord In the sense of "grant," takes the preposition *to;* in the sense of "agree," the preposition *with: We hope they'll accord the same courtesy to us/The text of the contract fully accords with the terms we discussed.*

accountant, auditor See AUDITOR.

account executive See SALESMAN.

accounts receivable Plural of *account receivable;* also, one word, *receivables;* the amounts currently due from customers: *They must make a greater effort to collect their accounts receivable/The receivables were given over to a collection agency/You can finance growth by using receivables, inventories, equipment, and other assets.*

accumulative See CUMULATIVE, ACCUMULATIVE.

acknowledge "Please acknowledge our payment" is an economical way of saying, "Please report the receipt of our payment," but *ac-*

knowledge is less aptly used in such expressions as "We acknowledge receipt of" (for "We have received") and "We acknowledge with thanks" (for "Thank you for"). See **STEREOTYPED LETTER PHRASES**.

acknowledgment The preferred spelling, but *-edgement* is also correct.

acoustics So spelled (*not* acc-). Takes a singular verb when it represents the name of the science of sound, a plural verb when it represents the qualities or the total effect of sound: *Acoustics is her specialty.* But (plural): *The acoustics are excellent.*

   The adjective is *acoustic* or *acoustical: an acoustic* (or *acoustical*) *achievement.*

acquiesce Takes the preposition *in: The question is whether management will acquiesce in the takeover.*

acronyms ABBREVIATIONS formed from the first letters or parts of words and pronounced as words. Most acronyms are represented by all capitals (ACTH, COMSAT, NASA, NOW); some by capitals and small letters (Amvets, Jaycees, Seabees); and others, which have acquired generic status, by small letters alone (laser, loran, radar, scuba, sonar). Abbreviations not pronounced as words are not acronyms (FHA, NBC, AMA).

activate, actuate Although the words are often interchangeable, activate is more common for "set in motion": *The engineer activated* (rather than *actuated*) *the generator. Actuate* is the better word for "move to action" or "motivate": *Most workers were actuated by a genuine desire to help their employer succeed.*

active voice, passive voice A statement may be expressed with the verb in the active voice or in the passive voice. The active voice is generally recommended, but the uses of the passive voice should not be overlooked.

   1. A verb is said to be in the active voice when its subject performs the action of the verb:

   I will sign the letter.
   The weather delayed construction.

   A verb is in the passive voice when the subject receives the action of the verb:

   The letter will be signed by me.
   Construction was delayed by the weather.

The passive voice is made by joining some form of the verb *to be* to a past participle *(is known, was persuaded, will be told).*

2. As a rule, the active voice is preferred for its simplicity, directness, and force. Compare:

PASSIVE: The canceled check *was returned* by us to you on Tuesday.

ACTIVE: We *returned* the canceled check to you on Tuesday.

PASSIVE: A lead mask resembling a venetian blind *is used* by the $20,000 machine.

ACTIVE: The $20,000 machine *uses* a lead mask resembling a venetian blind.

PASSIVE: The winner *is prohibited* by the contest rules from selling any part of the prize.

ACTIVE: Contest rules *prohibit* the winner from selling any part of the prize.

3. The passive voice is useful when the directness of the active voice would be harsh or tactless. See also **COURTESY AND TACT.**

ACTIVE *(overdirect):* We held up your order because of an unexpectedly heavy demand.

PASSIVE: Your order was held up by an unexpectedly heavy demand.

ACTIVE *(debasing):* Mr. Boris apparently failed to mark the appointment on his calendar.

PASSIVE: The appointment was not marked on Mr. Boris's calendar.

ACTIVE *(tactless):* You did not include the authorization form with your letter.

PASSIVE: The authorization form was not included in your letter.

4. The passive voice may permit more effective placement of important words.

ACTIVE: An apprentice copywriter created the advertisement.

PASSIVE: The advertisement was created by an apprentice copywriter. [The creator is named climactically at the end.]

ACTIVE: The company has already started construction of its new headquarters.

PASSIVE: Construction of the company's new headquarters has already been started. [The action taken receives emphasis at the beginning and the end.]

ACTIVE: We have expanded our work with local community development organizations over the past two years by using the general reserve fund.

PASSIVE: The general reserve fund has been used over the past two years to expand our work with local community development organizations. [The words at beginning and end avoid the self-centered "we."]

5. By putting emphasis on the receiver of the action, the passive

voice is useful when the performer is already known or is not important to the discussion.

The evolution of the theory of plate tectonics has been widely publicized. [The names of the publicizers are irrelevant.]

Purchased LPG and naphtha are processed into ethylene, propylene, and benzine. [The processor is the issuer of the statement and does not have to be identified further at this point.]

6. The passive voice helps the writer, consciously or not, to make indirect and unattributed statements. Often the practice can be justified as a way of preserving objectivity, as in a formal report, or protecting a source of information. In some instances, however, the passive voice is either a poor stylistic choice or a method of expressing ideas and opinions for which the writer does not wish to take responsibility.

A question has been raised as to the validity of the current practice. [Source tactfully omitted.]

The applicant is reported to have significant outstanding debts. [Source of credit information protected.]

Detailed figures are not considered necessary at this time. [An impersonal rendering of "I do not believe that detailed figures are necessary at this time."]

It was noted that housing starts rose by 23 percent. [A weak rendering of "Housing starts rose by 23 percent."]

7. The awkward "double passive" demands correction.

The seminars were asked to be given by top management itself. [*Improved:* Top management itself asked for the seminars.]

The company was informed by Mrs. Eisner's lawyer that she had been injured in the accident. [*Improved:* Mrs. Eisner's lawyer informed the company that she had been injured in the accident.]

ad, adv., advt.   Advertisement. *Ad* is a CLIPPED FORM, not followed by a period. The other forms are abbreviations, which require the period.

A.D., B.C.   1. Formally, A.D. (for *anno Domini*, "in the year of the Lord") is used only with a specific date and precedes the number: *died in the second century* (not *the second century A.D.*)/*died in A.D. 104* (not *104 A.D.*). A.D. is not used with current dates, and unless otherwise indicated, it is always assumed. Informally, A.D. follows the same usage as B.C., discussed below.

2. The restrictions that apply to the formal use of A.D. do not apply to B.C. (''before Christ''), which may follow or precede a specific date or may be used in naming a general period: *68 B.C.; B.C. 68; the first century B.C.*

See also **DATES**.

adapt, adopt   See **ADOPT, ADAPT**.

add, add.   To add is to make a sum; add. is the abbreviation of *address* or **ADDENDUM**. Neither is to be used for *ad* (advertisement).

addendum   Plural, *addenda*. 1. Latin for an addition to a legal document, book, list, etc.; similar to a **POSTSCRIPT** on a letter and denoting material inadvertently left out or material not at first intended or ready for inclusion. *Addition* is a good English substitute.

2. The grammatical distinction between the singular and plural forms should be carefully observed: *these addenda* (not *this addenda*)/*an addendum* (not *an addenda*)/*The addenda are* (not *is*) *part of the document.*

See also **PLURALS** 4.

additional   The simple *more* will do in some constructions: *For $20 additional ($20 more) you can have the deluxe room.* But (well used): *There is no additional* (or *extra*) *charge.*

additionally, in addition   Cumbersome substitutes for *also* or *besides: Additionally, the tenant requested (The tenant also requested)/In addition (Besides), we had no knowledge of what they were up to.* See also **IN ADDITION TO**.

address   The position in the ''memory'' of a computer where a particular item of information is stored; also the number or name that identifies the location.

address, forms of   See **FORMS OF ADDRESS**.

address block   See **ENVELOPE ADDRESS**.

addresses   1. Figures are used for building and house numbers, except for numbers through ten, which are spelled out when more formality is desired: *23 Houston Street; 3459 Demarest Avenue.* But (a choice): *2 World Trade Plaza* or *Two World Trade Plaza; 10 Dupont Circle* or *Ten Dupont Circle.*

2. Figures are also used for the names of numbered streets and av-

enues, though numbers through ten are better spelled out. Spelled-out numbers are always ordinals, but the ordinal endings are sometimes omitted when figures are used: *700 Fifth Avenue; 880 West 23rd Street* (also *880 West 23 Street*). But, to avoid elision of numbers: *1044 12th Avenue* (rather than *1044 12 Avenue*). See also **NUMERALS** 8.

3. Words like *street, avenue, boulevard,* and *drive,* are capitalized when part of the street name, but not—as in a running text—when they are separated from it: *77 Casper Road; 652 Hollingsworth Avenue* (but *the stores on the avenue* [referring to the same street]).

4. All the words in a street address are usually spelled out, but abbreviations like *St., Ave.,* and *Blvd.* may be used to save space when formality is not an important consideration. Single-letter compass points (N., S., E., W.) may be abbreviated before numbered street names written in figures, but are better spelled out before or after spelled-out street names: *330 W. 96th Street* (but *10 Park Avenue South*); *39 East Fourth Street* (rather than *39 E. Fourth Street*); *1012 North Michigan Avenue* (rather than *1012 N. Michigan Avenue*). Double-letter compass points following a street name are abbreviated and set without periods: *3109 14th Street NW; 1400 Fairview Avenue SE.*

See also **ENVELOPE ADDRESS** and **INSIDE ADDRESS**.

add up   Informal. 1. To come to a correct or acceptable total: *The figures don't add up.* 2. To make sense, to be plausible: *His explanation does not add up.*

add up to   Informal for "mean" or "imply": *Their answer adds up to a rejection of the offer.*

adequate   1. Sufficient, suitable. Sometimes encumbered by needless words: *not sufficiently adequate (insufficient* or *inadequate)/proved adequate enough (proved adequate).*

2. **PEJORATIVE** in the sense of "barely satisfactory": *Mr. Doe's performance in this position was adequate.*

ad hoc   Pronounced ad hock; Latin, meaning "for this" (particular purpose or need): *an ad hoc committee* [a committee organized for one case or purpose only; not a standing committee]/*an ad hoc financial adviser* [one who dispenses advice on a per case basis; not as a regular consultant]. Also, used in the sense of "informal": *The room, once furnished with homogeneous low tables and seating modules, today has a more ad hoc mien.*

ad hominem   Latin, meaning "to the man"; descriptive of an argument appealing to personal feelings and prejudices, as opposed to reason. Example: *This latest truce proposal is just another red herring. In effect, the union leadership would call off their lawbreaking tactics in return for the company's giving in to some extra demands. It is an attempt to get us to pay a bribe so that they will stop interfering with the livelihood of thousands of employees who want to work.* Compare **PEJORATIVE**.

adjacent   Means close to, but not necessarily adjoining: *adjacent to shopping, restaurants, and theaters.* Compare with **CONTIGUOUS** and **ABUTTING**.

administrate   A **LONG VARIANT** of *administer;* better avoided: *A small department is easier to administrate (administer, manage) than a large one/She was selected to administrate (administer) the program.*

administrator   Masculine or feminine; the *-or* ending does not denote gender.

administratrix   Plural, *administratrices.* A cumbersome and archaic synonym for a female **ADMINISTRATOR**; found only in legal use.

admission, admittance   Although the distinction is subtle, it seems worth observing.

Admission is access or the right to enter by invitation, payment of a fee, or otherwise: *an admission charge of $10.* The word also signifies appointment or acceptance: *admission to the bar/admission as evidence.*

Admittance carries with it not only the meaning of permission to enter physically, but also the suggestion that there is some qualification attached: *Admittance to the crowded hearing room was restricted to the press and the concerned parties.* But: *The thief gained entrance* (not *admittance*) *to the plant by scaling a fence.* [The thief cannot be said to have gained "admittance," for he wasn't *permitted* to enter; rather, he entered by stealth.]

admitted   Not to be used for "said" or "stated" unless a negative **CONNOTATION** is desired: *The witness admitted (stated?) he had been aware of the probability of a delay in completing the project.* Even a negative connotation, however, is softened by a word like "conceded" or "acknowledged": *The Bureau admitted that its inspection procedures were inadequate.* (Compare: *The Bureau acknowledged . . .*)

adopt, adapt   To *adopt* is to take, follow, or accept as one's own: *adopt a trademark; adopt a mascot; adopt a policy.*

   To *adapt* is to alter, make suitable, or become adjusted to: *The television series was adapted from a popular novel/We adapt our advertising to our market/The company has now adapted to the cut in freight service.*

adult   In some contexts, a EUPHEMISM for "obscene": *adult entertainment, adult movies, an adult bookstore.*

advance feedback   JARGON for information obtained in advance—from tips, inside information, consultations, existing data, etc.—to ensure a desired outcome. The information may be used in composing a message, formulating a policy, or planning some other action that will presumably bring some FEEDBACK: *Before setting the rate on the bonds, we must be able to sense the market. That's where advance feedback comes in.*

advance planning   Although it may be argued that all planning is done in advance, *advance planning* is not redundant when *advance* carries the sense of "early": *Our advance planning gave us a choice of options when the final decision had to be made.*

adverse, averse   *Adverse* describes that which is hostile or unfavorable to one's interests: *an adverse suggestion/adverse conditions. Averse,* however, indicates the opposition or reluctance of the subject; it takes the preposition *to: I am averse to such a suggestion/No one is averse to your making a legitimate profit.*

advertise   The common spelling; *advertize* is rare.

advertisement   Pronounced ad-*vurt*-iss-munt (preferred) or ad-ver-*tize*-munt.

advertising claims   See COMPARATIVE CLAIMS.

advice(s)   1. Used especially in banking and finance as a synonym for "notice" or "receipt": *We are crediting your account, as the enclosed advice shows/We did not receive advice of payment due/Advices of rent due are sent out on the last day of each month.*

   2. In other contexts, *advice* denotes either information or counsel and may therefore be ambiguous: *After inquiries among several brokers, our advice is that the shares you contemplate buying represent a sound investment.* [Does *our advice* mean "our counsel" or "the information we received"?]

3. *Advices* (plural) is formally used in the sense of information, especially from some distance: *advices from abroad/diplomatic advices.*

advisable   So spelled (-able, *not* -eable): *an advisable move.*

advise   Verb, pronounced ad-*vize;* not to be confused with the noun **ADVICE.** 1. *Advise* is a formal, sometimes stilted synonym for "inform," "notify," "write," or "tell": *We are unable to advise (tell) you when the certificate will be issued/Kindly advise (Please let us hear from you).*

2. *Please be advised that* marks the beginning of a formal notification. In ordinary correspondence, it is simply deadwood (see **WORDINESS** 2): *Please be advised that your order will be shipped on June 16 (Your order will be shipped on June 16).*

3. *Advise* is well used in the sense of to counsel or give advice: *We advise you to accept the offer/Our attorney has advised us not to answer the complaint/Borrowers are advised of their rights and responsibilities.*

4. *Advised,* meaning "considered" or "thought out," is acceptably used in the compounds *well-advised* and *ill-advised: I believe their action is ill-advised.*

—advise with. Stilted for "consult with": *Their insurance broker promised to advise with us (consult with us).*

advisement   Generally acceptable in the sense of counseling: *advisement services.* Formal, however, in the phrase "under advisement": *We shall take their proposal under advisement (We'll carefully consider their proposal).*

adviser, -or   The first spelling is preferred: *a financial adviser.*

advocacy   Active support given to a cause. The term denotes the work not only of a lawyer or lobbyist, but of any persuader. In *advocacy advertising,* the sponsor takes sides on some public issue, like oil pricing, tax policy, or industry regulation. In *consumer advocacy,* the intended beneficiary is the citizen as consumer. See also **CONSUMERIST.**

advocate   One who engages in **ADVOCACY;** a supporter or defender: *an advocate of reduced government spending, an advocate of the poor.* See also "patient advocate" at **OMBUDSMAN.**

ad-words   The frequency of certain words in advertising is more likely a sign of their effectiveness than of the paucity of the copywriter's vocabulary. The table that follows offers a random sampling. Some words, it will be seen, have a news peg *(announcing, introducing);* some promise savings or value *(cents off, free);* others relate to effectiveness of the product *(heavy duty, concentrated);* and still others have the appeal of quality or exclusivity *(crafted, personalized).* Often two or more of the ad-words appear in a single phrase. The star (*) before a listed word indicates that the word will also be found in the main entries.

AD-WORD	SAMPLE PHRASING
announcing	*Announcing* the new extra-strength solid Arrid
*better	A new and *better* way to earn high yields (Scudder)
cash rebate	$2.00 *cash rebate* with coupon
*cents off	15 *cents off* Heinz pickles
collection	The Benvenuto Cellini *collection* by Rolex
concentrated	*Concentrated* for closer shaves (Noxzema)
*crafted	Imagine owning a collection of bells created and *crafted* by 25 of the world's most famous porcelain houses.
dairy	Extra creamy *dairy* recipe (Cool Whip ''topping'')
discover	*Discover* Paradise on shore. And aboard. (Pearl Cruises)
exclusive	Eterna ''27'' Cream with *exclusive* Progenitin
extra	*Extra*-strength Tylenol / *Extra*-dry Arrid
famous	*Famous* Mighty Dog recipe
fight(er)	*Fights* colds 3 ways (Dristan) / Colgate—the cavity-*fighter*
free (exempt from)	Here's how to get tax-*free* interest (New York Muni Fund)
*free (without charge)	Buy new Trident Mints and get one pack *free*
fresh	Made *fresh* every day (Carvel ice cream) / Keep that *fresh*-dressed feeling all day (Carefree panty shields)
good news	*Good news* for dry hands (Jergen's) / *Good News* (Gillette disposable razors)
gourmet	*Gourmet* honey (Kodiak) / *Gourmet* coffees (the Bean Bag)
guaranteed	FNMA *guaranteed* mortgage-backed securities / Satisfaction *guaranteed* or your money back (Kraft)
hand	*Hand*-crafted solid wood children's chair / *Hand*-woven rattan sewing kit
heavy duty	For *heavy duty* dishwashing, start with Finish
homestyle	Progresso *Homestyle* Spaghetti Sauce
improved	*Improved* Bayer aspirin (with micro-thin coating)

introducing	*Introducing* the new Ford LTD. / —Diet Coke / —new Mildew's Gone / —unscented Bounce
light	Fritos *Lights* / Natural *Light* (Anheuser Busch) / *Lite* 'n' Natural spaghetti sauce (Mueller)
longer lasting	*Longer lasting* relief with Neo-Synephrine 12 Hour
maximum	*Maximum* strength Sucrets / *Maximum* fluoride protection / *Maximum* sinus medicine for *maximum* sinus pain relief
medicated	America's #1 *medicated* powder (Ammens) / *Medicated* Noxzema shave
money back	*Money back* guarantee (Value Line Investment Survey)
*natural	The all *natural* cooking oil from the seed of the sunflower (Sunlite)
new	*New* jumbo pak (Viva napkins) / Try *new* Chips de luxe (Keebler biscuits)
now	*Now* Purina is even better value
*number one	High Point's *No. 1* with me (Lauren Bacall)
off	30% to 50% *off* / Take an additional 20% *off* our low fashion clearance prices
100%	*100%* new Dristan / I feel good about *100%* corn oil (Fleischman's margarine)
*only	3 days *only* / Twin decanter set now *only* $8.95, was $15.00
personalized	*Personalized* Sheaffer pen and pencil set only 4.99
*plus	*Plus* 100 additional prizes
protection	Get unbeatable *protection* from Dial (soap)
*real	More *real* cheese for better taste (Chee-tos snacks)
refund	Send for your *refund* up to $1.00 / $1 *refund* offer
revolutionary	Two *revolutionary* new bandages from Band-Aid
rich	Coffee *Rich* (non-dairy creamer)
sale	4-Star White *Sale* / After-Christmas *sales* and clearance / Last days! 2-fer *sale*
save	*Save* 55¢ on Lilt and Perm / Snack and *save* 40¢ (Mr. Salty)
scientific(ally)	Keep healthy with these up-to-the-minute *scientific* facts (Barnard, the Body Machine) / A *scientifically* formulated skin care system (Mary Kay)
super	*Super* Suede (a fabric simulating suede) / *Super* values / *Super* dry Sure (antiperspirant) / *Super* Sure Shot (Canon camera)

*system	Clearasil products—the #1 *system* for better looking skin
tough	Discover how *tough* Glad 3-ply (trash bag) is
trust	*Trust* Colgate to make fighting cavities taste terrific / It's effective medicine you can *trust* (Dristan tablets)
ultra	*Ultra* Sense panty hose / *Ultra* Brite tooth paste / *Ultra* low tar Cambridge cigarettes
win(ner)	*Win* a resort vacation (Irish Spring sweepstakes) / Taste the *winner* (Heinz tomato catsup)
without a prescription	Now available *without a prescription* (Sudafed S.A. nasal decongestant)

affect, effect   To *affect* is to influence *(The weather directly affects power consumption)* or to simulate *(He affects a French accent)*. The noun *affect*, denoting feeling or emotion, is part of the vocabulary of psychology: *characterized by affects of guilt and remorse.*

To *effect* is to bring about: *The new manager effected striking changes in work assignments.* The noun *effect* signifies an outcome or result: *The weather has a direct effect on power consumption/What the effect will be, we do not yet know.*

—**affected.** Feigned, artificial: *an affected manner.*

—**affecting.** Influencing, moving: *a decision affecting thousands of workers/an affecting performance.*

—**affective.** Emotional. Not to be confused with *effective, resultful: affective language* (language appealing to the emotions); but: an *effective worker, effective advertising.*

affirmative, negative   JARGON when used for "yes," "no," "I agree," "I disagree," and similar expressions. "In the affirmative" and "in the negative" are affected and wordy: *The answer is in the affirmative (The answer is yes)/replied in the negative (refused, said "no").* See also POSITIVE AND NEGATIVE WORDS.

affluence   Pronounced *af*-loo-uns. Wealth, abundance: *a person of affluence, conditioned to affluence.*

—**affluent,** adjective. Pronounced *af*-loo-unt: *an affluent lawyer, the affluent society.*

affordable   Adjective favored by advertisers, possibly because its vagueness gives it broad appeal: *The home of affordable elegance* (W

& J Sloane)/*Surprisingly affordable* (Bermuda)/*Austin* [travel agency] *makes Britain affordable.*

Also a noun: *Introducing the affordables* (Ford).

AFL-CIO Abbreviation of American Federation of Labor-Congress of Industrial Organizations, a consolidation of the two largest American labor unions.

aforementioned, aforesaid JARGON, common in legal writing. If a choice must be made, the first is the less stilted, but there are alternatives: *the aforementioned property* (*this property, the Donnelly property,* etc.)/*the aforesaid Mr. Reeves* (omit *the aforesaid*). Compare ABOVE 2.

aftermarket 1. The market for a security after its initial offering by an underwriter: *After Monday's sellout of all 2 million shares, the aftermarket took over with enthusiasm.*

2. The market for spare parts needed for the repair of cars and other machines: *ready for major changes in the U.S. automotive aftermarket.*

Also, adjective: *aftermarket companies/the company's aftermarket strategy/sell a variety of aftermarket products and services.*

age, aged 1. *Age* (singular), *ages* (plural), and *aged* (pronounced as one syllable) are all correct when used for "of the age of": *Tommy, age* (or *aged*) *three/Tommy and Marie, ages* (or *aged*) *three and five/Henry Bentley, age* (or *aged*) *35.*

2. Except in formal usage, the words *age* and *aged* are usually dispensed with when the meaning is clear without them: *Children between three and five will be registered on Friday/The senior position went to Henry Bentley, 35, a graduate of Tufts.*

3. *Aged,* for "advanced in years," is pronounced *ay*-jid (two syllables): *the aged couple. Aged,* meaning "old," as in "aged cheddar" and "aged whiskey," is pronounced *ayjd* (one syllable).

—**teenaged:** *a teenaged* (pronounced -*ayjd*) *boy.*

—**teenager:** *a room full of teenagers.*

agency shop A union shop that may employ nonunion members, but only on the condition that they pay union dues. The arrangement helps nonunion workers benefit from the bargaining power of the union, but not at the expense of union workers. Compare CLOSED SHOP.

agenda A Latin plural meaning "a list of things to be done," *agenda* denotes especially the items to be taken up at a meeting. As a COL-

LECTIVE NOUN, *agenda* is acceptably used with a singular verb: *The agenda for the meeting was distributed beforehand.*

Agendas, the Anglicized form of *agenda,* is used to designate the programs for more than one meeting: *The agendas for the meetings of May 6 and May 20 are not in the files.*

See also PLURALS 4.

agenting   JARGON for "performing the work of an agent": *You'll learn editing, typography and design, literary agenting, circulation, advertising, and much more.* See also -ING.

aggravate   To make worse, or intensify in an unpleasant way: *The depressed market only aggravates the company's already weak financial position.* Also, informally, to irritate, vex, or annoy: *Don't aggravate me/Their complacency is aggravating.*

—**aggravation,** noun. A worsening state: *Further aggravation of the problem is expected.* Also, informal for "vexation": *Your aggravation over the delay is understandable/He should have my aggravation.*

aggressive   A PEJORATIVE sometimes when used for "pushy" or "combative," but *aggressive* has a desirable CONNOTATION in the sense of "bold" or "enterprising": *an aggressive marketing program.*

—**aggressively,** adverb: *working aggressively to turn the company around.*

agribusiness   That part of the economy devoted to agriculture and related products and services, including farm machinery; seed, feed, and fertilizer; and processing, storage, and distribution.

AID   The Agency for International Development; an agency of the U.S. Department of State, administering economic assistance to underdeveloped nations.

aid, aide   1. The words are synonymous, but *aide* is preferred for its suggestion of dignity and importance: *the commander's aide/an aide to the presiding judge/a nurse's aide. Aide* may also be helpful in preventing misunderstanding. A teacher's *aid* is either a person or a teaching tool, but a teacher's *aide* is necessarily a person only.

2. In most instances, the apt word is *assistant* or *helper: assistant to the president, laboratory assistant, carpenter's helper.*

AIDA   In advertising, an ACRONYM to help call to mind the essentials of an effective sales message: attract *A*ttention, arouse *I*nterest, create *D*esire for the product or service, and stimulate *A*ction.

aim In general usage, to aim is to direct one's efforts to a particular goal: *We aim to complete the installation in ten months.* Aim is informal, however, when it is used loosely for "intend": *I certainly aim to be there.*
—**aim at:** *The committee is aiming at 100 percent participation.*
—**aim for:** *We aim for the impossible.*

ain't A contraction of *am not, is not,* or *are not.* Nonstandard, but sometimes hard to avoid. "Aren't I" is found in the speech of thoroughly literate people, but only because "amn't I" and "am I not" are so awkward. In writing, there is more time to find satisfactory alternatives. *Ain't* is used, however, in both speech and writing to obtain a facetious or merely down-to-earth quality: *Tell me it ain't so/Ain't no reason to go anywhere else* [Wendy's]/*Some way we've got to find the money, which ain't going to be easy/Continental Produce Association—We ain't just fruit.*

air Acceptably used for "broadcast": *The program will be aired on the 22nd/The film will be aired by CBS.* Air is also used in the sense of giving utterance, especially to a negative idea: *will air their grievances.*

air rights Rights to the space above land owned by someone else. For instance, space above a rail yard is leased for the construction of a factory complex; builders of an office tower lease the space above a low adjacent building to ensure an unobstructed view.

a.k.a. Also known as. Common in legal papers, but also used otherwise, sometimes facetiously; it does not, however, have the negative CONNOTATION of "alias": *J. W. Goodman, a.k.a. Adam Smith, author of* Paper Money/*a fabulously wealthy Dallas construction tycoon Jake, a.k.a. "J.B.," Rampling/illustrated his talk with a handsome poster (a.k.a. visual aid), which refused to stay up.*
—**k/a.** Known as: *will sell at auction the premises k/a 165–21 Jamaica Avenue, Jamaica, N.Y.*

alarm To equip with an alarm, as a bell or siren, usually to discourage thieves and vandals: *Door alarmed. This exit to be used only in case of fire.*

albeit Pronounced awl-*be*-it. Meaning "though," "although," "even if," *albeit* is considered archaic by many: *The recruiters act as door openers for the qualified albeit unattached executives/We do not advertise in consumer media albeit many of our competitors do.*

alibi Adapted from the Latin meaning "elsewhere," an alibi is a legal defense that claims the accused was at another place when a crime was committed and is therefore innocent: *The jury apparently believed the defendant's alibi.* Informally, however, an alibi is any excuse: *How long are they going to use the alibi that skilled workers are hard to get?*

Also an informal verb: *I won't alibi/As expected, they alibied their failure.*

align, aline The words, meaning "to arrange in a line," are variant spellings, but the first is the more familiar and preferred: *The margins were not properly aligned.*

A-line Pronounced *ay*-line. Shaped like the letter A; a term describing a silhouette common in women's clothing.

all 1. Unnecessary when a statement is sufficiently inclusive without it: *Patrons* (rather than *All patrons*) *should have their tickets ready.* But (correct): *All merchandise has been marked down for this sale.*

2. When used as a pronoun, *all* is singular or plural depending on the sense: *All we want* (that is, *The one thing we want*) *is the normal discount.* But: *All are invited.*

See also **ALL OF; ALL READY, ALREADY; ALL RIGHT;** and **ALL TO-GETHER, ALTOGETHER.**

all- So hyphened when used as a prefix: *all-inclusive, all-out, all-star, all-purpose, all-time.* See also **HYPHEN** 2.

all-around, all-round 1. The words are interchangeable as adjectives: *an all-around* (or *all-round*) *administrator/an all-around* (or *all-round*) *plan.*

2. Not to be confused with the unhyphened *all around* and *all round,* which are interchangeable as prepositions and adverbs: *She walked all around* (or *all round*) *the property/From the tower, you can see all around* (or *all round*).

allege To state or claim before proof is legally established. In ordinary use, the word may give offense when the allegation is attributed to the reader or listener: *We have your letter about the alleged damage* (Better: *about the damage*)/*You allege* (Better: *You state* or *Your letter states*). But (well used): *The alleged shoplifter was apprehended as he left the store.* See also **COURTESY AND TACT.**

all of Idiomatically correct, but the *of* is superfluous except when a pronoun follows: *We had heard all* (rather than *all of*) *the arguments before*. But (no alternative): *All of them are to be commended*.

allotted, allotting So spelled (two *t*'s); but *allotment (allot + ment)*: *allotted 50 percent of the amount of their order/are allotting more space for storage/received an allotment of the discounted goods*.

all ready, already *All ready* means "entirely ready"; *already* means "by this time": *Everything is in place, and we are all ready for tomorrow's crowds*. But: *Our production so far this year has already exceeded our estimates*.

all right So spelled (two words). *Alright* is a misspelling, probably through a mistaken analogy with *already* (see **ALL READY, ALREADY**): *I feel all right* (satisfactory)/*All right* (Very well), *we'll do it if you say so/They were cheaters, all right* (without a doubt).

—**all-right,** adjective (slang): *It looks like an all-right proposition*.

all together, altogether *All together*, meaning "in a group" should be distinguished from *altogether*, meaning "entirely": *We were all together in the lobby when the bus arrived*. But: *The clause is altogether meaningless*.

Together, meaning "in harmony," need not be prefaced by *all: We stand together* (not *all together*) *on the issue of equal opportunity*.

aloha suite The facetious name for the quarters to which dismissed managers and professionals are assigned before their permanent departure. Here, isolated in a small office, they can use the telephones and dictate résumés. The term has become largely obsolete as companies turn more humanely to the use of **OUTPLACEMENT** firms or outplacement counselors within the company.

along the line(s) of See at **LINE**.

alphabet soup An informal characterization of the welter of abbreviations used for the names of organizations of all kinds: NCR, UV, LTV, PPG, IBM, RCA, HIP, UCLA, ASCAP, IRS, SBA, FRB, etc. See also **NAMES** 2.

already See **ALL READY, ALREADY**.

alright A misspelling of **ALL RIGHT**.

also Best used as a simple conjunction: *The store also carries women's wear/Simpson was also assigned a place on the personnel committee*.

Also is better not used as an introduction to a statement requiring the force of a conjunctive adverb (see **HOWEVER, THEREFORE, MOREOVER**): *Ridership on the line has reached the saturation point. Also, the route is heavily used by freight traffic.* (Substitute *Moreover* for *also.*)

Entirely acceptable is the placement of *also* at the beginning of an inverted sentence (see **SENTENCES** 3(c)): *Also included in the report were references to the effects on profits of recent price rises.*

alternate, alternative   *Alternate,* the adjective, means "occurring in turn," as in *on alternate days;* or "relating to every other," as in *sent to alternate names on the list. Alternate,* the noun, denotes a person who takes the place of another—a delegate, for example: *An alternate was chosen.*

Alternative, both as a noun and as an adjective, relates to a choice of one from two or more: *The alternative was to lose the account/Let me add a third alternative/Alternative procedures will be considered.*

Alternate is synonymous with *alternative* only in the sense of a voluntary substitution or free choice. Hence the last example above could as well read, *Alternate procedures will be considered.* But in a sentence such as, *There is no alternative to a written contract, alternate* is not a satisfactory synonym for *alternative* because the idea of a free choice is absent.

In substituting *alternate* for *alternative,* one must also be careful to avoid ambiguity: *A car pool and public transportation were used as alternate means of getting to work.* [Was the car pool alternating with public transportation? Probably not. The sense appears to require *alternative.*]

alternative, choice   An *alternative* is a choice limited to one of two or more possibilities: *If you want an alternative to taupe, try ecru/We were offered the alternatives of buying, leasing, or renting.* "No other alternative" is redundant: *We have no* (not *no other*) *alternative.*

A *choice* is a free selection of one or more: *The choices are ecru, tan, and taupe/We offer a choice of models/Among the many fresh vegetables, the menu offers you two choices* (not *two alternatives;* an alternative necessarily limits the selection to one).

alternative work schedule   See **FLEXTIME**.

altho   A **CLIPPED FORM** of *although.* See also **SIMPLIFIED SPELLING**.

although, though   *Although* is somewhat more formal than *though,* but with some exceptions the words are interchangeable.

1. Only *though* can be used in the expressions "as though" and "even though," and only *though* can be used at the end of a sentence: *Figures don't lie; in this case, we're a bit skeptical though.*

2. In other instances, *although* is often more favored at the beginning of a sentence: *Although unfavorable exchange rates hurt profits, sales were at record-breaking levels.* But: *Sales were at record-breaking levels, though unfavorable exchange rates hurt profits.*

3. Between single words and phrases, *but* makes a smoother link than either *though* or *although: He was looking for a small but* (rather than *though*) *profitable enterprise/They were still without complete stocks, but* (rather than *though* or *although*) *not without a great many enthusiastic buyers.*

alum A CLIPPED FORM of *alumnus* or *alumna;* sometimes useful in avoiding the awkwardness of differentiating male and female graduates: *March interviews with alums are used to help Rollins seniors in their job hunt.* See also ALUMNUS, ALUMNA.

aluminium Pronounced al-yoo-. British or Canadian for *aluminum: Alcan Aluminium Ltd.*

alumnus, alumna An *alumnus* is a male graduate; the plural is *alumni* (pronounced -nye). An *alumna* is a female graduate; the plural is *alumnae* (pronounced -nee). A group consisting of male and female graduates are *alumni: an alumnus of Williams/an alumna of Vassar/an alumni reunion/a gathering of alumnae/the New York University Alumni Federation.* See also PLURALS 4.

a.m., p.m. Also A.M., P.M. The lowercase letters are preferred in typewritten work because of the undue prominence of the full capitals. In print, small capitals (A.M., P.M.) are common.

The abbreviations are to be used only with figures: *10 a.m.,* or ten o'clock (but not *ten a.m.*).

The use of *a.m.* and *p.m.* without reference to a particular time is colloquial: *I'll see you in the a.m.*

Expressions like "10 *a.m.* in the morning" and "2 *p.m.* in the afternoon" are redundant. Correct: *Thursday at 10 a.m./Thursday afternoon at two o'clock.*

See also CLOCK TIME.

amanuensis A person employed to take dictation or to copy manuscript; a secretary. The term, though now archaic, is occasionally used with deliberate pretentiousness: *volunteered to be my amanuensis during my secretary's absence.*

ambiance Also *ambience*. Pronounced *am*-be-unce or (French) ahn-byahns. The atmosphere or surroundings: *understood the importance of a restaurant's ambiance/an agreeable ambiance for repose and study.*

ambiguity A statement should be phrased so that it does not lend itself to more than one interpretation. Even when it is possible to guess at the intended meaning, an ambiguous statement is, at best, sloppy and the effect can be ludicrous.

A rest period will not entirely succeed in eliminating tired employees. (*Improved:* A rest period will not entirely succeed in reducing fatigue.)

The new will will be ready for your execution in a few days. (Omit *your.*)

Carelessness aside, ambiguity can result from various faults in expression. Some examples follow.

1. AMBIGUOUS WORDS

We have not been able to develop any *positive* information about this company. (*favorable?* or *definite?*)

Their credit request will be treated with extreme *consideration.* (*caution?* or *solicitude?*)

2. MISPLACED SENTENCE ELEMENT (See also **POSITION OF MODIFIERS** 1.)

Thank you for the letter about the Hansen Cemetery Plot, which we are returning to you in this envelope. (*Improved:* We are returning to you in this envelope the letter about the Hansen Cemetery Plot.)

3. OMITTED WORD OR WORDS

The adoption of the bank's new name requires no action on your part—just continue to use your present checks and other forms until exhausted. (*Improved: . . .* until they are exhausted.)

4. SUPERFLUOUS WORD (See also **COMPARISONS** 1(b).)

Otto Salvatore. Piano and accordion instructor. All other instruments taught by experts. (Omit *other.*)

5. AMBIGUOUS PRONOUN REFERENCE (See also **PRONOUNS** 1(a).)

Let Roberts talk to Owen and get the details, and I will call *him* later. (*Improved: . . .* and I will call Roberts later.)

ameliorate *Ameliorate*, meaning ''to improve'' (a preferably simpler word), should not be mistaken for *lessen, relieve, alleviate,* or *miti-*

gate. One *ameliorates* (improves) working conditions, but lessens (or alleviates) the effects of a power breakdown.

amenable   Pronounced uh-*meen-* (preferred) or uh-*men-*. Agreeable, submissive. A prepositional phrase following is introduced by *to: Simpson was amenable to the suggestion.*

amenity   Pronounced, preferably, uh-*men-*. That which is agreeable or pleasant: *The amenities include twin washbasins.*

amend, emend   To *amend* something is to improve or change it: *amend the law/amend the offer.* To *emend*, applicable only to the written or printed word, is to correct by editing: *emended the text to make it more concise.*

Amex   ACRONYM for both the *Am*erican Stock *Ex*change (New York) and the *Am*erican *Ex*press Company.

amid, amidst   These are literary words; other prepositions are more suitable for general use: *amid (in) the confusion/there amid (with) her friends/amidst (among) the old scrapbooks/surviving amidst (under) the pressure of competition.*

among, between   1. *Among* is used when reference is made to more than two persons or things: *The award was divided equally among the three highest scorers.*

2. *Between* is used when the reference is to two parties or, in a group of more than two, to the members of the group in individual or reciprocal relationships: *An agreement was hammered out between the company and the union/Contracts between the Big Five will permit work on their joint project to begin on July 1/Dorman's—the cheese with the paper between the slices* (but not *between each slice;* see next paragraph).

3. *Between* cannot logically be followed by one singular noun: *The musicians asked for a rest after each set* (not *between each set*). But (plural noun following): *asked for a rest between sets;* or (two singular nouns following): *offered a choice between blue and red.*

4. Pronouns following *between* are invariably in the objective case: *between you and me* (not *you and I*); *between him and her* (not *between he and she*); *between the client and us* (not *between the client and we*). See also PRONOUNS 2.

5. Objects of *between* are joined by *and,* not *or: a choice between coal and oil* (not *coal or oil*).

amongst   Rare in American English; *among* is preferred.

amortize   Pronounced preferably with the stress on the first syllable (*am-*). To amortize a mortgage or other obligation is to retire it by making regular payments of interest and principal over a period of years. The book value of a fixed asset, like a machine, or of a patent or copyright is similarly amortized by gradually reducing its value at fixed intervals. **—amortization,** noun. Also pronounced preferably *am-*.

amount, number   *Amount* is used with sums and with things in bulk or in aggregate: *an amount of sugar, an amount of money, the amount of a purchase, an amount exceeding $50. Number* refers to a quantity of countable units: *a number of employees/the number of shares traded in a day/the number of miles per gallon of gasoline.*
—in the amount of. A wordy phrase for *of* or *for: payment of $4,500; check for* (not *of*) *$92.50;* but appropriate in formal use: *announced a bond issue in the amount of $150 million.*
   For the conventions governing the treatment of numbers and amounts, see NUMERALS.

ampersand   The sign & for *and.* Saves space in closely set reference data; also used in a company's official name or its common abbreviation, and occasionally in a textual title: *Tiffany & Co., Wiss & Lambert, AT&T/Notes & Comments.* The ampersand is not ordinarily used in a running text.

analogous   Meaning "similar." Takes the preposition *to: The situation is analogous to the one we faced five years ago.*

analyzation   A LONG VARIANT of *analysis: An analyzation (analysis) of the figures shows . . .*

and   1. As a link between ideas, *and* signifies their equality in value: *They're good at their trade, and they know it. And* does not make a suitable connective, however, when the ideas to be joined are not easily equated: *The company imports electronic components, and Elwood Thomas is the president.* Improvement is made by choosing a method of connection that establishes a relation between the disparate ideas or by putting the ideas in separate sentences: *The company, which imports electronic components, is headed by Elwood Thomas, president.* Or: *The company imports electronic components. Elwood Thomas is the president.*
   2. In a series, the sentence elements joined by *and* should be gram-

matically equivalent (see **PARALLEL STRUCTURE**): *From our Houston headquarters we supervise the drilling operation, the processing of the crude oil, and control the distribution system.* [The noun phrases *the drilling operation* and *the processing of the crude oil* are not the grammatical equivalent of the verb phrase *control the distribution system.*] Improved: . . . *supervise the drilling operation, the processing of the crude oil, and the distribution system.* [Three noun phrases follow the verb *supervise.*]

3. A clause beginning with *and* may effectively stand as a sentence, especially in informal writing: *Whatever the international financing problem, we can provide refreshing ideas. And because we have 10,000 people around the world, we can see that those ideas are efficiently translated into action.* [Better than a single sentence in which the two main parts are joined thus: . . . *refreshing ideas, and because we have . . .*]

and/or A formal expression used in law and commerce to denote either one or both of two possibilities: *secured by mortgages and/or other collateral; pay to David Harper and/or Marie Harper.* In ordinary use, a simple *and* or *or* is sufficient: *members of the bowling and chess clubs; service is available day or night.*

and etc. The *and* is superfluous. See also **ETC**.

and which The *and* is not applicable unless the clause beginning *and which* is joined to a preceding *which* clause: *It is a still developing situation, which* (not *and which*) *we are closely watching/The project entailed a cost overrun of $2 million, which* (not *and which*) *the government agreed to pay.* But correct: *The formula was one which we ourselves had developed in 1972 and which we later offered to other metallurgical producers (. . . which . . . and which . . .).*

anent Archaic for "about," "regarding," or "concerning": *your letter about* (not *anent*) *the removal of the wall hangings.*

angle Informal for "slant," a biased or other particular point of view: *What's their angle?* A prepositional phrase centered on *angle* is likely to be verbose: *He sees the idea from a different angle (He sees the idea differently).* See also **WORDINESS** 6.

ante Slang for the amount put up as one's share: *raised the ante to $10,000.* Also, with *up*, a verb: *ante'd up the $10,000.*

ante- A prefix meaning "before" or "in front of": *antecedent*, *ante-room*.

antedate To put a date earlier than the actual one on a document such as a life insurance policy in order to have it take effect before the date of execution. *Predate* is seldom used for *antedate* in the context just cited, but the two words are otherwise interchangeable in the sense of "to precede in time": *Her role as vice president for finance antedated (or predated) the company's expansion spree by at least ten years/An old ferry, predating (or antedating) the present bridge, carried most of the traffic between the two cities.*

anti- A prefix denoting opposition to, or counteraction. The HYPHEN is used only when the element following the prefix begins with *i* or a capital letter: *antitrust*, *antisocial*, *antidemocratic;* but *anti-institutional*, *anti-American*.

anticipatory subject See THERE IS, THERE ARE.

anxious Best used to convey worry or unease: *anxious about the outcome of the dispute/a few anxious moments. Anxious* is informal but not always apt, however, as a synonym for "eager": *anxious* (better, *eager*) *to serve you/anxious (eager?) to do what is right.*

anymore, any more *Anymore* is an adverb meaning "at the present time" or "from now on": *We don't use manual typewriters anymore/Please don't call anymore.*

Any more (two words) functions as a noun in the sense of something additional: *If you're referring to the shirts on sale, we don't have any more.* Only *any more* will do, also, when it is followed by *than*, and *any* carries the sense of "to any degree": *We don't like the arrangement any more* (not *anymore*) *than you do.*

Contrary to general opinion, *anymore* and *any more* can be acceptably used in other than negative contexts: *Do you do business with Allied Products anymore?/I wonder if Blakely knows what he's doing any more* (that is, *any longer*). But (unacceptable): *Heaven knows what will happen anymore.*

anyone, any one The joined form is used except when emphasis on *one* is desired: *Anyone will be glad to help.* But: *Any one of the three models is a good choice.* The same distinction applies to *everyone, every one;* and *someone, some one.*

anyone else's The correct possessive form. See ELSE.

anyplace   Also *any place* (two words). Informal for *anywhere: I'll meet you anyplace you say/Put the carton any place that's convenient.*

any time   Always two words: *Make the appointment for any time you wish/I'll see you any time.*

anyway, any way   Either term may be used for "anywise" or "in any manner": *We'll pack it anyway* (or *any way*) *you say.*
   Only *anyway* is used for "in any case" or "notwithstanding": *I'll call you anyway.*
   Only *any way* (two words) is used for "in whatever direction": *We find ourselves stymied any way we turn.*

anyways   Nonstandard for ANYWAY: *Anyway* (not *anyways*), *we decided to negotiate a settlement.*

anywheres   Nonstandard for *anywhere: We deliver anywhere* (not *anywheres*).

apathetic   Takes the preposition *toward: The client was apathetic toward* [but *indifferent to*] *the proposal.*

aperture card   A small coded card with a punched-out window holding one or more microfilm frames; especially convenient for the computerized retrieval of engineering drawings and other graphic materials.

apostrophe (')   A sign used to form the possessive case of nouns and signify certain other locutions.

   1. POSSESSIVE USES.   2. IN CONTRACTIONS.   3. BEFORE CERTAIN PLURAL ENDINGS.   4. WITH COINED VERBS.   5. MISUSES.

   1. POSSESSIVE USES.   (a) An apostrophe and *s* are regularly added to form the possessive case of singular nouns, indefinite pronouns, and plural nouns not ending in *s.*
   SINGULAR NOUNS: the company's policy, her brother's claim, Charles's interest, Jones's share
   INDEFINITE PRONOUNS: anyone's guess, everybody's business
   PLURAL NOUNS: men's shoes, women's clubs, children's playthings

   (b) To avoid an awkward sound, the apostrophe alone is added to form the possessive of plural nouns ending in *s* and some proper names ending in *s* or *z.*
   PLURAL: other companies' policies, her brothers' claims, ladies' suits, the Joneses' share, the Montgomerys' children

SINGULAR: Iroquois' dividend, Agassiz' headquarters, Willis' (or Willis's) share

(c) To show joint possession, only the last of two or more names is given the possessive ending if there is no chance of misunderstanding. Otherwise, the possessive ending is given to each name. Nouns assigning separate possession and those joined to possessive pronouns are also given their own possessive endings.

Sealy and Harper's bid *or* Sealy's and Harper's bid [joint bid]

Sealy's and Harper's bids [separate bids]

Sealy's or Harper's bid [separate bids]

Woodward's and our guarantees [joint guarantees]

damage to their company's and their stockholders' interests [joint interests; this meaning would not be so clear if the phrase read "damage to the company and their stockholders' interests"]

(d) The possessive ending is added to only the last member of a compound noun, whether hyphened or not.

the brother-in-law's claim

Lord & Taylor's downtown store

General Motors' decision

Henry Seastrom, Jr.'s, contribution

(e) Singular expressions of time often take the *'s* ending even though no possession is indicated: *a day's work, a month's pay, a year's planning.* The possessive ending is often omitted in the plural: *two days* (or days') *work, five years* (or years') *planning.*

(f) The use of an *of* phrase is sometimes preferred to the possessive ending with names of inanimate objects, but the possessive ending is characteristic of many idioms and is used whenever an *of* phrase would be unnecessarily wordy or awkward.

the corners of the desk [*rather than* the desk's corners]

the roof of the house [*rather than* the house's roof]

But: the factory's smokestacks [*rather than* the smokestacks of the factory]

Also: a stone's throw, a book's cover, the computer's capabilities, your money's worth

(g) A possessive noun or pronoun following the possessive *of* is accepted idiom: *a subsidiary of ours* (not *us*); *friends of Mr. Gray* (or *Mr. Gray's*). In some instances this double possessive helps to resolve ambiguity. "A portrait of Pembroke," for example, suggests that the portrait is a likeness of Pembroke; "a portrait of Pembroke's," on the other hand, denotes that the portrait is owned by Pembroke, but is not necessarily a likeness of him. See also **POSSESSIVE WITH GERUND.**

Care should be taken that the double possessive is not redundant: *The account was originally that of Mr. Klein* (not *that of Mr. Klein's*); also, better still: *The account was originally Mr. Klein's.*

(h) The apostrophe is often omitted after a plural noun ending in *s* when the noun is more descriptive than possessive: *General Motors cars, the employees lounge, Mothers Day, consumers rights.* The apostrophe is also omitted before the possessive *s* in some singular trade names, especially those of retail stores: *Gimbels, Wallachs* (but *Barney's, Beck's* [beer], *Bloomingdale's, Macy's*).

2. IN CONTRACTIONS. The apostrophe is used to substitute for omissions in contracted words or numerals: *isn't, they're, I'll, we've, Dancin'* (musical show), *nine o'clock (of the clock), Class of '86.* See also **CONTRACTIONS** in the main entries.

3. BEFORE CERTAIN PLURAL ENDINGS. With the exceptions noted in the next paragraph, the *'s* is used to form the plural of letters of the alphabet, numerals, signs, and words used as words: *the ABC's of investing; &'s that look like 8's; took the cash in 5's and 10's* (But: *in fives and tens*); *the 1980's; the 80's.*

The apostrophe is sometimes omitted when there is no chance of confusion. This exception applies particularly to financial writing: *Treasury 8s* (8 percent Treasury bonds); *the 1989s and 1990s* (bonds then due); *took the cash in 5s and 10s.* But *the A's and B's* (not *As and Bs*); *spelled with two t's* (not *two ts*); *uses too many I's* (not *too many Is*).

4. WITH COINED VERBS. Parts of certain coined verbs are formed with an apostrophe: *X'd out the unwanted sentence; O.K.'d the project; will stop COD'ing packages* [stop sending them COD].

5. MISUSES. (a) No apostrophe is used to form the possessive of *who (whose)* or of any of the personal pronouns *(ours, yours, its, hers, theirs).* These pronouns should not be confused with like-sounding contractions requiring the apostrophe: *who's* [*who is* or *who has*]; *it's* [*it is* or *it has*]; *they're* [*they are*].

(b) The apostrophe should not be used before the *s* ending of a simple plural noun: *Stores for lease* (not *Store's*)/*These are the papers to be signed* (not *paper's*)/*The Wilsons are expected at three* (not *Wilson's*). See illustration.

His and Her's Monogrammed Sweaters

Can your Data Processing and Word Processing systems talk to one another? Our's can.

Former Roger's Estate

Built in 1888
On 110-Plus Acres

Tune-up's Are Our Specialty.

Apostrophe 5 (Misuses).   A typesetter's nightmare.

appeal   1. In some phrases, *appeal* is JARGON for the power to arouse a particular kind of interest: *sex appeal, eye appeal, taste appeal.*

2. In advertising especially, the "appeal" is the promise of a message; the implied or stated benefits of a product or service, as opposed to its substance. A storefront dental clinic proclaims, "Now everyone can afford a beautiful smile." The appeal of Kreeger & Sons outdoor clothing is stated, "We sell warmth." Similarly, AT&T promotes familial closeness by long-distance telephone; Northwest Orient Airlines, the exclusivity of "Business Class"; and Sanka, relief from "coffee nerves."

3. Emotional appeals are rooted in the desire for love, admiration, security, approval, competitive advantage, relief from pain, etc. (see illustration). Rational appeals stress economy, performance, good value. Though appeals are most clearly evident in business messages, they are characteristic of ADVOCACY in any vocation, including law, politics, administration, and religion.

See also MOTIVATION.

appendix   Plural, *appendixes* (preferred) or *appendices* (pronounced

THERE is an air of insatiable
desire about Shalimar.

The inspiration for this classic
fragrance came from the story of a man
who loved a woman so deeply, that when she
died, every fiber of his being was devoted to
creating a monument to her memory.

Twenty thousand men labored daily
for twenty-two years to fashion marble into
the pinnacles, parapets and domed kiosks
we know today as the Taj Mahal.

The garden where their love grew
was called the Garden of Shalimar.

Shalimar, the most exquisitely
voluptuous perfume on Earth, by Guerlain.

Appeal (emotional)

-seez). Supplementary material, such as notes, research data, charts, and the like, added to a **REPORT** or book.

appositive   Ordinarily, an appositive—the explanatory equivalent of another word—is set off by commas, but there are exceptions. "The legator's son, John, is not named in the will" indicates that John is the only son; but "The legator's son John is not named in the will" may indicate that John is but one of two or more sons. See also **COMMA** 4(a).

appraise, apprise   The words are often confused. To *appraise* is to place a value on: *appraise an estate/appraise the damage*. To *apprise* (of) is a formal term for "inform" or "notify": *I want to be apprised* (not *appraised*) *of any changes/Apprise her of* (tell her) *the facts/They were apprised* (notified) *of the decision.*

appreciate   There is no question about the use of *appreciate*, meaning "to increase in price or value," as a share of common stock or a work of art. However, *appreciate* is probably overused in other senses: "We appreciate your patronage" treats the patronage as a favor, perhaps correctly so; but "we value your patronage" is usually more to the point. So, too, "We appreciate the difficulty," might better be stated, "We understand the difficulty''; and "We appreciate your letter"—like "THANK YOU for your letter"—is apt enough when the letter has given the respondent something to be grateful for, but not otherwise.

approximately About: *The work will take approximately (about) five days.* See LONG WORDS AND SHORT.

apt, liable, likely All three words denote probability, but there are distinctions.

Apt means "suitable," "inclined," or "quick to learn": *The phrase is apt/She makes an apt successor to Grimes/Given his talents, Daly is apt to charm the most implacable opponents of the plan/Toni is an apt pupil.*

Liable is used in the sense of openness to risk or disadvantage: *In case of default, the company will be liable for damages/In such a tense atmosphere, tempers are liable to erupt at any time.*

Likely, meaning "fairly certain," is without any special connotation: *A price increase is likely in the spring/The negotiations are likely to be concluded tomorrow.*

arbiter Though sometimes used for ARBITRATOR, the word *arbiter* usually designates a person respected for his or her judgments in some aspect of the arts: *an arbiter of fashion.*

arbitrator, mediator Both an *arbitrator* and a *mediator* are persons designated by the concerned parties to examine the issues in a dispute and find some formula for settlement. However, only the arbitrator's recommendations are binding.

area In its nonliteral sense, *area* is usually either unnecessary or imprecise: *Their interests lie in the area of power plant technology (Their interests lie in power plant technology)/The area of employee rehabilitation* (Better: *Employee rehabilitation*) *needs more converts/Several problem areas (Several problems) were discussed/My area (My specialty) is consumer motivation.*

—in the area of. Informal for "about": *We expect profits to be in the area of $200,000 (We expect profits of about $200,000).*

archaic English See at USAGES 5.

aren't I See AIN'T.

argument In persuasion, the use of *evidence* and *reasoning*. *Evidence* is the data from which one may arrive at a conclusion or judgment. It includes reports based on direct observation and the experience of others; facts and figures from the government or other reliable sources; the results of valid surveys, tests, and experiments; and specific details of construction or performance. Evidence may also include accepted truths (*favoritism in an organization breeds discontent/poor training increases the chance of error*) and opinions worthy of belief (see **CREDIBILITY**).

Reasoning from the evidence usually proceeds inductively or deductively—from a presentation of the data to the conclusion, or from a statement of the conclusion to the presentation of the supporting data. See also **ORDER OF PRESENTATION**.

arithmetic mean See **MEAN**.

around Informal for "about": *cost around fifty dollars/will be ready around Thursday.*

arrears Pronounced uh-*reerz.* "In arrears," a bookkeeper's term, is better avoided in consumer correspondence: *Your account is $60 in arrears (overdue).*

as *As* may be ambiguous when used for "since" or "because": *As sugar prices were about to rise, we increased our purchase orders.* [Was the second action a consequence of the first, or did the two actions merely coincide? "Because," "Since," or "At a time when" would make the meaning clear.]

As is sometimes superfluous: *elected as president* (omit *as*)/*As much as we needed the business, we felt that the credit risk was too great* (Better: *Much as we needed*).

For case of pronoun following *as,* see **PRONOUNS** 2(a).

as, like 1. As a conjunction, *as* is regularly followed by a subject and predicate: *Robards signed the contract as it was presented to him/Do as you are told. As* is also standard as a preposition when it relates to the taking of a particular role; it is then followed by a noun or pronoun, grammatically its "object": *She was trained as an economist/In Terry's absence, Campbell acted as manager* (Compare in meaning with: . . . *Campbell acted like the manager*).

2. *Like,* in the sense of "similar to," or "closely resembling," is regularly a preposition: *The material feels like velvet/He eventually became president, like his father.* But *like* is informal when it is used in place of the conjunction *as* in a comparison: *Winston tastes good like*

a cigarette should/The company no longer uses glass containers like they used to/The supervisor treated his workers like a mother might treat her wayward children. Like is also informal when it is used for *as if: Perry behaved like he owned the business/They sounded like they meant every word/It looked like they were out to gouge the public.*

3. *Like* is nonstandard as a substitute for the conjunction *as* when no comparison is involved: *One of the reasons I look like I do is Oil of Olay/The buyers jammed the store like we expected/Like I said, there'll be no deal.*

as, than   For case of pronoun following, see PRONOUNS 2(a).

as, that   *As* is nonstandard for *that* after such verbs as *know, say,* and *think: We don't know that* (not *as*) *we can put off the decision any longer.*

as always   Also, *as ever.* A COMPLIMENTARY CLOSE used in a personal letter or a very friendly business letter bearing a first-name SALUTATION.

ASAP   As soon as possible. An abbreviation common in office memos and telecommunications: *Please answer ASAP.*

as . . . as, so . . . as   In general usage, a double comparison begun with *as* requires a second *as: The tire is as good as, if not better than, the Michelin.* Or (smoother): *The tire is as good as the Michelin, if not better.* In informal usage, the second *as* is omitted: *The tire is as good if not better than the Michelin.* See also COMPARISONS 1.

In a negative comparison, *so . . . as* is somewhat more formal than *as . . . as: This plan is not so comprehensive as the earlier one.*

as best, as best as   Nonstandard for "as well as" or "the best": *They did as well as* (not *as best* or *as best as*) *they could.* Also correct: *They did the best they could.*

ascertain   Learn. See LONG WORDS AND SHORT.

as for   See AS TO.

as good . . . if not better   See COMPARISONS 1.

as how, as where   Nonstandard expressions for "that": *I see that* (not *as how,* or *as where*) *Continental has named a new chairman.*

As how is also nonstandard for "whether": *They did not know whether* (not *as how*) *their lease would allow for alterations.*

as if, as though The subjunctive *were*, with a singular subject, follows these expressions in formal usage, but not otherwise: *Perry behaved as if he were the head of the department.* But (acceptable in general usage: . . . *behaved as if he was*).

as if, like See AS, LIKE.

as much, if not more For this usage as well as *as much or more* and *as many or more*, see COMPARISONS 1.

as per See PER 3.

as regards See REGARDING, AS REGARDS.

asset A term best confined to the sense of "something of value" and not to be loosely used as a synonym for *benefit, advantage, help: Among our assets is a trademark familiar to almost everyone.* But: *Your cooperation would be a big help* (not *an asset*) *to us/Another benefit* (not *asset*) *of the plan is its simplicity.*

assistance Help. See LONG WORDS AND SHORT.

associate, partner An *associate* is a person closely connected with another in some business or other enterprise. A *partner* is, in addition, a principal in a business. Lawyers, for instance, may be associates but not necessarily partners in the firm. See also COLLEAGUE.

assume, presume Both words express a supposition; if there is any difference in meaning, it is that *presume* gives reason to believe there is evidence to support the supposition, whereas *assume* does not: *The figures assume an upturn in fall sales/Mr. Carneros is a large landholder and is presumed to be entirely creditworthy.*
—**assumption, presumption,** nouns: *Our plans are based on the assumption of economic recovery/The presumption is that the increase in Democratic strength will slow the federal efforts toward deregulation.*
—**assumedly, presumably,** adverbs: *Assumedly, our chances of landing the contract are as good as anyone else's/With good weather, we will presumably avoid the delays in delivery we encountered at this time last year.*

assure, ensure, insure All three words are interchangeable in the sense of making an outcome certain: *The contour chair assures* (also *ensures* or *insures*) *complete comfort for those suffering from lower-back problems.* In other usages, however, differences occur.

Only *assure* offers reason for confidence or peace of mind: *We assured the customer we would replace the damaged cylinder/Can you assure us of prompt delivery?*

Both *ensure* and *insure* are used to denote protection from harm: *Abundance now does not ensure* (or *insure*) *against scarcity later.*

Insure refers without exception to the protection of life and property against risk: *Every home should be insured against storm and water damage.*

asterisk The symbol * used as a reference mark after a statement for which a footnote, identically marked, is provided. Two and three asterisks are sometimes used for the second and third footnotes on a page; in formal writing, however, numbered references are preferred. Compare **DAGGER**. See also **REFERENCE NOTES**.

as to 1. *As to* (or *as for*) is legitimately used at the beginning of a sentence to emphasize the point being introduced: *As to* (or *As for*) *the design, we expect it will be approved soon.* Compare with: *We expect the design will be approved soon.*

2. Many sentences read more smoothly when *as to* is replaced by *of* or *about* or omitted altogether: *We spoke to the client as to (about) their plans/With the statement, he dispelled any thought as to (of) his retirement/They cannot decide as to whether* (omit *as to*) *the old machine needs replacing.*

See also **QUESTION AS TO**.

as well as 1. When two subjects are joined by *as well as*, the verb is not necessarily plural: *The store as well as its advertising agency was* (or *were*) *nominated for the award.* See **SUBJECT AND VERB** 2(c).

2. A pronoun following *as well as* takes the same case as the word to which it is linked: *Blaine as well as I* (not *me*) *insisted on the settlement/The invitation was for Sanford as well as me* (not *I*). See **PRONOUNS** 2.

as when, as where See **AS HOW, AS WHEN, AS WHERE**.

at about, at around The *at* is superfluous: *I'll see you about* (not *at about*) *one o'clock/The festivities begin around* (not *at around*) *noon.*

attached hereto, attached herewith *Hereto* and *herewith* are redundant. See also **STEREOTYPED LETTER PHRASES**.

attendee One who attends a meeting. Preferred in this sense over the more ambiguous terms *attender* and *attendant*, and sometimes over *participant* and *conferee*, which suggest an active role in the program.

attention Part of several **STEREOTYPED LETTER PHRASES**: *brought to our attention/has come to our attention/will receive our attention/referred to me for attention.*

attention line Part of the address on material the sender wishes to direct primarily to the organization and still ensure that it will be seen or attended to by a particular individual.

These are traditional styles:

Attention of Mr. Julio S. Ramirez
Attention Mr. Julio S. Ramirez
Attention: Mr. Julio S. Ramirez

In a letter, the attention line is typewritten below the **INSIDE AD-DRESS**; it usually begins at the left margin when paragraphs are blocked and is indented or centered when paragraphs are indented. The abbreviation *Att.* is better not used. (For position on the envelope, see **ENVELOPE ADDRESS**.)

The salutation following the attention line should be consistent with the company name, as *Gentlemen*, not *Dear Mr. Ramirez*; but see **SALUTATION** 2.

at the present time Either superfluous or verbose: *We are overstocked at the present time.* Better: *We are overstocked;* or, emphasizing a temporary condition: *We are at present* (or *now, currently*) *overstocked.* Compare **PRESENTLY**.

at this writing See **UP TO THE PRESENT WRITING**.

attorney-at-law, lawyer The terms are synonymous, but many lawyers prefer *attorney-at-law* or, less accurately, *attorney*. An attorney, though having the power of attorney and legally empowered to act on behalf of another person, is not necessarily a lawyer. Only the lawyer is legally empowered to prepare cases and represent a client in court.

at your earliest convenience A **STEREOTYPED LETTER PHRASE**. See also at **CONVENIENCE**.

audience Properly used not only for listeners and spectators or viewers, but for readers as well: *the growing audience for hobby magazines/prime-time television audiences.*

audit   To *audit* is to examine records or accounts for their accuracy and completeness. In academic practice one may also *audit* a class in the sense of attending it as an observer and listener rather than as a formally enrolled student. In business, because of possible misunderstanding, the substitution of *sit in on* or *observe* may be preferable, especially with relation to conferences and company training courses.

auditor, accountant   Both individuals examine or AUDIT accounts, but only the accountant also designs and installs accounting systems, interprets accounting data, provides tax services, and assists in financial planning. See also C.P.A.

author   Not generally accepted as a verb: *The legislation was authored (originated) by Senator Kalsky/Pace has authored (written) several articles on the subject.*

authoritative   So spelled and pronounced (-uh-tay-tiv): *an authoritative source.*

available   Takes the preposition *for* or *to*. Expressing purpose: *The room is available for staff meetings.* Designating the receiver: *The room is available to any employee group.*

averse   See ADVERSE, AVERSE.

avert, avoid   To *avert* is to prevent an unpleasant occurrence: *They can avert a lawsuit only by living up to the terms of the contract.* To *avoid* is to keep clear of, to shun: *By avoiding the meeting, they left the committee without a quorum.*

awhile, a while   Awhile means "for a short time." Hence "for awhile" is redundant: *We'll think about it awhile* (not *for awhile*). *For,* however, may precede *a while,* which means "a short time": *We'll think about it for a while.* Also correct: *Let's keep the offer open a while* (or *awhile*).

B

back, forward See PUT BACK, PUT FORWARD.

background The name often given to the introduction of a REPORT or that part of it dealing particularly with its origin and purpose.

back of, in back of Both are informal for "behind." Of the two, though, *in back of* is the more acceptable: *the parking lot in back of (behind) the building.*

bad, badly 1. Bad is well used as a complement to certain verbs: *look bad, feel bad (ill), taste bad, smell bad.*
 2. *Feel bad* and *feel badly* are both acceptable in expressions of distress or regret: *We feel bad (or badly) about their misfortune.*
 3. In other instances, *bad* is an adjective meaning "faulty"; and *badly*, an adverb meaning "in a faulty manner" or "very much": *The workmanship is bad/The lathe is working badly (not bad)/The tiling is badly in need of replacement.*

badge Acceptably used as a verb: *Only individuals registered and badged will be admitted to convention events.*

bad-mouth Slang for "speak ill of": *Sims is an expert at bad-mouthing his superiors.*

bail out To rescue from bankruptcy or other calamitous situation: *bailed out by their creditors/can't expect us to bail him out again.*
—bailout, noun: *asked the government for a bailout of a billion dollars.*

baker's dozen Thirteen; from the former custom of bakers giving an extra roll for every dozen purchased, a precaution against short weight.

balance, remainder, rest *Balance* is standard in reference to money or bookkeeping: *the balance of the debt/leaving a balance of $500/the balance of payments* (in international trade).
 For quantities other than money, general usage requires *remainder* or *rest: We have now used up the remainder (or rest) of the stock/Let's*

take the rest of the day off. In business, however, *balance* is acceptably used for *remainder* or *rest* in expressions like "the balance of the shipment" and "the balance of your order," but the approval does not extend to expressions like "the balance [for *rest*] of the day" and "the balance [for *remainder* or *rest*] of our conversation."

balanced sentence   See SENTENCES 3(c).

balancing act   An informal way of describing a skillful adjustment in terms or conditions to please all parties to a transaction: *It took a balancing act to work out the phrasing of the settlement.*

bailoon mortgage   A loan on property requiring generally that the principal be paid back in a lump sum at the end of the loan term. The mortgage may then be refinanced at the prevailing rate.

ball-park figure   Informal for "guess" or "estimate": *A million is just a ball-park figure.* Compare GUESSTIMATE.

baloney   Also *boloney;* informal variant of *bologna,* a type of sausage. Slang for "bunkum," "nonsense"; an expression of disagreement: *That's a lot of baloney.*

Band-Aid   The BRAND NAME for the small adhesive bandages made by Johnson & Johnson; used as a synonym for a makeshift solution to a problem: *Painting the facade is treating the crumbling building with a Band-Aid.* See also CAPITALS 23.

bank on   Informal for "depend on": *You can bank on it.*

bankroll   Informal for "available assets": *has a big bankroll.* Slang as a verb meaning to finance or underwrite: *The show was bankrolled by a syndicate of private investors.*

bar code   See UNIFORM PRODUCT CODE.

bargain   A PEJORATIVE in some comparative advertisements: *Compare Cascade with bargain dishwashing liquids.* See also COMPARATIVE CLAIMS.

based on   1. No objection to this usage so long as *based on* behaves like the participle (adjective) it is and modifies an expressed noun.

The award was *based on* past performance [modifies *award*].

No decision should be *based on* intuition alone [modifies *decision*].

Liberal company-paid benefit program and open salary *based on* prior experience and future potential [modifies *salary*].

2. As a preposition, however, *based on*—used in the sense of "on the basis of"—has its critics. For almost any sentence in which *based on* is employed as a preposition could be a smoother, more coherent sentence if the construction was changed.

Based on my understanding (As I understand it), the contract will be signed on Friday.

Based on our study (Our study shows that), the site has ample fresh water.

Based on my experience (In my experience), dual responsibility can only lead to trouble.

3. In some instances a phrase beginning *based on* also rates criticism as a **DANGLING MODIFIER.**

DANGLING: *Based on our projections, the building* is expected to be completed by January 1. [The initial phrase modifies the subject *building*, but what is "based on our projections" is not the *building*, but the date for the *completion* of the building.]

CORRECTED: *Based on our projections, completion* of the building is expected by January 1.

There are also simpler alternatives:

By our projection, the building will be completed by January 1.

We project completion of the building by January 1.

BASIC The ACRONYM for *B*eginner's *A*ll-purpose *S*ymbolic *I*nstruction *C*ode, a computer programming language.

basis Plural, *bases*, pronounced -seez. The foundation on which something rests: *The basis of the decision is clear/The bases of their decisions are yet to be explained.*

Basis presents no problem until it becomes a part of such phrases as "on the basis of" and "on the basis that," which are wordy and overworked: *On the basis of (From) these facts I conclude . . ./We deal only on a cash basis (for cash)/The stock is being split on a two-for-one basis (two for one)/On the basis of (Because of) increased competition, the company changed its advertising strategy* (or *The company changed its advertising strategy to meet increased competition).*

batch processing Computer processing of accumulated data; permits use of the computer when the workload is light. Withdrawals and additions to inventory may be processed in this way. Compare REAL TIME.

bath As in "took a bath" (suffered a financial reversal): *When interest rates rose, holders of bonds took a bath.*

bazoom Pronounced buh-*zoom*. A slangy EUPHEMISM for a woman's breasts. The term is common in the women's garment industry.

B.C. See A.D., B.C.

beat Informal for "surpass" or "excel": *In fall sales we intend to beat the competition/The new model beats anything we have yet offered.*

because An unambiguous substitute for "as" (see AS). See also REASON IS BECAUSE.

because of See DUE TO.

beep A short high-pitched sound, like the time signal on radio and television: *A few more beeps and the sale is recorded.* Also a verb: *As the laser beams read the coded bars, the scanner beeps to indicate that the message has been received.*

beeper The familiar name for an electronic PAGER.

before, in advance of See IN ADVANCE OF.

beg Archaic in such phrases as "beg to advise," "beg to inform," and "beg to remain," but still so used in some very formal diplomatic and official correspondence. See also STEREOTYPED LETTER PHRASES.

behalf See IN BEHALF OF, ON BEHALF OF.

being as, being that Nonstandard for "as," "since," "because," "inasmuch as": *Being as (Since) it was a holiday, we closed early/Hynes decided to make the concession being that (because) they were good customers.*

belabor See LABOR, BELABOR.

bench mark Also *benchmark* (one word). A surveyor's mark; a point of reference; anything serving as a guide, criterion, or measure: *The move threatened to upset the OPEC bench mark crude oil price/Their introduction of magnetic tape was a benchmark in the recording of sound/The prime rate, used as a benchmark for loans to businesses, has fallen three percentage points since July.*
—**benchmark,** adjective: *have joined forces in a benchmark study of media influence.*

benefited, benefiting Both spelled with one *t*: *benefited by the advice/was benefiting everyone.*

beside, besides Both are used in the sense of "except" and "in addition to," but *besides* is the more common word: *What advantage is to be gained besides* (or *beside*) *a few paltry dollars?/Besides* (or *Beside*), *they were prepared to offer a modest bonus.*

Beside (but not *besides*) has the additional meaning of "next to": *I sat beside* (not *besides* or *beside of*) *the host.*

best For its use in a comparison of only two things, see COMPARISONS 2(a).

best of any, worst of any Acceptable in informal usage: *It's the best of any* (or *worst of any*) *we've tried.* But (general usage): *It's the best one* (or *worst one*) *we've tried/It's the best* (or *worst*) *of those we've tried.*

best wishes An informal COMPLIMENTARY CLOSE to a letter.

bet Past tense of *bet;* also, rare, *betted:* They *bet* (rather than *betted*) *everything on the success of the venture and won.*

better 1. Informal for *had better: We better leave while we can.* 2. Used vaguely in COMPARATIVE CLAIMS by advertisers: *Tastes better.*

bettor A person who bets; preferred to *better*, a variant spelling.

between you and I Not so. *Between*, a preposition, requires that a pronoun complement be in the objective case. The rule poses no difficulty when the complement is a single pronoun *(between us, between them);* but it may give trouble when two pronoun complements are paired: *between you and me* (not *you and I*)/*between them and us* (not *they and we*)/*between her and him* (not *she and he* or *she and him*). See also PRONOUNS 2.

bi- Two, twice. Often confusing in the words *biannual* (twice a year), *biennial* (every two years), *bimonthly* (every two months), and *biweekly* (every two weeks). Hence the preference for expressions not prefixed by *bi-*: twice a year, semiannual, every other year, twice a month, semimonthly, and so forth.

bias, prejudice Just as one may be biased (or prejudiced) against, so one may be biased (or prejudiced) in favor of: *Biased against* (or *in favor of*) *the acquisition/prejudiced in favor of* (or *against*) *a single-story warehouse.* Because of the negative CONNOTATION of *bias* and *prejudice*, however, a positive view might better be expressed with positive words: *favor the acquisition/prefer the advantages of a single-story warehouse.* See also **POSITIVE AND NEGATIVE WORDS**.

bibliography   An organized list of written or printed sources dealing with a particular subject. When appended to a report, the bibliography includes all the sources cited in the report and any others the writer has found pertinent and wishes to recommend to the reader.

　　1. LISTING OF ENTRIES.　2. FORM OF ENTRIES.
　　See also **REFERENCE NOTES**.

　　1. LISTING OF ENTRIES.　(a) If the title "Bibliography" is considered too bookish, alternative titles are available, for instance, "References," "List of Sources," and "Works Consulted." A long list of entries may be subdivided by type of material, as "Books," "Periodicals," and "Government Documents."

　　(b) Entries are arranged alphabetically throughout the bibliography (or throughout each titled subdivision), with the author's last name first. In the instance of a work by more than one author, the names of the second and succeeding authors are better given in the normal order.

Christiansen, Roland C., Kenneth R. Andrews, and Joseph L. Bower.

　　(c) If an author is represented by more than one work, the author's works are usually listed in chronological order. In the entries for a second and succeeding work by the same author, the author's name may be represented by a solid underscore of ten spaces or a series of ten hyphens. For a work written anonymously for a "corporate author"—a company, association, bureau, periodical, or the like—the name of the issuing agency is listed in the author's position. If a work carries no author's name—individual or corporate—the name of the work is entered alphabetically in the author's position.

　　(d) The first line of each entry starts at the margin, but succeeding lines are indented a few spaces. All entries are uniformly single- or double-spaced; and at least in typewritten work, a single space is left between entries.

　　2. FORM OF ENTRIES.　(a) A bibliographical entry consists of data appropriate to the source, as the author's name, the title of the work, the facts of publication (place, publisher's name, and date); and possibly, also, the name of the series, the volume number, and, if the cited work is part of a larger work, the inclusive page numbers.

(b) Following the style of reference notes, titles of books are underscored or italicized; those of articles and chapters are put in quotation marks. Unlike the style of reference notes, however, which are written as a single sentence, periods separate the main divisions of each entry.

(c) Following is a demonstration of the style of bibliographical entries for various types of material. A comparison with the style of reference notes is suggested (see especially **REFERENCE NOTES** 3).

Botein, Michael, and David M. Rice. *Network Television and the Public Interest.* Lexington, Mass.: D. C. Heath, 1980.

Chavez, Lydia. "The Making of a Security Analyst." *The New York Times*, Jan. 31, 1982, sec. 3.

Forbes. "Cash Flow Made Easy." Feb. 2, 1981.

Future Systems, Inc. *World Environment & Satellite Communication 1978–2003.* Gaithersburg, Md., 1977.

General Electric Co. *1983 Annual Report.*

Industrial Relations Counselors, Inc. *People, Progress, and Employee Relations.* Fiftieth Anniversary Conference of Industrial Relations Counselors, Inc. Charlottesville: University of Virginia, 1976.

Leigh, James H. and Claude R. Martin, Jr., eds. *Current Issues and Advertising Research.* Ann Arbor: University of Michigan, 1979.

Pessemier, Edgar A. *Product Management: Strategy and Organization.* New York: John Wiley, 1977.

————, and P. Root. "The Dimensions of New Product Planning." *Journal of Marketing*, vol. 37 (Jan. 1973), pp. 10–18.

Time. "The Seeds of Success." Feb. 15, 1982.

U.S. Copyright Office. *Circular 61* (June 1977). Washington, D.C.: Library of Congress, 1977.

bid   Bid, meaning "to offer a price," has the same form for the past tense as for the past participle: *Speculators bid as much as $24 a bushel/They have bid $2 above the market price.*

biennial   Every two years. See also **BI-**.

Big Board   The New York Stock Exchange: *listed on the Big Board.*

big one   Slang for a thousand dollars: *made one hundred big ones ($100,000) on the deal.*

big ugly Familiar name for a SMOKESTACK COMPANY: *Only the big uglies have not yet been touched by the resurgence in the stock market.*

bimonthly Every two months. See also BI-.

biweekly Every two weeks. See also BI-.

biz Slang for *business*, especially the entertainment business: *That's show biz.*

black Sometimes capitalized. An often preferred synonym for NEGRO: *Meharry is the single largest educator of black physicians and dentists today/a largely Black community.*

black box The name given an electronic control device that will produce the desired results, although the mechanism itself may be kept a secret even from the user: *They bought an $8,500 black box called the Lexicon 1200 Audio Time Compressor/Expander and shrank each* Star Trek *episode by three minutes without losing a word of dialogue.* Also, a theoretical MODEL like that used in econometrics for forecasting economic behavior.

black market Any market in which goods or currency are traded in violation of legal restrictions, like those on price, supply, or distribution: *Russia forbids the importation of movies on video cassettes, but an active black market exists.* Compare GRAY MARKET.

blame on A generally accepted usage despite some preference for the somewhat more formal *blame (someone) for: Don't blame the delay on the factory* (or *Don't blame the factory for the delay*)/*The voters will blame the governor for the defeat* (or *The voters will blame the defeat on the governor*).

bleed In printing, to let an illustration overrun the margin and extend to the edge of the page; also an adjective descriptive of such treatment: *Let the illustration bleed into the gutter* [the margin against the facing page]/*a bleed advertisement/Now: bleed charges lowered again.*

bleep 1. The sound used in broadcasting to replace a censored word or phrase: *The epithet was obscured by a bleep.* Also, synonymous with BLIP, a verb: *bleeped* (or *blipped*) *out the offensive word.*

2. Imitative of any electronic sound, a BEEP: *Challenging supercharged games—everything that blinks, bleeps, and makes you feel like an electronic moron.*

blind advertisement   An advertisement, usually of the help wanted type, that conceals the advertiser's name and requires correspondents to write to a box number or other "blind" address.

blind notations   COPY NOTATIONS or IDENTIFICATION INITIALS that are included on the file copies of letters but omitted on the originals. Usually noted as bcc on the file, or carbon, copies.

blindsided   Subjected to an unexpected shock: *Here's a way to keep your pension plan from being blindsided by unrecognized business factors.* The term has its origin in sports where a player may be hit on an unguarded or "blind" side.

blip   1. A spot of light, as on a radar screen or similar monitoring device: *waiting for an age when paper pushing will be replaced by blips on a computer screen.* Also used figuratively: *The sales of the record hardly made a blip on the charts.*
   2. An error; a foul-up: *The country's August unemployment rate is being revised downward following the discovery of a blip in a new claims reporting system. . . . It was not clear where the reporting lapse occurred.*
   3. As a verb, synonymous with BLEEP 1.

blister pack   A type of packaging suitable for small articles to be sold at retail. The "blister" is created by a see-through plastic film molded to the shape of the article and secured to a cardboard backing.

blitz   A clipped form of the German *blitzkrieg* ("lightning war"), *blitz* has settled into the relatively peaceful sense of any intensive campaign: *a publicity blitz/the opening salvo in a Washington blitz to split the industry.*

block   A quantity of things treated as a unit, as *a block of stock.* Not to be confused with *bloc,* a group united in a political cause.

block style   Descriptive of several letter formats: the full block style, modified block style, and semiblock style. See LETTER FORM 3.

blond, blonde   As a noun, blond denotes a man, and blonde a woman: *He's a blond; she's a blonde, too.* As an adjective, *blond* is generally descriptive of persons and things, but custom favors *blonde* for women: *a blond male model/her blonde* (or *blond*) *hair.* But (descriptive of things): *a blond finish/blond mahogany.*

Brunet and *brunette,* used only of persons, are similarly differentiated.

blowup An enlargement of a picture or a document of any kind: *a blowup of the ad.* The verb is *blow up* (two words): *Let's blow up the photo to life size.*

BLS Bureau of Labor Statistics (U.S. Department of Labor).

blue chip Descriptive of the common stock of a large, long-established company with an excellent record of earnings. The stocks of IBM, Exxon, and Corning Glass are blue chips.
—**blue-chip,** adjective: *blue-chip stocks;* also descriptive of any investment of rare quality: *blue-chip properties/a blue-chip art collection.*

blue-collar Descriptive of a worker or workers who perform manual labor in rough clothing: a steelworker, plumber, electrician, auto mechanic, warehouseman, etc. Compare with GRAY-COLLAR and WHITE-COLLAR.

blue laws Local laws regulating the kinds of businesses that may operate on Sundays and the hours to be kept; also any laws concerned with enforcing moral standards.

blue-pencil To revise written material in the manner of an editor using the traditional blue pencil: *Feel free to blue-pencil my copy.*

blue ribbon A prize or symbol for excellence: *won a blue ribbon at the Heidelberg Fair/deserves a blue ribbon for its quality.*
—**blue-ribbon,** adjective: *a blue-ribbon panel of experts/a blue-ribbon winner.*

blurb A brief laudatory notice, as on a book jacket: *The blurb was a masterpiece of overstatement.*

board Short for "switchboard"; see also PBX.

board room Two words. A room in a brokerage office where customers can come to follow the prices of leading stocks as they are flashed electronically and in continuous movement in a long narrow strip for all to see. The name comes from the "board" on which price quotations used to be posted.

boardroom One word. The room in which meetings of an organization's board of directors are held: *an elegant boardroom on the 65th floor/boardroom politics.*

bodega Pronounced bo-*day*-guh. A grocery store found in Spanish-speaking neighborhoods.

body language Gestures and facial expressions which, alone or with spoken words, communicate thoughts and feelings. Thus a listener's crossed arms may suggest resistance to a speaker's message. See also **NONVERBAL COMMUNICATION.**

boiler plate Also *boilerplate* (one word). A newspaper term for preset plated copy, like the masthead; now used in business and legal practice to denote any routine, repeatable copy: *Many annual reports are just a lot of boiler plate/Using boiler plate, a storefront law office can prepare a simple will at relatively low cost/The storage unit holds a boiler-plate library of commonly used text.*

boiler room An operation, like that used in the sale of questionable stock, employing a bank of telephones to reach prospective buyers.

bona fide Pronounced *bo*-nuh-fide; also *bon*-uh-fide and bo-nuh-*fie*-dee. A Latin term for "in good faith" or "sincere": *a bona fide offer.* Also (rare): *The offer was made bona fide.*

bona fides Pronounced bo-nuh *fie*-deez. Formal and pretentious for "credentials," the term is grammatically singular: *His bona fides was* (not *were*) *impeccable/Having established his bona fides, he was admitted to the inner circles of corporate power.*

bond In finance, evidence of a debt on which a specified rate of interest is to be paid regularly until the bond **MATURES** and the face value is returned in full. Since a bond is a debt, the bondholder has a claim on the assets of the issuing company should it fail. Compare **STOCK.**

bonded warehouse A repository, vouched for by the government, for the storage of goods pending payment of customs duties or other taxes.

bond paper Also, simply, *bond.* A strong, durable paper made entirely or in part of rag pulp; used for documents and good quality stationery.

bond ratings **MOODY'S** basic ratings are, in descending order of quality, Aaa, Aa, A, Baa, Ba, B, Caa, Ca, and C. In April 1982, Moody's began adding the numerical modifiers 1, 2, and 3 in each rating classification from Aa through B. The 1 represents the higher end of the generic rating, 2 the midrange, and 3 the lower end of the generic rating. Examples: Aa1, Aa3, Ba3.

STANDARD & POOR'S grades are AAA, AA, A, BBB, BB, and B; and plus and minus signs are added to grades AA through BB (as AA +, AA, AA −, etc.).

The style of writing, when words are spelled out, follows the pronunciation. *Plus* and *minus* are spelled out; even so care must be taken not to use the hyphen in such a way that it may be mistaken for a minus: *A bond rated triple A; a triple-A rated bond; a single A minus* (or *plus*) *bond*. But *a double-B rated bond*, not *a double-B-rated bond* (the bonds are rated *double-B*, not *double-B minus*).

bonified A corruption of BONA FIDE. Not to be used.

booby trap Slang for a hidden or unsuspected hazard: *The action by the government had the effect of inserting a booby trap into every procurement contract.*

—**booby-trap,** verb: *They were booby-trapped into the costly project by a fast-talking promoter.*

book In publishing parlance, a magazine or any single issue: *preparing for the November book with a thirty-two-page advertising insert/put the book to bed* [sent the magazine to press]. Compare SHEET.

book-entry Adjective descriptive of securities for which computer records are kept, but no certificates are issued: *a book-entry transaction/book-entry securities.*

—**book entry,** noun: *Ownership of the securities is attested by book entry.*

bookkeeper, bookkeeping Spelled with two *k*'s (book + keep-): *needed a bookkeeper/a bookkeeping function.*

boondoggle A trivial or pointless activity: *called the project a billion-dollar boondoggle.* Also a verb: *The city council boondoggles while striking bus drivers stay off the job.*

boost In general usage, to raise (as a salary or dividend) or give a lift to: *boosted the annual dividend to $2/boosted their morale/boosted Patrick's candidacy.* Also a noun: *a boost in the dividend/gave the drive a needed boost.*

booster Informal for an active supporter: *one of the club's most enthusiastic boosters.*

borax house   Slang for a store, especially a furniture house, selling shoddy goods.

boss   Acceptable in general usage for *employer, supervisor, manager, foreman*, etc., though any one of these synonyms may be preferred for its special CONNOTATION.

both . . . and   See CORRELATIVES.

bottleneck   Any hindrance or obstruction to performance: *The bottleneck was caused by a malfunctioning conveyor belt/I was the bottleneck.*

bottom line   The last line of a financial statement, the net profit; and, by extension, a much overworked term for the culmination or definitive part of anything: *Capital investment decisions must not be made in the expectation of an immediate effect on the bottom line/The bottom line is that wage increases must be limited to seven percent/The bottom line in reducing community tensions is jobs/Let's start with the bottom line: Despite the fifty thousand remedies on druggists' shelves, there is no cure for the common cold/The bottom line for the traveler is that an agency is only as competent as the particular travel counselor you deal with.*

bottom out   To reach a low point from which a rise can be expected; often used in reference to the state of the economy and stock prices: *It is expected that the recession will bottom out in the late fall/Big Steel bottomed out at 21¼.*

bounce   1. Informal as a verb denoting the return of a check by the bank, usually for lack of funds: *The check bounced.* Also used transitively: *The bank bounced their $800 check.*
    2. Slang, to dismiss from employment: *bounced for taking too many days off.*

boutique   A small shop, sometimes contained within a larger store, specializing in select fashions and accessories. The word is strained in such usages as "book boutique," "health foods boutique," and "the firm having evolved into a classic research 'boutique.' "

brace   The symbol { or } used to group two or more lines of figures or words, especially in charts, tables, and mathematical formulas. The point of the brace faces away from the lines that are to be joined.

bracket creep   The phenomenon whereby increases in income, caused by inflation, propel the taxpayer into higher tax brackets even when there is no real rise in income: *a victim of bracket creep*. See also **IN-DEXING**.

brackets [ ] Sometimes called "square brackets" to distinguish them from **PARENTHESES** ("round brackets").
USES:

1. To enclose an addition to a text, especially a quotation, by someone other than the writer. The addition may consist of an explanation, comment, or correction. Parentheses are sometimes more convenient, but they can be mistaken for part of the original text. See also **SIC**.

In the words of the article, "Only one of the ten biggest coal companies [North American Coal] is independently owned and managed."

"This [the corruption of the poor by social paternalism] is precisely what has happened in the United States."

". . . and I for one will never let my country down." [Applause]

"In the past year renewals came to *30 percent over the preceding year*." [Emphasis added]

2. To enclose the missing parts of a date from a letter that is being transcribed: February 7 [1984].

3. To enclose a parenthetic statement already enclosed in parentheses.

(Cited by W. Allen Wallis in *An Ungoverned Society* [New York: Free Press, 1976])

brainstorming A technique of some business **MEETINGS** whereby the participants begin by putting forward ideas in rapid succession without discussion or analysis. The ideas are then sorted out, with some being discarded quickly while others are examined more closely for their possible value. Also, loosely, any rapid-fire exchange of views.

—brainstorm, verb: *First we talk to the broker and brainstorm with him to determine our common interests.*

brand name 1. The distinctive name given to a product or line of products, as Fritos, Ajax, Ivory, Del Monte, Calvin Klein, 3M. See also Trade Names at **CAPITALS** 23.

2. Owners of brand names like Kleenex, Coke, Xerox, and Sanka object with good reason to the generic use of those names, as in "a box of kleenex," meaning any tissues, and "a cup of sanka," meaning any decaffeinated coffee. One of the measures used to protect a famil-

iar brand name is to link the word *brand* to the brand name, as in "Sanka brand decaffeinated coffee," a formula repeated frequently in Sanka's television commercials.

3. Some advertisers misrepresent unfamiliar brands by using the term "brand" or "brand name" to give the impression that the names are well known and that the goods are of superior quality: *The brand name is on every garment/Men's clothing at half price—well-known brand names/Sale of brand-name television sets.*

Brand X The name once customarily assigned to the anonymous competitor with which an advertised product was compared. The fact that Brand X was chosen for its weaknesses invariably gave the advertised product the advantage. Competition has sharpened in recent years, however, and it has become practice to compare competing brands by name. See **COMPARATIVE CLAIMS** 2.

bread and butter Informal for "livelihood": *The brand-name goods are our bread and butter.*

—bread-and-butter, adjective: *a bread-and-butter sideline;* also expressive of thanks for hospitality extended: *a bread-and-butter note.*

break 1. A sudden downward movement in prices: *Stocks fell by eleven points before the break was halted.* 2. Informal for "advantage" or "happy chance": *Investors will get a break from the IRS if the new legislation becomes law/The manager's resignation was a break for Sloan.*

break down To analyze or consider by parts or classes: *The circulation was broken down to show both geographic and demographic characteristics.* Care must be taken, however, not to create a ludicrously ambiguous statement: *Readers were broken down by sex and age.*

—breakdown, noun: *The breakdown will show a circulation gain in large metropolitan areas.*

brief To instruct, inform, fill in, summarize: *I'll brief you about the meeting when I get back.* Also, as a noun, an abstract or synopsis; a memorandum summarizing the evidence or points in law for use in a legal proceeding: *a whiz at preparing a brief.*

briefing A concise oral presentation of information or instructions: *Grant provided the briefing/We were asked to attend a briefing on the new payroll procedures.*

bring, take *Bring* is properly used to denote action toward the speaker or writer; and *take*, to denote action away from the speaker or writer: *Please bring the draft of the contract with you/Now take the application to Window 3.* See also FETCH.

broke Informal for "without funds" or "bankrupt": *He's broke/If the company goes broke, the investors stand to lose the most.*

broker An agent or go-between: *a stockbroker, a real-estate broker.* But also used as a verb: *The sale was brokered (negotiated) by Huberth & Peters.*

brokering See -ING.

brown-bag it To bring one's lunch, usually a sandwich, from home; an expression of BLUE-COLLAR chic, exhibited boldly by would-be sophisticates: *I've been brown-bagging it.*

brunet, brunette See BLOND, BLONDE.

B school A graduate school of business, of which Harvard's is a prominent example: *Even the B schools can produce bad managers/A B-school degree practically guarantees a high starting salary.*

buck slip See ROUTING SLIP.

bug 1. A small, inconspicuously placed microphone for electronic eavesdropping: *A bug was suspected in the leak of information from the chief's office.* Also a verb: *suspected that the room had been bugged.*
2. Usually in the plural, a reference to fanciful creatures—kin to hobgoblins and gremlins—to whom problems, mechanical and otherwise, are often attributed: *The computer program will be all right once we get all the bugs out/The test for interviewers was found to have some bugs.*
See also DEBUGGING.

bulk In general usage, *bulk* may stand for "most" or "the major part"; it is especially appropriate when the mass rather than a countable number is involved: *The bulk of the work can be done by unskilled labor/We believe the bulk of our retailers will want to stock the bonus packs.* But (countable numbers): *Among the retailers polled, the majority* (rather than *bulk*) *indicated they would stock the bonus packs.*

bullet In printing, a bold dot (●) often placed before each of a series of coordinate paragraphs to give them prominence. See also ENUMERATION.

bullion Gold or silver considered in mass as distinguished from its value; also gold or silver in bars or ingots: *The bullion is kept in vaults secure even from an atomic blast.*

bump Informal for "oust" or "displace." 1. In airline practice, to deny, because of overbooking, the boarding privilege to an airline passenger with a confirmed reservation. FAA regulations require compensation and alternate arrangements for passengers so discommoded: *Three passengers were bumped from the flight to Atlanta.*
2. In industry, to replace a worker by one with more seniority: *The workers being bumped are precisely those with young families and heavily mortgaged homes.*

bunch A connected group of like things; a cluster: *a bunch of bananas.* Also, informal, a group of people: *a bunch of us.* But, nonstandard: *Is there anybody who couldn't use a bunch of cash?*

bundle 1. Slang for an indefinite sum of money: *We can save you a bundle/It's a big benefit for your employees that won't cost you a bundle/Lang Hancock made a bundle in iron ore.*
2. To offer a set of components or otherwise related products at a single price: *They're working on a bundled system, with software, printer, and data storage device combined in a package.*
—**bundling,** noun: *By bundling the whole system and selling it as a package, the company is able to take its profit up front.* Compare UN-BUNDLING.

burglarize Used without objection for "commit burglary": *burglarized the premises.*

burglary Breaking into and entering a premises to commit a felony. Compare with THEFT and ROBBERY.

burgle Informal for "burglarize": *What is there to burgle in an empty loft?*

burst In advertising, a synonym for FLIGHT. See also BUST.

bus The plural is *buses* (preferred) or *busses.*

businessman, businesswoman Both are also spelled as two words: *business man, business woman.* But: *business men and women* (not *businessmen and women*).

business English 1. A term used mainly to denote the correct use of English in business, with emphasis on such matters as grammar, word use, spelling, and punctuation, and sometimes also the form and composition of business letters.

2. Because of the JARGON and STEREOTYPED LETTER PHRASES associated with business English, the term is often used as a PEJORATIVE; hence, it is not uncommon for employees to be advised, "Avoid business English; write naturally, as if you were talking."

Business Reply Mail Preaddressed cards and envelopes on which postage is paid by the addressee when they are returned. A permit is required, and an extra fee is charged for each piece returned. The U.S. Postal Service prescribes the printed form to be used.

bust A corruption of the verb *burst (has burst, is bursting), bust* has many common meanings, all of them classified as slang or informal. Slang: *The pipe bust (burst); luckily, it busted (burst) after business hours/The sergeant was busted to patrolman (reduced in rank)/The con man was busted (arrested).* Informal: *I'm bust (without funds)/The company's bust (bankrupt)/No account executive wants his trades busted (canceled).*

—**bust up.** Slang for "destroy": *Shifting cargo can bust up manufactured goods like furniture and TVs—even damage trucks, trailers, and railroad cars themselves.*

but 1. Despite some academic strictures, a sentence may acceptably begin with the conjunction *but* (just as it may begin with AND). The result is a less formal but more emphatic statement than one in which the *but* clause is part of the preceding sentence: *In many jobs women have a decided edge. But great obstacles to advancement remain.* (Compare with: *In many jobs women have a decided edge, but great obstacles to advancement remain.*) See also HOWEVER 1 and 2.

2. As a preposition meaning "except," *but* is followed by a pronoun in the objective case: *They will accept anyone but him as arbitrator/I wouldn't give the task to anyone but her.* To avoid awkwardness, however, an exception is usually made when the *but* links a grammatical subject with an immediately following pronoun: *No one but I* (rather than *me*) *can make that decision/Anyone but she* (rather than *her*) *would have faltered.* In these instances the *but* is construed as a conjunction, which requires that the following pronoun take the nominative case, like the subject to which it is linked. See also PRONOUNS 2(a).

3. The *but* in *won't take but a minute* creates a DOUBLE NEGATIVE. Better: *won't take a minute* (or *will take only a minute*).

but that "Do not doubt," is followed by *that* or *but that: I do not doubt that* (or *but that*) *you are right*. After a negative other than "do not doubt," the *but* gives the expression a positive CONNOTATION: *I do not know but that you are right* (that is, *You may be right*). Compare: *I do not know that you are right*. See also DOUBT.

but what Nonstandard for BUT THAT: *I do not know but what you are right*.

buy Generally acceptable for "bargain" in the commercial sense: *At $5,200, the copier is a real buy*.

buyback See at GIVEBACK.

buzz Informal for a telephone call: *Give me a buzz*. Also a verb: *Buzz me when you get a chance*.

buzz session 1. A small discussion group, usually one of several formed by dividing a larger group. The purpose is to give everyone a chance for expression on a subject already presented to the entire assembly by the main speaker. At the end of a specified period, a representative chosen by each group may present its views or direct its questions to the platform.
2. Any small-group meeting devoted to a free discussion of a designated topic.

buzz word Also *buzzword* (one word). 1. A technical, or "insider's," term adapted to popular use. EXAMPLES: BOTTOM LINE, EXTRAPOLATE, INFRASTRUCTURE, REINDUSTRIALIZATION. Compare CODE WORD.
2. Also, a common term that has taken on new significance.

To whom can school administrators turn to keep struggling school systems afloat? Why, to corporations, of course. And indeed "corporate support" has become the new *buzz word* in the education community.

Fiber became a *buzz word* in the mid-1970s as nutrition researchers studied the link between low-fiber diets and diet-related illnesses.

by hand See at HAND.

byte In data processing, the rough equivalent of one typed character: *The basic model includes 128K* (about 128,000) *bytes of internal memory*.

C

C ROMAN NUMERAL for 100. Also the abbreviation of CENTURY (slang for $100).

©, c., C., cop. COPYRIGHT, as in *c. 1983*. In a printed work, the copyright notice takes the form: *Copyright © 1983*.

ca. CIRCA: *an oriental vase, ca. 1856*.

CAB Civil Aeronautics Board, an independent U.S. agency charged with promoting and regulating the civil air-transport industry, with particular regard to its commercial activities. See also FAA.

CAD ACRONYM for *c*omputer-*a*ssisted *d*esign, a system for the computerized drafting of architectural and engineering plans.

cadre Pronounced *kad*-ree. A group of trained personnel usually forming the nucleus of a larger group: *A cadre of top civil servants gave up certain rights to job protection in return for the chance to win bonuses for superior performance/By the spring of 1978, West had gathered a cadre of experienced engineers to build the Eagle* [microcomputer].

calculate To RECKON or make an estimate; to determine mathematically: *calculate the interest*. Also dialectal (see USAGE) for "think" or "suppose": *I calculate (think) we can always beat the competition*.

calculated risk A considered risk, one undertaken with some forethought: *Many contractors may take a calculated risk in not certifying to a known conflict of interest*.

can Slang, to dismiss or discharge (a worker). The informal word is *fire: canned him for absenteeism*.

can, may Traditionally, *can* denotes ability; and *may*, permission: *We can easily make the delivery on schedule/May I prepare a letter for your signature? Can*, however, is often and acceptably used in both senses: *Can I hear from you soon?/You can take your vacation anytime*.

The line between *can* and *may* is especially blurred in negative statements and negative questions: *You cannot* (or *may not*) *enter the office without knocking/Why can't I?* (preferred to *Why mayn't I?* and *Why may I not?* because of their awkwardness).

canceled, cancelled   The first spelling is preferred.

canned   Informal for "prepared in advance"; also "recorded" or "taped": *a canned editorial* [one provided by a trade association, for example, to be printed in some of the less independent newspapers without attribution]/*canned (recorded) music/canned applause* [applause added to the sound track of a recorded performance].

cannot, can not   *Cannot* is preferred.

cannot but, cannot help but   Both terms are rather forced, but the first is the stiffer of the two: *I cannot but feel that we could have been more generous* (Compare with: *I cannot help but feel that we could have been more generous*). But (a more natural alternative to both): *I cannot* (or *can't*) *help feeling that we could have been more generous.*

cannibalize   To strip a car, airplane, or other machine of usable parts for the repair of other equipment: *built their air fleet from cannibalized parts.*

can't seem   Informal for "seems unable," or "does not seem able": *They can't seem (seem unable, do not seem able) to agree on the correct procedure.*

canvass   So spelled (double *s*). To solicit orders, opinions, votes, etc.; to make a survey, to poll: *We'll canvass for orders house-to-house/Customers will be canvassed to determine their preferences.* Also a noun: *The recent canvass showed a general dissatisfaction with the cafeteria food.*

cap   1. A maximum limit or CEILING: *voted a cap of 50 percent [tax] on personal service income/put a cap on advertising expenditures.*
2. A capital letter. See CAPITALS.

capital   1. Any material assets; also the collective value of things owned: *The couple included a small portfolio of stocks and bonds among their capital.*
2. The amount needed to start an enterprise or remain in business: *had to raise enough capital to keep them going until they could realize the income from their patents.*

3. In accounting, the worth of a company after allowances have been made for the payment of all debts; the net worth: *The company's capital is well over $2 billion.*

capital, capitol   *Capital* (the city) is usually lowercased: *arrived at the capital in midafternoon. Capitol* (the building) is usually capitalized: *was received at the Capitol by members of both parties.*

capital gain (loss)   A *capital gain* is a profit realized from the sale of a plant, stock, real estate, or other capital asset. Tax rates generally favor long-term capital gains, that is, assets held for longer than the minimum period (usually six months) required by law.

A *capital loss* is incurred when an asset is sold for less than it cost. A capital loss can be deducted from a capital gain or in other ways be used to reduce tax liability.

capital goods   Also producer goods. All goods used to produce other goods; includes especially machinery, tools, and equipment. Capital goods contrast with *consumer goods*—food and clothing, for instance—which are bought to satisfy human wants.

capital-intensive   Descriptive of an industry or a particular company requiring a large amount of capital relative to labor or land: *The oil companies and the public utilities are capital-intensive.* Compare **LABOR-INTENSIVE.**

capitals   Also, for short, "caps," and from their historical position in the printer's type box, "uppercase" (u.c.); similarly, small letters are "lowercase" (l.c.).

To "capitalize" a word usually signifies capitalization of the initial letter only. The term "all caps" or "solid caps" is used when it is intended that all the letters in a word or words be capitalized.

Apart from the practice of capitalizing the first word of a sentence and the particular, or "proper," name of a person, place, or thing, the use of capitals is very much a matter of discretion. Where choice governs, the criteria of selection come down to taste, clarity, and consistency—the last necessarily sacrificed at times to the other two.

In many instances, management ensures some uniformity in capitalization by prescribing the style for names and titles within the company and for the special terms associated with its business. With good reason, for example, a law office will specify that *will*, standing for a testamentary document, be spelled with an initial capital.

1. Abbreviations. 2. Abstract nouns. 3. Calendar divisions. 4. Coined names. 5. Companies and institutions. 6. Derivatives of proper names. 7. First words. 8. Geographic references. 9. Government references. 10. Historical periods and eras. 11. Holidays and holy days. 12. Hyphened compounds. 13. Numerical prefixes. 14. Persons. 15. Political parties. 16. Racial and ethnic references; languages. 17. Religious references. 18. Single letters. 19. Streets and avenues. 20. Structures and landmarks. 21. Titles and headings. 22. Titles of office. 23. Trade names. 24. Transport.

1. Abbreviations. An abbreviation is normally capitalized when the word it stands for is capitalized, but many abbreviations of common names are also capitalized, as NNW (north northwest) and C/D (certificate of deposit). The abbreviations of academic degrees and professional certifications are always capitalized.

30° F.	RCA	Ph.D.
Feb. 20	Gen. H. C. M. Walker	C.P.A.

See also **ABBREVIATIONS** 3 in the main vocabulary.

2. Abstract nouns. In formal writing, abstract nouns representing ideals, concepts, and institutions are sometimes capitalized.

respect for Honor and Truth
before Fate steps in
the separation of Church and State
in the annals of Big Business

3. Calendar divisions. January, February/Monday, Tuesday/ Spring 1986 (*But:* spring, summer, fall, winter).

4. Coined names. The Big Board (New York Stock Exchange)/Fanny Mae (Federal National Mortgage Association)/the Bay State (Massachusetts)/the Miracle Mile (a street lined with exclusive shops).

5. Companies and institutions. (a) The names of companies and their distinctive shortened forms are capitalized. The article *the* before a proper name is not capitalized unless it is an integral part of the name.

Union Carbide Corporation, Union Carbide, Carbide
Chemical Bank, the Chemical, Chemical

Yale University, Yale
Metropolitan Opera House, the Metropolitan, the Met
the Sony Corporation. *But (article capitalized):* The Texas Company, The Custom Shop.

A plural common noun following the distinctive name of two or more companies is not capitalized.

the 3M and Mobil corporations
the Plymouth and Lerner shops

(b) The common-name substitute for an organization's name is customarily capitalized by those employed by the organization, but not necessarily by outsiders except in recognition of the organization's importance.

the Corporation/the corporation
the Company/the company
the Bank/the bank
the Museum/the museum
the Foundation/the foundation

(c) The names of departments and other subdivisions and their distinctive short forms are usually capitalized by those within the organization.

Data Processing Division, Data Processing
Personnel Department, Personnel
Corporate Trust Department, Corporate Trust

Outsiders are less particular about such capitalization except when the distinctive name is important to prevent confusion. Hence they are more likely to capitalize the name *Personnel Training Section* (or *Personnel Training*) than *Personnel Department;* and while they may be indifferent to capitalizing *Manufacturing Department*, they are likely to capitalize *Manufacturing* as its shortened substitute.

Within an organization, usage is divided on capitalizing such common-name substitutes as *department, division,* and *section.* Employees will, for instance, write "the Department," but "our department." An outsider would be inclined to lowercase *department* without distinction, as in "the department" and "your department."

6. DERIVATIVES OF PROPER NAMES. Words derived from proper names are usually capitalized.

a Californian	Keynesian economics
Swedish meatballs	Arabic (also arabic) numerals

Not capitalized are words long dissociated from their proper source-words.

macadam (after John L. McAdam)   china (porcelain ware)
mesmerize (after Franz Mesmer)   japanned (varnished)
venetian blinds   turkish towels

Some exceptions: Irish whiskey, Mendelian theory, Jersey cow.

7. FIRST WORDS.   (a) The first word of a sentence and of a formal quotation is capitalized. See also QUOTATION MARKS.

Ask yourself, "Where else can you get a better value?"

(b) The first word of a direct question within a declarative statement is capitalized. See also QUESTION MARK.

At this point you may well ask, If the cost of vanquishing inflation is so terrible, what is the cost of simply tolerating it?

(c) Following a COLON, the first word is capitalized if it marks the beginning of a full sentence. The article in a literary title following a colon is also capitalized.

The terms of the agreement were simple: We had to deliver the specified goods within 60 days.

Marketing in Turbulent Times: The Challenge and the Opportunities.

(d) A statement in PARENTHESES begins with a capital only if the parentheses stand outside the preceding sentence.

The last three stores in the chain were closed yesterday. (The others had previously been sold.)

But: . . . yesterday (the others had previously been sold).

(e) The first word of the SALUTATION and COMPLIMENTARY CLOSE of a letter is capitalized.

Dear Mr. Farnum   Very truly yours,
My dear Mrs. Dorsey   Yours sincerely

8. GEOGRAPHIC REFERENCES.   (a) Capitalized are the names or nicknames of continents, regions, mountains, oceans, countries, states, cities, and other geographic entities.

Asia	Germany	Chicago
the Near East	Argentina	the Big Apple
the Americas	Nigeria	Marin County
the Pacific Ocean	New Hampshire	Manhattan
the Rockies	the Wheat Belt	Federal Plaza

(b) Words like *ocean, river, lake,* and *mountain* are capitalized when they are part of a proper name, but seldom otherwise. When plurals of some of the same words follow a proper name, usage on capitalization varies.

the Snake River

the Ohio and Missouri rivers

the Great Lakes, the Finger Lakes

the Bering Sea, the Indian Ocean

the Rock of Gibraltar; the Rock [its familiar name] *[But:* the Strait of Gibraltar; the strait]

the Leeward Islands *[But:* the East River islands]

the Adirondack and Allegheny Mountains [each of the two names takes the plural anyway]

(c) Words like *state, city,* and *county* are capitalized when they immediately follow a proper name, but except in formal or official use they are usually lowercased when they precede a proper name or are separated from it.

GENERAL USE:

Washington State, *but* the state of Washington, the state

Kansas City, *but* the city of Kansas, the city

Dade County, *but* the county of Dade, the county

the village of Armonk, the village

Greenwich Village, *but* the Village (the shortened name of a distinctive neighborhood, not that of a political subdivision)

ALSO:

the state officials, the city council

payment of state and city taxes

the county offices

a meeting of the village supervisors

FORMAL OR OFFICIAL USE:

the State of New York, the State, the City of New York

the Incorporated Village of Armonk, the Village

the State officials, the City charter, the County offices

a meeting of the Borough supervisors

9. GOVERNMENT REFERENCES. (a) Words like *government, federal*, and *administration* are capitalized when they are part of a proper name or stand for the government in power. Lowercasing is favored when the words are only descriptive or are used in a general sense. Admittedly, the line between the usages is not always clear.

a department of the Federal Government

the Administration's measure

the British Government, the Government
the French Republic, the Republic

the Federal Aviation Administration
the Government Printing Office
the National Archives

a Federal grand jury   under Federal authority
the Federal budget   the Federal income tax

BUT ALSO:

the federal government
federal income taxes
government regulations
administration policies
a national referendum

(b) The full names of legislative, administrative, and other officially constituted governmental bodies are capitalized, but their common-name substitutes are capitalized only as a sign of their importance or the special respect due them.

an urgent meeting of the Cabinet
the U.S. Congress, the 98th Congress, the Senate, the House of Representatives, the House
the U.S. Supreme Court, the Court
the Treasury Department, the Department of State; the Department (*also* Treasury, State)
the Air Force, the Army, the Navy, the Armed Forces
the President's Council on Youth Opportunity, the Council
the New Jersey State Senate, the Senate; *also* the State senate, the state Senate, the senate
the Civil Court, the court; *but (in reference to the judge),* the Court declared
the New York Board of Health, the New York board of health, the board of health, the Board, the board
the Hempstead Public Library, the Hempstead public library, the library

(c) The distinctive names of government programs and official indexes are selectively capitalized.

Social Security   Gross National Product (*also* gross national product)
Medicare   Consumer Price Index (*also* consumer price index)
But (lowercase only): food stamps, energy grants, draft registration

10. HISTORICAL PERIODS AND ERAS.

the Industrial Revolution   the Great Depression
the Gay Nineties   the Era of Good Feeling
But: the atomic age, the age of lowered expectations, the office revolution

11. HOLIDAYS AND HOLY DAYS.

Christmas   Washington's Birthday
New Year's Day   the Fourth of July
Yom Kippur   Thanksgiving

12. HYPHENED COMPOUNDS.   Proper nouns and adjectives forming a hyphened compound are capitalized. See also Par. 21, "Titles
and headings."

the English-American connection
the president-elect
post-World War II
non-Catholics

13. NUMERICAL PREFIXES.   A noun or its abbreviation is usually
capitalized when it describes a following figure or letter. See also
NUMERALS 7(b).

Proposition 12   Room 4200
Certificate No. 1347   File 659-X2

Exceptions are made for minor literary references, as in a footnote:
vol. 2, page 6, line 5, note 3.

14. PERSONS.   Everett D. Sloan, Mary Kenworthy; Kathy, David,
Don. Such particles as *de, du,* and *della* are not ordinarily capitalized unless they begin a sentence or stand without a first name or
title: Alexis de Tocqueville, *but* De Tocqueville. Usage is divided
on the capitalization of *van* and *von:* Miës van der Rohe, but Robert
Van de Graaff. In all instances, the style used by the individual named
prevails.

15. POLITICAL PARTIES.   The names of the political parties, but
not their common-name substitutes, are capitalized. Also capitalized
are the names given the adherents of those parties.

the Republican Party (*or* Republican party), the party
the Democratic (*not* Democrat) Party (*or* party), the party
a Republican, a Democrat, a Conservative (*for party affiliation only*), a
   party member

16. RACIAL AND ETHNIC REFERENCES; LANGUAGES.

Caucasian, *but* whites, nonwhites
Negroes, *but* blacks *or* Blacks

Indian, Japanese, Arab, Arabic
Indo-European, Eurasian, Semitic
English, French, Sanskrit

17. RELIGIOUS REFERENCES.   (a) Names of religious bodies and
their creeds, and words descriptive of their members are capitalized.

Protestant, Catholic, Catholicism
Presbyterian, Presbyterianism, the Presbyterian Church
Hebrew, Hebraic, Judaism
Christian, Christianity; Islam, Islamic

(b) Names describing the Supreme Being, members of the Trin-
ity, and sacred writings are capitalized.

God, *but* a god, godlike
the Almighty, the Son, the Holy Spirit
Muhammad, the Messiah, Providence
the Bible (*but* Biblical *or* biblical)
the Ten Commandments
the Koran, Koranic; the Talmud, Talmudic

(c) A pronoun standing for the name of the Deity is usually
capitalized; exceptions are most likely when the pronoun is close
to its reference and no ambiguity is likely.

We deliver ourselves unto Him.
May God in his compassion look after us all. [Pronoun *his* close to the
name of the Deity.]
But: God, the minister said, loved the meanest of His flock. [A lowercase
h would make *his* ambiguous.]

18. SINGLE LETTERS.   The interjection *O* and the pronoun *I* are
always capitalized; so, too, any letter standing alone or part of a hyphened compound.

General Motors J cars   A-frame
rated B   I-beam
Model D   U-turn

19. STREETS AND AVENUES.   The words *Street, Avenue, Road,*
and the like are capitalized when they follow specific street names
or numbers. See also ADDRESSES 3.

Beale Street   Ocean Drive
Michigan Boulevard   79th Road
Cedar Lane   23d Street
Wall Street (*also, to the financial community,* the Street)
Fifth Avenue (*also, distinctively,* the Avenue)

20. STRUCTURES AND LANDMARKS.

the old Custom House   O'Hare International Airport
the Empire State Building   the Golden Gate Bridge
Peachtree Center   the Capitol
the Merchandise Mart   the Guggenheim Museum

21. TITLES AND HEADINGS. (a) By custom, the principal words of a title or heading are capitalized. Those words include the first and last words and all other words, except articles, and all prepositions and conjunctions of, usually, five letters or more. The first word of a subtitle following a colon is also capitalized.

Notice of Annual Meeting of Shareholders
Letter from the Chairman of the Board
Looking After the Consumers' Interests
Venture Marked by Success and Growth
What We Aim For
Retirement at Seventy: A New Trauma for Management

(b) Also capitalized are the parts of a hyphenated compound that would be capitalized if they were not part of a compound. However, usage is divided on capitalizing the second part of a compound numeral.

Pitfalls in Medium-Term Planning
Report of the Secretary-Treasurer
Church-in-the-Gardens Holds Bazaar
Mother-of-Pearl Collectibles
Paid-Up Insurance at Age 60
But: Proceedings of the Twenty-second Annual Meeting, *or* Proceedings of the Twenty-Second Annual Meeting

(c) Some publications specify initial capitals for all words in a headline.

Planning For Retirement At 55
Tips On Savings And Investments

22. TITLES OF OFFICE. (a) A title preceding a person's name is always capitalized.

General Grayson   Chairman Byrnes   Treasurer Reynolds

(b) A title of high public office, either standing alone or following the name of the officeholder is also capitalized.

the President   the Governor
Mr. Haynes, the Consul General

(c) A business title, either standing alone or following the name, is usually capitalized when the title refers to someone in the writer's organization, but seldom otherwise.

Within one's organization:
the Chairman
Mr. Carter, our Senior Vice President
Outside one's organization
the chairman
Mr. Carter, your senior vice president
See also INSIDE ADDRESS and ENVELOPE ADDRESS.

23. TRADE NAMES. (a) BRAND NAMES, TRADEMARKS, and SERVICE MARKS protected by patent or copyright are capitalized.

L'eggs (hosiery)	Vaseline Intensive Care
Crest (toothpaste)	Lilt Softperm
Complete (furniture polish)	New Freedom (sanitary pads)

(b) The name of a common product to which a trade name is appended is not usually capitalized except by the owner of the trade name: Campbell's soups (*but, in Campbell advertising,* Campbell's Soups), Bayer aspirin, Pond's cold cream.

(c) Generic names are not capitalized: a cola drink (*but* Coca-Cola *or* Coke), reserpine (a generic drug; *but* Serpasil, a brand name for the same drug).

24. TRANSPORT. The Metroliner, the Concorde, the Hellenic Star, the Chevrolet Citation. For the use of italics in such names, see ITALICS 1(a).

caption A short title or description accompanying a table, chart, picture, or other illustration; also, a heading or title of any kind.

captioned Identified by a caption: *a captioned photograph.* Also, JARGON; a reference, as in a letter, to the subject identified in the caption or SUBJECT LINE: *the captioned account (this account, the Brady account, the above account/the above-captioned policy numbers (the policy numbers listed above).* See also ABOVE 2.

CAR For *c*omputer-*a*ssisted *r*etrieval; a technology by which microfilm frames stored in cartridges can be accessed through a computer and displayed on a screen. Paper prints can also be made.

carat Abbreviated car. or c. Also, *karat,* abbreviated kt. or k. A unit of weight for precious stones and metals, equal to 200 milligrams. Not to be confused with CARET.

career, job   A career is one's lifework or PROFESSION. The word has a generally good CONNOTATION, suggesting status and permanence: *has not yet chosen a career*/"My Brilliant Career" [movie title]/*a career in management*. Compare VOCATION.

A job is a particular position: *sought a job as company treasurer*/*a job that pays well*/*a temporary job*.

"care" label   A government-required label on clothing stating what methods of cleaning can safely be used without harm to the fabric or garment. Usually accompanied by a FIBER LABEL.

caret   The symbol ∧ showing where an insertion is to be made in a line of written or printed matter. Not to be confused with CARAT.

carriage trade   Well-to-do patrons; a nostalgic reference to a clientele that would arrive in elegant horse-drawn vehicles: *The store still caters to the carriage trade*/*Swissair is convinced that its prosperity lies in going after the carriage trade of air travel*.
—**carriage-trade,** adjective: *Today's customers are a carriage-trade clientele, men and women comfortable in tailored suits during the week and chino pants on weekends*.

cartel   An association of independent enterprises formed to obtain a monopoly for its members through the control of production, pricing, and distribution. Cartels in domestic trade are not permitted by U.S. antitrust laws. Among international cartels, the Organization of Petroleum Exporting Countries (OPEC) is the most conspicuous example.
—**cartelize,** verb: *As cartelized markets give way to free markets, new opportunities are created for American business*.

case   Useful in such locutions as "in case of fire," "the case for the prosecution," and "the number of cases of influenza," but there is objection to its use as a substitute for the adverb *so,* or in a connecting phrase, where it is either unnecessary or cumbersome: *Pessimists in the trade forecast a trend away from luxury watches, but this was not to be the case (was not to be so)*/*Management wants to look into the case of the rising number of (look into the rising number of) complaints about poor workmanship*/*In the case of employees who do not enroll in the plan by October 1, the loan provision will not apply (The loan provi-*

sion will not apply to employees who do not enroll in the plan by October 1).

For grammatical case, see **PRONOUNS** 2.

cash flow Fluctuations in a company's cash position as a result of continuous changes in such contributory elements as depreciation, receivables, payables, and inventories. Not to be used, except perhaps facetiously, to denote ready cash: *Close attention to cash flow has given the company millions in cash that would otherwise have been sitting unproductive.* But: *The company does not have enough cash on hand* (not *cash flow*) *to meet the bank's note.* Also (facetious): *I'd lend you the sawbuck if my own cash flow wasn't already dried up.*

—**cash-flow,** adjective: *The bankcard enables the retailer to give customers speedy credit without assuming the credit risk or the cash-flow problems of an in-store credit system.*

casualty In an accident, a casualty includes any person injured, whether fatally or not: *Among the workers, the casualties were three injured and one dead.*

catalog, catalogue *Catalog* is preferred as a noun; *catalogue* as a verb: *Sears' catalog/catalogued* (rather than *cataloged*) *the reports.*

category So spelled (*not* cata-): *doesn't fit into any specific category* (class).

cats and dogs Low-priced stocks of highly questionable value: *a portfolio of cats and dogs.*

causative factor JARGON for "cause": *The causative factor (The cause) was the formation of mold spores in the filter.* See also **FACTOR.**

cautious optimism A trite but often necessarily guarded phrase: *The president expressed cautious optimism about the year-end figures/Cautious optimism has been voiced by the University of Michigan's econometric experts.* Finding substitutes for the phrase can present difficulties. To say, for example, that one is "guarded in his optimism" is to emphasize the reservation to the point of negating the optimism.

—**cautiously optimistic,** adjective phrase: *was cautiously optimistic in their assessment of the new line's impact on sales.*

caveat Pronounced *kay*-vee-ut (also *kav-* or *kahv-*). A formal term, from the Latin, for "warning" or "caution": *issued a caveat/added a ca-*

veat to the request. But **JARGON** as a verb: *Let me caveat that statement (issue the statement with a warning).*

caveat emptor Latin for "Let the buyer beware." The antithesis of *caveat venditor,* "Let the seller beware."

CD See **CERTIFICATE OF DEPOSIT.**

CEA Council of Economic Advisers. The three-member panel analyzes the economy and advises the President on economic developments. Publishes *Economic Indicators* (monthly) and an annual report.

CED The Committee for Economic Development, a group of business executives whose research and publications are influential in government and business.

ceiling A top limit or **CAP:** *a ceiling on prices/usury ceilings.* Antonym, **FLOOR.**

censor, censure *Censor* (verb or noun) relates to the prohibition of objectionable material, such as pictures and written or spoken words: *Luckily, the legal department censored the libelous copy before the advertisement appeared/The sponsor protested the network's attempt to censor the program/We do not want to become censors.*

Censure (verb or noun) relates to the expression of strong disapproval, although further action may also be taken: *In censuring the investment firm, the SEC stipulated that the company abstain from similar practices in the future/Censure is too lenient a punishment for a convicted embezzler.*

center A place of coordinated activity, ordinarily—but not necessarily—encompassing a number of stores, departments, or buildings: *Rockefeller Center, Roosevelt Field Shopping Center, Midtown Learning Center* (a college branch), *Citicorp Center* (the bank's main office). Also a vogue word: *Vacation Planning Center* (travel agency), *Pearle Vision Center* (eyeglasses), *Oster Kitchen Center* (an all-in-one kitchen blender and food processor), *Waldner's Resource Center for the Work Environment* (office supplies). Compare **COMPLEX.**

center around To speak of "centering around" is to ignore the meaning of *center* as a focal point. Correct idioms are *center on* (or *upon, in,* or *at*) and *revolve around* (or *about*): *Interest at the showing centered on the leisure clothes by Ralph Lauren/The trouble was centered in the computer's storage unit.*

centrex A telephone system through which incoming calls go direct to the extension of the party desired. This is possible because each extension has its own number. Callers not having the extension number may still reach their party through the company's switchboard by calling the company's listed number.

cents See NUMERALS 2.

cents-off coupon A coupon issued usually by the producer of a common household product, like soap or cereal, permitting the consumer to obtain from the dealer a reduction of a few cents or more from the regular purchase price. In turning the coupon back to the issuer, the dealer is allowed a nominal sum for handling in addition to the face value of the coupon.

century Slang for $100 or a $100 bill: *a century note/cost me a century*. Abbreviated C: *borrowed two C's*.

CEO Also c.e.o. CHIEF EXECUTIVE OFFICER.

certificate To authorize or license by issuance of a certificate: *No question of safety was raised when the FAA certificated the airliner/Wanted: certificated engineer*. Compare with CERTIFY and DEGREED.

certificate of deposit Abbreviated CD. A MONEY MARKET instrument earning a specified rate of interest over a stated period of time. CDs, also called time deposits, are subject to an interest penalty if redeemed before MATURITY.

certified check A check bearing the guarantee of the bank that funds to cover the check are on deposit and will be held until the check is paid.

certified mail A postal service that provides a receipt for the sender and a record of delivery at the office of address. In transit, the mail receives no special treatment, and no insurance is provided. Any mailable matter of no intrinsic value is accepted on payment of the first-class rate and the applicable fee. See also MAILING NOTATIONS.

certified professional secretary Abbreviated C.P.S. A professional title granted to qualified candidates who pass the nationwide examination given by Professional Secretaries International through its Institute for Certifying Secretaries.

certified public accountant   Abbreviated C.P.A. A professional title granted to qualified candidates who pass the examination and meet the educational and work requirements of the American Institute of Certified Public Accountants.

certified purchasing manager   Abbreviated C.P.M. A professional title granted by the National Association of Purchasing Management to members who pass the association's examination and otherwise qualify by reason of education and experience. Members must be recertified every five years until they reach age 55 or have fifteen years' experience.

certify   To give formal or official endorsement when certain standards have been met: *certify a check/a diploma certifying completion of the degree requirements/will certify to my qualifications.*

chair   Regularly used in such phrases as "chaired the meeting," "took the chair," and "the chair recognizes." However, there is some objection to the use of *chair* as a neuter substitute for the person occupying the chair: *Election of a chair will take place on February 28.* See also CHAIRMAN, CHAIRWOMAN, CHAIRPERSON.

chairman, chairwoman, chairperson   *Chairman* may signify a man or a woman. A female chairman is also called a *chairwoman,* but not a *chairlady. Chairperson,* a title designating either sex, is now customary in organization bylaws: *Committee chairpersons shall be appointed by the president.* To many, however, the term *chairperson* seems incongruous in referring to the actual holder of the office by name: *Robert Pastore will serve as chairperson (chairman)/The chairperson (chairwoman) is Sandra Mandel.* See also CHAIR.

Chapter 11   A section of the Federal Bankruptcy Act under which a company continues to operate with the court's protection against lawsuits while it tries to work out a plan for paying its debts: *There was still a chance that the creditors would throw the company into Chapter 11 proceedings.*

charge card, credit card   A distinction is made between cards like those issued by American Express and Diners Club, on the one hand, and Visa and MasterCard, on the other. The first, also called T & E cards (for "Travel and Entertainment") are "charge cards," requiring outstanding balances to be paid in full each month. The others are "credit cards," permitting bills to be paid either in full within a stated period, without interest, or in installments with interest added. Compare **DEBIT CARD**.

chartered accountant Abbreviated C.A. A member of a British institute of accountants granted a royal charter; the equivalent of a **CERTIFIED PUBLIC ACCOUNTANT** in this country.

charts If certain theorists are correct, the prevalence of pictures has made us less tolerant of words. However true that may be, there is no question that visual representations command attention and reduce the need for words.

Graphs and tables are used extensively to display numerical data. Although they are often referred to as charts, the term *charts* also includes diagrams, maps, outlines, checklists, and similar forms.

The versatility of charts permits them to be put on a chalkboard, projected on a screen, or enlarged and displayed on a stand. And just as a speaker addresses each chart as it is displayed, so it is important for the writer to make specific reference to each chart accompanying a report. The speaker, however, has the added responsibility of removing each chart from display after it has served its purpose; otherwise, it becomes a distraction.

See also **NONVERBAL COMMUNICATION** and **TABULAR SUMMARIES**.

cheap price A price is low, not cheap; however, one may refer to a cheap meal or cheap goods. But since *cheap* may mean *low* in either price or quality, or both, the word should be used with caution. Unambiguous: *For sale, cheap; late model Buick Skylark*. Ambiguous: *Cheap watches will be found in the costume jewelry department, main floor* (Better: *Low-priced watches*). Prudent avoidance: *Premiat tastes like French wine, but it is a whole lot less expensive* (better than *a whole lot cheaper*.) See also **CONNOTATION**.

check Followed by *for*, rather than *of*, before an amount: *Thank you for your check for* (rather than *of*) *$75*. But: *Have you received our check of May 11?*

check into (on, upon) Good idioms for "investigate" or "look into": *check into the reasons for the loss/check on the number of items in stock/check up on Whitney's whereabouts*.

checkless society See at **EFT**.

checklist Also *check list*. A list of points to be checked off, verified, compared, or otherwise used as a reminder or guide; especially useful in instruction manuals and routine printed forms. See illustration at **ROUTING SLIP**.

checkoff The automatic deduction of union dues from a worker's salary for remission to the union. In some states the written consent of the worker is required. See also **AGENCY SHOP**.

cheque Chiefly British for *check* (a bank draft). Also, in the United States, the characteristic spelling of some travelers' checks: *American Express Travelers Cheques, MasterCard Travelers Cheques*.

chic Pronounced *sheek*. A synonym, to be used with discrimination, for such terms as *elegant, stylish, modish, fashionable, sophisticated* (in dress or manner): *a chic costume/the chic new fashion coordinator*.

chief executive officer Abbreviated CEO or c.e.o. The person principally concerned with the overall direction of a business enterprise: *Mr. Ingalls is president and chief executive officer*.

chintzy Gaudy or cheap: *The publisher's Shakespeare series includes photographs from the productions, but the typography is chintzy/The chintzy furnishings in the lobby set the tone for the hotel*. Also, from *chinchy* (U.S. dialect), miserly: *chintzy with a dollar*.

chit A small note or voucher attesting to a debt or credit: *Account holders were given chits purporting to be good at least for partial redemption of their losses at some unspecified date*.

circumstances Despite some quibbling, both ''under the circumstances'' and ''in the circumstances'' are well used: *I don't know what we would have done in (or under) the same circumstances/Under (or In) no circumstances will we permit a change in the formula*.

cliches These are commonplace expressions so stale that they are usually better avoided. When, however, a set phrase provides the clearest and briefest and handiest way to state an idea, that may be good enough reason to use it. No doubt such a phrase can be drawn occasionally even from the list of threadbare expressions that follows. See also **STEREOTYPED LETTER PHRASES**.

back to square one	the handwriting on the wall
grin and bear it	there's no quick fix
a whole new ball game	lock, stock, and barrel
rest on one's laurels	bigger and better than ever

few and far between	conspicuous by its absence
short and sweet	more than meets the eye
a drop in the bucket	leave no stone unturned
head and shoulders above	by leaps and bounds
last but not least	you'll be glad you did
you owe it to yourself	touch all bases
the frosting on the cake	bursting with pride
coming up to the wire	no free lunch
bet your bottom dollar	and much, much more

—old clichés, tired clichés. Both are redundancies: *You're paid to have ideas, not to repeat tired clichés* (omit *tired*). See **WORDINESS** 3.

client   1. A buyer of professional services: *a Coopers & Lybrand client.* Also, a synonym for *customer,* sometimes preferred by stores catering to a high-class trade.
2. A **EUPHEMISM** for one who depends on another's patronage: *a welfare client.*

clientele   A **PREPOSSESSIVE WORD** for the body of customers of a retail store: *Bergdorf's clientele.* Buyers of professional services are more likely to be called *clients: our attorney's clients.*

climactic, climatic   The two are often confused. *Climactic* pertains to a climax or high point; *climatic,* to climate: *a climactic event,* but *a pleasant climate.*

clipped forms   A shortened form of a word; used in conversation and informal writing, but not in a formal presentation. Clipped forms are pronounced as they are spelled and, unlike **ABBREVIATIONS**, they are not followed by a period except at the end of a sentence: **CAP, DEMO,** dorm, lab, limo, **PROF, REP.**

clock in   To punch a time clock or otherwise record the time of one's arrival for work: *All employees are required to clock in.*

clock out   To record the time of one's departure from work: *clocked out at 4:03 p.m.*

clock time   1. 12-hour system. (a) The day begins at midnight (12 A.M.); and noon (12 P.M.) is the midpoint. Since *12 a.m.* and *12 p.m.* can be confounded, however, they are better expressed as *12 midnight* and *12 noon.* See also **A.M., P.M.**

(b) The use of A.M. with *morning*, P.M. with *afternoon*, and A.M. or P.M. with *o'clock* is redundant.

6 A.M. (*not* 6 A.M. in the morning)

2 P.M. (*not* 2 P.M. in the afternoon)

8 o'clock (*not* 8 o'clock P.M. *or* 8 o'clock A.M.)

But (correct): six in the morning, two in the afternoon, 8 o'clock in the evening

(c) Ciphers are not used after even hours except in a mixed series or tabulation: *11 a.m.* (rather than *11:00 a.m.*) But: *performances at 2:00, 3:30, and 4:45 p.m.*

(d) In formal writing, numbers expressing time are spelled out: *at ten-thirty o'clock on Wednesday morning, the twenty-third of June.*

2. 24-hour system. In the 24-hour system—used in Europe and by the U.S. Armed Forces—the hours and minutes are given a four-digit number, and the abbreviations A.M. and P.M. are not used. Thus 1240 (European usage, 12:40) means 40 minutes past noon. Midnight is either 2400 or 0000. The first minute past midnight is 0001, and 1 A.M. is 0100. In speaking, one uses the terms "O one hundred hours," "twelve hundred and forty hours," "twenty-four hundred hours," etc.

close corporation   Variant of *closed corporation,* one in which stock is held by a small group, with little or none available for purchase by outsiders.

close down   Also *shut down.* To stop operations completely. Though redundant, *down* is part of the idiom: *The factory was closed down for the regular two-weeks vacation period.*

closed punctuation   Also *close punctuation.* A style, now obsolete, in which all the lines of the mechanical parts of the letter end with a punctuation mark. See **LETTER FORMAT** 5.

closed shop   A union establishment, one whose workers belong to a union or agree to join the union after they are hired. Compare with **AGENCY SHOP** and **OPEN SHOP**.

close proximity   Redundant, but common in informal usage: *spoke of the negative effects when ads for competing products are placed in close proximity (close to each other, close together, in close order, in proximity).* See also **WORDINESS** 3.

clothe A verb, to dress. The *th* is pronounced as in *the*. Not to be confused with the noun *cloth* (the fabric), pronounced with a soft *th: The city ordinance required stores to clothe nude mannequins/The woman was clothed by Geoffrey Beene.*

clothes A plural noun (it has no singular), preferably pronounced *kloze: Clothes are* (not *is*) *a significant item in the family's budget.*

clout Informal for "power," "influence": *With Jones as your representative, you have clout in Washington/MasterCard gives you clout.*

C.L.U. Chartered life underwriter. A professional title conferred by the insurance industry's American Society of Chartered Life Underwriters: *Charles Dolan, C.L.U.*

clutter The proliferation of advertising, especially in commercial broadcasting, with the consequent frequent and prolonged interruptions in program continuity: *Television clutter will eventually be curbed by competitive pressures among the media.*

Co. The abbreviation of COMPANY is used only after a specific company name: *Tiffany & Co.* See also NAMES 2.

C.O.D. Also *COD* or *c.o.d.* Cash (or collect) on delivery. A condition of sale, customary in the absence of prepayment or credit.

codeword Also *code word.* A word or phrase in common discourse signaling some meaning not denoted by the term itself; usually a deliberately deceptive EUPHEMISM for an idea the user prefers not to express in direct terms:

> One question on the ballot will be whether to take a "job action." That is a codeword Federal unions use when they mean strike or slowdown, both of which are illegal, but not impossible, in government. *[Wall Street Journal]*

> When on the job less than two months, he [Alfred Kahn] shocked other administration officials by warning publicly of a "deep, deep depression" if inflation weren't harnessed. To placate rattled colleagues, he then substituted "banana" as a codeword for depression. *[Newsday]*

coequal Equal with another in rank, responsibility, or the like: *The partners are coequal in making financial decisions.* Also a noun: *The partners are coequals/She is a coequal with Roswell in financial decisions.*

cognizant   *Aware* will usually do: *We have been cognizant (aware) of the condition for some time.* See **LONG WORDS AND SHORT**.

COLA   ACRONYM for *cost-of-living adjustment*, a feature of Social Security benefits and of many wage contracts: *The union threatens to strike if the COLA is eliminated.*

cold type   A method of typesetting by which flat copy is prepared for reproduction without the need for cast metal forms (hot type). Also, the type so set, as by photocomposition or computer-assisted typewriter.

colleague   The term is most aptly applied to an **ASSOCIATE** in the professions, especially a member of the staff of a college or university. In business, one also finds colleagues working as biologists, chemists, economists, etc., but in most instances, *associate* or *co-worker* is the more appropriate term.

collectable, collectible   Although the words are essentially interchangeable, a division in usage has become discernible.

Collectable is now usually reserved for reference to a debt: *The outstanding amount is still collectable/Our collectables come to over a million dollars.*

Collectible is the more likely name for an article of value, collected sometimes as a hobby, but often as an investment or as a hedge against the falling value of currency. Collectibles include rare coins, stamps, books, antiques, and objets d'art: *We can obtain buyers for your collectibles.*

collective nouns   A collective noun is a noun that, in its singular form, names a group of people or things: *company, department, board* (of directors), *personnel, committee, clientele, jury, dozen, remainder,* etc. The use of a collective noun may raise the question whether it is to be treated as singular or plural.

1. A plural collective noun *(committees, juries)* regularly takes a plural verb, as one would expect; but a singular collective noun takes a singular or plural verb depending on the sense. The verb is singular when the group represented by the collective noun is referred to as a unit: *The committee meets tomorrow/The jury is still deliberating/The board has no jurisdiction.* The verb is plural when the singular collective noun refers to members of the group as individuals: *The committee were not all of the same mind/The jury of ex-*

perts are at each other's throats/The board were invited to the reception/Civilian personnel are prohibited from entering this area.

2. A grammatical inconsistency occurs when, say, a correspondent dictates "the company is" and then refers to the company as "they" rather than "it." The problem can be resolved with a plural verb ("the company are") or a singular pronoun ("it"), but not without some awkwardness. The better solution is usually to allow the inconsistency, a minor sacrifice to the cause of common sense.

CONSISTENTLY SINGULAR: The company is a large manufacturer of office equipment. We value highly our relation with it and recommend it to you without reservation.

CONSISTENTLY PLURAL: The company are a large manufacturer of office equipment. We value highly our relation with them and recommend them to you without reservation.

INCONSISTENTLY SINGULAR AND PLURAL: The company is a large manufacturer of office equipment. We value highly our relation with them and recommend them to you without reservation.

colloquial English See USAGES 2.

colon (:) A punctuation mark chiefly useful in anticipating a following statement.

1. AFTER WORDS OF INTRODUCTION. 2. MISUSE. 3. CONVENTIONAL USES. 4. CAPITAL FOLLOWING.

1. AFTER WORDS OF INTRODUCTION. A colon is used after an introductory statement to direct attention to a following list, amplification, explanation, or quotation. The introductory statement sometimes includes words like *these, below,* and *following.*

Please send us the following supplies and charge Account No. TD 437: [List follows]

The main reasons are these: First, we are understaffed. Second, . . .

Takeovers should be seen for what they are: a form of cannibalism.

The factors that contribute to the city's industrial development are still present: ample electric power, plentiful skilled labor, and access to markets in the Northwest and Canada.

A number of basic national problems are yet to be solved. Among them: energy, inflation, and a mountainous foreign debt.

With the temperature at a low 62°, Johnson explained: "You might think that's cold but it's not, when people are working."

2. MISUSE.   The colon should not needlessly interrupt a sentence that does not contain a distinct introductory element.

Among the basic national problems are [*not* are:] energy, inflation, and a mountainous foreign debt.

3. CONVENTIONAL USES.

(a) After a letter SALUTATION

Dear Mrs. Graham:

Gentlemen:

(b) In figures expressing time

9:45 P.M.

The malfunction was registered at 2:16:31 A.M. [Two colons: 16 minutes and 31 seconds after two o'clock]

(c) Between a title and subtitle

Industrial Organization: Theory and Practice

(d) In a footnote or bibliographical reference (see REFERENCE NOTES)

New York: Doubleday, 1983

4. CAPITAL FOLLOWING.   The word following a colon is usually capitalized when it begins a complete sentence.

This is how the plan works: First, you order a starter set. Then . . .

An uncapitalized letter is used when the expression following the colon is a subordinate sentence element or, if a full sentence, is very closely tied to the idea that precedes the colon.

We carry sizes to fit everyone: small, medium, large, and extra large.

All this may seem very difficult, but do not worry: the guidelines offer a simple alternative.

colored   Although *colored* remains part of the title of the *National Association for the Advancement of Colored People* (NAACP), the terms BLACK and NEGRO are favored as a racial description.

combine   Noun, pronounced *com*-bine. Informal for any joining of two or more companies to further their commercial interests. Also, variously, CARTEL, *pool, syndicate, trust,* or *monopoly,* although *combine* may have a more desirable CONNOTATION than some of its synonyms: *If the affiliation is effected, the resources of the combine will be close to a billion dollars.*

comer   Pronounced *kum*-ur. Informal for a person who shows exceptional promise: *She's a real comer.*

Comex ACRONYM for the *Com*modity *Ex*change Inc.: *The Comex has tightened the margin requirements for silver futures.*

comma (,) A punctuation mark for separating elements within a sentence. Except in conventional uses, the trend is to use commas only when they help the sense. Many commas, even those prescribed by the formal rules, are unnecessary.

1. BETWEEN MAIN CLAUSES. 2. IN A SERIES. 3. AFTER AN INTRODUCTORY ELEMENT. 4. TO SET OFF A PARENTHETIC ELEMENT. 5. FOR CLARITY. 6. CONVENTIONAL USES.

1. BETWEEN MAIN CLAUSES. A comma is placed before a coordinate conjunction linking the clauses of a compound sentence. Conjunctions in this class are *and, but, or, nor,* and *for.*

I was glad to assist in the survey of consumer preferences, *and* I hope your report will be well received.

The proposed merger suffered from an unfortunate convergence of events, *but* the basic conditions are still favorable to an agreement.

Note: The comma is often omitted when the linked clauses are short and simple.

The premium must be paid by April 1 *or* the policy will be canceled. [Comma omitted before *or*]

2. IN A SERIES. Commas are used between words and phrases in a series of three or more.

(a) Usage is divided on the need for a comma before the *and* or *or* linking the last two members of the series. The comma is usually omitted in informal and journalistic prose, but—to avoid confusion—it is advisedly included in such writing also when the last member of the series is a compound.

The freight company handled large tonnages of grain, coal, iron ore, limestone, lumber, and petroleum. [Last comma optional]

But: United in opposition were businessmen, union members, and minority and women's rights advocates. [Last comma necessary to avoid confusion]

(b) Two or more adjectives in a series are not separated by commas when each adjective is thought of as modifying the noun or nouns that follow. The test: If the adjectives can be read with *and*s between them, the commas are needed.

a conservative Wall Street investment house [No commas]

a hexagonal dark mahogany tea table [No commas]

But (commas): a prosperous, educated, sophisticated audience [That is, "prosperous *and* educated *and* sophisticated"]

3. AFTER AN INTRODUCTORY SENTENCE ELEMENT.

(a) A comma is placed between a subordinate clause and a following main clause.

When the system does not work, we are all losers.

However, a comma is placed between a main clause and a following subordinate clause only when there is a slight break in thought.

We are all losers when the system does not work. [No comma]

But: There the workers can rightly claim that capitalism is inefficient, because they make sure it is inefficient. [Comma marks a slight break, giving emphasis to the thought that follows.]

(b) A comma follows an introductory word or phrase (especially a long phrase) that is not closely woven into the fabric of the sentence.

With the introduction of the new model still many months away, the company was already being swamped by inquiries from prospective buyers.

For their part, U.S. officials are not ready to concede a defeat.

In short, Northbrook residents are very unhappy.

Furthermore, there is no way we could have anticipated the turn of events.

But (comma not necessary):

In every instance we found a willingness to cooperate.

At fifty he was not yet ready to retire.

(c) A comma follows an introductory phrase containing an infinitive, participle, or gerund—words formed from verbs, but serving other grammatical purposes.

To achieve genuine management-employee rapport, the company audits its progress once a year. [Introductory infinitive phrase]

Concerned about the division of authority, the management took prompt remedial action. [Introductory participial phrase]

By making a small concession now, we gain a big concession later. [Introductory prepositional gerund phrase]

4. TO SET OFF A PARENTHETIC ELEMENT.

Commas are used to separate expressions that are only incidental to the sense of the sentence.

(a) Commas set off mild interjections, words in direct address, appositives, interrupting connectives, and so-called *nonrestrictive modifiers*—that is, qualifying phrases and clauses that can be omitted without serious damage to the sense. (See also Paragraph 4(b) following.)

Yes, we are committed to the deal. [Mild interjection]

Here, Mrs. Fallon, are the details. [Direct address]

Mr. Stephens, the board chairman, was unavailable for comment. [Appositive] *But:* Board chairman Stephens was unavailable for comment. [No interruption, no commas]

In these circumstances, therefore, we are allowing the discount. [Interrupting connective] *But:* We are therefore allowing the discount. [No interruption, no commas]

A wide variety of sets, including Design Line decorative phones, is on display at these stores. [Nonrestrictive modifier]

The market was highly competitive, with prices severely depressed throughout most of the year. [Nonrestrictive modifier]

Coal, of which we have much, presents many environmental problems. [Nonrestrictive modifier]

(b) *Restrictive modifiers*—those that have a strong identifying function and cannot be omitted without damage to the sense of the sentence—are not set off by commas. Clauses beginning with *that* are always restrictive. Those beginning with *who* or *which* may be either restrictive or nonrestrictive, depending on the sense. Invariably restrictive phrases and clauses are read without a pause or change in tone.

We need an argument that management can accept. [Restrictive]

Women who are trained as managers are in relatively short supply. [Restrictive]

Any salesperson who brings in a million dollars' business a year deserves our respect. [Restrictive] *But:* Dave Elkins, who brings in a million dollars' business a year, deserves our respect. [Nonrestrictive; commas required]

Desks *which* (or *that*) are more than ten years old are bound to show signs of wear. [Restrictive] *But:* The desks, many of which are more than ten years old, are showing signs of wear. [Nonrestrictive; commas required]

A company nearing its golden anniversary should be preparing to celebrate. [Restrictive] *But:* The growth of the company, now nearing its fiftieth anniversary, shows no signs of slowing. [Nonrestrictive; commas required]

5. FOR CLARITY. A comma is used whenever it is needed to preserve the sentence sense.

(a) To mark an omission.

Some customers prefer a thirty-day charge account; others, an installment account. [The comma substitutes for the word *prefer*.]

(b) To set off a contrasting or antithetical element.

They are different, not better, than other carpets made by the same manufacturer.

The less informed the customer, the harder to make the sale.

(c) To prevent a mistaken reading if the comma were omitted.

During the year, Mobil drilled twenty-eight wells in the Gulf.

More and more, business is giving attention to the training of upper-level managers.

I can't recommend a condominium, any more than I can recommend private ownership.

6. CONVENTIONAL USES.

(a) To separate the parts of an address or date. However, when the day and month are given, the trend is to omit the comma after the year; and when only the month and year are given, to omit the commas altogether.

Our office is at 350 Park Avenue, New York, opposite the Waldorf.

The item is stocked in our Lexington, Ky., warehouse.

The contract of September 26, 1980, is still valid. [Second comma optional]

We can't find the July, 1983 issue. [Comma better omitted]

(b) To divide a figure into thousands. See also NUMERALS 7.

$1,250; 465,000; 3,526,755

(c) To punctuate the SALUTATION of an informal or personal letter.

Dear Perry,

(d) To set off a title or degree after a name.

Helen Ferris, director of merchandising, was present.

Meet Martin Cain, C.P.A., a good friend of ours.

The comma between a name and such appendages as Jr., II, Inc., and Ltd., though traditional, is being increasingly omitted.

David Gordon, Jr. (*or* David Gordon Jr.)

Anacomp, Inc. (*or* Anacomp Inc.)

Libra Bank, Limited (*or* Libra Bank Limited)

commence Pretentious for *begin: will commence (begin) proceedings/commenced (began) operations.* See **LONG WORDS AND SHORT.**

commentate To commentate is to act as a commentator. The verb, which may or may not take a direct object, should not be used for "remark" or "comment," but on any count it is clumsy and better avoided: *The genial actor was hired to commentate the fashion show (hired to give the commentary on the fashion show)/I wish to comment on* (not *commentate on*) *Jason's proposal.*

commerce, trade The distinction is a narrow one and not always observed. *Commerce* is the interchange of commodities and manufactured goods on a large scale, particularly within one's own country. *Trade* represents a similar exchange, but with international implications.

commercial An advertisement on radio or television. See also SPOT ANNOUNCEMENT and PROGRAM ANNOUNCEMENT.

commercial paper Short-term promissory notes of business firms with excellent credit records.

committee A COLLECTIVE NOUN treated as singular or plural, depending on the sense and sound: *The committee is only protecting its prerogatives.* [The committee is treated as a unit.] But: *The committee do* (or *does*) *not seem to have reconciled their differences.* [The reference is to the several members of the committee.]

common, mutual That which is *common* is shared by two or more persons or things: *a common interest in economic history/speak a common language.* That which is *mutual,* however, is reciprocal, or given and received in equal amounts: *share a mutual respect* [said of two persons respecting each other]/*a mutual arrangement* [as when the guests of either of two nearby resort hotels are permitted to share some of the facilities of the other].

The phrases "mutual friend" and "mutual acquaintance," though they violate the rule, are well established, probably because the "correct" word *common* might easily be misinterpreted for *vulgar.*

Common Market The popular name for the European Economic Community (EEC), an organization founded in 1957 to further the economies of the member nations, especially through the removal of trade barriers.

communication A versatile but often overworked word. 1. Appropriately used in the singular and plural to denote the sending and receiving of messages. In this sense, the idea of reciprocity is strong: *We have been in communication with the Federal Trade Commission* [Suggests an exchange of messages, but the form of the messages is perhaps deliberately kept vague]/*Communications regarding the purchase are now in progress* ["Negotiations" might raise unwarranted expectations].

2. A pretentious substitute for the more specific terms *message, letter, memorandum, telephone call*, etc.: *Please refer to our communication (letter) of the 10th/In a communication (telephone call) from the client, we were told* . . . In a nonspecific and nonreciprocal sense, "in communication with" can more simply be expressed "in touch with" or by some change in sentence structure: *They have been in communication (in touch) with us/We will be in communication with the buyer (We will contact the buyer).* See also CONTACT 2.

3. A common synonym for *rapport: We have excellent communication with our employees/They talk to each other, but there seems to be no communication between them.*

4. Vogue word for social discourse, with its supposedly residual therapeutic value: *A single membership fee opens the way for communication with others sharing your interests and goals.* The idea is also captured in this wry comment: *In communication, people express their true feelings and tell everything about themselves with complete honesty, holding back nothing except their last names.* [Judith Martin as "Miss Manners," *Washington Post* Syndicate]

5. In the plural, a common EUPHEMISM for press agentry, lobbying, publicity, advertising, and the like; and a convenient term for a variety of activities relating to the dissemination of information. A public relations firm may refer to its work as "communications." So, too, a company may more aptly call itself a "communications company" than an "advertising agency" when it provides not only a full range of advertising services, but publicity and merchandising services as well.

6. In the plural also, unexceptionable in the sense of communication technology or the general system by which messages are sent and received: *RCA's business is communications/a communications breakdown caused by a faulty circuit/a communications engineer.*

For the treatment of communication not as a word, but as a function or process, see COMMUNICATION FLOW (below) and the entries listed in the Classified Guide to Topics, Sec. V, immediately preceding the Dictionary.

communication flow   The direction in which messages flow within the organization.

1. MOVEMENT OF MESSAGES.   2. SIGNIFICANCE.

1. MOVEMENT OF MESSAGES.   (a) Downward communication is the flow of messages from the top of the corporate ladder to managers, supervisors, and workers. It includes orders, work assignments, procedures, performance evaluations, and policy statements.

(b) Upward communication is communication from workers to their superiors and from lower administrators to higher ones. It includes reports on work performance and problems, as well as evaluations, opinions, and suggestions regarding organizational practices and policies.

(c) Horizontal communication (also called lateral communication) is communication between people on the same level of authority in the organization. See also DOTTED LINE 2.

2. SIGNIFICANCE.   Importance is attached to the directional flow of messages because of its bearing on the way people in the organization work together.

In downward communication, for instance, not all types of messages to lower-level employees get the emphasis they deserve. There is an especial deficiency in communicating to employees the importance of their jobs and its relation to other jobs in the company.

The basic problem of upward communication is that people in managerial positions are more accustomed to giving directives than to LISTENING to what their subordinates have to tell them. The subordinates, on their part, are inclined to tell the boss what he wants to hear and only what they want him to know. They are especially not likely to give him any report that might reflect unfavorably on them or lead to decisions affecting them adversely.

Communication between peers provides needed coordination in the performance of their jobs. It is also necessary in giving them emotional and social support. A possible danger in horizontal communication, however, is that while it satisfies an important part of the participants' need for information, it may shut them off from the critical information available from the workers below them.

See also FEEDBACK.

commute   Used informally as a noun in the sense of "traveling as a commuter": *When she was hired at Lourdes, she moved from Manhattan to Bayside to shorten the commute.*

company   Followed, with some inconsistency, by a singular verb and a plural pronoun reference. See COLLECTIVE NOUNS 2.

company man   A worker in any position whose attitudes and behavior put him on the side of management. The CONNOTATION of the term is not always favorable. Loyal though he is, the company man may be viewed as lacking imagination and initiative or, worse still, as a sycophant.

company names   See NAMES 2.

comparable   The stress is on the first syllable.

comparative claims   1. Comparative claims—those using words like *stronger, safer, more economical*—are a staple of competitive advertising. When the comparisons are not completed (stronger than what? safer than what?) or are otherwise vague, they pass for PUFFERY and thus escape regulatory strictures.

> Nobody does it better than your Anchor Banker.
>
> Bounty [paper towels]—the quicker picker-upper.
>
> Arrid Extra Dry Powder Roll-On—goes on drier than anything.
>
> Bayer Aspirin—works faster.
>
> Hallmark, for those who care enough to send the very best.
>
> Taylor Champagne—America at its best.
>
> Cool Whip tastes fresh as homemade.
>
> Nobody else can do it like McDonald's can.
>
> Fights odor better so you'll feel cleaner [Shield Deodorant Soap].

The choice between buying a Plymouth Reliant K or a Chevy Citation becomes both simple and obvious when you look at the facts.

	Plymouth Reliant K 2 Door	Chevy Citation
Base Sticker Price*	$5,995	$6,386
Est. Hwy. EPA Est. MPG†	41 $\boxed{25}$	35 $\boxed{22}$
Passenger Seating	6	5
Resale Value	89.3%	84%

Comparative claims 2.   From a New York Air advertisement.

2. Once considered ungentlemanly, the practice of comparing an advertised product with competing products by name is now well established (see chart). The self-imposed but voluntary rules of the trade discourage comparisons that directly disparage a competitive product.

Reach out and touch someone—but do it for half of what Bell charges. [MCI Telecommunications Corp.]

Who'd ever believe a Rabbit could be beaten by a Pontiac?

compare to, compare with   Informally, the expressions are used interchangeably, but distinctions are made in general and formal usage.

Compare to is used to point out similarities: *The computer display unit can be compared to a television screen/He liked to compare his copy to David Ogilvy's. Compare to* is also used when things of different classes are compared: *His voice has been compared to a ship's horn.*

Compare with is used to emphasize differences, or in the sense of examining to determine differences or similarities: *No bread compares with ours in nutritional value/We asked an expert to compare the original print with the copy made by our patented process.*

The past participle *compared* is followed by either *to* or *with*: *Compared to* (or *with*) *their niggardly contributions to the Community Chest, ours are munificent.*

comparisons   1. INCOMPLETE COMPARISONS.   2. SUPERLATIVES.
3. COMPARATIVE FORMS.
See also **ABSOLUTE ADJECTIVES** and **COMPARATIVE CLAIMS.**

1. INCOMPLETE COMPARISONS.   (a) A word logically required to complete a comparison is sometimes omitted in informal usage. In the "Informal" examples below, the caret ($_\wedge$) shows where the omission occurs.

INFORMAL: At Aamco we fix only transmissions and we fix more of them than anyone $_\wedge$. [From Aamco advertisement]
GENERAL: At Aamco we fix only transmissions and we fix more of them than anyone else.
INFORMAL: She is one of the leading $_\wedge$, if not the leading designer of leisure clothes.
GENERAL: She is one of the leading designers, if not the leading designer, of leisure clothes.
INFORMAL: The results will be as good $_\wedge$ or better than you expect.

GENERAL: The results will be as good as, or better than, you expect.

Or (better): The results will be as good as you expect or better.

INFORMAL: I like the new layout as much ⸲, if not more than the old.

GENERAL: I like the new layout as much as, if not more than, the old.

Or (better): I like the new layout as much as the old, if not more.

(b) Not acceptable is an omission resulting in ambiguity or in a comparison of things that are not comparable.

AMBIGUOUS: The factory is closer to the freight station than the warehouse.

IMPROVED: The factory is closer to the freight station than to the warehouse.

ILLOGICAL: Tokyo's population is bigger than New York. [The things compared—population and New York—are not in the same class.]

IMPROVED: Tokyo's population is bigger than that of New York.

Or (better): Tokyo's population is bigger than New York's [*population* understood].

ILLOGICAL: The Sears Tower is taller than any building in the world.

IMPROVED: The Sears Tower is taller than any other building in the world.

Or: The Sears Tower is the tallest building in the world.

2. SUPERLATIVES. (a) Although the superlative is usually confined to expressions relating to more than two persons or things, there is some precedent—in informal usage, at least—for the superlative in a comparison of two: *Between Pepsi and Coke, I like Coke best/Hallmark will test both advertising campaigns and see which one produces the best results.*

(b) Informally, the superlative is also used for emphasis without reference to numbers: *He has the smoothest sales pitch/It's the greatest.* The superlative *most,* however, is standard in such expressions as *You are most thoughtful* and *They were most helpful.*

(c) A superlative is not to be completed by *other: The company racked up the greatest dollar sales volume that had ever been achieved by any other American company* (omit *other*).

3. COMPARATIVE FORMS. Adjectives and adverbs form their comparative and superlative degrees by the addition of *-er* and *-est* (*stronger, strongest*) or by the qualifiers *more* and *most* (*more willing, most willing*). Many words—especially those of one or two syllables—permit a choice. Such a choice is controlled by the sense as well as the sound. In a word ending in *-er* or *-est*, the emphasis is

on the quality denoted; in a word formed with *more* or *most*, the emphasis is on the degree.

NO CHOICE: Sales are coming faster as Christmas approaches.

They have grown more independent.

It's the earliest fall showing we have ever put on.

The company is growing most rapidly in the suburbs.

CHOICE POSSIBLE: We couldn't have had a prompter reply. [Emphasizes *prompt*—the quality]

No one could have been more prompt. [Emphasizes the degree]

She's the ablest candidate we have interviewed. [Emphasizes *able*—the quality]

Of the several candidates, she is the most able. [Emphasizes the degree]

compelled See COMPULSIVE WORDS.

compensating balance A minimum balance required to be kept in a borrower's bank account during the term of a loan from the bank. For a loan of $50,000, a borrower may thus have to maintain a compensating balance of $10,000.

compensation Usually used in the sense of reimbursement or recompense for a loss, *compensation* is pretentious for *wages* or *salary*. It has some utility, though, in denoting an inclusive payment for salary, commissions, bonuses, etc.: *a compensation package/compensation of $60,000, including fringe benefits.*

compile To compile is to bring together material from various sources; it is not a synonym for *write: compiled a record of the transactions.* But: *wrote* (not *compiled*) *a report of her investigation.* See also WRITE UP.

complected Nonstandard for *complexioned: a dark-complexioned model* (not *dark-complected*).

complement, compliment As nouns, the first denotes that which makes something complete; the second is an expression of praise or admiration. Thus, a blouse is a *complement* to a skirt; but one person pays a *compliment* to another person. The same distinction applies when the words are used as verbs. A blouse *complements* a skirt; one person *compliments* (praises) another.

complete Better not modified by *more* or *most*. See ABSOLUTE ADJECTIVES.

completely See TOTALLY, COMPLETELY, ENTIRELY.

complex A real estate development consisting of a number of adjacent buildings or a number of special facilities under one roof: *Detroit's Renaissance Center hotel and office complex/an indoor shopping complex in which J.C. Penney, Macy's, Gimbels, and Alexander's are the principal tenants/the huge Bellevue [Hospital] complex on First Avenue.* Compare CENTER.

complimentary close *Very truly yours* or other conventional expressions marking the end of a letter and placed several spaces below the letter body. The particular expression chosen is determined by the nature of the letter and the tone desired. Only the first word is capitalized. The complimentary close is omitted when the SIMPLIFIED STYLE of letter makeup is used. See also LETTER FORM 2 and FORMS OF ADDRESS 3.

Formal and deferential	Respectfully yours
	Respectfully
	Very respectfully
Merely polite	Yours truly
For general correspondence	Very truly yours
	Yours very truly
For more warmth	Sincerely yours
	Yours sincerely
	Sincerely
	Very sincerely
Informal*	Cordially yours
	Cordially
	Very cordially
Very informal and personal (usually with a first-name salutation)	As always
	As ever
	Fondly
In doubtful taste	Yours for more sales
	Yours for a successful meeting, etc.

*Other expressions acceptable in informal use are *Kindest regards, Kindest personal regards, Regards, Best wishes,* etc. These may form the complimentary close or the final statement in the body of the letter, followed by a comma or period and a complimentary close in the usual position. The expressions "I am," "We remain," etc., at the end of a letter are archaic and better omitted. See also PARTICIPIAL CLOSE.

compose, comprise Strictly speaking, the parts *compose* the whole, while the whole *comprises* the parts: *Those who compose the top management are the chairman of the board, the president, and the chairman of the Executive Committee.* But: *The top management comprises the chairman of the board, the president, and the chairman of the Executive Committee.*

In disregard of the "rule," however, *comprise* is regularly—and without stigma—used for *compose:* Four sections *comprise* (also *compose* or *make up*) the report.

composite index of leading indicators Also *leading index.* A figure issued periodically by the U.S. Bureau of Economic Analysis, combining the 12 "leading indicators" of economic activity. The indicators, which are changed from time to time, measure such factors as average factory workweek, new building permits, changes in initial claims for state unemployment insurance, corporate profits, etc.: *The leading index declined nine-tenths of 1 percent in August, breaking a string of four consecutive increases.*

compound connectives See WORDINESS 4.

compound numbers See HYPHEN 3.

compound words See HYPHEN 1 and PLURAL NOUNS 2.

comptroller See CONTROLLER.

compulsive words In ordinary discourse, such words as *must, requested, forced,* and *compelled* may smack of a rigid attitude, even coercion. Softer words are usually more productive if goodwill is to be preserved: *We are forced to refuse (We are sorry we cannot)/You are requested to submit to this office (Please send us).*

Exceptions can of course be made, as when a tactful approach has already failed or when the compulsion is upon the writer or speaker: *We must now insist that payment in full be made at once/The IRS requires that we send this information to them.* See also COURTESY AND TACT.

con Slang. To swindle, especially by first winning the victim's confidence: *They were conned out of thousands of dollars.* Also a noun: *The con was artful.*

—con man. A swindler; more particularly, a CONFIDENCE MAN.

concept, conception, etc. Possibly because it is an impressive word, *concept* is often used when *conception, idea,* or *plan* would be more suitable. A *concept* is an abstract notion developed from a study of particularities (as in the book title, *The Concept of the Organization*); a *conception* is a set of particulars applied to such a notion (Halston's conception of the twenties' look); an *idea* is, more generally, the product of thinking, as a thought or view *(advanced the idea of adding a line of children's wear); and a plan* is a scheme worked out beforehand *(the plan succeeded brilliantly).*

conceptual framework An idea or symbolic structure applied especially to a plan yet to be executed: *The conceptual framework of the organization is now in place.* When used simply for *framework,* however, *conceptual framework* is JARGON: *We hope to develop an employee relations program within the framework* (rather than *conceptual framework*) *of industrial democracy.*

conciseness See WORDINESS.

concrete words See ABSTRACT AND CONCRETE WORDS.

condo A CLIPPED FORM of *condominium.*

conferee See ATTENDEE.

confidence man A swindler who operates by first gaining the confidence of his victims. See also CON.

confidential An ON-ARRIVAL NOTATION placed on letters intended to be opened and read only by the addressee or some authorized person. Compare PERSONAL.

confliction Nonstandard for *conflict: disturbed by the conflict* (not *confliction*) *of interests.*

conglomerate A corporation, like I.T.T. and Textron, consisting of a number of companies, usually in different industries. *Conglomerate* is also a verb, meaning "to form into a mass," but it is not easily found in the analogous business sense of "to form into a conglomerate." But see CONGLOMERATION below and *conglomeratize* at -IZE, -IZATION 3.

conglomeration The process of becoming a CONGLOMERATE: *an accelerating movement toward conglomeration/an industry facing competition or conglomeration.*

connected with, in connection with, in this connection Wordy, awkward phrases that are better replaced with a simple preposition or omitted altogether.

They are having a problem *connected with the installation of (in installing)* the hung ceiling.

The company is now making studies *in connection with (of)* the feasibility of adding another shift.

We are replying to your inquiry *in connection with (about)* your order of July 9.

At some point the employee has to decide which option he prefers. *In this connection*, he is free to seek the advice of the Pension Committee. [Omit *In this connection*.]

connecting phrases Many connecting phrases are unnecessarily verbose: *in the course of (during) our investigation/subsequent to (after) your call/your check in the amount of (your check for) $120.* See also **WORDINESS** 4.

connive From the Latin for "to close the eyes," hence to wink at or pretend not to notice wrongdoing, or to be indulgent toward misbehavior (followed by *at*): *His assistant connived at the cashier's petty thieveries.* Also, to aid secretly, to conspire (followed by *with*): *The custodian was disciplined for conniving with the plumber in exaggerating*

connotation 1. The connotation of a word is its suggested meaning as opposed to its literal meaning. Synonymous words may differ in their connotation: compare *plan* and *scheme, government official* and *bureaucrat, stated* and *admitted.* In these instances, a primarily denotative word is set against a strongly connotative counterpart; but whereas the denotative word is essentially factual, the connotative word is overtly biased.

2. Connotative words permit the user to express feelings, attitudes, and opinions; at the same time they evoke a response (sympathetic or not) from the reader or listener. They also give a statement color and interest that might otherwise be lacking. The use of connotative words in literature is seldom questioned. Used responsibly, they also have an important function in business, law, politics, and wherever **ADVOCACY** is practiced. Generally, however, they are not suitable tools for the objective reporter in business or journalism.

3. The effectiveness of any particular connotation can be judged only in reference to the circumstances of its use and the audience

addressed. Words like *profit* and *competition*, for instance, carry different suggestions for different people. *Profit* sounds good to business executives and investors, but it sometimes irks consumers and workers. *Competition*, on the other hand, may suggest risk to an entrepreneur, especially one having to live with cheap imports; but it appeals to consumers who see it as a means of getting better goods at lower prices.

In other instances, the connotation of a word derives from the context in which the word is used. *Foreign*, for example, arouses distrust in such terms as *foreign-born*, *foreign ideas*, and *foreign agents*, but it is not unattractive in *foreign travel*, where the suggestion of the exotic is strong. Some connotations change. During President Carter's term of office, editors were citing the chief executive's inability to work with Congress as indicative of the need for a politician in the White House, and for a short time the word *politician* lost its derogatory suggestion.

4. By their connotation, words can ameliorate a situation (compare the dentist's "This will hurt" with "You may feel some discomfort"); they can mislead (Butterball turkeys and Mrs. Butterworth's syrup have butter in name only); they can create false images (a *blonde*, a *model*, an *heiress*); they can show favor or disfavor (as *new* vs. *untried*, *investing* vs. *spending*, *developing nation* vs. *backward nation*).

5. Choosing words for their connotation is an exercise in sensitivity, as these paired statements show:

What have you got on Darrin? [Suggests a desire for negative information.]

What can you tell us about Darrin? [Opens the way for an unbiased response.]

Soon the store will try a new gimmick to increase sales. [Suggests a cheap strategem.]

Soon the store will institute a new plan to increase sales. [The scheme is given dignity.]

American Express cards are accepted here. [Suggests passivity.]

American Express cards are welcome here. [Gives active encouragement.]

After six weeks of dickering, the terms were accepted. [Suggests petty bargaining.]

After six weeks of negotiation, the terms were accepted. [Raises the level of bargaining and suggests the greater skill of the negotiators.]

From our own factory, our 10-month midweight suits. [Suggests mass-produced clothing.]

From our own workrooms, our 10-month midweight suits. [Suggests a more intimate environment, with tailors giving individual attention to the garments they produce.]

Choose your toothbrush for hard or soft bristles. [Suggests the alternative of abrasion or mushiness.]

Choose your toothbrush for firm or gentle action. [Provides a seemingly better choice.]

See also **EUPHEMISM, PEJORATIVES, POSITIVE AND NEGATIVE WORDS**, and **PREPOSSESSIVE WORDS**.

consensus   So spelled (only one *c*). Collective opinion or agreement; hence "consensus of opinion" is redundant: *The consensus (not consensus of opinion) was that an extra dividend was unwarranted/It was hard to obtain a consensus on the long-range prospects of the economy.*

considerable   Informal as a noun: *worth considerable* (for *worth a considerable sum*)/*done considerable* (for *done a great deal*).

consistency   For treatment of needless shifts in sentence structure, see **SENTENCES** 4.

consortium   Pronounced kun-*sor*-she-um; plural, *consortia* (-she-uh). A group of financial institutions or large corporations joined in some undertaking, usually of international scope and requiring large financial resources: *a consortium of pipeline companies led by Northwest Alaskan Pipeline Co.*

construct   An intellectual synthesis or **MODEL**: *Their construct of the organization views it as a communication system/Let's begin with a construct of the process.*

consultant   1. A professional adviser: *a consultant on employee pension funds.* Also, infrequently, one who seeks information or advice from another: *My consultant* [advice-seeker] *wanted to know what steps could be taken to stem the attrition among their engineers.*

2. A prepossessive synonym for *salesperson: Mary Kay consultants* [sales agents] *are mainly younger married women.* See **PREPOSSESSIVE WORDS**.

consumerism   Also *consumer advocacy.* A social movement devoted to protecting consumer interests in such matters as product safety, honest packaging and advertising, and fair pricing.

consumerist   A proponent of CONSUMERISM. The CONNOTATION is not always favorable.

consumer price index   Abbreviated CPI. Issued by the Bureau of Labor Statistics, this index measures the changes in prices of about 400 goods and services sold in large cities throughout the country: *The consumer price index for the first nine months rose 4.8 percent.*

contact   1. No question about its use as a noun or adjective: *My contact* [personal connection] *at the agency is Mr. Sampson/Influenza is a contact disease* [a disease caused by physical association].

2. As a verb meaning "get in touch with," *contact* still bears the taint of association with commerce. It is a useful word, however, and has gained wide acceptance: *Should we need your services, we'll contact you/The police department warns that if you are approached in person or contacted by telephone by a stranger with any plan or scheme . . .*

3. The complaint that the verb *contact* is insufficiently specific is often well founded. Words like *write, telephone,* and *visit* are preferable when they can be conveniently used. But when a nonspecific term is needed, *let know* may serve as a pleasantly informal substitute for *contact: If we can be of help, please let us know* (rather than *please contact us*).

contents noted   A phrase without significance, usually part of a banal acknowledgment of an incoming letter: *Your letter received and contents noted.* See also **STEREOTYPED LETTER PHRASES.**

context   Best used in the sense of "what precedes and what follows": *The meaning of the word could have been obtained from the context.* In other uses, *circumstances* or *situation* will often serve as well or better: *Business is definitely improving. In this context (In these circumstances) the proposal to increase advertising expenditures makes sense.*

—in the context of. A wordy and overworked phrase, not always apt: *We learn in the context of (from) our experience/The conclusion of the report should be examined in the context of (along with) what we know about the writer.*

contiguous   Touching or abutting. A word useful in the description of property: *now available: three contiguous floors/the contiguous forty-eight states.* Compare ADJACENT.

continual(ly), continuous(ly) *Continual* means "repeated in rapid succession"; *continuous*, "unceasing": *There have been continual (not continuous) interruptions in production/The noise is continuous (unceasing).*

Continually and *continuously* are similarly differentiated: *He was continually (not continuously) devising new strategies/The air intake must operate continuously (not continually).*

continuation sheets The second and succeeding pages of a letter or memorandum. See LETTER FORM 6.

continue on The *on* is superfluous: *In defiance of progress, they continue (not continue on) in their old ways.* See also WORDINESS 3.

contractions 1. Contractions like *I'm, we'll, you're, don't,* and *haven't* are characteristic of speech, and although they are found in informal and general writing—particularly ordinary correspondence—they are avoided in long-form REPORTS and in contracts and other formal papers. See also APOSTROPHE 2 and 5(a).

2. The apostrophe is placed where the omission of a letter or letters occurs: *weren't* (not *were'nt*); *cont'd, nat'l, 'n'* (for *and*). Sometimes a single apostrophe is used even when omissions occur in several places: *shan't* (for *shall not*); *won't* (for *will not*), *'n* (for *and*), and *mf'g* (for manufacturing). But (correct): *Who'd've thought he'd resign.*

3. Contractions do not end with periods, but ABBREVIATIONS do: *contd., natl., mfg.*

contractual So spelled and pronounced; not *contractural: We keep our contractual obligations.*

contrarian In the securities market, a person who takes a position contrary to the prevailing or popular one. Also an adjective: *pursues a contrarian investment pattern.*

contrast Always used in expressions of difference, *contrast* is followed by *with*. An exception is made in the phrase "in contrast to": *We want you to contrast our $200 cash rebate with their $50.* But: *In contrast to our cash rebate of $200, they are offering only $50.* See also COMPARE TO, COMPARE WITH.

controlled circulation   A EUPHEMISM for "free circulation," a method used by some periodicals reaching select audiences and carrying a large volume of paid advertising. *Medical News* is such a publication.

controller   Also, less common, *comptroller*. Both are pronounced kun-*tro*-lur. An individual in charge of accounts or of the financial management of an organization.

convenience   Often misspelled *convience* (syllable omitted): *We are open for your convenience five nights a week.*
   —at your earliest convenience. A STEREOTYPED LETTER PHRASE, better replaced by a term that expresses less ambiguously the time for action: *at once, immediately, by* (date), *promptly, as soon as you can, when convenient.*

conventional wisdom   Overworked; but effective synonyms can be found: *The conventional wisdom (prevailing view) is that we are entering an age of scarce natural resources/Contrary to the conventional wisdom (accepted belief), mergers do not necessarily restrict competition.*

conversant with   Familiar with, as by study or experience. Better not used in the sense of mere recognition. Thus (no question): *They are thoroughly conversant with our plans.* But, not apt: *We are not conversant with the name on the letterhead* (Better: *not familiar with*).

converse   Most people just talk. See LONG WORDS AND SHORT.

convince, persuade   1. Though the words are synonymous, *convince* carries to a greater degree the suggestion of inducing belief by evidence or reasoning. *Persuade*, on the other hand, relates to inducement by any means, including emotional appeals.
   2. *Convince* is preferably followed by an *of* or *that* construction: *convince them of our sincerity/convinced us that the terms were the best we could get. Persuade* is preferably followed by an infinitive: *persuaded us to accept the terms.*
   See also PERSUASION.

cook the books   Slang; to tamper with financial records: *They discovered too late that the missing officer had cooked the books.*

co-op   CLIPPED FORM of *cooperative*. The hyphen in *co-op* is used to prevent mispronunciation: *a co-op arrangement/The building is now a co-op.*

Also a verb; past tense, *co-oped* (pronounced *-opped*): *Three-bed-room apartments in Manhattan rent for $2,000 a month if you can find one that has not been co-oped* [that is, one that is not being sold as a cooperative].

co-opt To preempt or take for oneself, as when a disputant or rival adopts the opposition's stand as his own: *In full-page advertisements boldly co-opting the U.S. Dietary Guidelines, General Foods put itself squarely on the side of good nutrition/In the dispute between ownership and management, control drifted inexorably into the hands of the managers, who were frequently able to co-opt one another and perpetuate their position.*

copy notation A notation on a business letter showing the names of individuals to whom copies are being sent. The notation is placed at the left margin two spaces below the last typed line excepting only the **POSTSCRIPT**. Some acceptable styles are shown below. The abbreviation cc (for "carbon copy") is retained even when the copy is made by machine. A "blind" copy notation (bcc) is one included on the copies, but omitted on the original. For convenience, it may be placed in the upper left-hand corner of the carbon copies. See also **DISTRIBUTION LIST**.

Copy to Mr. Alfred Cross, VP

Copy to Mr. Cross

cc: Mr. Cross

[Multiple copies (listed alphabetically):]

cc: R. D. Allen	cc: RDA
E. S. Craig	ESC
G. Patman	GP

[Blind copy notation:]   bcc: Mr. Friedman

[Copy carrying recipient's address and a reference to an accompanying enclosure:]

cc: Mr. Harry M. Dresser (1 copy, "Estate Planning")
10 Garden Square
Bradford, PA 16701

copyright One speaks of *a copyright* (noun), the exclusive right granted by law to reproduce a literary or other creative work. The two adjective forms are *copyright* and *copyrighted*, as in "a copyright work" or "a copyrighted work." However, the past tense form of the verb and the past participle are *copyrighted*, as in "copyrighted the work" and "was copyrighted in 1983."

Other related forms are *copyrightable* and *copyrighter*. The latter is not to be confused with *copywriter*, one who writes advertising copy.

For a note on the abbreviation of *copyright*, see ©, c., C., COP.

cordially, cordially yours　See COMPLIMENTARY CLOSE.

corporation　Always capitalized following a proper name: *Diamond International Corporation*. Not abbreviated except after a proper name: *Diamond International Corp*. See also CAPITALS 5(a) and 5(b) and NAMES 2(a).

correlatives　Paired conjunctions used to connect coordinate sentence elements: *both . . . and; not only . . . but* (or *but also*); *either . . . or; neither . . . nor* (see PARALLEL STRUCTURE). The members of the paired conjunctions belong immediately before the coordinate elements, shown in brackets in the following examples.

Participative management is a way *not only* [to get the industrial worker more involved], *but* [to make him more productive].

They wanted the credit for *both* [conceiving the idea] *and* [carrying it out].

Either [the address was wrong] *or* [the air express company was careless].

We wished *neither* [to bid on the whole job] *nor* [to accept the job as a subcontractor].

correspond　To communicate by letters, usually over a period of time; suggests a reciprocal activity. Not to be used for *write: We corresponded regularly during his tenure as chairman*. But: *I wrote* (not *corresponded*) *on April 8 and again on April 20*.

correspondence　Communication through an exchange of letters; also a body of letters sent or received. Not to be used for *letter: have been in correspondence with*. But: *in our letter* (not *correspondence*) *of July 21*.

correspondence secretary　An employee charged primarily with originating or answering letters or transcribing letters from dictated copy, often with the help of WORD PROCESSING equipment. Compare CORRESPONDING SECRETARY.

correspondent　1. A writer of letters.　2. In banking, a bank dependent for various services on a larger or more favorably located bank, with which it maintains a **COMPENSATING BALANCE.**

corresponding secretary An individual elected or otherwise designated to correspond with members of a fraternal organization, professional society, or similar body, as by sending notices of meetings and answering inquiries. Compare **CORRESPONDENCE SECRETARY.**

cosmetic Decorative or superficial, with no change in substance or function: *The change in design was purely cosmetic.*

cosmeticize To make a **COSMETIC** change: *They cosmeticized the old model and raised the price, but essentially it's the same car.*

cost Acceptably used as a transitive verb, meaning to estimate or figure the costs of: *Let's cost the program before we discuss it any further.* Compare **COST OUT.**
—**costing,** noun: *The aim is to standardize the costing* [the method by which the cost is arrived at].

cost-benefit analysis A statistical technique for determining which of several ways of achieving a given objective offers the greatest benefit in relation to cost: *Before the architects get carried away by pie-in-the-sky approaches to our building needs, we should call for some honest cost-benefit analysis.* See also **COST-EFFECTIVE.**

cost-effective Also *cost-beneficial.* Economical; providing benefits consistent with the money spent: *Wood is claimed to be the most cost-effective material for windows in private homes/The company has developed transmission techniques that may never be cost-effective/Environmental regulations? Yes, but they must be cost-effective* (or *cost-beneficial*).

costly 1. Expensive, with the implication of the quality and the importance or rarity of an object: *a costly 18th-century side table.*
2. High-priced; also expensive in the loss of time, energy, or other resources: *a costly redecorating job/a costly experience/a costly lawsuit.*

cost out More than the verb **COST** alone suggests, to *cost out* is to figure the total costs over the life of an object or program and thereby make possible a true comparison with the available alternatives: *When we costed out* [past tense] *the project, we realized there'd be no profit in it.*

cost-plus An amount equivalent to the actual cost, plus a fixed fee or percentage; an arrangement common in contracts let by the government: *The new fighter plane will be built on a cost-plus basis.*

cost-push Describing inflation caused by the pressure of increased costs, as of labor and raw materials. Compare DEMAND-PULL.

could of Illiterate for *could have* or its contraction *could've. Should of* and *would of* are similarly flawed: *They could have* (or *could've*) *sold more.*

council A deliberative body; not to be confused with COUNSEL. In some instances, also, part of an impressive name for a trade association or its propaganda offshoot (see PREPOSSESSIVE WORDS): *Council on Family Health* (established by pharmaceutical manufacturers who describe it as "a public service of the manufacturers of medicine")/*The American Council of Life Insurance* (the life insurance companies)/*The Advertising Council* (an association of advertising groups organized to promote PUBLIC-INTEREST ADVERTISING campaigns/*The Metropolitan Energy Council* (an organization of oil dealer groups formed to promote oil and counter "misinformation").

councilor Also *councillor.* A member of a COUNCIL or other deliberative body. Not to be confused with COUNSELOR.

counsel 1. Advice: *We value your counsel.* Also, an adviser, particularly an attorney-at-law: *We'll turn the matter over to our counsel.* 2. To *counsel,* the verb, is to give advice: *They counseled caution.*

counselor One who gives advice, a CONSULTANT; also an ATTORNEY (counselor-at-law). Not to be confused with COUNCILOR: *Her tax advisory service has fostered so much enthusiasm that she is now training other would-be counselors.*

counterfeit In its CONNOTATION, an improvement over FAKE, thereby qualifying it perhaps as a descriptive for higher-class merchandise: *Created by Wellington. Designer collection of the finest counterfeit diamonds.*

counterproductive EUPHEMISM for *injurious;* producing results contrary to a desired objective: *Your efforts on their behalf would only be counterproductive.*

couple of *Couple* for *couple of* is acceptable only in colloquial use, if then: *Just give us a couple of* (rather than *a couple*) *more days.*

couponing   The practice of issuing and redeeming manufacturers' coupons good for cash rebates at retail stores: *The latest converts to couponing are the wine brands/You see the couponing because people are becoming more price conscious.* See also -ING and DOUBLE COUPONS.

courier   A word associated with diplomatic pouches, *courier* has been borrowed for its CONNOTATION for the names of speedy parcel delivery services *(Purolator Courier Corp., Air Couriers International)* and those of local messenger services. Federal Express has a "Courier Pak" for overnight letter delivery.

courtesy and tact   1. In face-to-face encounters, courtesy usually requires nothing more than instinctive good manners. Writing—letter writing particularly—takes more conscious effort, putting on the correspondent the responsibility of being alert to both the need for courtesy and the opportunities to put that quality into words. The use of expressions like PLEASE, THANK YOU, and SORRY makes a good start; they constitute a language of courtesy that may be only superficial, but they still give civility to the most mundane messages.

> Thank you for your order of April 16.
> We appreciate your writing so promptly.
> I am sorry you lost your passbook, but don't worry; it can be replaced.
> We sincerely regret the trouble we caused you.
> Please be sure to call on us if we can be of help.

See also QUESTION OF COURTESY.

2. Tact, even more than courtesy, is an appreciation of the delicacy of a situation and requires an equally appropriate use of language. Expressions like "you CLAIM," "you NEGLECT to state," and "we MUST ask," though not meant to annoy, may so irritate the reader that a satisfactory response becomes all but impossible to obtain. A gratuitous word or phrase can also ruffle feelings when no offense is intended.

> I am patiently waiting to hear from the commissioner. [May I hear from the commissioner?]
> Please let us know whether you intend to send us this information. [Please let us know when we may expect to receive this information.]
> If you will send us a sample of your product, we will determine the benefit, if any. [. . . we will see what use we can make of it.]
> Contrary to your opinion, we do not believe that the fault occurred in the packing process. [Strike out *Contrary to your opinion.*]

Please accept our apologies if our error caused you any inconvenience. [We are sorry about the inconvenience we caused you.]

See also **LETTER WRITING** 3.

cover letter Also *covering letter*. A letter calling attention to a résumé, letter, or other enclosure. The cover letter not only serves as a record that the item was sent, but also gives a personal touch to what would otherwise be a routine act. See **RÉSUMÉS** 4. Also compare with **LETTER OF TRANSMITTAL** and **ROUTING SLIP**.

C.P.A. See **CERTIFIED PUBLIC ACCOUNTANT**.

CPI See **CONSUMER PRICE INDEX**.

CPM 1. In advertising, cost per thousand; a figure showing the cost of reaching each 1,000 of audience or circulation.
2. Also C.P.M. **CERTIFIED PURCHASING MANAGER**.

C.P.S. See **CERTIFIED PROFESSIONAL SECRETARY**.

CPU Central processing unit; that part of the computer in which the logic and arithmetic functions are performed.

craft 1. An occupation or trade requiring manual dexterity (dressmaker, carpenter, plumber, etc.): *It is not known whether the striking reporters will be supported by the craft unions.*
2. *Craft*, the verb, can mean to make by hand, but it is just as likely to be applied to anything presumably made or manufactured with care. Use of the term *hand-crafted* helps to preserve the distinction: *crafted of solid mahogany after a classic 18th-century design*. But: *hand-crafted by artisans in our own shop*. See **CONNOTATION**.

craft union A labor union limited to workers in the same **CRAFT**. Compare **INDUSTRIAL UNION** and **TRADE UNION**.

crank in To make allowance for some new element in a process; to take account of: *As the economy gets back to normal and both sides get down to bargain about wages, management will be able to crank in a lower rate of inflation.*

creative A synonym for *imaginative* or *original*, as in "creative accounting," "creative advertising," and "creative financing," *creative* is finding new applications in business, not all of them flattering: *The ethics of syndication are not to be considered beyond reproach. Anything is possible. Kickbacks and bill-paddings and creative accounting are rumored constantly.*

credential   As a verb, JARGON for "give official status to": *She was one of the many writers credentialed for Boston's 350th birthday celebration.*

credibility   In ARGUMENT, the sum of the qualities that make a statement of *fact* or *opinion* worthy of belief.

A FACT is most credible when it comes from a reliable source and is unambiguously stated, verifiable, and relevant.

An OPINION is most credible when it comes from a person qualified as an authority, when it relates to the specific area of expertise in which that person practices, and when it is not subject to personal bias. Those qualifications aside, an opinion is apt to be valued in direct proportion to the esteem in which the person giving the opinion is held.

credible, creditable   That which is credible is believable or plausible: *a credible statement, a credible witness.* That which is creditable is deserving of credit or commendation: *a creditable act.*

—**credibly, creditably,** adverbs: *spoke credibly* (in a manner that inspired belief)/*acted creditably* (in a manner deserving commendation).

credit card   See CHARGE CARD, CREDIT CARD.

creditworthy   One word. So, too, *creditworthiness: One of Mr. Corrello's primary responsibilities is monitoring the creditworthiness of customers around the world.*

crisis management   In public relations a term denoting the application of strategies to minimize the damage done to a company's IMAGE as a result of some unfortunate occurrence like a catastrophic accident, a public accusation of wrongdoing, or the closing of a plant. Remedial actions range from issuing news releases and writing speeches to lobbying.

criterion   A test or standard. The plurals are *criteria* (preferred) and *criterions: One criterion* (not *One criteria) is the ability to pay/The criteria* (or *criterions) have not yet been established.*

critique   Acceptable as a noun denoting a critical review, but it is better not used as a pretentious or inexact substitute for a word like *criticism, review, discussion,* or *analysis: We'd like a critique (an analysis) of our sales training program/The presentation was followed by a critique (discussion?) of the speaker's proposal.*

As a verb *critique* is new and occasionally useful, though jarring to some sensibilities: *Benson was asked to critique the report.*

CRT The TV-like cathode-ray tube that permits the visual display of data at a computer terminal or as part of a **WORD PROCESSOR** equipped for text editing.

crunch An overworked synonym for words like *crisis, confrontation,* and *squeeze: The credit crunch (crisis) is expected in July/Some of us were reminded of the crunch (recession) of 1973–74/The crunch (confrontation) with the union will come with the opening of the automated plant.*

cumshaw From the Chinese, a gratuity or present; sometimes a bribe or **PAYOFF**: *The cumshaw had become an inevitable part of their dealings with foreign politicians.*

cumulative, accumulative Although the words are synonymous, *cumulative* is often preferred in the sense of increasing, as in number or amount, by successive additions. Thus a *cumulative preferred stock* is a preferred stock on which declared dividends are allowed to accumulate for later payment; and *cumulative voting* is a system which permits a shareholder to multiply the number of shares held by the number of directors to be elected and to vote the entire number for a single director or divide the number among several.

Accumulative, like *cumulative,* may also refer to successive additions, as in *accumulative* [or *cumulative*] *pressures* and *accumulative* [or *cumulative*] *problems.* Only *accumulative,* however, is used in the sense of acquisitive or disposed to amassing money or things: *bric-a-brac appealing to accumulative wage earners/an accumulative instinct.*

curbstoning The practice of some field researchers, such as census enumerators, polltakers, and market surveyors, of faking their reports of interviews: *The unreliability of the survey could be traced to wanton curbstoning.* From the verb *curbstone,* meaning to operate on a curb or street, or without an office; and, derivatively, to work on chance impressions or hunches.

currently *Now* and *at present* are less formal. **PRESENTLY** is not a desirable synonym.

curriculum vitae Pronounced ——— *vee*-tee. Plural, *curricula vitae.* Latin for "the course of [one's] life." Also *vita,* pronounced *vee*-tuh. Academic **JARGON** for **RÉSUMÉ**; pretentious when used in business.

CUSIP Also *cusip.* **ACRONYM** (pronounced *kew*-sip) for Committee on

*U*niform *S*ecurity *I*dentification *P*rocedure (American Bankers Association). The CUSIP number on a stock certificate indicates the company issuing the stock as well as its class and type.

custom Meaning ''made to the specifications of the buyer,'' *custom* is still apt in such terms as *custom shirtmaker, custom tailor,* and *custom-built bookcases.* More often than not, however, the term is intended only to suggest exceptional attention to quality of materials or workmanship: *the Ford Custom 500/many custom details.*

customer See CLIENT.

customize To manufacture or alter to suit the needs of the individual buyer: *A Cadillac with a customized body.*
—**customization,** noun: *Automation technologies are bringing about a new era of customization.* See also -IZE.

customs 1. Takes a plural verb when it refers to the duties on imported or, infrequently, exported goods: *The customs are collected at the port of entry.*
2. Takes a singular verb when it refers to the government agency charged with collecting customs or to the procedures it follows: *Customs is very strict in controlling the entry of perishable goods/Customs at the airport has now been simplified.*

cutthroat HYPERBOLE for ''cruel'' or ''ruthless,'' as in *cutthroat competition.* The word is best used, if at all, in a way that avoids the commonplace: *The consumer electronics business has produced some fierce marketing wars, but none is likely to be so cutthroat as the struggle for control of the videodisc industry.*

cutting edge See EDGE.

cyclical Pronounced *sik*-lik-ul; also *sike*-. Generally preferred to *cyclic,* meaning ''periodic,'' as coinciding with fluctuations in the economy: *cyclical products* (steel and chemicals)/*cyclical stocks* (those of companies manufacturing CAPITAL GOODS)/*cyclical unemployment* (compare STRUCTURAL UNEMPLOYMENT). See also SECULAR.

czar Informal for a person having great authority, but not necessarily a tyrant: *czar of the transport union/a movie czar/the President's frustrated czar of wages and prices.* Compare TYCOON.

D

dagger The symbol †. Used like the ASTERISK for an occasional footnote reference when the more formal numerical system is not required. The double dagger (‡) may be used for a second footnote following a single dagger, but two single daggers (††) are more familiar and clearer. See also REFERENCE NOTES.

dais Pronounced, preferably, *day*-iss. Plural, daises (*day*-iss-iz). A platform for speakers or honored guests and diners. Compare with LECTERN and PODIUM.

D & B For Dun & Bradstreet, purveyors of credit and financial data to the business community: *a D & B report.*

dangling modifier The term describes a phrase that, if not thoughtfully used, remains grammatically disembodied from the rest of the sentence or attaches itself to the wrong word. The error often, but not always, involves a participle (the ''dangling participle'') and often, but not always, occurs at the beginning of the sentence.

> Using its strong financial position, the present Reed Division was acquired by Ace in 1981.

Because of the way the sentence is constructed, the idea in the phrase beginning *Using* refers to the subject *Reed Division*, but it wasn't the Reed Division that used its strong financial position; it had to be Ace. Hence the sentence should read:

> Using its strong financial position, Ace acquired the present Reed Division in 1981.

1. METHODS OF CORRECTION. (a) Recast the main part of the sentence so that the dangling phrase is given the proper word to modify. This method was used in the sentence cited above. Here is another example:

> DANGLING MODIFIER: In establishing Capital Funds, safety of principal was the main objective.
>
> CORRECTED: In establishing Capital Funds, we made safety of principal our main objective. [Modifies *we*]

The next sentence is corrected in the same way.

DANGLING APPOSITIVE PHRASE: An executive experienced in labor relations, it was felt he would do much to solve our problem.

CORRECTED: An executive experienced in labor relations, he was expected to do much to solve our problem. [Descriptive of *he*]

(b) Recast the dangling phrase to make clear the connection with the rest of the sentence.

DANGLER: The need for training doesn't end after being hired. [After *who* is hired?]

CORRECTED: The need for training doesn't end after an employee is hired.

(c) Recast the whole sentence to eliminate the dangling phrase.

DANGLER: By rearranging the present layout, more laboratory space would be available.

CORRECTED: Rearranging the present layout would make more laboratory space available.

2. EXCEPTIONS. Several types of phrases grammatically isolated from the rest of the sentence are permitted by usage.

(a) Absolute participle (a participle having its own subject).

A major demand having been won, the claimants backed off from major litigation.

They pondered the decision for a long time, *no one apparently knowing what to do*.

Although the absolute participle is grammatically sanctioned, the idea can usually be expressed in a less cumbersome way.

When they won their major demand, the claimants backed off from further litigation.

They pondered the decision for a long time; no one apparently knew what to do.

(b) Idiomatic phrase at the beginning of a sentence.

Strictly speaking, the interest was not due until June 16.

To tell the truth, no one realized the indirect effects the delay would have.

As a rule, refunds are paid within thirty days after the claim is approved.

(c) Sentence modifier (any independent phrase considered to affect the meaning of the whole sentence).

To judge from their past performance, the contractors deserve our confidence.

Considering that the suits are sewn entirely by hand, the prices seem reasonable enough.

dash (—) A punctuation mark providing an emphatic separation of sentence elements or signifying an abrupt change in the normal sentence pattern. On a typewriter the dash is made by a double hyphen (--).

The dash is not used with a colon or comma, but it is followed by a period or other end mark when it concludes a sentence. Dashes are best used sparingly; they should not take the place of more appropriate marks or serve as a substitute for carefully wrought sentences.

USES:

1. To mark a sudden break in thought.

They asked for—no, they demanded—the exclusive selling rights.

Insurers, lawyers, judges—all of them share the responsibility of controlling excessive claims.

As they say, a bird in the hand—. [*Also:* in the hand . . . (See **ELLIPSIS** 3.)]

2. To give prominence to a sentence element that might otherwise be put in parentheses.

Total payroll costs—wages, benefits, and applicable payroll taxes—exceeded $1.5 billion.

The Braun juice extractor. An absolute essential for anyone who likes his juices—vegetable or fruit—straight from the source.

The trend to electronic media has largely been the result of improved—and less costly—technology.

3. To emphasize a series of parallel sentence elements (see **PARALLEL STRUCTURE**).

Find out exactly what protection you now have—how much of the bills your basic plan will cover—how much this new Major Medical plan will cover.

4. To emphasize a final word or thought.

They did—what?

Mail the order card—now!

Those were the days when news was—news.

But our business is not locking customers' meters—it's selling gas.

5. To mark the omission of letters in a word.

The secret witness is a Mr. R———. (Long dash)

6. After an introductory phrase, to signify that the same words are to be understood before each member of a following series.

We therefore propose—

That . . .

That . . .

That . . . etc.

data Pronounced *day*-tuh or *dat*-uh. Information collected and used for analysis; the information, especially of a quantitative kind, fed to computers. *Data* is the plural of *datum*, a particular item of information. *Datum* is rarely used, but *data*, though plural in some formal usages, is regularly treated as a singular collective noun: *This data is incomplete; more data is needed.* But (formal usage): *The statisticians asked to review the report discovered an error in how the data were analyzed.*

data base The collection of specific types of information held in a computer and available for use by the owner or for sale to others: *a data base of 9,000 companies followed regularly by 300 brokers and their security analysts/a data base of advertising and marketing information gathered from 60 trade and professional journals, newsletters, newspapers, and magazines.*

—**data-based,** adjective: *The company pioneered in data-based publishing, which allows subscribers to call up data from the publisher's computer onto their own terminals.*

date 1. Informal for "appointment" or "engagement": *We have a date with the Board on Thursday/Greer and I have a date for lunch.*

2. Informal as a reference to a person, especially one of the opposite sex, with whom one has a social engagement: *My date didn't arrive until ten o'clock.* The word is not used to signify a business visitor or a person visited on business.

See also **DATES.**

dated 1. Old-fashioned, out-of-date: *The style is dated.*

2. Marked with a date, as a letter or memorandum, or perishable goods bearing the last date of sale, the date until which the consumer can expect the product to retain its freshness: *The letter is dated March 11/Milk sold in New York is dated.*

3. Redundant, as in the phrase "your letter dated May 8." Better: *your letter of May 8.* See also **WORDINESS** 3.

date line 1. On a letter with a printed heading, the first typewritten line. The month is spelled out, and a comma is placed between the day and year.

SCOTT ADVERTISING INC.
22 Meadow Lane
Dec. 10, 1983

(a) Begins at center

SCOTT ADVERTISING INC.
22 Meadow Lane
Dec. 10, 1983

(b) Ends at margin

SCOTT ADVERTISING INC.
22 Meadow Lane
Dec. 10, 1983

(c) Aligned with the L

Date line 2.   Optional positions with modified block style or semiblock style.

December 2, 19xx

See also **DATES**.

2. The position of the date line on the letter sheet varies. A "floating" date line is typed from 12 to 20 lines below the top edge of the sheet, depending on the length of the letter. A fixed date line is usually typed two or three lines below the last line of the letterhead. If the full block style or simplified style is used, the date begins at the left margin. If the modified block or semiblock style is used, the date begins (a) at or five spaces to the right of the horizontal center of the page, (b) in a position that will align the date with the right margin, or (c) in a position below a particular point in the letterhead (see figure). Centering takes time. Unusual arrangements in two or three lines smack of boondoggling. See also **LETTER FORM** 2–5.

3. Form letters often omit the date line or substitute a general date for an exact one, as September 19xx, Christmas 19xx, Spring 19xx.

dates 1. The name of the month is spelled out in the **DATE LINE** of a letter and in a running text. Ordinal numbers are not used for the days of the month: January 10, 19xx (*not* January 10th, 19xx). However, dates in context may be expressed in the style of *the third of August* or *your letter of the 3rd* (But: *your letter of August 3,* not *your letter of August 3rd*).

2. In in-house notes and informal memorandums, the names of the months are sometimes abbreviated, or the whole date is written numerically in the style of 4/6/83. The writer must be sure, though, that there is agreement on the order of the month and day. In American usage 4/6 is April 6; in foreign usage it is June 4.

3. In military and some other formal or official usages, dates are written in the style of 4 July 1983. In military correspondence, the abbreviation is 4 Jul 83 (not 4/7/83), and the abbreviations of all months consist of the first three letters (no period following).

4. In some formal invitations and legal documents (notably wills) the date is spelled out in full: July ninth, Nineteen hundred and eighty-three.

5. Other examples of styling:

in the thirties; the mid-Eighties; back in '75
in the 60's and 70's (*also* '60s and '70s)
in the 1980's (*also* 1980s)
1985–90 (*or* 1985–1990)
the March 1980 issue; dated May 12, 1982, and later

days of the week   The names of the days are usually spelled out. When, as in a table, abbreviations are required, uniform three-letter abbreviations may be used: *Mon., Tue., Wed., Thu., Fri., Sat., Sun.* Tuesday and Thursday are also conventionally abbreviated *Tues.* and *Thurs.* (rather than *Tu.* and *Th.*).

D.C.S.   Doctor of Commercial Science. See **FORMS OF ADDRESS** 1.

dead   Not usually subject to comparison. But for example of acceptable use, see **ABSOLUTE ADJECTIVES**.

deadbeat   Slang for a debtor who does not pay: *We will not sell to that deadbeat.*

deadwood   Superfluous words, as in "entirely eliminated" and "in close proximity." See also **WORDINESS** 3.

deal   1. Informal for "arrangement," "transaction," "bargain," or some indefinite quantity or degree: *A long-term deal (arrangement) for financing Chinese imports is now being negotiated/The deal (transaction) was mutually satisfactory/We got a good deal (bargain) on the trade-in/She has a great deal of (much) experience.* However, *deal* is not to be used for *many* or *numerous: The accord covers a great many* (not *a great deal*) *of the major steel carriers.*

2. Slang for "fuss" or "issue": *Why make such a big deal out of a small mistake?*

3. *Deal,* the verb, meaning "to do business," is thoroughly acceptable in general usage: *We deal with many important exporters/They will deal fairly with you.* The verb is informal, however, in the expression *We're dealing,* denoting a readiness to strike a bargain, as in the sale of cars.

dear   1. High-priced, expensive: *Lamb is dear, but beef is dearer.* Compare **COSTLY**.

2. A conventional part of the **SALUTATION** of letters addressed to individuals: *Dear Mr. Sampson; Dear Henry.*

dearly   At a high price: *We pay dearly for the leather we use/Their refusal to negotiate will cost us dearly.*

Dear Madam, Dear Sir, etc.   See **SALUTATION**.

debit   An accounting term, better understood by business people than by consumers: *The debit (charge) will appear on your next state-ment/We have debited (charged) your account.*

debit card   A "credit" card without the credit. Purchases are charged directly to the user's bank account. As a result, the customer loses the FLOAT allowed by the credit card—the thirty-day period during which there are no interest charges on new purchases.

debugging   1. The removal of flaws, as in a product design, a questionnaire, or a computer program: *At the start of the debugging, the question arose whether "fatal" flaws in the design were about to be revealed.*
   2. The dismantling of wiretapping devices: *When electronic eavesdropping was suspected, an expert in debugging was called in.*
   See also BUG.

debut   Pronounced duh-*byoo*, day-*byoo*, or *day*-byoo. Standard as a noun meaning "first public appearance": *The new Cadillac makes its debut in March.* As a verb, however, *debut* is considered by many to be non-standard: *The new Cadillac debuts in March/The first tea bags debuted at the 1906 St. Louis World's Fair/The manufacturer will debut his fashions at Neiman-Marcus.* Compare with PREMIER, PREMIERE.

decision-making process   Usually pretentious for *decision-making: We must cut the time of the decision-making process (the time for decision-making)/The chairman invariably takes an active part in the decision-making process (in decision-making)/We must pay more attention to the operation of the decision-making process (to the way decisions are made).* See also WORDINESS 2.

decorator   The favorable reputation of the interior decorator has been borrowed in the use of *decorator* as a general descriptive word: *decorator colors, decorator fabrics, decorator designs, decorator touches.* See CONNOTATION.

decruitment   EUPHEMISM for dismissal from employment: *Workers marked for decruitment may be temporarily assigned to special duties.*

deem   Stilted for *think, believe, suppose, consider, judge: We deem it advisable to protest the claim (We think it advisable; We believe you should; In our judgment, you should).*

de facto   Pronounced dee-*fak*-toe. Latin for "in fact"; descriptive of the exercise of power without actual legal authority: *In Dobson's ab-*

sence, Jordan is the de facto head of the enterprise/Europe's hectic airline ticket discount outlets are technically illegal. But last year alone this form of de facto deregulation saved international travelers $2 billion. Compare **DE JURE.**

defalcate Pronounced, preferably, dih-*fal*-cate. To use funds in violation of a trust; to embezzle. Nouns: *defalcation* (def-ul-*kay*-shun; *defalcator* (dih-*fal*-kay-tur).

definite, definitive Both words are used in the sense of "clear and explicit," but *definitive* has the added suggestion of conclusiveness or finality: *was definite about the time and place.* But: *has written a definitive (conclusive) history of the CIA.*
  —**definitely, definitively,** adverbs: *We are definitely committed to the purchase.* But: *Neither of the agencies could say definitively whether the building was covered by the Historic Preservation Act.*

definitize To put into specific terms; to define precisely: **JARGON**, perhaps, but concise and clear: *When we definitize the proposal, we'll lay it before the Board.*

deflation Any decrease in the general price level and corresponding increase in purchasing power. Compare **DISINFLATION.**

degreed **JARGON** for "possessing a college degree": *Wanted—men and women degreed in mechanical engineering.* See also **CERTIFICATE.**

degrees and certifications 1. An academic degree follows a name only when the degree is important in signifying the individual's competence in a specific field. Among academics, a doctorate such as Ph.D. (Doctor of Philosophy) or the title Dr. is commonly indicated. Lesser degrees (master and bachelor) are not. A medical degree (M.D.) or title (Dr.) invariably goes with the name.
  In business, a professional certification like C.P.A. (Certified Public Accountant) or C.L.U. (Chartered Life Underwriter) may be appended to the name. Except in the written signature, a business person with an honorary degree is free to use the title Dr. (if that is the degree) or to append the abbreviation to the name (as Alvin C. Forrester, LL.D.). The holder of an honorary doctorate may also be addressed *Doctor* or *Dr.* as a special mark of respect.
  2. Except in formal or ceremonial use, only the highest degree, if any, follows a name. In any listing of degrees, however, the order of academic degrees is lowest to highest, followed by honorary de-

grees in the order of bestowal and, finally, by professional certifications. Religious orders and theological degrees take precedence over
academic degrees.

Barnard W. Wald, Ph.D., D.C.S., C.P.A.

Gerald O. Hanahan, S.J., D.D., Ph.D., D.H.L.

Fenwick Marvell, A.B., M.S., Sc.D.

See also FORMS OF ADDRESS and SIGNATURE BLOCK 1.

dehire A EUPHEMISM for *dismiss* or *fire* (a worker): *The company gave only a handful of the dehired executives professional assistance in finding a job.*

de jure Pronounced dee-*joor*-ee. Latin for "by right, legally": *Hanson is the de jure head of the council, but Cribben holds the power.*

delamping See RELAMPING.

de luxe Also *deluxe*. Pronounced dih-*looks* or dih-*luks*. Luxurious, elegant. Much used, but still descriptive of a high level of refinement: *de luxe suites, deluxe interiors, deluxe treatment.* See also LUXE.

demand-pull Describing inflation caused by the pressure of high demand in the face of limited supplies. Compare COST-PUSH.

demo A CLIPPED FORM of *demonstration: man or woman needed for service demos and presentations/sale of demo models.*

demographic edition CLIPPED FORM, *demo.* An edition published simultaneously with the regular edition of a newspaper or magazine and especially edited for an audience with particular DEMOGRAPHICS, such as corporate executives, doctors, and educators: *Demographic editions are attractive to advertisers because they claim to give access to an upscale readership/They're spawning demos as fast as rabbits; Time already has seven.*

demographics A plural noun. Also *demography*. The statistics of population, including size, growth, distribution, economic status, and personal data. *Demographics show that there is almost no eighteen- to twenty-five-year-old audience for the Jerry Lewis brand of comedy and that nearly all the ticket buyers older than twenty-five bring their children with them.*

—**demographic,** adjective: *a demographic study.*

denotation The literal meaning of a word, as distinguished from its suggested meaning, or CONNOTATION.

depend Followed by *on* or *upon: The renewal of the offer depends on* (or *upon*) *its success.* Also: . . . *depends on whether it is successful* (but not . . . *depends whether it is successful*).

dependent The noun, but not the adjective, is sometimes spelled *-ant*, but there can be no mistake if the *-ent* ending is used for both: *The worker has two dependents* (or, infrequently, *dependants*). But: *The company is now wholly dependent* (not *dependant*) *on the output of their Fargo mill.*

depositary, depository Both words denote a place for the safekeeping of cash or other valuables. *Depositary*, however, is the more likely term for a person or institution, such as a FIDUCIARY entrusted with valuables for preservation or safekeeping: *The Sony Corporation's gains in the equity market here are shown by the American depositary receipts, now holding at a level three times as high as in February 1980.* But: *Several of the utility's depositories (rather than depositaries) accept payments directly from consumers/The Board of Education uses the building as a book depository* (rather than *depositary*). See also RE-POSITORY.

depreciate in value Redundant. Depreciate means "to lessen in value": *Even the best equipment depreciates* (not *depreciates in value*). See also WORDINESS 3.

depression A severe decline in economic activity. "While there is no standard quantitative definition of depression, it signifies a spell of high unemployment and idle industrial capacity lasting for several years and more likely to be marked by falling prices than by inflation" [Leonard Silk]. Compare RECESSION.

designer Descriptive of an article fashioned by a person with a reputation for quality and taste in the field; also suggestive of those attributes when no designer is named: *designer jeans/designer wallpaper/designer sheets and matching pillowcases.* Compare DECORATOR.

desk 1. Objection is now and then raised to the conceit of using notesheets imprinted "From the desk of —————." That the message was dispatched from a desk is superfluous, and the impersonal tone of the whole phrase smacks of petty officiousness. The name alone is sufficient.

2. *Desk*, as part of a name designating a post or station, is standard: *information desk/call desk/city desk.*

deskilling Simplifying a job by the introduction or extension of machine labor: *fear that computerization will bring about a "deskilling" of the operation, with individual workers performing only part of what used to be their entire job.*

detail However the word is used, it is acceptably pronounced with the emphasis on either syllable: *The manager was fussy about details* [noun]/*We will detail each expenditure* [verb].

detail man (woman) A person employed by a pharmaceutical or medical supply house to promote its products in calls on doctors, dentists, and other professionals who use or prescribe them.

develop This is the customary spelling. Despite support by some dictionaries, *develope* is rare and used at risk. *Develop* is acceptably used in the sense of gather or compile (as information): *The data on housing deterioration was developed at the request of Senator Burns.*

dial With the push-button telephone taking the place of the dial phone, *dial* (as in "Just dial 555-1234") must make room for other words that are superseding it. See, for example, TOUCH, PUNCH IN, PUNCH UP. *Dial* is still common, however, when the use of either a dial or push-button telephone is anticipated: *When you're away, you may be able to have all your calls reach you wherever you are—simply by dialing a special set of numbers and programming your day* [AT&T].

In general, problems presented by the use of *dial* may be solved by substituting the terms *call, phone,* and *telephone: Call 555-1234 any time between 9 and 5.*

—dial up. One *dials* a number, but *dials up* information to which the telephone provides access: *Right now, some people are participating in experiments that let them dial up news, weather, and other information on their home video screens* [AT&T].

dialectal terms See USAGES 5.

dialogue An overworked synonym for an exchange of ideas: *We have a continuing dialogue with our employees through personal contact, meetings, and our suggestion system/The community dialogue will help to determine whether the plant is to be built/I look at the meeting as a dialogue rather than a search for conclusions.* A simple synonym is sometimes more apt: *Our dialogue (talk) was held last Thursday/After a lengthy dialogue (conversation) with the foreman, Hynes agreed to go back to work.*

—one-sided dialogue. Communication marked by a failure to invite other views or to listen when other views are expressed; a facetious term for *monologue*.

See also TWO-WAY COMMUNICATION.

dichotomy Pronounced die-*kot*-uh-me. A division into two contradictory parts. The less pretentious word *contradiction* usually does as well or better: *Analysts sense a curious dichotomy between the worsening economic forecasts and the buoyancy of the stock market.*

dictated but not signed This offensive notation, placed on a letter signed by proxy, is happily now rare. See SIGNATURE BLOCK 5.

differ from, differ with To differ from is to be unlike or dissimilar: *We differ from our larger competitors only in size.* To differ with is to disagree: *They differ with us on the extent of the possible loss.*

difference, differential 1. A *difference* is a disparity or variation: *a big difference in salaries/no difference in quality/will iron out the differences in conference.* A *differential* is the degree or amount of difference, as in the rates charged for the transportation of two different cargoes over the same route, or wages paid to workers for the same kind of work done under different conditions: *The pressmen had earlier rejected an agreement on pay differentials drafted by their union representatives/We plan to offer transferred employees a rent differential to compensate for the higher residential costs in their new location/In broadening their menus, the limited-menu chains have made themselves vulnerable to intense competition from the coffee-shop chains because the price differential has been narrowed but the quality differential has not.*

2. *Differential* is misused as an elegant synonym for *difference: Please send us a check for the difference* (not *differential*).

different from, different than *Different from* has general acceptance, but *different than* is less formal and often makes a smoother sentence when a clause follows: *Our plan is different from Ryan's in several respects* (Less formal: *Our plan is different than Ryan's*)/*The designer's concept is different from* (or *different than*) *anything we've seen before.* Awkward: *We decided to use a different fabric from that which the designer specified.* Better: *We decided to use a different fabric than* (or *from the one*) *the designer specified.*

direct address For punctuation of words in direct address, see COMMA 4(a).

direct advertising Any advertising that permits the advertiser to control its distribution and select the individuals who will receive the message. Includes unmailed advertising (as HANDBILLS, store displays, and package inserts), as well as DIRECT-MAIL ADVERTISING.

direct-mail advertising Advertising in any form sent through the mails, but not including paid advertising in a newspaper, magazine, or other periodical. See also DIRECT RESPONSE ADVERTISING.

direct quotations See QUOTATION MARKS 1.

direct response advertising Any advertising, as by print, phone, or broadcast media, designed to obtain orders, sales leads, or other evidence of interest from prospective customers. See also MAIL-ORDER SELLING.

dis- A compound formed with the prefix *dis* is not hyphened, even when the second part of the compound begins with *s: dissatisfied, disservice, dissimilar*. Compare MIS-. See also HYPHEN 2.

disadvantaged A EUPHEMISM for the poor: *unemployment among the disadvantaged*. Also an adjective: *disadvantaged families*.

disassociate A LONG VARIANT of *dissociate*. Similarly, *disassociation* for *dissociation*.

disastrous So spelled; not *disasterous: a disastrous fire*.

disburse To pay out, to distribute money; not to be confused with *disperse* (scatter) or DISPENSE: *Window 3 disburses petty cash/The proceeds were disbursed in accordance with the donor's wishes*.
—**disbursement,** noun: *manages the disbursement of funds from the estate*.

disc, disk Variant spellings, but *disc* is preferred for the phonograph record; *disk*, in computer applications: *disk storage, floppy disks*.

discounter A retailer who regularly sells standard merchandise at a discount: *The basic appeal of the discounter is his low prices*.

discounting The practice of selling regular merchandise below established prices: *Large-scale discounting could become a threat to established marketing channels*. Compare OFF-PRICE RETAILING.

discriminate To act with prejudice; but, also, to differentiate or make a fine distinction. Where there is even a hint of ambiguity, a change in language is necessary: *In developing a promotion policy, we need to*

discriminate more carefully among workers in the same classification.
Better: *. . . we need to devise better competency tests among workers in the same classification.*

discuss One discusses something; hence *discuss* is properly followed by an object: *Let us discuss your investment needs.* The word is misused and awkward, however, in such a locution as, *As we discussed* (or *As discussed*), *the work will begin on April 16.* Better: *As we agreed* (or *As agreed*) . . .

discussant Academic JARGON, but sometimes a convenient synonym for a panelist or participant (in a discussion, of course). *Discusser* is not an easily accepted substitute because of the sound and suggestion.

disincentive Absence of reward. In many instances, the simple synonym *deterrent* is to be preferred: *Under the anti-inflation program, producers can expect tax disincentives to keep right on building/Import duties provide a prime disincentive for (deterrent to) the dumping of foreign goods/Closer monitoring of the quality of each worker's output would itself be a strong disincentive for (deterrent to) substandard performance.*

disinflation A slowing of the rate of inflation, particularly by some action of the government, as a tax increase or cuts in spending. Compare DEFLATION.

disinterested, uninterested Although the words are frequently used interchangeably, careful writers and speakers believe there is a distinction worth preserving. To be *disinterested* is to be impartial. To be *uninterested* is to be not interested. A good arbitrator should be a *disinterested* (not *uninterested*) listener and fact finder. But an *uninterested* (not *disinterested*) customer is a poor prospect for a salesperson's wares.

diskette A FLOPPY DISK.

dispense 1. To deal out; to prepare and distribute, as medicine by a pharmacist. Better not used for DISBURSE when funds are involved. But (correct): *dispense one's favors/dispense justice/dispense sodas and sundaes.*

2. *Dispense* is not synonymous with *send: We will see that your statements are hereafter sent* (not *dispensed*) *to your new address.*

—dispense with. To do without: *dispense with the formalities/dispense with frills.*

display advertisement See at CLASSIFIED ADVERTISEMENT.

dissociate   Preferred to DISASSOCIATE.

distribution list   A list of persons selected to receive something, as a copy of a letter or memorandum.

dividend, interest   In finance, a *dividend* is a share of the profits of a company paid to its owners or stockholders, usually at regular intervals: *dividends declared quarterly/omitted the April 1 dividend.* Also, less formal, a PAYOUT.

Interest is what a borrower pays for the use of money, such as that loaned by a bank or finance company. So, too, it is the money earned on, say, deposits in a savings account or invested in CERTIFICATES OF DEPOSIT or similar savings instruments. Bonds—certificates of debt issued by a government or corporation—earn interest too. Earned interest may be expressed in dollars: *accumulated interest of $6,565.25 since January 1.* Interest paid or exacted is also expressed as a percentage (the *interest rate*): *earns interest of 10.5 percent annually/charge 18 percent* [interest] *per annum on unpaid balances.*

The term *dividend* as a synonym for *interest* is often used by banks in their pronouncements to depositors: *Passbooks should be presented at least once a year for the entry of dividends.*

do.   The abbreviation of *ditto,* "the same as the above." In a table, usually preferred to the sign ″, which is more likely to be overlooked or misunderstood.

dock   To deduct, usually as a penalty, part of an employee's wages: *docked for time off the job.*

doctor   Abbreviated Dr. See FORMS OF ADDRESS 1.

documentation   See REFERENCE NOTES.

dollars   Not to be used after a figure prefixed by a dollar sign: *at a cost of $23 million* (not *$23 million dollars*). See also NUMERALS 2.

dollars and cents   For style of representation, see NUMERALS 2.

dollar value   *Dollar* is redundant when a dollar amount is given: *a gift with a value of $200* (not *a dollar value of $200*). But: *It was a collector's piece, and the dollar value fully reflected its rarity.*

done   Less formal than *finished* or *completed,* but care must be taken to avoid ambiguity: *The cement work will be done in February (completed? started? or started and completed?).* But (no question): *The report is done/We have done the necessary spadework.*

doorstopper Informal name for a business or research report big and bulky enough to hold a door open.

door-to-door See HOUSE-TO-HOUSE.

dope Slang for *information: What's the inside dope?*

dope sheet A "scratch sheet," or bulletin, giving information about the day's horse races; but also, in business, a small periodical providing timely official information for a selected group of employees or executives.

dotted line 1. Part of a STEREOTYPED LETTER PHRASE, "Sign on the dotted line," characterizing the place for the signature, especially on a purchase contract. "Sign" or "Sign where indicated" are usually satisfactory substitutes.

2. Indicative of positions on the same hierarchical level in an organization: *I don't expect to sit on top of a research and development pyramid. Instead, I'll be connected to Parsons by a dotted line from the side.*

double coupon CENTS-OFF COUPONS that retailers redeem for double their face value—a promotional device used primarily by the large grocery chains: *This week, double coupons.*

double dagger See DAGGER.

double-dipping The practice, among civil servants, of retiring on a pension and taking another government job at regular salary. The criticism implied by the word tends to obscure the fact that double-dipping is not illegal.

double negative 1. The use of two negatives to express a single negative idea is nonstandard: *We don't buy from them no more* (Correct: *any more*)/*We scarcely never use the back-room files* (Correct: *scarcely ever*).

2. Some double negatives, however, are well established idiomatically, with one modifying the other to give a positive idea special emphasis: *Don't believe they wouldn't do it* (That is, "Better believe they will do it.")/*We are not insensitive to our customers' feelings/Not for nothing are we fearful of the consequences/It would be imprudent not to attend the meeting.*

3. Double and triple negatives, with all their possibilities for confusion, are often found in official JARGON. Bad: *No lost time inju-*

ries that do not result in a medical expense should not be reported to the O.W.C.P. [U.S. Department of Labor]

double passive An awkward locution. See ACTIVE VOICE, PASSIVE VOICE 6.

double possessive An accepted mode of expression. See APOSTROPHE 1(g).

doubt The word is part of several troublesome phrases. 1. In negative statements, when no doubt exists, the favored expression is "do not doubt that." "Do not doubt but that" is also acceptable, despite the unnecessary *but;* however, "do not doubt but what" is generally frowned on: *The company has no doubt that* (or *but that;* not *but what*) *it will maintain its strong competitive position.* See also BUT THAT.

2. In positive statements, when doubt does exist, the expression is "doubt that": *I doubt that he will succeed.* When unbelief rather than just doubt is to be conveyed, the expressions are *"doubt whether"* or, less formal, *"doubt if": I doubt whether* (or *if*) *he will succeed.*

Dow Jones For Dow Jones & Company, publishers of *The Wall Street Journal* (every business day) and *Barron's* (weekly).

—Dow Jones average. Also *Dow-Jones average.* A reference particularly to the average of 30 leading industrial stocks selected by Dow Jones from stocks listed on the New York Stock Exchange. The average is quoted every half hour on trading days. Separate Dow Jones averages are also compiled for 20 selected transportation stocks and 15 selected utilities, and for the composite average of all 65 stocks.

downsize To reduce the size of an established product: *Hershey responded to increased costs by downsizing their chocolate candy bars/The downsized Chevrolet gets 36 mpg.*

downstream At a distance from realization, as a plant, a new product, a scientific breakthrough: *Some of the commercial applications of laser technology are still ten to twenty years downstream/We've been looking downstream on how to staff the new department for some time now—actually since last September.*

downtime The time during which a machine or factory is idle: *Since the accelerated maintenance program has been in effect, downtime has been reduced by 40 percent.*

downward, downwards The words are interchangeable as adverbs, but only *downward* is an adjective: *was projected downward* (or *down-wards*). But: *a downward* (not *downwards*) *trend*.

downward communication See at COMMUNICATION FLOW.

Dr. Doctor. See FORMS OF ADDRESS. 1. Also dr. (debtor): *N. S. Clark & Co., dr.*

due course Usually overformal, and occasionally vaguer than the sense requires: *We expect to hear from them in due course (in good time)/In due course we received (Soon; Not long after; Eventually).* Also offensive when it suggests a dilatory attitude: *We will attend to the matter in due course (as soon as possible? promptly?).*

due to No question arises about *due to* when used as a synonym for "attributable to," "caused by," or "the result of": *The rise in prices is due almost entirely to the inflated cost of materials/Their exaggerated estimate of earnings was due to gross miscalculations/That they succeeded so well was due to their genius in organization.*

Somewhat less favored is the use of *due to* as a preposition meaning "because of," "on account of," or "through": *Due to (Because of) unforeseen shortages of raw materials, profits dropped to 23 cents for the quarter/Deliveries will be late due to (on account of) the bad weather/Due to (Through) our insistence, we obtained reimbursement from the supplier.*

The difference between the two usages is almost invisible, however, and *due to* as a preposition appears to be firmly entrenched. The substitution of an alternative expression does not necessarily bring any improvement, anyway. In some instances, a solution to the problem (if there is a problem) is offered by a change in sentence structure, but then the writer risks changing the emphasis, too: *Due to (Because of?) recent cost pressures, backlists have also been taking a battering, leaving publishers more reliant on sales of far riskier new titles.* Compare: *Backlists have also been taking a battering from recent cost pressures, leaving publishers more reliant on sales of far riskier new titles.*

—**due to the fact that.** *Because* is simpler. See WORDINESS 4.

duly Rightfully; in a proper manner. Confined largely to legal and other formal documents, *duly* is stilted and unnecessary in ordinary use. Acceptably formal: *a meeting at which it was duly resolved/a duly constituted committee.* Unacceptably stilted: *Payment was duly made and acknowledgment received (Payment was made and acknowledged).*

dumping Exporting goods at a price below that charged by producers in the country of origin: *The dumping of Japanese television sets has virtually eliminated our domestic production.*

dump on Slang for "criticize," "find fault with": *Everybody wants to dump on the foreman.*

dumpster A large metal container for trash or garbage, commonly used by storekeepers and builders. It is so designed that the contents can be dumped mechanically into a trash removal truck or hauled away on a flatbed truck.

dun To ask insistently or repeatedly for payment of a bill: *We dunned them at least twice last month.* Also, a bill collector or an urgent request for payment: *employed as a dun/sent them a dun.*

durable goods Manufactured products with a relatively long life: automobiles, washing machines, furniture, industrial equipment, and the like; hard goods, as opposed to *nondurable* or soft goods, which include such items as clothing, textiles, draperies, and bed linens.

during the course of *During* is enough: *We discovered the error during the course of (during) our examination.* See also **WORDINESS** 4.

during the time that For short, *while*: *I'd like to have you call me during the time that (while) you are in the city/The accident occurred during the time that (while) we were preparing for our opening.* See also **WORDINESS** 4.

dyeing, dying The first relates to coloring (*dye, dyed, dyeing, dyes*); the second, to death (*die, died, dying, dies*): *Dyeing the fabric is risky/The era of the universally affordable private home is dying.*

E

each 1. As the modifier of a subject (*each one, they each*), *each* does not affect the number of the verb; a singular subject takes a singular verb, and a plural subject takes a plural verb: *Each visitor is provided with an ID badge/We each were given* (not *was given*) *a souvenir of the occasion.*

2. As a subject, *each* is singular except where the idea of plurality is strong. In doubtful cases, general usage leans to the singular; informal usage, to the plural. In informal usage, also, it is not uncommon to find a plural pronoun reference after a singular verb. (See also **PRONOUNS 2.**)

STRONG SINGULARITY: Among the platform guests, each was obviously conscious of his importance.

STRONG PLURALITY: Each of these managements have their own peculiar experiences.

DIVIDED USAGE [General]: The company has a sales force of ten. Each has complete control of his own accounts. [Informal]: . . . Each has complete control of their own accounts.

each and every Trite as well as wordy: *each and every sale item (every sale item)/each and every one of us (each of us; all of us).*

each other's Also *one another's.* A noun following either expression is plural: *read each other's* (or *one another's*) *résumés* (not *résumé*)/*respected each other's wishes/knew each other's preferences.*

eager See ANXIOUS.

earliest convenience See CONVENIENCE.

early on The *on* is not superfluous when the expression is used to mean early in a sequence of events: *Early on we recognized that we would have to deal with the question of cost.* But: *They got their bid in early* (not *early on*).

easy, easily Expressions like "take it easy" and "easier said than done" are standard, but usually a clear distinction is made between *easy* (the adjective) and *easily* (the adverb): *an easy assignment/not easy for me to say "no."* But: *moved easily* (not *easy*) *among people of power/won the contract more easily* (not *easier*) *than we imagined.*

econometrics A branch of economics that, aided by computer science, uses mathematical and statistical measures to determine the interaction of such variables as prices, wages, interest rates, etc., and their effect on the economy as a whole.

—econometric, adjective: *econometric studies.*

economic, economical *Economic* relates to economics or finance, or to the creation and management of material wealth by a country, a business enterprise, a family, or an individual: *War creates many economic problems/Cooperative buying is an economic response to high costs/A family's economic health is highly dependent on the economic health of the nation.*

Economical means thrifty, frugal, skillful in the management of money: *An economical person might yet survive such a decline in income/The most economical air conditioning systems are those individually controlled.*

economics As a singular noun, *economics* is the science dealing with the production, distribution, and consumption of goods and services: *Economics is a hard master for businesses and politicians alike.* In the plural (same form) *economics* refers to the various elements of which the ECONOMY of a country or business enterprise is composed: *The economics of the oil industry are* (not *is*) *hard for the layman to understand.*

economy 1. The economic system of a country, or the production and management of its resources: *The economy is improving/All economies are subject to the laws of supply and demand.*

2. *Economy,* not qualified by *an* or *the,* is synonymous with *thrift* or *frugality: We must practice greater economy/Economies can result from careful control of warehousing.*

edge Denoting the desirable qualities associated with keenness, *edge* is a versatile word now in danger of being overused in such phrases as "competitive edge," "leading edge," and "cutting edge": *How to write letters and reports that give you a competitive edge* [competitive advantage]/*Japan is now seen as simply the leading edge* [the forerunner] *of a broader economic challenge from Taiwan, South Korea, Hong Kong, and Singapore/We've always felt that Pepsi advertising has been on the* *cutting edge of* [has taken the lead in] *socioeconomic change; we think we are in tune with the American people.*

EDP   Electronic data processing.

effect   See AFFECT, EFFECT.

efficacy, efficiency   *Efficacy* is effectiveness in the sense of producing a desired result: *the efficacy of a plan/no question about the efficacy of the product.* *Efficiency*, however, is productiveness, a relative quality resulting from the skillful management of resources or from built-in productiveness, as of a machine: *the department's efficiency* (not *efficacy*)/*the efficiency of the printing unit.*

EFT   Electronic funds transfer. The funds are automatically debited or credited to a bank account according to a prearranged schedule or by current transactions originating at a computer terminal. Older citizens know about EFT through the monthly Social Security payments credited directly to their bank accounts. It is believed that the growth of electronic funds transfers will eventually lead to a "checkless [or cashless] society."

e.g.   Abbreviation of the Latin *exempli gratia,* "for example." Used in footnotes and for other reference purposes. In ordinary writing, less formal expressions are preferred, as, "for example," "for instance," "such as," and so forth: *See, e.g., "Statistical Spotlight" in the November 10* Forbes (Better: *See, for example,* . . .). See also REFERENCE NOTES.

800   The prefix signifying a WATS (toll-free) number.

either   1. One or the other. Although *either* is acceptably used when the reference is to one of more than two, that purpose is better served by *any one: Either of the pair will be satisfactory.* But: *Any one* (rather than *Either*) *of the several models will do.*

   2. *Either* in the sense of "both" is questionable even when there is no ambiguity: *Either of the applicants is qualified.* Better: *Both . . . are qualified/The samples were distributed on either side* (Better: *on both sides*) *of the street.*

   3. *Either* is normally considered singular, but exceptions are occasionally made when a following prepositional phrase produces a plural sense: *Either of the varieties are in plentiful supply.* See also PRONOUNS 3.

either . . . or See **CORRELATIVES**.

elegant variation 1. The prejudice against the obvious repetition of a word is understandable, but the use of a substitute, or "elegant variation," can lead to confusion. The passage following suffers from a misguided attempt to avoid the word *computer*.

> It is no longer necessary to communicate with the *computer* by using complicated *artificial* languages. *EDP equipment* now speaks English and it solves everyday problems. The *machine* has also become an effective tool for dealing with soaring office costs and lagging productivity.

In the revision below, *computer* is repeated several times, with good effect.

> It is no longer necessary to communicate with the *computer* by using complicated *computer* languages. *Computers* speak English and they solve everyday problems. *Computers* have also become an effective tool for dealing with soaring office costs and lagging productivity.

2. Repetition is never advisable when the words repeated are used in different senses: *It is our policy to sell our policies through independent insurance agents.* [Substitute *practice* for *policy*.]

eliminate A word with a less abrasive **CONNOTATION** is often helpful: *Three typists will be eliminated (dropped)/We must eliminate (remove) the source of the inefficiency/The reasons for the protest have now been eliminated (no longer exist).*
—**completely eliminated.** *Completely* is superfluous. See **WORDINESS** 3.

elite A size of typewriter type that prints twelve characters to the inch; smaller than pica, which prints ten characters to the inch.

ellipsis Plural, *ellipses* (pronounced -seez). A punctuation mark consisting of three evenly spaced periods (. . .).

1. An ellipsis is used to show the omission of one or more words within quoted material.

> According to Joseph Schumpeter, "Creative destruction is the essential fact about capitalism . . . a form or method of change [that] not only never is, but never can be, stationery."

If the ellipsis comes after a full sentence, the sentence stop is better retained.

> As Charles L. Schultze, onetime chairman of the Council of Economic Advisers, has stated:

Relying on regulations rather than economic incentives to deal with highly complex areas of behavior, as we do for control of air and water pollution and industrial health and safety, has a built-in dynamic that inevitably broadens the scope of regulations. . . . Social intervention becomes a race between the ingenuity of the regulatee and the loophole closing of the regulation, with a continuing expansion in the volume of regulations as the outcome. [The first period after *regulations* is the sentence stop.]

2. The omission of a line or more of poetry or of a paragraph or more of copied material is sometimes indicated by a full line of periods, thus:

. . . .

Asterisks may be used for the same purpose, but their prominence is distracting.

3. An ellipsis, like a DASH, is used to mark an unfinished statement. It is also used to slow up reading by separating the parts of a statement or to direct the eye from a heading to a following paragraph.

You know, an ounce of prevention . . .

Nytol can make you drowsy . . . so you can get to sleep.

BEEF . . .

. . . the food you're right to like.

4. An ellipsis is used as the equivalent of *etc.* in a shortened series or enumeration.

Number the pages in each chapter 1-1, 1-2, . . . 2-1, 2-2, . . . 3-1,3-2, . . .

else 1. Takes the possessive form *else's* after certain pronouns: *somebody else's problem* (not *somebody's else problem*)/*anyone else's superior*/*Who else's* (not *Whose else*) *address could it be?*

2. *Else* is used for emphasis in speech and informal writing, but is considered superfluous otherwise: *There was nothing else to do (nothing to do) but wait.*

elusive Not to be confused with *illusive*. See ILLUSORY.

emend See AMEND, EMEND.

emendation A literary term for the alteration of written work to effect improvement. Usually, a more common word or locution is available: *With all the suggested changes in the announcement, an emendation of the draft was necessary (a revision of the draft* [or *a redrafting*] *was necessary).*

emigrate, immigrate   The difference is in the point of view. One *emigrates* from a country or region to establish permanent residence in another. One *immigrates* to the country in which residence is established. An *emigrant* from Italy would be an *immigrant* to the United States, the first referring to the place of departure; the second, to the destination.

émigré   Pronounced *em*-ih-gray or (French) ay-mee-*gray*. An emigrant, particularly a political refugee: *Solzhenitsyn is a Russian émigré.* But (preferred): *Many Korean emigrants* (rather than *émigrés*) *have settled in New York.* See also **EMIGRATE, IMMIGRATE**.

empathize   To have **EMPATHY**; usually followed by *with*: *The successful saleswoman empathizes with her customers.*

empathy   Vicarious identification with others, "feeling as" they feel. Not to be confused with *sympathy*, "feeling for" others: *Her empathy is her strong point as a saleswoman.*

emphasis   Achieved by variety in sentence structure; see **SENTENCES** 3.

empirical   A scholar's word describing knowledge derived from observation, experiment, or practical experience; not relying on theory alone: *empirical research/empirical evidence/The executive's conclusions are largely empirical; not so the philosopher's.* The word is pompous in ordinary use: *The report is based on empirical research (based on first-hand knowledge/He has an empirical knowledge of his job (He learned his job from experience).*

employ   Except in the sense of to hire, *use* is to be preferred for its plainness: *employed (used) a Xerox/will employ (use) all our resources/believe we can employ (use) him more profitably in the front office.*

employe   Another, less common, spelling of *employee*. Both words are pronounced em-*ploy*-ee or em-ploy-*ee*.

employment tax   Also *payroll tax*. The federal tax levied on all employers to finance Social Security. The tax is equal to that deducted from each employee's wages, under the Federal Insurance Contributions Act (FICA). The employee's contribution of **FICA** taxes is reported annually to the **IRS** on the **W-2 FORM**.

enclose, inclose   *Inclose* is a variant of *enclose*, but *enclose* is preferred. So, too, *inclosure* is a variant of *enclosure*, but *enclosure* is preferred.

enclosed herewith   A STEREOTYPED LETTER PHRASE: *Our check is enclosed* (not *enclosed herewith*). See also WORDINESS 3.

enclosed please find   A STEREOTYPED LETTER PHRASE. *I am enclosing* and *enclosed is* are more natural.

enclosure notation   When an enclosure is to accompany a letter, a notation is made at the left margin below the signature block, or below the IDENTIFICATION INITIALS when they are used. If there is more than one enclosure, the number is indicated. Descriptions of the enclosures are desirable only if they are not adequately identified in the letter itself. The following styles are typical:

Enclosure	encl.
Enclosures 2	enc.
2 enclosures	3 encls.

Enclosure: Annual Report, 19xx

Encs: 1. "Profit Sharing"
     2. Management Letter No. 96

endeavor   In one syllable, *try*. See LONG WORDS AND SHORT.

ended, ending   *Ended* is used preferably in expressions of past time: *for the week ended last Saturday/profit for the six months ended June 30*. But: *for the week ending next Friday, the fourteenth*.

end notations   Conventional additions to a business letter following the IDENTIFICATION INITIALS. They include COPY NOTATIONS, ENCLOSURE NOTATIONS, and SEPARATE COVER NOTATIONS.

endnotes   See REFERENCE NOTES.

endorse, indorse   The first spelling is preferred. So, too, *endorsement* over *indorsement*.

end result   Redundant. See WORDINESS 3.

engage in   A less formal synonym is usually preferred: *doing, making, working on*, etc. In other instances, a slight recasting will save many words: *We are engaged in making a survey* (omit *engaged in*)/*The company is engaged in the importation of toys* (*imports toys*). See also WORDINESS 5.

enormity   Outrageousness; great in wickedness; moral excess: *The pub-lic was outraged by the enormity of the offense.* Not to be confused with *enormousness,* "immense in size": *He didn't quite realize the im-mensity* (not *enormity*) *of his success.* ["The enormousness of his suc-cess" has an awkward sound.]/*The enormous size* (not *enormity*) *of the organization is a constant source of wonder.*

enroll, enrol   The preferred spelling is *enroll.* The only past tense form is *enrolled: Ninety percent of the employees are enrolled in the plan.*

en route   Pronounced on-root. Suitable as a term in shipping, but "on the way" is a less formal substitute in other contexts: *The cargo is now en route to the Philippines.* But: *We'll stop in Atlanta on the way to New Orleans.*

ensure   See ASSURE, ENSURE, INSURE.

enthuse   To be enthusiastic; also, to express enthusiasm. The word is acceptable in informal usage only; many discerning writers and speak-ers avoid it: *Carmichael enthused about (was enthusiastic about) the improved quality/We are more enthused (enthusiastic) than ever.*

entirely   See TOTALLY, COMPLETELY, ENTIRELY.

entrepreneur   Pronounced on-truh-pruh-*noor.* One who starts and op-erates a business, assuming the inherent risks: *If our free enterprise system is to remain healthy, it must attract more entrepreneurs.* See also INTRAPRENEUR.
   —**entrepreneurial,** adjective; ENTREPRENEURIALLY, adverb. The length of the words alone suggests the need for simple synonyms: *There are a lot of people who are not going to want to work for a giant company because they have a high entrepreneurial spirit (have a high degree of initiative) and they're likely to feel submerged in that sort of environ-ment/We need to know how educational programs can be modified to prepare people for entrepreneurially defined work (for adventurous work in business?).*

enumeration   1. An enumeration is any use of words, numbers, or signs to specify items in a series. Because it tends to give writing a me-chanical quality, enumeration is best used sparingly in informal statements, but otherwise it has great value in giving the reader easy access to a unified and closely limited body of data: names, facts, steps, reasons, questions and answers, descriptive details, etc. It is

144 — MODERN BUSINESS LANGUAGE AND USAGE

especially useful in such material as instructions, procedures, and detailed statements of policy. Whether or not the items in an enumeration are paragraphed separately, the items in each set should be coordinate in thought and expression (see **PARALLEL STRUCTURE**).

2. In a running text, the enumeration may consist of two or more closely related points following a simple **TOPIC SENTENCE**:

> *My client and I agreed on two steps. First,* he would become more deeply involved in the planning process, leaving to others the management of people. And *second,* we together would undertake a campaign to get him elected a fellow of the principal professional society in his field . . .

As an alternative to *first, second,* and other verbal expressions (as, *in the first place, another, finally*), a run-in enumeration may employ numbers (1, 2, 3) or letters (a, b, c). The *-ly* endings on ordinals (*firstly, secondly,* etc.) are not recommended.

3. When items are listed, they too are usually identified by consecutive numbers (1, 2, 3 . . .) or letters (a, b, c . . .) or by such marks as the **DASH** (—), **BULLET** (●), paragraph or section sign (¶, §), or index (☞), or by prefatory words like *Fact* or *Item* repeated before each unit of information. Two examples:

(a) DASHES

The Equi-Claims computer system contains all the information the approver needs to make a claim payment decision. For example—
—Is this employee covered for that claim?
—Up to how much?
—With what deductibles?
—What are reasonable and customary doctors' charges?

(b) PREFATORY WORD

Here are the FACTS about us.
FACT: Amax is one of the world's leading natural resource companies, a Fortune 200.
FACT: Amax is multinational, multidivisional, broadly diversified.
FACT: Amax places strong emphasis on the financial area of corporate management. . . .

See also **PLAIN ENGLISH**.

envelop Pronounced en-*vel*-up. To envelop is to enclose, to surround, or to cover with a wrapping, but it is not to be used for the noun **ENVELOPE**, the paper wrapper in which a letter is sent.

envelope Pronounced *en*-vuh-lope or *ahn*-. For envelope sizes used in correspondence and method of folding letters to fit, see **LETTER FORM** 2, 7, and 8.

envelope address   To be deliverable, mail should bear a complete and accurate address and conform in all other respects to postal requirements. (See illustration.)

   1. ADDRESS BLOCK.   2. NOTATIONS.   3. RETURN ADDRESS.

   1. ADDRESS BLOCK.   (a) The address consists of the name of the person, department and/or organization—as the situation requires— and the full postal address, including the Zip Code. Where known, an apartment or room number follows the street address on the same line or, if space does not permit, on the next line. The last line bears the city and state names and the Zip Code. The official two-letter postal abbreviation should be used for the state name (see **STATE POSTAL ABBREVIATIONS**). See also **ADDRESSES**.

   If an **ATTENTION LINE** is used in the letter, it should also be placed on the envelope as part of the address block. The customary position is directly above the street address.

Carver Manufacturing Company
Personnel Department
Attention Mr. Raymond C. Peters
351 Park Avenue
New York, NY 10022

   (b) Optical scanners used by the U.S. Postal Service exclude the extreme margins, so the address should be placed within the "read zone," extending not lower than a half an inch from the

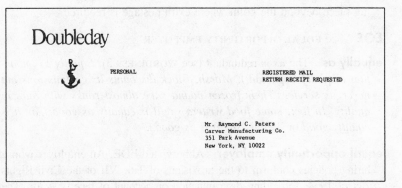

Envelope address

bottom of the envelope and not beyond an inch from the sides. For best appearance, the address should begin about five spaces to the left of dead center.

(c) A three-line address looks better if it is double-spaced. An address of four or five lines should be single-spaced; more than five lines should be avoided. A carryover line needed to avoid overrunning the right margin should be indented two spaces.

(d) If a window envelope is used, the letter should be folded so that at least a quarter of an inch of space shows above and below the address. In that way, the address will not be obscured if the letter slips inside the envelope. Of course, the number of lines in the address must be limited to the space available.

2. NOTATIONS. MAILING NOTATIONS—*Special Delivery, Registered Mail*, etc.—are typed in solid capitals under the stamp area and several spaces above the address. ON-ARRIVAL NOTATIONS— *Confidential, Personal, Hold for Arrival*, etc.—may be similarly typed above and to the left of the address on a line with the mailing notation, if any.

3. RETURN ADDRESS. If the envelope has no printed return address, the return address should be typed in the upper left-hand corner. If a printed return address does not already include the writer's name, the name or initials may be typed directly above it.

envelope notations See ENVELOPE ADDRESS 2.

envelope stuffer An enclosure accompanying a mailed letter, bill, or the like. Usually a printed advertisement, the stuffer has the advantage of traveling free as long as it does not increase the weight of the mailing piece beyond the point where extra postage is required.

EOE See EQUAL OPPORTUNITY EMPLOYER.

equally as The *as* is redundant (see WORDINESS 3): *Equally as important (Equally important), Marsh, Block discounts its commissions but never its services/Their frozen pound cake almost ranks with ours in quality. In fact, some food writers say it is equally as good (say it is equally good* or, better, *say it is as good).*

equal opportunity employer Abbreviated EOE. An employer whose hiring policies conform to the provisions of Title VII of the Civil Rights Act of 1964, forbidding discrimination on account of race or color. The phrase is common in job advertising, often with M/F appended to show that equality of treatment extends to both men and women under the affirmative action provisions of the Equal Economic Opportunity Act of 1972. The further addition of H (or Hc) and V signifies the inclusion of the handicapped and veterans: *Equal Opportunity Employer M/F/H/V.*

equivalent The noun is followed by *of;* the adjective, by *to: an investment that returns the equivalent of 24.2 percent if you are in the 50 percent tax bracket;* but (adjective): *an investment that returns a dividend equivalent to 24.2 percent.*

er, uh See **VOCALIZED PAUSE.**

ergonomics A **BUZZ WORD** for the art of designing tools and products for the way workers move and think, rather than forcing workers to adapt to them. One result: IBM's line of *ergonomic* furniture with pneumatic mechanisms that adjust backs and seats, a five-pronged chair base that prevents tipping, and molded backs that conform to the body.

err The pronunciation is *er* as in *her,* rather than *er* as in *error.*

erratum Latin for "error"; plural, *errata.* The term is used to call attention to the correction of an error in the editing or printing of a scholarly work. A list of such errors—labeled *Errata*—is usually made on an insert or an added page. In nonscholarly publications and in all ordinary uses, the terms *correction* and *corrections* are preferred.

escrow A deed, bond, money, or something else of value deposited with a third party until certain conditions are fulfilled: *put the money into an escrow account/required three months' rent to be placed in escrow at the Metropolitan Savings Bank.*
    —escrow holder; also *escrowee.* The third party by whom the escrow account is held.

ESOP The **ACRONYM** for *employee stock ownership plan,* through which employees are able to buy stock in the company for which they work.

especial(ly), special(ly) *Especial* has no use that cannot be filled by *special.* If a distinction is to be made, it is that *special* is more apt to be used as a synonym for "particular" *(has a special way with silk; comes with a special recommendation),* and that especial may be preferred in the sense of "outstanding" *(an especial occasion).*
    The adverbial forms *especially* and *specially* have similar distinctions. *Specially* relates to a particular purpose *(specially made tools; a specially trained crew); especially* relates to a particular degree *(espe-*

cially active; especially well versed in) or serves as a synonym for "particularly" *(asked especially for you).*

Esquire   Abbreviated Esq. See FORMS OF ADDRESS 1.

essential   For *more essential, most essential,* and *very essential,* see ABSOLUTE ADJECTIVES.

establishment   1. Pretentious for *store* or *business,* but sometimes preferred for its suggestion of elegance: *No store* (not *establishment) gives better value/Our business* (not *establishment) was founded in 1912.* But: *a Fifth Avenue establishment/an establishment catering to the Ivy League set.*

2. *Establishment* is well used in reference to an organized body, such as a government, political party, or church. Often capitalized, it is also a synonym for an elite group in any field that is not hospitable to new blood or contrary ideas: *maintains a large military establishment/work for the establishment* (or *Establishment)/will not surrender to establishment* (or *Establishment) values.*

esteemed   Too often part of an archaic letter phrase: *your esteemed favor (your letter)/our esteemed (valued) customer.* But *esteemed* is useful as a sincerely complimentary term: *our esteemed associate/ esteemed for her many contributions to management.*

estimation   The act of reaching a judgment; synonymous with *evaluation,* but better not used where *estimate* (for "approximation"), *opinion,* or *judgment* will suit the sense: *Any estimation* (or *evaluation) of the risk to workers should include a careful study of environmental factors.* But: *My estimate* (not *estimation) of the cost is close to a million dollars/In my judgment* (not *In my estimation), the lease can be concluded in a month.* See also LONG VARIANTS.

et al.   1. For the Latin *et alii,* "and others." Since only *alii* is abbreviated, only *al.* is followed by a period. *Et al.* is largely confined to legal documents and footnotes (see REFERENCE NOTES): *Maspeth Federal Savings and Loan Association v. Jan Dordau et al./Friedman, Gilder, Greenspan, et al.*

2. The "others" represented by *al.* (or *alii)* are usually other persons or business entities; so *et al.* should not be used where ETC. is more suitable: *heat, energy, fuel, chemicals, etc.* (not *et al.).*

etc.   Abbreviation of the Latin *et cetera,* "and other [similar] things."

Placed at the end of an incomplete enumeration, *etc.* is acceptable in reference material and in routine business writing: *The file holds orders, invoices, statements, receipts, etc.* Where more formality is desired, *etc.* is replaced by various locutions. Some examples:

> The file holds orders, invoices, receipts, and so forth.
> The file holds such records as orders, invoices, and receipts.
> The file holds orders, invoices, receipts, and other records.

Compare ET AL.

euphemism   The substitution of an agreeable or inoffensive word or phrase for one that is more precise, but disagreeable or blunt; also, the substituted word or phrase. Unquestionably, euphemisms can soothe feelings, promote harmony, and make persuasion easier, but carried too far, they become only evasions of the truth. Thus an auto manufacturer recalling cars to correct a defect that has caused many fatal accidents writes owners that it "may adversely affect vehicle control." A TV rerun of an old movie is called an "encore presentation." Public employees, forbidden by law to strike, engage in a "job action," which takes them away from their work just as effectively.

When the tobacco industry is disturbed by news of the most recent disclosures of the link between smoking and cancer, the traditional response is that "the findings are inconclusive." Entrepreneurs who shy away from "the gambling business" confidently put the same funds in "the gaming industry." Privately financed pressure groups, or lobbies, seek cover in the euphemisms "government relations" and "public affairs."

In other instances, an IRS bureau formed to receive complaints is named the Problem Resolution Program Office. So, too, public television stations hide their embarrassment in selling commercial time by calling it "enhanced underwriting," and NASA, the space agency, minimizes the astronauts' space sickness with the official name "space adaptation syndrome."

Meanwhile, a nuclear accident is an "event," the backward or underdeveloped nations are "the developing nations," and the failed program is "an incomplete success." Not to be neglected, the poor are the "disadvantaged," the prison guard is a "correction officer," the unemployed engineer is "unattached," and the fired executive is on "an indefinite leave of absence."

See also CONNOTATION.

evaluate   See VALUE, EVALUATE.

evaluation   See VALUATION, EVALUATION.

event   The phrases "in the event that" and "in such an event" are better shortened: *We intend to be prepared in the event that (if) the merger falls through.* Or: *We intend to be prepared should the merger fall through/In such an event (If so), it would be necessary to raise additional capital.* See also WORDINESS 4.

every, everybody, everyone   These words are followed by singular verbs, but later references to them are often, and unobjectionably, plural. See also PRONOUNS 3.

> Every customer receives a prize.
> Everyone here knows how much we appreciate their coming.
> Everybody seems interested in the offer. Certainly, they won't do better elsewhere.

everyday, every day   *Everyday* is an adjective: *an everyday occurrence, everyday tasks. Every day* (two words) is either an adverb or a noun. Adverb: *He calls on customers every day.* Noun: *Every day brings new opportunities.*

everyone, every one   See ANYONE, ANY ONE.

everyplace, every place   *Everyplace* is informal for "everywhere": *We looked everyplace for the missing report.* However, *every place* (two words) is acceptable in general usage as a noun phrase meaning "each place": *Every place on the program is now filled.*

every time   Two words: *The line was busy every time we called/They'll do it every time.*

evidence   See at ARGUMENT.

ex-   1. A compound formed by the prefix *ex,* in the sense of "former," is hyphened: *ex-ambassador, ex-secretary.* See also HYPHEN 2.

2. Expressions like "the American ex-ambassador" and "the corporate ex-secretary" are better phrased "the former American ambassador" and "the former corporate secretary."

exact same   *Exact,* an adjective, is nonstandard when used for *exactly,* an adverb: *We can offer the exact same terms (We can offer exactly the same terms). Exact same* (like *exactly the same*) can also be faulted as redundant; still, it may give emphasis to an otherwise lackluster statement: *At NBO you get the exact same merchandise for a lot less money.* But see also **WORDINESS** 3 and **ADVERTISING CLAIMS**.

exceed Although the expression "not to exceed" is characteristic of formal business and legal use, "not more than" is preferred in other contexts: *a sum not to exceed $5,000.* But (less formal): *a sum of not more than $5,000.*

except, excepting *Except*, meaning "but" or "excluding," is a preposition, and a pronoun following is in the objective case: *all except her* (or *him, me, them, us*). *Excepting*, meaning "excluding," is better not used for *except* unless it is preceded by *not: The proposal was made that all income, not excepting Social Security, be subject to income taxes.*

exceptionable, exceptional That which is *exceptionable* is open to objection: *exceptionable behavior.* Something *exceptional* is uncommon, better than average: *a diamond of exceptional quality.*

excessive feeling Conventional phrases like "best wishes" and "kindest regards" usually work well because they are polite without being effusive. When phrases are both trite and gushy, however, the effect is maudlin: *I offer my heartfelt congratulations/Your company is one of our most treasured customers/Our senior officers are bursting with pride.* See also **CLICHÉS**.

exciting Usually part of a catchphrase that excites nothing more than a bad case of apathy: *an exciting new fashion/an exciting sale/exciting work by master craftsmen.*

exclamation point (!) A punctuation mark used to add emphasis or express strong feeling. It is found with some frequency in advertising copy stressing sales, closeouts, and the like, but the mark is notably absent when the image of quality is important, and it is rarely called for in ordinary business correspondence or reports. Overdone: *Decorators! Collectors! Seize this opportunity! Sir Humphrey Davey*™ *Lantern . . . it cannot be improved upon! . . . Reliable! . . . Miners' lives depended on it!*

excuse, forgive, pardon One *excuses* a minor fault and *pardons* a more serious one. To *forgive* is to *pardon,* but *excuse* is less pretentious and it lacks *pardon's* suggestion of lingering ill feeling: *Please excuse our misspelling of the name/It's not easy to forgive such carelessness/We'll pardon his behavior this time.*

ex dividend   When a stock is sold "ex dividend," any dividend due is paid to the seller, not the buyer. Signified by the symbol *ex* (for "without") in the daily stock tables.

exec   CLIPPED FORM of *executive: They encourage their execs to take sabbaticals.*

execute   Relates to a formal action, as one in which an order is carried out or a document is made legally valid in a prescribed way: *We execute buy and sell orders promptly/A will was drafted, but it was never executed/The purchase contract is valid, but it can't be executed because of the financial default of the supplier.*

Execute is better not used when a simple word like *do* or *sign* adequately conveys the desired meaning: *The new manager's forte is getting people to carry out* (rather than *execute*) *his orders/Your order will be shipped* (rather than *executed*) *at once/Please sign* (not *execute*) *the form where indicated.*

—execution, noun: *Execution of the terms of the contract has now begun.* But: *Your signature on* (not *Your execution of*) *the form will be appreciated.* See also example of incongruous use at AMBIGUITY.

executive recruiter   Informally, HEADHUNTER. A firm retained by a large corporation to seek out qualified executives for specific job openings. Fees are paid by the hiring company. Compare EXECUTIVE SEARCH FIRM.

executive search firm   A company that enlists as clients job applicants whom it offers to assist with such general skills as self-evaluation and résumé preparation. Such a firm does not necessarily know of any specific job openings but requires payment in advance before services are rendered. Compare EXECUTIVE RECRUITER.

executive stationery   See LETTER FORM 1.

executor, executrix   In law, an *executor* is a person appointed by the maker of a valid will to carry out its provisions. Although the term applies to both sexes, there is an exclusively feminine form, *executrix;* but one would need a strong reason to use it, especially in the plural (*executrixes* or *executrices*).

exhilarate   So spelled (not *exhilerate*): *The meeting was exhilarating.*

exorbitant   So spelled (not *exhorbitant*): *exorbitant prices.*

exit interview   An interview given a departing employee to learn the reason for leaving, to determine if any corrective action is necessary, and to ease the pain if the departure is involuntary or clouded by dissatisfaction. See also VENTILATE 2.

expatriate The term is applied, without prejudice, to an American working abroad: *The employment of American expatriates in Europe will continue to decline as nationals learn to perform their jobs.*

expect Generally expresses anticipation, with either the probability or certainty of occurrence: *We expect the order any day now.* Only colloquially is *expect* used in the sense of "suppose": *I expect (suppose) there is an excellent reason for the delay.*

expedite Business JARGON, sometimes useful in routine messages, but a plain English substitute often carries more bite: *We're doing all we can to expedite (speed up) the delivery/Management has ordered us to expedite (rush) the installation.*
—**expeditious,** adjective: *expeditious (efficient, speedy, prompt) service.*
—**expeditiously,** adverb: *will answer your inquiries expeditiously (quickly, promptly, without delay).* See also LONG WORDS AND SHORT.

expense In accounting, to expense is to treat a disbursement as an expense fully deductible for tax purposes in the accounting year to which it applies. Tax regulations prescribe the kinds of disbursements that can be expensed. The alternative is to treat a disbursement as a capital investment that must be depreciated over a prescribed number of years. In some instances, the taxpayer is given a choice of methods, with the consequent possibility of tax savings: *The reported loss was the result of expensing interest costs of $10 million/For tax years beginning after December 31, 1981, you may elect to expense part of the cost of recovery property* [depreciable assets] *that would qualify for investment credit.* [IRS]

expert Since an expert is a person presumably qualified by skill and training, phrases like "qualified expert," "skilled expert," and "trained expert," are needlessly repetitive. See WORDINESS 3.

expertise Pronounced *-teez*. A convenient synonym for "expertness" or "special knowledge," but easily overused. Words like *skill, experience,* and *knowledge* often suit the sense as well or better: *Chrysler engineered the Reliant K with expertise gained from more than eleven billion owner miles of front-wheel drive/It's all backed by RCA's world-*

famous communications expertise/Despite her expertise as a consultant on leisure, she has not been able to find much leisure for herself/In the technology of energy, companies in electronics, mining, and shipbuilding have as much expertise as the oil industry, and in some cases, much more/My expertise is one of the resources Bache can bring to bear on any metal that's moving fast.

exploding bonus   A competitive device used by recruiters to hire away the most desired members of a college graduating class. The bonus offered is reduced by a stipulated sum for every day a candidate defers the decision to accept the offered position.

exploit   The verb (pronounced eks-*ploit*) has either a positive or negative CONNOTATION, depending on the sense: Positive: *All the company's other divisions will join us in exploiting the film* [publicizing the film to realize the greatest gain]/Negative: *They can hardly be accused of exploiting their workers* [using their workers selfishly or unethically].

—**exploitation,** noun: *experienced in film exploitation/the exploitation of illegal immigrants.*

ex post facto   Latin for "after the fact"; descriptive of something done in hindsight or to alter or set aside a previous condition: *an ex post facto law/an economist known for his ex post facto analyses of the administration's failures.*

exposure   In advertising, any observation of an advertising message. Because of the ephemeral nature of the medium, a broadcast message provides one exposure opportunity per viewer or listener. For a print advertisement, however, there may be a number of exposure opportunities for each reader.

extemporaneous   See IMPROMPTU.

extra   Something or someone in addition to what is usual: *The new Pontiac is loaded with extras/Mobil declared a year-end extra* [dividend]/*Five extras* [actors in nonspeaking roles] *were used for the single commercial.*

extraordinary   Pronounced preferably ek-*strawr*-; also *ek*-struh-*awr*-.

extrapolate   In statistics, to infer a value or quantity from data already known; now a BUZZ WORD for *estimate, guess,* or *project: From these* *figures we can extrapolate (project) an annual growth rate of 10 percent.*

eyeball   Slang. To fix one's gaze on: *eyeballed his opponent.* Also an adjective meaning "visual, using one's sight": *an eyeball inspection/land the plane under eyeball conditions.*

eyeball-to-eyeball   Informal and a bit worn for "face-to-face": *They met eyeball-to-eyeball.*

eye contact   The speaker's bridge to the audience. To establish eye contact is to look directly at the person spoken to, or—if a group is addressed—to shift attention now and then from one person to another or from one part of the audience to another. It is bad form and damaging to effectiveness to gaze at the ceiling or floor. In talking from notes or reading from manuscript, the speaker is expected to be sufficiently familiar with the content to look up at the audience for most of the time.

F

FAA Federal Aviation Administration. A division of the U.S. Department of Transportation with special responsibilities for air safety, air traffic control, and airport regulation. See also CAB.

facilitate Formal for *help, aid, ease,* etc.: *Miss Jessup will facilitate the opening of your account (will help you open your account)/The ring binder is designed to facilitate replacement of obsolete data (make it easy to replace obsolete data).* See also LONG WORDS AND SHORT.

facilitator An aide or assistant working principally as a coordinator: *The client is asked to choose a "facilitator," a company employee who is charged with overseeing the program after the consultants leave. The facilitator, usually a lower-middle manager, gets a separate round of intensive training.* See also AID, AIDE.

facility Used in the sense of a building or appurtenance, *facility* may be vague or ambiguous unless clarified in some way: *The company is constructing a new facility in Peoria* (a factory? warehouse? central computer installation?) See also ABSTRACT AND CONCRETE WORDS.

fact A statement expressed as a certainty, particularly one for which proof exists. Some modifying words add nothing to the sense: *The true facts are (The truth is)/It's an actual fact that (It's a fact that).* See also CREDIBILITY.
—**as a fact.** The correct idioms are *in fact, in point of fact,* and *as a matter of fact,* but any of them may be superfluous or be replaced by *actually: In fact* (not *As a fact*), *the decline in interest rates is now in its sixth consecutive week.*
—**in spite of the fact that.** Wordy for *although.*
—**owing to the fact that.** Wordy for *because.*
  See also WORDINESS 4.

factor 1. A factor is someone or something contributing to a result. It is therefore redundant to say "a CAUSATIVE FACTOR" (for "cause"). In other instances, too, *factor* may be either unnecessary or better replaced by a more exact word: *when you consider the efficiency factor* (omit *factor*)/*one of the many factors (steps) in the production process/another important factor (element) in media selection.* But (well used): *Of the many factors contributing to the success of the venture, the most important was superb leadership.*

2. In finance, a factor is an organization that undertakes to "buy" the ACCOUNTS RECEIVABLE of a company in exchange for credit services and working capital. The factor charges a fee based on the risk of loss in collecting the funds due. The work of the factor is called "factoring."

fact sheet   A summary of important background information about an organization, project, product, etc.; often distributed to the press when called together for some special occasion. A job RÉSUMÉ is a kind of fact sheet.

failed   In some contexts, too strongly negative: *You failed to (did not) specify/We failed to enclose (should have enclosed).* See also POSITIVE AND NEGATIVE WORDS.

fair trade   A EUPHEMISM for price-fixing, as in "fair trade laws," now illegal, which permitted a manufacturer to set the retail price at which its products should be sold by a wholesaler or retailer.

fait accompli   Plural, *faits accomplis.* Both are pronounced fet uh-*kawm*-plee. French for "an accomplished fact"; well established in the language of diplomacy, but also appropriate at times in business: *By showing mock advertisements, the agency elicits more candid reactions from a client than they could get if they presented the idea as a fait accompli.*

faithfully   A COMPLIMENTARY CLOSE, or part of one, found mainly in official correspondence; rare in the United States, less so in Great Britain.

fake   Normally avoided because of its bluntness, *fake* is at times a stylish substitute for such words as *simulated, imitation, artificial,* and *make-believe: fake furs, fake jewelry.* Compare FAUX.

fallout   Attending results or side effects, usually negative: *If the industry raises prices, it will have to deal with the political fallout/The tax changes affecting boat ownership is expected to produce little fallout among boat manufacturers.*

farther, further   In formal usage, *farther* is confined to expressions of physical distance, and *further* to those of degree or quantity in an abstract sense: *The site is farther from the highway than we would wish/The situation is further complicated by a lack of liquidity/We will go further than any competitor in meeting your demands.* In general usage, *further* is regularly used in both the physical and abstract senses: *Ryan will travel further* (or *farther*) *to see a client than anyone else we know.* But: *They are now further* (not *farther*) *from a solution than they were when they started.*

fast-food   Descriptive of restaurants, usually franchised, at which food is prepared and served quickly from a limited choice for take-away trade or consumption on the premises. McDonald's and Arby's are examples of fast-food restaurants.
—**fast food.** The type of food offered in fast-food restaurants; hamburgers, frankfurters, sandwiches, and the like: *specialize in fast foods.*

fast-track   To speed up, as construction, administrative and paper work, job advancement, etc.: *After all the delays on other projects, we are trying to fast-track this one/Groat was hired with the promise that he'd be fast-tracked.* Also adjective: *establish fast-track mechanisms for policy reviews.*
—**fast track,** noun: *It was understood that Woods was on a fast track to the presidency.* Also *fast lane: She was in the fast lane and moving up.*

fatal   Not logically subject to comparison. See **ABSOLUTE ADJECTIVES.**

fat cat   A person of wealth or privilege: *The fund-raiser was designed to attract the fat cats of the industry.*
—**fat-cat,** adjective: *Then it turned out that the new appointee had negotiated a fat-cat* (privileged) *contract for himself, including membership in a private club of his choice.*

fault   As a verb, sometimes criticized, but the usage is well established: *You can't fault* [blame] *the sales staff.*

faux   Pronounced *foe.* French for "false." A chic **EUPHEMISM** if it is not overused: *Ruffled blouses, embellished sweaters . . . plus faux jewels and gay dainties to wear with all this colorful garb/luxurious faux suede jackets.*

favor   Archaic as a synonym for *letter* and often stilted as a verb: *We have your favor (letter) of April 20/Please favor us with (let us have)* *a prompt reply/We have been favored with (have received) a letter from Brown & Co.* But (well used): *We appreciate the favor* [act of kindness]/*We favor* [approve, support] *the proposed change.*

fax The familiar name for high-speed facsimile transmission of printed pages, diagrams, sketches, and the like. Noun and verb: *Fax is easy. Fax is fast . . . And because you use the same phone lines to fax as you do to call, you pay the same low rates.* [AT&T]

faze Informal for *disturb* or *disconcert: Their action was unexpected, but it didn't faze us a bit.*

FCC Federal Communications Commission. An independent agency with broad powers over communications, including radio and television stations and broadcasting, and telephone, telegraph, and cable systems.

FDA Food and Drug Administration. A division of the Department of Health and Human Services, the *FDA* is responsible for ensuring the purity and safety of foods, drugs, and other potentially hazardous substances.

FDIC Federal Deposit Insurance Corporation. An independent agency that insures for up to $100,000 the individual accounts in all Federal Reserve member banks and qualifying state banks. The *FSLIC* performs a similar function for federal and qualifying state-chartered savings and loan associations.

featherbed To employ more workers than are needed for a particular task; a practice often protected by union contracts: *Conrail's labor force was more featherbedded than almost anyone in Washington suspected/If New York publishers could control the featherbedding, they would better be able to compete with suburban newspapers.*

feature Acceptable as a verb: *The suites feature 30-foot living rooms/All store brands are featured in this sale. Featured,* however, is superfluous in such a phrase as ''the featured speaker'' when only a single speaker is on the program.

(the) Fed A CLIPPED FORM of Federal Reserve Board.

federal Capitalized when part of a proper name (Federal Power Commission), but usage is divided when it serves as a simple adjective referring to the national government: *a federal* (or *Federal*) *statute/federal* (or *Federal*) *income taxes.* See also CAPITALS 9.

federalese   JARGON common to the federal government; a kind of OF-FICIALESE.

feedback   1. Adapted from communication technology, *feedback* in general use is the response returned to a message source, where it may be evaluated and acted upon. Conversation, for instance, may bring feedback in the form of a voiced response, a question, a comment, or the like. The feedback from a written message may come in a letter, a coupon reply, or a phone call; or there may be no overt response at all, which itself may carry some significance. In any case, feedback tells the communicator how the message is being received and what adjustments in "output" are to be made to help ensure a successful outcome.

2. *Feedback* is JARGON when it is loosely used to denote a simple response: *We wrote to Davis, but we haven't got any feedback yet (reply, answer, response).*

feedforward   A derivative of FEEDBACK, *feedforward* is JARGON, but it picturesquely describes the technique of cuing the reader or listener to the points that follow. The phrases below, excerpted from a short talk, show how the listener is led to anticipate each point in turn. The key words (in italics) are a virtual outline of the talk.

Let's begin by talking about the *causes* of the present stalemate. . . . The *effects* of these conditions are very much in evidence. . . . Now, what do I propose as a *remedy?* Let me make *three suggestions. First,* . . . *Something else* I would do is . . . *Finally,* . . .

feel   Often, a word too weak for the sense and better replaced by *believe* or by a flat statement: *I feel that the work is progressing satisfactorily (I believe that* . . . or, stronger, *The work is progressing satisfactorily).*

feel good, feel well   See at GOOD 2.

female, male   Useful in making sexual distinctions, especially for purposes of record, but not ordinarily to be used as synonyms for *woman* and *man: a female (or male) model/a male patient/female employees/a male sanctuary.* But: *The department employs as many women as men* (not *as many females as males*)/*Our customers are largely upper-class women* (not *females*)/*A man* (not *male*) *is more likely to have the lifting strength for the job.* See also SEXUAL BIAS.

FET   Federal excise tax.

fetch To go to a specified place for something and return with it: *I'll fetch you a hand calculator/Please fetch me that photograph.* The word is more favored by the British than by Americans, who seem to convey the meaning adequately with **BRING.** In commodity markets, however, *fetch* is a standard synonym for "sell for": *Steers are fetching a good price in the Kansas City market.*

fewer, less *Fewer* regularly denotes quantity in countable units: *We have fewer employees than we had a year ago/Fewer complaints suggest greater satisfaction.*

   Less denotes quantity in a collective or abstract sense: *less time, less money, less weight, less experience. Less* is also appropriate in statements expressing periods of time, sums of money, percentages, and measures of distance, weight, and the like: *less than five days, less than $25, less than ten miles, less than 40 lbs, less than 18 years old.*

   When the distinction between *fewer* and *less* is blurred, it is comforting to know that (a) misusing *less* is better than misusing *fewer,* and (b) *less* is often used informally for *fewer* anyway. Thus the erroneous use of *less* in "experienced less accidents" and "needed less salespersons" will attract little notice, but the misuse of *fewer* in "costs fewer than $10" could well raise an eyebrow or two.

FHA Federal Housing Administration, an agency of the U.S. Department of Housing and Urban Development (HUD). It insures loans and mortgages issued by private lending institutions for homes and multiple-housing units.

"fiber" label A government-decreed label on fabrics describing the fiber content (polyester, cotton, wool, etc.), including the percentages of each fiber when fibers are combined. The labels also próvide separate information about the fiber content of various parts of a garment, as shell and lining. See also **"CARE" LABEL.**

FICA ACRONYM for *Federal Insurance Contributions Act.* FICA taxes are employment taxes, of which half is paid by the employer and half by the individual employee through payroll deductions. Self-employed persons, also subject to the Act, are taxed at another rate and make quarterly payments based on anticipated earnings for the tax year. See also **EMPLOYMENT TAX.**

fiduciary 1. Relating to confidence and trust, usually characterizing an arrangement by which an agent holds property and funds in trust for someone; also, in this sense, *fiducial: a fiduciary* (or *fiducial*) *relationship; a fiduciary contract; a fiduciary possession/We are trying to make the foundation a model of fiduciary responsibility.*

2. A person or agent occupying such a position of trust: *The bank acts as a fiduciary for pension funds.*

field, in the field of   Either term may be superfluous: *an executive in the clothing field (a clothing executive)/experienced in the field of warehouse management (experienced in warehouse management)/a nonprofit research organization in the field of marketing (a nonprofit marketing research organization).* See also WORDINESS 2.

FIFO   See LIFO, FIFO.

figurative language   Words used symbolically rather than literally; a mode of expression using "figures of speech." If the figure is original, the result is greater color or force than could be achieved with words that mean exactly what they say. The most common figures of speech—such as *simile* and *metaphor*—involve comparisons between unlike things. In a simile, the comparison is made with the use of *like* or *as.*

> The bag that works like a can. [Hefty Steel-Sak trash bags]
>
> Brody is as friendly as a hairshirt.
>
> There are times when facts—like spinach and taxes—have to be faced with fortitude. [U. S. Steel]

In a METAPHOR, the symbolic comparison is made without the use of *like* or *as.*

> Satellite communications are allowing radio to transform the world into an enormous room. [M.S. Kaplin, *Omni*]
>
> There is no international lender of last resort that provides a safety net without holes. [Adam Smith, *Esquire*]
>
> Changing one's mind straightforwardly on an issue after taking office is one thing, but doing toe-dances around a semantic Maypole is to invite skepticism about the meaning of a promise or commitment. [Sydney H. Schanberg, *The New York Times*]

See also HYPERBOLE.

figuratively   Not to be taken in a LITERAL way: *started a trade war/when his fragile empire started to crumble/saw their resources melt under the heat of competition.* See also FIGURATIVE LANGUAGE above.

figure   Informal for "think" or "believe": *We figure the painters will finish the job by Tuesday.*

figurehead A person with authority in name only: *The manager's only a figurehead; if you want to sell to the company, see his uncle.*

figures See NUMERALS.

fill Literally, to make full or occupy to capacity. This meaning is contradicted in the statement, "The pianist was able to fill Alice Tully Hall to a respectable capacity," which implies that the hall was somewhat less than filled. However, the meaning of *fill* is preserved in expressions like "only partly filled," "nearly filled," and "filled to overflowing."

fin Slang for a five-dollar bill; half a SAWBUCK: *asked to borrow ten, but settled for a fin.*

finalize Often cited as bureaucratic JARGON, *finalize* is now firmly established in business, though a little thought will produce a common synonym without the bureaucratic sound: *It has taken much longer than anticipated to finalize (conclude) these arrangements/They expect to finalize (sign) the contract tomorrow/The FDA has never finalized (fixed) this standard for the compound.*

finagle Pronounced fih-*nay*-g'l. Informal for "deceive" or "trick": *finagled them into signing a 10-year service contract/finagled his way into the confidence of the boss.*
—**finagler,** noun: *He's a finagler and not to be trusted.*

finance, financier *Finance,* the noun, is a general term covering the management of funds: *a student of finance/experienced in finance.* *Finance,* the verb, is especially appropriate when large sums are involved, but it is also useful in dealing with smaller sums entailing loans and credit: *The bank will finance the purchase/We've financed you long enough.* Only facetiously is *finance* used for "pay for": *Okay, I'll finance the lunch.*
    Financier is a term reserved for a person who handles financial matters of some substance. It does not apply to a lender of small sums.
    See also FUND, FINANCE.

finding(s) The plural is generally used to denote a conclusion reached after an investigation: *Our findings point to the need for resumption of the Denver-San Francisco route/The auditor's findings shocked the financial community.* A clearly singular sense, however, calls for the singular form: *The auditor's finding of fraud shocked the community/ The jury came back with a finding of not guilty.*

fine print In a contract, the small details or particulars likely to be overlooked by the accepting party: *a provision relegated to the fine print/buried in the fine print/Most signers fail to read the fine print.*

fine tuning The adjustment, as of a price or plan, to a precise degree of tolerance: *Hammering out a rate that appeals to both the supply and demand sides of the market requires a lot of fine tuning.*
—**fine-tune,** verb: *helps you fine-tune your investment strategy.*

fire Informal for "dismiss" or "discharge" (a worker): *fired for incompetence.*
—**light a fire under.** Apply pressure to: *If you don't light a fire under them, you won't get delivery.*

fire up To excite, fill with enthusiasm, make productive: *fired up with the idea of winning/designed to fire up our salespeople/techniques for firing up dead typewriters* [an appeal to writers].

firm Principally a noncorporate business, as a partnership or proprietorship. Loosely, however, the term denotes any business enterprise: *the firm I work for/the firm name/several accounting firms.*

first-class mail Primarily letter mail. Pieces weighing over twelve ounces should be sent by first-class zone-rated **PRIORITY MAIL.**

firstly, secondly, etc. The *-ly* ending on ordinal numbers is acceptable, but superfluous. *First, second, third,* etc. makes a simpler **ENUMERATION**. The practice of writing *firstly* to begin a series and continuing with *second, third,* etc. has no apparent advantage.

fiscal Derived from the Latin word for "treasury," *fiscal* is truest to its origins when it refers to the finances of a government: *The opposition party urges conservative fiscal policies.* The term "fiscal year," used by corporations and other enterprises to denote a fixed twelve-month span in the management of their money, irrespective of the calendar year, has its roots in government, which extracts part of the earnings for taxes. Large companies also use *fiscal* as a term relating to finance in general: *The draconian fiscal measures are designed to improve their position in the credit markets.* Still, in most instances, *financial* is the more appropriate word: *financial necessity/the chief financial officer/a financial plan.*
    See also **FINANCE, FINANCIER.**

fiscal policy The program by which a government uses its powers of taxation and spending to carry out its economic objectives: *a prudent fiscal policy/a fiscal policy directed to making jobs by stimulating industrial output.*

fix　A versatile word used informally as a noun or a verb: *What a fix* (predicament) *to be in/The money was a fix* (bribe)/*He said, "I'll fix* (take revenge on) *you"/The deal was fixed* (unlawfully arranged)/*The loose binding can be fixed* (repaired).

—fix up.　Also informal: *fix up* (repair) *the cellar wall/fix up* (put in order) *the room/fix up* (put together) *a nice bouquet/fix you up* (provide you with) *the right truck for your business.*

fixer　One who makes general repairs or remedies difficult situations; but also a derogatory term for a person who gets others out of trouble by shady, if not illegal, means.

flack　An informal **PEJORATIVE** for press agent: *employed a flack to put their story over.* Also a variant of **FLAK**.

flagship store　The principal unit or showpiece in a chain of stores under the same management: *the site of their new flagship store.*

flak　Also, less commonly, **FLACK**. Informal for *criticism* or *complaints: getting a lot of flak from our dealers.*

flammable　Easily ignited. Synonymous with, but much preferred to *inflammable*, which is often mistaken for *nonflammable*, fireproof: *Flammable substance—do not use near heat or flame.*

flat　1. Not subject to variation: *a flat rate.* 2. Neither up nor down, dull: *Sales for the 3d quarter were flat compared with the same period last year.* 3. Without qualification: *a flat refusal.* 4. In bond transactions, a *flat sale* is one that cedes to the buyer 100 percent of the next interest payment.

flaunt, flout　To *flaunt* is to display ostentatiously: *flaunt one's wealth/flaunt one's knowledge.* To *flout* is to scorn, scoff at, be contemptuous of: *flouted the accepted rules of conduct/made the mistake of flouting the advice of his banker.*

Flesch formula　See at **READABILITY**.

flesh peddler　A **PEJORATIVE** for a recruiter of executive personnel: *The idea of recruiters as flesh peddlers—that's gone.* Compare **HEAD-HUNTER**.

flextime   Also *flexitime*. An alternative work schedule permitting employees to choose their work times within stated limits.

flight   In broadcast advertising, a series of commercials for a single product or service during a given number of weeks. The advertiser will usually schedule a series of flights punctuated by breaks during which the commercials are suspended: *Pere Pat is running a four-week flight on five stations in a heavy schedule starting October 22.*

flip chart   A large pad or loosely bound volume whose pages can be flipped in sequence to reveal charts or other data in synchronization with a speaker's oral presentation; also any large pad, usually mounted on an easel, for presenting key points in words or pictures. The material can be prepared in advance or drawn in by the speaker, using a crayon or felt marker while talking.

floating date line   See at DATE LINE.

float   Funds in suspension, including checks not cleared, travelers checks not cashed, and credit purchases not yet billed and paid for. The lapse in time enables the holder of the funds to realize interest on them: *In the past, the* [advertising] *agencies themselves were frequently late paying the media and "playing the float" with the clients' money.*

floor   A bottom limit: *a floor under wages*. Antonym, CEILING.

floppy disk   Also a *diskette* and, familiarly, a *floppy*. A thin, resilient plastic disk with a magnetic "memory"; used with a minicomputer to store and read data or instructions. The disks are predominantly 5¼ or 8 inches in diameter.

flounder, founder   To flounder is to move clumsily; to founder is to become disabled and possibly, as in the instance of a ship, to go down. The division in meaning is not always clear-cut, and less ambiguous terms might well be sought: *They're still floundering (thrashing about) in a sea of red ink/One program that appears to have foundered (run into trouble) is Lockheed's, whose Missile Systems division now has only a handful of quality control circles.*

flout   See FLAUNT, FLOUT.

flunky   Also *flunkey*. Used disparagingly for a person performing menial duties: *Title or not, he was just a flunky for the big man*. Also a flatterer or toady: *an obsequious flunky*.

flush 1. In printing, descriptive of copy aligned vertically at the margins, with no indentions: *set flush*.

2. Having a great deal of money, affluent: *feeling flush*.

flustrated Nonstandard. A blend of *flustered* and *frustrated: appeared flustrated (flustered)*.

—**flustration,** noun. Also nonstandard: *showed his flustration (frustration)*.

focalize Borrowed from optics, an awkward synonym for the verb FO-CUS, meaning to concentrate attention: *We should focus* (not *focalize*) *on more immediate goals*.

focus 1. The principal parts of the verb are spelled *focused* (or *focussed*), *focusing* (or *focussing*) and *focuses* (or *focusses*): *Attention was focused* (or *focussed*) *on the terms of financing*. See also **FOCALIZE**.

2. *Focus*, the noun, is well used in the sense of "center of interest": *The committee's focus is the long-term solution to the problem*.

focus group In marketing, a group of some eight or ten persons brought together to discuss a product, an advertising campaign, or just their needs as consumers. One session of several hours permits a marketer to obtain a relatively cheap qualitative evaluation of the marketplace for anything from a breakfast cereal to a surgical instrument. Use of the focus group is in contrast to the quantitative research methods by which hundreds or thousands of people are methodically surveyed.

fold Informal for "go bankrupt" or "go out of business": *When the company folded, we were left with an unpaid account of $10,000/The show folded after three weeks on the road*.

folk, folks *Folk* (singular), meaning "people" or "of the people," is fully accepted in general usage: *city folk, country folk, folk art*. The plural, however, is only informally used as a homey expression for parents, relatives, people in general, or those addressed: *The folks down home will really appreciate this remembrance from you/You folks up there can use some of our sunshine/Dear Folks* (letter **SALUTATION**).

following *Next* or *after* may do as well or better: *the following day (the next day)/following (after) the merger*.

—**the following.** Regularly part of a formal introduction to a list or statement: *Please enter our order for the following/Mr. Drew left the following instructions/Consider the following*. The introduction ends with a **COLON**.

follow up, follow-up The verb is not hyphened, but the noun and adjective are: *They promised to follow up the complaint/There was no follow-up/We sent a follow-up letter.*

font A full set of type in one size and face. Should a typesetter use a mismatched letter, the term "wrong font" (abbreviated wf) is used to call attention to the error.

foot Informal for *pay: Who'll foot the bill?/Current taxes don't even come close to footing the expected costs of the improvement.* Compare FOOT UP.

footnotes See REFERENCE NOTES.

foot up To add a column of figures and put the total at the bottom: *When she footed up the bill, the total came to $189.76.* Except in this narrow sense, *add* is preferred: *Let me add those figures again.*

forced See COMPULSIVE WORDS.

forceful, forcible *Forceful* means full of force, effective, or powerful: *a forceful speaker. Forcible* means accomplished by force: *forcible entry.*

fore- A prefix denoting *before* in time or space, as in "the foregoing statement," "the foreseeable future," and "in the forefront."

forecast The preferred past tense form is *forecast: Their economist correctly forecast* (rather than *forecasted*) *the rise in demand.*

forego, forgo Although the terms are interchangeable, *forego* is best used in the sense of going before, and *forgo* in the sense of abstaining or doing without. Hence "the foregoing [preceding] statement" and "a foregone conclusion"; but "will forgo [give up] his commission."

foresee Sometimes mistakenly spelled *forsee* because of a false analogy with *forgo* (see FOREGO, FORGO): *The trouble could not have been foreseen.*

foreword So spelled (*-word*, not *-ward*). A short statement prefacing a book or long report. Some texts may have both a foreword and a preface as, for instance, a foreword by someone other than the author and the author's preface following. Regardless of any foreword or preface, a long text will have an introduction, whether so-called or not, and whether separated from the text or an integral part of it. Compare FORWARD. See also REPORTS 1.

for free   Informal for "free" or "free of charge": *Subscribe now and the first issue is yours for free.*

forgive   See EXCUSE, FORGIVE, PARDON.

formal English   See USAGES 3.

former, latter   "The former" is the first of two; "the latter" is the second of two: *We received bids from Allied Power and Consolidated Utilities, but we gave the order to the former* (or *the latter*).

If three or more are named, the first is referred to as "the first" or "the first named," or the name is repeated; and the last is referred to as "the last" (not "the latter") or "the last named," or the last name is repeated. Repetition of the name is usually preferable: *We received bids from Allied Power, Consolidated Utilities, and Benson Electric, but we gave the order to the first* (or *last*). Or: *. . . we gave the order to the first named* (or *last named*); or (preferred): *. . . we gave the order to Allied* (or *to Benson*).

form letter   A letter that can be reproduced and distributed to any number of addressees. It may or may not be "personalized" with an INSIDE ADDRESS, SALUTATION, and SIGNATURE. See also GUIDE LETTER.

forms of address   Business etiquette, no less than social etiquette, requires the observance of certain forms in the use of titles and designations, and in the phrasing of letter salutations and complimentary closes. The forms chosen depend on the sex, position, and rank of the addressees. Within limits, some alternative forms are permitted.*

1. COMMON TITLES AND DESIGNATIONS.   2. INDIVIDUALS JOINTLY ADDRESSED. 3. ADDRESSING PUBLIC OFFICIALS.

See also DEGREES AND CERTIFICATIONS.

1. COMMON TITLES AND DESIGNATIONS (alphabetically arranged).

Doctor.   When a person is addressed as *Doctor* or *Dr.*, the initials of the doctorate (M.D., Ph.D., D.V.M., etc.) do not follow the name. When the initials follow, no title precedes.

Dr. Evelyn T. Kaye *or* Evelyn T. Kaye, M.D.

---

*The practice of omitting such courtesy titles as *Mr.* and *Miss* in addressing individuals is not generally recommended, but the writer has little flexibility when a name gives no clue to the appropriate sexual designation (e.g., *H. N. Farber, Marion Debray, Leslie Gorman*). The SALUTATION is then styled in the same way, as *Dear H. N. Farber,* or omitted altogether.

Dr. Timothy L. Shannon *or* Timothy L. Shannon, Ph.D.

The title is usually abbreviated in the inside address and envelope address, but it is often spelled out in the salutation. Only in familiar use, however, is the title *Doctor* used in the salutation without a following surname.

Dear Dr. Kaye *or* Dear Doctor Kaye
But (familiar only): Dear Doctor

Esquire. This title, seldom used in the United States, is limited to men and women engaged in such professions as law, architecture, and diplomacy. The title or its abbreviation *Esq.* is used only after the full name, and never when the name is preceded by another title. *Esquire* or *Esq.* is included in the envelope address, but not in the salutation, where the appropriate courtesy title precedes the name.

Donald M. Tyler, Esq.   Mary A. Hinds, Esquire
Dear Mr. Tyler   Dear Miss Hinds

Honorable. *The Honorable* or its abbreviation *Hon.* is a title of distinction used in addressing an elected or appointed public official. It is followed by the full name, without a courtesy title; or, in oral address, by the courtesy title and the surname.

The Honorable Ray S. Kline *or* Hon. Ray S. Kline
But not The Honorable Kline *and not* Hon. Kline
In oral address only: The Honorable Mr. Kline
The courtesy title, not *Honorable*, is used in the salutation.

The Honorable Harvey Stone   The Honorable Lauren Y. Hart
United States Senate   Governor's Committee on Consumer
                               Affairs

Dear Senator Stone   Dear Mrs. Hart

Jr., Sr., II, 3d, etc.   Such designations are treated as part of the name and do not take the place of the usual courtesy title or the appendage of an academic degree or professional rating. A comma before the designation is optional.

Mr. Henry S. Romney, Jr. *or* Mr. Henry S. Romney Jr.
Rev. Raoul Dunlop 2d, D.D.
David Williams II, Esq.

Madam. Pronounced *mad-*um. A courtesy title used in the salutation of a formal letter addressed to a married woman or a woman of rank or title. In order of decreasing formality: *Madam, My dear Madam, Dear Madam.* Used also with a title of office, as *Madam Secretary* (cabinet officer). Plural, *Mesdames* (pronounced may-*dom*).

Madame. Pronounced *mad*-um or muh-*dam*. A French form of *Madam;* abbreviated *Mme.* Plural, *Mesdames* (pronounced may-*dom*), abbreviated *Mmes.* A courtesy title corresponding to *Mrs.* and used with the surname in addressing a foreign married woman. Used also with a woman's full name or surname alone as a mark of respect for rank or achievement: *Madame Curie, Madame Maria Callas.*

Mesdames. Plural of *Madam, Madame,* and *Mrs.;* abbreviated *Mmes.* Used in addressing a professional partnership of women (Mesdames Lavin and Cantor) or two or more women individually (Mesdames Pearl Avery and Beatrice Croy). The corresponding salutations are *Ladies, Mesdames,* or *Dear Mesdames.* (See also Sec. 2, "Individuals jointly addressed," following.)

Messrs. Plural of *Mr.* Used in addressing two or more men associated in their own business or profession: Messrs. Bell, Huntley, and Cross. The customary salutation is *Gentlemen,* but see also Sec. 2, "Individuals jointly addressed," following.

Messrs. is not to be used before a corporate name consisting of the names of individuals: Abraham & Straus (*not* Messrs. Abraham & Straus).

Miss. A courtesy title used in addressing an unmarried woman or a married woman who goes by her maiden name (but see also *Ms.* below). The plural is *Misses* (see Sec. 2, "Individuals jointly addressed," following).

Miss Lisa Miller
Dear Miss Miller

Mr. A courtesy title used in addressing a man. For the plural, see *Messrs.* above.

Mr. Rex D. Carver
Dear Mr. Carver

Mrs. A courtesy title used in addressing a married woman or a woman using her married name (but see also *Ms.* below). In business usage, the title is followed by the woman's given name. For the plural, see *Mesdames* above.

Mrs. Eleanor A. Bayer
Dear Mrs. Bayer

Ms. Pronounced *miz.* A courtesy title particularly useful in addressing a woman whose marital status is unknown. *Ms.* is also preferred by some single women, married women using their maiden names, and other women who consider their marital status irrelevant. The plural of *Ms.* is the same as the singular. As a relatively new title, *Ms.* produces mixed feelings even among women, some of whom would prefer that the user err, if need be, on the side of *Miss.*

Ms. Carrie R. Palmer
Dear Ms. Palmer

Professional designations. When initials designating a professional certification are added to a name, a courtesy title precedes the name.

Ms. Annie T. Cross, C.P.A.   Mr. Robert Ball, C.L.U.
Dear Ms. Cross   Dear Mr. Ball

Professor. The title may be abbreviated *Prof.* in the address block, but not in the salutation. When *Dr.* or another title is used as a substitute for *Professor* in the address, the specific professorial title may be added on the second line.

Professor Daniel Robinson
Dear Professor Robinson

Prof. Harvey N. Gitlin
Dear Professor Gitlin

Dr. Seldon F. Frame
Professor of Economics

Dear Dr. Frame

An assistant professor, associate professor, or adjunct professor of any rank is addressed as *Professor.* If, however, the full title follows the name in the address block, the name is preceded by *Dr.* or other applicable courtesy title, but the title *Professor* may still be used in the salutation. It is well to note, too, that some professors, especially those in the lowest rank, do not have doctorates, and that in some colleges and universities, the use of a title like *Mr., Miss, Ms.,* or *Mrs.* for all professorial ranks is traditional.

Professor Samuel E. Cordry *or* Mr. Samuel E. Cordry
                                Adjunct Assistant Professor
                                of Accounting

Dear Professor Cordry   Dear Mr. Cordry *or*
                                Dear Professor Cordry

Reverend. *The Reverend* precedes the full name of the clergyman in the address block. In business or informal correspondence the title may be shortened to *The Rev.* or *Rev.* The title *The Rever-*

end Dr. may be followed by the last name alone. In the salutation, the title *Reverend* is not used; instead, the clergyman's name is preceded by the appropriate courtesy title, as *Mr. (Miss, Mrs., Ms.), Dr., Father, Rabbi, Chaplain.*

The Reverend Paul Green		Mr.	
The Reverend Dr. Green	Dear	Father	Green
The Rev. Paul Green		Dr.	
Rev. Paul Green		Rabbi	

2. INDIVIDUALS JOINTLY ADDRESSED.   When a single letter is addressed to two or more persons, questions arise about the order of names and the matching of titles and salutations. Regardless of a person's sex or marital position, an official, professional, or other distinctive title takes precedence over a simple title of courtesy *(Mr., Miss, Mrs., Ms.).* When titles have approximately the same standing, the order is determined by seniority or custom (as *Mr. and Mrs.; Miss Teresa Danby and Mr. Howard Fellows*). As a way to avoid awkwardness—or simply as a matter of preference—the joint addressees may be listed, rather than linked by *and.*

Dr. Helen B. Donaldson
Mr. Roderick N. Donaldson
Dear Dr. and Mr. Donaldson

Representative styles covering several different situations are shown below.

(a) Same Surname—Married Couples

Mr. and Mrs. John B. Trent	Dear Mr. and Mrs. Trent
Dr. John B. Trent and Mrs. Trent	Dear Dr. Trent and Mrs. Trent
Dr. Mae Trent and Mr. John B. Trent	Dear Dr. Trent and Mr. Trent
Drs. John B. and Mae Trent	Dear Doctors Trent
The Hon. and Mrs. John B. Trent	Dear Mr. and Mrs. Trent
The Honorable John B. Trent and Mrs. Trent	Dear Senator and Mrs. Trent
	Dear Governor and Mrs. Trent Etc.
The Hon. Mae Trent and Mr. John B. Trent	Dear Mrs. [Senator, Governor, etc.] and Mr. Trent

(b) Same Surname—Men

Messrs. Perry and Harmon Sloan	Dear Messrs. Sloan

Mr. Perry Sloan and Mr. Harmon Sloan	Gentlemen
Dr. Perry Sloan Mr. Harmon Sloan	Dear Dr. and Mr. Sloan

(c) Same Surname—Women

Misses Edna and Doris Smith	Dear Misses Smith
Ms. Edna Smith Ms. Doris Smith	Dear Ms. Smith
Professor Edna Smith and Miss Doris Smith	Dear Mesdames Smith
Mrs. Edna Smith and Miss Doris Smith	Dear Mrs. Smith and Miss Smith

(d) Different Surnames—Men and Women

Ms. Holly T. Rand Ms. Carla McDowell	Dear Ms. Rand and Ms. McDowell
Mr. Peter L. Travis and Mr. Ronald Potok	Dear Mr. Travis and Mr. Potok Gentlemen
Miss Terry Guest and Mr. Robert O. Dant	Dear Miss Guest and Mr. Dant
Dr. Gladys Weems and Mr. Henry Noonan	Dear Dr. Weems and Mr. Noonan

3. ADDRESSING PUBLIC OFFICIALS. The forms that follow (see chart) cover the principal offices of the federal, state, and local governments. In adapting the forms to other offices and titles, these principles apply:

(a) The more important the office, the more formality in the form of address.

(b) In most instances, a person may be addressed by his or her official title, as *Senator* —— ——, *Judge* —— ——, *Lieutenant* —— ——. Where the title of office cannot conveniently be used in this way, the full name may be prefixed by an appropriate courtesy title (*The Honorable, Dr., Professor, Mr.,* etc.) and followed by the title of office (*Member of the Assembly, Attorney General, Director of the Budget,* etc.).

(c) The salutation will employ the official or courtesy title, as *Dear Judge Smith, Dear Professor Jones, Dear Mrs. Brown.* Where greater formality is desired, the forms *Dear Sir* and *Dear Madam* are almost invariably correct.

(d) The complimentary closes *Very truly yours* and *Sincerely yours* also meet practically all needs.

FORM OF ADDRESS	SALUTATION	COMPLIMENTARY CLOSE
Ambassador, American		
The Honorable _____	Sir (Madam)	Very truly yours
_____	Dear Mr. (Madam) Am-bassador	Respectfully yours
American Ambassador		
(in Central or South America)		
The Honorable	Sir (Madam)	Very truly yours
Ambassador of the United States	Dear Mr. (Madam) Am-bassador	Respectfully yours
Ambassador, foreign		
His (Her) Excellency	Excellency	Very truly yours
Ambassador of (Country)	Dear Mr. (Madame) Ambassador	Sincerely yours
Ambassador, English		
His (Her) Excellency	Excellency	Very truly yours
The Right Honorable	Dear Mr. (Madam) Am-bassador	Sincerely yours
Ambassador of Great Britain		
Assistant Secretary		
(cabinet level)		
The Honorable _____	Sir (Madam)	Very truly yours
	My dear Sir (Madam)	Sincerely yours
_____	Dear Sir (Madam)	
Assistant Secretary of (De-partment)	Dear Mr. (Miss, Mrs., Ms.) _____	
Associate Justice		
(Supreme Court)		
Justice _____ _____	Sir (Madam)	Very truly yours
The Supreme Court	My dear Sir (Madam)	Sincerely yours
	Dear Mr. Justice	
	Dear Justice _____	
Cabinet officer		
The Honorable _____	Sir (Madam)	Very truly yours
	My dear Sir (Madam)	Sincerely yours
_____	Dear Sir (Madam)	
Secretary of (Department)	Dear Mr. (Miss, Mrs., Ms.) _____	

FORM OF ADDRESS	SALUTATION	COMPLIMENTARY CLOSE
Chairman, Congressional Committee		
The Honorable _____ _____	Dear Mr. (Madam) Chairman	Very truly yours Sincerely yours
Chairman, Committee on (Name) United States Senate (or U.S. House of Representatives)	Dear Senator (Mr., Miss, Mrs., Ms.) _____	
Charge d'Affaires, American*		
_____ _____, American Charge d'Affaires	Sir (Madam) Dear Mr. (Miss, Mrs., Ms.) _____	Very truly yours Sincerely yours
(in Central or South America)		
_____ _____, United States Charge d'Affaires	Sir (Madam) Dear Mr. (Miss, Mrs., Ms) _____	Very truly yours Sincerely yours
Charge d'Affaires, foreign*		
Mr. (Miss, Mrs., Ms.) _____ _____ Charge d'Affaires of (Country)	Sir (Madame) Dear Mr. (Miss, Mrs., Ms.) _____	Very truly yours Sincerely yours
*In the instance of a temporary replacement, add *ad interim* to the title.		
Chief Justice of the U.S.		
Chief Justice The Supreme Court The Chief Justice of the United States	Sir (Madam) Dear Mr. Chief Justice	Respectfully yours Very truly yours Sincerely yours
Commissioner		
The Honorable _____ _____ Federal Trade Commission	Dear Sir (Madam) Dear Mr. (Miss, Mrs., Ms.) _____	Very truly yours Sincerely yours
Congressman, -woman		
The Honorable _____ _____ The United States House of Representatives	Sir (Madam) Dear Sir (Madam) Dear Mr. (Miss, Mrs., Mr.) _____	Very truly yours Sincerely yours
Consul, American		
_____ _____, Esq. American Consul at _____	Sir (Madam) Dear Sir (Madam) My dear Mr. (Miss, Mrs., Ms.) _____	Very truly yours Sincerely yours

FORM OF ADDRESS	SALUTATION	COMPLIMENTARY CLOSE
Consul, foreign		
_____ _____, Esq.	Sir (Madame)	Very truly yours
The Belgian Consul	Dear Sir (Madame)	Sincerely yours
	Dear Mr. (Miss, Mrs., Ms.) _____	
Governor of a State		
The Honorable _____ _____	Sir (Madam)	Respectfully yours
Governor of (State)	Dear Governor _____	Very truly yours
		Sincerely yours
Judge (below Supreme Court)		
The Honorable _____ _____	Sir (Madam)	Very truly yours
Judge of the _____ Court	Dear Judge _____	Sincerely
Mayor		
The Honorable _____ _____	Dear Mayor _____	Sincerely yours
Mayor of (City)		
Military Officers*		
General _____ _____, USA	Dear General _____	Very truly yours
(Post)		Sincerely yours
(Address)		

*(1) The letter and envelope address use the officer's official title, as *Lieutenant General George H. Smith,* but the salutation drops the modifier: *Dear General Smith.* So, too, any reference to the officer in writing or speaking: *the General,* or *General Smith.*

(2) The title may be abbreviated in the inside address, but not in the salutation. In the inside address, as on the envelope, the title and name are always followed by the abbreviation of the branch of service:

USA (Army)   USCG (Coast Guard)   USN (Navy)
USAF (Air Force)   USMC (Marine Corps)

Minister, diplomatic		
The Honorable _____	Sir (Madam)	Very truly yours
_____	Dear Mr. (Madam) Minister	Sincerely yours
American Minister		
(in Central or South America)		
The Honorable _____	Sir (Madam)	Very truly yours
_____	Dear Mr. (Madam) Minister	Sincerely yours
Minister of the United States		
Minister, foreign		
The Honorable _____	Sir (Madame)	Very truly yours
_____	Dear Mr. (Madame) Minister	Sincerely yours
Minister of (Country)		

FORM OF ADDRESS	SALUTATION	COMPLIMENTARY CLOSE
President		
The President The White House	Sir Mr. President Dear Mr. President	Respectfully yours
Representative (U.S.) See "Congressman, -woman."		
Senator (U.S.)		
The Honorable _____ _____ United States Senate	Sir (Madam) Dear Senator _____	Very truly yours Sincerely yours
Senator (State)		
The Honorable _____ _____ The Senate of (State)	Sir (Madam) Dear Senator _____	Very truly yours Sincerely yours
Speaker (House of Representatives)		
The Honorable _____ _____ Speaker of the House of Representatives	Sir Dear Mr. Speaker Dear Mr. _____	Very truly yours Sincerely yours
Vice President		
The Vice President United States Senate	Sir Mr. Vice President Dear Mr. Vice President	Respectfully yours

formula   The PLURALS are *formulas* and *formulae* (pronounced -lee). *Formulas* is preferred in ordinary use; *formulae*, in technical use: *The formulas for the dyes are a closely guarded secret/Each issue shows you how to use such formulae as regression analysis to estimate the future values of common and preferred stocks, debenture bonds, and other equities.*

formulate   A simpler word may better express the meaning: *formulated (made) plans/formulate (form) an opinion/will formulate (set down) our ideas on paper.* See also LONG WORDS AND SHORT.

forte   In the sense of a strong point, pronounced preferably *fort: Her* *forte is placing talented people in responsible corporate positions.* Not to be confused with the musical term *forte* meaning "loud" and, without exception, pronounced *for*-tay.

forthcoming, forthright *Forthcoming* is correctly used in the sense of "about to appear" and "approachable," or "affable": *her forthcoming debut/a forthcoming fellow.* Too often, however, it is mistakenly used for *forthright,* which means "candid," "open," "aboveboard": *As I recall, your reaction was that we had been quite forthcoming and that our proposal was of real interest to you.* [Substitute *forthright* or *candid.*]

for the reason that Because. See WORDINESS 4.

fortuitous Unplanned, occurring by chance, not necessarily with happy results, though the word is used loosely for *fortunate* or *lucky: Our meeting was entirely fortuitous (accidental) and regrettable.* But: *Our meeting was fortunate* (not *fortuitous*); *Tom gave me a good sales lead.* [*Fortunate* is used because the sales lead was the result of a lucky meeting, not merely an accidental one.]
—**fortuitously,** adverb: *My acquaintance with Mr. Brian began fortuitously (accidentally) with a visit to my nephew.*

Fortune 500 *The Fortune Directory of the 500 Largest Industrial Corporations.* Gives information about products, plants, sales, assets, and net profits. Published annually in May as a section of *Fortune* magazine: *a Fortune 500 corporation* (one listed in the directory; evidence of size or standing).

forward Not to be confused with *send.* Something is *forwarded* when it is transmitted by the receiver to a third party: *Miss Grimes is away, but I'll forward your letter to her.* But: *We'll send* (not *forward*) *our check promptly.* Compare FOREWORD.
—**forward on.** The *on* is superfluous: *If you get the information, please forward it* (not *forward it on*) *to Ray.* See WORDINESS 3.

forward, forwards The words are interchangeable as adverbs in the sense of "to the front," but *forward* is preferred: *The demonstrator stepped forward* (or *forwards*). In other senses, as adjective or adverb, only *forward* is correct: *the forward compartment/a forward waiter/a contract for forward (future) delivery/asked to come forward/look forward to meeting you.*

forward planning   The phrase is not redundant if one distinguishes between planning for the immediate future and planning for implementation at some time in the future. The latter is *forward planning: instituted a set of formal procedures for capital budgeting and forward planning.* [*Planning* alone would not describe the objective as clearly.]

for your information   Except for occasional use to smooth the connection between sentences, the phrase is a superfluous introduction to a statement of fact: *For your information, the lease was signed yesterday* (omit *For your information*). See also WORDINESS 2. Entirely reasonable, however, is the use of the phrase in the sense of "for your files" or "for you to know but not to act on": *A copy of the complaint is enclosed for your information.* See also FYI.

fourth-class mail   Also parcel post. For packages weighing from 1 to 70 lbs.

fractions   See NUMERALS 5.

frame of reference   A set of ideas or data to which other ideas or data may be compared for any latent significance. An overworked phrase, it is better not used when the simple word *guide* will do: *Last year's sales and production figures provide a good frame of reference for this year's.* But: *We'll use their report as a guide* (rather than *frame of reference*) *in preparing our own.*

FRB   The Federal Reserve Board; the FED.

freebie   Slang for something given free with the purchase of a good or service: *For the airlines, the day of the promotional freebie is over.*

free gift   Although *free* is superfluous, the usage is entrenched among advertisers who have learned the magic of the word: *Explore* Discover *and get a free gift.* Outside advertising, *gift* is not enhanced by the adjective: *The sample was a gift* (not *a free gift*). See also FOR FREE.

free lance   A self-employed person, usually an artist or writer, who accepts assignments from a number of organizations: *works as a free lance.*
—free-lance, adjective: *a free-lance artist.* Also a verb: *I free-lanced for a while before joining BBDO.*

free lunch   Voguish term for "something for nothing," popularized in the axiom, "There's no such thing as a free lunch."

fresh   1. In advertising, a descriptive word often used for processed foods and fruit drinks from which all but the vestiges of the original products have been replaced by extenders, preservatives, and flavor enhancers: *Tastes fresh as homemade* [Cool Whip].

2. A EUPHEMISM for "clean" or "odor-free": *Comfortable fresh protection for every day* [Carefree Panty Shields]/*Now every bathroom can be fresh* [Befresh, a toilet bowl deodorizer]/*Rainbow-fresh Yes* [Yes, a laundry detergent and fabric softener].

Friday   See GAL/GUY FRIDAY.

fringe benefit   Originally a supplement to wages, such as medical insurance or a pension, the meaning is now extended to include any unanticipated benefit: *My suntan? That was a fringe benefit of my business trip to Phoenix.*

front office   Figuratively, an organization's policymakers: *The front office doesn't see it our way*/*I'll have to take it up with the front office.* In the same sense, the "front office" is more likely to be secluded than placed near the door or in some other position where it would be too easily accessible (see OPEN-DOOR POLICY 2).

frost belt   Also *Frost Belt*. Another name for SNOWBELT.

FSLIC   Federal Savings and Loan Insurance Corporation. Compare FDIC.

FTC   Federal Trade Commission. The U.S. agency charged with administering antitrust and consumer protection legislation.

-ful   Nouns ending in *-ful* usually form their plurals by the addition of *s: spoonfuls, tablespoonfuls, handfuls, cupfuls, glassfuls.*

full block style   A letter format in which all the lines of the mechanical parts and body of the letter begin at the left margin. See also LETTER FORM 3.

function   As a verb, *function* is better not used when a simpler or more exact word can be found: *also functions (acts) as a receptionist*/*saw that the machine was functioning (working) properly*/*the effect on morale of an executive who functions (is given duties) below his capacity.*

functional   Descriptive of something that serves its purpose, often implying an absence of ornamentation or frills. The modifier *very* tends to weaken the effect: *The municipal airport is a very functional facility, with excellent ground transportation* (omit *very*).

fund, finance   1. To *fund* is technically to set aside capital, the income from which is to be used over a period of time for a specific purpose;

to *fund* is also to convert a debt into a long-term obligation with an arrangement for fixed payments. To *finance*, however, is to obtain or supply funds or credit. A pension or bond issue is *funded*, but construction or developmental projects are customarily *financed*. If this distinction is not always observed, possibly it is because *fund* and *funding* have a better CONNOTATION than *finance* and *financing*. Thus donors are sought to "fund" (finance) the work of penurious artists, and the "funding" (financing) of hospital wings is the full-time work of professional money-raisers.

2. The noun *fund*, meaning money available for a specific purpose, is subject to none of the restrictions placed on the verb. A *fund* finances the work of penurious artists; hospitals raise *funds* for new facilities; and companies set aside *funds* for expansion.

See also FINANCE, FINANCIER.

funny money Slang for counterfeit money: *are stuck with the funny money to the tune of at least $6 million a year.*

further Well used for *additional*, as in "a further argument," and for *moreover*, as in "Further, we want to emphasize our continuing commitment to a fair labor policy"; but also tending to stiltedness in some expressions: *We shall write to you further in this connection (We'll write to you again)/Further to your request (Going back to your request/With further reference to your offer, we believe . . . (Again referring to your offer, we believe . . .)*

See also FARTHER, FURTHER.

future plans *Future* is superfluous: *our plans* (not *future plans*) include. See WORDINESS 3. But compare, also, FORWARD PLANNING.

futurist Also *futurologist*. A general scholar who anticipates the future from a study of past and present movements; not to be confused with specialists like security analysts, budget officers, and marketing managers, on the one hand, and charlatans like seers and clairvoyants, on the other. *The "information revolution" that futurists have long predicted has arrived.*

—futurism. The art or science of predicting: *the Hudson Institute, a citadel of futurism.*

FYI The abbreviation of FOR YOUR INFORMATION; a notation sometimes placed on a copy of a letter or other document, or on a ROUTING SLIP sent to an interested party.

G

G Abbreviation of *grand*, slang for a thousand dollars: *lost 5 G's on the deal.*

GAAP ACRONYM for *g*enerally *a*ccepted *a*ccounting *p*rinciples. See also at INFORMATION OVERLOAD 2.

gal/guy Friday Also *G/G Friday*, or *Friday* alone. (*Girl/man Friday* is discriminatory in language and now rare.) The term denotes a clerk or secretary assigned to or qualified to perform a variety of office tasks. From "Gal Friday," coined by Broadway columnist Walter Winchell. Well established as a job category in help wanted advertisements: *Fridays (typing required), PR, from $16,500.* [Employment agency advertisement]

game Slang for a business or occupation, usually a highly competitive one: *the insurance game/the advertising game.*

game plan JARGON for *strategy: We identify your assets, pinpoint your career options, and develop a complete game plan for getting you a maximum number of interviews/If defense contractors know what the game plan is going to be, they can prepare themselves to meet the military's needs.*

GAO See GENERAL ACCOUNTING OFFICE.

garnishee Also *garnish*. To take by legal authority a debtor's wages or other money or property. The process is called *garnishment. He didn't realize he had agreed to have his wages garnisheed* (or *garnished*). A *garnishee* (noun) is the person subject to garnishment: *It is not pleasant to be a garnishee.*

GATT ACRONYM for *G*eneral *A*greement on *T*ariffs and *T*rade. An agreement of the world's great trading nations to promote free international trade; also the body subscribing to the treaty. Formed in 1947 with 23 nations as members (88 by 1982), *GATT* continues its work in the face of recurring waves of PROTECTIONISM.

gauge Pronounced *gay*-j. A variant spelling of the noun, but not of the verb, is *gage: a gauge* (measure) *of profitability*. Also, *a gage of profitability*. But: *will gauge* (not *gage*) *their determination*. Not to be confused with **GOUGE**.

gear up To get ready, as by putting equipment in place or a process into motion: *The money market funds are gearing up to compete against the federally insured money market accounts now offered by banks and thrift units.*

gender, sex 1. *Gender* is a grammatical term; thus the *gender* (not *sex*) of the pronoun *she* is feminine. *Sex*, however, is a characteristic of living things: *The application was filled in by an S.T. Greaves; the sex* (not *gender*) *is not indicated.*

2. Despite the distinction above, *gender* is often used synonymously with *sex*, possibly because of some of the negative connotations of *sex: The appointment was thought to have been unduly influenced by her gender/It was felt that the gender of the insured is an unfair criterion for setting rates.* In many instances, it is possible—even desirable—to substitute other words for *gender* and *sex: partial to the feminine gender in choosing secretaries (partial to women)/was hard to tell the sex of the caller from the voice on the phone (was hard to tell whether the caller was a man or a woman).*

See also **SEXUAL BIAS** and the use of the terms "merged gender" and "sex-distinct" at **UNISEX**.

General Accounting Office Headed by the U.S. Comptroller General, the GAO audits the accounts of all federal agencies and departments and assists Congress in all matters relating to the handling of public funds.

general English See **USAGES** 1.

general public Not necessarily redundant. See **PUBLIC(S)**.

general rule Redundant, but in common use: *as a general rule (as a rule, in general)*. See also **WORDINESS** 3.

generalist A person with a broad business background, able to apply to the problems of a business organization a liberal understanding of its structure and aims. Antonym, *specialist*.

generation A class of manufactured goods having its origins in a preceding class: *a new generation of IBM computers/Mergenthaler was the first company to produce a third-generation digital typesetter.*

generic Descriptive of a class, as of unbranded goods usually sold at a lower price than the branded kind: *generic drugs* (e.g., aspirin, not Bayer's or others similarly identified)/*generic foods and household items* (e.g., canned peaches, tissues, laundry detergent, *not* Del Monte peaches, Kleenex, Tide). See also **BRAND NAME**.

gentleman Although *man* is preferred in ordinary use, *gentleman* survives as a mark of social or political distinction and for its **CONNOTATION** of elegance: *a real gentleman/gentlemen's apparel/the gentleman from the 22d District* (congressman)/*Gentlemen* (sign on a rest room). But: *a man's suit/the man from Glad* (brand of plastic wrap)/*the man in the street* (the average person)/*the men's room*. Compare **LADY**.

Gentlemen A common salutation in letters and public address. See especially **SALUTATION** 2.

gentrification The process by which property in decaying neighborhoods is taken over and rehabilitated for middle-class residential use— a cause of some resentment by the displaced poor.

gerund See **POSSESSIVE WITH GERUND**.

get See **OBTAIN, GET**.

gibe See **JIBE, GIBE**.

GIGO Rhymes with *why go;* **ACRONYM** for "garbage *in*, garbage *o*ut," a facetious reference to the fact that the information obtained from a computer can be no better than the information fed into it. The abbreviation is imitative of LIFO and FIFO, systems of inventory accounting (See at **LIFO, FIFO**).

gilt-edge Also *gilt-edged*. Of excellent quality, as an investment instrument: *a gilt-edge stock*.

gimmick Slang. A questionable promotional strategy; an innovation of little worth added to heighten the attraction of an offer: *just a gimmick to camouflage the increase in price/used an array of gimmicks that helped liquidate the store's inventory/The gimmick is a bubble-gum dispenser sewn into the front of the child's overalls*.

gimmickry The use of a **GIMMICK**: *doesn't have to resort to gimmickry*.

girl Informal and demeaning when used in reference to a secretary, stenographer, clerk, or similarly placed female employee. It is also biased, since the male counterpart is not called a "boy": *If your girl will call my girl when you're ready, we'll arrange a meeting.* See also SEXUAL BIAS.

girl/man Friday See GAL/GUY FRIDAY.

giveaway Informal. 1. Something given without charge: *offered a pocket calendar as a giveaway.* 2. Descriptive of a television game show in which prizes are given. 3. The accidental exposure of information: *The smile was a dead giveaway.*

giveback Informal. A return to the employer of a benefit won by a union in past contracts; a concession ("buyback") demanded by the employer to counter a rise in wages asked by the union: *The negotiations are stalled on the issue of givebacks.*

given name Synonymous with, but less favored than *first name,* which is more generally understood. *Christian name,* another synonym, is seldom used because of its religious connotation.

gizmo Also *gismo* (pronounced giz-mo). Slang. All or part of a mechanical device, the name of which is unknown or forgotten: *What's this gizmo for?*

glamour, glamor Both words are pronounced *glam*-mur. Although the *-or* ending is characteristically American, *glamour,* as an attribute of fashion, continues to be favored.
—glamorous, glamourous, adjectives. The first is preferred.

glitch Computerese for a machine malfunction or program failure; analogous to the bug and gremlin of a less sophisticated age: *A glitch snuffed out the computer tabulations.*

GNP GROSS NATIONAL PRODUCT.

gobbledygook Also spelled *gobbledegook.* A term popularized by Texas Congressman Maury Maverick in his battle against bureaucratic JARGON, and since extended to include jargon of whatever origin. For examples, see OFFICIALESE.

gofer Pronounced *go*-fur. Slang for a person who, in addition to more responsible duties, is asked to "go for" coffee and run similar errands.

go-getter An informal term, now out of date, for an ambitiously active person: *a real go-getter.*

go-go   In the stock market, a term for "fast-moving," "volatile," "speculative"; especially applicable in a rising market: *go-go stocks/a go-go mutual fund/the go-go days of the early 1970s.*

golden handcuffs   Descriptive of a company's offer to give valuable employees money or other benefits several years in the future to ensure their continued service; another name for "the ties that bind." Compare GOLDEN HANDSHAKE.

golden handshake   A financial arrangement designed to cushion the involuntary departure of employees through no fault of their own: *The terms of the golden handshake deals ranged from a few months' pay for relatively new workers to full pension benefits and generous bonus arrangements for those nearing retirement.* Compare GOLDEN HAND-CUFFS and GOLDEN PARACHUTE.

golden parachute   A large cash settlement, part of a special termination agreement sheltering high officers of a company who are forced to leave, usually after a TAKEOVER by another company. Also a GOLDEN HANDSHAKE.

gold mine   A CLICHÉ for any source of big profits: *The store is a gold mine.*

gold plating   The ornamentation or other additions to things that can function without them; a term used especially to describe the defense establishment's outlays for equipment and systems that provide little if any additional effectiveness: *According to its critics, the new X-19 back-up inertial guidance system is just gold plating.*

golf ball   The familiar term for the spherical printing element first used in IBM Selectric typewriters and now adopted, sometimes in modified form, in other, similar machines.
   —**golf-ball,** adjective: *With the Telexmaster connected to your golf-ball typewriter, the telex tape is punched while you wait.*

good   1. In some expressions, an archaic and unnecessary mark of politeness: *We would like to hear from your good bank (from you)/On May 28 we returned to your good selves (returned to you)/They are one of our good clients.* [In other circumstances, would they be "one of our bad clients"?]
   2. *Good* is well used after the so-called "linking" verbs, which include *be, feel, smell, sound,* and *taste: It's good to have you with us/*

I feel very good about the promotion/The proposal sounds good. "Feel well," however, is regularly used in the sense of "not ailing": *He didn't feel well and quit work early.*

3. Except facetiously, the adjective *good* is not used for the adverb *well.* Nonstandard: *You did good* (for *You did well*).

good will Also *goodwill* (one word). The hyphened form *good-will* is now rare. Although no rules require it, *good will* appears to be favored for the noun, and *goodwill* for the adjective: *sought the good will of their neighbors/a goodwill gesture.*

goof Slang. A careless error: *an inexcusable goof.* Also, to make such an error: *We goofed.*
—**goof off.** To waste time: *They discovered that the driver was goofing off.*
—**goof up.** To botch or perform ineptly: *The retoucher goofed up the photo.*

go public 1. To make available for sale to the public the stock of a corporation that was formerly held by a relatively few insiders.
2. To make revelations of internal dissension, dissatisfaction, or wrongdoing; an action taken by a person privy to the information: *To make matters worse, he decided to go public with his charges of management incompetence.*

got, gotten Both words are past participles of *get* (We have *got* [or *gotten*] over our timidity); but only *got* is correct when the meaning of the verb is "have" or "must": *I've got the lease in my pocket/No one has got to contribute.* In the same constructions, *got* can be omitted for a somewhat more formal effect: *I have the lease in my pocket/No one has to contribute.* See also **OBTAIN, GET.**

gouge Pronounced *gowj.* To extort or charge excessively: *gouged by the driver who took us from the airport/guard against gouging.* Compare **GAUGE.**
—**gouger,** noun: *will not deal with gougers.*

graduate One "graduates from" or "is graduated from" a school or college, but the idiom "graduated college" is nonstandard.

graffiti Plural of the Italian *graffito,* "writing on a wall," but commonly used as a singular noun to describe the defacement of public places by crude drawings or inscriptions: *The graffiti were* (or *was*) *removed with caustic chemicals.*

grammatical agreement   For agreement in number, see **SUBJECT AND VERB**; for agreement in case and number, see **PRONOUNS** 2 and 3.

grand   Slang for a thousand dollars; abbreviated G: *will cost a grand.*

grandfather clause   In a statute, a provision exempting existing products or conditions that do not meet the new regulations: *The building* [destroyed by fire] *was protected by a grandfather clause exempting it from the need for sprinklers.*
—**grandfather,** verb: *grandfathered the legislation* (prevented it from applying retroactively).

grapevine   An informal or secret source of information: *The grapevine has it that the treasurer is about to be bounced/Following the company's bad first quarter, Wall Street has now drawn some solace in gleanings from the Polaroid grapevine.*

gratuity   Useful for its **CONNOTATION** when *tip* seems vulgar: *All gratuities are included in the room rate.*

graveyard shift   A night work shift, or the crew on such a shift, running usually from midnight to 8 A.M.: *worked the graveyard shift.*

gray, grey   The first spelling is preferred: *gray hose, a gray suit.*

gray-collar   Descriptive of workers falling between **WHITE-COLLAR** and **BLUE-COLLAR**; for example, supervisors and foremen who do no heavy work themselves, but oversee such work by others.

gray market   A market in which trading, though not illegal, is unethical: *Taking advantage of changes in currency rates, unorthodox distributors of 35mm cameras have created a gray market in which prices to dealers are 10 to 20 percent below those available from the American distributing arms of foreign manufacturers.* Compare **BLACK MARKET**.

grease   Slang, usually with *hand* or *palm*, to bribe: *greased the hand of the inspector.* Also a noun: *shared in the grease.*

greenlining   The socially approved practice of banks investing in housing and other community development needs; a reversal of the heinously regarded **REDLINING**.

gremlin   See **GLITCH**.

grievous   So spelled (not *grievious*) and pronounced *gree*-vus: *a grievous occasion; grievous news* (causing grief or pain).

gripe session   Informal for a meeting at which complaints are aired: *turned the occasion into a gripe session.*

gross national product   Abbreviated GNP. The total market value of all the goods and services produced by a nation's economy during a given year or other specific period.

ground   Usually plural; well used for "basis" when a prepositional phrase follows: *had grounds for apprehension/refused to testify on grounds of self-incrimination.* But (singular): *One ground for complaint was summarily dismissed.* See also BASIS and ON THE GROUND(S) THAT.

ground zero   This is the target of a nuclear bomb and the center of the explosion—literally, "the end." Through a grim disregard of its real meaning, the term is being used as a synonym for "the starting point," "nothing," and "square one": *The poll showed that the candidate had jumped from ground zero* (from nothing) *to within ten points of the incumbent/We're starting the magazine from ground zero* (from the ground up)/*What a mistake! It's now back to ground zero* (back to square one).

guarantee, guaranty   1. The words are interchangeable in the sense of an agreement by which one party assures another of the assumption of a certain responsibility or standard of performance: *The manufacturer's guarantee* (or *guaranty*) *was printed on the package.* As verbs, too, *guarantee* is more common than *guaranty: The contractor guaranteed* (rarely *guarantied*) *his work in writing.*

   2. In finance, *guaranty* (so spelled) is the customary term for the promise made by one person (the *guarantor*) to assume responsibility for another person's debt in case of default.

guess   Standard in the sense of conjecture or estimate: *We can only guess at the results/I wouldn't want to guess what figure they have in mind.* Informal, however, for *think* or *suppose: If they insist on those specifications, I guess we'll have to oblige.*

guesstimate   So spelled (double *s*). Informal blend of *guess* and *estimate: just a guesstimate* (rough approximation). Compare BALL-PARK FIGURE.

guest speaker   A guest speaker is an outsider invited to address an organized group, or a speaker who fills in for or supplements the work of another. Unless there is some significance in the "guest" relationship, however, the word is better omitted: *Our speaker* (rather than *guest speaker*) *is Mr. Parsons.*

guide letter A sample letter from which individual copies—with or without appropriate changes and insertions (as dates and amounts)—can be made as required. Useful in dealing with frequently recurring situations, guide letters can be classified and stored in ordinary files or loose-leaf books, or on magnetic tapes or disks for use with word-processing equipment. Compare FORM LETTER.

guideline A suggested government policy for dealing with wages, prices, or other matters of public concern. Although a guideline is not legislated, sanctions can usually be invoked to obtain compliance. Loosely, a guideline is also any guide to future action: *If refunds are to be made equitably, our salespeople will need some guidelines.*

guide paragraphs Stock paragraphs that can be selected, altered, and combined to create texts for many different needs, as collection notices, answers to inquiries, and forms that must be adapted to different classes of recipients and to situations differing in details. The stored paragraphs are keyed and indexed for easy access by computer or otherwise. Compare GUIDE LETTER.

H

H Also Hc. Handicapped. See EQUAL OPPORTUNITY EMPLOYER.

hackneyed phrases Phrases worn out through use, lacking in interest and force; CLICHÉS. See also STEREOTYPED LETTER PHRASES.

had better Well used in expressions denoting advisability, but the *had* is sometimes omitted in informal usage: *Miles had better accept the offer while he can/You had better* (or *You'd better*) *go.* But (informal): *You better go.*

had ought, hadn't ought Nonstandard: *They hadn't ought (shouldn't) have left without notice.*

had rather, would rather Both phrases express preference, but the first is rarer and more formal than the second. *They would rather* (Formal: *had rather*) *do without than patronize such an unscrupulous seller.* The contracted form is the same for both expressions: *I'd rather, he'd rather, they'd rather,* etc.

half Well used in the expressions "buy *a half* share" and (somewhat less formal) "buy *half a* share"; but there is an excess of words in "buy *a half a* share," "buy *half of a* share," and "buy *a half of a* share." See also "Fractions" at NUMERALS 5.

hallmark A mark or stamp placed on an article to attest to its genuineness or distinctive quality; now also used, not always satisfactorily, as a synonym for any distinguishing characteristic: *One hallmark of (problem associated with?) high technology development is the difficulty of pricing advanced systems.* But, more apt: *His hallmark, simplicity . . . the fashion line that's pared down, beautifully basic.* [Calvin Klein]

hand A participant in any activity; more particularly, one who works at manual labor: *an extra hand/hired five more hands.* Also synonymous with *skill: had a fine hand for portraiture.*
—**by hand.** A notation placed on a letter or envelope that is to be delivered in person by the signer, a messenger, or anyone else.

—come to hand. Business-letter JARGON: *Your letter has come to hand (We have your letter).*

—hand you herewith. Formal but apt in reference to something hand-delivered with the letter in which the phrase appears: *We hand you herewith an authenticated copy of . . .* In other instances, ''We are enclosing'' is more appropriate. See also STEREOTYPED LETTER PHRASES.

handle Used FIGURATIVELY as something to be grasped or seized, as an opportunity, but with some imaginative turns of sense: *Dayton doesn't seem to have a firm handle on* (control of) *the problem/What's the selling handle* (the pitch, sales approach)?/*The track's handle* (the total amount wagered during a given period) *reached an all-time high.* Informal: *Don't fly off the handle* (lose your temper). Slang: *Their rep will call. He sports the handle* (name) *of Dinty.*

handout 1. A NEWS RELEASE, especially one consisting of background information and given to reporters at the event to be publicized. 2. An advertising circular given out by hand. 3. Relevant material distributed to a group gathered for a lecture or other kind of meeting. 4. A PEJORATIVE for a subsidy to business, public assistance to an individual, or any funds sought without thought of repayment: *a government handout/not asking for a handout/a supporter of most business subsidies including the tobacco and nuclear power handouts.*

hands-on 1. Permitting manual use or examination: *a hands-on opportunity to try the new small computers/a hands-on course in auto repair/Just as the general practitioner who made house calls is a dim memory, so is the hands-on corporate leader who rose through the ranks learning every aspect of the business before managing it. [Business Week]*
2. Also, loosely, a fad word for practical, down-to-earth, participatory: *a hands-on meeting/a hands-on training seminar.*

hang, hanged, hung *Hanged* and *hung* are both the past tense and past participial forms of *hang,* but *hanged* is used only in reference to capital punishment: *hanged for his crime.*
In general usage, *hang* and *hung* refer to mere suspension: *The picture was hung from the wall molding.* Informally, however, *hung* is also used for *hanged: He should be hung for such behavior.*

hangar Pronounced like *hanger: The cargo was stored in the Lufthansa hangar* (airport shed).

hanging indention   Also *hanging paragraph*. A style of paragraphing in which the first line is set flush with the left margin and succeeding lines are uniformly indented about five spaces. "Hanging-indented" business letters are set in this manner, but the eccentricity can be distracting. See illustration.

```
            Dear Mr. Quimby:

            Most people do not generally xxxxx xxxx xxxx
                  xxxx xxxxxx xxxx x xxxx xxxxxxx xx xxx
                  x xxxx xxxxxxx xx xxxxxx xx xxx xxxxx xx
                  xxxx xx xxxx.

            Whether you are concerned xxxx xxxxx xx xxxx
                  xx xxxxxxxxxx xx xxxx xxxxxx xxxxxxx xxx
                  xxxxx xx xxxxxxx xxxx xxx xxxxxx.

            If there is a problem xxx xxxxxxx xx xx xxxx
                  xxxxxxxx xxxxx xx xxxxxxxx x xxxx xxx
                  xxxx xxxxxxx xx xx xxxxxx xxxxxxx xxxx
                  xx xxxxx xxx.

                              Sincerely,
```

Hanging indention

happenstance A blend of *happening* and *circumstance*. Informal for a chance occurrence: *I was at the meeting by the oddest happenstance.*

happy An effusive synonym for *pleased* or *glad*, either of which is usually better suited to the expression of positive feelings in corporate writing: *We're happy (glad) to learn that you are interested in a demonstration . . .*

hard copy Written or printed copy that is readable as opposed to, say, a voice recording or computer-encoded data, which must be processed in some way to produce words and numbers.

hard data Information based on FACT and therefore reliable: *Hard data on personnel turnover are difficult to come by, even in the occupations of highest demand.* See also DATA.

hard goods See DURABLE GOODS.

hard landing A recession. Compare SOFT LANDING.

hardly never Nonstandard for *hardly ever: Kirby hardly ever* (not *hardly never) buys from us.*

hard sell Informal for a loud, aggressive, or abrasive effort to persuade or sell; often used to promote highly competitive goods and services: *We expressly avoid the hard sell.* Opposite of SOFT SELL.
  —hard-sell, adjective: *We'll take a hard-sell approach/Their advertising is very hard-sell.*

hardware In electronic data processing, the central processing unit and peripheral equipment, as opposed to the SOFTWARE, or programs necessary for their operation.

harmonization Not to be used for *harmony* or *accord: His mandate was to plan cultural programs abroad and ensure harmonization (accord) with foreign policy objectives and priorities.* See also -IZE, -IZATION.

have a nice day A tiresome CLICHÉ, no doubt soon to be replaced by some other cliché, while the old-fashioned "Good-day" will retain its simple sincerity. See illustration.

have before me Part of a pompous acknowledgment of an incoming letter: *I have before me your letter of August 10 (I have your letter of August 10).* See also STEREOTYPED LETTER PHRASES.

TO OUR GUESTS

Due to the water shortage,
we will serve ice water
only on request.

Have a nice day

THE MANAGEMENT

Have a nice day

hawk To peddle merchandise in the streets, especially by calling out. The term is also used to denote any crude selling effort: *They hawk their wares at street fairs and flea markets.*

headhunter An informal name given to an EXECUTIVE RECRUITER: *The headhunters are already getting résumés from the squeezed out AT&T execs.* See also FLESH PEDDLER.

headings 1. Heads and subheads are especially characteristic of reports, manuals, and other writing intended to explain or instruct. Used with discretion, they help to organize the text and make reference easy. Sometimes they are taken directly from an OUTLINE, from which the numbering scheme may also be carried over.

Heads bearing the same relation to each other are treated typographically the same, as by the position of the heads, the use of spacing, and the style of type: all caps, caps and lower case, italic, boldface, etc.

See also ENUMERATION and TITLES OF WRITTEN MATERIAL.

2. The most common types of heads, in order of descending importance, are the *centered head*, the *sidehead*, the *run-on head*, and the *run-in head*. The terms *first-*, *second-*, *third-*, and *fourth-degree head* are also used to denote the order of subordination.

CENTERED HEAD

A centered head, usually also a main heading, is set squarely between the margins.

Sidehead

A sidehead is set at the left margin as a separate line.

Run-in Head. A run-in head is indented, forming a continuous line with the paragraph to which it belongs. A period is placed between the head and the first word of the following text.

<u>A run-on head</u> consists of a few words forming an integral part of the first sentence of a paragraph and emphasized by underscoring or other means.

MARGINAL HEAD   Another type of head is the marginal head. This is set in the margin, opposite the beginning of the paragraph to which it belongs. It is particularly attractive with single-spaced copy.

There is double spacing between paragraphs and no indention for the first line.

headquarter To establish headquarters or provide headquarters for. Although not universally accepted, the usage is common in business: *The new company will headquarter in Los Angeles/We headquartered Danvers close to the territory he serves.*

headquarters Any center of operations. The noun is found only in the plural, but—depending on the sound and sense—it occasionally takes a singular verb: *Our headquarters are located in Philadelphia.* But: *The company's headquarters is a former private estate.* See also **COLLECTIVE NOUNS.**

head-to-head Up close: *Let's talk head-to-head.* Also used in a competitive sense: *Another writer, who often goes head-to-head with Mr. Barnes in direct-mail testing, charges a fee of $7,500 for a basic mailing package.*

head up Informal for *head* in the sense of either "take a position of leadership" or "put a heading on": *Stipes was asked to head up the committee/You can head up the column, "News from the Grapevine."*

healthy, healthful The words are interchangeable in the sense of conducive to good health: *Phoenix has a healthful* (or *healthy*) *climate*.

Healthy is well used in the sense of having good health or indicating a sound physical and mental condition: *a healthy child/a healthy muscle tone/a healthy respect for authority*.

Healthful is well used to describe something wholesome or health-giving: *healthful exercises/healthful fruit juices*. Even in these senses, however, *healthy* seems to be taking over: *healthy exercises/healthy fruit juices*.

hear Although *hear* is often used in the sense of "learn," *learn* is the more appropriate word when a written source is mentioned: *We are glad to learn* (rather than *hear*) *from your letter that* . . . But: *We have heard some very good news about you* [this even though a written medium may have been the source of the information].

heat up Informal. To accelerate; also, to become worse: *Enthusiasm is heating up/With the money supply rising, the mild inflation is likely to heat up.*

hence Formal for "from now," "therefore," and similar locutions: *The subject will come up for discussion two weeks hence* (Less formal: *in two weeks*)/*It's not only the most powerful computer we ever made, it's also the most reliable. Hence* (Better: *That's why*) *we can back it up with an unprecedented guarantee.*

he or she An awkward expression that can usually be avoided: *If any person desires to protest the granting of this application, he or she has a right to do so if he or she files a written notice of his or her intent with the Regional Director (Persons desiring to protest the granting of this application have the right to do so if they file a written notice of their intent with the Regional Director).* See also SEXUAL BIAS 4.

hereby By this means; by this act, decree, document, etc. Found in official and legal documents, but not suited to general use: *I hereby renounce all title to/By the powers vested in the board, the chairman is hereby authorized* . . . But (overformal) *I hereby make application for the position of* . . .

herein, herewith Stilted expressions, better avoided: *the provisions herein (these provisions)/enclosed herewith (enclosed)/sending you herewith (enclosing).*

hereinafter, hereinbelow JARGON for "after this," "in a later part," "below": *the provisions hereinafter referred to (referred to below).*

hereinbefore JARGON for "before this," "earlier in this message": *the condition hereinbefore stated (the foregoing condition).*

here's Contraction of "here is." Although formal grammar requires "here are" when the noun following (actually, the subject of the verb) is plural, informal usage favors "here's": *Here's four great ways to tour a great country. Britain.* [Pan Am]

hereto Stilted and often superfluous: *Attached hereto (Attached, Here) is our check.* See also THEREAFTER, THEREBY, ETC.

her's No such word; the possessive form of *her* is *hers* (no apostrophe): *Matching monogrammed sweaters, His and Hers* (not *His and Her's*). See APOSTROPHE 5.

hesitate As in "please do not hesitate." In those rare instances when the reader of a letter is judged to be truly shy about responding, as by requesting assistance or registering a complaint, the injunction not to hesitate serves a legitimate purpose. Otherwise, the expression is meaningless and should be omitted: *If we can be of help, please do not hesitate to let us know (please let us know).*

heuristic Pertaining to learning through one's own resources, as experience, investigation, intuition, or trial and error: *took a heuristic approach to problem-solving.* See BUZZ WORDS.

HHS The U.S. Department of Health and Human Services. Principally concerned with health care and Social Security. Formerly, the Department of Health, Education, and Welfare, but education is now separately administered in the Department of Education.

high, highly Although *high* may be used as an adverb, it cannot usually be substituted for *highly: rising high in her profession* (but not *rising highly*). Both *high* and *highly* are used as parts of adjective compounds, but they are seldom interchangeable: *a high-class store, a high-priced product, a high-spirited reunion.* But: *a highly regarded account, a highly motivated employee, a highly visible position.*

highflier A stock that experiences a sharp rise in price, usually with a countervailing decline; also any speculative or improvident venture: *known as an investor who specialized in highfliers.*

high-pressure Characterized by harassment or unnerving force: *high-pressure selling/a high-pressure job.* The converse of *low-pressure: a low-pressure (easygoing, relaxed) approach.*

high profile A state of public conspicuousness, sometimes sought, sometimes not. People in communication and the arts usually thrive on a high profile. A company may develop a high profile by its advertising, publicity, and proclivity for making news. The Mobil Corporation maintains a high profile by its well-advertised positions on public issues, especially those affecting the oil industry.

high-tech Also hi-tech. 1. A shortened form of HIGH TECHNOLOGY: *High-tech industry has long dipped into academe's brain pool for the superstars of science.*
2. For a time, a home furnishings style that adapted industrial and commercial products to domestic uses, as gym lockers in the bedroom, a wire-caged factory lamp over the dining table.

high technology Descriptive of technologically advanced industrial activity in such fields as computers, semiconductors, telecommunications, aerospace, and genetic engineering: *High technology is as much a resource for this country as oil in the ground is for Saudi Arabia.*
—**high-technology,** adjective: *a high-technology company.*

high-wire act A risky venture: *warned that the program was too much of a high-wire act, too much of an all-or-nothing gamble.*

hike In the sense of "increase," acceptable as a verb or a noun: *hiked the price by 20 percent/a hike of 3 cents a quart.*

hire A *hire* is informal for a worker, especially a newly employed one: *We had six hires this month/Dave is one of the new hires.*

hired gun 1. A PEJORATIVE for a newly employed executive whose presence is viewed with apprehension by the veterans: *Mr. Bradshaw's arrival was marked by the replacement of several high-priced people by a new cadre of hired guns.*
2. Someone brought in temporarily from outside the organization to lend his or her special skills to a special objective: *The clear winners in this takeover war so far have not been the main combatants but their hired guns—their investment bankers, law firms, and public relations agencies/For these hired guns* [authors and other creative talent for the motion picture industry] *the center of Los Angeles is Beverly Hills.*

historic, historical Despite the similarity of terms, there is a point of difference. *Historic* is descriptive of something that makes or contributes to history; *historical,* of something concerned with history: *Last year's 20 percent growth rate looks like a peak to some analysts, but is decidedly below its historic rates.* Also: *a historic event, a historic decision.* But: *The unemployment rate is already high by historical standards.* Also: *a historical display, a historical account.*

hitherto Overformal, if not old-fashioned: *an offer we had hitherto (until now) ignored/had hitherto (previously, until then) been employed by Textron.*

hit list 1. A list of choice prospects for a seller's services or wares; a term used especially in credit work: *When the hit list was complete, it was sent to the bank, which then mailed form letters offering its credit card.*

2. A list of persons or things marked for unfavorable action of some sort: *Companies carrying advertising on the offending shows will be put on the hit list, and consumers will be urged to boycott their products/Also on the hit list* [taken off the federal budget] *were government-financed books, pamphlets, and assorted audio and visual materials.*

HMO Health maintenance organization; a medical group providing comprehensive health care services to an individual for a fixed fee.

hold for arrival See ON-ARRIVAL NOTATIONS.

holdup Because of its association with robbery, *holdup* might better be avoided when the sense is "delay": *a holdup (delay) in delivery/ blamed the strike for the holdup (suspension) of production.*

holistic Relating to the whole; a BUZZ WORD that emphasizes the distinction between the study of an entirety and the study of its parts: *holistic medicine* (dealing with the whole person)/*a holistic approach to organizational structure* (a study of the effect of the parts on the whole).

home, house A *home* is any lived-in quarters. What realtors offer is a *house* or *apartment.* If they advertise "Homes for sale," they are only projecting the image of the house to an occupied state. See also CON-NOTATION.

homely Since the word means homelike, domestic, informal, simple, familiar, and—contrarily—crude, ugly, and unprepossessing, *homely* should be used with care. No problem: *homely virtues; a homely mutt.* But, ambiguous: *her homely appearance (ugly? domestic? informal?).*

homogeneous, homogenous These words should not be confused. *Homogeneous* (pronounced ho-mo-*jee*-nee-us or -*jen*-yus) means similar or marked by harmony. *Homogenous* (pronounced ho-*moj*-uh-nus) is a biological term relating to a correspondence between parts or organs as a result of common descent: *a homogeneous* (not *homogenous*) *group of executives.*

homogenized Uniform in composition or structure. *Homogenized milk?* Yes. But also: *Southland's corporate computer has turned the neighborhood grocery into a homogenized marvel. [The Wall Street Journal]*

honorable Abbreviated *Hon.* See FORMS OF ADDRESS 1.

honorarium Plural, *honorariums* or *honoraria.* A voluntary sum paid to a professional person for services not requiring payment; also, when the term *fee* might seem crass, a payment to a professional person of a sum agreed on in advance for some extraordinary service, like making a speech, conducting a seminar, or merely attending a function to which the recipient of the honorarium lends his or her name and prestige.

hope Acceptable phrases are "in hope of," "in the hope of," and "in hopes of," but the first two are preferred. *Hoping* alone, however, often permits a smoother locution: *She stopped at the office in the hope of* (rather than *in hopes of*) *finding that the morning mail had arrived.* (Or: *She stopped at the office hoping to find that . . .*) "In the hope that" and "in hopes that" are also acceptable: *The promotional budget was raised in the hope that more intensive promotion would reinforce brand preference.*
—hoping to hear from you. A stereotyped letter closing, often followed by *I am* or *I remain.* More natural: *Please let me hear from you/May we have your answer soon/I'm looking forward to your reply.* See also PARTICIPIAL CLOSE.

hopefully Fully acceptable in the sense of "with hope" or "in a hopeful manner": *We entered into the agreement hopefully.* Purists object, however, to using the word in the sense of "it is hoped" or "I (we) hope": *Hopefully, the arrangement will turn out well.* Despite the objection, however, the usage is entrenched, no doubt because it serves a need.

horizontal communication   Also *lateral communication*. See at COM-MUNICATION FLOW.

host   1. Informal as a verb: *The city will host the A.M.A. convention/The symposium was hosted by Professor Arthur Sterling of Columbia.*
  2. In some contexts, *host* rather than *hostess* is regularly used as a noun denoting a woman: *The campaign will be inaugurated by a concert at which Ruth Lewis Farkas, former Ambassador to Turkey, will be the host/Miss Francis is co-host of Channel 4's "Prime Time."* But: *She was a most gracious hostess as she greeted her guests/A hostess is stationed at the entrance to the dining area.*

hot line   A best-selling merchandise group: *Home computers are one of the hottest lines in years.* Also *hotline*, a telephone number, usually toll free, for direct communication for emergencies, complaints, and other special purposes. Example (from product wrapper): *Questions about Ivory Soap? Call us toll free: 1-800-543-1745 (Ohio: 1-800-582-0345).*

hotshot   Slang. Flamboyantly skillful or aggressive: *a hotshot salesman.* Also a person fitting that description: *a hotshot from Detroit.*

hot type   See COLD TYPE.

house agency   Also *in-house agency*. An advertising agency owned by a company in some other field for the purpose of producing and placing its own advertising. It receives the customary agency discounts from the media, but it is barred from membership in the American Association of Advertising Agencies.

house brand   See PRIVATE BRAND.

house organ   A periodical published by an organization for its own employees, patrons, shareholders, or the like. Also called *house publication* and, depending on its readership, *employee publication, shareholder publication*, etc.

house-to-house   A term applied to canvassing for orders, votes, opinions, and so forth by personal visits to the home. With a prevailing mix of private homes and apartment dwellings, however, *door-to-door* is the more inclusive term: *a house-to-house (or door-to-door) salesperson.*

however   1. *However* is better avoided when it suggests an obstacle to the fulfillment of a favor or concession already granted: *Thank you for your check. However . . .* (Better: *Thank you for your check. Under the terms of the purchase . . .*)/*You are certainly entitled to the refund. However . . .* (Better: *You are certainly entitled to the refund. You will receive it as soon as . . .*). See also **COURTESY AND TACT**.

2. *But*, used in place of *however*, makes for less formality and smoother reading. Stiff: *We weren't going to put any new money into the plant. With orders coming in so fast, however, we've changed our mind*. Less formal: *We weren't going to put any new money into the plant, but with orders coming in so fast, we've changed our mind*.

3. *However* should be placed where it most clearly emphasizes the contrasted elements.

Our competitors can survive a prolonged dearth of machine orders. We, however, cannot. [Contrast between "Our competitors" and "We."]

Low retail inventories gave us hope of an upsurge in demand. We were not prepared, however, (*or* However, we were not prepared) for the bad weather that continued to hold sales down. [Contrast between "Low retail inventories gave us hope" and "We were not prepared."]

4. Barring the need for alternate punctuation, *however* is set off by commas (see examples in Paragraphs 2 and 3 above). But when *however* begins the second clause of a compound sentence, it is preceded by a semicolon: *We thought the deal was set; however, a new problem has now arisen*. See also **SEMICOLON** 1.

huckster To sell, peddle, or haggle over: *huckstered us into buying a carload*. Also a **PEJORATIVE** for salesperson, advertising copywriter, or promoter of any kind: *the huckster you see in their television commercials*.

—**huckstering,** noun: *Broadcasters scrutinize commercials to see if the huckstering is in good taste*.

human, human being The use of *human* for *human being* is well established despite some preference for the latter in formal usage. On all levels, however, *human* is appropriate when a contrast is desired with nonhuman living things: *For humans, living under water for extended periods presents great technological problems*. But (contrast with an inanimate thing): *You see, a machine can't love making a cigar. But a human being can*. [Primo del Rey]

human capital A **PREPOSSESSIVE** term for public or private funds invested especially in improving health and education. Also, the personal talents and skills that can be used to further economic development (see **HUMAN RESOURCES**).

human resources The sociologist's term for the talents and abilities of people; now adopted by business as an impressive name for *personnel* and the broad range of related administrative activities. The *director of human resources*, for instance, is usually concerned not only with the day-to-day functions of hiring, grading, testing, training, and evaluating, but also with labor negotiations and industrial relations. See also **HUMAN CAPITAL.**

hustle A verb used in many senses and on several levels of dignity. General usage: *He hustles* (hurries) *to work at 6 a.m./The usher hustled* (prodded) *the tardy patrons into the theater.* Informal: *I'm not hustling you* (exerting pressure)/*He hustles ladies' clothing on a Fifth Avenue corner* (sells by high-pressure methods). Slang: *hustles "gold watches" for ten dollars apiece* (sells by questionable or illegal means).
    —**hustler,** noun: *That boy will go far; he's a real hustler* (a fast worker)/*earns a precarious living as a hustler of cheap jewelry* (informal for *aggressive merchandiser*)/*picked up as a hustler* (slang for *swindler* or *streetwalker*).

hype Slang. A noun denoting excesses in methods of promotion: *needs a lot of hype to get attention/angry at the way music is swallowed up in show biz and hype.* Also a verb: *We'll hype the ad budget and cover TV with a barrage of 30-second spots.*
    —**superhype,** noun. **HYPE**, intensified: *engaged in superhype for a film that has nothing going for it.*

hyperbole A nonliteral form of exaggeration, effective if it is apt.

> The administration boldly predicted that our economic ills would soon be cured by the treatment of the long knives.
> One view is that the management is playing a fiscal Russian roulette— a dangerous and disingenuous gamble in which there are no sure winners.
> Such measures can bring only delight to those who wish to eviscerate the program.
> The momentum of short-run economic, financial, and budget forces is creating the conditions for an economic Dunkirk.

See also **METAPHOR.**

hyperbolic deadwood Some modifiers of measures and amounts provide a cheap form of exaggeration, but add nothing to the sense: *The* *warranty is good for 90 days or a* full *4,000 miles.* Also: *save* big *dollars*/large *quarter-acre plots/a* full *quart.* See also **WORDINESS** 2.

hyphen (-)   A punctuation mark linking the parts of certain compound words, including some prefixed words and compound numbers. For the use of the hyphen to divide a word at the end of a line, see **WORD DIVISION**. Also, compare **DASH**.

The trend is to reduce the number of hyphens by writing compound words as solids *(shortcut, paperwork)* or as two words *(real estate, consulting engineer).* Common compounds are listed in the dictionary.

1. COMPOUND WORDS.   2. PREFIXED WORDS.   3. COMPOUND NUMBERS.   4. SUSPENSION HYPHEN.   5. OTHER USES.

For the use of capitals in hyphened words, see **CAPITALS** 12 and 21(b).

1. COMPOUND WORDS.   (a) A compound is usually hyphened when it consists of two or more words modifying a following noun; but the compound is not hyphened when it follows the noun and the words composing it retain their separate force.

a part-time secretary	*but* a secretary working part time
no-par-value stock	*but* a stock with no par value
a large-scale operation	*but* an operation on a large scale
fire-retardant material	*but* a material that is fire retardant
a one-time concession	*but* a concession for one time only
a well-known lawyer	*but* a lawyer well known for

(b) A hyphen is placed between the parts of an improvised compound. Many such compounds contain a preposition.

hand-to-mouth	passenger-miles
right-of-way	land-poor
out-of-doors (*but* outdoors)	go-getter
ready-to-wear	lean-to (a shed)
free-for-all	pay-as-you-go

(c) A compound is not hyphened if it is unlikely to be misread or misunderstood without hyphening.

income tax payment	carbon monoxide poisoning
soft goods outlook	a per diem allowance
high school graduate	a not very eager customer
Latin American countries	a copper mining venture
a bluish green shade	an unusually long season

But: a blue-green shade (*not* a blue green shade)

a no-win situation (*not* a no win situation)

the New York-Washington corridor (*not* the New York Washington corridor)

2. PREFIXED WORDS. A hyphen follows the prefixes *all-, ex-* (meaning *former*), *quasi-,* and *self-.* A hyphen also follows a prefix consisting of a single capital letter and any prefix to a capitalized word. In other instances, a prefix (or suffix) is joined to the root word without using a hyphen except when misreading or difficulty in reading may result.

all-important	T-square
ex-chairman	U-turn
quasi-corporation	un-American
self-employed	Afro-American

Also: co-op (not coop), *but* cooperative

anti-intellectual, *but* antiprogressive

re-cover (cover again), *but* recover (get back)

shell-like (not shelllike), *but* businesslike

But (not hyphened):

antiaircraft	preeminent
biennial	reemploy
intercompany	reenter
intradepartmental	reevaluate
multiaddress	reinvest
overambitious	semiskilled
postdate	ultramodern
prearrange	undermotivated

3. COMPOUND NUMBERS. (a) When written as words, compound numbers under a hundred are hyphened.

twenty-five   sixty-six   forty-two

one hundred and twenty-five

two thousand fifty-three

(b) Numerals compounded with other words to form adjectives are usually hyphened.

a 400-page prospectus, but a prospectus of 400 pages

a 12-point plan   a five-year-old child

But: a 15 percent mortgage, a $10 million enterprise

(c) A spelled-out fraction takes a hyphen, but never more than one.

two-thirds   five-sixths   three-sixteenths
thirty-five hundredths   five and seven-eighths
twenty-three and one-half [Only *one-half* is the fraction.]

The hyphen is often omitted from simple fractions not modifying a following noun.

They were given a one-half share.
But: Their share was one half.

(d) Hyphens are used with dates to show a time span and with compound numbers relating to a decade or similar period.

1985-1990

Jan. 1-June 30

the nineteen-eighties (*also* the nineteen eighties)

(e) When a hyphen is used to show the omission of intermediate figures, at least two digits of a figure containing two digits or more are carried over; however, digits are not omitted from hyphenated telephone numbers.

1985-89 (*not* 1985-9)
pp. 6-9, 22-28, 121-34
Tel.: 555-2623-2624-2625

4. SUSPENSION HYPHEN.   When a series of compound words have a common base, a comma follows each ''suspended'' member of the series.

odd- and even-lot trades
two-, three-, and four-family houses
20-, 25-, and 30-year debentures

5. OTHER USES.   Hyphens are also used:

(a) to divide a serial number

Soc. Sec. No. 085-26-4754

(b) to show syllabication

lin-e-age (ancestry)

(c) in respelling a word letter by letter

Ronzoni is spelled g-o-o-d.

(d) to form a LEADER (as a substitute for dots)

Proceeds from sale - - - - - - - $21,500.

(e) to prevent ambiguity

imported flannel slacks (the flannel slacks are imported)
imported-flannel slacks (only the flannel is imported)

hyphen, hyphening Short variants of *hyphenate* and *hyphenation: hyphened* (or *hyphenated) the word/marred by an excess of hyphening* (or *hyphenation*).

hypothecation The pledging of property to a creditor as security for a loan. Although there is no transfer of title, the creditor can sell the property in case of default. In the purchase of securities on MARGIN, the hypothecation agreement gives the broker the right to use the securities as collateral in borrowing funds.

I, we 1. Ordinarily, *I* represents the individual, and *we* the organization: *I enjoyed meeting you/I will see to it that you receive the proper notification/We do understand your needs/We are sorry about the mixup.*

2. Use of both *I* and *we* in the same message is not necessarily inconsistent: *I* [the individual] *assure you that we* [the organization] *will observe your instructions very carefully.*

3. Use of expressions like "our company" and "Blank & Co." to avoid *I* or *we* makes stilted sentences and puts distance between the writer and reader: *Our company has developed (We have developed)/The Magnus Corporation has received (We have received).* Similar fault is found in the use of *it* and the passive voice to avoid personal reference to the writer: *It is believed (I believe)/Your cooperation is appreciated (We [I] appreciate your cooperation).* See **ACTIVE VOICE, PASSIVE VOICE.**

4. The use of *I* is often governed by the authority of the writer. The higher the position and the better the reputation, the greater the justification and need for the first personal singular pronoun. When the authority is weak, however, there is greater inclination on the writer's part, and greater justification, for resorting to the corporate *we.* For instance, a department junior answering a letter not personally addressed to him might write "We are pleased to learn" or "It is a pleasure to learn" rather than "I am pleased to learn."

5. The *I*—and *we*—can be overdone, of course, with a resulting monotony or impression of conceit. For this reason the writer should be wary of putting an *I* or *we* at the start of several successive sentences or paragraphs and should in other ways mute the references by varying the sentence patterns.

I am, I remain Archaic lead-ins to the **COMPLIMENTARY CLOSE** of a letter, as in "With all good wishes, I am, Very truly yours." Better omitted. See also **PARTICIPIAL CLOSE.**

ICC Interstate Commerce Commission. A federal regulatory agency having jurisdiction over railroads, trucking companies, and other carriers engaged in interstate commerce.

I.D. Identification; an identification card or other document establishing proof of identity: *Please show your I.D. at the gate/A customer who wishes to pay by check must have some I.D.*

idea See at CONCEPT, CONCEPTION, ETC.

identification initials For purposes of record, initials are typewritten on a business letter to identify those who have had a part in its making. The initials are placed at the left margin, two spaces below the signature block. The styles vary.

rd	FPM/RD
fpm:rd	FPM:rd

1. A single initial or unpunctuated set of initials, usually lowercased, identifies the typist.

2. When the letter signature is that of the writer, the writer's initials may be omitted. If included, they precede the typist's initials. If the signer's name is not typewritten below his or her signature, the name may be typed out in full before the typist's initials.

Frank P. Mooney:rd

3. When the letter bears the signature of someone other than the writer, initials representing the signer, the writer or dictator, and the typist are typed in that order. The notation is simplified when a single letter is used for each name.

fpm:ess:rd *or* msd

4. Many executives preferring a "clean" letter appearance specify that initials be placed on carbon copies only. See COPY NOTATION.

identity The essential character by which something is known or recognized: *They haven't taken the time to examine and define their store's identity.* Compare IMAGE.

idle Correctly used in general English as a transitive verb: *The power breakdown idled two thousand workers.* But (more formal): *Two thousand workers were idled by the plant breakdown.*

i.e. 1. Abbreviation of the Latin *id est*, "that is." Occasionally used in technical papers and footnotes, but plain English is otherwise preferred: *The industry claimed that because of "adverse selection"—that is* [rather than *i.e.*], *only the most flood-prone would take out policies—rates would be inordinately high. What were the hired hands to do? If they wanted to hit homers and be memorialized in candy bars* *(that is* [rather than *i.e.*], *keep their jobs), they had to settle for a less-than-competitive wage.* See also **THAT IS**.

2. The abbreviation *i.e.* is often mistakenly used for *e.g.*, "for example". Wrong: *Senate Bill 2292—allows deduction on state income tax for all state-mandated insurance premiums (i.e., auto insurance).* [*e.g.*, not *i.e.*, is called for because auto insurance is given as an example, not as an explanation or elaboration.] See also **E.G.**

if A conditional that, for reasons of tact, is often better avoided: *We are sorry if the delay caused you any inconvenience (We are sorry for the inconvenience).* See **COURTESY AND TACT**.

if, whether 1. *If* is standard in simple conditional statements: *Please let us know if you want us to hold the goods for you/We'll see if any call from Miss Dunn was received.*

2. *Whether* is generally preferred when it is followed by an expression with *or*, an expression of doubt, or an **INDIRECT QUESTION**: *I do not care whether they place an order or not/We doubt whether he will attend/Holmes wanted to know whether the invoice had been paid.* See also **WHETHER OR NOT**.

3. In informal usage, *if* is far more common than *whether*, regardless of the type of sentence: *I don't care if they come or not/We doubt if he knows the cost/Ask her if she'll be there.*

if and when This and similar phrases *(when and if; if, as, and when)* serve a legitimate purpose in fixing particular conditions, as for the delivery of goods or securities, but they are not to be used thoughtlessly when *if* or *when* alone will do: *If* (not *If and when) the tax bill is signed, we will surely see a drop in sales/Kramer said he'd worry about the consequences when* (not *when and if) they came.*

iffy Informal. Conjectural; marked by doubt or uncertainty: *an iffy question/see the trend in steel production as still very iffy.*

ill See **SICK, ILL**.

illusive Also *illusory* (pronounced il-*loos*-uh-ree or il-*loo*-zhuh-ree). Deceptive, unreal: *Earnings are illusive* (or *illusory) because inventory profits are overstated.* Not to be confused with *elusive,* "evasive," "hard to define or realize": *an elusive answer/an elusive idea/in search of elusive profits.*

image The perceived character of an individual, organization, culture, or the like; a determinant of attitude and action. Although advertising and public relations may seek to develop a uniform image of a company, the image remains subjective, varying with the experiences of the person making the judgment. Literally, therefore, it is people who have an image of, say, General Electric; but in common usage, it is likely that one will speak of General Electric's image, as if the image belonged to the company.

IMF See **INTERNATIONAL MONETARY FUND.**

imitation See at **FAKE.**

immigrate See **EMIGRATE, IMMIGRATE.**

imminent, impending The words are interchangeable in the sense of about to occur or likely to occur, both suggesting an event hanging menacingly: *A lawsuit is imminent* (or *impending*). Compare **PENDING.**

impact As a verb, **JARGON** in the sense of "to affect," "to have an effect on": *The accident impacted traffic across the bridge/Expenditures for research will impact on* (affect) *future earnings.* As a noun, *impact* is acceptable without qualification: *The decision to close the plant will have a serious impact* (effect) *on employment in the town.* See also **AFFECT, EFFECT.**

impact mitigation The effort made by some large companies in small towns to cushion the effect of their presence on the economy of the area. Forms of aid to the localities include direct grants, prepayment of local taxes, and planning services offered for the benefit of all citizens, not just their workers.

impact statement A statement detailing the environmental, economic, or other effects of a proposed undertaking. In many instances such a statement is required by law before any necessary permits can be issued.

implement 1. To provide the means to ensure a given result; to carry out: *The president proceeded immediately to implement the board's action/It is a good idea, but how can it be implemented?*

2. Loosely used in the sense of taking some simple action better described in more specific terms: *I will implement your request for a new desk (I will order you a new desk).*

—**implementation,** noun: *The implementation of the board's action will not be easy.* But (pretentious): *The implementation of your order for a* *new desk will take a few days (Getting you a new desk will take a few days).*

imply, infer 1. Although *infer* is often used for *imply*, the distinction in meaning is observed by careful writers and speakers. To *imply* is to suggest, intimate, or state indirectly; to *infer* is to deduce, to conclude from the evidence: *Barry implied* (suggested) *that the offer might be withdrawn/This report implies* (states indirectly) *that moving the plant would be uneconomic.* But: *We infer* (deduce) *from Barry's remarks that the offer might be withdrawn/From a reading of the report, one infers* (concludes) *that moving the plant would be uneconomic.*

2. *Imply* used for *infer* is nonstandard: *I don't care what he implied from my remarks* (Use *infer*).

importantly See MORE (MOST) IMPORTANTLY.

impossible Not logically subject to comparison. See ABSOLUTE ADJECTIVES.

impromptu, extemporaneous An *impromptu* speech is one given without preparation. An *extemporaneous* speech is allowably synonymous, but it is used more often in the sense of "without overt preparation," that is, prepared in advance, but delivered without notes.

in, within See WITHIN.

in accordance with Simpler connectives are usually available: *in accordance with your instructions (as you instructed)/in accordance with your request (at your request)/in accordance with the law (under the law)/in accordance with trade custom (following trade custom).* See also WORDINESS 4.

in addition See ADDITIONALLY, IN ADDITION.

in addition to A singular subject followed by a phrase beginning *in addition to* normally takes a singular verb: *Some new merchandise, in addition to the leftovers of the season before, was included in the sale.* But see also SUBJECT AND VERB 2c.

in advance of *Before* is simpler, but it does not always have the same force: *It's hard to tell how the public will respond to a new stock issue in advance of* (rather than *before*) *any announcement.* But: *Word of the new stock issue was out before* (rather than *in advance of*) *the official announcement.*

inadvertence   Pronounced in-ad-*vur*-tence. Also *inadvertency* (-en-see). A useful EUPHEMISM for words like *carelessness, oversight, error,* and *mistake: We regret our inadvertence/Please excuse the inadvertency.*

inappropriate   A CLICHÉ when used to turn aside questions to which the unvarnished answer would be indiscreet, embarrassing, or incriminating: *It would be inappropriate to comment at this time.*

inasmuch as   Two words, as shown; but *since, as,* or *because* is simpler: *Inasmuch as (Since) I wasn't going anyway, I returned the tickets to the treasurer.*

inaugurate   To begin in a formal way: *Ceremonies marking the company's fiftieth anniversary will be inaugurated with a gala dinner at the Century Plaza.* Compare INITIATE.

in back of   See BACK OF, IN BACK OF.

in basket   The desk receptacle for incoming mail. Also *in-basket,* descriptive of a new situation not yet taken care of: *an in-basket problem.*

in-basket technique   Describing a method of management training and testing. The trainees are given a sheaf of letters and memorandums encompassing a variety of administrative problems and are asked to reply to them in writing within a specified time.

in behalf of, on behalf of   There is a distinction. To speak *in behalf of* is to speak for, as an advocate; to speak *on behalf of* is to speak as the agent for. Similar distinctions are found in the statements, "The party was held *in behalf of* the Children's Shelter" and "Simms agreed to approach the IRS *on behalf of* his client."

Inc.   Abbreviation of INCLOSURE and INCORPORATED.

incentive marketing   A strategy designed to increase sales by the offer of premiums and prizes to dealers, salespersons, or consumers.

incidentally   So spelled *(-ally),* but the next to the last syllable *(-al-)* is barely voiced *(-dent'*lee).

inclose   See ENCLOSE, INCLOSE.

inclosure   Abbreviated *inc.* or *incl.* A variant of the more common ENCLOSURE.

incomes policy   A course of action by which the government would control prices by making increases in income from wages and other sources contingent on increases in **PRODUCTIVITY**: *With the return of economic health and high employment, an incomes policy will be needed to preserve a noninflationary trend.*

incomplete comparison   See COMPARISONS 1.

incorporated   With its abbreviation *(Inc.)*, always capitalized following a proper name. The comma, formerly standard in separating *Incorporated* or *Inc.* from the name preceding it, is now often omitted: *The Signal Companies, Inc.* But: *Wheelabrator-Frye Inc./Magic Chef Incorporated/Lane Wood Incorporated.*

incredible, incredulous   *Incredible* is unbelievable; *incredulous* is disbelieving, skeptical: *an incredible story.* But: *an incredulous audience.*

incumbent   Stilted as an adjective: *It is incumbent upon them to resist the offer.* Better: *They have an obligation to resist the offer.*

indent   As a noun, a shortened form of **INDENTION**; pronounced *in*-dent: *an indent of five spaces.*

indention   An alternate form of *indentation*, the spacing between the margin and the start of a written or printed line: *specified an indention (or indentation) of five spaces.* See also **LONG VARIANTS**.

index   Plural *indexes* (preferred) or *indices* (pronounced *in*-duh-seez).
   1. An alphabetical list of items, with page references, placed at the end of a volume in which the items are treated; also, any file or systematic reference.
   2. A measure or indicator of some phenomenon, as in economics: *the cost of living index/an index of industrial activity/the composite stock-market index.* Also a verb: *Under the old contract, wages were indexed to the cost of living* (were adjusted to meet changes in the cost of living index).
   3. In printing, a symbol (☞) pointing to a paragraph or section. Also named a "fist" or "hand."

indexing   Also, less commonly, *indexation.* In economics, the practice of adjusting such factors as Social Security entitlements, wages, and interest to changes in price indexes (see **INDEX** 2): *There is no guarantee, of course, that even indexing would stiffen the government's spine against inflation.*
   —tax indexing. A reform measure that would ensure that taxpayers

whose incomes go up with inflation are not automatically thrown into a higher tax bracket: *As a simple matter of equity, it would seem that tax indexing to eliminate this unlegislated bracket creep ought to have universal support* [Senator Robert Dole]. See also **BRACKET CREEP**.

indirectness   See **WORDINESS** 7.

indirect question   A question restated to form part of a declarative statement. It is not enclosed in quotation marks and is followed by a period, not a **QUESTION MARK**: *They asked where she had previously been employed* (The direct question was something like *"Where were you previously employed?"*).

indirect quotation   Words not directly quoted are not enclosed in quotation marks. See **QUOTATION MARKS** 1(c).

indicia   A Latin plural, pronounced in-*dish*-ee-uh (singular, *indicium*). Identifying marks; in postal use, a form printed on bulk mail as a substitute for stamps. In the latter sense, *indicia* is regularly treated as singular, and *indicias* as plural: *The indicia has been approved for presorted first-class mail/We have several indicias for our different classes of mail.* See illustration.

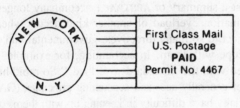

First Class Mail
U.S. Postage
PAID
Permit No. 4467

Indicia

indorse, indorsement   Variants of *endorse* and *endorsement;* uncommon, but acceptable.

in due course   See **DUE COURSE**.

industrial union   A labor union whose membership consists of workers in a particular industry, whatever their trade or craft; for instance, the United Auto Workers and the Amalgamated Clothing Workers. Compare **CRAFT UNION**.

infer   See **IMPLY, INFER**.

inferior figure   A character set slightly below the type line, as in $C_2H_{30}O_5$ (hydrocortisone). Compare **SUPERIOR FIGURE**.

in excess of Overelaborate for "more than" or "over": *They expected to invest in excess of (more than) $25 million in the structure/Checks in excess of (over) $100 must be approved by the assistant manager.*

inflammable Easily set on fire. See FLAMMABLE.

influence Pronounced with the stress on the first syllable: *promised to use his influence* (noun)/*cannot influence the result* (verb).

info CLIPPED FORM of information; no period following: *Our info was wrong.*

informal English See USAGES 2.

information overload 1. An excess of messages demanding attention, with resulting confusion and loss of efficiency. The condition occurs when people in an organization operate under the belief that "letting everybody know" is a management ideal. The condition is made worse when executives permit themselves to be overwhelmed by the clutter. Some, in self-defense, have an assistant, or "gatekeeper," limit the number and kinds of messages coming to their desks. They may also decree, like Winston Churchill, that messages be confined to one page or that a summary or ABSTRACT accompany longer ones.

2. Information overload of another kind occurs when an organization is subject to so many directives, governmental and otherwise, that it cannot cope with them. In accounting, for example, the profession is concerned with the "standards overload." So rapid has been the acceleration of generally accepted accounting principles (GAAP) that small firms especially have difficulty in keeping up with them, observing them, or even finding them relevant to their operations. [Source: Vincent C. Ross Institute of Accounting Research, New York University]

infrastructure The underpinning of a society: its basic facilities (as transportation, communication networks, public utilities), as well as the education, skills, health, and technical sophistication of its people: *Such large-scale industrial development requires an elaborate infrastructure/In rural areas we do not have an intellectual infrastructure from which we can instantly summon a manager, top engineer, lawyer . . .* [E. F. Schumbacher]
See also BUZZ WORD.

-ing A noun suffix denoting acquisition of the qualities of the noun to which it is added. Current specimens include AGENTING, *brokering, lawyering, newslettering, parenting.*

in hopes that   See HOPE.

in-house   Originating within an organization or confined to it: *an in-house publication* (a HOUSE ORGAN)/*an in-house economic adviser* (not an independent consultant)/*an in-house computer operation.*

in-house agency   See HOUSE AGENCY.

initial   As an adjective, *first* is simpler and more forceful: *In taking office, his initial (first) task was to reduce the company's debt.* See LONG WORDS AND SHORT. For the verb, there is no adequate synonym: *was asked to initial the memo.*

initials   See NAMES 1 and IDENTIFICATION INITIALS.

initiate   Correctly used in the sense of taking an innovative first step, but a simple synonym is usually preferable: *will initiate (start) production on the new line of trucks next August/initiated (began) the Key Lecture Series in 1973.* Compare with COMMENCE and INAUGURATE.

in length, in number, in size   Such expressions are often redundant: *The frontage on Pine Street is 120 feet in length* (omit *in length*)/*Those who attended were few in number (Few attended)/The package was not as large in size as I thought* (omit *in size*). See also WORDINESS 3.

in lieu of   The *lieu* is pronounced *loo*. Stilted for "instead of"; often misused for "in view of": *Many customers take the cash bonus in lieu of (instead of) merchandise.* Misused: *In lieu of (In view of, Because of) their intransigence, they stand to lose the order.*

innovate   Acceptably used in the sense of starting something new: *innovated the use of museum-quality art in office decor/talked about the inability of some companies to grow and innovate.*
   —innovative, adjective: *a talent for starting innovative magazines* [magazines unlike those already on the market].

innovation   An innovation is something new; to speak of a "new innovation" is redundant: *Trip Talk is the exciting new travel innovation that lets you be easily and instantly understood anywhere in the world* (omit *new*). See also WORDINESS 3.

in number   See IN LENGTH, IN SIZE, IN NUMBER.

input   A name for anything put into a system to achieve a result, *input* may legitimately include work, power, or data: *The help you get from the computer can be no better than the input.* Often, however, *input* is simply **JARGON**, taking the place of a more traditional but also more exact term: *Your inputs (ideas) will be welcome/We should get some input (suggestions) from Henry/If the input (the planning? the participation?) is good, the return on the investment should prove favorable.*

—inputted. Verb, past tense; well used in a technical sense: *The trouble is that they inputted* (put into the system) *a lot of faulty data/Once inputted to a magnetic medium, the words can be printed by electronically actuated inkjet printers at the rate of 100 characters a second.*

in re See **RE, IN RE**.

in receipt of See **RECEIPT**.

in reference to See **REFERENCE**.

in regard to See **REGARDING, AS REGARDS, ETC.**

in reply to See **REPLY**.

in respect to, with respect to 1. *With respect to* is preferred when the sense is "concerning" or "regarding." The reason is that *in respect to* may be taken to mean "in deference to": *With respect to (Concerning) the proposed delivery date, we have serious reservations.* But (ambiguous): *They were obviously not going to do anything in respect to our urgent plea for delivery.* (Substitute *with respect to* or, better, *about* for *in respect to.*)

2. As the examples show, both *in respect to* and *with respect to* are apt to be unnecessarily pretentious: *your letter with respect to (about) our recent order.*

in-service courses Classroom instruction given to workers to improve their present skills or teach them new skills. See also **TRAINEE**.

inside address That part of a letter, usually placed above the salutation, giving the addressee's name and full mailing address. See also **ADDRESSES**.

1. A letter addressed to an organization consists of the organization's name, the department name or room number, if applicable, and the mailing address. The state name can be spelled out, conventionally abbreviated, or abbreviated in the official two-letter post-office style (compare with **ENVELOPE ADDRESS**).

Superior Steel Corporation
Engineering Department
1500 Penn Square
Pittsburgh, PA 19102

2. When a letter is addressed to an individual, the name is preceded by a courtesy title (*Mr., Miss, Mrs.*, etc.) and followed by the business title or department and the business affiliation and address. The business title and department are often omitted, especially when they would make the address longer than four or five lines. If the title is used, it may be placed on the same line as the individual's name only if it does not awkwardly protrude.

Mr. James E. Wright, Treasurer
Superior Steel Corporation
1500 Penn Square
Pittsburgh, PA 19102

Ms. Ellen C. Brody
Personnel Department
Spartan Chemicals, Inc.
300 Elmora Avenue
Elizabeth, NJ 07202

See also **LETTER FORM** 3–5 and **FORMS OF ADDRESS.**

inside of The *of* is usually superfluous: *We asked Williams to look inside* (rather than *inside of*) *the casing. Inside of* is better used in expressions of time: *should finish the job inside of an hour.* Preceded by *the, inside of* is standard: *We examined the inside of* [that is, the inner surface of] *the casing/The inside of the building* [as opposed to the outside] *is not yet completed.* See also **OF** 1.

insider An officer, director, or principal stockholder of a large corporation, usually one coming under the jurisdiction of the SEC; also any person with access to confidential information: *It is suspected that accelerated trading in the stock was triggered by insiders.*

insightful JARGON, better avoided: *insightful conclusions (revealing)/an insightful analysis (penetrating)/an insightful executive (discerning).*

insignia Pronounced in-*sig*-nee-uh. A badge or emblem signifying membership, rank, authority, etc. *Insignia* is the plural of *insigne* (pronounced in-*sig*-nee), but it passes for the singular as well: *The official insignia* (or *insigne*) *has not yet been designed.* The plural form *insignias* is also acceptable: *The insignia* (or *insignias*) *for the guards' uniforms are to be delivered on Thursday.*

in size See **IN LENGTH, IN NUMBER, IN SIZE.**

insofar as So spelled (two words). *To the extent that* is not shorter, but it is somewhat plainer: *We expect to fill their requirements insofar as (to the extent that) our facilities permit.*

in spite of the fact that   A less cumbersome expression is preferred: *Anderson was willing to go in spite of the fact that the mission was probably futile (despite the probable futility of the mission)/In spite of the fact that (Although) it was not the lowest bid, it was readily accepted.* See also WORDINESS 4.

instant   Abbreviated *inst.* Archaic. Of the present month: *Your letter of the 10th instant (Your letter of the 10th,* or *Your letter of* [say] *July 10).* Analogous expressions, also archaic, are ULTIMO and PROXIMO.

institute   Overformal for *originate, establish,* or *begin: instituted (began) an inquiry into* (Also: *inquired into*)/*instituted (established) a procedure for.* Compare INITIATE.

institutional advertising   Broad-gauge advertising promoting a company's philosophy, policies, aims, etc. The purpose is to advance the reputation and objectives of the organization rather than to engage in any direct selling effort.

inter-, intra-   Easily confounded, *inter-* is a prefix meaning "between" and *intra-,* "within": *an interoffice memorandum* (a memorandum for transmission between offices). But: *intracompany affairs* (matters concerning the company alone, not other companies or the public)/ *Intercompany trade* (not *intracompany trade) is growing very rapidly. For example, General Motors is working with Isuzu and Suzuki and is planning to import its low-end models from Japan.*

interactive   Descriptive of a computer system by which a user at an input-output terminal is able to enter data and receive a direct response. The term is similarly applicable to the telephone, VIDEOTEX, and cable television connections that permit viewers spontaneously to participate in opinion polls or order goods shown on the screen.

interest   See DIVIDEND, INTEREST.

interface   To juxtapose complementary entities to achieve a desired result: *The LEO III interfaces with Pitney Bowes postal meters.* Used at first as a reference to the function of computer adjuncts, *interface* is now popular JARGON in describing people working together: *We need representatives who can interface confidently with business executives/The candidate will report directly to an executive vice president* *and interface with senior management in the company's investor relations activities.*

Also a noun: *The interface between the social worker and the client has been weakened by an intolerable government bureaucracy.*

in terms of Words like *for*, *of*, and *by* help make neater sentences: *The advertising is useful in terms of (in) building goodwill/When we think in terms of (of) the cost, the project is one big sinkhole/Only a modest expenditure in terms of (for) research is required/They are way out of line with the industry in terms of (in) their salaries and promotion policies.* Sometimes a sentence must be recast: *In terms of managing the economy, the control of consumer credit is not where the problem is. (The problem in managing the economy is not in the control of consumer credit.)* See also WORDINESS 4.

international company A company doing business in more than one country. For a finer distinction, see MULTINATIONAL COMPANY.

International Monetary Fund Abbreviated IMF. A Washington-based organization providing credits as needed to any of its member countries (146 in 1982) having trouble paying their foreign debts. The fund operates like a bank and makes decisions on loans only after negotiations on changes in economic policy that must be followed by a nation requesting funds.

interoffice letter See MEMORANDUMS.

interpersonal Between persons: *interpersonal behavior/interpersonal communication*. The word is often superfluous: *Degan's interpersonal feuding with his subordinates is criticized* (strike out *interpersonal*)/*Since I had that long talk with Macready, our relations* (not *interpersonal relations*) *have improved markedly.* But (necessary to meaning): *They were asked to find a candidate with stronger interpersonal skills* (skills in dealing with individuals).

interpretative A LONG VARIANT of *interpretive: prepared a series of interpretive* (rather than *interpretative*) *graphs.*

intestate See TESTATE, INTESTATE.

in the amount of Ordinarily, a simple *for* or *of* makes a good substitute: *a charge in the amount of (of) $50/a check in the amount of (for) $27/posted profits in the amount of (of) $10.4 million for the quarter.* However, the long phrase is preferred for its formality, especially in banking practice, when large sums are involved: *loans in the amounts of $2 million and $3.6 million.*

in the area of   See AREA.

in the course of   During. *In the course of (During) our search, we consulted records going back ten years/The error was discovered in the course of (during) a routine examination.* See also WORDINESS 4.

in the event that   See EVENT.

in the field of   See FIELD.

in the line of   See LINE.

in the nature of   See NATURE.

in the process of   Wordy or superfluous: *We are now in the process of collecting data (We are now collecting data)/In the process of investigating (While investigating) the complaint, we came across . . .* See WORDINESS 4.

in the way of   Usually superfluous: *No one sees much in the way of improvement ahead (No one sees much improvement ahead).*

in this matter, in this regard   Stilted and often superfluous, especially at the end of a sentence when the reference is self-evident: *As soon as we have more information, we'll write you again in this regard* (omit *in this regard*)/*Thank you for your cooperation in this matter* (omit *in this matter*). See also WORDINESS 2.

into   Vogue word for "taken up" or "engaged in," as a hobby, specialty, or product line: *Now she's into pottery/It's a big company; they're into telecommunications, paper manufacturing, and office furniture.*

in toto   Latin for "entirely" or "as a whole." Better avoided: *The terms required that we take the factory output in toto (that we take the entire factory output).*

intrapreneur   An ENTREPRENEUR working within an established organization: *But major corporations are also . . . discovering that some of their best people want to operate within the company as "intrapreneurs." This provides an environment that nourishes new ideas and lets people develop successful new businesses under a protective corporate tent.* [John Naisbitt]

inversion, in sentences   See SENTENCES 3.

investor relations   A newer, more impressive name for stockholder or shareholder relations; a change prompted by the growing influence of large institutional investors—banks, insurance companies, mutual funds, etc.—representing the financial interests of large numbers of people.

in view of the fact that   Since; because: *In view of the fact that (Since) we have already placed the order* . . . See WORDINESS 4.

invite   The noun, meaning an invitation of sorts, is slang: *Six ad agencies get invite from Schlitz* (newspaper headline referring to Schlitz's invitation to the agencies to bid for its advertising account)/*No invite— no contribution.*

IOU   For "I owe you," an informal acknowledgment of a debt, usually on a slip bearing the amount and a signature or initials. Also any promise to pay: *accepted my IOU.*

I remain   See I AM, I REMAIN.

irrefutable   Pronounced ir-*ref*-yuh-tuh-b'l or ir-rih-*fyoo*-tuh-b'l. Incontrovertible: *irrefutable evidence.*

irregardless   DOUBLE NEGATIVE. An unacceptable corruption of *regardless: irregardless of (regardless of, no matter) what you say.*

irrelevant   So spelled, and pronounced ir-*rel*-; not *irrevelant.*

irreparable   The stress is on the second syllable (ir-*rep*-). Not capable of being repaired: *irreparable damage.*

irrevocable   The stress is on the second syllable (ir-*rev*-). Not retractable: *an irrevocable decision.*

IRS   Internal Revenue Service (U.S. Department of the Treasury).

issue-oriented advertising   A form of INSTITUTIONAL ADVERTISING concerned with some public issue in which the advertiser usually has a partisan interest. Also called *public-issue advertising.*

is when, is where   Phrases better avoided in definitions, where they create awkwardness: *A consumer cooperative is when a retail business is owned and operated by some or all of its customers (A consumer cooperative is a retail business owned and operated* . . .)/*Amortization is where a debt is gradually retired (is the gradual retirement of a debt) by regular payments of both principal and interest.*

An exception is made for *is when* in a statement relating to time, and for *is where* in a statement relating to place: *Noon is when the merchants shutter their shops and take their siesta/California is where most American wines are produced.*

it The so-called "preparatory" *it* (*it is, it was,* etc.) often creates a weak and unnecessarily impersonal statement: *It was suggested (They suggested)/It has been found (We have found)/It is noted (I note)*/But (well used): *It was a nice day/It was good to see you/It's easy to be complacent/It is they who are at fault* (Compare, for emphasis, with: *They are at fault.*) See also **THERE IS, THERE ARE.**

For the avoidance of ambiguity when *it* is used as a simple pronoun, see **PRONOUNS** 1.

italics Abbreviated *ital.* Italic is a slanted typeface differentiated from the customary vertical type called "roman" (abbreviated *rom.*).

> *This is italic.*
> This is roman.

In manuscript and typewritten work, italics are indicated by underlining.

Special conventions govern the use of italics in professional and scholarly papers. Business is less insistent on observing the formalities. Thus a rule prescribing italics may be ignored, or **QUOTATION MARKS** may be used instead; but usage should never be so relaxed that it poses a threat to the sense.

> *Ike* will be the feature attraction of Thursday night's ABC lineup. [Italics differentiate the TV movie from the person.]

1. TITLES.   2. WORDS, LETTERS, ETC.   3. FOREIGN WORDS AND PHRASES.   4. LEGAL CASES.   5. FOR EMPHASIS.

1. TITLES.   (a) In running texts and **REFERENCE NOTES**, italics are used for the titles of books, plays, motion pictures, television shows, periodicals, newspapers, long poems, musical compositions, and works of art; and for the distinctive names of ships, trains, planes, and spacecraft. An initial article *(a, an, the)* is not italicized unless it is accepted as an integral part of the title.

> Leavitt's *Managerial Psychology*
> a revival of *My Fair Lady*
> the success of *Star Wars*
> starred in *Saturday Night Live*
> advertised in *Cosmopolitan*

the Sunday *Times*
quoted from Dante's *Inferno*
singing *Row, Row, Row Your Boat*
choreographed *Ondine*
de Kooning's 1949 canvas *Attic*
the tanker *Shin Aitaku Maru*
took the *Palatino* overnight to Florence
in a Boeing 727 called *Leadership 80*
the spectacular *Viking* landings on Mars

(b) Practice varies in italicizing the city appellation in a news-paper name even if it is part of the masthead. Words like *maga-zine, weekly*, and *monthly* are not capitalized if they are not part of the publication name. The article *the* may be capitalized and italicized if it appears in the name on the masthead or cover.

the *Daily News*
The Wall Street Journal or the *Wall Street Journal*
The New York Times or the New York *Times*
The Times of London
Time magazine
the *Atlantic* monthly
the *Harvard Business Review*

(c) The name of a short work, like a poem, a chapter in a book, or an article in an encyclopedia or magazine, is not italicized, but enclosed in **QUOTATION MARKS**.

2. WORDS, LETTERS, ETC. Words, letters of the alphabet, and— less frequently—figures are italicized when used for reference, not for their intrinsic meaning.

The word *hangar* was misspelled. [*But:* The plane was still in the hangar.]
The *s* is not correctly aligned.
The *7* and *2* were transposed.

3. FOREIGN WORDS AND PHRASES. Only words and phrases not assimilated into English are italicized. The dictionary is not always helpful in identifying such terms, but it may be assumed that a common foreign term need not be italicized.

a chic costume
a forte rendering of the national anthem
an ex officio member of the committee
the chargé d'affaires
laissez-faire policies

But: Lancôme's *certificat spécial,* valued at $10
not considered *de rigueur*
filled with *Weltschmerz*
and make it *mucho pronto*
a long parody of *le roi s'amuse*

4. LEGAL CASES. In a running text, the names of legal cases are italicized: ". . . cited *Benedict v. Ratner* in the brief." However, footnote references to the same cases are not italicized.

Benedict v. Ratner

Jaspan v. Philadelphia Electric Co.

See also REFERENCE NOTES 3.

5. FOR EMPHASIS. In most copy, italics for emphasis are used very sparingly. A notable exception occurs in advertising, where italics vie for attention with solid caps, boldface, and other typographical treatments.

its, it's *Its* is the possessive form of *it; it's* is the contraction of *it is* or *it has: The company will celebrate its tenth anniversary.* But: *If it's* [it is] *priced right, buy it/It's been* [It has been] *a good year.*

it's me Although formal grammar prescribes a nominative case pronoun after the verb *be* (*it's I, it is I*) the objective case *me* is regularly so used in both speech and writing. Differences of opinion are more pronounced on the similar use of *her, him, us,* and *them* after *be,* but the "correct" forms—shown in parentheses in the examples below—do not necessarily represent an improvement: *When we want advice, it's him (he) that we go to/It was them (they) all along/The next victims will be us (we).* But (an uncontroversial alternative): *We will be the next victims.* See also PRONOUNS 2.

-ize, -ization Verb and noun suffixes respectively.

1. Adding *-ize* to an established word, or part of one, is common: *legalize, modernize, subsidize, containerize, sanitize.* The trend extends to trade terms and slogans: *Texize, Sanforize, Simonize/It pays to Midasize.* However, a newly coined word ending in *-ize* may be merely a poor substitute for a perfectly satisfactory word in the standard vocabulary: *the need to quantitize (quantify)/scheduled to concertize (play, sing) at Carnegie Hall/will prioritize (give priority to) your order.*

2. The noun suffix *-ization* may add nothing to the sense of the original word: *an analyzation (analysis) of the proposal/a summarization (summary) shows/seeking harmonization (harmony) with/full utilization*

(use) of our resources/will bear scrutinization (scrutiny). See also **LONG VARIANTS**.

3. New coinages with the *-ize* or *-ization* ending are usually classified as **JARGON**: *conglomeratize, strategize/boutiquization, sanitization*.

J

jargon Jargon is, in a sense, shoptalk; but it is also shoptalk turned into gibberish. The need for specialized vocabularies in business and the professions is undeniable. When *input,* for instance, is used to describe the data entered into a computer, the term aptly fills a need that would otherwise be unmet. When, however, a teacher tells about seeking "inputs" from students, the term is deflected from its original meaning and becomes a poor substitute for words like *answers, advice, suggestions,* and *information*—all more familiar and more precise. In other instances, jargon is the expression of muddled thinking, in prose that is inflated, pompous, and abstract.

> EXAMPLE: The delegation to purchasing personnel of the responsibility of validating vendors' payments does not provide the necessary control, i.e., that division of duties such that the work of one employee can validate the work of another, and also will provide a signal to supervision when an error, either by accident or design, is introduced into the operating process.

> TRANSLATION: Vendors' invoices should not be approved by the same people who made out the purchase orders, because this permits more errors to slip through and increases the chance of falsification.

> EXAMPLE: The networking software package operates independently of microcomputer hardware, net and operating system, providing true file server capability for multi-user network environments.

> TRANSLATION: The networking software package makes it possible for small computers to communicate with each other.

> ANOTHER EXAMPLE, FROM A WORLD BANK MANUAL: Change in the ecology of an area induced by a new development project may have a profound, if indirect, impact upon human health as a result of effects upon biologic vectors, or the spread of intensified breeding of certain insects and aquatic species that provide a vehicle for the completion of the life-cycle of some important parasites and viruses that afflict man.

> TRANSLATION: A development project may change a local environment and unexpectedly cause more people to become sick.

Granted that the last "translation" is oversimplified, the fault appears to be more the original author's than the translator's. See also **PLAIN ENGLISH** 1 and **READABILITY**.

jawbone To attempt to persuade by talk or pressure, a device sometimes used by a President to thwart price increases thought to be detrimental to the economy.
—**jawboning,** noun: *When jawboning fails, legislation will force the issue.*

jibe, gibe To *jibe* is to agree or be in harmony with; to *gibe* is to jeer or taunt. That dictionaries give *jibe* as a variant of *gibe* only adds to the confusion and is best forgotten: *The figures jibe* (agree)/*They gibe at* (taunt) *him for preaching the work ethic. Gibe is also a noun: He withstood their gibes.*

job See **CAREER, JOB**.

job, position A *job* is any occupation, but where dignity counts, *position* has a better **CONNOTATION**: *The job has been open for several weeks/The job title is assistant controller.* But: *My former position was that of assistant controller.*

job action A **EUPHEMISM** for a strike or slowdown. The workers involved avoid the latter terms when there are statutory or contractual prohibitions against such conduct: *threatened a job action if no contract was signed by midnight on Sunday.*

job hopping Also *job-hopping.* The practice of flitting from job to job in an effort to improve one's personal standing, as measured by prestige and income: *Job hopping by executive personnel is now rightly perceived as having a deleterious effect on a company's ability to engage in long-term planning/In an industry where job-hopping is the norm, some computer companies are considering ways to strengthen employee loyalty.*

job sharing The sharing of one full-time job by two workers, both of whom work part time and share responsibilities for the job. Compare **WORK SHARING**.

join together *Together* is superfluous: *The cutouts were joined* (not *joined together*) *with rubber cement/Now we will all join* (not *join together*) *in a tribute to our late leader/When two businesses join forces* (rather than *join together*) *for the benefit of both, the chances for success are bright.*

Jr., Sr., II, etc. See FORMS OF ADDRESS 1.

judgment, judgement The first spelling is preferred. Both words, however, are pronounced *juj*-ment (not *juj*-uh-ment). See also OPINION, JUDGMENT.

jungle FIGURATIVELY, a heavily competitive or confusing environment. "It's a jungle out there" is a business CLICHÉ. Compare RAT RACE.

junket A PEJORATIVE for a trip taken by a public official at the taxpayers' expense. However, the word is also used without prejudice for any trip, as by a businessman or author, for speeches and public appearances. Also a verb: *junketed to Sun Valley for a conference on mortgage financing.*

junk food A PEJORATIVE for packaged food with appealing taste but low nutritional value, often well advertised; includes soft drinks, candy bars, gooey cupcakes, and similar snacks.

junk mail A PEJORATIVE for unsolicited mail advertising, especially that sent under third-class bulk rates.

junky Also *junkie*. Drug-culture slang, only sometimes denoting a person with a benign addiction: *Scores of specialty shops have sprung up to supply sophisticated gadgetry to home-media junkies.*

justified copy Typed or printed copy with an even right-hand margin, except for paragraph endings; gives a professional look to house organs, bulletins, instructions, etc. prepared for reproduction on office machines.

K

K For kilo (Greek for 1,000). 1. Often preferred to the Roman numeral **M** to prevent confusion with "million": *Deli, East End . . . $40K down/Wanted, chief financial officer. Salary $50K + .*

2. A measure of computer storage capacity, or "memory": *Model 16 comes with 128K bytes (128,000 characters) of Random Access Memory (RAM) that can be expanded to 512K* [Radio Shack]/*American companies aimed for the best 64K RAM device on the smallest possible silicon chip.*

k/a See A.K.A.

key account A large account of critical importance: *Under our system of large-account management, one person has full-time responsibility for servicing a single key account.*

keyboard capability A term that, more than "typing ability," describes the skill needed to operate a word processor or computer terminal: *The new information management professional comes to the job with keyboard capability, among other qualities.*

key opinion makers See OPINION MAKERS.

kickback Slang for money illegally paid to a person to influence a purchase or other decision that holds the potential for profit: *solicited a kickback.*

kick off Informal for *begin: We'll kick off the celebration at 2 p.m.* Noun, *kickoff: Several movie stars will be present for the campaign kickoff.*

kind As an adjective, often trite and inappropriate: *We are pleased to have your kind order.* [The order was not given out of kindness.] But (well used): *Your kind words are appreciated.*

kind enough to, so kind as to The first expression is preferred, though both are stilted and may convey some sarcasm: *Please be so kind as (Please be kind enough) to reply promptly.* Better: *May we hear from* *you promptly,* or *We'd appreciate your prompt reply,* or (more blunt), *Please reply promptly.*

kindly Well used in senses 1 and 2, tolerated in sense 3, and better avoided in sense 4. 1. Kind, tender, helpful: *a kindly person/a kindly gesture.* 2. With kindness, out of kindness, sympathetically: *kindly disposed to/spoke kindly of/kindly overlooked my embarrassment.* 3. A stilted synonym for *please: Kindly sign the authorization/Kindly keep moving/Kindly refrain from smoking.* 4. Mistakenly used in the phrase "We kindly ask," which immodestly attributes kindness to the writer or speaker.

kind (sort) of, kinds (sorts) of In general usage, *kind* is treated as singular and *kinds* as plural: *We prefer this kind of program/We prefer these kinds of programs.* Colloquially, however, *kind* is often treated as plural: *We prefer these kind of programs/Those kind of arrangements always cause trouble.* Sort of and sorts of are used analogously, but convey disparagement: *this sort of person, these sorts of persons.* But (colloquial only) *these sort of persons.*

kind of a, sort of a The *a* is omitted in general usage: *The terminal is a kind of typewriter* (Informal: *The terminal is a kind of a typewriter*)/*What sort of executive is she?* (Informal: *What sort of an executive is she?*)

kiting Writing a check for an amount greater than the balance in the account to take advantage of the time elapsing before collection; also, fraudulently raising the face value of a check by altering the figures. **—kite,** noun. The check so issued or altered: *didn't know he was given a kite.* **—kite,** verb. To issue as a kite: *kited the check.*

kitsch A vulgarized work of any of the arts: *The "antique" table, with its ornate carving and fake wormholes, is pure kitsch.*

klutz Slang. A clod, a dull-witted person: *afraid of seeming like a klutz.*

knit, knitted Both are acceptable as past participles, but *knit* is favored as a simple adjective: *The sweaters are knit* (or *knitted*) *in Ireland.* But (preferred): *knit goods, a knit jacket.*
   Knit is also a noun: *fashionable knits.*

knockdown Informal for a reduction in price: *pays cash and orders big to get a knockdown in the price.* Also an adjective descriptive of an article like furniture, the parts of which are easily assembled or disassembled: *a knockdown bookcase.*

—knock down, verb (two words). To declare as sold at an auction sale, usually by the strike of a gavel: *The colonial chest was knocked down at $2,400.* Also, informal, to earn: *knocks down $750 a week.*

knockoff Informal for an imitation of a competitor's product: *a knockoff of Rubik's Cube/trying to protect its Oil of Olay from competitive knockoffs.*

know-how Informal: *Her know-how* (experience, skill, ability) *will be a big asset to us.*

L

labeled, labeling Preferred to *labelled* and *labelling*, which are also correct: *indistinctly labeled/a labeling error*.

labor, belabor To *labor* (a point) is to treat in exhaustive detail; to *belabor* is to harp on or repeat insistently: *If I labor the point, it is to prevent the possibility of misunderstanding.* Compare with: *Not satisfied with belaboring the point over the telephone, he drew up a lengthy memorandum to make certain that no details were lost.*

labor-intensive Describing a business or industry requiring large expenditures for labor in relation to its needs for capital or land. The clothing industry is an example. Compare CAPITAL-INTENSIVE.

ladder Metaphorically, a series of steps in the organizational hierarchy: *the executive ladder.* Too often used tritely, as in "climbed the ladder of success." See also TRACK, an analogous but more recent usage.

lade To load cargo. The past tense is *laded;* the past participle, *laded* or *laden: The stevedores laded the ship at night/The cargo ship was laded (or laden) at night. Laden* is also a simple adjective meaning "burdened" or "filled": *carts laden with fruit/a report laden with fresh ideas.*

Ladies Also *Mesdames.* A courtesy title used in addressing two or more women jointly. See FORMS OF ADDRESS 2.

lady Used in titles *(Lady Diana);* as a symbol of refinement *(conducted herself like a lady);* a EUPHEMISM for a sexual companion *(my lady);* and in some religious and commercial names *(Our Lady of Mercy/Ladies of Charity/Lady in Waiting* [maternity clothes]/*the Avon lady/Lady Devon, Inc./Ladies' Home Journal/landlady).* These, however, are exceptions, for *woman* and *women* are usually used when no special connotation is desired: *The First Women's Bank; The Women's City Club; Young Women's Christian Association; Woman's Day* (magazine); *a young woman* (though proud parents may still refer to a maturing daughter as "a young lady"). Compare GENTLEMAN.

lag To hold back, as an obligation due: *The policy is to lag salaries one week to prevent the need for retroactive adjustments resulting from raises, job changes, and other payroll changes.* Also, to fall behind, as an economic factor: *Leading copper issues have lagged the market, their prices hardly reflecting underlying values.*

lagged reserves A Federal Reserve Board policy permitting banks to peg their required reserves to the level of deposits on their books at some specific time in the weeks past: *proposed elimination of the lagged reserves requirement.*

lagniappe Pronounced *lan*-yap or lan-*yap*. A small gift given with a purchase at a retail store. Also, any unexpected small gift or gratuity, as the chocolate mint left on the pillow each night at some hotels.

laissez-faire Pronounced *less*-ay-fair. French for "let (them) do"; the doctrine that government should not interfere in economic affairs: *Even ardent believers in laissez-faire grant that government must have a role in protecting property rights, especially their own.*

land To gain or win. The usage is well established: *landed the account.*

landlady The general preference for *woman* over LADY notwithstanding, *landlady* is still the choice for a female landlord.

landmark An event marking a new stage or turning point: *Passage of the bill was a landmark for the banking industry.* Also an adjective: *a landmark bill/a landmark decision.*

land-office business A trite but convenient expression for a thriving big-volume business; from "land office," a government office for registering sales and transfers of public land: *The store has done a land-office business since it opened.*

land-poor Owning much land, but unable to improve it or profit from its use.

large number In a word, *many: Despite the weather, a large number (many) of our trucks are on the road.*

last, latest Although the words are synonymous, *latest* offers better security against ambiguity when the meaning wanted is "last until now": *Manet's last work/the defaulted company's last annual report.* But: *Gucci's latest scarves/the latest issue of Barron's.*

lateral communication   See at COMMUNICATION FLOW.

lateral move   A switch from one job to another, but without any appreciable improvement, if at all, in pay or status: *By encouraging the mobility myth as a work incentive, top management is able to use lateral moves to disguise even a demotion.*

Latin words   Some Latin words like *agenda, data, ultimatum, index,* and *media* have been so thoroughly assimilated in English that they are rarely thought of as foreign. Other terms like *ad hoc, quid pro quo,* and *sine qua non* are more easily recognized as Latin, but they survive at least partly because English does not have comparably terse or felicitous synonyms. Still other Latin terms hang on because they are part of the tradition of law *(bona fide, ad rem, prima facie)*, literary scholarship *(circa, ibid., sic, supra)*, or science *(in vitro, carnivore)*. Finally, there are the terms for which good English synonyms are available: *in re* (regarding), *in toto* (entirely), and *ad interim* (meanwhile).

Latin words and abbreviations in common use are not italicized except when, as in the paragraph above, they are used as examples (but see ITALICS 3). The plural forms of Latin and other foreign terms are shown at PLURALS 4.

latter   See FORMER, LATTER.

launder   To process illegally obtained funds in a way to prevent identification of their source by law enforcement and taxing agencies. The funds are eventually invested in legitimate enterprises: *built the hotel with laundered money/testified that when the money appeared "clean," it was withdrawn* [from bank accounts] *by those for whom it had been laundered.*

laundry list   Informally, any list of things to be done: *Mr. Harwood presented the employers with a laundry list of the union's demands/The President was said to be compiling a laundry list of the legislative proposals he was going to present to the Congress.* Compare SHOPPING LIST.

lawyering   See -ING.

lay, lie   In their ability to confuse the user, these words rank high. But the best approach to their correct use is to understand that the first takes an object and the second does not.

1. To *lay* is to put (something) down. The something—the grammatical object of the verb—must always be present: *Please lay the carton* [object] *on the floor.* To *lie* is to rest or recline; it is not followed by an object: *The carton lies* [no object] *on the floor.*

2. The difficulty of choosing between *lay* and *lie* is compounded by their grammatical peculiarities. Both the past tense and past participle of *lay* is *laid: We laid* (put down) *the carton on the floor/We have laid* (put down) *the carton on the floor.* But the past tense of *lie* is *lay,* and the past participle is *lain: The carton lay* (rested) *there all day/The carton has lain there all day.*

3. In informal usage, *lay* is frequently used, intentionally or not, for *lie* or *laid: The carton lays* (for *lies*) *on the floor/We lay* (for *laid*) *the carton on the floor.*

layaway Denoting the practice whereby a merchant accepts a deposit for merchandise to be held until the full price is paid, thus ensuring that it will be available to the buyer for a reasonable time at the agreed price: *layaway plan/layaway merchandise.*

lay off To temporarily suspend employment: *laid off a dozen workers.* Noun, layoff: *an anticipated layoff.*
—on layoff. Temporarily unemployed: *a dozen workers on layoff.*

lead, led *Led* is the past tense of *lead* (pronounced *leed*): *We now lead the competition in sales/Morton led her supporters into the conference room. Lead* (pronounced *led*) is the metal: *a high lead content.*

leader Spaced dots or hyphens leading across the page, as in an index or table. Where there is more than one row, the marks are aligned vertically. Example:

Retail stores 419
Catalog stores 284

leading indicators See COMPOSITE INDEX OF LEADING ECONOMIC INDICATORS.

leak To disclose (information) indirectly or without official sanction: *Someone must have leaked the news to the press.* Also used intransitively: *Word of the management changes soon leaked out.*

lean on Informal. To exert pressure, as on an officeholder, a debtor, a business. The kind of pressure varies from the polite to the illegal: *He doesn't like to be leaned on.*

lease   To lease is to occupy property as a lessee or to grant the use of the property as a lessor (see LESSEE, LESSOR). Thus both the tenant and the landlord contract to lease (or let) the same property, the first paying rent and the second receiving it. See also LET 1.

leave, let   *Leave alone* and *let alone* are interchangeable; but without the word *alone*, *leave* and *let* have different meanings. To *leave* is to allow to remain: *Please leave the file where it is/I'll leave the key with the doorman.* To *let* is simply to allow or permit: *Let the guests of honor go first/We'll let our attorney settle the matter.*

lectern   A stand, with a rest for papers, provided for the convenience of a speaker: *asked that a microphone be placed on the lectern.*

led   See LEAD, LED.

legs   Informally attributed to a product that "moves" or sells. In movie parlance, a picture with legs is one with the power to attract audiences week after week. Books with legs are those that virtually "walk out of the store."

lend, loan   As a verb, *loan* is preferred to *lend* in business usage. Even those who are partial to *lend*, however, sometimes balk at the use of *lent* (the only correct form of the past tense and past participle) and use *loaned* instead: *will loan* (or *lend*) *them the money/loaned* (or *lent*) *them the money.* Loan, the noun, offers no such choice: *a loan for 30 days/The typist is on loan* (borrowed) *from the credit department.*

length   Pronounced *len*-gth. See also IN LENGTH, IN NUMBER, IN SIZE.

less, fewer   See FEWER, LESS.

less, lesser   Both are comparative forms of *little*, but *less* relates to amount, whereas *lesser* relates to value, rank, or importance. One speaks of *less* profit, *less* absenteeism, *less* work, but of a *lesser* prize, a company of *lesser* means, a *lesser* position. The term "lesser price" is wrong because what is needed is the comparative not of *little*, but of *low: a lower price*. So, too, the expression is "a smaller [not *lesser*] company," in relation to size; and "fewer [not *lesser*] people" in relation to number.

lessee, lessor   A *lessee* is a tenant, one who leases property from the *lessor*, or landlord. See also LEASE.

let   1. To rent or lease: *The agent let the house for $1,000 a month.*

Also intransitive: *The house lets for $1,000 a month.*   2. To assign for work, especially after competitive bidding: *The maintenance contract was let to a local firm.* See also **LEAVE, LET.**

letter form   The distinctive form of the letter permits some variations, but the field for change is relatively narrow. The changes that occur are mainly evolutionary, adapting gradually to shifts in custom and the drive for efficient processing. Within such limits, however, large businesses find it advantageous to prescribe the mechanical standards governing their own letters.

   1. PAPER.   2. LETTERHEAD.   3. LETTER   FORMATS.   4. ME-CHANICAL PARTS.   5. PUNCTUATION.   6. CONTINUATION SHEETS.   7. ENVELOPES.   8. FOLDING.

   See also **FORMS OF ADDRESS** and **LETTER WRITING.**

   1. PAPER.   The standard letter sheet is of white bond paper measuring 8½ by 11 inches or, less commonly, 8 by 10½ inches. The weight is rated 20 lbs., occasionally 24 lbs. Lighter 16-lb. papers are used for large-volume correspondence and branch-office mail, and 13-lb. paper for foreign airmail and file copies.

   Officers' letters and other high-level correspondence are customarily written on "executive" stationery measuring 7¼ by 10½ inches or the "monarch" size, 7½ by 10 inches. Half-sheets, 5½ by 8 inches, are handy for brief letters and notes. With new typewriter technologies, erasing qualities are not as important as they used to be, but the greater the cotton fiber content, the sturdier the paper is and the better it looks and feels. When a blank (unprinted) sheet is used, the side from which the watermark is intended to be read offers the better typing qualities.

   2. LETTERHEAD.   The **LETTERHEAD** customarily bears the business name, full mailing address, and telephone number. Other data may include the company **LOGOTYPE,** the telex or cable reference, and the name of the department or the name and title of the individual using the letterhead. Nonessentials are best excluded. Within the same organization, different letterheads may serve different needs, as executive letters, sales letters, internal correspondence, and so forth. Because of the importance of the letterhead in company communications, its design is a proper concern of top management, and skilled professional talent is employed for the purpose.

   3. LETTER FORMATS.   The letter format generally conforms to one of several currently acceptable styles. Among these, which are de-

FULL BLOCK STYLE

```
Date                 August 9, 19xx

Inside               xxx xx xxxxxxxx
address              xxx xxxx xxxxxx
                     xxx xxxx xxxxxx

Salutation           Dear xxx xxxxxxxx

Message              xx xxxxxx xxx xxxxxx xxx xxxxxx xxxxxxx
                     xxxxx x xx xxxxxxx xxx xxxxxx xx xxxx

                     xxxxxx xxx xxxxxxx xxx x xxxxxx xxxxx
                     xxxxxx x xxxxxx xxxxxxx xx xxxx
                     xxxxxxx xxx xxxxx

                     x xxxxxx xxx xxxxxxx xxx xxx
                     x xxxxxx xxx xxxxxx xxx xxxx

Complimentary        Very truly yours
close

Signature            Denise Cunningham
```

SIMPLIFIED STYLE

```
Date                 October 11, 19xx

Inside               xx xxxx x xxxxxx
address              xxx xxxx xxxx
                     xxxxxxx xxxx xxxx

Subject line         BRIARCLIFF ESTATES

Message              xx xxxxxxx xxx xxxxxxx xxx xxxxx xxxxxx
                     xxx xx xxxxxxx xxx xxxxxx xx xxxxxxx
                     xx xxxxx xxx xxxxxx xxx xxxxxxx

                     x xxxx xxxxxx xxx xxxx xxxxxx xx xxxxxx
                     x xx xxx x xxxx xxxx x xxxxxx xxx xxx
                     xxx xxxx xx xxxxxx xxx xxxxx

                     xx xxxxxx xx xxxxxxx xxx xxxx xxxxxx
                     x xx xxxx x xxxxxx xxx xxxxxx xxxxx
                     xxxxxxx xxx xxxxx xxx xxxxxx
                     xxxxxxx xxx xxxxxxx xxx xxxx
                     xxxxxx xxx xxxxxxx xxx xxxx

Signature            JAMES McGHEE - CONTROLLER
and title
```

SEMI-BLOCK STYLE

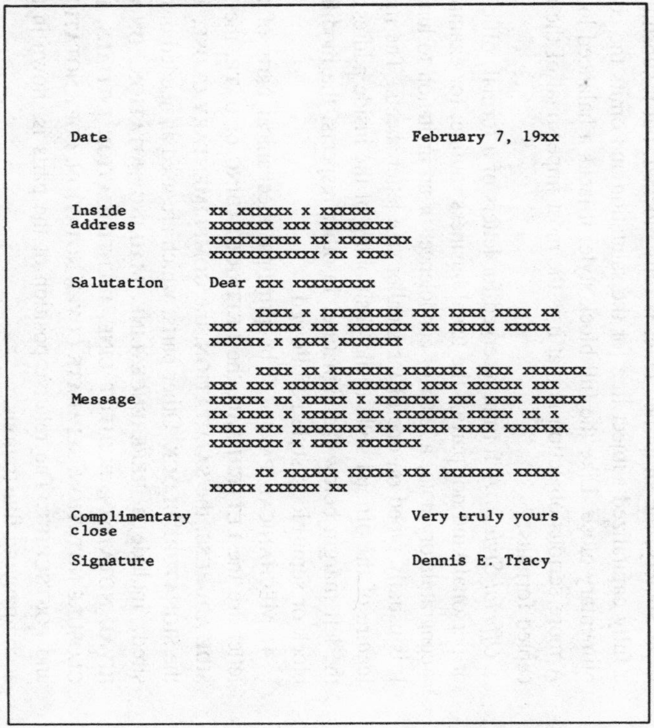

OFFICIAL STYLE

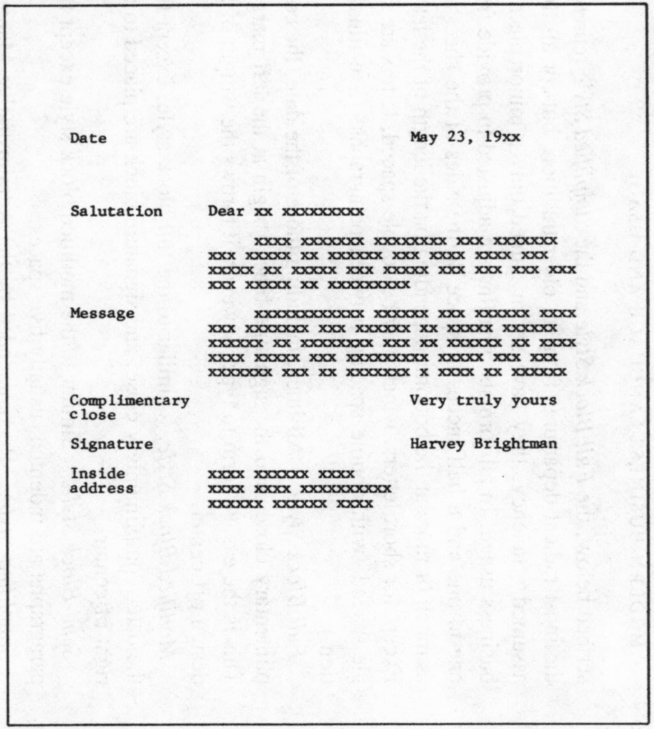

Letter form 3. Four styles of makeup

scribed below, the *Full Block Style* and the *Simplified Style* represent the most radical departures from an older tradition, but for all their assumed efficiency, they have so far gained only a minor place in business usage. In all formats, margins are adjusted to provide from one to one and a half inches of space on the sides of the sheet and as much or more at the bottom, depending on the length of the letter. Except for short letters, which may be double-spaced, letters are single-spaced, with double spacing between paragraphs. (See illustration.)

Full Block Style. All lines, including those of the date, the complimentary close, and the signature block, begin at the left margin. This is the easiest form to type; however, it throws the weight of the design off center.

Modified Block Style. Similar to the full block style, except that the date, complimentary close, and signature block are placed to the right of center.

Semi-Block Style. Similar to the modified block style except that paragraphs are indented, usually five spaces.

Simplified Style. Recommended by the Administrative Management Society, the simplified letter is fully blocked, but it substitutes a fully capitalized subject line for the salutation and omits the complimentary close. Like the full block style, it lacks a balanced look. A more serious objection is that it is the most impersonal of the accepted formats.

Official Style. A format reserved for letters of a formal, official, or personal kind not part of the usual business routine; for example, a congratulatory note, a letter of condolence, or an invitation to lunch. It is usually typed on one of the smaller size letter sheets. The main feature of the official style is the positioning of the inside address at the left margin below the signature. In other respects, the modified block or semi-block style is followed.

4. MECHANICAL PARTS. The principal mechanical parts of the letter are the LETTERHEAD, the LETTER HEADING or DATE, the INSIDE ADDRESS, the SALUTATION, the COMPLIMENTARY CLOSE, and the SIGNATURE BLOCK. Other parts, which are used as needed or desired, include a REFERENCE LINE, MAILING NOTATION, ON-ARRIVAL NOTATION, SUBJECT LINE, IDENTIFICATION INITIALS, ENCLOSURE NOTATION, SEPARATE-COVER NOTATION, COPY NOTATION, and POSTSCRIPT. The relative position of the parts is shown in the accompanying illustrations.

5. PUNCTUATION. Except for a period following an abbreviation, *open punctuation* requires no punctuation at the ends of the lines of the mechanical parts of the letter. In *mixed punctuation*, only the salutation and complimentary close have end punctuation: a colon

```
                                  March 28, 19xx

                                  File No. 5555B


CERTIFIED MAIL
RETURN RECEIPT REQUESTED

Harrison Insurance Co., Inc.
Claims Department
2843 Pilgrim Boulevard
Portland, OR  97208

Attention Mr. Sean S. Finley

Gentlemen:

This section of a letter set in the Modified Block
Style shows the position of the date, reference line,
mailing notation, inside address, attention line, and
salutation...
```

```
                                  August 20, 19xx


Ms. Courtney M. Wilson
Marketing Director
White Dairy Corporation
524 Walnut Street
Cincinnati, OH  45202

Dear Ms. Wilson:

              FALL BROADCAST SCHEDULE

     This is a section of a letter set in the Semi-
Block Style showing the date, inside address,
salutation, and subject line...
```

Letter form 4. Upper parts of the letter

after the first (a comma in personal letters), and a comma after the second. This style is favored by most organizations. In *closed punctuation*, now practically extinct in this country, the ends of all the lines constituting the date or heading, inside address, salutation, and complimentary close are punctuated.

6. CONTINUATION SHEETS. When a letter requires more than a single page, the second and following pages are numbered. The

. . . .

```
        This section of a letter set in the Modified Block
        Style shows the complimentary close, signature block,
        identification initials, and enclosure notation.

                                        Very truly yours,


                                        George C. Keeler
                                        Securities Division

gck:lm

Enc:  Release form
```

_____

. . . .

```
        This section of a letter is set in the Semi-Block
        Style and shows the complimentary close, signature
        block, identification initials, and copy notation.  All
        paragraphs are indented.

                                        Very truly yours,


                                        Ronnie Carson

cc:  Mr. D. M. Heller, V.P.


        The postscript, if one is needed, is placed here.  The
        initials P.S. are not necessary.
```

Letter form 4.   Lower parts of the letter

number, along with the name of the addressee and the date of the letter, is placed at the top of each sheet. If a reference line appears under the date on the first page, it should also be placed in relatively the same position on succeeding pages. (See illustration.) The paper of the continuation sheets should be of the same quality as that used for the first sheet, or at least have the same weight, color, and texture.

7. ENVELOPES. Business favors the "long" No. 9 or No. 10 envelope, the first measuring 3⅞ by 8⅞ inches, the second 4⅛ by 9½ inches. The smaller No. 6¾ envelope, measuring 3⅝ by 6½ inches, however, is suitable for a single standard-size letter sheet or half-sheet. Executive stationery is accommodated by an envelope usually measuring 3⅞ by 7½ inches. The quality of the envelope paper should match that of the letter sheet.

For the form and placement of the mailing address, see **ENVELOPE ADDRESS** in the main entries.

8. FOLDING. To fit a No. 6¾ envelope, a standard-size letter sheet is folded once from the bottom to about a half inch from the top, and then twice across. To fit the same envelope, a half-sheet held long side up is folded twice horizontally. Full-size sheets are also folded twice across to fit the longer envelopes. When folded, the sheets are tucked into the envelope fold-first.

See also **WINDOW ENVELOPE** in the main entries.

letterhead   A term used to signify either the letter sheet, including the printed **LETTER HEADING,** or the printed letter heading alone. See also **LETTER FORM** 1 and 2.

Mr. Bromberg   -2-   November 15, 19xx

Mr. Bromberg
November 15, 19xx
Page 2

Letter form 6.   Styles of headings on continuation sheets. The second is especially suitable for letters set in the Full Block and Simplified styles.

letter heading In the absence of a **LETTERHEAD** bearing a printed address, the heading on a letter must be supplied. This consists of the mailing address of the sender and the date, arranged usually in three lines and placed in approximately the same position that would otherwise be occupied by the **DATE LINE** alone. The telephone number may be added on a separate line.

527 Marquette Avenue
Minneapolis, MN 55402
April 23, 19xx
Tel: (612) 555-6740

letter of transmittal A letter that formally conveys a **REPORT** to the person or group for whom it is intended. It may serve simply as a record of the submission of the report, or it may include data that would otherwise be included in the preface to the report itself; for example, the authorization for the report, its purpose and scope, and an expression of willingness to review the findings with the reader. Compare **COVER LETTER**.

letter report A short **REPORT** or **MEMORANDUM** set in **LETTER FORM** and extending over one or more pages. As in other reports, the text is often broken up by **HEADINGS** and **ENUMERATIONS**.

letter writing The most personal of written messages in business, the letter nevertheless presents a strange contradiction between conventionality and individuality. Its conventionality is most evident in the **LETTER FORM** and in the persistence of stereotyped language. Its individuality is most evident when correspondents rise, as they often do, above the temptation to treat routine matters in a routine way and give their writing the freshness, directness, and cogency that effectiveness requires.

1. GENERAL ORGANIZATION.   2. POINT OF VIEW.
3. LANGUAGE.

1. GENERAL ORGANIZATION.   (a) The letter is usually most efficient when it concentrates on one topic. Treating several topics in a letter creates the possibility that the letter will have to be passed to several persons for attention, with resulting delays or neglect. A letter treating more than one subject also complicates the filing procedure for both the sender and the receiver.

(b) The basic letter has an opening, a core, and a close. The opening introduces the subject, the core provides the particulars, and the close asks for a response, offers help or assurance, or in some other way brings the letter to a fitting conclusion. The opening and close are likely to be paragraphed separately from the core, except when the letter is very short. The core, though, is the main part of the letter and takes as many paragraphs as required.

THE BASIC LETTER PATTERN

Dear Mr. Stevens:

OPENING

You asked about our experience with Roselawn Landscaping, Inc..

CORE

Our contract with Roselawn goes back to April 19xx, when our Tarrytown Laboratories were completed. The work includes regular seasonal care of our three acres of landscaped property, as well as resodding and replacement of shrubbery as needed.

We have been completely satisfied with the regularity and quality of the work done and have a high regard for the management and its staff.

CLOSE

Our contact at Roselawn is Mr. George Gruber, the general manager.

Very truly yours,

Long letters dealing with complex subjects may present formidable problems of organization. See **ORDER OF PRESENTATION.**

(c) Some letters have too little content to require any conscious effort at organization. As the examples below suggest, however, they may generally follow the basic letter pattern.

Dear Mrs. Field:

Here is your refund check for $20.56. We're sorry you had to remind us of it.

Sincerely,

Gentlemen:

Will you please let us have a copy of your company's Annual Report for 19xx. Thank you.

Very truly yours,

Dear Mr. Davis:

We have an opening for an assistant marketing manager here in our main office. If you are still interested in a position with us, we'd like to have you come in for an interview. I suggest you call me for an appointment.

Very truly yours,

Gentlemen:

The item in yesterday's *Times* about your training program in community relations intrigues us.

We'd appreciate having any more information you can give us or putting us in touch with an individual in your company who would be willing to share your experience with us.

Very truly yours,

2. POINT OF VIEW.   A letter is addressed to a single person even when it is duplicated and sent to many. The use of the pronoun *you* is therefore preferable to impersonal references to "people," "our customers," "the purchaser," and the like. Rightly or wrongly, the presence of the *you* is also taken as a sign that the substance of the letter is directed to the reader's interests. See also **"YOU" VIEWPOINT.**

The enclosed pamphlet is designed to help its readers (*designed to help you*).

As requested (*as you requested*), we are returning . . .

When people buy (*When you buy*) a Dynast product, they (*you*) are assured . . .

Credit is a businessman's (*is your*) most valuable asset.

3. LANGUAGE.   (a) Letter language varies from the familiar to the formal, depending on the subject and the reader-writer relationship.

A good letter sounds as if the writer is talking directly to the reader without affectation. Even when a letter is dictated, however, there is invariably a strong temptation to fall back on stock expressions. See also **STEREOTYPED LETTER PHRASES.**

STEREOTYPED

Dear Mrs. Harmon:

Pursuant to your communication of recent date, we are enclosing herewith the Summary of the Annual Stockholders Meeting of Excelsior Pictures Corporation. The empty envelope which you returned to us should have contained same.

As advised by you, we are changing your address on our records to read as this letter is directed.

Regretting the inconvenience caused in this matter, we are,

Very truly yours,

NATURAL

Dear Mrs. Harmon:

Here is the Summary of the Annual Stockholders Meeting of Excelsior Pictures Corporation. This is the report that should have been enclosed in the envelope you received from us. Please excuse the oversight.

We have changed your address as you requested.

Very truly yours,

(b) Making the letter sound natural is only one aspect of letter language. Another relates to the attitude and feelings conveyed to the reader. See also **COURTESY AND TACT.**

OFFENSIVE

Dear Mrs. Delman:

We have your letter about the service you say you received at our Hingham store. On the day about which you complain, we had our annual inventory clearance, and naturally you should not expect the same kind of service you would normally be entitled to.

We hope you will understand our position and have better luck next time.

Very truly yours,

CONSIDERATE

Dear Mrs. Delman:

We are glad you wrote to tell us about the service you received at our Hingham store. On the day you mention, we had our annual inventory clearance, but even that should not excuse the conditions you encountered. Please accept our apologies and the assurance that we will try to do better next time. We do value your patronage and, even more, your good opinion of us.

Sincerely yours,

level Often overworked, with awkward results, in the sense of rank or position: *The meaning of the report can be found on several levels (The report can be interpreted in several ways)/My level of concern is our dealerships (Our dealerships are my concern)/Such a decision is best made at the local level (best made locally).*

liable See APT, LIABLE, LIKELY.

liaison So spelled (two *i*'s) and usually pronounced *lee*-ay-zon (not *lay*-). A connecting link. Use of the word is not confined to the military: *served as liaison between the parties during the delicate merger negotiations.*

lieu French for "stead." *In lieu of* is JARGON for "instead of" or "in place of": *took merchandise in lieu of cash.* Some persons confuse *in lieu of* with *in view of*: *We will be forced to begin collection proceedings in view of* (not *in lieu of*) *their nonpayment.*

lieutenant An AIDE; borrowed from the military in somewhat the same fashion as TROOPS: *The Chairman always talks the issue through with his top lieutenants.*

lifestyle Also *life style* and *life-style*. An omnibus word now used to denote everything from one's general way of living to diet and sexual behavior: *With the war, their lifestyle was oppressively changed/The only way to lose weight is to make really big changes in your life-style/We create an image in terms of life style, personalities, tempo, and mood /You can light your room to suit your lifestyle/The treatment promises to change the lifestyle of arthritic patients/Here is multipurpose furniture that fits your lifestyle/Few diseases have altered basic lifestyles as much as herpes.* See also ABSTRACT AND CONCRETE WORDS.

LIFO, FIFO Systems of inventory valuation. Under LIFO *(last in, first out),* items received last are shown on the balance sheet at the cost of those received first during an accounting period. In FIFO *(first in, first out),* items received first are shown at the cost of those received last. The decision regarding the choice of method is a complex one, involving economic conditions, rulings of the IRS and, in the instance of publicly owned companies, the SEC. For a parody abbreviation, see GIGO.

lift The numerous and contradictory meanings of *lift* are not usually confused when the word is used in context: *the Fed's lifting* (removal) *of the borrowing surcharge/the lifting* (raising) *of interest rates/lifted* (paid off) *the mortgage/lifted* (plagiarized) *the passage from Adam Smith.*

like A pronoun following the preposition *like* is in the objective case: *a woman like me* (not *I*)/*Like them, we sell only at retail* (not *Like they*)/*They are like us* (not *we*) *in many ways.* See also AS, LIKE and SUCH AS 2.

—would like to. The phrase "I would like to" or "We would like to" is a wordy introduction that can easily be dispensed with: *I would like to thank you for (Thank you for)/We would like to take this opportunity to announce the opening (We are opening)/We would like to inform you that the check has now arrived (The check has now arrived).*

likely When used for "probably" (an adverb), *likely* is preferably preceded by a qualifying word like *very* or *most: They are very likely pleased by the turn of events/The loss most likely occurred while the goods were in transit.* When, however, *likely* is used as an adjective, a qualifying word is not needed: *a likely* (improbable) *story/a likely* (suitable) *location for a warehouse/not likely* (apt) *to concede defeat.*

limited The meaning is "restricted" or "confined." Still, the dignified CONNOTATION of *limited* probably accounts for its use in expressions where small, few, or insufficient would be more accurate: *limited funds, limited resources, limited quantities.* See also LTD.

linage Pronounced *line*-ij; also occasionally spelled *lineage*, but not to be confused with *lineage*, pronounced *lin*-ee-ij, the synonym for *ancestry.*

Linage is the number of lines in a newspaper advertisement or the number contracted for: *We are increasing our linage in the* Tribune *next year.* In display advertising, lines are traditionally counted and charged at the rate of 14 to the column inch, regardless of the size of type used or the number of lines set. Thus an advertisement 2 columns by 10 inches fills 280 lines. In classified advertising, a line is measured by the depth of the publication's standard type size and is usually charged at a rate based on a specified number of words or letters to the line.

line 1. Well used to denote a class of merchandise, credit availability, or a trade or occupation: *a* (credit) *line of $20,000/a line of women's coats/What's his line?*

2. Slang for a story or excuse believed to be untrue or exaggerated: *They gave us a line about wanting to be fair to their other customers.*

—along the line(s), in the line of. Wordy, vague, and awkward phrases; better avoided: *We worked along the line (on the assumption) that the order would eventually come through/The applicant said he was looking for a job along the lines of a salesman (looking for a job as a salesman)/They wanted to see something in the line of copiers (They wanted to see a copier).*

listening "Listening," it has been said, "is the other half of talking." A key to successful COMMUNICATION, listening encompasses not only hearing, but also interpreting, evaluating, and reacting to what is said. Effective listening techniques center on such questions as: What is the speaker trying to say? Am I listening without bias or preconception? What are the speaker's biases, sources, personal background, and motives? What has the speaker left out? What has the speaker said that is of value to me and how can I use the information most profitably? Many companies offer training in listening skills to their employees, and packaged courses are available. See also TWO-WAY COMMUNICATION.

literally In a literal or exact sense; not to be confused with *virtually,* PRACTICALLY, *almost,* or *in effect: We literally* (without exaggeration) *made a million dollars on the sale.* But: *We virtually* (not *literally*) *drowned the opposition.*

literature Well established as a reference to printed material of any kind, including advertising and promotional pamphlets: *Write for literature.* When practicable, however, a more specific term is preferred: *prospectus, report, catalog, illustrated booklet,* etc.

litigious Pronounced li-*ti*-jus. A term that grows in usefulness with the propensity to engage in legal proceedings: *Moreover, society is becoming increasingly litigious, and an employee whose firing has been well planned is less likely to sue.*

live Originally, in radio and television, a show broadcast at the time of the performance; not filmed or taped. However, the term is now often corrupted to mean only that the performance was given in the presence of a "live" audience, not just the production crew; or, as in the instance of a news broadcast. that the segment was taped earlier for re-broadcast at a more convenient time. Shows with "live" legitimately in the title for the first broadcast retain the title when the shows are repeated months or years later: *Saturday Night Live; Live from the Met; Live from Lincoln Center.*

live one Slang. A prospective customer for one's goods or services: *The ad produced a dozen live ones/Here's a live one coming through the door.*

loan See LEND, LOAN.

loan shark Slang for a person, often with underworld connections, who lends money at usurious rates.

lobby A group representing some public or private interest for the purpose of influencing legislation. Methods may include advertising and publicity as well as direct contact with legislators: *the gun lobby/the oil lobby.* Also a verb: *lobbied the state legislature to permit gaming/ formed a committee to lobby vigorously for the measure.*
——**lobbyist.** A person who engages in lobbying: *a lobbyist for the milk producers.*

locate Now that the quibbling about this word has ceased, it is acceptable in all of the following senses: *locate* (establish, place) *the factory near the main railroad line/locate* (find by searching) *the source of the rumor/expect to locate* (settle) *in Denver.*

lock in To ensure a stable rate of return by the purchase of bonds or long-term bank savings certificates, on which interest is fixed for the term of the instrument: *Consumers wanting to lock in high interest rates are putting their savings in longer term time deposits.*
——**lock in to:** *Maybe you want to lock in to our high-yield municipal bond trust fund.*

lockout The exclusion of employees from the workplace as a protest against their demands; in effect, a strike by the employer: *The lockout became ineffective when the ousted employees were permitted by law to apply for unemployment insurance benefits.*

log A record, or a book in which a record is kept. In the office, typical logs consist of chronological lists of telephone calls made or received, and names of visitors.

Logotype

logo Pronounced *lo*-go. Short for **LOGOTYPE**.

logotype Pronounced *law*-guh-type or *log*-. An organization's name and/or symbol in the characteristic style used in its letterhead or advertising. *See illustration.*

long term Antonym of **NEAR TERM**.

long variants In some instances, two words with the same stem have essentially the same meaning, but one of them is capriciously lengthened by a prefix, suffix, or otherwise. The long word may be more impressive, but the short word is simpler and more direct. See also **-IZE, -IZATION** and **LONG WORDS AND SHORT**.

COMPARE:

administer	*administrate	indexing	*indexation
advance	advancement	interpretive	interpretative
*alternate	alternative	limit	limitation
analysis	*analyzation	maturity	*maturization
connect	interconnect	mingle	intermingle
denounce	denunciate	note	notation
*dissociate	disassociate	orient	*orientate
distinct	distinctive	origin	origination
estimate	*estimation	*preventive	preventative
except	excepting	prudent	prudential
filter	filtrate	*recur	reoccur
first	*firstly	*recurrence	reoccurrence
*flammable	inflammable	*revaluate	reevaluate
*hyphen	hyphenate	summary	summarization
imagination	imaginativeness	systemize	*systematize
indecision	indecisiveness	use	*utilize
indemnity	indemnification	visit	*visitation
*indention	indentation		

*Starred words are treated in the main vocabulary.

long words and short   Long words are often useful for their CONNO-
TATION or their precision, but short words are easier to read and un-
derstand, and they usually carry more force. See also LONG VARI-
ANTS.

1. The bias in favor of short words should not be exercised at the
expense of clarity and accuracy. To *end* an investigation, for instance, is not necessarily to *complete* it. Though *end* and *complete*
are synonyms, the longer word may well be the more exact one for
the purpose.

2. A long word is more likely to be pompous or abstract than a
short synonym.

assistance	→ help	impecunious	→ poor
converse	→ talk	modification	→ change
demonstrate	→ show	remuneration	→ pay

3. Several short words may convey meaning more plainly than one
long word.

ascertain	→ make sure
determine	→ find out
effectuate	→ bring about
eliminate	→ cut out
exacerbate	→ make worse
simultaneously	→ at the same time

4. A long word may be chosen because of the failure to think of
a short one. The following list is intended to reduce that probability.
The paired terms, though, are not always interchangeable.

accomplished	done	conception	idea
acquire	get	concerning	about
additional	more	conclusion	end
adjacent	next	consequently	so
aggregate	total	cooperation	help
alleviate	ease	currently	now
approximately	about	deleterious	harmful
ascertain	learn	demonstrate	show
assistance	help	determine	find out
attributable	due	detrimental	harmful
cognizant	aware	directive	order
commence	start	disbursement	payout
communicate	write, speak	eliminate	cut out

employment	use	magnitude	size
encounter	meet	majority	most
endeavor	try	minimum	least
espousal	support	modification	change
evidenced	shown	numerous	many
exacerbate	make worse	objective	aim
exhibit	show	obtain	get
expeditious	fast	optimum	best
extinguish	put out	peruse	read, study
facilitate	ease	predominantly	mainly
formulate	make	presently	soon
identical	same	purchase	buy
illumination	light	remittance	check, payment
inadvertency	error	remuneration	pay
inaugurate	start	replete	full
indication	sign	subsequently	later
initial	first	substantiation	proof
institute	set up	sufficient	enough
inundated	flooded		

loophole Some defect in a law or contract—usually by ambiguity or omission—that makes evasion possible: *The loophole was not wide enough to prevent prosecution for tax evasion.*

loose Pronounced *loos*. Not securely fashioned; not to be confused with *lose* (pronounced *looz*), to cease having: *The peg is loose.* But: *We must not lose the account.*

loose sentence See SENTENCES 3(a).

loot Slang. 1. Money, obtained not necessarily by dishonest means: *When they offered $4,000 for the old car, we took the loot and used it for a down payment on a new limo.* 2. The samples, printed material, and other goods given away at a convention or trade show: *At the door you could pick up a large plastic bag to hold the loot.*

loss leader An article, sold at a very low price, perhaps at a loss, in the hope that the patrons it attracts will also buy other goods at regular prices.

lot A specific quantity or batch, often of a particular kind or quality: *will sell the lot for $5 apiece/offered several lots of natural ranch mink skins.*

—a lot of, lots of. Informal for "much" or "many": *a lot of work, a lot of confidence/lots of people, lots of luck.*

loud, loudly Both words may be used as adverbs, but *loud* is favored with verbs like *sing* and *talk: sang loud/talked louder/the person who can shout loudest. Loudly,* somewhat more formal, is thoroughly at home with other verbs: *Insisted loudly/announced loudly/boasted loudly/banged loudly on the door.*

Loud is the only accepted form for the simple adjective (*a loud laugh, loud talk*) and for the predicate adjective. In the latter usage, *loud* follows a verb but describes the subject: *A doorbell should be loud/The siren only seems loud.*

loud and clear A CLICHÉ used adverbially: *I hear you loud and clear (I understand you completely)/As a company spokesman, the actor comes through loud and clear in terms of believability (. . . the actor is very believable).*

lowball To understate, as a quotation or estimate, in an effort to make a sale which will eventually cost the customer more than he anticipated; a practice found especially in the automobile business: *Some insurance brokers lowball* [underestimate premiums].
—lowballing, noun: *Lowballing is their specialty.*

lowercase Abbreviated lc. Small letters (as a, b, c), not CAPITALS, or uppercase: *set in lowercase/a typewriter without lowercase letters.*

low pressure See at HIGH PRESSURE.

low profile A state of discreet inconspicuousness, assumed when contrary behavior would bring about or aggravate hostility: *Since his gaffe, Kronk is keeping a low profile/The company's policymakers and publicists will keep a low profile until the suit is settled.*

low-tech Informal for "low technology," a reversion to manual work and machine processes that have a minimum impact on the environment as, for example, marketing soft drinks in returnable bottles and designing buildings to take advantage of outside light and air. Compare HIGH-TECH.

Ltd. Abbreviation of *Limited*, used chiefly in the British Commonwealth. The common equivalents in the United States are *Corp.* (for *Corporation*) and *Inc.* (for *Incorporated*): *Northern Telecom Ltd./ Canadian Pacific Enterprises Ltd.* In 1982, following regulations of the

COMMON MARKET, of which Britain is a member, the designation for a British *public limited company* (a corporation whose shares are publicly traded) was changed from *Ltd.* to *PLC*, and the *private limited company* (a privately held company or a PLC subsidiary) was given the designation *Ltd.;* thus *Barclays Bank PLC* (formerly *Barclays Bank Ltd.*), but *Barclays International Ltd.* (a subsidiary).

luncheon   A formal word for "lunch." Best used for a special social or business gathering at which lunch is served: *a luncheon in honor of the retiring chairman*.

luxe   Sumptuousness, extravagance, elegance. Usually, but not necessarily part of the phrase DE LUXE: *Pure luxe reigns here* [Bloomingdale's]/*stayed at one of Tokyo's luxe hotels*.

luxuriant, luxurious   *Luxuriant* (lush, flourishing) should not be misused for *luxurious* (rich, opulent): *a luxuriant beard/a luxuriant penthouse garden*. But: *luxurious furs/a luxurious setting for their objets d'art*.

M

M The ROMAN NUMERAL for 1,000. Also, from *mega-*, of Greek derivation, the abbreviation for 1 million. To avoid confusion, the metric K (for *kilo*) is preferred to the Roman numeral in some contexts. See **K**.

macroeconomics, microeconomics *Macroeconomics* is the study of the whole economy, including total employment, national income, and gross national product. In contrast, *microeconomics* is the study of the economics of a particular industry, company, product, or individual.
—**macroeconomic, microeconomic,** adjectives: *The current macroeconomic policies have helped move the world toward protectionism, partly because high interest rates have resulted in slower growth and higher unemployment.*

Madam See FORMS OF ADDRESS 1.

Madame See FORMS OF ADDRESS 1.

Mad Ave. An epithet for "Madison Avenue," a New York street closely associated with the advertising business: *The 15-page document was compiled by McCollum-Spielman, a communications research organization that wields influence along the jungle highway that has become known as "Mad Ave."* [Eric Pace]

magnate Pronounced *mag*-nate or *mag*-net. A person of great importance and influence, especially in business or industry: *a steel magnate.* Compare with MOGUL and TYCOON.

magnet Used in compounds like "magnet store" and "magnet school," *magnet* is intended to suggest a center of interest, with the power to draw to it activities of a particular kind. *Magnet* is used in the same sense as a simple noun: *a magnet for cultural development in the area/a magnet for talented people.*

mailing notations Mailing notations like *Registered Mail*, *Certified Mail*, and *Special Delivery*, or ON-ARRIVAL NOTATIONS like *Personal* and *Confidential* are placed directly above the INSIDE ADDRESS of the letter and separated from it by a line space. The notation is usually typed in full capitals. See also LETTER FORM 3 and ENVELOPE ADDRESS.

mail-order selling   A sales method through which orders are solicited by letters, circulars, and catalogs sent directly to prospective customers, and orders are in turn received by mail or telephone.

mainframe   Descriptive of the central processing unit of a large computer: *Our new HP 3000 Series 44 gives you mainframe power for the price of a small system.*

mainstream company   A large and successful company with an impressive record of growth in earnings and occupying a prominent place in the economy.

mainstreaming   The practice of absorbing a certain number of educationally or physically handicapped persons into the regular work force. Adapted from educational JARGON for placing handicapped children in classrooms with other children of the same age.

majority, minority   A *majority* is more than half of a given total; a *minority* is less than half: *won a clear majority, with a vote of 56 to 42.* See also PLURALITY.

male, female   See FEMALE, MALE.

Mammon   The false god named in the New Testament (see, for example, Matthew 6:24). Also, sometimes lowercased, a personification of riches, material wealth, and greed: *Compared to him, Mammon was a philanthropist/worshiped Mammon* (or *mammon*).

management-by-objective   Abbreviated MBO. A concept of management whereby company officers methodically establish numerical goals for their performance and are then expected to meet them; includes planning, budgets, and written policy objectives: *Seat-of-the-pants banking is being replaced by management-by-objective.*

manager   A man or woman in charge of some activity. The "man" in *manager* has nothing to do with gender; it is derived from the Latin *manus,* meaning "hand."

manageress   A female manager, as of a theater or hotel. Of British origin, the term is not used here.

maneuver   So spelled, and pronounced muh-*noo*-ver. The British spelling *manoeuver* is not used here: *It was a clever maneuver* (scheme)/*It took a lot of maneuvering* (skillful management) *to come out as well as we did.*

manufacturer   Abbreviated *mfr.*, not MFG: *Price $256, less $100 rebate from mfr.* (not *mfg.*)

many a   Construed as singular. See PRONOUNS 3(b).

marathon talks   Talks extending over a long period without a break; a term often used in describing the crucial stages in labor negotiations: *The agreement was reached after 17 hours of marathon talks.*

margin   In finance, a loan by the broker to enable a financially responsible customer to buy securities by making only a partial payment. The customer is then said to have a margin account. An interest charge is levied for the loan. See also HYPOTHECATION.

marginal   Just above the lowest limit of acceptability or viability: *a marginal profit/a marginal enterprise.*
—**marginally,** adverb. Barely: *The company's earnings per share for the three months ending February 28 were but marginally better than for the same period a year ago—$1.97 compared to $1.93.*

margin call   A request from the broker that the MARGIN customer put up more cash to cover a decline in the value of the securities held by the broker as collateral for the broker's loan.

margin head   See HEADINGS.

margin requirement   The minimum amount the customer is required to put up to finance new purchases of securities on MARGIN. The requirement, expressed by a percentage, is set by the Federal Reserve Board and has varied from 40 percent upward.

markdown   A reduction in the selling price of an article, usually expressed as a percentage of the former selling price: *Markdowns of 30 to 50 percent.* Compare MARKUP.

marketing   It's just a step from marketing (selling) goods and services to marketing (placing, finding jobs for) people: *Now there's a firm that can market you fast/When it comes to marketing people into new jobs, we are the leaders.* [Robert Jameson Associates]

market share   The percentage of the total market for a product reached by a particular maker or brand: *Xerox was ready to cut copier prices further to fight stiff Japanese competition and build market share.*

markup   The difference between the price paid for an article and the price it is sold for. Computed as a percentage of the *selling price,* as it usually is, the markup on an article bought for $10 and sold for $15 is 33⅓ percent. Assuming the same prices, the markup on the *cost* is 50 percent. Compare MARKDOWN.

mart   A store or some central location where business is transacted: *sought a fast-food restaurant for the shopping mart.* Also, as used by journalists, a financial market, such as a stock or commodity exchange: *Coal strike sends mart into decline/Marts closed for holidays.*

materiel   Also *matériel.* Both pronounced muh-teer-ee-*el.* The equipment, machines, and supplies used in any organization, but especially by the military. Not to be confused with *material,* the name for any matter from which something is made: *The company is a prime supplier of weapons, ammunition, and other materiel to the army.* But: *The delivery of construction materials has been speeded up.*

matrix organization   The first word is pronounced *may*-triks. A small group organized to set strategies for a larger working group: *uses matrix organizations to tackle temporary problems requiring expertise from several parts of the company.*

mature   1. To become due, as a promissory note or a bond: *The note matures on April 15.* 2. To develop fully: *Once such a store has matured, it has remarkable powers of survival.* 3. Fully developed or slow in growth, as the economy or some segment of it: *The amateur camera market in the United States is now fairly mature/Many of the company's products are in the mature food categories: coffee, cereals, gelatin.*
—**maturity,** noun: *The maturities of the bonds run from 1995 to 2010.*

maturization   JARGON for maturation, "the process of becoming mature": *The maturization (maturation) of the steel industry.*

maven   Pronounced *may*-vin. The Yiddish word for an expert: *You don't have to be a fashion maven to explain their success with women's suits.*

maximize   To increase to the greatest possible degree. The word is not logically subject to modification as by "greatly" or "further": *With* *another million in advertising, we can maximize* (not *further maximize*) *our profit.* But (assuming an increase has already been effected): . . . *we can further increase our profit.* Compare **OPTIMIZE**.

—maximization, noun: *the maximization of profits.*

may be, maybe *May be* (two words) is a verb form: *They may be late/Collins may be pretending. Maybe* (one word) is an adverb meaning "perhaps": *Maybe we ought to consider their bid.*

M.B.A. Master of Business Administration. See **DEGREES AND CERTIFICATIONS**.

MBO **MANAGEMENT-BY-OBJECTIVE.**

M.D. Doctor of Medicine: *John S. Streitz, M.D.* See also **FORMS OF ADDRESS** 1.

mean Average. Also *arithmetic mean.* A number derived by dividing the sum of a set of quantities by the number of quantities in the set. The mean of ten quantities totaling 65 is 6.5. Compare **MEDIAN**.

meaningful Overworked and often vague: *The risks in the long-term bond market are still meaningful* (dangerous?)/*meaningful* (useful? significant?) *work/a meaningful dialogue* (a helpful exchange of views?)/*a meaningful relationship* (a **EUPHEMISM** for a sexual partnership). But (used in its original sense of "having meaning") *The industry is so amorphous that meaningful figures are hard to come by.* Also: *a meaningful sentence/a meaningful declaration.*

means Takes a plural verb when it signifies money or property: *Their means are underestimated/Her means are evident in the way she lives.* In the sense of a way or ways to an end, *means* takes a singular or plural verb, depending on the sense: *Not every means of accomplishment is acceptable/All means are being exerted to clear up the question promptly/There's nothing wrong with winning if the means are honorable.*

meantime The correct expression is *in the meantime* or *meanwhile: In the meantime* (not *Meantime* alone), *we'll hold the goods for your instructions/Meanwhile* (not *Meantime*), *wholesale prices went up.*

measures See **NUMERALS** 1. See also **IN LENGTH, IN NUMBER, IN SIZE**.

mechanical In printing, a clean **PASTE-UP** of type proofs and artwork exactly positioned for reproduction.

media Plural of MEDIUM.

media event According to cynics, a pseudo-event. A promotional happening arranged primarily to obtain media coverage, and hence free and presumably favorable publicity for the organization, person, or activity being promoted. Common types of media events include formal openings, cocktail parties, dedication ceremonies, award ceremonies, and testimonial dinners. In addition to the principals and the media representatives, current celebrities usually fill out the guest list.

median The middle value in a set of numerical values arranged in ascending order. In a distribution of 45, 62, 64, 69, and 73, the median is 64 (the third of the five figures). In less obvious instances, a mathematical formula is applied. Compare MEAN.

mediator See ARBITRATOR, MEDIATOR.

medium 1. Plural, *media* or *mediums*. (a) A mode of communication, as print, radio, television; also a particular newspaper, magazine, or broadcasting station, which in advertising parlance is more accurately termed a VEHICLE.

  (b) *Media*, singular, is nonstandard: *Television is a medium* (not *a media*) *of vast potential/The medium* (not *media*) *we chose was the* Washington Post.

  (c) *Medias*, plural, is nonstandard: *Of all the mass media* (not *medias*), *television is the most influential.*

  2. *Mediums* is the preferred plural for an item, like money or a bank draft, used for exchange or transfer: *mediums of exchange.*

—the medium is the message. An aphorism coined by Marshall McLuhan to denote the inescapable influence of a medium apart from its content. His thesis was that any new technology (the medium)—whether it be printing, television, or computers—creates a new environment and alters our perceptions, our behavior, and our culture. Those changes are the real message of the medium.

meet The CLIPPED FORM of *meeting,* in the sense of a race or other athletic contest; but *meet* has not caught on as the name for a meeting for discussion or learning.

meetings Meetings are superior to written communication in that they provide face-to-face contact and usually an opportunity for questions and discussion. Standard formats for large-group meetings include the

BRIEFING, BUZZ SESSION, FORUM, LECTURE, PANEL DISCUSSION, SEM-INAR, SYMPOSIUM, and WORKSHOP.

The effectiveness of a meeting may be enhanced by the use of visual and audiovisual aids. These include chalkboard, charts, demonstrations, models, motion pictures, overhead projector, records, and tapes. See MULTIMEDIA.

Formal meetings are organized around an AGENDA. In many meetings—certainly those that are legally or officially prescribed—PARLIA-MENTARY PROCEDURE is followed and MINUTES are kept.

meet up with Informal for "become acquainted with" or "be introduced to": *If you're surprised by these revelations, it's time you met up with the* Columbia Journalism Review.

meet with Idiomatically correct for "to meet for discussion or consultation" and in some other senses: *After the reception, we will meet with* (join in discussion) *several West German business leaders/This plan protects you if you meet with* (suffer) *an accident/The new company did not expect to meet with* (experience) *such fierce competition.* However, the *with* is superfluous when *meet* alone conveys the sense: *When I meet her, I expect we'll talk about plans for our print advertising.*

megabuck Slang for a million dollars: *It was the kind of deal where some oil sheik slaps you on the back and starts talking in megabucks.*

MEGO In public relations, an ACRONYM for "*My Eyes Glaze Over*," denoting the boredom resulting from subjection to a communication overload: *The publicity blitz was so overpowering that the event itself found the public suffering from a severe case of MEGO.*

melon Informal for an extra dividend or a share of profits or winnings: *Stockholders were expecting a melon and they were not disappointed.*
—cut a melon. Slang: *It was agreed that the melon* (gain, winnings) *would be cut five ways.*

meltdown A melting of the reactor core in a nuclear power plant and, by extension, any catastrophe: *If Congress insists on following its present inflationary policy, there's going to be a real meltdown.* See HYPER-BOLE.

memento Pronounced me-*men*-toe (not mo-). Plural spelling, -*tos* or -*toes*. A keepsake or souvenir: *The medallion is a memento of the prime minister's visit.*

memo   CLIPPED FORM of *memorandum*.

memorandum report   A short report set in the mechanical style of a memorandum. See **MEMORANDUMS**.

memorandums   *Memorandums* is the preferred plural form of *memorandum;* the alternative plural is *memoranda*. The CLIPPED FORMS are *memo* (singular) and *memos* (plural). Another name for a memorandum is *interoffice letter*, and for memorandums collectively, *office correspondence*.

   1. A memorandum is essentially a letter or short report sent to someone in one's own organization. The format, however, is less personal than that of a letter and less formal than that of a report (see illustration). The occasional addition of a SALUTATION and COMPLIMENTARY CLOSE simply recognizes the need for more warmth than the form of the memorandum ordinarily supplies.

   2. The language of the memorandum, like that of the report, is largely matter-of-fact and with special attention to conciseness and clarity. Trade and professional jargon are used without inhibition. However, an easy familiarity may mark at least the beginning of the memorandum, and there and elsewhere the pronoun "I" is used unselfconsciously.

   3. Charts, tables, footnotes, and text passages broken up by heads and subheads are as likely to be found in a formal memorandum as in a formal report.

   See also **LETTER WRITING** and **REPORTS**.

menial   Pronounced *meen*-yul. Servile or of low status: *menial work/ started in a menial job*.

mental attitude   *Mental* can be inferred from the context and is therefore superfluous: *a healthy attitude* (rather than *a healthy mental attitude*) *toward his work*.

mentality   Mental capacity or intelligence; often used disparagingly: *I can't understand that kind of mentality*.

merchandize   A variant and rarely used spelling of *merchandise: the new season's merchandise/will merchandise the line aggressively*.

Mesdames   Plural of *Madam, Madame*, and *Mrs*. See **FORMS OF ADDRESS** 1 and 2.

Messrs.   Plural of *Mr*. See **FORMS OF ADDRESS** 1 and 2.

MEMORANDUM

DATE: September 25, 19xx

TO: Miss Enid Carpenter/229 Leasing

FROM: David Drewes/450 International

SUBJECT: Visit to Mr. Elwood Fisher, Treasurer
RM-Europa, Inc.

I called on the subject today at his World Trade
Center address to discuss the services of our
International Division. Mr. Fisher said he was
well satisfied with his present banking relationship and had no desire to change. During the
conversation, however, I learned that the company
has an interest in a number of cargo vessels and
has its own trucking fleet in this country. I
frankly don't know the particulars about his
financing of these operations, but it occurred to
me that there might be some business there for
our Leasing Division. Because of your concern with
that area, I am passing this information on to
you to do with as you wish.

I found Mr. Fisher very cordial, and know he has a
high opinion of the Bank.

David Drewes

DD:ab
Copy to Mr. A. R. Sohmer
Vice President

Memorandums.   Example of form and language

metaphor   A nonliteral comparison, in which one thing is given the attributes of another, unlike thing. Also any use of **FIGURATIVE LAN-
GUAGE:** *The high winds of inflation make it harder to bring the economy down to a smooth landing/The chief executive is moving beyond*

trimming the fat to building muscle in product development and marketing.

—mixed metaphor. An incongruous comparison, to be avoided: *The ship of state has been derailed.*

M/F Male and/or female. See EQUAL OPPORTUNITY EMPLOYER.

mfg. Abbreviation of *manufacturing: Morescot Mfg. Co.* Often confused with *mfr.*, the abbreviation of MANUFACTURER.

Mickey Mouse Slang descriptive of something frivolous or inconsequential; a term of belittlement: *Mickey Mouse tasks/has 1,001 Mickey Mouse solutions to 1,001 tasks/consider ethics a Mickey Mouse course.*

micro 1. Relating to that which is small and characterized by detail: *To understand problems of capital formation and slow productivity, we have to probe more at the micro level.*

2. CLIPPED FORM of *microcomputer*, a small computer for personal use in business or the home.

microeconomics See at MACROECONOMICS.

microfiche Pronounced -feesh. Plural *-fiche* or *-fiches.* A postcard-size sheet of microfilm bearing many pages of material in greatly reduced form; convenient for catalogs, manuals, and similar documents that are kept up-to-date through page changes. Selected pages can be projected to reading size, or enlarged and reproduced on paper. *Instead of spending $29.00 to print a 1000-page 3-part report, you'll spend only about $1.00, the price of 9 microfiche.* [Kodak Komstar microimage processor]

microfilm Film bearing small photographic images of documentary material. Depending on the intended use, microfilm can be processed in rolls or cartridges, or made up in strips to be filed in transparent jackets. Large engineering drawings can be reduced and mounted on indexed APERTURE CARDS that can be filed and retrieved manually or by computer.

microform A general term for the print-to-film transference of documentary material in greatly reduced size.

micrographics The science of reducing documents to a small fraction of their size, usually on film, for ease of storage, reference, and transmission.

middle manager A midlevel management position, such as foreman or supervisor, below the rank of vice president: *One out of three middle managers are estimated to have résumés in circulation.*

mighty Informal for "very": *mighty slow/mighty pleased.* Acceptable without reservation, however, for "potent," "with great force": *struck a mighty blow for free enterprise.*

mil Slang for a million dollars: *needs five mil to finance the production.*

mileage Informal for "use beyond the ordinary," referring figuratively to matters other than transportation: *We can get more mileage out of the TV ad by using the sound track in radio spots.*

militate, mitigate Words often confused. To militate is to work (against); to mitigate is to make less severe: *The continuing high interest rates militated against the marketability of a new bond issue/ Government loans will help to mitigate the disastrous effects of the flood.*

mind-set JARGON for a fixed or stubborn opinion: *Before the incident, management's mind-set was that the backup systems would prevent a serious malfunction.*

minimal, minimum 1. As an adjective meaning lowest or very small in quantity or degree, the two words are synonymous, but ambiguity is possible: *for a minimal* (or *minimum*) *fee/requires a minimal* (or *minimum*) *effort.* But (ambiguous): *The monthly cost of $2.50 is minimal for this comprehensive protection.* [Does *minimal* mean "very low" or "the lowest available" from the offering company or any other company?] Unambiguous: . . . *is the lowest for which this comprehensive protection can be obtained anywhere.*

   2. Only *minimum* denotes a base legally or voluntarily imposed. Thus *a minimum fee* and *a minimum wage* represent formal commitments to a particular figure.

   3. *Minimum,* but not *minimal,* is also used as a noun: *for a minimum of $10/a minimum of service.*

minimize To reduce to the smallest possible degree. Since the meaning is absolute, the word is not subject to modification: *Action now will considerably minimize our losses* (Omit *considerably,* or substitute *reduce* for *minimize*).

minority See MAJORITY, MINORITY.

minus   1. In mathematics, less, denoting subtraction. A following verb is singular: *Ten minus three does not equal six.*

2. A loss or deficiency: *Brady's part in the program can be counted a minus.* Compare PLUS 2.

3. Informal in the sense of lacking: *He arrived minus his notes.*

minuscule   So spelled (not mini-) and pronounced *min*-uh-skyool. Tiny: a *minuscule* profit.

minute   Pronounced *min*-it in the following senses.   1. A single item in the MINUTES of a meeting: *a minute recording the standing ovation given Mr. Linton.*

2. To *minute* (the verb) is to make a record in the minutes of a meeting: *In the absence of the secretary, Miss Farr was asked to minute the meeting.*

minutes   The official record of the proceedings of a meeting, as of a board of directors, a committee, or other formally organized body.

1. CONTENT.   2. ORDER.   3. STYLE.   4. FORMAT.

1. CONTENT.   The minutes include the following information, with those modifications dictated by the circumstances, bylaws, or statutory requirements.

(a) Name of the group.

(b) Date, time, and place of meeting.

(c) Kind of meeting (regular or special); and, if special, the purpose for which the meeting was called.

(d) Number of members present. If the number is small, the names of those present or absent are given instead.

(e) The names of the presiding officer and secretary, or their substitutes.

(f) A record of the disposition of the minutes of the preceding meeting, as read and adopted, reading dispensed with, or adopted after some discussion and/or emendation.

(g) A record of reports submitted and their disposition. Unless appended, a report is briefly summarized in the minutes.

(h) A record of all resolutions and main motions, and of whether carried or not. Those carried are cited in full.

(i) Time of adjournment.

(j) Secretary's signature.

A summary of the discussions relating to main motions and reports is not required, but may be included for the record and for the benefit of those not present.

2. ORDER. Minutes of a formal or statutory meeting are recorded in the order in which the business of the meeting is transacted. Those of other meetings, including informal conferences, may be arranged chronologically or by subject.

3. STYLE. (a) The language of minutes is strictly reportorial, without interpretation or embellishment. Descriptive words, as in "our *distinguished* guest," "read an *excellent* report," and "spoke *vehemently*" are out of order.

(b) Minutes are divided between those that employ such stilted expressions as "pursuant to," "upon motion duly made," and "the directors named therein," and those written in plain English. The trend is to the looser style, regardless of the formality of the meeting or the nature of the AGENDA.

4. FORMAT. Marginal or side HEADINGS are used to identify the subjects covered in the meeting. Subjects regularly dealt with are best reported under the same headings each time, as "President's Report," "Report of the Subcommittee on Productivity," and "New Business." Use of enumerations and an outline format make for easy reference, especially when changes or corrections are called for in future meetings.

minutia Pronounced my-*nyoo*-shuh or my-*nyoo*-she-uh. A *minutia* is a small detail. It is not to be confused with the plural *minutiae* (-she-ee), which the sense almost invariably requires: *The minutiae* (not *minutia*) *of the job are wearing her down.* See also PLURALS 4.

mis- A compound formed with the prefix *mis* is not hyphened, even when the second part of the compound begins with *s: misspell, missent, misshapen.* Compare DIS-. See also HYPHEN 2.

mischievous So spelled, and pronounced *mis*-chuh-vus (not mis-*chee*-vee-us): *a mischievous act.*

mishmash Pronounced *mish*-mash or *mish*-mosh. Informal for a hodgepodge, a mixture of unrelated things: *The scheme was a mishmash of hopes and phony logic.*

Miss Plural *Misses.* A courtesy title. See FORMS OF ADDRESS 1. Also (no capital), a common noun denoting a girl or young woman: *a miss who knows what she wants.*

misses Indicative of a range of clothing sizes for smaller women:

available in sizes for misses and women. Also, *Misses,* plural of MISS (see FORMS OF ADDRESS 2).

mitigate See MILITATE, MITIGATE.

mixed metaphor See at METAPHOR.

mixed punctuation A style observed in punctuating the inside address and other mechanical parts of business letters. See LETTER FORM 5.

Mmes. Abbreviation of MESDAMES.

mobile See MOVABLE, MOBILE.

mobility The ability of a person to move relatively freely from one job to another: *O'Hare feels that a certain amount of mobility is necessary for advancement/The personnel department's mobility unit is a kind of clearinghouse that matches job openings to the skills of staff members who want another job within the company.* See also UPWARD MOBILITY.

mobility pool A EUPHEMISM for employees designated for dismissal: *assigned to the mobility pool.*

mode Vogue word, often JARGON, used roughly in the sense of capability or manner of performance: *the Royfax* [copier] *with a reduction mode/a plane that can be used in an offensive mode (used offensively in combat)/when the gear was set in the reverse mode (was set in reverse)/had been operating in a failure mode (operating at a loss)/sets the pace in state-of-the-art cameras with an entirely new program mode (with entirely new operating features)/intellectualized the American dream as a kind of planning mode (as a model for future action).*

model A representation of an object, process, or system by means of a diagram, a replica, or a verbal or mathematical formula. Economic models use equations to help predict actions of the economy from what has happened in the past.

modified block style See LETTER FORM 3.

modifiers See DANGLING MODIFIERS and POSITION OF MODIFIERS. For compression of modifiers, see WORDINESS 6.

module A standard of measurement: *sees a movement away from mere attendance at the workplace and toward paying people for modules of work done.* Also, a structural component that can be used with com-

patible units as the need for greater size or capacity occurs: *furniture modules/whole houses assembled from modules.*
—**modular,** adjective: *a modular computer system.*

mogul Informal for a rich and powerful person in business or industry: *a media mogul.* Also a **TYCOON,** a **MAGNATE.**

mom-and-pop Relating to a small, local, family-run enterprise: *gave them an edge on the failing mom-and-pop stores.*

monetarism A doctrine that would bring order to the business cycle by increasing or decreasing the amount of money in circulation as the state of the economy required. Milton Friedman, a Nobel prizewinner in economics, is well known for his contributions to this theory.
—**monetarist** An adherent of monetarism.

money market The market for short-term, low-risk, highly liquid forms of credit, including Treasury bills, **COMMERCIAL PAPER,** and corporate debt securities.
—**money-market,** adjective: *money-market fund, money-market account, money-market instrument.*

moneys Also *monies.* The term, plural of *money,* refers to the mediums of domestic and foreign exchange, as well as to money in any form used within a country for specific purposes: *the moneys of foreign countries/the moneys* [from a number of different sources] *available for investment. Moneys* is better not used as a pretentious substitute for words like *money, sums,* and *funds: debated the question of monies* (funds) *allocated by the government for job development programs.*

Moody's The familiar name for Moody's Investors Service, publishers of detailed and constantly updated information on the organization, financial structure, and investment instruments of companies here and abroad. See also **BOND RATINGS.**

moonlight Used informally in the sense of working at a spare-time job: *Some workers have been forced to moonlight to maintain the standard of living they want/Police officers have been moonlighting as taxi drivers.*

morale Pronounced muh-*ral.* The spirit of an individual or group: *Her morale is at a low point/Worker morale is high.* Not to be confused with *moral* (pronounced *maw*-rul or *mahr*-ul): *the moral* (lesson) *of the story/a moral* (ethical) *decision.*

more (most) importantly   Usage favors *more (most) important* (a reduction of "What is more [most] important"): *More important, the February sales figures show a sharp upturn/Perhaps most important,* The Journal'*s editorial content provides an environment where readers read. And trust.*

more than one   Followed by a singular verb: *More than one credit executive has failed* (not *have failed*) *to heed the signs of lagging collections.*

mortgage   So spelled, and pronounced *mawr*-gij. A document by which property is pledged as security against a loan. The borrower continues to use the property during the term of the loan. See also **BALLOON MORTGAGE**.

mortgagee   A bank or other holder of a **MORTGAGE**, or lien, to secure a debt on property. Not to be confused with **MORTGAGOR**.

mortgagor   The individual or entity that mortgages, or pledges, property against the repayment of a loan. Not to be confused with **MORTGAGEE**.

most   1. A colloquial substitute for *almost;* better avoided. *Almost* (rather than *Most*) *everyone agrees/Almost all* (rather than *Most all*) *of the order is completed.* But (correct in other usages): *Most workers accept the plan/We had the most profitable year in our history.*

2. Standard as a substitute for *very* in expressions like "They were most helpful." See also **COMPARISONS** 2(b) and 3.

mother firm   An innovative company, from which in time many key employees leave to form their own companies, carrying with them the knowledge they acquired from their mentors. Mother firms do not like the compliment paid them and are often in the courts to prevent or punish the misappropriation of technological secrets.

motif   Pronounced mo-*teef*. Also, occasionally, *motive* (mo-tiv or mo-*teev*). A recurring element as a theme or design in some creative work: *Warner has licensed the use of Superman motifs to more than a hundred manufacturers/The interior of the car has a nautical motif.*

motivation   The want, need, or drive underlying behavior. In business, it is commonly taken for granted that people are motivated by the desire for money or profit. But that is only one of the factors explaining why people work or choose one path in preference to another in their work, lifestyle, and satisfaction of their needs.

In 1954 A. H. Maslow developed a theory in which people were viewed as being motivated by a hierarchy of needs, beginning with the most elementary: (1) physiological needs (the need for food, shelter, rest); (2) safety needs (protection against danger, threat, and deprivation); (3) social needs (the longing for association and acceptance); (4) ego needs (those related to one's self-esteem and the search for status, recognition, and appreciation); (5) self-fulfillment needs (the realization of one's potential, continued self-development, and being creative in the broadest sense).

Depending on the individual and the stage of life, such factors as curiosity, expectations, education, personal values, and self-confidence all play a part in motivation.

movable, mobile   Both that which is *movable* (also *moveable*) and that which is *mobile* can be moved from place to place, but *mobile* implies an ease of movement absent in *movable: a movable partition/movable displays/movable lockers*. But: *a mobile generator/a mobile health clinic/a mobile consumer testing laboratory.* The term "mobile homes" is entrenched, but most such homes are more accurately described as "movable homes."

Mr.   A courtesy title. See **FORMS OF ADDRESS** 1.

Mrs.   A courtesy title. See **FORMS OF ADDRESS** 1.

Ms.   A courtesy title used in addressing a woman, regardless of marital status. See **FORMS OF ADDRESS** 1.

much   For use before a past participle, see **VERY, VERY MUCH.**

much thanks   See **THANKS MUCH.**

multimedia   Employing more than one medium to present a message. Effectiveness is heightened when several senses are engaged simultaneously, as by lecture and overhead projector; or live action, recorded music, and slides: *introduced the line with a rousing multimedia show for buyers.*

multinational company   Also *transnational company.* A company having production facilities or other fixed assets in various countries, yet subject to the decisions by the nationals of the parent organization. An international company may well be a multinational company, but *international* is also descriptive of any company doing business in foreign countries: *Now, ironically, some of the U.S. multinational com-*

panies find themselves calling for a more compassionate policy toward Mexico.

Also, *multinational,* noun: *Until recently the multinational was perceived in the third world as a tool of capitalist oppression, but now many analysts see the growth of these companies as part of the development process itself.*

muni Pronounced *myoo*-nee. Plural *munis* (-neez). CLIPPED FORM of *municipal bond(s);* also *municipal(s): Tax-free munis at 8 percent are worth 16 percent if you're in the 50 percent tax bracket.*

Murphy's Law The name for an axiom of unknown origin: "If anything can go wrong, it will."

must 1. *Should* or some other locution is usually less abrasive (but admittedly weaker) when necessity or obligation is to be shown: *You must (You should) submit your application in duplicate/A stamped return envelope must accompany your request (Please enclose a stamped return envelope with your request).* See also COMPULSIVE WORDS.

2. Acceptable as an adjective in the sense of obligatory; *must legislation/must reading/on the must list.*

mutual See COMMON, MUTUAL.

My dear—— See SALUTATION.

myself 1. Often misused for *I* or *me* when part of a compound subject or object, possibly because of uncertainty over the correct use of these PRONOUNS: *Henry and myself (I) will attend/The committee thought Dunphy and myself (I) could help/We'll keep the secret between you and myself (between you and me,* or *between us)/As for Kane and myself (me) we just don't agree.*

2. Correctly used as an intensive form of *I* or to refer to it reflexively following a verb: *I myself am not convinced* [intensifier]/*I gave myself three days to complete the report* [reflexive].

N

'n A common contraction of *and;* the **APOSTROPHE** following the *'n* is usually omitted: *Sweet 'n Low* [sugar substitute]/*Brown 'N Serve Swift Premium Sausage/Hot'n Juicy Wendy's Old Fashioned Hamburgers/Books 'n Things* [bookshop].

n.a. Not available. The abbreviation is used in tables to explain the absence of a figure. Also n/a, "no account," in banking, and "not applicable," used to answer a question, as on a questionnaire or other form.

name brand A well-known, usually nationally advertised, brand of goods. Stores that advertise "name brands," and even "famous brand names," without revealing the names, may be offering—deceitfully—only obscure **BRAND NAMES:** *Despite predictions that supermarkets would reduce the number of name brands they stock, the study showed that lots of brands besides those that are No. 1 and No. 2 in their categories are apparently still very much alive.*

names Observing the etiquette of names is both a common courtesy and a sign of regard for the person or organization named.

    1. INDIVIDUALS.   2. ORGANIZATIONS.

   · See also **CAPITALS** for the capitalization of names, and **FORMS OF ADDRESS** for the use of names and titles in letters.

    1. INDIVIDUALS. (a) A person is ordinarily addressed in the style he or she prefers, as evidenced by the name on a letterhead or in an official listing, as *George Stevens, George R. Stevens, G. R. Stevens, G. Ronald Stevens, Geo. R. Stevens,* and so forth. In a letter address, the name is preceded by *Mr., Miss, Mrs., Dr.,* or other appropriate title.

    (b) In a letter addressed to a personal friend, or one who signs a letter with the first name, the salutation should carry the first name (as, *Dear Jerry*), and the letter should be signed with the first name of the sender (as, *Phil*).

    (c) The proprietary "our" before an individual's name *(our Mr.*

Smith) is considered bad form and should be omitted. However, there is no objection to the use of "our" before a job title: *our controller; our vice president for sales.*

(d) The article *a* before a name has some value in suggesting that the person is unknown to the writer or speaker: *We received a call from a Miss Jones.* The article is discourteous, however, when used in the presence of the person named: *A Miss Jones is here to see you.*

2. ORGANIZATIONS. (a) The name by which an organization is addressed follows the style preferred by the organization as indicated by its letterhead, advertising, or *Standard & Poor's Register of Corporations: Chase Manhattan Bank; BayBank Harvard Trust Co.; Peat, Marwick, Mitchell & Co.; Columbia Gas Corporation, Inc.; WICOR, Inc.* For convenience, words like *Company, Corporation,* and *Incorporated* may usually be abbreviated when they follow a long name: *American Natural Resources Corp.*

(b) In context, a shortened version of the company name may be used if the full name has been used before in the same document, or if the reference is otherwise unmistakable: *Chase; Columbia Gas; Peat, Marwick.*

(c) When one writes for one's own organization, accepted styles of reference include *we* and—more formally—*the Company, the Bank, Exxon,* and the like. Expressions like "our company," and formal pronouncements like "Exxon believes" (for "we believe") usually sound pretentious.

(d) Some well-known organization names, especially long ones, acquire clipped or familiar forms common in informal usage: *the Fed* (Federal Reserve Board); *Manny Hanny* (Manufacturers Hanover Trust Company); *Fanny Mae* (after the abbreviation FNMA, for Federal National Mortgage Association).

narrowcasting The practice of directing broadcast programs to special audiences (night workers, teachers, women in the home) or audiences with special interests (religion, sports, rock music): *wondered whether a 1 a.m. to 5 a.m. television news program wasn't carrying narrowcasting to an extreme.*

NASD See NATIONAL ASSOCIATION OF SECURITIES DEALERS.

NASDAQ Also *Nasdaq.* Pronounced *naz*-dak. ACRONYM for the *Na*tional *A*ssociation of *S*ecurities *D*ealers *A*utomated *Q*uotations. *The Wall*

Street Journal and other newspapers offer daily **OVER-THE-COUNTER** quotations supplied by the *Nasdaq* system.

National Association of Securities Dealers   Abbreviated NASD. An organization empowered by the SEC to regulate members' operations in the **OVER-THE-COUNTER** securities market.

natural, naturally   1. Both words are favored for their appealing **CON-NOTATION**, but they are often misleading. Hair dyes and cosmetics are touted for the ''natural look'' they impart, and a ''pasteurized process American cheese food,'' containing among other ingredients a preservative and artificial coloring is described as ''naturally good.''

2. The extent of the obscurity surrounding the words *natural* and *naturally* is demonstrated in the labels of two brands of mineral water. Perrier is described as ''Naturally Sparkling Mineral Water'' and Saratoga as ''Natural Sparkling Mineral Water.'' In the first, *naturally*, an adverb, modifies the adjective *sparkling*, thus denoting that the effervescence is natural. In the second, however, *natural* is an adjective that can only modify the noun *water*, denoting that the water is natural, but leaving it to the linguist to infer that the effervescence is added by the bottler.

nature   It is hard to create a concise sentence when *nature*, in the sense of ''form'' or ''kind,'' is used in a prepositional phrase: *The offer was in the nature of a free pack for every ten packs purchased (A free pack was offered for every ten packs purchased)/We were attracted to the topographical nature of the site (attracted by the topography of the site)/The meeting was of a secret nature (was secret)/We expected that their reply would be positive in nature (would be positive).* See also **WORDINESS** 4.

near term   Synonymous with ''near future'': *The near term holds promise for substantial improvement in earnings.* Antonym, *long term*.

—**in the near term.** **JARGON** for ''soon'': *I'm not at all optimistic that we'll see commercially viable electric automobiles in the near term (soon).*

necessary   ''It is necessary that'' is a mild though clumsy substitute for ''must,'' but there are alternatives. Compare: (a) *You must (or should) make claims promptly;* (b) *It is necessary that claims be made promptly;* and (c) *Please make claims promptly.* See also **COMPULSIVE WORDS, IT IS,** and **THERE IS (ARE).**

negative Indicative of denial or lack of positive qualities: *a negative response/a negative personality/negative feelings.* Also a EUPHEMISM, as in "a negative success" (for "failure"). See also POSITIVE AND NEGATIVE WORDS.

—**in the negative.** JARGON: *The answer was in the negative. (The answer was no.)*

neglect In expressions like "We neglected to send you" and "You neglected to tell us," the CONNOTATION is unusually harsh. See also COURTESY AND TACT 3.

neglect, negligence Though the words are usually interchangeable, *neglect* is more often used in the sense of oversight, whereas *negligence* is likely to refer to habitual neglect and, especially in law, the result of not taking reasonable precaution: *a neglect of protocol.* But: *sued for negligence.*

Negro Plural, *Negroes.* Always spelled with the initial capital. However, *black* as an ethnic designation is not usually so capitalized.

neighborhood Informal in the sense of "approximately" or "about": *cost in the neighborhood of $10,000/a population in the neighborhood of a half million.* See also VICINITY.

neither 1. Not either one (of two). Usage is divided on *neither* as a reference to one of more than two, but the question is hardly worth agonizing over when *none* so satisfactorily serves the purpose: *Neither of them* [two persons] *is authorized to sign checks.* But questionable: *Neither of the three qualifies as an expert* (No question: *None of the three qualifies as an expert*).

2. When a prepositional phrase comes between *neither* and a following verb, the verb is correctly singular, but exceptions are made in informal usage, especially when the sense is felt to be plural: *Neither of us is ready for the test/Neither of the copies completely fills* (informal: *fill*) *our needs.* See also PRONOUNS 3.

neither . . . nor See CORRELATIVES.

nepotism Literally, "the favoring of nephews," nepotism is the partiality shown to friends and relatives by those in a position to dispense patronage: *shocked by such blatant nepotism.*

net income Also *net earnings.* The difference between income from sales and the outlay for goods and expenses over a year or other fixed period. The term *net income* is often preferred to *net profit* because it has a better CONNOTATION in some quarters; besides, *net income,* when it is negative, can also represent a *net loss*—a term to which *net profit* would not apply.

networking The technique of acquiring and using mutually beneficial contacts for business advancement; a term born out of the needs of aspiring women and men lacking experience on the upper rungs of the career ladder: *started a networking klatch for businesspeople to meet, exchange cards, arrange deals and perhaps hunt for a new job.*

news Always used with a singular verb: *The news has been good/News is the principal feature of the weekly bulletin.*

New York City In a mailing address the correct form is *New York, NY* (not *New York City* alone or *New York City, NY*). See also ENVELOPE ADDRESS.

news releases 1. The news release (also *press release*) is a notice sent to the press and broadcast media to publicize some event of more than parochial interest. In large companies the releases are prepared by the PUBLIC RELATIONS staff, or the work is turned over to a firm engaged as public relations counsel on a regular basis.

2. Subjects for news releases are as varied as a company's activities. For instance:

Special events

Staff appointments, promotions, and awards

Sales, earnings, new products and services

Speeches by company personnel

New policies and procedures affecting the company's various "publics"

New facilities, new stock issues, acquisitions, and changes in corporate structure

Corporate philanthropy; participation by the company in community affairs

3. The release is written in the factual style of the traditional news story, answering the questions Who? What? Where? When? and Why? or How? A characteristic feature of the writing is that while each paragraph adds new details, the story can be cut off after any paragraph without damage to the sense. It is expected that the newspaper or other medium using the story will edit it to suit its own require-

ments; and that—if the event is of sufficient interest—it will cover the event with its own staff.

Sometimes the release is accompanied by a FACT SHEET, a chronology, a biography, or the like. Photographs and drawings may also be part of the news package.

4. The form of the news release may be described as follows:

HEADING: Includes the source of the release and the address; also the name of the individual, with telephone number, to whom inquiries can be directed.

HEADLINE (optional): A line or two summarizing the story.

RELEASE DATE: The date of release appears either in a dateline at the start of the first paragraph (as, *Chicago, June 11*) or separately, above the headline (as, *For Immediate Release* or *For release after 4 p.m., April 3, 19xx*).

COPY MECHANICS: Copy is double spaced, with indented paragraphs and one-inch margins at sides and bottom. Caps and lower case are used, except for the headline, which is commonly set in solid caps. The word *more* at the bottom of a page indicates that copy is carried over to a following page. Pages after the first are numbered at the top. The end of the story is usually marked by one or more number signs (#). Pages are stapled in the upper left-hand corner.

See illustration.

N.G. Also *n.g.* Abbreviation of "no good," signifying either a deficiency in quality or an invalid statement or document.

NHTSA Pronounced *nit*-suh. ACRONYM for the *N*ational *H*ighway *T*raffic *S*afety *A*dministration (see at **RECALL NOTICE**).

nice Well established in the sense of pleasant, attractive, or appealing: *a nice day/a nice costume/a nice location*. It is an even better word, however, in its more exact applications: *a nice* (subtle) *distinction/a nice* (close) *correlation/a nice* (skillful) *try*.

nickel The metal and the coin; so spelled (not *nickle*): *gone like the nickel candy bar/raised the price of gasoline by a nickel a gallon*.

nickel and dime business A business dealing in many low-figure transactions; the term is sometimes used disparagingly: *Started as a nickel and dime business in a sparsely populated state, the New Mexico brokerage house now finds the promised growth a reality.*

HOFFMANN-LA ROCHE INC.

NUTLEY • NEW JERSEY • 07110

January 20, 1982

Contact: Public Relations Department
          (201) 235-3315

For Immediate Release

Ann Sullivan, Ph.D. has been appointed director of pharmacology I
and associate director of experimental biology, Pharmaceutical Research
and Development Division, Hoffmann-La Roche Inc., Nutley, New Jersey.
In her new position, Dr. Sullivan will be responsible for the scientific
management of preclinical drug research for Roche pharmaceutical products.

Dr. Sullivan joined Roche in 1969 as assistant biochemist, biochemical
nutuition, Pharmaceutical Research and Development. Following several
promotions, she became director of pharmacology II in 1979. She received
a B.A. degree in biology, College of Notre Dame of Maryland; an M.S. degree
in biological sciences, Northwestern University, and a Ph.D. degree in
biochemistry, New York University.

A member of numerous professional organizations including the American
Society for Pharmacology and Experimental Therapeutics and the American
Institute of Nutrition, Dr. Sullivan serves on the Executive Committee of
the Obesity Center, St. Luke's Hospital Center, New York, and holds an
adjunct appointment at the Institute of Human Nutrition, Columbia University.
In addition to Dr. Sullivan's many honors, she is an experienced lecturer
and writer who has published more than 90 scientific articles and abstracts.

Dr. Sullivan lives in Cedar Grove, New Jersey.

####

PHARMACEUTICALS • FINE CHEMICALS • VITAMINS • DIAGNOSTICS

Nielsen For A. C. Nielsen, a company engaged in measuring media audiences and advertising effectiveness. Also, more particularly, the name for the company's rating ("the Nielsen") of a television program based on the size of the viewing audience. The figures, statistically projected from relatively small samples, are highly regarded for their accuracy and become the basis for time charges imposed on advertisers by stations and networks.

One audience measure is the "rating," representing the percentage of American households with television sets watching a particular program. A second measure is the "share," or the percentage of all existing television sets actually in use at the time and tuned to a particular station. Thus on a particular Tuesday evening, it was reported that a television drama seen on CBS-TV from 8 to 11 P.M. drew an average 28.3 rating and a 41 share. A far less successful three-hour drama seen on NBC-TV on a Thursday evening drew a 12.4 rating and a 20 share. The relative standings of the top ten or twenty television programs are reported weekly in many newspapers.

nil   Nothing; zero; NAUGHT: *claimed that the influence of the federal deficit on interest rates is virtually nil.*

nite   SIMPLIFIED SPELLING of *night;* not ordinarily recommended.

No.   The abbreviation of *number* is always capitalized and followed by a period. It is used only immediately before a figure; it is omitted with street ADDRESSES: your account No. 63-467. But: *Your account number is 63-467/Please let us have your claim number* (not *claim No.*)/*The address is 70 Wilshire Boulevard* (not *No. 70*).

The number sign # is confined to merchandise tags, crate markings, and similar routine uses.

no doubt but that   The expression is well established, though usage favors *no doubt that*. See also DOUBT.

no-frills   Without the usual amenities; stripped to the bare essentials: *no-frills flights to Europe/offering no-frills merchandising at substantial savings.*

nohow   Nonstandard for "not by any means," "not at all"; often part of a DOUBLE NEGATIVE: *We can't do it nohow (There's no way we can do it).*

noise   In communication technology, a distortion in the quality of a signal as it is transmitted from sender to receiver; a term now in general use to describe any disturbance in a system, including a loss of meaning from the misuse or misinterpretation of language or other code: *Every* [Federal Reserve] *funds rate movement is not a reliable signal, of course. Reserves supplied may deviate from target day to day, imparting some "noise" to the funds rate signal.* [John M. Davis]

noisome   Not to be confused with *noisy*. That which is noisome is foul or disgusting. Even when used correctly, the word is likely to be misunderstood: *a noisome* (foul) *odor*. But (ambiguous): *a noisome quarrel* (loud? *or* disgusting?).

nominal 1. In name only: *the nominal head of the department.* 2. Bearing a person's name: *bought 2,000 nominal shares of Digital for a client* [not in a STREET NAME]. 3. Minimal; descriptive of a mere token: *offered a nominal price/has only a nominal value* (but see NOMINAL PRICE and NOMINAL VALUE below). Not to be used for "low," which, though nonspecific, has a closer relation to the actual value: *The low* (not *nominal*) *bid caused the seller to withdraw the offering.*

nominal price The price at which a stock is quoted—sometimes the last recorded price—when the stock has not been recently traded and therefore has no current price. See also NOMINAL 3.

nominal value The book or par value of a stock as opposed to the price at which the stock is currently quoted. See also NOMINAL 3.

nominal wage The nominal wage represents actual earnings, not earnings measured in purchasing power. The latter is the *real wage: Their nominal wages, the union claimed, had not risen, but their real wages were down as the result of inflation.*

non- Words beginning with the prefix *non-* are not hyphened: *nonassignable, nonferrous, nonnegotiable, nonpayment, nonprofit, nonstandard, nontaxable, nonunion, nonvoting.* See also HYPHEN 2.

nondurable goods See DURABLE GOODS.

none See NO ONE, NONE.

nonessentials See WORDINESS 1.

nonperforming loan A EUPHEMISM for a failed loan due either to the borrower's bankruptcy or the inability to pay interest and principal when due: *The sharply lower earnings reflected the adverse impact of losses from the collapse of Penn Square Bank and other nonperforming loans/Nonperforming loans fell slightly to $737 million in the fourth quarter.*

nonprofit See NOT-FOR-PROFIT.

nonrestrictive modifiers Not set off by commas. See COMMA 4.

nonstandard English Also *substandard English.* See USAGES 4.

nonstructured Also *unstructured*. Loosely organized: *Creative people work best in a nonstructured environment.*

nonverbal communication Communication without words, as by pictures, signs, dress, and BODY LANGUAGE. Much of the IMAGE people have of the world is formed by nonverbal means, and it is by nonverbal means that people present themselves to others. Frequently, however, nonverbal communication takes place at such a low level of awareness that not even the sender and receiver are conscious of its presence.

no one, none *No one* is invariably treated as singular: *No one is sure of the result. None,* though also singular in form, is usually construed as plural, and especially so when it is followed by a plural noun: *We had our choice of machines, but none were suited to our needs/None of the directors are in favor of the merger.* But (singular sense): *None of the directors was more stubbornly opposed to the merger than Stanford.* Also (singular noun following): *None of the dampness has come through the wall.* See also PRONOUNS 3.

no place, noplace *No place* is well used in the sense of "no room": *There's no place to store the records. Noplace,* however, is informal for "nowhere": *He's going noplace.* The DOUBLE NEGATIVE "not going noplace" is nonstandard, though it is sometimes used facetiously.

normalcy A well-established synonym for "normality": *looks forward to a return to normalcy.*

nosh From the Yiddish; informal for a snack or tidbit: *a nosh before dinner/the Bagel Nosh, the Posh Nosh* (names of eating places). Also a verb: *Don't nosh when you're on a diet.*

no show See at SHOW, SHOW UP.

no sooner than Not *no sooner when: No sooner had the meeting been arranged than* (not *when*) *it had to be postponed.*

no such a The correct idiom is *no such: No such title exists.* See also SUCH.

not Best placed directly before the sentence element it is intended to modify. Confusing: *All items are not on sale.* Better: *Not all items are on sale.* See also POSITION OF MODIFIERS.

not as, not so In a negative comparison, *not so* is sometimes preferred to *not as: The plan is not so* (or *not as*) *daring as we had at first believed.*

note   To note is to write down or make a note of, but *note* is not to be used for "mark." Correct: *We have noted your change of address.* But: *We have marked* (not *noted*) *our records accordingly.*

not-for-profit   An emphatic variant of *nonprofit: does business with schools, associations, and other not-for-profit organizations.*

not only . . . but also   See CORRELATIVES.

not operational   See OPERATIONAL.

not to exceed   Overformal for "not more than": *We propose to invest a sum not to exceed $2 million* (Less formal: *We propose to invest not more than $2 million*).

not too   This or any similar use of a negative before *too* is informal, creating the sense of "mildly," "not very," or "not at all": *He was not too enthusiastic about the idea/Bunker doesn't know too much about the transaction/We didn't think the first quarter would be too terrific.* AMBIGUITY resulting from the use of *not too* is a common risk: *I can't say too much for his leadership.*

not to worry   A modish but usually facetious substitute for "don't worry": *What about inflation? No problem. Energy crisis? No sweat. The worst is over. Productivity? Not to worry. Improvement will come from the exploitation of new technologies.*

novelize   To fashion into a novel, usually from a movie or television script: *The movie was later novelized by the writer of the screenplay.* **—novelization,** noun: *a novelization of* Battleship Galactica.

NOW   The ACRONYM for *n*egotiated *o*rder of *w*ithdrawal, a check drawn on a savings account in a commercial or savings bank. NOW accounts, unlike regular checking accounts, pay interest.

nowhere near   Informal for "not nearly": *The building is nowhere near finished.*

nowheres   Nonstandard for "nowhere": *The end of the demand was nowhere* (not *nowheres*) *in sight.*

null and void   Legal JARGON. Without legal force or validity: *The contract was declared null and void.*

number [the grammatical concept] The number of a verb—singular or plural—is determined by the number of the subject. The number of a pronoun is determined by the number of its antecedent, the word it stands for. Simple though the rules sound, they lead through a maze of grammatical constructions and special cases. Fortunately, common sense usually prevails. See SUBJECT AND VERB and PRONOUNS 3.

For use of figures, see NUMERALS.

number [the word] 1. "The number" is followed by a singular verb; "a number," by a plural verb: *The number of imported trucks has* (not *have*) *not increased dramatically*. But: *A number of our trucks are* (not *is*) *due for replacement*. See also COLLECTIVE NOUNS.

2. *Number* is used informally for a person or thing selected for some particular characteristic: *She's a smart number/It's one of our fastest selling numbers/It's the number featured in our latest catalog.*

3. The plural *numbers* is used informally for "figures" or "profits": *What are the numbers?/The company posted a profit of $110 million for the first quarter. The numbers at midyear are expected to be as good/It's a fine company showing some good numbers/Advertisers are holding their fire until they see our numbers* (audience statistics).

—by the numbers. An idiom meaning "by price" or "with the financial considerations in mind": *They operate strictly by the numbers/There's more buying by the numbers and more centralized control.*

number one Also No. 1, #1, and 1. Informal for "first," "most preferred," or "most important": *They're number one with us/Avoiding acid burns is industry's No. 1 safety problem.* In advertising, a much-used claim, less likely to sound trite if the point of primacy is specific and important: *We limit our stock to No. 1 name brands/Number one in Diesel automobile sales* [Oldsmobile]/*At Ford quality is job 1/Hertz is #1 for everyone/America's #1 discount brokerage firm* [Charles Schwab & Co.]/*It's no wonder American was chosen #1 for domestic travel by members of the Airline Passengers Association/Europe's #1 bottle of beer* [Kronenbourg]/*The No. 1 imported German beer* [Beck's].

See also COMPARATIVE CLAIMS.

numerals In general, numbers are better expressed in figures than in words for ease of reading, reference, and calculating. Figures are indispensable in tabulations and in designating exact numbers and amounts. For typographic appearance, however, short isolated numbers are sometimes spelled out in a running text.

1. MEASURES. 2. DOLLARS AND CENTS. 3. SPELLED-OUT NUMBERS. 4. NUMBERS IN SERIES. 5. FRACTIONS. 6. TABULATED FIGURES. 7. PUNCTUATION. 8. ORDINAL NUMBERS. 9. ROMAN NUMERALS. 10. NUMERICAL PLURALS. 11. UNIT SYMBOLS AND WORDS.

For other uses of numbers, see CLOCK TIME, DATES, and STREET ADDRESSES.

1. MEASURES. (a) Figures are used to designate exact units of distance, time, weight, dimension, or capacity, whether expressed in whole numbers, percentages, degrees, proportions, or otherwise.

7 miles	200 horsepower	3 carats
3:30 A.M.	72° Fahrenheit	72 points
12 tons	25 percent	voted 4 to 3
18′ by 25′	.38 caliber	1/4 share

(b) A measure used as a unit modifier is expressed in figures. The adjective compound formed by the figure and the following word is usually hyphened (see also HYPHEN 3(b)).

a 7-hour day	12-percent bonds
a 48-story building	an 80-degree turn
a 50-mile trip	a 10-point gain

(c) In exact work, a cipher is used before or after a decimal point.

measures 0.0394 inch	extended from 10.7 to 11.0 centimeters
averaged 0.232 percent	weighs 2.0 carats
interest at 0.875 percentage points above the London interbank rate	

2. DOLLARS AND CENTS. (a) Exact amounts, including market quotations are ordinarily expressed in figures and, in the instance of a million dollars or more, in figures and words.

$5 a box	quoted at 63¼
$22.50 each	$30 million
sale priced at $499	$425.7 million

(b) The decimal point and ciphers are omitted after an isolated even-dollar amount. An exception is occasionally made in exact work, when the ciphers are added.

a check for $34 in payment of
featured at $81 each

But (in exact work): raised the dividend to $2.00

(c) Within a sentence, isolated amounts under a dollar are represented in a variety of ways.

39 cents	0.7 cent (in exact work)
39¢	five cents (for amounts under 10¢)
$.39 (uncommon; but see Par. (d) below)	a nickel, dime, quarter, half-dollar

(d) In a series containing mixed amounts (dollars and cents), all the figures are shown with a dollar sign and two decimal places.

at $14.25, $22.50, and $35.00 (*not* $35) each

in those years dividends rose from $.75 to $1.00 to $1.50

In a series containing cents and even-dollar amounts, the figures are expressed in cents and dollars, without the decimal.

sold in 50¢, $1, and $5 sizes

(e) In a series of figures representing all cents or all dollars, the cents sign or dollar sign is repeated with each figure, but in an informal coupling of like figures joined by *and* or *or*, the word *dollars* or *cents* follows only the last.

in denominations of $100, $500, and $1,000

installments of $10 or $15 a month (*not* 10 or $15); *but (correct):* installments of 10 or 15 dollars a month

priced at 10¢, 25¢, and 50¢ (*not* 10, 25, and 50¢)

cost 25 and 50 cents each

(f) In some representations of figures, the dollar sign is omitted, possibly at times because it is considered crass, but more often because it gets in the way, especially when—as in a catalog or sale advertisement—many figures are quoted in close order.

Now 5,000. The Maximilian Mink that's regularly 6,250.

Barbara Sheets. 5.99. Twin flat or fitted, reg. 9.95

Salary 50K [see κ in main vocabulary]

When dollar signs are omitted, ciphers are normally used after even-dollar amounts of one or two digits; in other instances, the dollar sign is used before an even-dollar amount, but omitted before a mixed amount.

Now 6.90, regularly 12.00 (*not* regularly 12)

Reg. $7, now 5.75 (*But:* Reg. 5.75, now 4.25)

3. SPELLED-OUT NUMBERS. (a) A number that begins a sentence

is regularly spelled out. An exception is sometimes made in informal writing when the figure consists of not more than three or four digits.

Fifty dollars is not excessive.
Ten thousand employees are affected.
HEADING: Twenty Years Later
INFORMAL: 1983 was a very profitable year.

If the initial number cannot conveniently be expressed in words, the sentence should be revised.

AWKWARD: Nineteen eighty-three was a very profitable year.
RECAST: The year 1983 was very profitable.

(b) A number paired with an initial spelled-out number is also spelled out if convenient.

Twenty or thirty dozen should be ample. (*Better than* Twenty or 30)
But: Fifty or 150 people—any number can be accommodated. (*Better than* Fifty or one hundred and fifty)

(c) A simple number under 100 is often better spelled out if it is followed by a figure that is part of a compound modifier.

thirty 25-cent candy bars
But: 24 25-cent candy bars (rather than twenty-four 25-cent candy bars)
four 3-day holidays
seventy 2-bedroom apartments (*or* 70 two-bedroom apartments)
three ¼-inch layers (*but* 3 half-inch layers)

(d) When a number is expressed in words, a following unit of measurement should also be spelled out.

six feet (*or* 6 ft., *but not* six ft.)
twelve dozen (*or* 12 doz., *but not* twelve doz.)

(e) Round numbers and indefinite numerical expressions are usually spelled out. A round number exceeding a million is commonly expressed by a figure and a word.

hoped to obtain a thousand new accounts
nearly three hundred companies
would take a million dollars
increased threefold
a hundred and one excuses
in the sixties and seventies
60 million viewers

a budget of $2.7 million
a federal deficit of $40 billion

(f) An unofficial "rule of ten" prescribes the use of words for isolated numbers of ten or below, but usage is divided.

met three times in the past week
will take five men to move the cargo
used to cost ten cents
earnings in six figures
had two breakdowns in four years
ordered eight copies (*also* 8 copies)
must respond within nine days (*also* within 9 days)

(g) In formal price quotations, checks, and legal documents—but not otherwise—amounts are often expressed in both words and figures (note initial capital).

redeemable at One hundred fifty-six dollars ($156.00) each
agrees to pay Two hundred thirty-three and 50/100 dollars ($233.50)
Nineteen hundred fifty-two and 65/100 (Dollars) [amount on check]

4. NUMBERS IN SERIES. (a) In a sentence containing a series of two or more numbers, all members of the series are expressed uniformly, preferably in figures.

packed in cartons of 12, 24, and 144 (*or* one dozen, two dozen, and a gross)
lengths of 8 and 12 feet (*not* eight and 12 feet)
have 27 distributors in Pennsylvania, 14 in Maryland, and 6 in Delaware

(b) When two or more series of numbers are interposed, the series are sometimes more easily differentiated if the members of one of them are put in words.

Among the 100 leading stocks, 21 were up by three to four points, 40 were up by two to three points, 25 were up by one to two points, 6 gained less than a point, and 8 were down by a fraction. [*Compare:* Among the 100 leading stocks, 21 were up by 3 to 4 points, 40 were up by 2 to 3 points, 25 were up by 1 to 2 points . . .]

But (no problem): Such a combination would create the nation's third largest railroad, with assets of nearly $5.5 billion and 19,000 miles of track in 21 states. The Chessie-Seaboard merger would be No. 2, with assets of $6.6 billion and a 27,000-mile system in 22 states.

5. FRACTIONS. (a) Except for isolated fractions that can be written in one or two words (*a half, two thirds*), fractions are written in

figures. Use of the fractions on a typewriter is discouraged because they are too small to read easily, especially on copies, and because they must often be supplemented by other fractions typed in full figures. When full figures are used, a space is left between the full figure and the fraction. Fractions are not given ordinal endings.

6 1/2   5/16 share (*not* 5/16ths)
5 1/2 by 10 7/8 (*not* 5½ by 10 7/8)

(b) When a whole number is spelled out, an appended fraction is also spelled out.

two and a half stories (*not* two and ½ stories)

(c) Expressions like "a million and a half workers" raises the facetious question, "What does a half worker look like?" Although the meaning is clear, some purists might be happier with the equally clear but stiffer "one and a half million workers." See also **HALF**.

For the hyphening of fractions, see **HYPHEN** 3.

6. TABULATED FIGURES.   (a) Whole numbers are aligned on the right, and decimals on the decimal point. Fractions, parentheses, and ordinal numbers overhang.

1,256	I	10.50
942	IV	102.84
785	LII	65.72
16	242	21st
7½	(92)	22d
144	112	23d

(b) A zero figure is indicated by the word *None* or by a cipher (but no decimal) to the left of the decimal position; a missing figure is indicated by a dash or by the abbreviation n.a. (not available).

January	$1,485.00
February	219.50
March	0
or March	None
April	897.16
May	—
or May	n.a.

(c) When amounts of money are tabulated, a dollar sign is placed before the first figure and the figure below the underline (the total). In both instances, the position of the dollar sign is governed by the first digit of the largest amount. Plus and minus signs are aligned in the same way.

$ 75	− 6.2%
124	+20.9
3,465	+10.3
793	− 1.2
$4,457	

(d) In a mixed column of even-dollar amounts and dollars and cents, a decimal point and two ciphers are placed after the even-dollar amounts. In a column having mixed decimals of two or more places, the ciphers are omitted. In a column having single decimals, a whole number is followed by a decimal and a cipher.

$23.25	4.1	32.6
4.00	2.315	14.3
19.46	11.	9.0
15.84	7.24	12.6

(e) Disparate figures are usually aligned on the right, but occasionally they are aligned on the left or centered.

Earnings before taxes	$6,292,264	$6,292,264	$6,292,264
% of net sales	9.0%	9.0%	9.0%
Shares outstanding	52,741	52,741	52,741
Number of employees	1,053	1,053	1,053

7. PUNCTUATION. (a) Commas are used to separate exact figures into thousands, millions, etc.

2,456
234,044
16,954,223

(b) Serial numbers, including house numbers, room numbers, catalog numbers, order numbers, and policy numbers are set solid. Exceptionally, however, patent numbers are punctuated by commas, and other serial numbers are occasionally broken by spaces or hyphens.

7525 Patterson Avenue	Invoice No. 33324
Room 2463	Policy No. 67544321
Cat. No. 4521B	Account No. 209531

But: U.S. Patent 2,341,165
Account No. 234 7795 534
Soc. Sec. No. 935-26-4754
File No. 334-BH

(c) The comma is often omitted in isolated numbers of four digits: 1500 shares, an order for 1600 dozen, a bonus of $2000.

8. ORDINAL NUMBERS. An ordinal number shows the order or rank of an item in a series.

(a) Ordinal numbers are written as follows. The suffix *d* (as in *2d* and *3d*) is preferred to *nd* or *rd* (as in *2nd* and *3rd*). In **AD-DRESSES** the ordinal ending is often omitted to save keystrokes.

WORDS: first, second, third, fourth, fifth, sixth, seventh, eighth, ninth . . . eighteenth . . . twenty-third . . . seventy-fifth, etc.

FIGURES: 1st, 2d, 3d, 4th, 5th, 6th, 7th . . . 16th . . . 39th . . . 84th . . . 103d . . . 165th, etc.

IN ADDRESSES (optional): 2419 82 Avenue

(b) Figures are ordinarily used for ordinal numbers of *10th* or more. Figures are used exclusively for ordinals in reference material (footnotes, tables, etc.) and in the numbered names of military units. Ordinals under *10th* are spelled out before the name of a month and in any formal context. See also **ADDRESSES** and **DATES**.

on the 15th floor
But: on the second floor
3d ed. (in footnote)
77th Division (military)

85th Congress
the 26th of October
But: the ninth of October
29 West 72d Street

(c) When one of two closely placed ordinals is *10th* or more, both are expressed in figures.

the 7th through the 18th volumes

9. ROMAN NUMERALS (see chart). Roman numerals are used to designate:

(a) Major topics in outlines and some texts.

I. Prospects for growth
II. Source of gains per capita output

(b) Volumes in a series or set.

A Treatise on Money, Vol. II (*also* Vol. 2)

(c) Pages in a preface (in lower case Roman).

page iv, page xii

(d) Persons, including historic figures.

Henry Ford II, Edward VI

(e) Dates on a cornerstone or other architectural feature.

MCMLXXXI (1981)

---

1. I	11. XI	21. XXI	101. CI
2. II	12. XII	22. XXII	102. CII
3. III	13. XIII	30. XXX	200. CC
4. IV	14. XIV	40. XL	400. CD
5. V	15. XV	50. L	500. D
6. VI	16. XVI	60. LX	600. DC
7. VII	17. XVII	70. LXX	900. CM
8. VIII	18. XVIII	80. LXXX	1,000. M
9. IX	19. XIX	90. XC	2,000. MM
10. X	20. XX	100. C	5,000. $\overline{\text{V}}$

10,000. $\overline{\text{X}}$
100,000. $\overline{\text{C}}$
1,000,000. $\overline{\text{M}}$

Numerals 9:   Guide to forming Roman numerals

10. NUMERICAL PLURALS.   (a) The plurals of figures are formed by the addition of *s*, sometimes by an apostrophe and *s*. When numbers are expressed in words, the plurals are formed like those of other words (see **PLURALS** in the main vocabulary).

the 1980s (*also* 1980's)   in twos and threes (*not* two's and three's)
Treasury 8s (*also* 8's)

(b) The choice of the singular or plural in a numerical expression depends on the idiom.

(1) Simple amounts: two hundred (*not* two hundreds); forty thousand; six million dollars; 3.5 million dollars (*but* 3.5 millions of dollars).

(2) With *several:* several hundred; several thousand dollars; several thousands of dollars.

(3) With *many:* many hundreds of dollars (*not* many hundred dollars); many thousands of customers.

(4) With *by the:* Sell them [units of sale] by the yard, by the dozen, by the hundred. *But (large numbers)*: by the yards, by the dozens, by the hundreds.

(5) With *by* or *in:* Sold in pairs; measured in inches; multiplied by thousands.

11. UNIT SYMBOLS AND WORDS.   A symbol joined to a figure is repeated with each figure in a pair or series. (See also "Dollars and cents," Par. 2(e) above.)

> 10′ by 12′
> 2″ x 4″ x 12″
> 9°–34°C

But: A unit of measurement expressed in a word or its abbreviation need not be repeated in the same circumstances.

> 10 by 12 feet
> 2 x 4 x 12 in.
> 9 to 34 degrees centigrade

NYSE   The New York Stock Exchange; also the BIG BOARD.

O

objet d'art   Plural, *objets d'art*. Both pronounced *aub-zhuh-dahr*. A valuable art object: *Every item for sale is an objet d'art.*

oblige   Archaic and usually superfluous in such business-letter phrases as "and oblige" and "kindly oblige": *Kindly send us the details and oblige (Please send us the details).* See also **STEREOTYPED LETTER PHRASES.**

oblige, obligate   *Oblige*, but not *obligate*, is used in a free expression of gratitude for a favor. Usually, however, the thought can better be expressed in a less formal way: *Please oblige us by returning (Will you please return) the copies you do not need/We are obliged to you (Thank you) for your kindness.*

Either *oblige* or *obligated* is used to express compulsion or constraint: *We are obligated (or obliged) by law/The contract obligates (or obliges) you to give us 30 days cancellation notice.*

obscene profits   A CLICHÉ characterizing an extraordinarily favorable balance sheet by a large company, especially at a time when the market it serves feels imposed upon by high prices: *In those years auto companies enjoyed the "obscene profits" that were so often the target of attacks by Congress, Naderites, and Harvard professors.*

obsolete   Better not used as a verb because of the awkwardness it creates: *Satellites are obsoleting much of our wired telephone system (Satellites are making much of our wired telephone system obsolete)/Fuel prices and federal regulations have obsoleted the 707 and DC-8 (have made the 707 and DC-8 obsolete)/Only Aquarius plugs into any IBM or Olivetti electronic typewriter, so there's no need to obsolete (junk) useful equipment.*

obtain, get   *Get* is simpler, but *obtain* is better in suggesting success in gaining possession of something through planned effort: *I obtained a copy of the document from the registrar's office. But: I got the form at the bank.*

obvious, obviously   These words may be overassertive or lacking in tact and should be used with caution: *It is obvious (The facts suggest) that a change is needed/Obviously (Apparently) you were not acquainted with our policy.* See COURTESY AND TACT.

occasion   So spelled (two *c*'s, one *s*).

occurrence   So spelled (two *c*'s, two *r*'s).

of   1. Usually informal and superfluous when it follows another preposition: *If they'd get off of their butts, maybe we'd get some work done.* (In general usage, omit *of*.) See also INSIDE OF, OUT OF, and OUTSIDE OF.

2. Some "of" phrases can be compressed with good effect: *some of the banks (some banks)/all of the workers (all the workers)/many of the government's regulations (many government regulations).* See also WORDINESS 6.

3. The wordiness and formality of an "of" phrase can often be converted to a simple adjective modifier: *the policy of the bank (the bank's policy)/the touch of the master (the master's touch).* But see APOSTROPHE 1(f) for comment on the "inanimate possessive."

4. *Of* is nonstandard when used for *have: He should of reported the incident.* A contraction, however, will preserve the grammatical integrity of the sentence. Correct: *He should've (for should have) reported the accident.*

of between, of from   The *of* is superfluous: *at a cost* (not *cost of*) *between $20,000 and $30,000/in lengths from* (not *of from*) *10 ft. to 12 ft.*

off-board   See OVER-THE-COUNTER.

office correspondence   See MEMORANDUMS.

office park   A landscaped COMPLEX of office buildings: *Blue Hill . . . establishing the standards for office parks in the future.*

official correspondence   A loose term confined usually to letters on official business written by persons elected or appointed to public office, and in this sense contrasted with letters these persons may write without official sanction or in their capacities as private individuals. Not to be confused with the OFFICIAL STYLE of letter makeup.

officialese   Government JARGON, at least partly the result of attempts to cover all cases and close all loopholes. Whatever clarity is achieved usually resides in the minds of the promulgators, and citizens are left to rely on the uncertain interpretations of other officials and an eager army of lawyers and accountants.

SAMPLE:

Except as provided in Paragraph B of this section, applications, amendments thereto, and related statements of fact required by the commission shall be personally signed by the applicant, if the applicant is an individual.

MEANING:

If you are an individual, you must sign your own application.

Some officialese is not so easily translated. According to *Time*, President Carter's Council on Wage and Price Stability (COWPS) received twelve hundred calls a day from corporate controllers and finance officers anxious to learn the meaning of the newly instituted pricing regulations. Sample sentence:

The program-year rate of price change is the sales-weighted average of the percentage changes of a company's product prices measured from the last calendar or fiscal quarter completed prior to October 2, 1978, through the same quarter of 1979.

See also **PLAIN ENGLISH** and **READABILITY**.

official style   A letter format for executive correspondence of a personal or informal official sort. The principal departure from other formats is the placement of the inside address at the left margin *below* the signature. See **LETTER FORMAT** 1 and 3.

off of   See **OF** 1.

off-price retailing   The cut-rate merchandising of branded goods obtained from the suppliers' overstock, irregulars, or seasonal remainders. Different from *discounting*, by which retailers sell merchandise at reduced prices made possible by lower **MARKUP** and savings in overhead.

off the books   Without a record, as a cash transaction which presumably is not reported for tax purposes. Such transactions are the mainstay of the **UNDERGROUND ECONOMY**: *makes deals off the books.*
   —off-the-books, adjective: *an off-the-books transaction.*

off-the-record   Confidential, not for publication: *an off-the-record interview.* Also an adverb: *I'll give it to you off-the-record* (or *off the record*).

off-the-wall Slang for "unconventional": *an off-the-wall decision.* Also an adverb: *The decision came off-the-wall* (or *off the wall*).

of the opinion 1. "I think" or "I believe" is less pompous than "I am of the opinion," but such a substitution is not always possible: *Mr. Evans said the SEC was of the opinion that no new regulations were needed to protect money market investors.* [To say that the SEC—a government agency—"thought" or "believed" does not make the best use of those words.] But: *We don't think the SEC needs any new regulations* (better than *We are of the opinion that . . .*).
2. *Opine,* as a substitute for "be of the opinion of" or "believe," is archaic, if not whimsical: *Connors opined (thought) that he would need more time/But I do opine (believe) that the restriction will eventually be lifted.*

O.K., OK, okay Informal expressions of approval: *The estimate is O.K.* (or *OK* or *okay*). Also verbs: *O.K.'d* (or *OK'd* or *okayed*) *the proof.*

old boy network Informal for a group of men bound together by school, business, or political ties: *outbid by a member of the old boy network.* The idea, if not the precise term, has been emulated by career-minded women in such organizations as All the Good Old Girls in Minneapolis and the Women's Career Network Association in Cleveland. See also **NETWORKING**.

older, elder See **ELDER, ELDEST**.

ombudsman A person employed by an organization to investigate the complaints of customers or employees and attempt to reconcile differences in an impartial way. Some hospitals have an analogous position, "patient advocate." In the IRS, "problem resolution officers" deal with some types of complaints by taxpayers.

on See **UPON, ON**.

on account In partial payment: *sending you a check for $200 on account.*

on account of 1. Nonstandard as a conjunction: *They withdrew their bid on account of they found other sources of supply* (substitute *because*). 2. As a preposition, synonymous with "because of," which is preferred: *The fair was postponed on account of* (better, *because of*) *inclement weather.* See also **DUE TO**.

on-arrival notation On a letter, the word "Personal" or "Confidential.'' A letter is marked *Personal* (not *Private*) when it is intended to be opened and read only by the person addressed. It is marked *Confidential* to indicate that it may be opened and read by anyone authorized to do so. *Personal and Confidential* if not redundant, is a contradiction in terms. Like a MAILING NOTATION, the on-arrival notation is placed at the left margin two lines above the inside address. If the letter requires both a mailing notation and an on-arrival notation, the one is placed directly above the other. Solid capitals are used. See also LETTER FORM 3 and ENVELOPE ADDRESS.

on behalf of See IN BEHALF OF, ON BEHALF OF.

one 1. Superfluous in some constructions: *The task is not an impossible one (is not impossible)/The decision is one that should not be made hastily (The decision should not be made hastily).*

2. As an indefinite pronoun, *one* may present some stylistic difficulties. Used once, it can help express a generalization in a formal but graceful way: *One should be able to mail a letter across town with the assurance that it will be delivered the next day.* If consistency requires that *one* be repeated, however, the result can be awkward: *What one does with one's time is one's own business/If one asks for a Coke by name, one is entitled to a genuine Coke.* Abandoning such consistency can result in the exclusion of a whole gender: *What one does with his own time is his own business/If one asks for a Coke, he is entitled to a genuine Coke.* A more rational solution to the problem is to avoid the pronoun *one* altogether and phrase the statement with words like *people* or *you*: *What people do with their time is their own business/If you ask for a Coke, you are entitled to a genuine Coke.* See also SEXUAL BIAS.

one of the . . . if not the See COMPARISONS 1.

one of those who This and similar constructions usually call for a plural verb: *It is one of those bureaucratic rules that defy* (not *defies*) *logic/She is one of a group within the organization who give* (not *gives*) *their time to worthy causes.* In informal usage, however, the main subject may carry the singular sense to the second verb: *He is one of those executives who still believes in the old virtues.*

one-on-one See ONE-TO-ONE.

oneself, one's self The forms are interchangeable, but the first is preferred: *have confidence in oneself/take it on oneself* [assume the initiative].

one-to-one   Relating to the pairing of individuals in complementary roles for discussion, debate, instruction, and the like. *One-on-one* is used synonymously especially but not necessarily when there is some suggestion of conflict. Both words are overworked and sometimes superfluous: *The study showed that managers spend less than an hour a week in one-to-one (personal) contact with their subordinates/Instruction is given on a one-to-one basis (Individual instruction is given)/When Hynes withdrew, the bidding became a one-on-one contest between Goldsmith and Romano* (omit *one-on-one*).

ongoing   JARGON for "continuing" or "current": *an ongoing review of insurance needs and options/dedicated to an ongoing dialogue on creative currents in contemporary architecture/expressed concern about the ongoing investigation into buying practices.* Analogous to UPCOMING.

on-line   Linked to a central computer, as a terminal through which information can be fed or retrieved instantaneously: *Series 1: an information processor with on-line capability.* See also REAL-TIME, a synonym.

on line   In production: *Military systems are now so complex that it takes at least two or three years to put them on line.* Compare ON STREAM.

only   The best insurance against AMBIGUITY is to place *only* next to (usually *before*) the word it is intended to modify. Ambiguous: *Trucks only in right lane* [Does that mean that trucks are restricted to the right lane or that trucks are the only vehicles allowed to use the right lane?] Clear: *Only trucks in right lane* or *Trucks in right lane only.* Compare also: *Smith only signed the letter* (he did not dictate it)/*Smith signed only the letter* (he signed nothing else)/*Only Smith signed the letter* (Smith's was the only signature). See also CORRELATIVES.

on-site   On the premises; not elsewhere: *on-site inspection/an on-site rental office.*

on stream   Descriptive of a product being produced for the market after going through the various stages of development: *By the time the plane comes on stream, it is likely to be obsolete/Gas production will continue to increase as proven reserves come on stream.* Also, "in the process of completion": *The company enters the market with superb new mines and facilities either recently completed or on stream.*

on the basis of, on the basis that   See BASIS.

on the ground(s) that *Because* is shorter: *refused to sell on the ground(s) that (because) the offered price was too low.* See also **GROUND** for use with prepositional phrase following.

on-the-job training Training given a worker while actively performing the work for which he was hired; not classroom instruction. See also **TRAINEE**.

on the order of *About* or *approximately* makes a simpler sentence: *The amount offered for sale was on the order of (about) four thousand tons/It will take on the order of (approximately) a thousand workers to staff the completed offices.*

on the part of See **PART**.

onto, on to *Onto* is a simple preposition meaning "to a position on." It suggests somewhat more movement than *on* alone: *The workers loaded the bales onto the barge/The applause started as soon as the speaker stepped onto the platform.* In the expression *on to,* the *on* is an adverb modifying a preceding verb, and only *to* is the preposition: *The chairman went on to the next order of business/Management was concerned that they might not hold on to their sales lead.*

opaque 1. Not permitting light to pass through; not transparent or **TRANSLUCENT**: *an opaque screen.* Also dull, not reflecting light: *an opaque finish* (applied to paper or a wall, for instance). 2. Obscure, not clear; also dull, unintelligent: *opaque writing/an opaque* [facial] *expression.*

OPEC ACRONYM for the *O*rganization of *P*etroleum *E*xporting Countries, a **CARTEL**.

open-door policy 1. A policy by which opportunities for trade within a particular nation are extended to all other nations on equal terms. 2. A policy extending to employees free access to management; a concept of personnel relations often proclaimed, but usually practiced only selectively. See also **SUGGESTION SYSTEM**.

open-end Without a definite limit, as on duration or amount, but not without the possibility of some qualification: *an open-end mortgage/open-end credit/an open-end mutual fund* (one without a fixed capitalization).

open-end question A question, usually part of a questionnaire, that does not restrict the answer to certain given alternatives (as *yes* or *no*), but permits a free response. Example: *As a telephone subscriber, what is your opinion of the use of the telephone to obtain magazine subscriptions?*

open house   An occasion provided for attendance by anyone or, more customarily, by selected groups, at a celebration of some kind, as an anniversary, the opening of a new plant, a preview of an exhibition: *open house on Thursday, April 10, from 10 to 4.*

open letter   A letter addressed to an individual, but published or broadcast for the information of others. Also, any advertisement set up as a letter and published as a **FLIER** or in a newspaper or magazine.

open punctuation   A style of letter makeup in which the punctuation is omitted from the ends of the lines of the inside address and the other mechanical parts of the letter. See **LETTER FORM** 4.

open shop   A business establishment whose workers are not required to join a union. Antonym of **CLOSED SHOP**.

open stock   Denoting merchandise normally sold in sets, like china and flatware, but also offered by the piece for additions and replacements: *available in open stock.*
—**open-stock,** adjective: *an open-stock pattern.*

open window   The incentive offered a company's employees to resign or retire; provides a way to reduce excessive staffing and open opportunities for younger, fresher men and women: *More and more managers seem to agree that it is easier to let employees jump through open windows than to try shoving them out the door. [Time]*
—**open-window,** adjective: *Kodak's open-window plan.*

operational   Complete, installed, or repaired and fit for use: *The Ithaca plant, completed in July,. is now fully operational/The robot welders will be operational in time for the model changeover.* Compare **OPERATIVE**.
—**not operational.** Sometimes used as a **EUPHEMISM** to hide an embarrassment: *For visitors* [to the billion-dollar Disney Epcot Center] *this past weekend, the excitement was tinged by the frustration of going back and forth among exhibits, only to be told they were "not operational," as the Disney hosts had been instructed to describe breakdowns. [The New York Times]*

operative   1. In working order, functioning; has a more general application than **OPERATIONAL**: *The new policy is now operative/Two of the* *lathes are not operative* (meaning "not in working order"). Better not used pretentiously for *operating: The escalator is not operative* (Better: *not operating* [idle, not in use, not working]).

    2. JARGON for "controlling" or "exerting force or influence": *When the Freedom of Information Act was passed, the operative word was "freedom."*

operator 1. One who deals in securities, real estate, and the like, often spectacularly: *a Wall Street operator.* 2. Informally, a clever or unscrupulous manipulator: *I'd be wary of his promises; he's quite an operator.*

opine See OF THE OPINION 2.

opinion See OF THE OPINION 1.

opinion, judgment An opinion is a belief for which there may or may not be supporting evidence: *In my opinion, the decision is a bad one/The company will seek a legal opinion.*

    A *judgment* invariably implies careful assessment based on evidence: *Her associates respect her judgment/It is our attorney's judgment that they have met the terms of the agreement.*

opinion maker Also, more selectively, *key opinion makers.* Those members of society who, by reason of their position and access to the media, have a disproportionately large influence on public opinion. They include public officials, members of the press and broadcast media, educators, and persons prominent in the arts and sciences.

opportunity In many instances, an unnecessarily pretentious word: *Thank you for giving us the opportunity to (Thank you for letting us) quote on your order/If the opportunity arises (If the chance comes).* But see examples of appropriate use at OPTIMIZE.

optimize To make the best or most effective use of: *Now that fashion is favoring leather, we should optimize our opportunity.* Not to be confused with MAXIMIZE, "to the greatest degree": *The new advertising campaign should help us maximize* (not *optimize*) *our sales.*

    —**suboptimize.** JARGON, to make less than the best use of: *I fault the company for suboptimizing one of the world's greatest growth opportunities.*

optimum Not necessarily best, but best in the particular circumstances: *Their employees work under the optimum conditions* [considering, say, the age of the plant and the resources available]/*To present the collection to the public under optimum conditions, we felt that our first obligation was to identify and catalog each item.*

opus Pronounced *o*-pus. A creative work, as of literature or music. The plurals, rarely used, are *opera* (pronounced *o*- or *op*-) and *opuses* [not to be confused with *opera* (plural, *operas*), a distinctive form of musical presentation]: *Publishers are scrambling for the Australian author's new opus. Opus* is also used sarcastically at times in reference to a minor production of any kind: *By the time you put the finishing touches on that opus* [an earnings forecast], *we'll already have the actual figures.*

orchestrate Business JARGON for meticulously arranging or managing the efforts of a number of persons or organizational units to obtain a desired result: *The publicity attending the opening of the plant was beautifully orchestrated by the public relations department.* Synonymous with CHOREOGRAPH.

order, in sentences See POSITION OF MODIFIERS and SENTENCES 3.

order of presentation At REPORTS 2 several patterns of organizing data are shown. Such planning is required for all messages of some length and complexity. Finding an overall plan, however, is just the beginning, for each paragraph and section also needs some scheme of presentation.

The chart on pages 310–11 is a guide to the common rhetorical orders and the purposes they serve. Almost invariably several orders are used in concert within the same passage.

ordinal numbers Numbers indicating position in a series, as *first, second, third, ninety-third.* See also NUMERALS 8.

organizational communication The meaning of the term is usually restricted to COMMUNICATION between members of the same organization individually and in groups. Such communication involves all the means and avenues by which messages are sent and received, the language used, and the steps taken to ensure its effectiveness in carrying out management's aims. See also COMMUNICATION FLOW.

orientate A LONG VARIANT of *orient*, to adapt or become adjusted: *Our people are not yet orientated (oriented) to the change in management philosophy.*

ORDER OF PRESENTATION

ORDER	DESCRIPTION	APPLICATION
Acceptability	Ideas known to be acceptable are followed by others that are likely to meet resistance. The theory is that once the communicator expresses ideas in harmony with those held by the reader or listener, acceptance of other ideas from the same source is more probable.	A common technique in persuasion.
Complexity or familiarity	Ideas progress from the simple or familiar to the complex or unfamiliar.	Especially useful in description or technical exposition which may challenge the reader's or listener's understanding.
Fixed order	A division into particular functions or topics is prescribed on the basis of precedent or experience. For an example, see AIDA in the main vocabulary.	Suitable for use in repetitive types of messages, as sales, collections, answers to complaints, minutes, proxy solicitations, periodic reports.
General to specific	A general statement is followed by such supporting details as definition, historical data, description, example, or comparison.	The most common way of treating explanatory material and appeals to reason. Useful in the development of paragraphs and larger units.
Importance	Ideas are taken up progressively from most important to least important or from least important to most important. The first order is helpful when the span of attention is short; the second, when a climactic effect is the primary consideration.	Necessary in presenting any series of data of equal rank, for example, advantages, disadvantages, causes, results, conclusions, recommendations.

Pattern	Description	Comment/Usage
Pairing	Consists of juxtaposing causes and effects, problems and solutions, questions and answers, advantages and disadvantages; elements in a comparison; etc. The paired items may be treated individually (one to one) or collectively (set to set).	An arrangement easy to compass and easy to follow; suitable for a wide range of messages and their parts: instructive, descriptive, or persuasive.
Primacy	This is the order of "first things first." A letter or report usually begins by identifying the subject or purpose. Instructions accompanying an unassembled machine will identify the parts and provide a guide to assembly, operation, and repair, probably in that order.	Needed to some degree in every type of message.
Space	Progression follows a directional pattern, as from east to west or north to south, or from the center to the periphery, from a distance to close up, from front to back.	Used in descriptions of objects, displays, real property, floor plans, sales territories, routes, and so on.
Specific to general	Facts or details of any kind are cited to justify a following generalization or conclusion.	Effective in getting attention or for a change in pace. Also useful when the conclusion would be less acceptable if stated before the supporting data.
Step-by-step	A variation of the order of time (see below). Consists of a progressive series of steps or actions leading to a desired result.	A standard method of presenting instructions, procedures, processes, and other material detailing a specific order of accomplishment.
Time	Events are chronicled in the order of their occurrence; or, inversely, the events are reviewed beginning with the most recent and moving progressively backward in time.	Useful in tracing activities or transactions, and in giving autobiographical data, as in a "who's who" or a job application (see RÉSUMÉS).

—orientation, noun: *a two weeks' orientation program/discusses the difficulties of the American worker's orientation to Japanese methods.*

oriented Adapted to; directed to; a voguish word, often superfluous: *entrepreneurially oriented companies/a management-oriented book (a book for managers)/a consumer-oriented magazine (a consumer magazine).*

OSHA Pronounced *oh*-shuh. ACRONYM for *O*ccupational *S*afety and *H*ealth *A*dministration, an independent U.S. government agency.

OTC Also O-T-C. See OVER-THE-COUNTER.

other For use in comparisons, see COMPARISONS 1 and 2(a).

our For proprietary use, as in *"our* Miss Lynch" or *"our* company," see NAMES 1(c) and 2(c).

ours No apostrophe: *Ours* (not *Our's*) *is a family business/The pleasure is ours* (not *our's*). See APOSTROPHE 5(a).

out Informal in such usages as *We're out ten dollars* [without a sum previously possessed or counted on] and *The bonus is out* [removed from consideration].

outlines Before writing a short paper, as a letter or memorandum, it is usually enough to have in mind a list of items to be covered or make some jottings on paper. For an extended report or speech, a more formal outline will be needed. Such an outline is prepared after the research has been done and some thought has been given to the significance of the data and its relation to the purpose at hand.

1. DIVISION OF THE PARTS. 2. NUMBERING SCHEMES. 3. OUTLINE LOGIC.

See also REPORTS 2 and ORDER OF PRESENTATION.

1. DIVISION OF THE PARTS. The outline begins with a statement of purpose and a division of the topic into its main parts. The list that follows shows the purpose and main parts of a proposal to management.

I. Purpose: To explore new ways of finding qualified applicants for clerical jobs.
II. Recent company experience
III. Experiences of selected companies
IV. Problems encountered and solved
V. Recommendation

The second step is to divide and subdivide the main parts, as in this treatment of Topic II above.

II. Recent company experience
    A. Sources of applicants
        1. Agency referrals
        2. Employee referrals
    B. Attrition record

2. NUMBERING SCHEMES.   The excerpted outline above employs a traditional numbering scheme: Roman numerals for first-order topics, capital letters for second-order topics, and Arabic numerals for third-order topics. Fourth- and fifth-order topics, if needed, are indicated by lowercase letters and parenthesized Arabic numerals respectively.

A decimal system is often preferred by engineers and scientists. This is a model:

1. First-order topic
    1.1 Second-order topic
    1.2 Second-order topic
        1.21 Third-order topic
        1.22 Third-order topic
        1.23 Third-order topic
            1.231 Fourth-order topic
            1.232 Fourth-order topic
    1.3 Second-order topic
2. First-order topic
    2.1 Second-order topic
    2.2 Second-order topic

3. OUTLINE LOGIC.   (a) Apart from putting topics in a logical sequence, a good outline also shows their relative rank. An outline that does not properly differentiate between main and subordinate topics fails in this respect.

CONFUSING:	IMPROVED:
I. Types of accounts	I. Types of accounts
II. Fiduciary	A. Fiduciary
III. Estates	1. Estates
IV. Guardianships	2. Guardianships
V. Trusts	3. Trusts
VI. Custodian	B. Custodian
VII. Agency	1. Agency
VIII. Banking Division	2. Banking Division

IX. Bank safekeeping   3. Bank safekeeping
X. Accommodations   C. Accommodations

(b) The division of a topic usually presumes two or more subtopics. An exception can be made when a single subtopic is used to signify an example.

This:

A. Number of employees: 160

Or this:

A. Number of employees
 1. 106 full time
 2. 54 part time

Rather than this:

A. Number of employees
 1. 160

But (acceptable):

A. Public service advertising
 Ex.: General Electric

(c) A reasonable consistency is expected in the phrasing of topics. Topics are written as either phrases or whole sentences, but usually not both in the same outline. Phrases are easier to work with, but even they require some uniformity in dealing with co-ordinate topics (see **PARALLEL STRUCTURE**).

Faulty (phrasing of subtopics varies in form):

C. Advantages to the company
 1. Proximity to warehouse
 2. Markets are diversified
 3. Storage space increased
 4. Stabilizing production

Improved (subtopics uniformly phrased):

C. Advantages to the company
 1. Proximity to warehouse
 2. Diversification of markets
 3. Increase in storage space
 4. Stabilization of production

Acceptable (run-on phrases in sentence outline):

B. The Mail Department prepares a cash report for the cashier.
C. The cashier examines each check for
 1. Postdating
 2. Name of payee

3. Signature

4. Agreement of written and figure amounts

out of 1. Informal for "from a position in": *The sales staff work out of the main office.* 2. The *of* is superfluous when *out of* is used in the sense of "through" or "outside of": *could see out* (rather than *out of*) *the window.* See also **OF** 1(a).

out-of-pocket Descriptive of a small expenditure in cash: *Now I'm a dollar out-of-pocket/an out-of-pocket expense.*

outplacement The practice of helping unwanted or unneeded employees find other jobs. Employers often engage "outplacement companies" to perform this service for them: *has 16 years of outplacement experience.*

outreach Describing an organization's extension of services to persons and places beyond its normal range of activities. Examples: using a mobile van to bring health services to the elderly; providing schools with educational materials as part of a company's marketing or public relations program. The word is also found in such phrases as "operation outreach," "an outreach program," and "provided $400,000 for outreach."

outside of 1. The *of* is superfluous when *outside* is used as a preposition relating to physical space or scope: *the storage space outside* (rather than *outside of*) *the building/the property is outside* (rather than *outside of*) *the town's jurisdiction.* But (*outside* used as a noun; no question): *the outside* (the facade) *of the building.* See also **OF** 1(a).

2. Standard in the sense of "except for": *Outside of Krensky, I know of no other supplier.*

outsourcing Particularly in the auto industry, the practice of subcontracting the manufacture of components that can be more cheaply produced elsewhere—sometimes in another country.

outstanding Still existing: *an outstanding* (unpaid) *debt/capital stock outstanding* (in public hands)/*many outstanding* (unresolved) *questions.*

over Standard for "more than"; but its use in an unfavorable numerical comparison can be confusing. Well used: *The value was over a million dollars.* But (confusing): *Our return was over 10 percent below the figure we anticipated* (Better: *Our return was below the figure we anticipated by more than 10 percent*). Compare **IN EXCESS OF.**

overkill Any excessive remedy, action, or reaction: *The FDA must be persuaded not to meet the consumers' complaints with regulatory overkill.*

overlook, oversee For clarity, it is best to confine *overlook* to the sense of "fail to notice" and let *oversee* serve for "supervise." Ambiguous: *The foreman overlooked* (Better: *oversaw* or *supervised*) *the men working in the interior court.* But (unambiguous): *The foreman was inclined to overlook minor infractions.* See also OVERSIGHT.

overly Well used for "excessively," but the combining form *over* is preferred for its conciseness and smoothness: *overly valued* (better, *overvalued*)/*overly confident* (better, *overconfident*).

oversell To sell overaggressively or by exaggerated claims: *They made the mistake of overselling the deodorant qualities of the soap/The public was oversold on the movie, as exhibitors soon learned from the disparaging comments of their patrons and disappointing revenues.* See also OVERSOLD.

oversight The word has two diametrically opposed meanings: (1) inattention or an error due to inattention, and (2) watchful care or supervision. When the context does not make the meaning immediately clear, a synonym should be used. No question: *Please excuse the oversight/An oversight committee will examine the way the contracts are let.* But (confusing or incongruous): *The process requires careful oversight* (Better: *careful supervision*). See also OVERLOOK, OVERSEE.

oversold Descriptive of an excess of sales, with its consequent effects. An oversold securities market results in a drop in prices; an oversold theatrical performance results in the inability of ticket holders to gain admittance; an oversold manufacturer will be unable to fulfill all his commitments for delivery. See also OVERSELL.

over-the-counter Abbreviated OTC or O-T-C. 1. Descriptive of stocks and bonds sold "off-board," or outside an official stock exchange. See also NASDAQ. 2. Also descriptive of drugs sold legally without a doctor's prescription and, in fact, any convenience goods sold at retail: *Over-the-counter business accounts for half the company's sales.*

　—**over the counter,** an adverbial phrase: *The stock is sold over the counter.*

owing Due; not paid: *The customer paid $3,000, leaving $1,200 still owing.*

　—**owing to.** See DUE TO.

P

PABX Private automatic branch exchange (telephone switching system): *Western Electric is only one of many domestic suppliers of PABXs.*

pack A small package or a collection of small items in a single package: *a pack of Wrigley's gum/Now in convenient six-packs* (fruit juice)/*the Marlboro hardpack* (box). Also, as part of a **TRADE NAME**, *pak: Flavor-Pak* (a paper bag)/*United's Nite Pak* (air express).

package Any combination of separate elements composing a whole: *an entertainment package* (dinner and show)/*a benefits package* (bonus, insurance, pension, etc.). Also a verb: *specializes in packaging parties* (assuming charge of all the details). See also **PACKAGER**.

package deal 1. The offering for sale of a combination of products or packages at a special price. EXAMPLES: *Get 3 for the price of 2/The 8-ounce size is free when you buy the large 32-ounce size/Buy the cosmetics kit and get the carry-all bag (a $15 value) for $5.95.*
2. An arrangement obliging a buyer to purchase something he may not want in order to obtain the goods he does want.

packaged goods Also *package goods.* Items, such as food, drink, proprietary drugs, and toilet articles enclosed in a box or other container for convenience of display and sale at retail; goods not sold loose or in bulk: *His experience in packaged goods led him to Bates and work on Colgate's Rapid Shave as an account executive.*
—packaged-goods, package-goods, adjectives: *a packaged-goods company/a meeting of package-goods executives.*

packager A producer of services requiring a combination of skills and talents: *a packager of television shows/a book packager/enjoys a reputation as a packager of fashionable Washington parties.* See also **PACKAGE**.

package store A common **EUPHEMISM** for a store that sells bottles of wine and liquor for consumption off the premises.

pager Also, informally, a *beeper.* A small electronic call instrument, usually carried on one's person, that emits a sound alerting the carrier to the fact that a telephone call has been received. The person paged can then obtain the message by getting in touch with his or her office or answering service. Some models have a display panel showing the telephone number at which the caller can be reached directly.

pair 1. A set of two corresponding things (as curtains, end tables, theater tickets) or an object consisting of two interdependent parts (as pliers, tongs, scissors). *Pair* is treated as singular or plural depending on whether the pair is thought of as a unit or two separate units: *An extra pair of shoes is enough for a short trip* (But: *The pair* [two persons] *are prosperous*)/*This pair of scissors needs sharpening* (But: *These scissors* [one pair] *need sharpening*).

  2. A number exceeding one is regularly followed by the plural *pairs*, though informal usage permits *pair: two pairs of contestants/five pairs of hosiery*. But (informal): *two pair of shoes*.

pamphlet So spelled (not pham-). A small printed folder or unbound booklet: *decided to put the instructions in a pamphlet accompanying the product.*

pant A modish singular for the plural "pants," a pair of trousers [origin, *pantaloons*]: *Pant, $49* [Bloomingdale's]; ordinary usage: *Pants, $49*. However, the term *pant suit*, as well as *pants suit*, a woman's suit of coat and trousers, is standard. Compare SLACK.

paperback A book with soft covers: *issued as a paperback*. Also, descriptively, *paper* or *bound in paper: cloth, $10.95, paper $4.95/school edition, bound in paper, $1.95.*

paperhanger Slang. A professional passer of bad checks: *a reputation as a paperhanger.*

paper pusher A PEJORATIVE for a person whose time is largely occupied with PAPERWORK.

paper pushing A PEJORATIVE for tasks requiring PAPERWORK: *The company, which started as a photographic papermaker, is now preparing itself for the age when paper pushing will be replaced, in part at least, by electronic blips on a computer screen.*

paperwork Also *paper work*. Routine clerical tasks, sometimes suggesting work of greater importance; also any work with letters, reports, and other written documents.

paradigm Pronounced -dim or -dime. Originally, a table used as an example of all the inflectional forms of a verb or noun. Now, also JAR-GON for any carefully delineated example or model: *a paradigm showing the effect of market forces on disposable income/The Carle Place store was a paradigm of discounters.*

parallel structure 1. The use of comparable, or coordinate, grammatical forms for sentence elements that are comparable, or coordinate, in thought: *available in white, aqua, and lemon/as useful in the home as in the shop/The site is secured. The plans are ready. The money is available.*

2. Violations of parallel structure occur when sentence elements that ought to be expressed in like grammatical forms are not, with resulting awkwardness or lack of clarity.

Knowing the answer is better than *to guess it (guessing it).*

Expansionary monetary policies will scarcely result in lower interest rates in Germany, but rather *increase the flow of capital and weakening the mark (and weaken the mark).*

Telemarketing, as a result, *can increase sales, profits, and give you a better share of the market (can increase sales, profits, and market share* [or] *can increase sales and profits, and give you a better share of the market).*

3. An article, preposition, or other word should be repeated, if necessary, to make clear the relation between the parallel sentence parts.

The board voted to acquire the building site and [to] appropriate funds for its development.

Our representative spoke to the owner and [the] manager. [Two persons]

Siemens products range from household goods to microprocessors and [from] nuclear plants to computers.

See also CORRELATIVES.

parameter Pronounced puh-*ram*-. Borrowed from mathematics, JAR-GON when used in the sense of the limits imposed by legal, political, geographic, or other factors. Other words may be simpler and more apt: *Within the parameters* (limits) *of the new ruling, they still expect to operate at a profit/If we must function within those narrow parameters* (limits), *we'll adapt/All I'm asking for is a vote on a broad parameter* (issue?), *the spending target/When you're accountable to mil-*

lions of stockholders, your performance is measured by different parameters (criteria?) *than those used in a hospital.*

paraprofessional A nonprofessional assistant to a member of a PROFESSION, as a paraprofessional in nursing or law.

parcel post See FOURTH-CLASS MAIL.

pardon See EXCUSE, PARDON.

parentheses ( ) Plural of *parenthesis*. In speaking—as for proofreading—*parentheses* is shortened to *parens* (pronounced puh-*renz*). The short singular form is *paren*. 1. Parentheses are used to enclose explanatory matter, editorial references, and letters or numbers identifying the elements in a series.

New 12-month bills are issued on the Tuesday following the auction (Wednesday, if Tuesday is a bank holiday).

Funds are also provided for the Ford Foundation-Rockefeller Foundation population research awards program (see page 46).

Congress reacted (some say overreacted) to such abuses by passing the 1976 Tax Reform Act (TRA).

Approached from the air, São Paulo resembles Chicago, with hundreds of towering buildings and traffic-charged expressways. (Actually, the population of São Paulo is three times that of Chicago.)

Expected capital expenditures could be broken down by amounts (a) to replace existing capacity, (b) to meet environmental needs, and (c) to expand capacity.

A complete sentence within parentheses begins with a capital and ends with a period only if it is outside the sentence it follows. Compare the second and fourth examples above.

2. Parentheses are used to enclose confirming figures, a practice confined mainly to legal documents: *at an annual rental of Nine thousand four hundred and fifty dollars ($9,450.00).*

3. In a financial statement, parentheses enclose figures representing a loss or other negative value.

	QUARTER ENDED			
	Mar. 31	June 30	Sept. 30	Dec. 31
Earnings (loss) per share	$3.03	$(.06)	$(.95)	$1.29

parenthetic expressions   For punctuation, see COMMA 4(a) and PA-RENTHESES.

parliamentary procedure   The rules regulating the conduct of formal deliberative bodies: governmental, corporate, and social. The basic purposes are to maintain decorum, ensure the orderly transaction of business, and determine the will of the majority, while safeguarding the rights of minorities to express their views.

Parliamentary procedure is followed in meetings of boards of trustees and the annual meetings of shareholders, as well as those of corporate committees legally accountable for their actions. However, parliamentary procedure is not well adapted to the meetings of less formally constituted groups since it does not allow for the spontaneity and free expression so valuable in ordinary discussion. Further, parliamentary procedure is based on a system of "motions" that almost invariably requires a statement of the action recommended before discussion takes place. The discussion is then confined to the merits of the motion and tends to neglect a more thorough analysis of the problem and other possible solutions.

part   "On the part of" is more simply expressed by words like *by, from,* and *among: It was disappointing to see the low turnout on the part of (by) the women workers/They welcomed the show of confidence on the part of (from) the audience/The preference for vests is strong on the part of (among) young executives.*

partially   See PARTLY, PARTIALLY.

participial close   A participial phrase that merges into the COMPLIMEN-TARY CLOSE of a letter, with or without a linking expression like "I am" or "I remain." A complete sentence, independent of the complimentary close, makes a stronger ending: *Anticipating the pleasure of hearing from you, I am (I anticipate the pleasure of hearing from you soon)/Assuring you of complete satisfaction (We assure you of complete satisfaction).* See also STEREOTYPED LETTER PHRASES.

particular   Often superfluous: *in this particular instance (in this instance)/the particular size (the size) we wanted/at this particular time (at this time, now).*

partly, partially   Although the words are synonymous, *partly* is better used in reference to part of the whole: *The order is only partly complete/The error is partly my fault/The tract is partly wooded. Partially,* on the other hand, is preferable in denoting a limitation in state or condition: *After six months, her training is only partially complete/We employ many partially disabled workers.*

party The word is well established in reference to a person on the telephone and to one engaged in a legal proceeding: *I have your party now/He is a party to the contract.* As a general synonym for person, however, *party* is slang: *He's a tough party (person) to deal with/The party (woman) with him attracted much attention.*

party selling A method of selling embraced by Mary Kay and Tupperware, among others. The company sales agent brings together a number of prospective purchasers in a neighbor's home, where the products are demonstrated, small gifts are offered, and orders are taken. The social milieu provides a relaxed atmosphere for selling.

passed, past *Passed* is a form of the verb *pass: Fully 90 percent passed the test/We have passed the site many times. Past* is a simple adjective *(past experience)*, an adverb *(past due)* or a preposition *(walked past the store).* See also **PAST.**

passive voice See **ACTIVE VOICE, PASSIVE VOICE.**

past Redundant when used with another word relating to the past: *the past history (the history) of the project/our past experience (our experience)/their past achievements (their achievements).* See also **PASSED, PAST.**

paste-up Also *pasteup.* A collage of drawn or printed materials pasted on a flat surface for reproduction on a copier or by some other method. In offset printing, also called a **MECHANICAL.**

patron A customer, particularly a regular customer, of a retail store: *Most of our patrons charge their purchases.* Also, a benefactor or supporter: *a patron of the arts/a patron of the Smithsonian Institution.*

patronize Expressions like "buy from" and "trade at" are plainer, but *patronize* has a **CONNOTATION** of refinement that is at times useful: *Our advertising should leave no doubt that we are appealing to women who patronize the finer stores.*

pay When the sense is "discharge a debt" or "remunerate for goods or services," the past tense is *paid: We paid (not payed) that bill last month. Payed* is the past tense of *pay,* meaning to let out a line by slackening, or to coat—a boat, for example—with pitch or waterproofing.

payoff   Informal: *expected a payoff* (bribe)/*Now, here's the payoff* (climax, end result; analogous to the **BOTTOM LINE**)/*The payoffs* (rewards) *of a good presentation are invariably immediate.*

payola   Slang. Originally the payment of a bribe to a disc jockey for favoring the music of a particular recording company, the term has been broadened to mean a bribe or bribery of any kind: *can't swing the deal without plenty of payola.*

payout   A dividend or dividends, including any extras: *a payout of $4.50 a share for the year.*

payroll tax   See **EMPLOYMENT TAX.**

PBX   Private branch exchange. A switchboard or, simply, "board," through which telephones in a place of business are interconnected.

P.C.   Professional corporation; a form of incorporation adopted by many physicians, as well as lawyers, accountants, and members of other professions: *Milton H. Schlachman, M.D., P.C.*

P/E   PRICE-EARNINGS RATIO.

pecuniary   Pertaining to money; financial. The term is usually limited to small private transactions: *a pecuniary interest/of pecuniary value.* But: *the organization's financial* (not *pecuniary*) *affairs.*

peddle   To hawk; to sell wares by traveling; to sell in small quantities. Sometimes used as a **PEJORATIVE**: *peddles housewares for a living/arson rings that peddle their services to businessmen.*
    —peddler, noun: *started as a peddler of dry goods.* Pejorative use: *a peddler of small favors.*

pejoratives   Words that denigrate or disparage. Pejoratives are common when argument turns from reason to emotion. Because they appeal to prejudice, they can arouse strong feelings. But for the same reason, they need to be used with care if they are used at all, for they can just as easily turn people against the user as against the person or thing that is denigrated.
    When a business proposal is disliked, it is called *simplistic, impractical, theoretical, utopian, visionary,* a *half-baked doodle,* a *harebrained scheme.* When people get in the way, they are called

obstructionists, malcontents, naysayers, zealots, pantywaists. The Republican candidate for governor of New York, accused of being a "Reaganite," returned the compliment by calling his Democratic opponent a "fast-talking lawyer." Critics of government regulation have their own pejorative vocabulary.

> Government regulation has *mushroomed* into a vast *shadow industry.* . . . *Bureaucratic sprawl* is just the tip of the iceberg. Worse, regulation often represents an *impersonal machine, impervious to control or reason.* And it is becoming a career for the thousands upon thousands of government employees who *design Byzantine systems of rules, demands, and compliances* for a living. . . . This "new class" of *powerful bureaucrats* is peopled by Federal civil servants and their counterparts in state and local government, by the *mushrooming* body of *powerful unelected legislative staffs,* and by a broad spectrum of *"public interest" professionals.* [Rawleigh Warner, Jr., in *Dun's Review* (emphasis added)]

See also **CONNOTATION** and **AD HOMINEM.**

pending 1. As an adjective, pending means "awaiting settlement or disposition," but without the threatening connotation of **IMMINENT** or **IMPENDING:** *An award in the case is still pending.*

2. As a preposition meaning "until" or "while waiting for," *pending* smacks of **JARGON,** but the alternatives do not necessarily offer improvement: *The work was delayed pending issuance of the building permit (until the building permit could be issued)/We'll withhold judgment pending receipt of (until we get) their check.*

penny The name for the one-cent coin: *short by one penny/a roll of pennies.* Also acceptably used for "cent" to emphasize a trifling sum: *costs but a few pennies.*

penultimate Next to the last. The word is often an affectation, but it should not be misconstrued for "last": *on the penultimate day of the month* (the next to the last day of the month, as August 30).

people **JARGON** when used as an attributive in certain compounds to contrast the attention given to people with that given to technical or operational matters: *His colleagues credit him with good people skills/Savings banks are people banks.* See also **PEOPLE, PERSONS.**

people, persons *People* refers to an indefinite group, large or small: *We see many people every day/People believe our ads/Several people were still waiting for their baggage. Persons* is used to single out individuals from a group: *We have had compliments from several persons/Three persons were injured.* However, neither *people* nor *persons* should be used when the group can be identified more specifically as, say, customers, workers, readers, spectators, etc.: *Many travelers* (rather than *people* or *persons*) *were inconvenienced/More sanitation workers* (not *persons*) *are to be hired/The event is planned as a great tribute to performers* (not *showpersons*) *of the past.* See also **PERSON**.

per 1. Latin for "through," "by," or "each." Formal usage sanctions expressions like **PER DIEM**, *per annum*, **PER SE**, and *per bearer*.

2. General usage sanctions such expressions as "per day," "per year," and "per dozen," but the *per* is usually better replaced by a simple article: *$10 a day/6 percent a year/$12 a dozen.*

3. In many other instances *per* is stilted and should be avoided: *as you ordered* (not *as per your order*)/*following your instructions,* or *as you instructed* (not *per* [or *as per*] *your instructions*).

perceive An unnecessarily learned word for "see" or "observe." *Perceive* is best used to suggest not only visual awareness, but mental understanding as well: *He is convinced that consultants are important because they are perceived as important.* [Robert Sherrill]/*If you* [the company's chief executive] *smile and look confident about what you're doing, people will smile back at you—and assume things are going well. Remember—you are perceived as a mirror image of "how the company is doing."* [Ronald Hoff]/*It is one of several industries that perceive interest rates as their biggest problem.* But: *As I walked through the reception room, I perceived (observed) Mr. Walker's visitor waiting to be called/If you will only examine the record, you will perceive (see) that our growth in sales has been maintained.*

—**perception,** noun: *She admitted sadly that her perception of the situation had failed her.* But: *In addition, there is a perception (impression?) among advertisers that the word "new" simply doesn't arouse consumers the way it once did.*

percent Also *per cent.* The symbol % is best confined to charts and tables. 1. Rate per hundred: *The vote was 67 percent for and 33 percent against/The bond yields 14 percent.* 2. Nonstandard in the sense of profit: *There's a good percent (profit) to be made on the deal.* See also **PERCENT, PERCENTAGE**.

percent, percentage 1. **PERCENT** is always preceded by a specific figure, as "20 percent of the gross"; percentage denotes a general amount, as "a percentage of the gross," "works for a percentage."

2. A *percentage point* is not the same as *1 percent*. For example, if interest at 10 percent goes up *2 percentage points*, it rises to 12 percent; but if interest at 10 percent goes up by *2 percent*, the interest rises to 10.2 percent (10 plus 2 percent of 10).

3. When *percent* and *percentage* are used as subjects, the noun following (or understood to follow) determines whether the verb will be singular or plural: *A 50 percent markup seems fair/What percentage of our workers are covered by dental insurance?* (Also, in the same context: *Over 90 percent* [of our workers] *are covered)/A percentage of the gate has been pledged to the Red Cross.* See also **PERCENTAGE**.

percentage 1. Better not used as a general synonym for *part: An increase of five cents a pound would compensate for only a small part* (rather than *percentage*) *of our loss.* See also **PERCENT, PERCENTAGE**.

2. Informal in the sense of *advantage: There's no percentage in offending a good customer*.

perception See at **PERCEIVE**.

per diem Pronounced pur *dee*-um or pur *die*-um. Latin for "by the day": *a per diem allowance/paid on a per diem basis.* Also, a daily expense allowance: *a per diem of $200*.

perfect Not to be qualified by *more* or *most*. See **ABSOLUTE ADJECTIVES**.

period (.) 1. The period signifies a full stop. It follows a declarative sentence, an indirect question, or a mild command or exclamation.

The company's new retail outlet is expected to be ready in October. [Declarative sentence]

I wondered what they would think of the proposal. [Indirect question]

Please sign your name at the bottom. [Mild command]

Hurray. We won. [Mild exclamation]

2. A sentence does not have to be grammatically complete to end with a period. It just has to express a unit of thought that, with other like units, expresses the idea to be communicated.

You'll spend two weeks in training. Shaping your skill. Earning a part-time income. Getting ready for the opportunities to come.

For more about sentence "fragments," see **SENTENCES** 2.

3. Periods are conventionally used after numbers or letters stand-

ing alone in an enumeration. Periods are not used after numbers or letters in parentheses.

   I. Topic
      A. Subtopic
      B. Subtopic
         1. Third-order topic
            (a) Fourth-order topic
            (b) Fourth-order topic

For other uses of periods, see **ABBREVIATIONS** and **ELLIPSES**.

period of time　Redundant: *within a reasonable period of time (within a reasonable time)*. Similar redundancies: *within a period of a year (within a year)/within 30 days' time (within 30 days)/at this point in time (at this point, at this time, at present, now)*. See **WORDINESS** 3.

periodic sentence　See **SENTENCES** 3(b).

peripheral　In computer terminology, an adjunct to the basic computer, as a printer, word processor, or additional storage: *said the acquisition would allow the company to offer total systems and peripherals to the intermediate computer systems market.*

perk　Short for **PERQUISITE**: *Company perks were severely reduced and several company cars were sold.*

permit　Better not used in such timid and superfluous introductions as "Permit me to say" and "Permit us to state." The statement should stand on its own: *Permit me to say how sorry I am (I am very sorry)/Permit us to state our view in favor of the plan (Here's why we favor the plan)*. See also **WORDINESS** 7.

perquisite　A benefit—real or psychic—that one receives in addition to salary or otherwise considers due as a right or privilege. Examples: a stock option, bonus, car or chauffeured limousine, membership in an exclusive club, select office space, executive dining room privileges. Informal, **PERK**.

per se　Pronounced pur *say* or pur *see*. Latin for "in or by itself": *The court pointed out that the tie-in sale did not per se (by itself) violate the law.*

person　The overuse of *person* is a consequence of the movement against **SEXUAL BIAS** in language. **CHAIRMAN** was an early casualty. Now *per-*

son is often needlessly or superfluously used as a sign of nondiscrimination: *Miss Haynes is spokesperson (is spokeswoman, speaks) for the Commission/Delivery persons will please use the service entrance (All deliveries should be made through the service entrance)/Cashier person wanted/The deli person (server?) will take your order.* The facetious use of *person* has also been noted: *Here is our critic person Jeffrey Lyons* [WCBS-AM radio]. See also **HE OR SHE** and **PEOPLE, PERSONS**.

personal 1. Capitalized; a notation placed on letters intended to be opened and read only by the person addressed. See **ON-ARRIVAL NOTATION**.

2. Used commercially in the sense of "for one's own use" and as a **EUPHEMISM** for "small": *a personal computer/personal-size Ivory.*

3. Redundant when used in some phrases: *a close personal friend/for personal oral hygiene* [legend on toothbrush].

See also **WORDINESS** 3 and **PERSONALLY**.

personalize To give (something) a personal quality, as to print the user's name on a letterhead, to inscribe the user's name on a pen or his initials on a tie, to fill in the name and address of the recipient on a form letter. With the help of the computer, the last-named use is carried to a ridiculous but not necessarily unprofitable extreme when the addressee's name is introduced several times in the body of a sales letter by the use of such phrases as "Your name has been selected, Mr. Jones," "You see, Mr. Jones," and "Mr. Jones, we'll be waiting to hear from you."

personally Often superfluous: *I will be there personally with my associates/Personally, I think* . . . But (acceptable): *I will attend to the matter personally* (not through a surrogate)/*Personally, I approve the idea, but I must consider the wishes of my partner* (difference emphasized).

personnel The body of individuals employed by an organization or one of its parts; often misspelled *personal* either through carelessness or the failure of one dictating to place the stress clearly where it belongs—on the last syllable.

1. A **COLLECTIVE NOUN**, *personnel* is singular when it is construed as referring to employees as a unit, and plural when it is construed as referring to employees as individuals: *The company's personnel is now*

at top strength. But (plural): *Our sales personnel are chosen largely for their personal qualities.*

2. *Personnel* is more abstract and less personal than designations like *workers, employees, engineers, lab assistants: We are lucky to have such fine personnel* (better, *such fine men and women*) *working for us.*

3. Not to be used in reference to specific members: *Five employees* (not *Five personnel*) *were cautioned about their lateness/They're the kind of people* (not *personnel*) *we want.*

persuade   See CONVINCE, PERSUADE.

persuasion   The use of ARGUMENT and APPEALS to bring about a desired RESPONSE. Effectiveness also depends on proper MOTIVATION and the degree of mutual confidence and respect already existing between persuader and persuadee.

Persuasion is not always overt, but it is essential to all communication. Its absence can be assumed when a message is too weak or misdirected in thought or feeling to achieve its purpose.

For persuasion in reports, see REPORTS 3.

PERT   The ACRONYM for *p*rogram *e*valuation and *r*eview *t*echnique, a method used by management to oversee large-scale projects. The procedure includes the formulation of a specific sequence of actions necessary to reach a desired goal and provision for effective scheduling and cost control.

Peter Principle   "In a hierarchy, every employee tends to rise to the level of his incompetence"—a way of saying that those who do a good job at one level are promoted eventually into jobs for which they are unfit. The principle is expounded in *The Peter Principle: Why Things Always Go Wrong* by Laurence J. Peter and Raymond Hull.

Ph.D.   Doctor of Philosophy, an academic degree. See FORMS OF ADDRESS 1.

phenomenon   Any perceived occurrence.   1. The plurals are *phenomena* (preferred) and *phenomenons*. Too often *phenomena* is mistakenly used as the singular, with *phenomenas* as the plural: *The seesawing market is an interesting phenomenon* (not *phenomena*). But (correct): *The phenomena of this period were rising prices, rising unemployment, and rising interest rates.*

2. *Phenomenon* is better not used when a simpler or more specific

word is available: *Armid's entry into the market is a phenomenon* (an *event*) *that deserves watching/The report cites all sorts of phenomena (facts) that could help in our planning.*

phone   Now acceptable for "telephone" (noun or verb) in all but formal or historic usage: *Use my phone/We'll phone* (or *telephone*) *tomorrow.* But: *At the time, the telephone* (rather than *phone*) *was still a novelty.*

phonogenic   Pronounced *-jen*-ik. A coined word, by analogy with *photogenic,* for a person with a pleasing voice: *a great need for telephone clerks with phonogenic voices.*

phony   Also *phoney.* Informal in its various grammatical functions and senses: *The Picasso is a phony* (not authentic)/*The guy's a phony* (an impostor, or an insincere person)/*phony nutritional claims* (fake).
   —phony up. Also *phoney up.* Slang: *phonied up* (faked) *the statistics.*

photo   CLIPPED FORM of *photograph: supplied a photo.* Not ordinarily used as a verb; but see SHOOT.

photocomposition   A keyboard typesetting (COLD TYPE) process through which type characters selected from the desired FONTS are projected onto photographic film from which printing plates are made. Contrasts with older, "hot type" methods by which metal characters have to be formed by linotype or similar process and set in place mechanically.

pica   Pronounced *pike*-uh.   1. A size of typewriter type that prints 10 characters to the inch, often preferred to the similar ELITE size for legibility in reports, executive correspondence, and material to be set for reproduction.
   2. In printing, a unit of size equal to 12 points or one sixth of an inch: *a paragraph indent of 3 picas.*

picture   1. Informal for "situation" or "circumstances," but a more specific word is usually to be preferred: *The picture (outlook) is not all dark/We'll look into the supply picture (problem)/Thus for a minimum capital investment, the hotel can greatly improve its profit picture (improve its profit outlook).*
   2. Informal for "photocopy": *Please make me a picture of this* [letter, contract, invoice, etc.].
   —get the picture. Informal: *Do you get the picture? (understand the situation?)*

piggyback To add one thing to another that is already complete in itself: *Our solution to the lack of time was to piggyback the computerized data search on a writing task already included in the course.*

Also an adjective: *has devised a piggyback sampling system for magazines* [samples encased in a slim box glued to the inside cover of a magazine].

pilot 1. Experimental, as in "pilot study," "pilot project." Often a EUPHEMISM for *test*, a word that is likely to inspire less confidence.

2. A prototype for a television series: *The pilot was run without fanfare during the summer.*

pink slip A notice of discharge from employment, particularly one enclosed in the employee's pay envelope: *received their pink slips on Friday.*

pipeline Figuratively, any channel for information, product distribution, stages in a process, etc.: *After the plant opens, it will take about three months to fill the pipeline to the dealers' shelves/With recent breakthroughs in high technology, the pipeline is full of such new composites as graphite- and carbon-reinforced polymides.*

pitch Slang. A HIGH-PRESSURE sales talk; a spiel: *must develop a pitch that will sell/came to public attention through her pitch for the Revlon perfume Charlie.* Also a verb: *pitched for Revlon.*

pitchman A PEJORATIVE for a person engaged in advertising or public relations, or anyone else who speaks for a company, product, cause, etc.: *A pitchman for the company said that the program would be a breakthrough in television presentations.*

pix Slang for movies or still pictures: *The pix are the best part of the report.*

placard Pronounced *plak*-erd. A notice, usually on heavy paper, for public display; a POSTER: *put placards in store windows.* Also a verb: *placarded the town.*

place As a verb, acceptably used in several distinctive business senses, all relating to putting something, with care, in a particular position: *We'll place* (invest) *the funds in short-term Treasury notes/The loan was placed with* (obtained from) *the Midland Bank/We'd like to place* (find employment for) *her where her managerial talents will be most useful/The book was placed with* (sold for publication to) *Doubleday.*

plain English The kind of English almost everyone wants everyone else to use; now also a goal in the movement, reinforced by state laws, to rewrite standard consumer contracts in language the ordinary citizen can understand. Documents relating to loans, credit, leases, and insurance are especially affected. See also JARGON and READABILITY.

Using plain English in consumer contracts requires reconciling such language with the more exact terminology found in the statutes themselves. When the two are at variance, the court's decision is governed by the language of the applicable statute. That may help to explain why there has been no serious movement to require plain English in contracts entered into with business clients.

The most noticeable changes in the new contract forms are (1) the absence of legal JARGON, and (2) the use of headings and enumerations to mark clearly the various provisions of the document. A fringe benefit is a probable reduction in the number of words.

1. ABSENCE OF JARGON. (a) Terms used in a document are clearly defined, as in this section from a personal auto policy:

"Family member" means a person related to you by blood, marriage or adoption who is a resident of your household. This includes a ward or foster child.

"Occupying" means in, upon, getting in, on, out or off.

"Trailer" means a vehicle designed to be pulled by a

1. Private passenger auto; or

2. Pickup, panel truck, or van

It also means a farm wagon, or farm implement while towed by a vehicle listed in 1. or 2. above.

(b) The words *you* and *we* replace terms like *the insured* and *the insurer* or *the debtor* and *the creditor;* and even the pronouns are defined:

The words *you* and *your* refer to the person or persons who applied for the account. *We, us* and *our* relate to State National Bank.

(c) JARGON is replaced by plain English.

OLD PHRASING: Debtor has good indefeasible, marketable title thereto and will warrant and defend same against all claims. Debtor is not to, and will not attempt to, transfer, sell, or encumber the collateral or use it for hire or in violation of any statute or ordinance.

NEW PHRASING: You guarantee you have good and clear title to the collateral and won't sell or dispose of it. You'll pay taxes and insurance premiums on the collateral, keep it in good repair and free from all other liens or claims against it. You'll also let us inspect it at reasonable times. You'll notify us in writing if anything happens we should know about— for instance, major damage to the collateral.

2. HEADINGS AND ENUMERATIONS. Documents in plain English look like a detailed outline. The use of HEADINGS and subheadings, ENUMERATIONS, and indentions show the relation of the parts (see figure).

plan Better followed by an infinitive than by a gerund phrase beginning with *on: We plan to test the product thoroughly* (Rather than: *We plan on testing . . .*).

—plan ahead. Although *ahead* is superfluous, its absence may be felt strongly enough to warrant its inclusion: *How are you going to succeed if you don't plan ahead?* But: *Planning* (not *Planning ahead*) *is their strong point.*

—future plans. *Future* is clearly superfluous: *What are your plans* (not *future plans*)?

See also ADVANCE PLANNING and CONCEPT, CONCEPTIONS, ETC.

plaque Regularly so spelled (not *plague*) and pronounced *plak*. A plate or tablet inscribed as an identifying or commemorative piece, usually hung on a wall. The spelling *plak* is found in commercial use as part of a trade name and possibly to prevent mispronunciation: *We will be happy to work with you in designing a plak to fit your specific needs.* [Virginia Plak Ltd.]

plastic A familiar characterization of a credit card: *With one piece of plastic, banks can now offer a variety of services.*

plateauing Moving from one job to another, but with little change in the level of responsibility: *Managers who move about are, I suspect, more readily frustrated and anxious about the prospects of plateauing than are managers who stay put.*

platform In a bank, the open area, not necessarily raised, set aside as the officers' work space: *You'll find Mr. Egan on the platform.*

PLC Public limited corporation. See LTD.

please See COURTESY AND TACT.

—please be advised. A STEREOTYPED LETTER PHRASE: *The blue-*

OLD FORM

1. **CASH ADVANCE PROGRAMS.** Customer hereby directs State Bank to treat any overdraft of his/her checking account maintained at State Bank effected by any means set forth below, exceeding **$10** in amount, as a request for a cash advance ("Advance") in the exact amount sufficient to cover such overdraft. Any such Advance shall be credited to Customer's said checking account. If Customer does not maintain a checking account at State Bank, and requests for Advance(s) are effected in the manner described in subparagraphs (iii) and (iv) below, such Advances shall be debited to Customer's Revolving Credit Account, hereunder.

A request for an Advance may be effected in any of the following ways: (i) a check drawn by Customer, or by anyone authorized by Customer to sign checks on his/her behalf, on Customer's checking account maintained at State Bank; (ii) a request on a State Bank transfer voucher or by an ordinary letter from Customer instructing State Bank to deposit such Advance in Customer's checking account; (iii) authorization of Customer to defer an indebtedness created under charge card plans of others; (iv) by drawing drafts on form(s) provided by State Bank, if State Bank has extended Check Credit privileges to Customer, or; (v) the use of a Card, by Customer or an authorized user ("User") thereof, issued by State Bank to Customer, upon Customer's request, for use in an automated cash dispenser or teller or in accessing in any other manner Customer's checking account maintained at State Bank. The use of any Card referred to above, and the rights and responsibilities of Customer or any User thereof, shall be governed by the terms and conditions of this Agreement, to the extent applicable to the use of such Card(s) by the terms hereof, and of any other Agreement pertaining to the use of such Card(s), the terms of which are incorporated by reference and made a part hereof.

NEW FORM

HOW TO USE YOUR PRIVILEGE CHECKING ACCOUNT. You may use your Account to get automatic cash loans (Advances) in any of the following ways:

- **Overdrawing Your State Bank Checking Account**
  (1) **By writing a check.** If you write a check that is over $10 more than you have in your checking account, we will treat this overdraft as a request for an Advance in the exact amount of the overdraft. We will honor overdrafts by anyone you authorize to sign checks for you.
  (2) **By using a State Bank Cash Machine.** If you use your State Bank card or State Bank's Master Charge or Visa Card in a State Bank Cash Machine to withdraw money from your checking account, we will treat any overdraft of **$10** or more as a request for an Advance in the exact amount of the overdraft. We will honor overdrafts by anyone you authorize to use your card.
  (3) **By any other way you can use your checking account.** Any way you overdraw, the Advance will be deposited in your checking account and charged to your Privilege Checking Account.

- **Requesting A Transfer To Your Checking Account**
  We will treat as a request for an Advance, any State Bank transfer voucher or an ordinary letter from you instructing us to deposit an Advance in your State Bank checking account.

- **Using Your Check Credit Privileges**
  If we give you Check Credit Privileges, any checks you draw on the forms we provide will be treated as requests for an Advance.

Plain English. Section of a consumer contract before and after adoption of New York State's "Plain English" law *prints you inquired about will be ready on Thursday* (rather than *Please be advised that the blueprints . . .*).

plug Informal for "mention favorably": *I'm not here to plug anything.* Also informal as a noun: *The plug in the* Time *story can't hurt us.*

plug-compatible Machine components and MODULES that can be integrated into existing equipment made by the same or another manufacturer: *National Semiconductor offers units plug-compatible with IBM Series 4300 computers.*

plurality 1. In a contest, a number greater than any other in the set. When three or more alternatives are presented, the plurality may be less than half; more than half is a MAJORITY: *With four candidates in the race, only a plurality was required to win.* 2. The number of votes by which a competitor wins over the closest rival: *won by a plurality of thirty-two votes.*

plurals Almost all nouns undergo some change in the plural.

1. COMMON ENDINGS.   2. COMPOUNDS.   3. PROPER NAMES.
4. FOREIGN WORDS.

For special cases, see also ABBREVIATIONS 5, APOSTROPHE 1 and 3, and NUMERALS 10.

1. COMMON ENDINGS.   (a) The plurals of most words are formed by the addition of *s* or *es: files, menus, radios; sashes, taxes.*

(b) A final *y* following a consonant is changed to *i*, and *es* is added: *copies, cities, thirties;* but (*y* preceded by a vowel): *attorneys, surveys, forays.*

(c) An *f* or *fe* ending is changed to *v*, with *es* following: *halves, selves, wives;* but (exceptions): *beliefs, proofs, wharfs* (or *wharves*).

(d) Some nouns have the same form in the singular and the plural. Many of them, but not all, end with an *s* or *z* sound; and some that end with a silent *s* in the singular have a voiced ending in the plural.

headquarters	aeronautics	chassis (*sing.,* -see; *pl.,* -seez)
proceeds	economics	
scissors	mathematics	corps (*sing.,* kohr; *pl.,* kohrz)

2. COMPOUNDS.   (a) When a noun comprises two or more words, only the key word takes the plural form: *letters of credit, attorneys-at-law, points of view, provost marshals, trade unions, assistant attorneys general.*

(b) When the two words composing a compound are equally

significant, both are plural: *women delegates, secretaries-treasurers, professors emeriti.*

(c) When a noun is joined to a preposition or adverb, the noun is given the plural ending: *passersby, runners-up, goings-on.* However, when none of the words composing a compound is a noun, the last word is given the plural ending: *sit-ins, go-betweens, run-throughs, come-ons.* See also **HYPHEN.**

3. PROPER NAMES. (a) The plurals of proper names, including those ending in *y*, are formed by the addition of *s* or *es*. Names with the suffixes Jr., II, 2d, etc., usually add the plural ending to the surname, though it may be appended to the suffix in informal usage.

the Adamses   the Walter Kennedys
the Cohens   the Henry Lucases
the Philip Bradys Jr. [*or, informal:* the Philip Brady Jrs.]
But: owns two Mercedes [no change in plural]
the new Mercurys

(b) When two or more persons are addressed by title, only the titles are plural.

Mr. and Mrs. Daly
the Drs. Greenfield [two or more doctors by that name]
the Reverends Palmer and Courtney
the Misses Conley and Bragg

See also **FORMS OF ADDRESS** 2.

4. FOREIGN WORDS. Many words of foreign origin have only the foreign plural *(strata, stimuli)*; others have an Anglicized plural but retain the foreign plural as well *(tempos, tempi; indexes, indices).* Where both forms exist, the Anglicized plural is usually preferred in ordinary use, while the foreign plural is usually confined to some scientific or other specialized use.

The starred words in the following table are treated in the main vocabulary.

SINGULAR	ANGLICIZED PLURAL	FOREIGN PLURAL
*addendum	addendums	addenda
*agendum (also, preferred, agenda)	agendas	agenda (rare)
*alumna	——	alumnae (-nee)
*alumnus	——	alumni (-nye)
analysis	——	analyses (-seez)
apparatus	apparatuses	apparatus (same as singular)

SINGULAR	ANGLICIZED PLURAL	FOREIGN PLURAL
automaton	automatons	automata (rare)
axis	——	axes (*ak*-seez)
basis	——	bases (*bay*-seez)
bureau	bureaus	bureaux (rare)
cactus	cactuses	cacti
candelabrum	candelabrums	candelabra (preferred)
cello	cellos	celli (*cheh*-lee)
crisis	——	crises (-seez)
*criterion	criterions	criteria (preferred)
curriculum	curriculums	curricula
datum (also, preferred, *data)	——	data
diagnosis	——	diagnoses (-seez)
emphasis	——	emphases (-seez)
*erratum	——	errata
focus	focuses	foci (-sigh)
*formula	formulas	formulae (-lee)
*graffito (also graffiti)	——	graffiti
hiatus	hiatuses	hiatus (rare)
*honorarium	honorariums	honoraria
hypothesis	——	hypotheses (-seez)
impediment	impediments	impedimenta
*index	indexes	indices
indicium	indicias	*indicia
insigne	insignias	*insignia
matrix (*may*-trix)	matrixes	matrices (-seez)
maximum	maximums	maxima (rare)
*medium	mediums	media
memorabile (rare)	——	memorabilia
minimum	minimums	minima (rare)
*minutia	——	minutiae
nucleus	nucleuses (rare)	nuclei (-klee-eye)
oasis	——	oases (-seez)
opera (musical drama)	operas	——
*opus (a literary or musical composition)	opuses	opera
[No singular]	——	paraphernalia (sometimes takes singular verb)
*phenomenon	phenomenons (rare)	phenomena

SINGULAR	ANGLICIZED PLURAL	FOREIGN PLURAL
prospectus	prospectuses	——
residuum	residuums	residua
serum	serums	sera
status	statuses	——
stigma	stigmas	stigmata
stimulus	——	stimuli (-lie)
*stratum	stratums	strata
synopsis	——	synopses (-seez)
tempo	tempos	tempi (-pee)
thesis	——	theses (-seez)
ultimatum	ultimatums	ultimata
virtuoso	virtuosos	virtuosi (-see)

plus Plural, *pluses.* A versatile word calling for special care only in uses 3 and 4.

1. Adjective, "being in addition": *a plus factor/rated a B-plus.* Used only informally, however, in the sense of an increase beyond normal expectations: *In Del Monte products, you get quality plus.*

2. Noun, "an added advantage": *should be regarded as a plus/a plan with many pluses.* The term "extra plus" must be regarded as **HYPERBOLE:** *Having the bar in the well-lit lobby is an extra plus for women residents.*

3. Preposition, "in addition to": In arithmetic expressions, *plus* is followed by either a singular or a plural verb: *Two plus two is* (or *are*) *four.* When, however, the words joined by *plus* are not numerals, a following verb normally takes the number of the subject: *The payments plus the interest come to $456.75.* [The subject *payments* is plural.] Any resulting awkwardness can be avoided by ignoring the rule or by substituting *and* for *plus: The dividend plus the extras comes to $4 per share* [The subject *dividend* is singular. The alternatives are "The dividend *plus* the extras come to $4 a share" and "The dividend *and* the extras come to $4 a share."]

4. Conjunction, "besides," "also." This is an informal usage found mainly in advertising copy. Even so, it is more easily acceptable when followed by a phrase than by a clause. Phrase [following first sentence]: *We have the only big, comfortable 747s flying to and from Ireland. Plus the most flights to Ireland and the best connections between Ireland and Britain or the Continent.* Clause [following first sentence]:

Poof (insecticide) *is not toxic to humans. Plus a small can around the kitchen lasts for months.*

p.m. For "push money," a bonus offered by a manufacturer or distributor to retail salespersons to promote the sale of their own brands over those of competing brands; often given without the knowledge of the store proprietors. The practice is unethical and unfair to consumers who, ignorant of the duplicity, may be persuaded to buy inferior or overpriced goods.

For P.M. in expressions of time, see A.M., P.M.

podium A DAIS, especially one used by a musical conductor.

point in time See at TIME.

point of fact The phrase "as a point of fact" is wordy for "in reality," "actually," or "in fact": *As a point of fact (In fact), we have already agreed to the terms.*

point of purchase Abbreviated POP (pronounced pee-oh-pee). A marketing term for the place, usually a retail store, where goods are sold to the consumer: *Some advertising is most effective at the point of purchase. Point-of-purchase advertising,* often provided by the retailer's suppliers, includes special displays, counter cards, posters, streamers, SHELF-TALKERS, etc.

point of view See VIEWPOINT.

points In mortgage financing, a measure of the amount paid to a mortgage company in addition to the interest charged. A point is a one-time fee equal to one percent of the mortgage. Thus a 4-point fee on a $50,000 mortgage comes to $2,000.

pointy-headed Informal for "lacking brains." Often joined prejudicially to words like *liberal* and *do-gooder.* See also PEJORATIVES.

POP See POINT OF PURCHASE.

portentous So spelled, and pronounced *-ten*-tus (not *ten*-shus). Awesome, sometimes ominous: *These are portentous times.*

portfolio 1. The securities and other instruments owned by an individual, a financial house, or other organization; also the list of such investments: *a diversified portfolio/a portfolio worth $2 million.*
    2. A book or portable case containing samples of the work of a

copywriter, artist, or photographer, among others; also the name for the collective work of such a person: *asked to see her portfolio/carried his portfolio to the interview/a dazzling portfolio developed over a long career.*

position 1. A financial commitment or investment, especially in the commodities market: *an initial position in wheat/closed out several positions.*

2. The place occupied by an advertisement in any print or broadcast advertisement, at top of page, inside front cover, sports section, 9 p.m. station break, and so on.

3. To position a product is to give it a distinctive place in the market alongside its competitors. Whereas, for example, most bottled waters are cheap substitutes for unpotable tap water, Perrier entered the American market by *positioning* it as a high-image imported water to be used as a mixer or as a beverage in its own right. Compare REPOSITION.

4. In personnel JARGON, to position is to fill a job vacancy: *The company will concentrate on positioning the new operation with trained real-estate people.* See also JOB, POSITION.

—in a position. Wordy for *able: We are not in a position (not able) to enter into a franchise arrangement now/As soon as she was in a position (able) to act, she bought the shares.*

position of modifiers 1. The intended sense of a sentence is best conveyed when modifiers are placed as close as possible to the words they modify.

AMBIGUOUS: Mexico will get a $450 million credit to buy U.S. farm products *from 26 banks.*

IMPROVED: Mexico will get a $450 million credit *from 26 banks* to buy U.S. farm products.

AMBIGUOUS: Mr. Bono passed on your request for credit *to me.*

IMPROVED: Mr. Bono passed on *to me* your request for credit.

AMBIGUOUS: She would be in dire straits if she were to lose what she now has *by improvident investment.*

IMPROVED: She would be in dire straits if she were to lose *by improvident investment* what she now has.

AMBIGUOUS: *If possible,* I would enjoy your company for lunch next week.

IMPROVED: I would enjoy your company for lunch, next week *if possible.* [The comma also helps.]

2. A long modifying phrase or clause following the subject may

unnecessarily separate the subject from its predicate verb. The fault can be corrected if the sentence is recast or divided to form two sentences.

LONG INTERVENTION: The company's restructured operations, adapted to the market section we serve, are shown in the following chart.

IMPROVED: The following chart shows the company's restructured operations, adapted to the market section we serve. [The subject is shifted from *operations* to *chart*.]

LONG INTERVENTION: These rates, which include allowances for depreciation of fixed assets, guard services, and health services, which were not previously recognized in the accounts, closely approximate our actual cost.

IMPROVED: These rates closely approximate our actual cost. They include allowances for depreciation of fixed assets, guard services, and health services, which were not previously recognized in the accounts.

See also **CORRELATIVES, DANGLING MODIFIERS, ONLY,** and **SPLIT INFINITIVE.**

positive From its original meaning of "certain," positive is now acceptably used to express affirmation: *gave a positive answer/took a positive step to acquiring ownership.*

positive and negative words The desire to use words with a good CONNOTATION may require a choice between positive words and negative words. *Positive words* are affirmative and reassuring: *can, benefit, pleased, efficient, promptly. Negative words* suggest denial and may otherwise create discomfort or aversion: *cannot, loss, delay, sorry, unfair, unfortunately.* The difference between positive and negative words is not necessarily one of substance. "We are open till 5 P.M." and "We close at 5 P.M." have essentially the same meaning, but the one is an invitation and the other a warning.

See also **COURTESY AND TACT.**

1. As the last illustration suggests, a negative statement can sometimes be turned into a positive one by a simple reversal of terms.

NEGATIVE: The garment will not be ready before Thursday.

POSITIVE: The garment will be ready on Thursday.

NEGATIVE: It's a mistake to buy a car without first looking into the cost of a personal bank loan.

POSITIVE: It's a good idea to look into the cost of a personal bank loan before buying a car.

NEGATIVE: A company that is stingy with fringe benefits for its employees operates at a competitive disadvantage in the labor market.

POSITIVE: A company that provides its employees with a full range of fringe benefits has a competitive edge in the labor market.

2. Sometimes it takes not just a change of language to avoid a negative statement, but a change in point of view as well. See also "YOU" VIEWPOINT.

NEGATIVE: We hope there will be no recurrence of this unfortunate delay in filling your order.

POSITIVE: We'll certainly be more careful about filling your future orders promptly.

NEGATIVE: You failed to tell us if you will be at the meeting.

POSITIVE: Will you please let us know if you will be at the meeting.

NEGATIVE: This matter does not come within our jurisdiction.

POSITIVE: This matter comes within the jurisdiction of the Department of Labor.

See also ACTIVE VOICE, PASSIVE VOICE 3.

3. Negative words may unwittingly reveal the user's insecurity.

NEGATIVE: I hope this letter answers your question without adding to the confusion.

POSITIVE: If you still have a question, by all means let me know.

4. When complete avoidance of negative words is either not politic or not possible, it may still be practical to soften them or reduce their number.

NEGATIVE: Please accept our apologies for the inconvenience you suffered through our unfortunate mistake.

IMPROVED: Please accept our apologies for the inconvenience caused you.

Or, when the context permits: Please accept our apologies.

5. When a positive word cannot be found to provide an apt replacement for a negative word, a word with a neutral connotation may yet work an improvement. In answers to customers' complaints, for instance, it would be better to make reference to "your letter" than to "your complaint"; and words like "your experience" or "the treatment you received" might prove more calming than a reference to the precise form of mistreatment the customer has written about.

positively   See ABSOLUTELY, POSITIVELY.

possession For rules governing the formation of the possessive case of nouns and pronouns, see **APOSTROPHE** 1.

possessive with gerund The gerund is an *-ing* form of a verb *(going, doing, taking)* used as a noun. A noun or pronoun modifying the gerund is sometimes possessive in form: *Dave's going* (not *Dave going) was a surprise.* The possessive form is avoided, however, when the resulting locution would be awkward and when the modifier of the gerund rather than the gerund itself receives the emphasis.

POSSESSIVE FAVORED:

We will appreciate *your* returning the damaged part.

Kline's boasting was one of his less attractive qualities.

GM's closing of the plant was understandable.

DIVIDED USAGE:

We were surprised to hear of *Robinson's* (or *Robinson*) getting the contract.

The *pipe's* (or *pipe*) bursting was only a minor disaster.

We object to a *worker's* (or *worker*) quitting his job without notice.

POSSESSIVE AVOIDED:

We object to *workers* quitting their jobs without notice.

It was a case of *enthusiasm* getting out of hand.

The chances of the *president* being voted down were slim.

possibly Redundant when used with *may: They hinted that they may* (not *may possibly) change their plans.* See **WORDINESS** 3.

postal card, postcard A *postal card* is a government mailing card with the postage imprinted on the face. A *postcard* is a private mailing card, which requires a stamp or a postage-paid imprint requiring a permit. A double postcard is folded to allow one panel to be used for reply. The size of postcards is regulated by the U.S. Postal Service.

postindustrial Relating to a time when the production of goods will be superseded in importance by the professional and technical knowledge that makes production possible: *A "postindustrial" society ruled by experts is a myth.* [Morris Janowitz, University of Chicago]

postscript 1. A postscript is usually avoided in ordinary correspondence on the theory that a well thought-out letter should not need one. On the other hand, the postscript receives so much attention that it is often deliberately used, particularly for an important point in a sales or collection letter.

2. The letter postscript begins a couple of spaces below the last typed line. The first line is indented only if the paragraphs are also indented. The abbreviation P.S. (and P.P.S. for a second postscript) is optional. The postscript should be hand-initialed by the signer of the letter. See also **LETTER FORM** 3.

posttesting See **PRETESTING**.

posture Vogue word for "attitude": *What's your posture regarding Mr. Bly? Posture* is better used in the sense of a frame of mind or bias affecting action: *Our posture toward the visit of Mr. Albers will be correct but cool/Now that the Mayor has taken a conservative posture toward budget increases, he has won a new constituency in the business community.*

PR Abbreviation of **PUBLIC RELATIONS**.

practical, practicable The distinction is sometimes elusive. *Practical* means useful, not theoretical; also, experienced through practice: *a practical solution/a practical thinker/practical instruction.*

Practicable, on the other hand, means feasible, capable of being effected or put into practice: *The plan seems practicable/After work was started, the project was abandoned as not practicable* [that is, *not feasible; not practical* would have changed the meaning to *not useful*].

practically 1. Best used in the sense of "in a practical manner" or "from a practical point of view": *A doer rather than a dreamer, she thinks practically/Practically, it would be wise to offer a modest contribution to the campaign.*

2. *Practically* is not a good synonym for "almost" and is especially to be avoided when the statement it introduces is contrary to fact: *They were gone almost* (rather than *practically*) *an hour/They almost* (not *practically*) *succeeded in their caper.*

3. *Virtually* is preferable to *practically* in expressing the idea of "essentially" or "in effect, if not in fact": *The work is virtually* (rather than *practically*) *complete/There is virtually* (rather than *practically*) *no call now for nonelectric typewriters.*

precede To come (or go) before. So spelled (not -ceed): *will precede you to the platform.* But compare **PROCEED**.

precedence So spelled, and pronounced prih-*see*-dens or *press*-ih-dens: *takes precedence over the earlier directive.*

précis Pronounced *pray*-see or pray-*see*. Plural, also *précis*, but pronounced *pray*-seez or pray-*seez*. A concise summary of the important data in an article, report, or other text. *Summary* and **ABSTRACT** are the more common terms.

predate See at **ANTEDATE**.

predilection So spelled, and pronounced *pred*-uh-(or *pree*-duh-)lek-shun. An inclination or disposition: *a predilection toward venturesome investments.*

preface See at **FOREWORD** and **REPORTS** 1 (chart).

prefer Usually completed by *to* or *instead of: I prefer the desk calculator to the hand-held one/We prefer acting on the information we have instead of waiting for a lucky break.* However, when *prefer* is followed by an infinitive, it may be completed by *rather than* and another infinitive: *We prefer to act rather than wait.* [The *to* before *wait* is understood.] But (also acceptable): *We prefer to act instead of waiting/We would rather act than wait/We prefer acting to waiting.* See also **RATHER THAN**.

preferable Accented on the first syllable *(pref-)* and followed by *to*, not *rather than: We consider selective price increases preferable to a flat across-the-board increase.*

prefixed words A hyphen does not usually separate the parts of a prefixed word *(antedate, macroeconomics, multimedia, subcontractor, underemployed).* But see **HYPHEN** 2 for exceptions.

prejudice See **BIAS, PREJUDICE**.

prejudice words See **PEJORATIVES**.

premier Pronounced *pre*-me-ur or prim-*eer*. First in rank or importance; also the first in time: *our premier line of upholstery fabrics/the premier actor of his generation/the premier showing.*

premiere Also *première*. Pronounced prim-*eer* or prum-*yair*. 1. The first presentation of a public performance, as a movie, play, trade show: *attended the premiere of Burlington's "Fabrics Ahoy" at the Waldorf.*

Also, in the theater, descriptive of the leading lady: *the premiere danseuse*.

2. Informal as a verb: *The show will premiere on January 28.*

premise 1. To premise is to state a supposition from which a logical conclusion can be drawn. The word is often used when *assume* would be more apt and less pretentious: *What he is premising (assuming) is that one or more of his market positions will fully justify his confidence in them/In seeking additional capital, they are premising (assuming, counting on) a fourfold increase in demand for their products.*

2. As a noun, used only in the plural in referring to a building or part of one: *put up the premises for sale/vacate the premises.*

premium "At a premium" means both in short supply (*Office space is at a premium*) and at a price above what would ordinarily be expected (*Fall wheat was in demand and sold at a premium*). To "put a premium on" is to place a high value on: *We put a premium on innovation.*

pre-owned See PREVIOUSLY OWNED.

preparatory to Pretentious for "before": *I'll phone you preparatory to (before) leaving.*

preplanning A benign REDUNDANCY for "planning" or "preparation" to emphasize, intentionally or not, the idea of work that must be done beforehand: *Successful magazine startups don't just happen. They are the result of much preplanning.* But: *Our planning (rather than preplanning) for the advertising campaign will include an extensive study of the client's distribution network.* See also FORWARD PLANNING.

prepositions 1. At end of sentence. The idea that a sentence must not end with a preposition has only limited application: The preposition is better not placed at the end when it is awkward there.

> BAD: They asked what conditions we'd sell the serial rights to the book *under.*

> BETTER: They asked *under* what conditions we'd sell the serial rights to the book.

In many instances, the end is the most natural place for the preposition.

> His is the only side of the story I'm acquainted *with.*
>
> What is the customer complaining *about?*
>
> They're the kind of client we're aiming *for.*
>
> It's not an organization we'd want to compete *against.*

2. Omitted preposition. A second preposition may be needed to preserve idiomatic usage.

> INCORRECT OMISSION: I appreciate Mr. Nelson's confidence and support *of* this study. [*Confidence* and *support* take different prepositions.]
>
> BETTER: I appreciate Mr. Nelson's confidence *in* and support *of* this study.

If the last construction seems a bit heavy, it can be avoided, e.g., "I appreciate Mr. Nelson's support of this study," or "I appreciate Mr. Nelson's support and his confidence in this study." In the latter sentence, *support* stands alone, and the prepositional phrase applies only to *confidence*.

3. Double preposition. Two prepositions are not always better than one: *at a cost of from $8 to $10* (omit *from*). See also OF 1.

4. Unintentional repetition. Sometimes a preposition is unintentionally repeated: *To what do we owe this pleasure to?* (Omit the first or last *to*.) But for the intentional repetition of a preposition to make clear the relation between parallel sentence parts, see PARALLEL STRUCTURE 3.

For the substitution of a simple preposition for a connecting phrase, see WORDINESS 4.

prepossessive words* Just as PEJORATIVES create a bias against someone or something, so prepossessive words create a bias in favor. Unlike EUPHEMISMS, however, they are not substitutes for disagreeable synonyms, but appeal instead to a predilection or favorable opinion already entertained by the reader or listener. Invariably emotive, they are intended to arouse such feelings as sympathy, patriotism, security, love of fine things, and respect for traditional values.

> Pendleton fabrics, made in the rugged proving ground of the Pacific Northwest.
>
> The European handling characteristics of the Mark T/A tires are maintained on wet and dry road surfaces.
>
> Strange how many modern ideas in car design have come out of an ancient town in Bavaria. [Audi]
>
> To reduce a kid's fever fast, Bayer has just what the doctor ordered.
>
> Think of the Hickey-Freeman suit as an investment in your future.
>
> Taylor's Champagne. America at its best.

---

*The term "prepossessive words" is borrowed from Edward J. Kilduff's *Knowing and Using Words* (Harper, 1941). It seemed like the most apt term for the kind of words described.

My husband and I hunt almost every weekend during the season. It brings us closer together because we both share a love for the outdoors. Being a member of NRA is like belonging to a large family. We are people who share common interests like environmental conservation and wildlife preservation. [Sandra Curry, quoted in an advertisement of the National Rifle Association of America, *Time* magazine]

preprint   A copy printed in advance; especially a copy of a forthcoming advertisement sent by the advertiser to distributors and salespeople for their information—a way of igniting interest and ensuring preparedness for the anticipated response.

prescreen   Though *screen* itself suggests a preliminary weeding out or classification, *prescreen* is useful in describing the first of several steps in the process. A list of prospective customers, for example, may be prescreened by reference to their residential address (or ZIP Code), business status, or type of list from which their names were obtained. Then, after an initial solicitation, the names of those responding favorably may be turned over to a credit agency for a final determination of their financial responsibility.

   Prescreen should not be used when only a single screening is involved: *Candidates for the program are screened* (not *prescreened*) *to determine their entry level.*

presenter   A celebrity, usually from fashion or entertainment, employed as a media spokesperson for a product or service. The ranks have included Danny Kaye (Polaroid), Frank Sinatra (Chrysler), Lauren Bacall (High Point), and John Houseman (Smith Barney).

presently   Soon; in a short time. Because the word is often taken to mean "now" or "at once," it is better avoided altogether: *Judge Dane is presently* (at present? soon?) *hearing arguments in the case/Foster is currently* (rather than *presently*) *the company's counsel.*

present time   Redundant. See TIME 1.

present writer   See WRITER.

press agent   A person engaged to obtain favorable publicity for an individual or organization, sometimes through advertising, but more often through press releases, "tips" to columnists, and planned events. For synonyms with better connotations, see EUPHEMISM.

press agentry   The work of the PRESS AGENT; often used as a PEJOR-

ATIVE: *The press agentry included parading a live lion through the hotel lobby.*

press release   See NEWS RELEASES.

presume, presumption, presumably   See ASSUME, PRESUME.

pretesting   Testing in advance to determine the potential of, say, a trainee, a questionnaire, the market for a new product, and so forth. Contrasts with *posttesting,* which measures actual performance, as on the job or in the marketplace.

pretty   Informal for "somewhat," "moderately": *is pretty well informed/gets pretty tired/works pretty hard.* Better not used in contradiction to a following adjective or adverb: *had a serious* (not *pretty serious*) *accident/worked diligently* (not *pretty diligently*).

preventive, preventative   The former is preferred to its LONG VARIANT for simplicity and ease of pronunciation: *a rust preventive.*

previously owned   Also *pre-owned.* A EUPHEMISM for used or secondhand: *many previously owned Cadillacs to choose from.*

previous to   Pretentious for "before": *Previous to (Before) coming to us, she was an engineer with Boeing/We could not have provided the figures previous to (before) today.*

price-earnings ratio   Abbreviated P/E ratio. The current market price of a company's stock divided by the annual earnings per share. Thus a stock selling for $100 and earning $10 a share has a price-earnings ratio of 10. The P/E ratio, usually included in newspaper stock quotations, is regarded as a measure of a stock's value.

price tag   A picturesque rendering of "price": *The price tag is a mere $53.* Also a perverse way of expressing the kind of figure not usually found on a "tag": *carries a price tag of $100 million for the first year alone/and the price tag for all this luxury is a mere $200,000.*

pricey   High-priced: *At $300,000, the lavish fashion show was a pricey advertisement for the line.* The comparative and superlative forms are *pricier* and *priciest: A case in point is Hong Kong's invasion at the pricier end of the market.*

prime rate   Also "the prime." The publicly announced interest rate a bank charges on loans to its best corporate customers. In practice, the rate may be somewhat lower than the prime on short-term credits.

principal, principle As an adjective, *principal* stands for "chief," "foremost," "highest in rank or worth": *the principal negotiator/the principal advantage/the principal sum*. As a noun, *principal* denotes a person or organization in a key position; the main body of assets in an estate; or the funds in an interest-bearing account in a bank, mutual fund, etc.: *the principal* (chief party) *in the transaction/the principal* (corpus) *of the estate/withdrew the dividends, but left the principal untouched.*

Principle is used only as a noun. It stands for a rule, basic truth, or ethical standard: *a principle of the law of liability/a matter of principle/a principle on which the company was founded.*

printout The printed data or message representing the output of a computer, word processor, or similar machine.

priority mail For first-class mail weighing over 12 ounces and packages not exceeding 70 pounds. Rates vary according to weight and delivery zone.

prioritize JARGON for "to give priority to": *The city's energy code prioritizes residential users/There was some question as to how the department would prioritize its services if its budget were cut.* See also **-IZE, -IZATION.**

prior to More simply, *before: We always check the buyer's credit prior to (before) filling an order/The number of errors was far greater prior to the installation of the new inventory system (before we installed the new inventory system).*

Private Not to be used for "Personal" on a letter intended to be opened and read only by the person addressed. See also **ON-ARRIVAL NOTATION.**

private brand Also *private label* or *house brand*. The BRAND NAME adopted by a particular dealer or distributor for some or all of the goods it sells. Kenmore, a name adopted by Sears for many of its electric appliances, is such a brand. Goods bearing private brands are often made or processed by large companies that sell the identical goods under their own names.

private sector Collectively, businesses and institutions privately owned or run, as opposed to government-controlled enterprises (the *public sector*): *Public-sector jobs are only a high-cost palliative until jobs in the private sector can be enlarged.* [Marvin R. Feldman]

privatization   Turning over to private interests certain enterprises and functions heretofore under government control: *There is a knee-jerk reaction that privatization is always better* [New York's Sanitation Commissioner Norman Steisel on a failed program that allowed private towing companies to remove abandoned cars from the city's streets]/*One proposed change echoing the privatization theme of the Administration would allow nursing homes to have themselves inspected by the Joint Commission on Accreditation of Hospitals* [a nongovernmental organization dominated by health-care providers] *rather than by a state agency under federal supervision.*

proceed   To move forward. So spelled (not -cede), and pronounced pro-*seed: Proceed slowly.* But, *procedure,* not *proceedure: The procedure is simple.* Compare **PRECEDE.**

proceeds   Noun, plural only; pronounced *pro*-seeds. Funds realized from a sale, investment, or other source. It is not always clear whether the proceeds represent total revenue or the net sum after costs are deducted: *The proceeds of the bond issue came to $120 million/The authors will share the proceeds of the sale of the film rights to the book/The entire proceeds of the performance have been pledged to the Actors Fund.*

process   To process is to subject to a special course of treatment: *The metal is processed by heat infusion.* To process, in the nonmanufacturing sense of "to subject to a particular procedure" or "to deal with," is on less sure ground; but objections notwithstanding, the usage is well established: *Your application will be processed immediately/Your order is now being processed.*
—in the process of.   Usually superfluous: *We are now in the process of renovating our old warehouse (We are now renovating . . .).* See **WORDINESS** 2.

procure   Pompous for **OBTAIN, GET:** *We will be glad to procure (obtain) the tickets for you.*

procurement   Also *buying, purchasing. Procurement* is usually reserved for reference to the acquisition of everything needed to run a large-scale industry or governmental enterprise: *in charge of procurement for the Navy.*

producer goods   A synonym for **CAPITAL GOODS.**

product identification code   See **UNIFORM PRODUCT CODE.**

productivity Roughly, the value of wealth created in relation to the expenditure of money, labor, energy, and other forms of input: *reported a decline in manufacturing productivity/productivity in the nonfarm sector/cut plant personnel by 10 percent without loss of productivity.*

product mix The various products made or carried by a company and their relation to each other. A compatible blend is usually sought, though there are some notable exceptions: *They felt that General Electric's product mix came closest to their own.*

product placement The business of the PRODUCT PLACER: *Product placement has become so common there are even seminars about it.*

product placer An entrepreneur who represents certain brand name products and arranges with producers of movies and television shows to use them as props in their productions. As a result of a product placer's efforts, for example, the script for the film *Rocky III* was amended to include a Wheaties scene, in which Rocky advises his young son to eat the "breakfast of champions" if he wants to grow up big and strong.

profession An occupation requiring advanced academic study and, usually, accreditation by some legally or otherwise formally constituted body: *chose accounting for her profession.* Calling any trade or vocation a profession demeans those callings more worthy of the name: *is a carpenter by trade* (not *by profession*). Used, though, in the manner of "a member of the barbering *profession,*" the term is facetious. But also see PROFESSIONAL.

professional One who excels in any kind of work, not necessarily a PROFESSION: *She's a real professional/The robbery is unquestionably the work of professionals.* Also descriptive of any work done for pay or of any work well done: *requires a professional carpenter/expect their typists to do professional work.*

professional ratings See FORMS OF ADDRESS 1.

professor Abbreviated *Prof.* See also FORMS OF ADDRESS 1. The shortened form *prof (hired a former prof)* is used only informally.

profile A biographical sketch; also a demographic representation of a particular group, as a magazine audience, showing age range, income, type of employment, home ownership, and similar data: *issued a profile of the new chairman/the subject of a* New Yorker *profile/a profile of* Good Housekeeping *readers.* See also LOW PROFILE.

profile matching In advertising, the practice of selecting **MEDIA** that reach audiences exhibiting characteristics similar to those of prime buyers of the products to be sold. A particular medium may thus be selected on the basis of geographical coverage and such other audience attributes as age, sex, income, home ownership, **LIFESTYLE**, and the like.

profit center A part of a company's business, as a subsidiary or a product line, that contributes significantly to the company's profits: *wants an executive with a proven record in managing an international company's profit center/such programs as those offered by SuperStation WTBS, Ted Turner's profit center.*

pro forma Latin, "as a matter of form." 1. Normal, routine, not exceptional: *a pro forma hearing before the Board/a pro forma selection.*
2. In finance, descriptive of a financial statement using assumed data to show in advance the effect of hypothetical events: *a pro forma income statement hypothesizing the merger of the two companies.*

program A set of instructions prepared for computer use. See **SOFTWARE**.

program announcement An advertisement, or "commercial," in a broadcast program sponsored in whole or in part by the advertiser. Compare **SPOT ANNOUNCEMENT**.

programmer Also *programer.* One who designs the instructions, or "programs," for use in computers.

progressive tax A tax at a rate that increases with the amount taxed. The federal income tax is progressive in that, up to certain limits, the rates are higher on large incomes than on small. A *regressive tax,* on the other hand, places a disproportionately large burden on low incomes.

prohibit Preferably followed by the preposition *from: was prohibited from entering the premises* (rather than *was prohibited to enter the premises*).

promulgate A pretentious rendering of "proclaim" or "put into effect"; more suited to use by government than by business: *when we promulgated (established) this procedure* (or *put this procedure into effect*).

pronouns Although pronouns are essentially noun substitutes, they often raise questions that nouns do not. Is it clear what the pronoun—*it,* for example—stands for? Is the nominative or objective case to be used—*I* or *me?* *she* or *her?* *they* or *them?* Is the pronoun—say, *none* or *everyone*—to be treated as singular or plural, masculine or feminine? Such are the questions addressed here.

1. REFERENCE.   2. CASE.   3. AGREEMENT IN NUMBER.

1. REFERENCE.   (a) The antecedent of a pronoun—the word it stands for—should be unmistakable.

Grant told Henderson that *he* had misjudged the situation. [Who's *he?*] *Better:* Henderson, Grant told him, had misjudged the situation. *Or (the alternative interpretation):* Grant conceded to Henderson that he had misjudged the situation.

Don't take the life out of your rugs with harsh detergents. Let us do *it* with our steam cleaning process. [Do what? Take the life out of your rugs?] *Improved:* . . . Let us clean them with our steam cleaning process.

Mrs. Farrell had an account at our 34th Street branch *which* was closed last April. [Was it the branch or the account that was closed?] *No question:* Mrs. Farrell's account at our 34th Street branch was closed last April.

In the new Sears catalog, *they* feature some very competitively priced merchandise. [Does *they* relate to Sears or catalog? The difference may be slight, but the effect is not only ambiguous but awkward.] *Better:* The new Sears catalog features some very competitively priced merchandise.

(b) A pronoun should not refer to a word that is only implied or to a word that is so far away or so grammatically inconspicuous that the reference is not immediately clear.

Thorson had known he might be criticized for his decision, but still *it* distressed him. [Whatever word *it* stands for must be inferred.] *Better:* . . . but still the *criticism* distressed him.

The glass and aluminum structure, notable for its landscaped plaza and shopping arcade was completed only a year ago. Now, with the offices completely rented, the owners have decided to sell *it* to a realty syndicate for cash. [*It* is a long way from its antecedent, *structure.*] *Better:* . . . the owners have decided to sell the *building* to a realty syndicate for cash.

The cafeteria's management is so attuned to the tastes of our employees that *it* enjoys a remarkably enthusiastic patronage. [*It* would be more closely associated with *cafeteria* if *cafeteria*, rather than *management*, was the subject of the sentence.] *Better:* Thanks to its management, the cafeteria is so attuned to the tastes of our employees that it enjoys a remarkably enthusiastic patronage.

(c) In some instances, pronouns like *it, this, that,* and *which* refer to the general idea of a preceding clause instead of to a particular word. This usage is acceptable only if it does not result in vagueness or awkwardness.

The manufacturer was aware of the defects in the product, but did nothing about *it*. [About what?] *Better:* . . . but failed to take corrective action.

The number of discount brokers is growing, *which* presents a problem for the traditional Wall Street firms. *Smoother:* The growing number of discount brokers presents a problem for the traditional Wall Street firms. [See also WHICH.]

Yesterday Bailey's announced the closing of their Wilshire Boulevard store. *This* was unexpected. [Was it the announcement or the closing that was unexpected?] *Better:* This announcement (*or,* The closing) was unexpected.

In some other instances, the pronoun referring to a preceding idea (rather than a specific word) is amply clear.

Dawson wants a 20 percent commission. *That*'s all right with us.

I'd like to arrange a meeting with the client for Thursday afternoon. If *this* is all right with you, please let me know.

(d) The pronouns *you* and *they* are used only informally in a general sense.

In a brokerage office, *you* often have to work overtime. *More formal:* In a brokerage office, overtime work is often required.

They say *you* can't sell to the company unless *you* know somebody there. *More formal:* It's said that a salesman has to know someone in the company in order to do business with them.

They really go for our canned chili in Texas. *More formal:* There's a big market for our canned chili in Texas.

2. CASE.   Case refers to the inflectional forms that show the relation of a noun or pronoun to the rest of the sentence. Whether as grammatical subjects or objects, all nouns have the same form for both, but many pronouns do not, and a choice must be made.

(a) The form of the pronoun depends on its use within the sentence. A subject takes the nominative form (*I, we, he, she, they, who*). The object of a verb or object of a preposition takes the objective form (*me, us, him, her, them, whom*). The pronouns *it* and *you* have the same form for both the nominative and objective case. Problems arise only in unusual constructions.

They wanted to know *who* would chair the meeting. [Subject of the verb *would chair*]

We wish we knew *whom* she had in mind. [Object of the verb *had*]

They are in business longer than *we* (are). [Subject of the verb *are* (understood)] Informal only: . . . *longer than us.*

I hope you like it as much as *I* (do). [Subject of the verb *do* (understood)] Informal only: . . . *as much as me.*

Folger gives them as much business as (he gives) *us.* [Object of the verb *gives* (understood)] But, change in meaning: Folger gives them as much business as *we* (give them). [Subject of the verb *give* (understood)]

We'll talk with anyone but *him.* [Object of the preposition *but* (see BUT 2)]

See also **BETWEEN YOU AND I, IT'S ME, MYSELF**, and **WHO, WHOM.** For the possessive case, see **APOSTROPHE.**

(b) Pronouns joined by *and* or *or* take the same case.

You and he (not *you and him*) make an excellent team. [Subjects of the verb]

Either *he or they* (not *he or them*) will be notified. [Subjects of the verb]

They blamed neither *me nor them.* [Objects of the verb]

It's up to *her and me.* [Objects of the preposition *to*]

Between *you and me* (not *you and I*) . . . [Objects of the preposition *between*]

3. AGREEMENT IN NUMBER. (a) The number (singular or plural) of a pronoun is regularly the same as that of its antecedent.

When the *machine* failed, we had *it* repaired.

Daly and Rowan decided to pool *their* resources.

See also **ONE OF THOSE WHO** and **SUBJECT AND VERB.**

(b) The following pronouns are regularly construed as singular: *one, any, anyone, each, everyone, everybody, someone, somebody, no one, nobody, many a, either,* and *neither.* See, however, **NO ONE, NONE.**

One of them *is* (not *are*) sure to know the answer.

Everyone is expected to contribute *his* share.

Either of the models will do if *it is* guaranteed by the manufacturer.

Neither man was aware that *he was* being considered for the position.

Many a woman wishes she had this choice. [The subject is *woman,* not *many.*] But: *Many women wish they* had this choice.

Sometimes though the sense dictates the use of a plural pronoun with a singular antecedent. See also Rule (d) below and **COLLEC-TIVE NOUNS** 2.

Everyone was entitled to a fair share of the proceeds, and we made certain *they* (rather than *he*) got it.

(c) When two singular antecedents of a pronoun are joined by *or* or *nor*, the pronoun reference is regularly singular. When one of the antecedents is singular and the other plural, the pronoun reference usually agrees with the nearer one. But if the application of the rule results in awkwardness or distortion, the remedy is to suspend the rule or rephrase the sentence. The rule can also be breached in informal usage provided there is no damage to the sense.

Neither Mr. Kent nor Mr. Smith will express *his* preference. [*Informal:* will express *their* preference]

Neither the president nor the engineers in charge *have* revealed their plans.

Mr. Trump or Miss Pryor—whichever is on duty—will notify the Security Division when *he* or *she leaves*. [*Better:* . . . when *they leave; or, better still:* . . . upon leaving.]

They want either Dryfoos or me to assume the responsibility and discharge it in the best way possible [". . . in the best way *we can*" would distort the meaning].

(d) When a singular antecedent can be taken as masculine or feminine, choosing a pronoun reference permits several alternatives. The least attractive is the use of *he or she*. Other possibilities are the use of a plural pronoun reference or avoidance of the problem by rephrasing the sentence. Compare:

If anybody calls, get *his* name and telephone number.

If anybody calls, get *his or her* name and telephone number.

If anybody calls, get *their* name and telephone number.

If anybody phones, get the caller's name and telephone number.

Get the name and telephone number of anybody who calls.

See also **SEXUAL BIAS**.

(e) When a pronoun has a collective noun as its antecedent, the pronoun is singular or plural depending on the sense. See also **COLLECTIVE NOUNS**.

The staff did *their* best.

No company treats *its* workers more generously.

proof of purchase   Part of a package design—a trademark, word, slogan, or other product identification—which may be redeemable for cash

Proof of purchase

or merchandise when cut out and sent to the manufacturer under the conditions specified on the package or in an advertisement. See illustration.

propaganda   A PEJORATIVE for information, news, or rumor intended to influence public opinion for or against a person, institution, or cause— often without attribution of the source. Except for some INSTITUTIONAL ADVERTISING, advertising is not ordinarily considered propaganda.

proper names   see NAMES and CAPITALS.

prophecy, prophesy   The first, a noun, is pronounced -see: *The prophecy was realized.* The second, a verb, is pronounced -sigh: *Having prophesied success, he worked to achieve it.*
—self-fulfilling prophecy. Though apt at times, the phrase has fallen victim to overuse: *When the widely circulated newsletter predicted a sharp decline in stock prices, the prediction inevitably became a self-fulfilling prophecy.*

proposition   1. As a noun, acceptable in general usage for a carefully stated business proposal: *The proposition, as offered, has considerable merit.* But (informal only): *The investigation will be a tough proposition (will be difficult)/First novels are risky propositions (are gambles) in the marketplace.*
   2. As a verb, *proposition* is invariably confined to informal or colloquial use: *Let's proposition them about taking the lease (Let's talk to them about . . .).*

proprietary   An adjective denoting ownership by a person or group, whether by physical possession or by a trademark or patent; not a public facility or in the public domain: *proprietary medicines, proprietary hospitals, proprietary rights.* Also a noun: *a proprietary* (a proprietary medicine).

protectionism   A policy engaged in by a national government to protect domestic industry by limiting imports of certain goods, usually by levying import duties: *Protectionism would be brought back with a vengeance if Congress were to pass labor-backed domestic-content legislation requiring automobiles sold here to be built primarily of parts made in this country.*

—**protectionist,** adjective: *The protectionist steps already taken by Western governments have been aimed primarily against Japanese automobile exports.*

proved, proven   Although the words are synonymous, *proved* is sometimes preferred as a past participle; *proven*, as a simple adjective: *They have proved their point/The store is a proven success.* It must be conceded, however, that the phrase "proved reserves" conveys the idea of proof more strongly than "proven reserves" when referring to oil and minerals in the ground.

provided, providing   1. Both words are conjunctions meaning "on the condition (that)," but *provided* is preferred in that sense: *We will accede to the terms provided* (rather than *providing*) *they are also made applicable to our competitors.* In a simple condition, *if* is better still: *We'll go along with the idea if* (rather than *provided*) *you do.*

2. Only *providing* is correctly used as a present participle or adjective in the sense of "furnish" or "stipulate": *Our bank is providing the necessary forms/We'd like a contract providing a link between our volume of sales and our advertising allowance.*

proximity   "In proximity to" is better expressed by "near" or "close to": *in proximity to (near) the freight depot.* "In close proximity" is redundant. See **WORDINESS** 3 and 4.

proximo   Abbreviated *prox.* Archaic for "in the month following this one": *will be due on the 15th proximo* (will be due on [say] August 15). Compare with **INSTANT** and **ULTIMO**.

proxy   A person or agency authorized to act for another; also, the written authorization itself, as a shareholder's voting right: *act as a proxy/was present by proxy/voted my proxy/the proxies held by management.*

pseudo-event   See at **MEDIA EVENT**.

public   1. The people as a whole. As a **COLLECTIVE NOUN**, it is treated as singular or plural, depending on the sense: *The public* [collectively] *is not yet aware of the effects of the law/The public* [as individuals] *are not fools.*

2. Any group of people with some common interest: *the reading public.* In public relations, especially, the plural *publics* represents a number of different communities of interest: *The publics we serve include customers, suppliers, and shareholders.*

public information   Information issued to the PUBLIC through word-of-mouth, NEWS RELEASES, pamphlets, advertising, and so forth; a function of PUBLIC RELATIONS.

public-issue   Also *public-interest.* Relating to matters of public concern, as import restrictions, the environment, energy, food additives: *public-issue advertising* (also *issue-oriented advertising*)/*a public-interest lobby.* See also ADVOCACY.

public relations   Abbreviated PR. A function encompassing a wide range of activities designed to build rapport between an organization and its many constituencies (see PUBLIC 2); includes participation in community affairs, news of company activities, plant tours, etc. Sometimes euphemistically called *public information,* especially by such nonprofit practitioners as college and universities, churches, and philanthropic organizations.

public sector   See at PRIVATE SECTOR.

puffery   The use of a claim so trite, vague, or obviously exaggerated that it is deemed to be harmless: *When you buy from the best, you get the best* (Castro Convertibles)/*Greatest sale in the world* (Sherry-Lehmann, wine and spirits merchants)/*When you're picky about raisin bran, pick the best* (Post). Also: *miraculous new cleaner/sensational savings/the opportunity of a lifetime/never before and never again.* See also COMPARATIVE CLAIMS.

punch   To strike the digits on a push-button telephone: punch 555-1234. But see DIAL.

punch in, punch up   See TOUCH, PUNCH IN, PUNCH UP.

punctuation   See under the names of particular marks: APOSTROPHE, BRACKETS, COLON, COMMA, DASH, ELLIPSIS, EXCLAMATION POINT, HYPHEN, PARENTHESES, PERIOD, QUESTION MARK, QUOTATION MARKS, SEMICOLON.

For punctuation of numbers, see NUMERALS 7.

purchase   Buy. See LONG WORDS AND SHORT.

purpose   The phrases "for the purpose of" and "with the purpose of" make unnecessarily long locutions: *visited the factory for the purpose of finding (to find) the cause of the trouble/bought the novelty T-shirts with the purpose of using them (to use) as premiums.* See also WORD-INESS 4.

pursuant to   Legal JARGON for "according to": *We are taking this action pursuant to (under) Article XII of the contract/Pursuant to your request (As you requested, Following your request, At your request), we have put up for sale the premises at 14 River Street.*

push money   See P.M.

put   Part of a number of useful idioms: *Put across* (deliver acceptably) *an idea/put up with* (endure) *inconvenience/put upon* (imposed on) *by one's friends.* Also (informal): *put in* (devote) *time/put one over on* (outmaneuver, deceive) *a competitor/stay put* (remain stationary).

put back, put forward   To *put back* (or *move back*) an engagement or other event is to reschedule it for a later time. To *put forward* (or *move forward,* or *move up*) the engagement or event is to reschedule it for an earlier time. Contrarily, to *move back* a clock is to set it for an earlier time; and to *move* it *forward* is to set it for a later time. The common mnemonic device relating to adjustments in clock time at the beginning and end of daylight savings time is *"spring* forward, *fall* back."

Q

qualitative Pronounced *kwahl*-uh-tay-tiv. Relating to quality: *a qualitative measure/qualitative research/qualitative methods.* Compare QUANTITATIVE.

quality circles Denoting a management technique originated in Japan and adopted in some modified form by American companies. The *quality circles,* small groups of employees trained to spot and solve production problems in their areas, meet regularly and become involved in management decisions that help to increase productivity and reduce costs: *The company's quality circles solve problems from how to increase silicon wafer yields to how to avoid acid burns, the industry's No. 1 safety problem.*

Q and A Question and answer, one of several methods of ENUMERATION; useful in simplifying messages that inform or instruct. See illustration.

quantitative Pronounced *kwahn*-tuh-tay-tiv. Relating to quantity or expressed as a quantity: *quantitative data/quantitative analysis.* Compare QUALITATIVE.

quantitize JARGON for *quantify;* to determine a quantity and express it in numbers: *Would you want to quantitize* (better: *quantify* or *estimate*) *the anticipated shortage?* See also -IZE, -IZATION.

quasi- The prefix, meaning "resembling" or "to some degree," is followed by a hyphen: *a quasi-public corporation, quasi-judicial, quasi-military government.* See also HYPHEN 2.

question See at COMPLAINT.

question and answer See Q AND A.

question as to 1. An awkward phrase. *As to* can usually be replaced by a simple preposition: *There was no question as to (about) their intentions/All questions as to (of) procedure should be referred to the secretary/The ad raised a question as to (of) taste.*

A mailbox is a ballot box when you return your proxy

Q What *is* a proxy?

A It's a ballot that enables you to vote for – or against – your company's management But if you don't sign it, date it, and mail it, your proxy is a useless piece of paper

Q When will I get my proxy?

A In the next few weeks It will come to you in the mail with your proxy statement and the Notice of Annual Meeting

Q What's the difference between a proxy and a proxy statement?

A A proxy is a printed card that lists the items to be voted on, with boxes where you may mark your votes A proxy *statement* is a booklet that sets forth the issues on which you will vote, along with information about your company and its directors The first page of the booklet is the Notice of Annual Meeting

Q Does a proxy count as a vote for management if it's not returned?

A No A proxy that is not returned doesn't count either way

Q When should I mail my proxy?

A Promptly after you receive it, to assure that it arrives in time to be counted by the inspectors of election for the Annual Meeting

Q Do I have to pay postage to return my proxy?

No Your proxy will come to you with a postage-paid envelope

Q Can I change my vote later?

A Yes If you attend the Annual Meeting you can change your vote during the meeting if you wish Or you can change it by mail before the meeting

Q When and where is the Annual Meeting this year?

A On Thursday May 3 at 10 a m in the ballroom of the Alameda Plaza Hotel in Kansas City Mo Your management sincerely hopes that you will come if you can

Q and A [Mobil Corporation]

2. When *question* is followed by an appositive clause beginning *whether, where, when*, etc., no connecting words are needed: *The question whether* (not *as to whether*) *the fault is theirs is now moot.* When, in the same circumstances however, *question* is preceded by *any, some*, or other indefinite modifier—leaving some doubt about the nature of the question—a connective like *as to, of*, or *about* helps to convey the uncertainty: *There is some question as to* (or *of* or *about*) *how they arrived at the figure.*

question mark (?) 1. A question mark is placed at the end of a direct question, but not after an INDIRECT QUESTION, which is followed by a period: *Have you placed your order yet?/When is the plant expected to be in production?* But (indirect question): *The reporter* *wanted to know when the plant would be in production.* See also **QUESTION OF COURTESY.**

2. A question mark follows a question that is part of a declarative statement. The first word of the question is given an initial capital if it follows the declarative statement, but the first word of the declarative statement is not so capitalized when it follows the question: *We wanted to ask, What next?/What next? we wanted to ask.*

question of courtesy A request phrased as a polite question. It is followed by a period, not a question mark: *Will you please sign and return the enclosed card./May we have your answer soon.* Compare **RHETORICAL QUESTION.**

questions, solicited It is sometimes considered a mark of courtesy to ask at the end of an explanatory letter if the reader has any questions. In a reply to an inquiry, an offer to answer further questions may also serve as a defense against the possibility that the reply does not adequately serve the reader's needs. Current practice, however, discourages the solicitation of questions as a mere convention or for want of any other way to end the letter gracefully. The feeling is that idle invitations of that sort only stimulate unwanted correspondence.

queue To line up messages, as for computer processing or response to incoming telephone calls: *Some masochists use the telephone hold button to joyfully queue long lists of callers.*

quick fix A deceptively easy remedy: *threatens to generate a profusion of quick fixes for various wounded sectors of the economy.*

quid pro quo Latin, "something for something"; an equal exchange or **TRADE-OFF:** *Management examined the union's wage demands for signs of a quid pro quo/While approving the requests in principle, the Administration could demand as a quid pro quo that the Europeans and Japanese loosen their import restrictions/Broader coverage against catastrophic illness would be offered as a quid pro quo to those beneficiaries picking up some of the first-dollar expense.*

quite 1. Used traditionally in the sense of "entirely" or "fully": *quite satisfied/quite ready/not quite enough.* Also acceptable in the less extreme sense of "somewhat" or "rather": *priced quite reasonably/are quite alike/seems quite strong.*

2. The expression *quite a* is also used in several dissimilar senses: an indefinite quantity *(quite a few, quite a lot);* considerable *(for quite*

some time); and, informally, of extraordinary quality *(quite a sales-man, quite a book).*

quiz To interrogate; to question persistently: *When Harding became evasive, he was quizzed about his seeming memory lapses.* Because of its negative **CONNOTATION,** *quiz* is not a good substitute for *ask* in the ordinary sense: *We asked* (not *quizzed*) *Niles about her progress.*

quotation marks Double quotation marks ("/") are used at the beginning and end of a direct quotation. Single marks ('/') are used for a quotation within a quotation.

> Somewhat less than favorably impressed by Yale's newly built Gothic-style library, the financier commented, "There should be a sign over the entrance that says, 'This is not the Yale Library; the Yale Library is inside.'"

1. Direct quotations.   2. Titles.   3. Words in a special sense.   4. With other punctuation.

1. Direct quotations.   (a) Quotation marks enclose the exact words of the speaker or quoted writer, and no other words.

> Ewing offers the most terse definition: "Planning is to a large extent making things happen that would not otherwise occur."
>
> Explaining the lag in cataloging, the official said, "The government is putting out material faster than it can keep track of it."
>
> The release states that the Department "will try to induce relevant industries to act accordingly."
>
> He spoke with some irony of the "establishment banks."

A direct quotation may also be "broken," or interrupted by the words of the quoter.

> "Remember, we're in a hall of mirrors," Mr. Beckett told the graduates. "To succeed you must avoid the trap of being overly dazzled by your own image."

(b) Usage is divided in the treatment of long quotations. Preferably, a long quotation (not dialogue) is single-spaced, with an extra margin of five spaces on the left. An extra space above and below the quotation also helps to set it off from the rest of the text. No quotation marks are used unless they are part of the quoted material.

> From time to time, it is suggested that the [regulatory] agencies possess some mystical insight called "expertise." The "expertise" of regulatory

agencies is surely one of the greatest fictions since the "divine right of kings." Most agency members are appointed because they want a job and know a senator or other influential politician. If they have had some experience in the field in which the agency operates, that is as likely to be disqualifying as the contrary. It is difficult to acquire experience in any field without having been employed, so it is only the occasional academician who is able to claim any knowledge of a field without incurring opposition to appointment as being tainted by "conflict of interest." [Lee Loevinger]

Alternatively, long quotations can be set in the same fashion as the rest of the text, and quotation marks are then used. When, however, the quoted passage consists of two or more paragraphs, the marks are placed at the beginning of each paragraph but at the end of only the last.

Jack Anderson, who has never been called a mouthpiece for the right wing, addresses the situation in these terms:

"Another tax rebellion, not unlike the insurrection that brought down the British tyranny 202 years ago, is sweeping America. But the tyrant under attack is no George III conspicuously ensconced on his throne; it is the anonymous government clerk seated in his cubicle.

"In his pettifogging way, the bureaucrat has gained control over our destiny so unobtrusively that we didn't realize we were oppressed. So gently, prosaically, gradually and invisibly did he tighten the bonds that we never appreciated the extent to which we were caught in his grip. . . .

"But the laws have multiplied, each ensnarled in red tape and regulations until the bureaucrat can find a legality to any decision he chooses to make. This is bringing back the horror of whimsical rule, albeit by a clerk rather than a king." [Washington *Post*, July 4, 1978]

2. TITLES.   (a) In a running text, quotation marks are used to enclose minor titles, such as those of the chapters or sections of a book, and the titles of articles, reports, monographs, poems, and other short literary works: Raskin's article, "The Big Squeeze on Labor Unions"/the sixth chapter, "Role Performance in Groups"/refer you to page 6 of the bank's pamphlet, "Trusts and Wills"/an amusing poem, "Time Out," by Robert Gordon.

(b) Although major titles—those of books and magazines, particularly—are conventionally italicized in textual references, some writers and publications prefer the more convenient quotation marks: in the current issue of "Newsweek"/quoted in the Sunday "New

York Times"/a review of Barbara Tuchman's "A Distant Mirror." See also ITALICS 1.

3. WORDS IN A SPECIAL SENSE.   Quotation marks are used to enclose words used as words or words used facetiously or in a special sense; but they are less favored for nicknames, slang, and familiar expressions.

Even the term "full employment" raises numerous questions of definition and measurement.

The telephone was then considered a "miracle" of twentieth-century technology.

The swindler insisted that his "ethics" prevented him from naming his accomplice.

The old idea of the "melting pot" is now in disrepute.

But: Bertie (not "Bertie") proved very friendly/As a salesman, he was a real hotshot (not "hotshot")/The few that succeeded really hit the jackpot (not "jackpot").

See also ITALICS 2.

4. WITH OTHER PUNCTUATION.   (a) Closing quotation marks are placed *after* a comma or period, *before* a colon or semicolon, and either *before or after* a question mark or exclamation mark, depending on whether the punctuation mark belongs to the quotation alone or to the whole statement.

According to Caffrey, "The rosier the news, the higher-ranking the official who announces it."

"Such errors happen all too often," observed Mr. Simms.

He gave me my "orders": Take a vacation.

She wants an office with more "living space"; she'll get it.

"What does all this mean?" asked Biller. [But, question mark following quotation marks: Is the word "indexing" or "indexation"?]

The crate was marked "Fragile!"

(b) When a quotation is interrupted by "he said" or a similar element, a comma and a quotation mark are placed at the point of interruption and a comma, semicolon, or period are placed after the interrupter, depending on the structure of the quotation.

"All too often," observed Mr. Solomon, "Companies falsely assume that executives feel secure in their jobs." [A comma follows the interrupter when the quotation takes a comma or no punctuation at all at the break.]

"Some colors and patterns work," she said; "others don't." [A semi-colon follows the interrupter when the quotation takes a semicolon at the break.]

"Nobody expected a profitable operation in Italy this year," Mr. Terzian explained. "The fact that we have so far succeeded is due in good part to the effective help from our partners abroad. [A period follows the interrupter when the break in the quotation marks the division between two sentences.]

quote Informal for "quotation" or "quotation mark": *This is a direct quote/Put the word in quotes.* Also, general English as a verb: *Please don't quote me/He quoted the last paragraph of our letter/Here is what they demand. I quote.*

quote, unquote 1. "Quote" and "unquote" mark respectively the beginning and end of a spoken word or passage belonging in quotation marks. The terms are indispensable in dictated copy. In ordinary speech, however, a more natural way of denoting the beginning and end of a quotation is to use such phrases as "The passage reads" and "end of quotation."

2. The phrase "quote, unquote" spoken at the beginning of a quoted word or passage, and leaving the listener to infer the end of the quotation, is informal: *He says it's a question of quote unquote business morality.*

R

®   Registered (with the U.S. Patent and Trademark Office). The sign of a registered **TRADEMARK**.

racket   1. An illegitimate business or fraudulent scheme: *The office is a front for a loansharking racket/What's their racket?*

    2. Slang for any occupation or business: *What's your racket? Mine's real estate.*

racketeer   One who engages in a **RACKET** (Def. 1).

rag   Slang for "newspaper": *works for an evening rag.*

rag trade   Also *rag game*. Informal for the ladies' garment industry: *works in the rag trade.*

rain check   1. By analogy with the rain check familiar to patrons of outdoor sporting events, a voucher given a customer by a retail store, permitting—within a limited time—the purchase of an out-of-stock item at the advertised (sale) price.

    2. Part of a polite turndown of an informally offered invitation to lunch or other occasion: *Thanks, I'll take a rain check.*

raise   Preferred to *rise* in the sense of an increase in pay: *asked for a raise in pay* (rather than *rise in pay*)/*won a pay raise of 12 percent.*

RAM   The **ACRONYM** for **RANDOM-ACCESS MEMORY**.

R & D   Research and development: *needs an infusion of millions in R & D funds/spoke of the need for more support for R & D.*

random-access memory   Abbreviated **RAM**. A computer feature permitting the temporary storage of data and access to it in any order, regardless of the sequence in the storage unit. Compare **ROM**. See also **K** 2.

rarely ever   See **SELDOM EVER**.

rate   Informal for "deserve": *rates a recommendation/thought she rated a promotion.*

rather   It is incongruous for *rather*, meaning "somewhat," to modify an adjective expressing strong feeling: *a rather delightful meeting/a rather astonishing feat* [omit *rather* in both instances].

—had rather. See HAD RATHER, WOULD RATHER.

rather than   1. When preceded by a locution beginning with *more*, the *rather* is superfluous: *If you're more interested in what an information system can do rather than in how it works, come to INFO 84* [omit *rather*]. See also PREFER.

2. A question arises whether *rather than* should be followed by an *-ing* verb form or some other grammatical form. Since *rather than* is a conjunction, the user must look to see what two sentence elements it is joining and make sure they are compatible: *The management prefers to seek a permanent arrangement with an interior designer rather than make* (not *making*) *its own decisions every time an office layout problem presents itself.* [The words joined are *seek* and *make;* an alternative is *prefers seeking . . . rather than making . . .*] See also PARALLEL STRUCTURE.

ration   Both the noun and the verb are pronounced either *rash*-un or *ray*-shun.

rationalization   In psychology, the use of an acceptable but not necessarily the underlying reason to justify one's behavior. Consumers, for instance, may "rationalize" their purchase of margarine by telling themselves that the absence of animal fat makes it a healthful substitute for butter. The real reason, however, may be the price, which is often less than half that of butter.

The producers of margarine sense the psychology of the consumer and take advantage of it by almost invariably stressing the health properties or "buttery" taste in their national advertising. What the advertising does is called "rationalizing the APPEAL." A Mercedes advertisement—to cite another example—stresses workmanship and performance. But for many buyers who could as easily accommodate to a far less expensive car, the unadmitted MOTIVATION for buying the Mercedes is that it will be seen by neighbors and friends as a symbol of their material success. The advertisement serves its purpose, however, because it helps the self-conscious buyer resolve the conflict between desire for the car and the difficulty of explaining an essentially egoistic purchase.

rat race   Informal characterization of intensive competition or the heavy demands of a job: *It was a rat race, but we got the contract/I was sales manager of the company, but it will be a long time before I go back to that rat race again.*

re Also *in re. Re* is pronounced *ree*. Latin for "in the matter of." A familiar term in legal proceedings, but better not used in the body of a letter or report, and unnecessary when used in the SUBJECT LINE of a letter: *our letter in re the debt (our letter about the debt)/Re: Marathon Mutual Fund* [omit the *Re;* or, if a substitute is desired, use *Subject*].

reaction Well used for "response," but too often it is only a loose synonym for a more accurate word: *opinion, impression, feeling, attitude,* etc.: *Our reaction to (impression of, opinion of) Drury was quite favorable/Despite their disappointment with the results, their reaction to (attitude toward) the policy has not changed.* But (good choice): *Our shareholders' reaction to the proposal was not unexpected.*

readability   1. The concept of readability has gained currency through the invention of a number of formulas for determining the ease of reading any given passage. The measures of readability common to all formulas are sentence and word length, short being more readable than long.

2. One of the best known tests is the Flesch Readability Formula. Essentially, this test coordinates the average number of words per sentence and the average number of syllables per word with a conversion table to produce a score. Scores range from 0 for "very hard" to 100 for "very easy." A score of 65 is considered standard, the level you might expect in the *Reader's Digest.* Elementary-level writing is near the top of the scale; scientific writing, near the bottom. (See illustration.)

3. Business has welcomed readability formulas because they translate a highly complex verbal pattern into a numeral, something a business executive is used to dealing with. As if to mute any unwarranted enthusiasm, however, it has been pointed out that Lewis Carroll's famous nonsense poem *Jabberwocky* rates 90+ on the Flesch scale. This sort of anomaly has raised questions about the usefulness of the readability formulas generally. For instance:

How do you define readability?

Do sentence and word length account sufficiently for the variables that determine ease of reading?

How valid is a formula that takes no account of the degree of

VERY DIFFICULT	STANDARD	VERY EASY
Under the long-term cyclical program the Committee considers and, in its discretion, may make awards or allotments to certain members of senior management, including directors who are employees of Mobil or any subsidiary, with respect to certain periods of years. Payment of such awards and allotments is contingent upon attainment of standards of minimum growth in the consolidated net earnings per share of Mobil and its subsidiaries during designated performance periods in an amount to be fixed by the Committee at the conclusion of each performance period. Such standards may be reduced at the end of a performance period where the prescribed standards have not been met if Mobil's performance, when compared to competition is judged to have been superior to competition. ["Notice of Annual Meeting." Mobil Corporation]	One exercise in communication is to stand in front of a group and present an idea. It's a skill that most supervisors and executives need. Yet few get a chance to really practice it. The Supervisory Management Program provides an opportunity. Program members make a presentation and get a usually mild critique from the group. But the communication feedback process is really made complete by the fact that Trupiano [the instructor] videotapes the entire presentation. In private, he or Baldwin [the manager of training] shows the speaker the videotape and offers a professional critique of his or her delivery. "It's kind of painful to sit there and watch yourself," noted one former group member. And also instructive. ["Learning To Be Boss," in *Venture*, a house publication of the American Natural Resources System]	Fall's arrival is a signal to think of football, autumn leaves—and getting ready for winter. The fall months are a good time to prepare for winter's cold that will soon send up your heating bills. There are ways to keep your heating bills down and save energy dollars. One, make sure your heating system is working well. Two, keep the cold out. Third, keep as much of the heat inside your home as you can. Four, avoid overheating your home. These four steps will help you reduce heating costs this winter, and you will still be comfortable. [*Customer News*, Consolidated Edison Company of New York]

Readability.   Three samples of company prose graded on the Flesch Scale of Reading Ease.

background information, interest, and motivation a reader brings to the passage?

4. Such questions notwithstanding, the readability movement has undoubtedly had a beneficial effect on a great deal of business and government writing. "Plain language" laws regulating consumer contracts are being passed in state capitals; companies are holding classes in readable writing; and the federal government—not omitting the IRS—is turning its attention to producing intelligible forms and instructions.

Ironically, though, a writer does not have to use a calculator to produce readable prose. Words and sentences do not have to be measured arithmetically. And the time saved is probably better spent on content, the organization of material, and making good sense.

For other articles relating to readability, see ACTIVE VOICE, PASSIVE VOICE; JARGON; LONG WORDS AND SHORT; PLAIN ENGLISH; and SENTENCES 1.

reading notice An advertisement typeset to resemble the editorial content of the publication in which it appears. The reading notice is customarily identified as an advertisement in the heading; or, in the instance of a short, closely set announcement of only a few lines, by a dash and the abbreviation *Advt.* following the last word.

reading rack A stand providing free take-away reading matter for workers in offices and factories. Topics usually relate to such matters as safety, health, economics, and educational opportunities: *The reading rack needs replenishing.*
—**reading-rack,** adjective: *reading-rack literature.*

read zone The area on an envelope within which the address should be placed if it is to be picked up by the U.S. Postal Service's optical scanners. See ENVELOPE ADDRESS 1.

real, really *Real* is an adjective: *real sheepskin/a real pleasure. Really* is an adverb: *really difficult/a really pleasurable experience.* Informally, however, especially in conversation, *real* is frequently used for *really: I'll see you real soon/We had a real good laugh/Nobody's real sure of the results.*

real estate 1. Also *realty.* Landed property, including the improvements on it: *owns a great deal of real estate/realty worth millions.*

2. In exceptional instances, *real estate* may denote any area or sur-

face, including a very small one: *What makes the Mann 4800* [lithographic] *system so attractive to the semiconductor industry is that it can produce lines that are as narrow as 1.25 to 2 microns wide, which means that the same circuit need only occupy one quarter the real estate required by the older machines.*

3. The adjective is not necessarily hyphened: *a real estate operation* (or *a real-estate operation*).

real interest rates   The spread between actual interest rates and the inflation rate: *This recovery won't be as weak as economists were projecting six months ago, but high real interest rates and the lower inflation rate will prevent it from being any more robust.*

real time   1. The actual time required for a radio or television performance, without additions or subtractions to allow for commercials or to meet the broadcaster's time requirements.

—**real-time,** adjective. Computerese signifying that instructions given to a computer are processed simultaneously: *The Equitable real-time system provides up-to-the-minute claims information with the touch of a button.* Compare **BATCH PROCESSING.**

realtor   A dealer in real estate; a real estate broker. Also (capitalized), a member of the National Association of Realtors by whom the word is registered with the U.S. Patent and Trademark Office.

realty   Synonym for **REAL ESTATE.**

real wage   See **NOMINAL WAGE.**

ream   1. A standard quantity of 500 sheets of paper packaged primarily for letterheads, typescripts, and copiers. A *printer's ream,* also called a *perfect ream,* consists of 516 sheets to allow for waste.

2. The plural *reams* is informally used in the sense of any large quantity of paper product: *dictated reams of notes.*

reason is because   Though acceptable in informal use, the phrase is redundant. General English calls for the phrase "the reason is that." Informal: *The reason they stick with cable TV advertising is because they find it productive.* General usage: *. . . is that they find it productive.* Or (smoother): *They stick with cable TV advertising because they find it productive.*

recall notice   A letter or public statement from the manufacturer advising owners of one of its products that a safety defect exists and that the product should be returned for repair or exchange. The "recall" may be mandated by some government agency, such as the National Highway Traffic Safety Administration (NHTSA) or the Food and Drug Administration (FDA).

recap CLIPPED FORM of *recapitulate* or *recapitulation: I'll recap* (summarize) *the events of the day for you/At the end of his talk, he thoughtfully provided a recap* (summary) *of the main points.*

receipt Characteristic of some STEREOTYPED LETTER PHRASES: *We are in receipt of (We have received* or *We have) your request/Receipt is acknowledged of (We have) your letter of* . . . See also PENDING (receipt).

receivables See ACCOUNTS RECEIVABLE.

recent date See RECENT LETTER 3.

recent letter 1. An informal reference suitable when correspondence between two parties is infrequent and there is no question about the letter referred to. In most business situations, however, a more exact reference is preferred: *your letter of April 5* (or, in referring to a preceding year, *your letter of April 5, 19xx*).

2. Referring to "your recent letter" when the delay in response has become an embarrassment is an old dodge. In such a circumstance, a reference to the subject may permit omission of the date, as in, "your inquiry about the B100 line printer."

3. The alternate "letter of recent date" is stereotyped. See STEREO-TYPED LETTER PHRASES.

recession A mild DEPRESSION, more particularly defined by the National Bureau of Economic Research as "a recurring period of decline in total output, income, employment and trade, usually lasting from six months to a year and marked by widespread contractions in many sectors of the economy."

reckon 1. In general English, to count or compute, and with *on*, to depend or rely: *We'll reckon* (count) *the receipts for the period October 10 to 16 inclusive/We can't reckon* (rely) *on Jim's help any longer.*

2. Informal for "guess" or "suppose": *I reckon we'll just have to live with that decision.*

record As used in "our records show" and "on consulting our records, we find," *record* provides a factual basis for the statement that follows, but the official tone is sometimes annoying. Usually, the specific facts are enough: *The signed agreement was mailed on March 6/We received the shipment on July 18*. However, the phrase "we have no record of receiving" is an acceptable substitute for the kind of flat denial—"we have not received"—that may become embarrassing if there has been a foul-up at the writer's end.

recordkeeping As a noun, equally acceptable as one word or two: *simplifies recordkeeping* (or *record keeping*). But (adjective): *her record-keeping* (or *recordkeeping*) *duties*. See **HYPHEN** 1.

recur, recurrence Preferred to their **LONG VARIANTS** *reoccur* and *reoccurrence*.

recycle 1. To renovate or convert to a different use, as an old building; also to process and reuse waste, as paper, cans, bottles. See **RESOURCE RECOVERY**.

2. To retrain or redeploy people with obsolete skills or diminished capacities. In this sense, *recycle* is an insensitive word for a humane practice, as when stenographers and typists are *recycled* (Better: *retrained*) to operate word processing machines, or an aging salesman, no longer able to carry sample cases, is *recycled* for (Better: *transferred to*) showroom duty.

red herring The familiar name of the preliminary prospectus a company must, by law, make available to prospective buyers before it can publicly offer a stock issue. Similarly, the notice required in New York and other states outlining a preliminary plan by a landlord for conversion of rental housing to a cooperative or condominium. A statement printed in red ink on the cover of the prospectus cautions that a sale cannot take place until sanction is given by the Securities and Exchange Commission or the appropriate state authority.

redlining The practice, attributed to some banks, of refusing mortgages for homes and businesses in certain areas, usually those populated by the economically disadvantaged.

red tape Originally, the tape used to bind official documents in England; now, any bureaucratic forms or procedures that impede action: *You can't get a building permit without a lot of red tape.*

redundancy 1. The use of more words than the sense requires: *an account in four-figure proportions (an account in four figures)*. See **WORDINESS** 3.

2. Repetition to give emphasis or guard against the possibility of an error in the transmission of a message: *A reprint of the catalog is not—repeat "not"—needed/His name is Heins, h-e-i-n-s.*

3. In technology, the use of one or more backup systems to prevent the possible failure of a mechanical or electronic function: *The plane's four independent hydraulic systems provide plenty of redundancy/The Nonstop is designed to run for years without stopping. It employs two processors for redundancy and has a built-in battery to provide backup in power failures.*

4. In British usage, a EUPHEMISM for the layoff of "redundant" or unneeded workers: *Widespread redundancies have been announced by the Lucas car component group in Birmingham.*

reevaluate   See REVALUATE.

reference   1. A source that will attest to the character, creditworthiness, or other qualifications of a person or organization: *asked for bank references.* Also a statement attesting to such qualifications, as "a letter of reference."

—have reference to. Wordy for "refer to": *We particularly have reference to (refer to) their liability for any damage incurred.* See WORDINESS 5.

—in reference to. Stilted and wordy for "about": *your letter in reference to (about) our order.* Other phrases in the same category are "with reference to," "relative to" and "in relation to." See WORDINESS 4.

2. *To reference* is JARGON meaning to provide documentation or to identify by coding: *The report was not referenced* (documented with sources)/*The cards should be referenced* (coded for reference).

—reference back. Redundant for "search (one's records) for": *We referenced back to (looked up) the loan agreement.*

reference line   1. A notation consisting of a file number, contract number, policy number, or other exact reference placed on routine letters or other forms for convenience of reference.

2. If the place for the notation is not shown in the printed heading by some such phrase as "File No." or "Please refer to," the reference is customarily typewritten below the date. In a letter, the reference is carried over on the CONTINUATION SHEETS, if there are any.

3. The reference line is not used in a letter when the need for a distinctive or personal appearance takes precedence over ease of refer-

ence. However, the same data is incorporated into the body of the letter, usually close to the beginning.

See also **LETTER FORM** 3.

reference notes In any report or article, it is customary to give the sources of quotations and the authorities for the facts and opinions cited. Ordinarily, such references are few and can be conveniently woven into the text. In other instances—especially in research papers and articles in technical or professional journals—the citations are too many or too precise to be treated casually and must therefore be formally documented. This is done in notes placed at the bottom of the pages in which the references occur *(footnotes)*, or in a single list at the end of the paper or chapter *(endnotes)*. A **BIBLIOGRAPHY** may or may not be appended.

Endnotes not only avoid the distraction of footnotes, but make typing easier; they also, with some modifications, perform the function of a bibliography without requiring the preparation of a separate list.

Styles of reference notes vary with the field of inquiry, the publication, and in-house requirements. In general, however, the usages in business, as described below, follow closely those of the social sciences.

1. CONTENT. 2. NUMBERING. 3. STYLE OF ENTRIES. 4. OTHER CITATION SYSTEMS. 5. REFERENCE ABBREVIATIONS.

1. CONTENT. (a) Reference notes consist of precise documentation of source material or references to other relevant studies. With the reference notes, the writer may include an occasional explanatory note, consisting of a peripheral comment on some point in the text. Explanatory notes are distracting, however, and should be avoided where possible.

REFERENCE FOOTNOTE (source material)

[1]*Economic Report of the President*, January 1982 (Washington, D.C.: Council of Economic Advisers, 1982), pp. 96, 102.

REFERENCE FOOTNOTE (supplementary material)

[2]See, for example, C. Burke Tower, "High Court to Rule on Interrelated Competition in Sylvania Case," *Marketing News*, December 31, 1976, p. 7.

EXPLANATORY FOOTNOTE

[3]What little evidence we have on recent automation of clerical and

management work suggests that it does not greatly change the distribution of skill levels.

(b) References to books show the author and title; edition, series, or volume, if applicable; facts of publication (place, publisher, and date in parentheses), and page number(s). References to material in periodicals are usually confined to author, title of article, name of publication, volume (in the instance of a learned journal), date, and page number(s). See examples in Sec. 3 below.

2. NUMBERING. All notes are numbered consecutively to the end of the paper or chapter. In the text, the reference number immediately follows the statement or passage to be documented, and the corresponding note is prefixed by the same number. A quick succession of reference numbers should be avoided; several citations can be combined in one note, if necessary. Although reference and note numbers are traditionally raised above the line, other equally acceptable number treatments are more convenient (see figure). In any case, notes are usually single-spaced, with double spacing between each note.

Numbered reference in text:

to the point where this essential production phenomenon has strong implications for a marketing strategy[12]. They suggest that firms . . .

[or]

to the point where this essential production phenomenon has strong implications for a marketing strategy (12). They suggest that firms . . .

Numbered notes:

[12] William D. Guth, "Toward a Social System of Corporate Strategy," *Journal of Business*, July 1976, pp. 374–78.

[or]

12. William D. Guth, "Toward a Social System of Corporate Strategy," *Journal of Business*, July 1976, pp. 374–78.

[or (for endnotes)]

12. William D. Guth, "Toward a Social System of Corporate Strategy," *Journal of Business*, July 1976, pp. 374–78.

Reference notes 2.   Styles of numbering.

3. STYLE OF ENTRIES.   Notes are deliberately terse and make use of common abbreviations. Latin words and abbreviations are held to a minimum. Each note is punctuated as a single sentence, and succeeding references to the same source are reduced to the barest essentials, as

[4] Innis, p. 86.

Should a note refer to the work cited in the immediately preceding note, the author's name may be replaced by the Latin *Ibid.*

[5] Ibid., p. 86. [In the same place, but on page 86]

[6] Ibid. [In the same place; same page reference]

If the author is represented by more than one work, a later reference names the work as well as the author. If the title of the work is long, a shortened form is usually preferred.

[7] Vogel, *Lobbying,* pp. 162–64.

As in other types of material, underlining is used for the names of books and periodicals (see ITALICS 1). Names of shorter works—reports, articles, and chapters—are put in QUOTATION MARKS.

Following are examples of notes from various types of sources.

BOOKS

[8] Yoram Wind, *Product Policy: Concepts, Methods, and Strategies* (Reading, Mass.: Addison-Wesley, 1981), p. 82.

[9] Mark Powers and David Vogel, *Inside the Financial Futures Market* (New York: John Wiley, 1981), pp. 162–64.

[10] Barry Bosworth and others, *Capital Needs in the Seventies* (Washington, D.C.: Brookings Institution, 1975), p. 19. [More than two authors]

[11] Allen Sinai and Roger E. Brinner, *The Capital Shortage: Near-Term Outlook and Long-Term Prospects,* Economic Study Series No. 18 (Lexington, Mass.: Data Resources, August 1975), pp. 20–21. [Volume in a series]

CHAPTERS AND ARTICLES IN LONGER WORKS

[12] Rosabeth Moss Kanter and Barry A. Stein, "Life in the Middle: Getting In, Getting Up, and Getting Along," in *Life in Organizations,* ed. Rosabeth M. Kanter and Barry A. Stein (New York: Basic Books, 1979), pp. 225–41.

[13] David O. Green, "Interim Reports," in *Handbook of Modern Accounting,* ed. Sidney Davidson and Roman L. Weill (New York: McGraw-Hill, 1977), pp. 5–2 to 5–21.

ARTICLES IN PERIODICALS AND NEWSPAPERS

[14] N. R. Paul and others, "The Reality Gap in Strategic Planning,"

Harvard Business Review, vol. 56 (May–June 1978), pp. 124–25. [Volume numbers are given for learned journals.]

[15] Bro Uttal, "Life After Litigation at IBM and AT&T," *Fortune*, Feb. 8, 1982, pp. 58–60.

[16] Lydia Chavez, "The Making of a Security Analyst," *The New York Times*, Jan. 31, 1982, Sec. 3, p. 1.

[17] "Careening Credit," *The Wall Street Journal*, Nov. 17, 1981, p. 26. [Unsigned article]

PAMPHLETS

[18] Harry H. Long, *Interregional Migration of the Poor: Some Recent Changes*, U.S. Government Printing Office, Bureau of the Census Series, No. 73, 1978, p. 23.

[19] General Electric Corporation, *1983 Annual Report*.

[20] U.S. Department of Health, Education, and Welfare, *Affirmative Action/Vocational Rehabilitation: A Resource Guide for Employers*, 1978, pp. 14–17. [Corporate author]

OTHER SOURCES

[21] U.S. Congress, *Report of the Senate Commission on Immigration and Refugee Policy* (Washington, D.C., March 1, 1981). [Congressional report]

[22] "Maternal and Child Health Care Act," *Hearings before the Subcommittee on Health and the Environment of the House Committee on Interstate and Foreign Commerce on H.R. 12937*, 94th Cong., 2d Sess. (Washington, D.C., June 16, 1976), p. 132. [Congressional hearing]

[23] FCC v. Midwest Video Corp., 440 U.S. 689 (1979). [Case at law. The reference is to Volume 440 of the official records of the United States Supreme Court, page 689. Because of the many technicalities of legal citations, the reader is referred to *A Uniform System of Citation: The Bluebook*, 13th ed. (Cambridge, Mass.: Harvard Law Review, 1981).]

[24] New York State Electric Co., 21 P.U.R., 3d 276 (N.Y. Public Service Comm'n 1961). [An administrative case of a regulatory body. The reference is to the unofficial *Public Utilities Reports*, Third Series.]

[25] Fred G. Steingraber, "Improving Productivity in the U.S.: The Real Strategic Challenge," an address to the Manufacturing Services Seminar, Los Angeles, Calif., Oct. 27, 1981.

[26] Personal interview with Miss Ryan at her office, March 15, 1983.

[27] Letter to the author from Joseph M. David, president of Star Enterprises, Inc., Feb. 26, 1984.

4. OTHER CITATION SYSTEMS.   In business and technical writing there is a growing trend to the elimination of footnotes and endnotes,

and the substitution of a citation system linked to the **BIBLIOGRA-PHY**. In one such system, a parenthetic reference in the text gives only the author's last name and the page number(s) for a work listed alphabetically by author in the bibliography. For example:

> on the fear of disclosure of information that might affect the competitive advantage of a company (Kearney, 10–12).

If the bibliography lists more than one work by the author, the necessary distinction in the text reference is made by adding to the author's name a shortened title of the work cited or the date of publication, as (Kearney, *Public Disclosure*, 10–12) or (Kearney, 1975, 10–12). Another choice is to assign consecutive numbers to the items in the bibliography, making it possible to abbreviate the reference in the text to the number of the work and the page number(s) in one of these ways: (12, pp. 10–12) or (*12*, 10–12).

5. REFERENCE ABBREVIATIONS.   Following are some of the most common abbreviations and words used in reference notes and bibliographies. Where a choice is indicated, the trend is to substitute the English usage for the Latin.

anon.	anonymous
c., ca.	About: c. 1896 (exact date unknown)
ch., chs.; chap., chaps.	chapter(s): ch. 3, chaps. 4 and 5.
cf. *(confer)*	compare: cf. Dalton, p. 48; but "compare" is preferred.
Cong.	Congress
Cong. Rec.	Congressional Record
ed., eds	editor(s), edition(s), edited by: C. L. Barnhardt and others, eds., 3d ed., ed. Alfred G. Smith.
et al.	and others: Flora Carpenter et al.; but "and others" is preferred.
f., ff.	and the following page(s): See pp. 24 ff. The inclusive pages are preferred: See pp. 24–27.
fn.	footnote: See fn. 27. *See also* "n" below.
fig., figs.	figure(s)
GPO	Government Printing Office
H. Doc.	House [of Representatives] Document
H.R.	House of Representatives
H. Rept.	House Report
H. Res.	House Resolution

ibid. *(ibidem)*	in the same work cited in the preceding footnote: Ibid., p. 24. The writer's last name is preferred: Graham, p. 24.
(infra)	not an abbreviation; "below" is preferred.
l., ll.	line(s): l. 15, ll. 26–40. Because of possible confusion with the number 1 or 11, the word is better spelled out: line 15, lines 26–40.
L.C.	Library of Congress
loc. cit. *(loco citato)*	in the passage cited: Brown, loc. cit. The page reference is preferred: Brown, p. 125.
n., nn.	note(s): p. 45, n.2 (also, when the page has only a single note: p. 12n). Preferred to "fn."
n.d.	no date (date of publication not indicated in work): Esme & Co., "Personal Financial Strategy," n.d.
op. cit. *(opere citato)*	in the work cited: Perrine, op. cit. Usually superfluous.
p., pp.	page(s): pp. 126–28.
par., pars.	paragraph(s)
(passim)	here and there (scattered references): pp. 25–38 passim. (The Latin *passim* is not an abbreviation.)
pseud.	pseudonym
rept., repts.	report(s), reprint(s)
S.	Senate [U.S.]
S. Doc.	Senate Document
sec., secs.; sect., sects.	section(s): sects. 4–6.
ser.	series (singular and plural): Ser. 95.
S. Rept.	Senate Report
S. Res.	Senate Resolution
(supra)	not an abbreviation; "above" is preferred.
v., vs.	against. The "v." is preferred in legal citations.
vol., vols.	volume(s): vol. 3; in 3 vols.

reference of pronouns See PRONOUNS 1.

reflation A deliberate termination of DISINFLATION by the government. Designed to remedy economic distress, reflation is usually marked by tax cuts, increased government spending, and lowered interest rates. Compare DEFLATION.

regard 1. *Regard*, not *regards*, is used in the expressions "in regard to" and "with regard to," but for restrictions on the use of these phrases see **REGARDING, AS REGARDS, ETC.**

2. As a verb meaning "consider," *regard* is regularly followed by *as*: *We regard it as a privilege* (rather than *We regard it a privilege* or *We regard it to be a privilege*).

regarding, as regards, etc. Such expressions are usually better expressed by the simple prepositions *about, of,* or *for: We have your letter in regard to (about) the May 21 delivery/With regard to (For) the Haynes order, we have not yet set a completion date/Their ignorance regarding (of) the penalty for late filing will cost them hundreds of dollars.* See also **WORDINESS 4.**

regards An expression of good wishes, remembrance, affection, or esteem: *Give my regards to Bill and May.* Also used in such expressions as "Kindest regards" and "With kindest regards" immediately before the **COMPLIMENTARY CLOSE** of a letter, or as the complimentary close itself. Although *regards*, in the sense mentioned, can be overused, it does give a personal touch to a letter that might otherwise seem mechanical.

registered mail The safest way to send a letter or any article of value by mail. A registry fee must be paid in addition to the first-class rate. See also at **MAILING NOTATIONS.**

regressive tax See at **PROGRESSIVE TAX.**

reimburse To reimburse is to repay money spent or compensate for losses incurred; the word is not to be used in the simple sense of "pay": *Salespersons are reimbursed for meals and travel expenses/The insurance company reimbursed them for the water damage.* But: *We will pay* (not *reimburse*) *you for the goods we ordered when we get your bill.*

—reimbursement, noun: *They sought reimbursement for the water damage.* But: *When we deliver goods, we expect payment* (not *reimbursement*).

reindustrialization A Carter administration proposal to revitalize American industry with government help—a step prompted by the weakening of the country's productive capacity through a long period of overuse and underdevelopment. The plan never went to Congress for action.

reinvent To apply new thinking and technology to the making of a machine that was already considered to be technically advanced: *Oil shortages required that we reinvent the car.*

REIT Plural REITs. ACRONYM for *r*eal *e*state *i*nvestment *t*rust, an investment vehicle through which small investors are able to pool their money and compete with large investors in the real estate market. Many REITs foundered in the early 70s, but the trusts have recently made a comeback under strict federal regulation.

relamping Replacing present lamps or bulbs with others to increase or decrease lighting or to save energy. Analogous to *delamping*, the removal of excess or redundant lighting: *This department has taken great pains to reduce the lighting in public structures through relamping and delamping.*

relative to, in relation to See at REFERENCE 1.

relevant So spelled and pronounced (not *revelant*): *Janowski makes a relevant point.*

remain The expression "I (we) remain" forming the close of a letter, as in "Hoping to hear from you soon, I remain," is archaic. See also PARTICIPIAL CLOSE.

remainder What is left over: *Williams & Co. will take half our production; Simmons will take the remainder* (or *rest*). Also, plural only, leftover stock sold at a discount: *publishers' remainders.* See also BALANCE, REMAINDER.

remaining balance Though redundant in other senses, the term is well established to denote a balance in an account following an earlier subtraction: *Thank you for your check for $400 to be credited to your installment account. You now have a remaining balance of $1200* (But also: *Your present balance is $12.00*).

remediate LONG VARIANT of *remedy* (the verb): *Many were victims of learning disabilities that were not remediated (remedied) in school.*

remunerate Pay. See LONG WORDS AND SHORT.

render Give. See LONG WORDS AND SHORT.

rep Informal for a sales representative or agent, usually one who works as an independent contractor for a number of different companies: *a* *media rep/prefers reps to an in-house sales staff.* Also a verb: *The advertising agency will rep 53 Chinese technical journals.*

replace   See SUBSTITUTE, REPLACE.

reply, response   *Reply* is simpler than *response* and synonymous with *answer;* but *response,* synonymous with *reaction,* is necessarily used when the answer is of a general kind or is made in some way other than by words or overt action: *We appreciate your reply* (or *answer*) *to our request for information about . . .* But: *The free offer did not meet with a good response* (not *reply* or *answer*). Also: *The only response* (or *reaction*) *we wanted was the goodwill of the television audience.*
—in reply to, replying to. Commonplace ways of beginning a letter. See STEREOTYPED LETTER PHRASES.

repo   Pronounced *ree*-po. Plural, *repos* (-poze).   1. CLIPPED FORM of *repossession,* referring to goods taken from the purchaser for nonpayment of installments due: *Used cars, including some repos.*
2. Short for "repossession agreement," an arrangement through which institutions use temporarily idle funds to buy short-term Treasury bills from a securities dealer and at the same time contract to have the dealer buy back ("repossess") the bills at a higher price in a stipulated number of days.

reports   Probably the only characteristic common to all reports is that they purport to make a statement about a topic on which the writer has some special knowledge. In other respects they vary markedly. Some are as brief as a paragraph; others are as long as a book. Some are contained in a letter or memorandum; others are formal documents, complete with REFERENCE NOTES and exhibits. Some touch on a single item of concern; others treat in detail a subject as large as a corporation's financial structure. Some are primarily informational; others are prescriptive or analytical.

Because of the many types of reports and their physical differences, any generalizations about them must be made with caution.

1. CONTENT.   2. ORDER.   3. TONE.   4. STYLE.   5. DISPLAY.

1. CONTENT.   (a) Since the justification for a report is the information it brings to the reader, it is expected that the information will be accurate and sufficiently balanced to guarantee its usefulness.

(b) The amount of information may depend on regulatory requirements, like those of the IRS or SEC. In other instances, the authority of the writer has an important bearing on how much detail need be given and to what degree the opinions of the writer are welcome. The greater the degree of the writer's expertness—the more credibility he or she enjoys—the greater the flexibility allowed in the presentation and documentation of facts.

(c) When the situations treated by reports become repetitive, management ensures getting the kinds of reports it wants by providing either a printed fill-in form or a list of topics for a writer to take up in sequence, using the topics as headings. This assembly-line method is not likely to win points for creativity, but it scores high on efficiency.

(d) Of necessity, a long report will have many features that are absent in a shorter one. Although some of those features are mere trappings, others help to make reference easy and strengthen the presentation (see chart).

2. ORDER. Factors that determine the order of data in a report include the purpose of the report and the receiver's interest in the subject and attitude toward it. In any long report, an initial summary of the findings is usually desirable. But the full statement of conclusions and recommendations, especially if contrary to the reader's expectations, are better held to the end so that the supporting data that precedes it will have time to work on the reader's mind. The formats in the accompanying chart are adaptable to many needs, but see also **ORDER OF PRESENTATION** in the main vocabulary.

3. TONE. Unlike letters, reports are only occasionally permitted to be informal and personal. The longer reports, especially, require objectivity, with little or no personal reference to the writer.

But being objective does not leave the writer helpless to affect the reader's judgment. Writers whose purpose it is to interpret as well as report will surely have a well-developed point of view as a result of their research. The persuasiveness of the report is then determined by the evidence at hand and the manner in which it is presented.

The excerpt below is a section of a study on the effects of government regulation on American industries.* Ultimately, the weight of the evidence will suggest that the economy suffers from overregulation, but these measured paragraphs near the beginning are useful in establishing an objective basis for later judgments.

*From Jules Backman's "The Problem of Regulation," in *Regulation and Deregulation,* ed. Jules Backman (Indianapolis: Bobbs-Merrill, 1981), pp. 8–10.

Content of Long-Form Reports

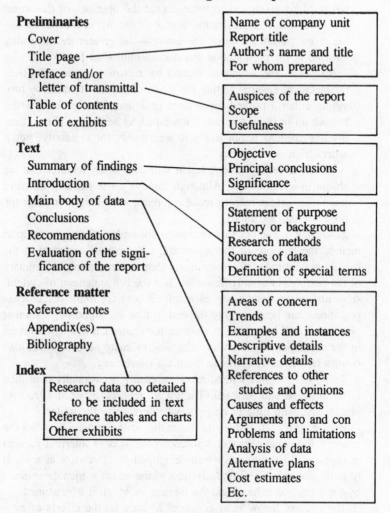

Preliminaries
Cover
Title page
Preface and/or
   letter of transmittal
Table of contents
List of exhibits

> Name of company unit
> Report title
> Author's name and title
> For whom prepared

> Auspices of the report
> Scope
> Usefulness

Text
Summary of findings
Introduction
Main body of data
Conclusions
Recommendations
Evaluation of the signi-
   ficance of the report

> Objective
> Principal conclusions
> Significance

> Statement of purpose
> History or background
> Research methods
> Sources of data
> Definition of special terms

Reference matter
Reference notes
Appendix(es)
Bibliography

Index

> Research data too detailed
>   to be included in text
> Reference tables and charts
> Other exhibits

> Areas of concern
> Trends
> Examples and instances
> Descriptive details
> Narrative details
> References to other
>   studies and opinions
> Causes and effects
> Arguments pro and con
> Problems and limitations
> Analysis of data
> Alternative plans
> Cost estimates
> Etc.

Reports 1.   Adjustments in content and order are made to suit the purpose of the report.

I.	**V.**
A. Subject	A. Background
B. Discussion	B. Present method
C. Conclusion	C. Proposed method
	D. Analysis of benefits
II.	E. Conclusion
	F. Recommendation
A. Statement of problem	
B. Recommendations	
C. Supporting data	**VI.**
	A. Summary
III.	B. Purpose of report
	C. Relevant data
A. Objective	D. Significance of the data
B. Proposal	E. Conclusion
C. Anticipated results	
D. Recommendation	
IV.	**VII.**
A. Problem defined	A. Statement of problem
B. Alternative solutions weighed	B. Division of the problem into its main parts
C. Recommendation	C. Defining the issues
D. Implementation requirements	D. Conclusions
E. Initial procedure	E. Recommendations

Reports 2. Some basic report formats

The nature and scope of the new regulatory agencies have changed dramatically in the past decade. Instead of controlling a market or an industry, the new agencies deal with the conditions under which goods are produced or a particular function of a company; they cut across industry lines. Because of their thrust, these activities have been described as "social regulation" in contrast to "economic regulation" for the earlier regulation of industries. Economic regulations "govern the conditions of doing business" in an industry and usually cover all operations while social regulations "dictate some of the operating conditions required of a wide range of industries."[4] To a large extent, the new regulatory agencies are concerned with some phase of the quality of life.[5]

An important distinction between the older and newer regulatory agencies is found in the legislation under which they operate. Professor George A. Steiner has noted:

"A . . . dimension of the new regulation is that legislation is lengthy and specific. Government regulatory legislation in the past established broad policies, with comparatively little specific guidance, and gave the regulatory agency wide powers to set detailed regulations in conformance with the public interest and the policy guidelines drawn by the Congress. Today's legislation tends to be lengthy and detailed. The EPA, for example, administers statutes that run into hundreds of pages of detailed specifications. The Clean Air Act sets specific pollution-reduction targets and timetables and leaves the EPA little discretion."[6]

These regulations have been embodied in such laws and agencies as the Truth in Lending Act (1969), Clean Air Act (1970), Occupational Safety and Health Act (1970), Environmental Protection Agency (1970), Consumer Product Safety Commission (1972), Employee Retirement Income Security Act (ERISA) (1974), and Equal Employment Opportunity Act (1964). The agencies established to administer these laws have assumed an ever-increasing role over the activities of the companies involved. Because of the far-reaching nature of the regulations, the impact of the federal government is enormously greater than it was formerly. This may be illustrated [in the figures for] industrial illnesses and accidents in which OSHA is involved . . .

"In 1976 one of every 11 workers in private industry suffered from an accident or illness related to the job; 4,500 workers lost their lives from such causes. The Bureau of Labor Statistics estimated that over 39 million workdays were lost in the private sector in 1976 because of nonfatal occupational illnesses or accidents."[7]

---

[4]*Economic Report of the President,* January 1978 (Washington, D.C.: Council of Economic Advisers, 1978), p. 206.

[5]On January 16, 1980, the Occupational and Health Administration (OSHA) announced for the first time comprehensive regulations to protect employees from exposure to substances that are strongly believed to cause cancer in the workplace. [*The New York Times,* January 17, 1980]

[6]George A. Steiner, "New Patterns in Government Regulation of Business," *MSU Business Topics,* Autumn 1978, p. 56.

[7]*Economic Report of the President,* January 1978, p. 209.

4. STYLE. (a) The use of "I" is common in an informal report, but unlikely in a formal report unless the writer is expected to make judgments on the strength of his or her authority as an expert. In staff reports, references to the writer are avoided by the use of flat statements of fact and expressions like "the facts show" and "investigation revealed." At other times objectivity is served by passive constructions like "it was learned" and "it is recommended." Experience suggests, however, that when references to the writer cannot or should not be avoided, the simplest substitutes for "I" are "the writer," "the investigator," "the reporter," "the analyst," and similar names. "We" is fairly standard when a committee is named as the author. See also ACTIVE VOICE, PASSIVE VOICE.

(b) Words are selected for their informative value, and expressions indicating hasty judgments, bias, or extremes of feeling are avoided: *It is obvious that employees are disregarding the safety regulations* (Better: *The accidents cited indicate a pattern of disregard for the safety regulations/There is no question that a sound research program is needed* (Better: *Management personnel we spoke to recognized the need for a sound research program*).

(c) A business report may necessarily be technical, but it need not be dull. Apart from the interest inherent in the subject and the data supporting it, the writer can enliven the prose in many ways. See, for instance, ABSTRACT AND CONCRETE WORDS; READABILITY; and SENTENCES.

5. DISPLAY. The appearance of the report says as much about the source (or writer) as the content says about the subject. Certainly, the layout and display can help materially to make reading easy and heighten the effect of the narrative.

(a) HEADINGS
A variety of heads can relieve the solid blocks of text and show more clearly the relation between the parts.

(b) WHITE SPACE
Adequate margins are needed to frame the page. If the text is single-spaced, it is especially important that the length of the lines be limited and that space be left between paragraphs. Important paragraphs can be set in a few spaces from the side margins. An open typographic effect is better than a crowded one.

(c) ENUMERATION
The scattered listing and numbering of related points (as de-

scriptive features, reasons, advantages) helps to break up a solid text.

(d) GRAPHIC DEVICES

The graphic representation of points made in the text can contribute to clarity and visual appeal. Graphic devices include spot tables, charts, diagrams, models, and—if the subject permits—drawings and photographs.

See also **HEADINGS** and **ENUMERATION** in the main vocabulary.

reposition   In marketing, to give a product and its advertising a new and distinctive character; to change the marketing strategy of a company or product in relation to the competition.

Town & Country, once a magazine for dowagers and debutantes, has been repositioned as a service magazine for people with money. ["A service magazine talks to people as if they were really human beings"—David A. McCann, the publisher.]

Diners Club International is now going into Phase 2 of its repositioning effort, which started last year with the introduction of the Double Card, one credit card for business and one for entertainment. Compare **POSITION** 3.

repository   A place where something is stored, usually for a long time, as a warehouse, a library, a museum, or a vault. See also the synonymous terms **DEPOSITARY, DEPOSITORY**.

repro   Pronounced *ree*-pro. **CLIPPED FORM** of "reproduction proof."
1. A blemish-free proof of printed material from which faithfully reproduced copies can be made, usually by some photomechanical process.
2. Any copy suitable for reproduction: *They wanted a repro of the cover design/If the pages are typed with a carbon ribbon, we can use them for repros.*

reprographics   Also *reprography*. A name encompassing all methods of office copying and record reproduction. Includes heavy-duty printing systems as well as systems for making photocopies, slides, transparencies, and microfilm: *in charge of reprographics.*

requested   See **COMPULSIVE WORDS**.

require   The plainer *need* is often more appropriate: *I'll need your signature on the requisition/Helmut needs a good talking to.* But: *The order form requires your signature.* Also: *We're going to require* (more formal than *need*) *at least two more floors in the main building.*

reside Formal for "live": *The chairman resides at the Waldorf Towers.* But: *They live* (rather than *reside*) *in the suburbs.*

residuals Payments made to certain participants of a taped TV performance or commercial announcement: *still earning residuals on his appearances in* Kojak.

resolutions 1. A resolution is a formal statement by an officially constituted body, such as a board of directors, a committee, or an assembly. The purpose is to put on record some action of the group or to perform some ceremonial function: express appreciation, convey regret or congratulations, commemorate an event, and so forth.

2. Resolutions vary in degree of formality, depending on the nature of the business and the mental disposition of the group. The simplest formal resolution consists of an enacting or resolving statement.

RESOLVED, That the vacancy left by the resignation of Wendell Raines, secretary of the Finance Committee, be filled by Carolyn Jason.

3. Other formal resolutions begin with the reason or reasons for the resolution and follow with one or more resolving clauses.

WHEREAS, . . . , and

WHEREAS, . . .

RESOLVED, That . . . ; and

RESOLVED FURTHER, That . . .

When a resolution consists of several or more reasons and resolving clauses, the form can be simplified in this manner:

WHEREAS, it is in the best interests of the Society that its annual meeting be conducted in such a manner that

1. . . . . ; and

2. . . . .

NOW, THEREFORE, BE IT RESOLVED, That the following procedures be adopted:

1. . . . .

2. . . . .

3. . . . .

4. Many resolutions, including the ceremonial kind, are seldom so formal and may use not a single *Whereas* or *Resolved.* A resolution on the death of a board member, for instance, will combine a tribute to the deceased, including a summation of his work and

achievements, and an expression of regret at his passing. Any formalizing touches, if any, may include a preamble,

> Resolution of the Board of Directors of the LMN Financial Corporation, on the death of Simon S. Brewer II.

and a line at the end,

> Adopted by the Board of Directors, October 11, 19xx.

5. Conventionally, *Whereas, Resolved, Be it resolved*, and similar phrases are set in solid capitals; and the *That* following *Resolved* begins with a capital.

resource   Educational JARGON, descriptive of someone or something able to offer support or help: *resource person, resource learning center, resource function/the most comprehensive resource book in its field*. See also HUMAN RESOURCES.

resource recovery   Recycling, or putting waste materials to use, as burning garbage to produce electricity, reprocessing used paper to make more paper, and reclaiming the metal in tin-coated and aluminum cans. See RECYCLE 1.

respectfully   Alone or in expressions like "Respectfully yours" and "Yours respectfully," a COMPLIMENTARY CLOSE limited to formal or official use.

respective, respectively   These words are occasionally needed for clarity, but are otherwise pretentious and superfluous: *Dyson and Kollman took their places* (not *their respective places*) *around the large table/Those present were* (not *were respectively*) *John Harriman, Delia Pauling, Henry Reese, and Glenda Waring*. But: *The shipments to Sears and the May Company were scheduled for January 12 and February 4 respectively*. [*Respectively*, meaning "each in the order mentioned," is needed to sort out the names and dates.]

Respectively yours   A crude misspelling of *Respectfully yours*, a COMPLIMENTARY CLOSE.

rest   See BALANCE, REMAINDER, REST.

restaurateur   So spelled (not *restauranteur*), and pronounced res-tur-uh-*toor*. The owner or manager of a restaurant.

restrictive and nonrestrictive modifiers   For definitions and punctuation, see COMMA 4.

résumé Pronounced *rez*-oo-may and, for convenience, commonly written without the phonetic marks. A summary of qualifications submitted to an employer by a job applicant. Compare CURRICULUM VITAE.

résumés Submission of a résumé is the customary way to seek consideration for a job. The résumé is submitted on the applicant's own initiative or in response to a help wanted advertisement. The immediate purpose is to obtain an interview.

A necessary preliminary to writing the résumé is an objective review of one's background and qualifications and a corresponding survey of the market for one's particular talents. Job applicants find it helpful to talk with friends, business acquaintances, and career counselors and to engage in some creative study, using business publications, career guides, and other library materials.

1. THE PRESENTATION. 2. JOB OBJECTIVE. 3. QUALIFICATIONS. 4. COVER LETTER. 5. TROUBLE SPOTS.

1. THE PRESENTATION. A résumé faces keen competition and close inspection. Its first objective is to get to the right person and gain his or her favorable attention.

(a) The résumé should preferably be addressed to the individual with responsibility for the job desired. The name may be obtained from a friend who works for the company, a business news item, a trade or professional directory, or by a telephone call to the company ("I'm addressing a letter to your marketing director . . ."). It is important to get the full name, correctly spelled, and the exact title.

(b) If only a few résumés are being mailed, they can be typed individually. The more common practice is to prepare a master copy—neat and correct in every detail—from which 50 or 100 copies can be made and sent out as the list of prospective employers is expanded. Offset printing, available from local shops, insures the best reproduction qualities. The résumé should be used only as long as it is current. A cover letter (see Par. 4 below) is better typed personally or done on a word processor to look as if it had been.

(c) Many persons with experience in these matters recommend that the résumé be confined to one side of a single sheet. Others with similar experience feel that, so long as the qualifications are pertinent and concisely stated, the employer will tolerate—even welcome—a second sheet. At the other extreme, a sparsely filled sheet suggests a deficiency of qualifications.

(d) The form of the résumé is best described by the term "fact sheet." The name of the applicant, and the address and telephone number are put at the top of the page. Data is then classified and listed under appropriate headings. The **HEADINGS** can be underscored or set in solid caps. Adequate margins, indentions, and space between items or sets of items will make a good display and improve **READABILITY**.

(e) Except perhaps for a summary statement at the beginning, the data are usually expressed in phrases and fragmentary sentences. This technique permits compression of the material and speeds reading. Some samples:

M.B.A., Wharton School, University of Pennsylvania, 19xx.

Seven years of experience in controller's department.

Established procedures to determine cost factors and profitability of prospective projects.

2. JOB OBJECTIVE.   Some authorities consider it desirable to formulate, in not more than a few lines, a statement of the job objective, and place it prominently above the list of qualifications. An example:

Product manager; packaged foods experience; prepared to take charge of consumer research, packaging development, new product planning, marketing, and product improvement.

Problems arise, however, when the candidate is young and has not yet a clearly defined job objective, or when the job objective is at variance with the qualifications offered. It may be preferable, in those instances, to leave any reference to a career goal to the cover letter (see Par. 4 below).

3. QUALIFICATIONS.   (a) Fitness for the job is shown by a detailed account of education, training, and job experience. Relevant off-the-job experience and interests, and personal qualifications, may be added. Main headings for the various types of data vary with the individual's background and the job sought. These headings from one résumé are merely suggestive:

Career Objective

Experience with the ABC Corporation

Previous Work Experience

Professional Affiliations and Activities

Education and Training
Personal Data

(b) Items are listed in the order of importance, with the most important first. This order applies both to main topics and supporting details. Younger applicants are usually advised to put their education ahead of experience, if any, and more mature workers to start with their job experience. The order of importance also makes it practically mandatory to list jobs held and schools attended in reverse chronological order, so that the last job held, the highest degree received, and the last school attended take precedence over others.

(c) Details relating to education will include at least schools attended and the highest certificate or degree, with the date awarded. Depending on the relative importance of the data, the applicant may also indicate awards and honors; course-related fieldwork and research reports; and participation—or better, leadership positions—in extracurricular activities. Ordinarily, though, the longer the time since graduation and the greater the amount and importance of the job experience, the less emphasis on the school record.

(d) Job experience includes jobs held, with dates, descriptions of duties, and noteworthy job-related accomplishments. This part of the résumé may also note professional memberships and certifications, speeches, publications, and participation in important company-offered seminars and training opportunities. For a person with considerable work experience, this section will be the longest in the résumé, and it will probably be advisable to classify and list the data under several headings.

(e) Personal qualifications are ordinarily placed last. The specifics may be hard to deal with and require much thought before they are put in the résumé. Some information employers used to require as a prerequisite for an interview—age, color, and religion, for instance—can no longer be legally requested. Age is important, of course, but the list of schools and jobs and the associated dates will give the employer a fair approximation. And any applicant can volunteer whatever personal data may be advantageous in getting an interview. That includes age as well as marital status, general disposition and health, languages other than English, birthplace, and so forth.

(f) References are not necessary in the résumé and the subject need not be mentioned. A possible exception occurs when the applicant can offer the name of a well-reputed figure in business, law, or politics, for example, that may make an interview more certain. Otherwise, references are best left to such time as the employer asks for them.

4. COVER LETTER.   (a) A "cover" letter is considered an essential accompaniment of the application. The letter is important not only because it can make a timely, direct, and personal appeal to the reader, but also because it affords the opportunity to adapt to the needs of the particular company addressed. Those needs can be surmised from information in such sources as the company's last annual report, published articles, and data in MOODY'S and similar business services. If the résumé is a response to a help wanted advertisement, the covering letter permits the applicant to deal directly with the job specifications in the ad.

(b) Like other letters with a primarily persuasive purpose, the cover letter needs a strong opening, and a close pointed to action.

Dear Mr. Greidler:

Your company is well known for its effective use of direct-response advertising. During my seven years' experience in that field, sales of the products in my charge tripled, while the cost per sale was cut in half. I would like to do as well or better as a member of your staff.

. . . .

An interview will, I am sure, be a good investment of your time. Please phone or write. I will bring with me a portfolio of my direct-response campaigns to show you.

Sincerely yours

See also AIDA, LETTER FORM, and LETTER WRITING.

5. TROUBLE SPOTS.   The résumé often brings the applicant face-to-face with some sticky problems that provide an unmatched, though not always appreciated, experience in business communication.

(a) Bragging.   Understandably, all applicants want to put their experience in the best light. This is done by selecting only those accomplishments that can be shown to be job-related, and then using fact and reason rather than bald assertion. Data showing rapid advancement in a company, for example, tells much more about the applicant than any number of claims of "outstanding achievement" and "extraordinary potential." The danger of overstatement is especially strong in the cover letter, where the ability to satisfy the specific employer's needs must be persuasively addressed. There the applicant, who is barely familiar with the job and the company, takes needless risks of irritating the employer with statements like "I am convinced I can improve your competitive position" and "Your search for an assistant credit manager is now ended." Caution dictates a more reasoned approach, for instance, "I am sure I can carry over to your company my long and successful credit experience in the textile field."

(b) Negativism.   A résumé and the cover letter are self-advertisements. There is no place in them for mentioning the absence of qualifications, as "I don't have any practical experience in selling, but . . ." A positive approach will omit such confessions and concentrate on the qualifications one does possess, using words like *completed, succeeded, accomplished, wrote, won, obtained, led,* and *organized.* See also **POSITIVE AND NEGATIVE WORDS.**

(c) Salary.   Once an applicant's credentials have been established, salary becomes a relatively minor issue. It is better discussed in the interview than mentioned in the application, where a relatively low or unrealistically high figure may rule out an interview.

(d) Career change.   An applicant who has followed one career path may wish to change to another. To anticipate any question, the applicant can give a valid reason for the change and show how education and experience already obtained can prove advantageous in the desired position. An employer often wants the fresh point of view an applicant can bring to the job. Many college teachers, for example, are having success in transferring their skills to research, training, and counseling positions in industry.

(e) Gaps in employment record.   There is some question whether gaps in the job chronology should be explained in the résumé. The gap is not likely to deter an employer from giving an interview to an otherwise qualified candidate. If the gap results from unrelated work, the time period can be accounted for in a section on "Additional Experience"; otherwise, any question about it can be answered at the interview.

retainer   A preliminary fee paid to secure the services of a professional person, such as a lawyer, architect, or business consultant: *paid her a retainer of $10,000.*

—on retainer. Engaged; descriptive of a professional person who has been paid a preliminary fee for services to be rendered.

retread Used as a PEJORATIVE to denote a worker with unneeded skills who has been retrained for a new job: *The department is a dumping ground for retreads.*

retrofit Pronounced *ret*-ro-fit. 1. To put back into an earlier condition: *The main power station has been retrofitted to burn coal* [the fuel it was originally designed to use].

2. To refit an old model, incorporating improvements made in later models: *For $15 million, the airline can retrofit their DC-8s for another decade of service.*

return address See ENVELOPE ADDRESS 3.

return mail The next mail: *Please send us your check by return mail/We fill all orders by return mail* [the next outgoing mail after receipt of the order]. Too often "by return mail" is merely a stereotyped phrase that is not to be taken literally. More apt are terms like "promptly," "at once," "immediately." "We are sending you by return mail" is gibberish for "We are sending you in the next mail," since no "return" is involved. See also STEREOTYPED LETTER PHRASES.

revaluate To make another valuation. Preferred over *reevaluate*, but not over *revalue*, which is synonymous: *In view of the storm damage, it was necessary to revaluate* (or *revalue*) *the entire stock.* See also VALUE, VALUATE.

—revaluation, noun; preferred over *reevaluation: The prospective buyers asked for a revaluation of the inventory.*

See also LONG VARIANTS.

revenue enhancement A EUPHEMISM for taxation: *Each side is advocating a different mix of budget cuts and new "revenue enhancements," once known as taxes.*

reverend Abbreviated *Rev.* See FORMS OF ADDRESS 1.

reverse engineering The practice of buying a competitor's product or obtaining it from a friendly customer of a competitor, and taking it apart to see how it works. Engaged in principally by semiconductor, computer, and instrument companies as a means of remaining competitive. Opinion on the ethics of the practice is divided.

revert back   Redundant because "back" is implicit in the meaning of *revert: After his death, the title to the property will revert* (not *revert back*) *to* . . .

revocable   Pronounced with the accent on *rev-*. Similarly, *irrevocable* is pronounced ir-*rev-* (accent on the second syllable): *The decision is revocable/irrevocable*.

rhetoric   The artful or persuasive use of language in speech and writing: *skilled in rhetoric/took several courses in rhetoric* (as in composition and speech). Unfortunately, the original meaning is often lost and the term takes on a **PEJORATIVE** coloration in such phrases as "racial rhetoric," "capitalistic rhetoric," "should lower the level of rhetoric," and "just a lot of rhetoric."

rhetorical question   A question to which an answer is not expected or which points to only one answer. It is usually followed by a question mark: *How are we to know what our competitors are thinking?/Did you ever see such enterprise?* Also: *Did you ever see such enterprise!*

right-to-work law   A law, in some states, forbidding the requirement of union membership for getting or holding a job. See **OPEN SHOP**.

ring   Informal. A telephone call: *Give me a ring.* Also a verb: *I'll ring you tomorrow.* Analogous to **BUZZ**.

risk management   A comprehensive term for the insurance business and the administration of insurance needs. Includes evaluating the risks inherent in any enterprise, providing insurance coverage of the right kinds and in the right amounts at the right price, and overseeing insurance purchases.

roadblocking   The practice of running the same television commercial at the same time on all major networks so that escape by the viewer is difficult, if not impossible: *We'll run all our network advertising in roadblocking fashion and add 223 spots during the week on seven cable systems.*

robbery   The taking of property by force or threat. Compare **BURGLARY** and **THEFT**.

robotics   The science of designing and using remote-controlled machines to take the place of workers in complex or hazardous work procedures; an advanced form of automation. In some instances, the same system can be adapted to the production and assembly of a variety of products.

role playing A training device by which two or more members of a group act out a relationship in front of the rest of the group. Lessons from the experience are drawn and discussed. When faults in behavior are observed, as they usually are, the situation can be reenacted to incorporate the lessons learned. Salespersons, complaint clerks, and personnel interviewers, among others, are trained in this way. Videotape may be used to record performances for analysis and discussion.

roll over To substitute one security for another by a transfer of funds; also to issue a new security of the same kind and amount for a maturing one: *can roll over his credits in the company's pension plan by placing them in an Individual Retirement Account (IRA)/asked the bank to roll over the certificate of deposit.*

—**rollover,** noun: *specified a rollover of the maturing certificate of deposit.*

ROM In data processing, the ACRONYM for *read-only memory,* consisting of the instructions the computer uses for repetitive tasks. The computer can read instructions in *ROM,* but *ROM* cannot receive data for storage. Compare **RANDOM-ACCESS MEMORY (RAM).**

Roman numerals See NUMERALS 9.

ROP Pronounced ahr-o-pee. Run-of-paper. Used to signify that a newspaper display advertisement is to be placed in any position, at the discretion of the newspaper; opposed to ''preferred position,'' which the advertiser can specify and buy at a premium.

round file Facetious for ''wastebasket'': *Don't keep your reader guessing or he might file the letter away even before he finishes it—in the round file.* [Malcolm Forbes]

route Commonly pronounced *root* when used in reference to a road, highway, or line of travel. The pronunciation *rout* (as in *trout*) is at least equally favored when the word refers to a fixed course of movement, as by a deliveryman, door-to-door salesperson, or trash collector.

routing slip Pronounced *root-.* A small printed form used by one person to direct a letter or other material to a second person for attention or action. In addition to spaces for the date and the names of the trans-

---

COMMANDER PRODUCTS, INC.

Referred to _____

By _____

Date _____

For—

_____ Action   _____ Noted and returned

_____ Advice   _____ Previous correspondence

_____ Approval   _____ Recommendation

_____ Checking   _____ Report

_____ Conference   _____ Reply

_____ File   _____ Reply (prepare)

_____ Memo (prepare) _____ Signature

           _____ Your information—return

Routing slip

mitter and the individual addressed, the slip usually includes a checklist of possible actions to be taken and a space for remarks (see illustration). Also *buck slip*.

RSVP Abbreviated from the French for "Please reply"; often used on invitations. The use of "please" with RSVP is redundant: *If you plan to attend, please RSVP by calling 555–2371* (omit *please*, or rephrase to "please call 555–2371"). See also **WORDINESS** 3.

run A simple synonym for "manage," "operate," "oversee": *His widow now runs the business.* See **LONG WORDS AND SHORT**.

runaround 1. In printing, type set in narrow lines on either side of an illustration or other inset.
2. Tactics of delay, often involving a deceptive response: *giving us the runaround.*

runaway Out of control; characterized by steep increases, as in price: *runaway prices/a runaway market.*

rundown A summary or a brief report of particulars: *Let's have a rundown of your talk with Sattler.*

run-in head See **HEADINGS**.

run-of-paper See **ROP**.

S

sabbatical A leave of absence with pay. Traditionally a teacher's **PER-QUISITE**: now occasionally extended to executives and professional personnel in business.

sack Slang. To fire, dismiss from one's job: *was finally sacked.*

sacrilegious So spelled, and pronounced sak-rih-*lee*-jus; often mis-spelled through confusion with *religious: thought that changing the product's century-old formula would be sacrilegious* (irreverent, pro-fane).

safe deposit box See VAULT, with which it is sometimes confused.

safety net Used by President Reagan to signify the subsistence mea-sures designed to protect the poor from budget cutbacks; now also used in the general sense of a safeguard: *A mineral supplement that supplies 100% of the U.S. recommended daily allowances cannot hurt and may act as a safety net for those who eat haphazardly/Because national in-troduction of a product may involve outlays of millions of dollars, test markets are a safety net under mass-marketers' slender high wire.*

said Legal JARGON for "aforementioned" or "previously specified": *the said property/the said claimant.* In ordinary discourse, *the, this,* or *these* is preferable: *The tenant was ordered to vacate the premises* (rather than *the said premises*) *by July 1.* See also AFOREMENTIONED, AFORE-SAID.

salable Usually so spelled and, less frequently, *saleable: a salable* (or *saleable*) *product.* But *salability* has no alternative spelling: *insists on salability first.*

salary, wage Both a salary and a wage are amounts paid to a worker on a regular basis. *Salary,* however, is the customary name given to the stipend of a **WHITE COLLAR WORKER** or executive, while *wage* (or, plural, *wages*) is applicable to a manual worker who is paid at an hourly or daily rate.

sale   Something "for sale" is available for purchase; something "on sale" is available for purchase at a special price: *house for sale*. But: *On sale at 2 pairs for $8, regularly $5 each.*

salesman   Whether the title is *salesman, saleswoman*, or *salesperson*, there is a latent prejudice against the association with sales. Hence the substitution of such ego-enhancing titles as *account supervisor, account executive, representative*, and **CONSULTANT**. See also **SEXUAL BIAS**.

salon   Pronounced suh-*lon;* French, sah-*lawn*. An elegant shop; also any commercial establishment devoted to fashion: *a salon patronized by some of the best-dressed women in Washington*. Also *a beauty salon, a dress salon, a fur salon.*

salutation   The conventional word or phrase of greeting in a letter, as *Gentlemen, Dear Mr. Bettman, Dear Barry*. Among the standard letter formats, the salutation is omitted only in the **SIMPLIFIED STYLE**.

The salutation is correctly placed at the left margin above the first line of the letter or the subject line, if there is one. Except when open punctuation is used, the salutation is usually followed by a colon, though a comma is appropriate after a first-name salutation.

See also **LETTER FORM** 3–5 and **FORMS OF ADDRESS**.

1. IN ADDRESSING INDIVIDUALS.   2. IN ADDRESSING ORGANIZATIONS.   3. IN FORM LETTERS.

1. IN ADDRESSING INDIVIDUALS.   (a) Acceptable salutations in a letter to a man or woman are shown below in the order of decreasing formality. The most common forms in ordinary business use are starred.

Dear Sir	Dear Madam
My dear Mr. Gordon	My dear Madam
*Dear Mr. Gordon	*Dear Miss (Mrs., Ms.) Gordon
Dear Phil	Dear Phyllis

(b) When a letter is addressed to an individual by his or her official title rather than by name—a course to be followed only when the name is not known and cannot be obtained—the salutation is *Dear Sir* or *Dear Sir or Madam*. If the choice is unappealing, the salutation can be omitted.

(c) For the salutations of letters to individuals jointly addressed, see **FORMS OF ADDRESS** 2.

2. IN ADDRESSING ORGANIZATIONS.   (a) When the organization includes men and women, as almost all do, the salutation *Gentlemen*

is no longer inviolable, though it is still common. *Ladies and Gentlemen* is literally correct, but it has few converts; and inventions like *Dear Persons* and *Dear Gentlepeople* have even fewer. Fortunately, not much is lost if the salutation is omitted. As in the simplified style of letter makeup, a SUBJECT LINE can be used in its place. See LETTER FORM 3.

(b) A letter to an organization of women, such as the Ms. Foundation, the First Women's Bank, and the Daughters of the American Revolution, takes the salutation *Ladies* or *Mesdames*.

3. IN FORM LETTERS. Since form letters are not bound by the traditions of personal letters, salutations can be found to meet any particular need, as this selection shows:

Dear Friend	Fellow American
Dear Customer	Fellow Worker
Dear Reader	To Whom It May Concern
Dear Member	To the Person Concerned
Dear Colleague	Dear Brother (fraternity)
Dear Student	Dear Sister (sorority)

same 1. Well used as an adjective *(the same day, the same size)* and as a pronoun in such a context as, "The children were bequeathed $10,000 each; the brother received the same" (that is, "the same amount").

2. JARGON when used as a pronoun with or without *the* in the sense of the aforementioned person or thing: *We have your check and thank you for same (Thank you for your check)/When the invoice is received, the same (it) is forwarded immediately to the Accounts Department for payment.*

S & L Savings and loan association; a financial institution that provides a place for savings as well as funds for financing primarily home mortgages. When such a bank is federally chartered (others are organized as corporations), it is known as a federal savings and loan association and must belong to the Federal Savings and Loan Insurance Corporation (FSLIC).

S & P The abbreviation of STANDARD & POOR'S CORPORATION.

saving, savings 1. Saving is used as a singular noun in such a phrase as "a saving of $10." Informally, the plural *savings* is also treated as singular in the same context: *A savings of $10 a pair is considerable.*

2. As an adjective, *saving* takes the sense of "redeeming": *a saving*

feature. Otherwise, the plural is used: *a savings account/the Franklin Savings Bank.*

savvy Slang as a verb, noun, and adjective: *I savvy* (understand) *his motives/political savvy* (understanding); *has lots of savvy* (practical wisdom)/*a savvy* (well-informed, sensible) *executive.*

sawbuck Slang for a ten-dollar bill: *lent him a sawbuck.*

SBA Small Business Administration. An independent federal agency.

scab An informal derogation for a strikebreaker or a person who refuses union membership.

scam Slang for a bogus scheme: *the victim of a scam.*

scare tactics Methods, not necessarily illegal, to frighten a person or group into doing something in the interests of the user of the technique. For example, the manufacturer of certain branded prescription drugs claims that dispensing generic equivalents—though allowed by state laws—will expose druggists to malpractice suits.

scenario Originally the outline of the plot of a motion picture play, now a vogue word for a hypothetical series of related events, a projected master plan: *The scenario of a successful commodity campaign is to close out positions as soon as you recognize that you are on the wrong side of the trend/The whole idea of planning assumes the possibility of a choice between alternative feasible scenarios* [Wassily Leontief]/*In the absence of information, people are always going to fill in the gaps with the worst possible scenario.*

scheme Words like *plan* and *proposal* have a better CONNOTATION: *He came in with a scheme (plan?) to double our profits/Their scheme (proposal?) would have cost us thousands of dollars.*

schlock From the Yiddish, slang for shoddy merchandise: *a dealer in schlock/such schlock!* Also an adjective: *a schlock merchant* [one who deals in schlock].

screen See PRESCREEN.

scrumptious So spelled (not *scrumptuous*). Slang for "delectable, very satisfying," usually descriptive of food: *scrumptious meals with wine/scrumptious hamburgers.*

search company See EXECUTIVE RECRUITER.

seasonable, seasonal *Seasonable* is "suitable to the season": *seasonable weather*. *Seasonal* is "relating to the season": *a seasonal business* [furs, fuel oil]/*seasonal employment*.

seasonally adjusted A qualification found on some data relating to economic trends. It signifies that a figure or figures have been statistically adjusted to avoid distortions caused by recurring patterns of change, as by climate or holidays. With such an adjustment, however, it is possible to translate, say, the number of housing start-ups in November—a traditionally slow month—into an annual rate.

seat-of-the-pants Informal. Descriptive of an unplanned or badly directed operation with a high potential for failure: *Seat-of-the-pants banking is being replaced by management-by-objective.*

SEC Pronounced ess-ee-see. Securities and Exchange Commission. An independent federal regulatory agency.

second-class mail A classification reserved for newspapers and periodicals which have the required permit from the U.S. Postal Service.

secretary Abbreviated *sec.* or *secy.* See also CPS.

sector JARGON for a part or section of the economy; often superfluous or better replaced by a more specific term: *The government sector (The government) must do its part by lowering business taxes/Housing development is best left to the private sector (to private investment)/A showdown is looming over the entrance of the big accounting firms into the lucrative sector (practice) of business consulting.*

secular Occurring over the long term. In statistical analysis, "secular trends" are used to forecast the growth rate of various industries. Compare CYCLICAL.

secure, obtain Unless the subtle difference in meaning is preserved, *secure* is just a pretentious synonym for "obtain" or "get." *Secure* is well used, however, to convey the idea of obtaining with certainty or sureness: *After many suits and countersuits, we finally secured possession of the premises.* But (no need to stress idea of sureness): *The new tenant can obtain (rather than secure) the key from the agent on the premises.* See also PROCURE and OBTAIN, GET.

seed money Money invested in starting a project: *In return for its contribution of seed money, the network will have first rights to televising the taped productions.*

seeing that Less formal than "considering that," "since," and "as," but there appears to be no valid objection to its use: *Seeing that the work was proceeding so slowly, we decided to obtain more help/The results might have been expected, seeing that they had absolutely no previous experience.* Not to be confused with *seeing as* and *seeing as how*, which are nonstandard. See also AS HOW, AS WHERE.

seems apparent A redundancy usually followed by awkward phrasing: *It seems quite apparent that it is feasible (It seems quite feasible) to computerize the reports.* See also WORDINESS 3.

seem(s) unable Well used in general English: *They seem unable to control the situation.* Compare CAN'T SEEM.

see where Informal for "see that": *I see where (see that) Bolton has found a new president.*

segment Part or portion; sometimes responsible for a needlessly pretentious phrase: *Our research into the attitudes toward the company shows they've had some success with the managerial segment that reads their ads (the managers that read their ads).* But (no question): *We'll start by sending the mailing to only a small segment of the list.*

segmentation of market In advertising, the division of the market for a product into the various groups and subgroups that compose it; a key to the effective selection of media and the choice of advertising AP-PEALS. Segmentation also affects marketing generally. A retail store, for example, will not only create separate departments for particular classes of goods, but also target the goods to particular categories of customers as determined by, say, age, income, or tastes. In a home electronics department, products may be arranged to appeal, separately, to young people, men, and women. In a shop focusing on maternity clothes, the pregnant lawyer having to argue a case in court may be viewed as requiring a different sort of maternity clothes than the pregnant woman caring for two children at home.

seldom ever Informal for "seldom" or "seldom if ever": *We seldom (or seldom if ever) require overtime work.* But (informal only): *We seldom ever require overtime work. Rarely ever* is similarly informal for "rarely" or "rarely if ever."

self- Takes a hyphen whenever the word following has a meaning of its own: *a self-made executive, a self-sealing envelope, a self-serving* *statement*. But: *selfhood, selfless, selfsame*. See also **HYPHEN** 2, as well as *self-* entries immediately following -**SELF**, -**SELVES**.

-self, -selves   See **MYSELF** for the use of this and other reflexive pronouns.

self-addressed   As in "A self-addressed envelope is enclosed for your convenience in replying." Some critics object to the word on the ground that an envelope cannot address itself; others find the phrase in which the word appears to be stereotyped or wordy. Some alternatives: *The enclosed envelope is for your reply/Please use the convenient enclosed envelope.*

self-adhesive   Describing some material, as paper or cloth, backed by an adhesive and applied by light pressure only: *self-adhesive address labels.*

self-employed   Engaged in remunerative work for oneself, not as an employee: *a self-employed financial consultant/a self-employed* [also **FREE LANCE**] *artist.*

self-fulfilling prophecy   Like many other **CLICHÉS**, this one is occasionally the most apt expression for the thought: *Confident, like all seers, that superstitious humanity remembers only the forecasts that prove correct, he expects investors to heed his advice and thus make his prophecies self-fulfilling.*

self-liquidating   Describing an investment, as in a toll bridge, that will be paid back out of income.

self-liquidating premium   An article offered to the consumer at cost as an inducement to buy the primary product of the advertiser; for example, a 20-piece set of stainless flatwear offered for $9.85 and three "proofs of purchase" of Quaker Puffed Wheat.

self-mailer   An advertisement, usually folded, designed to be mailed without an envelope. A panel on the face provides space for the address and postage. See also **POSTCARD**.

sell   Informally used as a noun denoting the act of selling: *believes in the soft sell/finds that the hard sell works/Both the cartoon and the caption get you right into the ad's straightforward, sensible sell.*

sell off   To dispose of a stock of goods by price reductions: *We decided to sell off our entire line of designer wallpaper.*

sell out To sell the entire inventory, as of goods, tickets, and the like: *The house is sold out/We're selling out our stock of last season's models.* ["Selling out our entire stock" is more emphatic, even if redundant. See WORDINESS 3.]

—**sellout,** noun: *The show is a sellout.* Also, informal, a betrayal: *Submitting to their demands would be a sellout of people who have given us their trust.*

sell short To sell for delivery at a later date, as securities, commodities, or foreign exchange that the seller does not own but hopes to buy before the delivery date at a price on which he can make a profit. Also, in common parlance, to underestimate the value of: *Don't make the mistake of selling Smithers short.*

selling handle See at HANDLE.

semantics The study of meaning, especially the meaning of words and their effect on human behavior. The word is often loosely used, as in the phrase "It's only semantics" to suggest a manipulative motive in a particular use of language. Though plural in form, semantics takes a singular verb: *The semantics of the word "profit" makes an interesting study.* For examples of semantics in practice, see CONNOTATION.

semi- Preferably pronounced *sem*-ee. Half; occurring twice during a given period: *semiannual, semimonthly.* Also, "having some of the characteristics of": *semiretired, semifinals.* The hyphen is usually found only before a proper noun or a word beginning with *i: a semi-Chicagoan; semi-integrated.* See also BI-.

semiblock style See LETTER FORM 3.

semicolon (;) The semicolon is less frequently found in business writing than in literary writing, perhaps because its use is not clearly understood and perhaps because the substitution of the period is, in most instances not only possible but also helpful in reducing sentence length (see SENTENCES 1). Anyway, a drop of the voice and a pause in dictation are as characteristic of an oncoming period as of a semicolon, and a period is what the transcriber usually supplies if no instructions are given.

1. The semicolon is used between grammatically complete statements either not joined by a connecting word or joined by one of the "heavy" connectives like *however, therefore, furthermore,* and *accordingly.* The semicolon thus shows a close relation in thought that

would not be so apparent if a period were used. And unlike the period, the semicolon gives the reader a sense of anticipation.

We have reached the end of the road; we are beating against the gates of an occluded frontier. [George Gilder]

Currently, the maximum rate applied to the first $50,000 of long-term capital gains is 25 percent; the proposal would increase the rate to 35 percent.

SBA loans may be for as long as ten or fifteen years; however, working capital loans are limited to six years.

2. The semicolon prevents misreading when placed between coordinate sentence elements of which at least one is already internally punctuated by commas.

The company has plants in Schenectady, New York; Moline, Illinois; Topeka, Kansas; and San Jose, California.

Electronics and Space Systems includes four classes of products and services: electronic components; electronic systems, equipment, and services; computer-based and analytical services; and spacecraft.

The structure can be relatively simple, utilizing a sole partnership, a proprietorship, or a corporation; or quite complex, involving corporations with sophisticated capital structures, limited partnerships, or any combination of these.

seminar   A meeting or series of MEETINGS in which a select group, led by an authority in the field, study in depth a subject of shared interest. Also, loosely, any small-group meeting for the exchange of ideas.

send a signal   See SIGNAL.

senior citizen   A EUPHEMISM for an elderly person. The term is offensive to many individuals so-called, but it is hard to know what terms can be substituted for it without giving similar offense. Suggestions include *a senior, an elder, an elderly* (or *older*) *person, a mature man* (or *woman*). The task of finding synonyms is usually easier in a particular context, where a term like *pensioner, retired worker, emeritus,* or *grandparent* may better describe the subject.

sentences   Overtly, a sentence is any word or word group beginning with a capital letter and ending with a period. In practice, however, the sentence is controlled by certain principles of grammar and **RHETORIC**. Aspects of sentence-making not treated here will be found principally at **SUBJECT AND VERB, POSITION OF MODIFIERS,** and **AC-TIVE VOICE, PASSIVE VOICE.**

1. LENGTH.   2. COMPLETENESS.   3. ORDER.   4. CONSISTENCY

1. LENGTH.   (a) Short sentences are easier to read than long ones and are likely to convey a thought more clearly. **READABILITY** studies show that an average of seventeen to twenty-two words per sentence provides a satisfactory range for most nontechnical prose.

(b) Technical and legal prose is biased toward relatively long sentences at least partly because of the complexities they deal with and the assumption that the reader is equipped by training to deal with such writing. Lawyers are particularly reluctant to shorten sentences because periods often separate main points from their restrictive elements and can lead to misinterpretation.

(c) A long sentence with a complex structure or too much to say is hard to follow:

> The threatened industries of the past always turn to politics to protect them from change because failure demands finance, and a government preoccupied with the statistics of crisis will often find itself subsidizing problems, shoring up essentially moribund patterns of economic and social activity, creating incentives for unemployment, inflation, family breakdown, housing decay, and municipal deficits, making problems worse by making them profitable.

Even this statement, however, becomes tolerable when the several main ideas are sorted out and separated by periods.

> The threatened industries of the past always turn to politics to protect them from change. Failure demands finance. A government preoccupied with the statistics of crisis will often find itself subsidizing problems, shoring up essentially moribund patterns of economic and social activity, creating incentives for unemployment, inflation, family breakdown, housing decay, and municipal deficits, making problems worse by making them profitable. [George Gilder]

The last sentence is still long by ordinary standards, but the use of **PARALLEL STRUCTURE** eases the way through it. The sentence also benefits from the attention focused on it by the two sentences preceding it. The second sentence, with only three words, has special force.

2. COMPLETENESS.   (a) A grammatically complete sentence has at least one subject and one predicate: *Cabot produces gas and oil.* Many sentences, however, are not complete in the strict sense. An

imperative sentence regularly omits the subject: [You] *Subscribe now.* Exclamatory sentences and answers to questions need no subject or predicate: *Hurrah!/What a day!/Will we concede? Never.* Other so-called fragmentary sentences are acceptable when they are used as a stylistic device with the aim of either creating a mood or chopping up thoughts for easy assimilation (see also **PERIOD** 2).

Sunset . . . and the end of another perfect day on the water. Now it's back to the Marina, with a helping hand from Raytheon electronics on the bridge and, surprisingly, in the galley, too.

No other machine can live up to such a lifetime performance record. No car. No truck. No train. No bus. Nothing else in the world. [The Boeing 727]

When the big movies come, HBO people see them, with no cuts and no commercials. Right in the comfort of their own homes. Movies like *Animal House, Jaws 2, Grease,* and *Yanks.*

(b) Catalog copy consistently consists of short fragmentary sentences.

66-3. Cuisinart DLC-7 Food Processor with Bonus! Similar to the DLC-8, only with a larger feed capacity. With special large workbowl and powerful motor that's incredibly quiet. Pulse on–off control, feed tube and dough mixing blade. 250.00. DLC-050 bonus kit, reg. 60.00 value.

(c) Except in the instances already cited, it is bad form for a sentence fragment to be indiscriminately punctuated as a sentence. The fragment should either be joined grammatically to the sentence to which it belongs or converted into a whole sentence.

The landlord offered a month's free rent. Hoping to lure tenants. *(Hoping to lure tenants, the landlord offered a month's free rent.)*

For a while the profession was in the doldrums. Because no new talent was being developed. *(For a while the profession was in the doldrums because no new talent was being developed. Also, two sentences: For a while the profession was in the doldrums. No new talent was being developed.)*

3. ORDER. Using a variety of sentence patterns helps to liven a text and put emphasis where it is needed.

(a) The natural order puts the main idea at the beginning of the sentence. A sentence so constructed—a *loose sentence*—can usually be ended at some point before the period. In each of the following sentences, the period in brackets shows where the sentence can be ended and still make sense.

We have begun a search for a new controller [.] to replace Ken Hyman [.], who is leaving in January.

Commodity speculation is probably not for you [.] if you are nervous [.] or slow to act.

The Boeing 747 has changed her shape [.] to help airlines keep down costs.

(b) A change from the loose sentence is offered by the *periodic sentence*. Here the main idea is suspended, so that the period cannot be placed at any point except the end.

With Ken Hyman leaving in January, we have begun a search for a new controller.

If you are nervous or slow to act, commodity speculation is probably not for you.

To help airlines keep down costs, the Boeing 747 has changed her shape.

Periodic sentences are somewhat more formal than loose sentences and are best used sparingly if they are not to sound strained.

(c) A *balanced sentence* is one in which elements similar in rhythm and nearly equal in length are juxtaposed for emphasis. Used occasionally, a balanced sentence makes an effective counterpoint to the more conventional loose and periodic sentences.

If he knew nothing about the broadcasting business, he knew everything he would have to know about managing a business for profit.

Delude ourselves that we have won the battle, and we may well lose all that we have gained so far.

To ask the question is to answer it.

(d) In the *inverted sentence*, a word or phrase is taken from its normal position in the sentence and placed at the beginning, where it receives more than ordinary emphasis. In the following examples, the normal order is shown in parentheses.

Cautiously, the new line was introduced. (The new line was introduced cautiously.)

Not for everyone is the risk of commodities futures. (The risk of commodities futures is not for everyone.)

Price was the magnet that drew the crowds. (The magnet that drew the crowds was price.)

Basic and long distance service we shall continue to provide under regulation. (We shall continue to provide basic and long distance service under regulation.)

4. CONSISTENCY. Sentences are smoother when they do not needlessly shift from one type of construction to another.

Two years later the Supreme Court overruled its earlier view and the Northern Securities Company was declared illegal. [Shifts from active voice to passive voice. Better: ". . . and declared the Northern Securities Company illegal."]

While the dollar soared to its highest level in 11 years, gold falls $15 an ounce. [Shifts from past tense to present tense. Better: ". . . gold fell $15 an ounce."]

She was asked about the "old girls" networks and could she form a chapter in her company. [Shifts from indirect to direct question. Better: "and whether she could form a chapter in her company."]

We all like to go shopping. It gives you a feeling of power to roam through a store and make buying decisions. [Shifts in person from *we* to *you*. Better: "We all like to go shopping. It gives us a feeling of power to roam through a store and make buying decisions."]

A common inconsistency, generally accepted in business usage, occurs when a company refers to itself by name and then by the pronoun *we*—a switch from third person to first.

Gannett believes in the freedom of the people to know and pursues that freedom in every communications form we are in . . .

A similar inconsistency, also generally accepted, is using *company* with a singular verb *(is)*, but a plural pronoun reference *(they)*. See **COLLECTIVE NOUNS** 2.

separate   So spelled (not *seperate*). Verb (pronounced -rate): *We can't easily separate the charges.* Adjective (pronounced -rit): *They traveled in separate cars.*

separate cover   "Sending you under separate cover" expresses the idea precisely, but fresher expressions are available: *sending you separately/sending you in another envelope/sending you by parcel post.*

separate-cover notation   When material mentioned in a letter is being sent separately, a notation on the letter serves as a reminder to the secretary and may specify the method of delivery and/or the number of envelopes or packages. The notation occupies the position of the EN-CLOSURE NOTATION, or the line below it, if both notations are needed. See also **LETTER FORM** 4.

EXAMPLES:

Federal Express/2

Separate cover: Parcel Post

Separate cover: "Information for Bidders"

separated   In personnel practice, a EUPHEMISM for "discharged" or "dismissed": *Mr. Hager was separated on August 16.* Compare TER-MINATED.

serendipity   A sometimes apt word, but easily misused and not always understood. Serendipity is the faculty of making fortunate accidental discoveries: *But how much longer must they depend on management's serendipity?/The serendipity Mr. Strand enjoys was earlier demonstrated in the success of the restaurants at the World Trade Center, including the highly rated Windows on the World.*

—**serendipitous,** adjective: *a serendipitous creative director/had a serendipitous advantage/Still, the pleasures of the neighborhood are largely serendipitous.*

serial numbers   See NUMERALS 7.

series   For numbers in series, see NUMERALS 4. For the punctuation of a series of words or phrases, see COMMA 2 and SEMICOLON 2.

service, serve   To *service* is to maintain or repair, almost invariably some object: *We service what we make/Our trucks are serviced regularly/The typewriter needs servicing.*

Serve is used more generally in the sense of providing service or benefits for something or someone: *The bank serves* (not *services*) *many wealthy customers/Con Edison serves the entire metropolitan area.* But: *Video Masters services* (makes repairs in) *all of Cook County.*

service mark   Abbreviated SM. A registered name used to identify a distinctive service to customers; analogous to a TRADEMARK, which identifies a product. "Assured Reservation" and "Express Service" are service marks of the American Express Company.

set, sit   1. To set is to put (something) in place; to sit is to rest on something. *Set,* a transitive verb, takes an object; *sit,* an intransitive verb, does not. To confound matters further, the past tense or past participle of *set* is *set,* but that of *sit* is *sat: They set* (also, *have set*) *the carton on the floor.* But: *The carton sat* (also, *has sat*) *on the floor all day.* Exceptions: *The sun sets; a hen sets* (or *sits*) *on her eggs; a coat sets* (or *sits* [that is, it *hangs*]) *comfortably.*

2. The mistaking of *set* for *sit,* especially with reference to things,

is sufficiently common to make the usage informal: *The shipment of fresh vegetables set* (for *sat*) *in the sun all day.*

set back   Postpone. See **PUT BACK, PUT FORWARD.**

sex, gender   See **GENDER, SEX.**

sexual bias   The Women's Movement has brought, among other results, an awareness of the sexual bias in language. References to jobs and people, for example, must not exclude or discriminate against either sex. Avoiding such bias sometimes strains one's ingenuity and mastery of syntax, but the language is adaptive and one need not become irrational about the subject (see, for example, **PERSON** and **ONE**).

1. There is no objection to a word like *chairman, salesman, Congressman,* or *workingman* when it specifically refers to a man; nor to a word like *chairwoman, saleswoman, Congresswoman,* or *working woman* when it refers to a woman. When, however, a title having a common gender is needed, words like *chairperson, sales representative, member of Congress,* and *worker* are available.

2. When examples involving individuals are cited, bias is avoided when they include a representation from both sexes, as: *Mary Smith buys a house . . . ; Mr. Blair, with a growing family, faces a different insurance problem than the widow or widower.*

3. The problem of pronoun reference may arise after the use of a common name like *employee, typist, executive, receptionist, manager,* or *plumber.* If the typist and receptionist are referred to as *she* and the manager and executive as *he,* sexual bias—or at least typecasting—may be presumed. Several corrective courses can be mentioned.

(a) Plural usage. Making the common names plural permits the use of plural pronoun references, all of which will have a common gender: *executives who pride themselves* (rather than *an executive who prides himself*)/*when receptionists arrive at their stations* (rather than *when a receptionist arrives at her station*).

(b) Change in sentence structure to bypass the need for a sexually oriented pronoun. Biased: *A typist trained to work on an ordinary typewriter will find her skills inadequate for the operation of a word processor.* Change to: *A typist's skills will prove inadequate for the operation of a word processor.*

(c) Substitution of *the* for the pronoun: *A secretary will at times be unable to complete the assigned work* (rather than *her* or *his assigned work*).

(d) Use of *you*. This method is well suited to manuals and instructions and, in fact, any message addressed directly to the reader or listener: *You are expected to phone in when you must miss work* . . . (rather than *An employee is expected to phone in when he must miss work because of illness*).

(e) Use of alternate pronouns (see **HE OR SHE**). Because of its awkwardness, this is often the least attractive choice, but there is no objection if it is used occasionally, and then only when another mode of expression would not do as well: *The person chosen to fill the vacancy will be one who has already proved his or her worth in another job with the company.*

shall, will   There are few occasions to use *shall*, especially since the former distinctions between *shall* and *will* are now seldom invoked. See also **SHOULD, WOULD**.

1. *Will* is regularly used to express simple future time: *I will be there/You will be pleased with the results/She will not sell the property/They will not be deterred.*

2. *I shall* or *we shall* to express simple future time is found in formal usage only: *I shall call you/We shall see what we can do.*

3. The use of *shall* to express simple future time in the second and third persons *(you, he, she, it, they)* is not sanctioned. Nonstandard: *You shall be expected on Thursday/The President shall sign the measure, as Mr. Hart predicted/Many experts shall be asked for their opinions.* [Substitute *will* in all examples.]

4. *Shall*, regularly used in questions, is more formal than *should*: *Shall I call the repair service?/Shall Herbert and Finch be consulted first?*

5. *Shall* is regularly used in laws, rules, and regulations to denote obligation or compulsion: *This law shall become effective ninety days after its passage/The amounts received under this agreement shall in no instances exceed the maximum credit/Employees shall not engage in fund-raising on company premises.*

shan't   A contraction of *shall not;* rarely used, and likely to be taken as an affectation when it is: *I shan't (won't, will not) be there.* See also **SHALL, WILL**.

shape   Informal for "condition"; a more specific term may be preferred: *The company's books are in good shape (are accurate, up-to-date)/Considering the shape he's in (his physical condition), I'd question his ability to do the job.*

shape-up The practice of assembling workers from which the hiring boss or union representative chooses the day's crew. The term is especially applied to the hiring of longshoremen.

shareholder Synonymous with *stockholder*, but preferred by many stock exchange brokers and listed firms because of the suggestion of participation in the management and the profits. *Shareowner*, another synonym, is valued for its suggestion of proprietary interest.

sheet An informal, sometimes derogatory, term for a tabloid or other newspaper or periodical: *a trade sheet with a controlled circulation of 11,000/has a reputation as a scandal sheet.*

shelf life 1. The length of time a perishable product may be kept on a store shelf before deterioration affects its salability. Many products, like milk and cheese, are stamped with the "last date of sale," often by legal mandate. Other longer-lasting products also carry notices like "Best used before [date]."
2. Also used FIGURATIVELY: *Selling movies is different than selling soap. You've got a product with a short shelf life—sometimes a movie opens and closes in two weeks—and no return business to speak of.*

shelf registration A procedure, made available in 1982, that lets a company obtain approval from the Securities and Exchange Commission to issue debt certificates (bonds) to the public and then wait for a financially propitious time to offer them for sale.

shill Slang. One who poses as a customer; a decoy, usually for a street vendor or confidence man.

shirt-sleeve 1. Describing a person in a responsible position who deals directly and informally with people and problems: *a shirt-sleeve executive/a shirt-sleeve analyst.*
2. Plain, practical: *shirt-sleeve English/a shirt-sleeve approach to management.*

shop A tongue-in-cheek put-down of a workplace, especially one devoted to highly professional activity. Thus a skilled and well-paid person in advertising or law might refer to "my shop" or speak of "setting up shop." Also acceptably used as a transitive verb: *shop* (buy from) *the better stores.*

shopping list Used as HYPERBOLE: *The trade representative came to* *this country with a $200 million shopping list for advanced military hardware.* Compare **LAUNDRY LIST**.

shoptalk   Talk about one's work; also the language, including the **JARGON**, used in such talk: *Their shoptalk bores me.*

—talk shop, verb phrase: *There's hardly a lunch when they don't talk shop.*

shortened words   See **CLIPPED FORMS**.

shortfall   **JARGON** for a shortage, an amount less than anticipated or necessary: *Reductions in refinery capacities could lead to shortfalls in domestically produced supplies/A shortfall in revenues will mean a cutback in services.*

shot   A photograph; also a single uninterrupted sequence of motion picture film or videotape: *Let's take several more shots/I like that shot best/She fluffed her lines and the shot had to be retaken.*

should, would   1. *Should* is used to express an obligation, a condition, or an expectation: *They should know better/If the order should not materialize* (less formal, *does not materialize*) . . . */The plane should get in at 10 a.m.*

2. *Would* is used to express a polite request: *Would you do me a favor?* However, formal usage sometimes prefers *should* in the first person: *I should appreciate* (less formal, *would appreciate*) *hearing from you.* [*Will,* lacking the conditional aspect of *would,* is more direct, more forceful in a request: *Will you do me a favor/I will appreciate hearing from you.*]

3. *Would* expresses habitual action, but it is more poetic than businesslike in expressing a wish: *She would drop in occasionally to review her account/Would that it were so* (Less formal: *I wish it were so*).

4. Unless the user deliberately wishes to show timidity, *would* is superfluous in expressions like ''I would prefer'' and ''We would suggest.'' See also **WORDINESS** 7.

should of   Illiterate for ''should have.'' See **COULD OF**.

show, show up   *Show up* is a good idiom meaning to arrive, usually unexpectedly or after some delay: *showed up at four o'clock. Show,* in the same sense, is informal: *The guest of honor finally showed.*

—no-show. Informal for a person who is expected but does not come: *When the meeting was called, there were six no-shows.*

showed, shown   *Shown* is preferred to *showed* as the past participle of *show: was shown to be an ideal medium/had shown the customer several models.* But (past tense): *We showed the customer several models.*

shrink   The past tense is either *shrank* or *shrunk*, but *shrank* is preferred: *Profits shrank/The garments shrank in washing. Shrunk* is the only acceptable form of the past participle: *Profits have shrunk/The garments had shrunk in washing.*

shut down   To stop operations—a sense not always conveyed by *shut* alone: *The plant was shut down on May 1/The No. 2 furnace was shut down for repairs.*
—shutdown, noun: *The shutdown is scheduled for May 1.*

sic   Latin for "thus" or "so." The term is put in **BRACKETS** within a quotation to indicate that a preceding word or phrase—copied without change from the original—is not an error in transcription: *The memorandum distinctly says that "a verbatum [sic] report is not necessary."* [*Verbatim* was misspelled in the memorandum.]

SIC   Abbreviation of **STANDARD INDUSTRIAL CLASSIFICATION.**

sick, ill   1. Although *ill* is considered the more refined word, *sick* aptly describes a person suffering from nausea. *Sick* is also the acceptable term in certain standard idioms: *sick pay, sick leave, called in sick, reported sick.* Mild synonyms include *unwell, not well,* and *indisposed.*
2. *Sick* is descriptive of mental illness, often when a **PEJORATIVE** meaning is intended: *He must be sick.*

sick-in   Also *sick-out.* A labor practice whereby a group of employees "call in sick" and fail to appear for work; sometimes engaged in when an antistrike law (affecting public employees) or a contractual obligation prevents a formal strike.

signal   Overworked in the sense of "sign" or "message," especially when used in a political context: *The Administration cited the leading index as a signal of approaching recovery/Your vote in favor of the measure will send a signal to Washington.*

signature   1. Used figuratively in the sense of "character": *With a second generation of office buildings now completing its transformation, Third Avenue is developing a distinctive signature.*

2. In printing, a folded set of printed pages—commonly 32—which are joined by sewing or pasting to form a book. *The signatures are ready and waiting to be bound.*

signature block That part of a letter, below the COMPLIMENTARY CLOSE, which includes the written signature and the typewritten name of the signer. See also LETTER FORM.

1. Three or four spaces are left between the complimentary close and the typewritten name of the signer. A professional degree or rating (M.D., M.E., C.L.U., etc.) may be added to the typewritten name, but not to the written signature. The signer's title or department affiliation is typed on a separate line if it is not carried on the letterhead.

Very truly yours

Jan Stromberg

Jan Stromberg
Vice President

Very truly yours

A. Harrison Schulz

A. Harrison Schulz, C.P.A.

Very truly yours

Carroll McIvor

Carroll McIvor
Secretary to Miss Peterson

2. If the company name appears on the letterhead, it is not included in the signature block. If the letterhead does not include the company name, the name is typed in all capitals below the complimentary close and aligned with it. In the instance of a company name so long that it would overrun the right margin, the name is aligned on the right with the right margin, and the complimentary close is centered above it. A typewritten signature, if added, is aligned with the complimentary close.

Very truly yours

CAPITAL ENTERPRISES INC.

Henry S. Carver

Henry S. Carver
Credit Department

Very truly yours

SIMPLEX DATA PROCESSING CORPORATION

Omar N. Barker

Omar N. Barker

3. When the department affiliation, title, or name of the signer is printed on the letterhead, the information is not typed in the signature block. Such data can also be omitted when the writer and reader are close associates and the signature can be readily identified. See also **IDENTIFICATION INITIALS** 2.

4. Except in personal correspondence, a letter signed with the first name only should have the full name typed below it if it is not printed on the letterhead. A first-name signature invariably follows a first-name salutation.

5. When, in the absence of the writer, a secretary or assistant signs the writer's name, the initials of the signer are inconspicuously placed below the right side of the signature.

Harriet Peterson
c. m.

The phrase, ''Dictated but not signed,'' is not to be used.

See also **IDENTIFICATION INITIALS** 3.

sign in, sign out   Analogous to **CLOCK IN, CLOCK OUT**.

signed, sealed, and delivered   Complete, done, accomplished. A **CLICHÉ** used particularly to mark the completion of the formalities of a contract, but also used figuratively: *Here's the agreement—signed, sealed, and delivered* (tidily complete)/*The company's doom is now signed, sealed, and delivered.* [*Sealed* alone would make more sense in this context.]

simile   See **FIGURATIVE LANGUAGE**.

simoleon   Slang for ''dollar'': *That will cost you two simoleons.*

simple words   See **LONG WORDS AND SHORT**.

simplified (letter) style   See **LETTER FORM** 3.

simplified spelling   The movement to bring the spelling of words into harmony with their pronunciation has not made much headway elsewhere, but simplified spelling is common in trade names and signs: *Dairy-Lite, Pure-Pak, Lo-Cal, Kwik, Dunkin' Donuts, Lipton's Flo-Thru* *tea bags, Riteway Laundry, TRIX* (cereal)/*to the Thruway, No Thorofare, Go Slo.*

simplistic Oversimplified; a disparaging term: *seeking simplistic solutions to complex problems/just another simplistic explanation of their extraordinary success/full of naive ideas and simplistic plans.*

simulated See at FAKE.

since Preferred to *as* in casual expressions. See AS 2.

Sincerely Also *Sincerely yours* and *Yours sincerely.* A COMPLIMENTARY CLOSE less routine than *Very truly yours.*

sine qua non Pronounced *sin*-nay kwah nohn or *sigh*-nee kway non. Latin for "without which not," meaning an "essential element": *An improved economy is the sine qua non of improved retail sales/When he arrived, he was clutching that sine qua non of upward mobility, a master's degree in business administration.*

sing To make prose "sing" is to give it an impressive or pleasing effect. Though trite, the word still—unexplainably—is used by some writers themselves: *How to create copy that sings* [blurb for a course in advertising copywriting]/*The report is workmanlike, but it doesn't sing.*

Sir Plural *Sirs.* A very formal SALUTATION confined to official and diplomatic correspondence. Also formal when used with *dear: Dear Sir(s); My dear Sir(s).*

sitcom Television lingo. A situation comedy: *loaded prime time with their inane sitcoms.*

site Usually a noun, meaning "place" or "location": *the construction site/on-site construction.* But also a verb *(siting, sited, sites)* meaning to locate or put in place: *decided to site the building on land once used as a farm/declared the siting of the factory would depend on the tax concessions obtained.*

sit-in Informal. A protest strategy by workers and others, who illegally occupy premises in an effort to win their demands or, at the least, call attention to their cause.

sizable Also *sizeable.* Rather large: *A sizable (or sizeable) order.*

size Often redundant: *The size of their private offices is minuscule (Their private offices are minuscule).* See also IN LENGTH, IN NUMBER, IN SIZE.

-size, -sized As part of a compound, *-size* is less formal than *-sized: a medium-size car* (also, somewhat more formal, *a medium-sized car*). However, only *-sized* will do when the compound follows the verb: *The car is medium-sized* (But also: *The car is of medium size*).

slack A pair of trousers for informal wear; not part of a suit. Usually plural *(slacks),* but as in the instance of **PANT**, the singular is gaining ground: *The slack is made of pure wool. $65.* (More common: *The slacks are made . . .*)

slant (the punctuation mark) (/) A diagonal line, technically a "virgule," also called a "slash," "shilling," and "solidus"; used specifically:

1. To separate the parts of an abbreviation: S/H (shareholder); R/E (real estate); C/D (certificate of deposit).

2. To show alternatives or the omission of words like *and* or *or: the owner and/or tenant; five flights daily to Fort Lauderdale/St. Pete; savings in the secretarial/clerical payroll.*

3. To separate the lines of a poem or a literary title when the lines are run together: *The lines are from Tennyson, "Theirs not to reason why/Theirs but to do and die."* Also: *Center the title on two lines, Demographic Dynamics/in America.*

slant (the word) To give a particular bias to: *The report is obviously slanted* (biased). Also a noun: *The slant of the story is prejudicial to our case/Her slant* (point of view) *is worth having.*

slave A drudge: *a wage slave/a slave in the typing pool/a slave driver.* Also a verb: *while she slaved away at the office.*

sleeper Something that achieves success unexpectedly or after a slow start: *Exhibitors who had reluctantly booked the film were pleasantly surprised to find they had a sleeper.*
—sleeper effect. *One thesis holds that disagreeable ads have a "sleeper effect" in which consumers forget the commercial itself but remember its message.* [The Wall Street Journal]

slew Informal for a large number or amount: *the maker of Addressograph machines and a slew of other office products/achieved second place in beer sales with a slew of ads from the McCann-Erickson team.*

slippery Informal for "elusive," "deceitful," "unreliable": *a slippery fellow/a slippery conceit.*

slo SIMPLIFIED SPELLING of *slow;* its use is confined mainly to traffic signs.

slow, slowly Often thought of only as an adjective, *slow* is also an adverb. As such, it is characteristic of certain idioms and usually found in less formal usage than *slowly: Go slow/Drive slow/Take it slow/The trains have been running slow.* But (more formal): *Proceed slowly/For the greatest enjoyment, sip it slowly/We drove slowly through the extensive plant grounds.*

Slow, the adjective, is not interchangeable with *slowly: Turnover is slow/It's a slow day/The slow deliveries are costing us money.*

slush fund From *slush,* the refuse grease from a ship's galley. A fund raised, as by an office staff for entertainment or other small pleasures. Also a fund to bribe public officials or engage in other corrupt practices.

slush pile The unsolicited manuscripts in an editorial office: *Her first book was discovered in the slush pile; the others were invited or came in recommended.*

smarts Plural only; slang for intelligence, brains: *Put all your smarts to work and pretty soon you'll be the one executive searchers are searching for* [Fortune]/Sometimes used in an unfavorable sense: *He has a bad case of the smarts* (shows his intelligence ostentatiously).

smokestack company A company in some heavy industry, as automobiles, steel, cement, and forest products; familiarly, a BIG UGLY.

smokestack stock The stock of a SMOKESTACK COMPANY. Traditionally, such a stock follows the business cycle, rising in prosperous times and falling in recessions.

snap Informal for something easy to do: *Getting the financing was a snap.*

Snowbelt Also *Snow Belt.* See at SUNBELT.

snow job Slang. An attempt to persuade through insincere talk or flattery: *gave us a snow job.*

so 1. A proper beginning for a sentence: *So we started a training program for our instructors.* 2. Used only informally as an intensive: *They were so accommodating.* 3. In the sense of "in order that," *so* is somewhat less formal than *so that: The rebate is to be continued for* *another two weeks, so* (or, more formal, *so that*) *dealers can dispose of their old stock.*

soap opera Also *soap*. Informal for a radio or television daytime serial stressing a sentimental domestic theme; also applied as a **PEJORATIVE** to any broadcast program with a similar tone. The name derives from the circumstance that the early radio serials were largely sponsored by soap companies: *Dallas set a pattern for evening soap operas/At midday the soaps are in command.*

soft Weak, not firm; characterized by slow demand and/or falling prices: *The soft market was partly attributed to Citibank's announced rise in its prime rate/Newsstand sales have been soft for a good many magazines this year.*

soft goods Dry goods: textiles, clothing, and related merchandise; not to be confused with **SOFTWARE**. Compare **DURABLE GOODS**.

soft landing A gentle slowing of the economy. Similarly, a plunge into a recession is a "hard landing." *Administration policymakers insist that a soft landing is still possible if restraints are placed on wage and price increases.*

soft sell Informal for a low-keyed sales or promotional effort: *a master of the soft sell/a professional hawker not given to the soft sell.* Compare **HARD SELL**.

software The programs or built-in instructions by which computers perform their routines; contrasted with **HARDWARE**, the machines themselves: *The company would protect their old customers' substantial investment in 16-bit Eclipse software and would offer prospective buyers at least the possibility of savings in software development.*

soldiers **JARGON** for employees loyally and actively engaged as a disciplined group in important work, often sales-related: *We have three hundred soldiers in the field/Our soldiers benefit from an array of support services.* Compare **TROOPS**.

solicited questions Discouraged in ordinary correspondence; see **QUESTIONS, SOLICITED**.

solid caps See **CAPITALS**.

some Informal for "somewhat": *The market is ruled by the expectation that interest rates will come down some in the next few weeks.* But (general usage): *The International Monetary Fund is helping somewhat* (rather than *some*), *but the prospects for agreement are not good.*

someone, some one   See ANYONE, ANY ONE.

someplace   See SOMEWHERE, SOMEPLACE, SOMEWHERES.

something else   A trite slang expression for an unusual person or thing: *Manischewitz wine—it's something else/HBO is something else/Our head of manufacturing—he's something else.*

sometime, sometimes; some time   *Sometime* means "at an indefinite time," but *sometimes* means "occasionally": *Call me sometime* (not *sometimes*) *next week.* But: *Sometimes* (not *sometime*) *we have to go into the capital market for funds.* Neither word should be confused with *some time* (two words), meaning "a period of time": *Some time passed before the results were known/We have followed the practice for some time.*

some way   Usually so written (two words): *We wish there were some way we could help.*

somewhat   See SOME.

somewhere, someplace; somewheres   *Somewhere* is in general usage; the synonym *someplace* is informal: *We'll find the right location somewhere* (informal, *someplace*). *Somewheres* is nonstandard: *I know I met him somewhere* (not *somewheres*).

SOP   Pronounced ess-oh-pee. Standard operating procedure. A procedure, usually in writing, prescribing the way in which some recurring task or problem is to be handled.

sophisticated   A description commonly applied to machines, tools, and technology to signify a high degree of complexity and refinement: *The robots support the most sophisticated assembly line in car manufacture today.*

sorry   Usually part of a proper response to news calling for sympathy and regret, but the user must be sorry about the right thing. "I'm sorry to have your letter," written in response to a complaint, seems to deplore the fact that the complaint was sent. What is usually meant is "I'm sorry to learn from your letter that . . . ," or "I'm sorry about . . ."

sort of a See KIND OF A, SORT OF A.

sort(s) of See KIND (SORT) OF, KINDS (SORTS) OF.

sound out Well established in the sense of seeking opinions or attitudes: *Let's sound out our sales staff.*

space grabber Informal for a person who greedily seizes opportunities for publicity; a celebrity: *Our spokesman should be a real space grabber.* Applied also to an organization or event benefiting from a great deal of publicity: *As a space grabber, their annual fall showing has no equal in the fashion world.*

speak to Formal and a bit strained when used in the sense of addressing a subject, rather than a person: *I will now speak to* (address) *the question of the proposed merger.* But (acceptable without qualification): *I will speak to Mrs. Danzig.*

spec CLIPPED FORM of *speculation, speculator,* and *specification: We'll take it on spec/The specs have all the tickets/Let's see the specs.*

special assignment Often a EUPHEMISM for "inactive status" or for the transfer of an executive to a desk in an unused office until his or her retirement from the company: *was placed on special assignment.*

special delivery For prompt delivery of any class of mail from the post office of destination to the receiver. Special fee applies. See also MAILING NOTATIONS.

special handling Assures faster in-transit handling of third- and fourth-class mail. The extra fee does not cover special treatment after the mail reaches the post office of destination. But see SPECIAL DELIVERY.

special(ly) See ESPECIAL(LY), SPECIAL(LY).

specie Pronounced *spee*-she or *spee*-see. Metallic currency; coin, especially gold or silver: *to be paid in specie.*

spectrum A broad well-articulated range of related ideas or things: *covers the whole spectrum of human communication.* The simple word *range* is often more suitable to the sense: *employs a wide spectrum (range) of training methods.*

speechify To speak in public; but the word has the CONNOTATION of orating pompously, at length, or vituperatively: *When we invited him* *to say a few words, we didn't know he was going to speechify.* Also used facetiously: *I expect to speechify for ten minutes.*

spell out   Well used in the sense of stating in explicit detail: *Have them spell out the terms of the agreement.* However, modifiers like those in "spell out *in detail*" and "spell out *fully*" are redundant. See WORD-INESS 3.

spiel   Pronounced *speel.* Slang. A garrulous discourse, as of a circus barker or high-pressure store demonstrator: *Her spiel drew a crowd in seconds.*

spinoff   Also *spin-off.* 1. In finance, the divestiture of part of a corporation and the transfer of part of its assets to its shareholders in order to form a new company. In this sense, both Primark Corporation and Wicor, Inc. are *spinoffs* of the American Natural Resources Company and the local Bell operating companies are *spinoffs* of AT&T.

2. Any by-product, as of an existing enterprise, product, or technology. A successful television series may thus spawn another (a *spin-off*) in which a minor character in the first becomes the star of the second. Similarly, video games are a *spinoff* of the microcomputer.

—**spin off,** verb (two words): *The company was spun off from its parent in 1983.*

split infinitive   Occurs when an adverb element is placed between the *to* and the verb forming the infinitive, as in "to hastily decide." If the split infinitive gives any cause for concern, it is not that a grammatical principle is thereby violated, but that the smoothness and clarity of the sentence may be at stake. Unsplit infinitive: *It was thought that Carson would be able to deal with the situation more effectively* (Better than: . . . *to more effectively deal with the situation*). Split infinitive: *To really appreciate the Peugot, you have to drive it* (Better than: *Really to appreciate the Peugot* . . .). Split infinitive: *The Mobility Unit is designed to effectively tap the bank's internal labor force, fulfilling its policy of promoting from within* (Better than: . . . *is designed to tap effectively the bank's internal labor force* . . .).

In some instances, a split infinitive is as good as an unsplit infinitive, and in other instances, not splitting the infinitive requires drastic change in phrasing. Divided usage: *We cannot hope to materially improve the situation,* or *We cannot hope to improve the situation materially.* Split unavoidable: *They expect to more than double their profits in five years* (The poor alternative: *In five years they expect to increase their profits more than twice over*).

split run A reference to the splitting of the press run of a newspaper or magazine into two or more parts, each part remaining essentially the same except for the substitution of one piece of copy for another occupying the same space in the publication. The split run is commonly used to test the effectiveness of advertisements, where a change in, say, the headline, APPEAL, or illustration will produce measurably different results. An analogous technique is adaptable to cable television.

spokesman, -woman, -person 1. An individual who is authorized to speak for a person, product, or organization: *A spokeswoman for the Society said the organization wanted to study the government's order before taking an official position*. See also PERSON.

2. Large companies regularly employ well-known personalities to speak for them in their advertising. Robert Young and Karl Malden, after long careers in films and television, became *spokesmen* for Sanka and American Express respectively. Synonymous with PRESENTER.

spoonfuls Not *spoonsful*. See -FUL.

spot announcement Also, informally, *spot*, as in "spot TV." An isolated broadcast advertisement inserted between breaks in a local or network show, or between shows. Compare PROGRAM ANNOUNCE-MENT.

spot cash Payment in cash made immediately on contracting for merchandise or on delivery: *We pay spot cash for your old jewelry*.

spot market A market in which commodities not under contract are bought and sold for immediate delivery and cash payment. *Spot prices—the prices on the spot market—fluctuate with supply and demand*.

spot shortages Shortages in some places, but not in others: *Spot shortages of heating oil are now being reported*.

spotty Uneven: *Retail business was spotty last week* (good in some stores or areas, and normal or poor in others).

spouse On applications and in other formal usages, often a convenient term for a marriage partner, referring either to the husband or wife. In most instances, however, the more natural terms are *husband, wife,* and *husband or wife: her former spouse (husband)/a man's spouse* *(wife)/where the spouse (husband or wife) is the beneficiary.* Not much choice: *The association has filled the Boca Raton Hotel and Club with 900 members and their spouses.*

square one As in the expression "back to square one"; a CLICHÉ for "the beginning," suggesting the failure or futility of what has already been done.

squeeze Pressure: *the squeeze on urban spending/the squeeze on credit markets* (also *the credit "crunch"*)/*Ease the cash squeeze. Squeeze* is slang only when the pressure is applied to force some concession, as the payment of a debt or a bribe: *put the squeeze on them.* Also a verb: *squeezed them for payment.*

Sr., Jr. For treatment of these and similar designations, see FORMS OF ADDRESS 1.

staffer Informal for "staff member"; the term is especially common among editorial personnel on newspapers and magazines: *a staffer with the Chronicle/several of our staffers.*

stagflation A mixture of economic stagnation and inflation: *With stagflation, one can expect the government's economic policies to be ambiguous.*

Standard & Poor's Corporation Financial publishers well known for the *S&P Composite Index* of 500 leading stocks, issued daily, and the *S&P Corporation Services*, which provide in loose-leaf form detailed and constantly updated information on the structure, management, and financial performance of corporations and other organizations offering investment opportunities. S&P's BOND RATINGS are also much valued.

standard industrial classification Abbreviated SIC. A detailed classification, federally sponsored, of all product lines. Each line is identified by a 4-digit code. Eases the task of finding sources of supply and targeting sales campaigns. SIC 3692, for example, is the code for storage batteries.

standpoint Synonymous with *point of view* and VIEWPOINT, but often cumbersome: *From the consumer's standpoint (For the consumer) the current deflation has definite advantages/When any new product is introduced, we have to be concerned about it from a safety standpoint (have to be concerned about its safety).* See also WORDINESS 6.

start up   Although the *up* may seem superfluous, *start up* is a good idiom when used in the sense of starting an enterprise, a machine, a procedure, or the like: *Starting up the operation will take a lot of cash/We're nearly ready to start up the assembly line/Start up the engine.*

—**start-up** (or **startup**), noun and adjective: *Housing start-ups are beginning to accelerate/Start-up costs are yet to be determined.*

stat   A CLIPPED FORM of *photostat* or *Photostat;* a positive or negative photographic copy of written or graphic material made on a Photostat machine. *Stat* is sometimes used also to denote a photocopy made by any means. Compare XEROX 3.

statement   A declaration as of principle or taste, often found in the phrase "a fashion statement" and in other references, particularly to art and design: *In a season of color and shape explosion, the muted statement of this offering* [of women's clothing] *is serenity. Assertion* is used in the same way: *It's a collection of updated classic forms that make a quiet yet firm assertion that clothing should be seen, noted and, most of all, appreciated and enjoyed.* [Nines by Southwick]

state of the art   The furthest point reached in the development of a science, process, technique, etc. Overuse has by now made the expression commonplace, especially in advertising: *Until there are advances in the state of the art, costs will remain prohibitive/Zenith's new set contains patented features that have enhanced the state of the art/The building offers the state of the art in luxury accommodations.*

—**state-of-the-art,** adjective: *We are seeking an individual to become involved in a state-of-the-art manufacturing project/The world's smallest, most convenient voice recorder—state-of-the-art technology in its most elegant expression* [Norelco].

state postal abbreviations   To facilitate the optical scanning of mail, the U.S. Postal Service has devised two-letter abbreviations for the fifty states, as well as the District of Columbia, Guam, Puerto Rico, and the Virgin Islands. As intended, these are rapidly taking the place of the former conventional abbreviations even in nonbusiness mail. Anyone using the postal abbreviations, however, had better take care to use them correctly, for they are easily confused. MA, for instance, is Massachusetts, not Maine (ME) or Maryland (MD), and MO is Missouri, not Montana (MT). See also ENVELOPE ADDRESS 1.

Alabama	AL	Kentucky	KY	Ohio	OH
Alaska	AK	Louisiana	LA	Oklahoma	OK
Arizona	AZ	Maine	ME	Oregon	OR
Arkansas	AR	Maryland	MD	Pennsylvania	PA
California	CA	Massachusetts	MA	Puerto Rico	PR
Colorado	CO	Michigan	MI	Rhode Island	RI
Connecticut	CT	Minnesota	MN	South Carolina	SC
Delaware	DE	Mississippi	MS	South Dakota	SD
District of Columbia	DC	Missouri	MO	Tennessee	TN
Florida	FL	Montana	MT	Texas	TX
Georgia	GA	Nebraska	NE	Utah	UT
Guam	GU	Nevada	NV	Vermont	VT
Hawaii	HI	New Hampshire	NH	Virginia	VA
Idaho	ID	New Jersey	NJ	Virgin Islands	VI
Illinois	IL	New Mexico	NM	Washington	WA
Indiana	IN	New York	NY	West Virginia	WV
Iowa	IA	North Carolina	NC	Wisconsin	WI
Kansas	KS	North Dakota	ND	Wyoming	WY

stationary, stationery *Stationary* (spelled *-ary*) means "not moving," "in a fixed position": *a stationary engine/The copier will remain stationary. Stationery* (spelled *-ery*) is writing materials: *ordered imprinted stationery/running out of stationery.*

stationery See LETTER FORM 1.

statistics Considered singular when it stands for the name of the science of collecting, organizing, and interpreting numerical DATA: *Statistics is* (not *are*) *not well served by practitioners with flabby minds.* Considered plural, however, when it stands for the numerical data: *The statistics show* (not *shows*) *a decided upswing in the last month.*

A *statistic* (singular) is a datum, a particular figure: *The statistic is of little significance.*

status Pronounced *stay*-tus or *stat*-us. 1. Condition; relative position or standing: *the current status of the project/a position of unknown status/enjoyed his status as acting manager.* 2. Prestige: *The job doesn't pay much, but it gives the occupant status.*

status quo   Pronounced *stay*-tus kwo or *stat*-us kwo. Latin for "existing condition": *Their argument was just a handy rationale for maintaining the status quo/The status quo could no longer be tolerated/He could see the status quo yielding to the new imperatives.*

steno   CLIPPED FORM of *stenographer*.

stereotyped letter phrases   The commonplace expressions characteristic of business correspondence.

1. As with all CLICHÉS a distinction must be made between those that are used mechanically and those that are, in the words of Fowler (see Bibliography), "chosen deliberately as the fittest way of saying what needs to be said." Business correspondents should be comforted by this distinction. So much of the language they use is necessarily repetitive that the problem is not just avoiding stereotypes, but finding good ones to take the place of the bad ones.

Bad stereotypes are simply those that are not "the fittest" for what must be expressed. *At your earliest convenience,* for example, is not only overpolite, but also vaguer than *as soon as you can, at your convenience, promptly,* or *at once. I wish to acknowledge receipt* is flawed by wordiness and a formality inappropriate to ordinary correspondence (compare *I have received*). Yet *I acknowledge receipt* seems entirely suited to, say, a letter from an attorney serving official notice of the receipt of a document, such as a will or a deed. Similarly, *Please feel free,* introducing an offer of help, may well be a mechanical substitute for the more simple *Please;* but if the writer senses a reluctance by the reader to accept the invitation, *feel free* seems entirely apt.

2. In some instances, an organization prescribes particular phrases because they offer a security not assured by the language the writers for the company may choose spontaneously. Thus a credit correspondent may be instructed to write *Mr. ———— is known to us as the president of the XYZ Corporation* instead of the better styled but less cautious *Mr. ———— is the president . . . ;* and *We believe the UVW Company deserves confidence* may be recommended over the more direct *We believe you may deal confidently with the UVW Company.* The prescribed phrases will quickly become stereotypes, but the desired limits of responsibility are preserved.

3. Generally, the common business-letter expressions that stand up best are the most simple and natural.

STEREOTYPED	NATURAL
Kindly advise	Please let us know
Your letter of recent date	Your recent letter
Under date of April 9	On April 9
Subsequent to receipt of	After we receive
As per your instructions	As you instructed
Reference is made to	We refer to
Attached hereto	Attached is
The said property	This property
Kindly redeposit same	Please redeposit the check
The accounts hereinbelow set forth	The following accounts

stet 1. Latin for "let it stand"; a notation in proofreading to nullify a previous correction.

2. Also used by editors and writers as a transitive verb: *The supervisor first struck out the offensive word, then inexplicably stetted* (reinstated) *it/I don't know why the editor keeps stetting my deletions* (restoring the deleted elements).

sticker shock The familiar term for the shock the buyer experiences on examining the itemized price notice posted on the side window of a new car: *thought the car would command a large market once the sticker shock wore off.*

stiff Slang. To withhold a tip for a service that usually commands one: *stiffed the waiter.*

still continue The *still* is redundant (see **WORDINESS** 3): *Timmons continues* (not *still continues*) *to serve as an adviser.*

sting A scheme to defraud by duping a gullible victim: *The target of the sting was highly knowledgeable in art, but utterly naive in financial matters.*

—sting operation. A plan designed to entrap suspected lawbreakers by involving them in a simulated criminal scheme: *The headquarters of the government's sting operation was a hotel room, complete with concealed microphones and TV cameras.*

stock In finance, a share in the ownership of a corporation. The two kinds of stock are common and preferred. Owners of common stock are paid dividends only after owners of preferred stock—on which the dividends are fixed—have received theirs. Although they take a greater risk, however, only owners of common stock can vote at annual meetings. They also stand to profit more through rising dividends and capital appreciation. Compare BOND.

stockholder   See SHAREHOLDER.

stockist   British for a retailer or distributor who stocks goods: *For a list of stockists, contact Burberrys.*

stonewall   To put up stubborn resistance in answering, especially in the face of damaging accusations: *He can only stonewall for so long.*
—stonewalling, noun: *Stonewalling is out of the question.*

storefront   Used to denote or describe a suite of offices or other facility, not a store but occupying premises with a store facade: *conducted their law practice in a storefront opposite the courthouse/a storefront dental office.*

storyboard   A sequence of cartoonlike drawings with captions, serving as a draft for a proposed film or television commercial. Also a verb: *storyboarded the commercial.*

straightedge   A rigid flat ruler.

strait, straitened   These words—not *straight* or *straightened*—relate to confinement or constriction: *a straitlaced* (prudish) *supervisor/in desperate financial straits/puts us in a straitjacket* (confines our freedom of decision)/*in straitened circumstances* (experiencing financial hardship).

strata   Plural of STRATUM.

strategic planning   A management concept concerned with the ways in which a company's resources can be used most advantageously to ensure the success of the enterprise in the long range: *With political crises abroad and an unclear economic outlook at home, companies are placing more emphasis on strategic planning/Our strategic planning is directed to maintaining our edge in laser technology.*

stratum   Pronounced, preferably, *stray-*. Plural, *strata;* sometimes *stratums*, but not *stratas*. A layer: *went through several strata of rock before striking water.* Also, a level or category in some organizational hierarchy: *The upper stratum* (not *strata*) *of executives was taken by surprise.* See also PLURALS 4.

(the) Street   The New York financial district, of which Wall Street is the center of activity: *The word on the Street was that interest rates were peaking*.

street addresses See ENVELOPE ADDRESS.

street name Stocks or bonds held for a client by a broker in the broker's name are said to be carried in a "street name." The practice facilitates trading of the securities and permits them to be used as collateral for the purchase of other securities on margin.

structural unemployment Unemployment resulting from changes in technology, consumer tastes, government policies, and the like. With the spread of computerization and ROBOTICS, for example, a large number of workers are unemployed because their skills no longer match business needs. Compare cyclical unemployment at CYCLICAL.

structured Planned, organized, or regulated; descriptive of work or a work environment. Considered JARGON by some. *In an efficient office, clerical jobs are highly structured* (organized)/*Our compensation packages are structured* (planned) *to provide employees with the best financial rewards in the industry*/*Their "working groups" are like the Japanese "quality circles," but somewhat less structured* (less tightly organized)/*Some companies have set up informal programs to bridge the gulf between male bosses and female subordinates. Continental Illinois favors a structured* (formal) *approach with seminars that have so far involved 250 of its managers*. The antonym is UNSTRUCTURED.

subject and verb The requirement that the subject and verb agree in number causes little trouble except when the subject is either obscured by other words or is itself in a form that makes the number uncertain.

1. INTERVENING WORDS.   2. COMPOUND SUBJECTS.   3. SUBJECT FOLLOWING VERB.   4. SPECIAL USAGES.

See also PRONOUNS 3.

1. INTERVENING WORDS.   Agreement of the subject and verb is not influenced by any words that come between them.

The purpose of these actions is (*not* are) to restore the company's credit.

The effects of the legislation are (*not* is) evident.

No amount of goodwill and faith is (*not* are) likely to restore the former relationship.

We want to know what the impact of those regulations is going (*not* are going) to be five years from now.

2. COMPOUND SUBJECTS.   (a) Subjects joined by *and* are followed by a plural verb. However, two singular subjects representing the same thing take a singular verb.

Capital and character are necessary assets for any successful entrepreneur. [Plural verb following two subjects]

The president and chief executive officer has only recently taken office. [Singular verb following two subjects representing the same person]

(b) Singular subjects joined by *or* or *nor* take a singular verb, and plural subjects so joined take a plural verb. When, however, one of the subjects is singular and the other plural, the verb usually agrees with the nearer one. If the result is awkward, the best remedy is recasting the sentence or deliberately violating the rule.

One model or another is sure to please. [Alternative singular subjects]

The statements or the invoices are all we need. [Alternative plural subjects]

Several pictures or *a single large mural is contemplated.* [Alternative singular subject closer to verb]

Or: A single large mural or *several pictures are contemplated.* [Alternative plural subject closer to verb]

Or: Several pictures or *a single large mural are contemplated.* [Rule violated: alternative singular subject followed by a plural verb]

(c) A singular subject compounded by a phrase beginning with such words as *with, together with,* and *as well as* generally takes a singular verb, but the sound or sense is occasionally improved by a plural verb.

Henry's plan, with all its faults, is (*not* are) better than anything we have now.

The visiting dignitary, as well as his secretary and aides, *are* to be accommodated at a local hotel. [The sense is plural]

The exterior planning, including the landscaping, footpaths, roads, and parking lot is (*or* are) the responsibility of the architect.

3. SUBJECT FOLLOWING VERB.   (a) A subject agrees in number with the verb even when the verb precedes it.

Fortunate *are* the *managers* who can keep regular hours. [*Managers* is the subject.]

Here *is* the perfect *solution.* [*Solution* is the subject.]

(b) When *it* and *there* are used as temporary "fillers" for the real subjects, *it*—but not *there*—is always followed by a singular verb. See also IT and THERE IS, THERE ARE.

It is the directors who will be held responsible. [*It* is the "filler"; *directors* is the real subject of the verb *is*.]

There is no way we could enter into such an arrangement. [*There* is the "filler"; *way* is the real subject of the verb *is*.]

There were at least forty applicants for the position. [*There* is the "filler"; *applicants* is the real subject of the verb *were*.]

4. SPECIAL USAGES. (a) A plural subject used in a singular sense has a singular verb: *Eight hours is the normal workday.*

(b) A singular collective noun takes either a singular or a plural verb, depending on the sense: *The staff meets every Tuesday.* But: *The staff are all enthusiastic about the extra holiday.* See also COLLECTIVE NOUNS.

(c) A singular subject takes a singular verb even when a following complement is plural, and a plural subject takes a plural verb even when the following complement is singular: *The best feature of the exhibit was the oils/The first prize is a Chevrolet and $5,000 in cash.* But: *The architects were the firm of Cambridge Seven Associates.* [Plural subject and verb with singular complement (*firm*).]

(d) A verb following a relative pronoun as subject (*who, which, that*) is singular if the pronoun refers to a singular noun or pronoun; the verb is plural if the pronoun refers to a plural noun or pronoun: *Anyone who knows us trusts us* [*Who* is singular because it stands for *anyone*, a singular pronoun.]/*Those who know us trust us.* [*Who* is plural because it stands for the plural pronoun *those*.] See also ONE OF THOSE WHO.

subject line Used in routine letters as a substitute for a REFERENCE LINE, the subject line is customarily typewritten two spaces below the SALUTATION. When paragraphs are blocked, the subject line begins at the left margin. When paragraphs are indented, the subject line may be similarly indented or centered between the side margins. Typical forms:

Subject: Employee Pension Plan
Reference: Policy No. K234567
Your letter of April 19, 19xx
Estate of Julian Hendricks

Introductory words like *Subject* and *Reference* are better not abbreviated. See also LETTER FORM 2–4.

suboptimize   See at OPTIMIZE.

subpoena   Also *subpena*, but *subpoena* is preferred for both the noun and the verb. In either spelling, the word is pronounced suh-*pee*-nuh, and the plural ending of the noun is *-nas*. The principal parts of the verb are shown in the following phrases: *have been subpoenaed/ thinking of subpoenaing the records/if he subpoenas our client.*

subsequent(ly)   Later: *in a subsequent (later) message/subsequently (later) we decided.* See also LONG WORDS AND SHORT.

subsequent to   After: *subsequent to (after) our conversation.* See also WORDINESS 4.

substantiate   So spelled and pronounced (not *substantuate*). To support with evidence: *asked them to substantiate their claims.*

substitute   To substitute, meaning ''to put in the place of,'' is followed by the preposition *for*, not *by: The 6.3-ounce tube was substituted for the 7-ounce size.* It is *replace*, meaning ''to supplant,'' that takes the preposition *by: The 7-ounce tube was replaced by the 6.3-ounce size.*

Similar restrictions apply to the prepositions following *substitution* and *replacement: The substitution of nylon for* (not *by*) *silk was started as a wartime necessity/The replacement of silk by nylon was started as a wartime necessity.*

subterranean economy   Another name for the UNDERGROUND ECONOMY.

such   1. Informal as an intensive: *They're such a reliable source of supply.*

2. Stilted when used as a pronoun: *When the customer asked for a pair of spats, I wasn't sure we had such (any)/We like the mutual funds and believe such (they) are admirably suited to the needs of many investors.*

—**no such.**   Not to be followed by *a* or *an: There is no such* (not *no such a*) *tenant in the building.* Compare KIND OF.

such as   1. Idiomatic but awkward when followed by a verb phrase: *The offer will be open only to such buyers as have clearly expressed their interest in our products.* Better: *The offer will be open only to those buyers who have clearly expressed their interest in our products.*

2. When a preposition is needed, *like* may make a less formal or less awkward sentence than *such as: We need such workers as Carl*

(We need workers like Carl)/They plan to diversify into several related fields, such as oil and coal (like oil and coal)/You will find many uses for laminations in an industry such as yours (like yours)/That's difficult even for an admirer such as me to guarantee (even for an admirer like me to guarantee.)

suggestion Sometimes used as a EUPHEMISM for "complaint" or "grievance": *We welcome your suggestions/As a result of our customers' suggestions, we are liberalizing our cash refund policy.*

suggestion system A procedure by which employees submit ideas for improving their work or the workplace. Ideas relating more broadly to the company's products and operations may also be encouraged. Cash awards are usually given for the suggestions accepted.

Sunbelt Also *Sun Belt*. Both terms are also lowercased. The states of the South and Southwest, and California. Geographically, the antithesis of the Snowbelt, those states in the North, Northeast, and Midwest.

sunrise industry An industry in the early stages of growth, as genetic engineering, aerospace, and telecommunications.

sunset industry Also *mature industry*. An industry that has, at least temporarily, reached the limit of its growth, as steel, railroads, shipbuilding.

sunset law A law containing a provision limiting its life to a specified period: *Nearly everyone agrees that sunset laws are the best way yet devised for curbing the growth of the bureaucracy.* A program or agency is "sunsetted" when it automatically comes to an end at the specified time, unless it is kept alive by new legislation.

sunshine law Any law requiring that regular meetings of government bodies be open to the public.

super Slang for "superior," "first-rate": *Henning has done a super job.* Also used, as part of a compound, to connote size or power: *supertanker, supermarket, Super Suds, super-strength Elmer's Glue-All.*

superhype See at HYPE.

superior figure A number or character raised slightly above the type line: *Studies by Michael Levine[3] and William Jordan[4] showed that . . .* [footnote references]/*The resulting crystals are of a high purity, with a density of 1000 cm^{-2}/*[a]*Included in the Metropolitan Region for the first time* [footnote to a figure in a chart].

superlatives   See COMPARISONS 2 and 3.

supersede   So spelled (not *supercede*): *The old regulation has been superseded* (replaced).

supply-side   Descriptive of an economic philosophy that views taxes and government spending as major constraints on economic effort and investment. It advocates, instead, tax reductions of a kind that would spur research and investment in plant and production: *supply-side economics/government support for supply-side policies.*
   —supply-sider. One who subscribes to supply-side theories: *A supply-sider, Mr. Johnson is also a pragmatic administrator.*

supposed to   Not *suppose to: The desks were supposed to arrive on Thursday.*

surprised   Tactless when the word puts the reader on the defensive: *We are surprised to learn about the damage (We are sorry to learn . . .)/We are surprised that we have not yet received an answer to our letter (May we have an answer to our letter).* See also COURTESY AND TACT.

suspension points   A series of three or more periods used primarily to denote an omission in quoted copy. See ELLIPSIS.

swap   Informal in ordinary usage as a noun or verb meaning "exchange": *an even swap/swapped stories about the old days.* In finance, however, *swap* is generally accepted as a trade term: *If you're thinking of swapping bonds for the tax advantage, come to Oppenheimer. Swap* is also standard in describing certain currency transactions. These include *currency swaps* and *swap agreements,* both relating to the exchange of currencies between two nations at the official exchange rate in times of emergency.

sweat equity   Ownership or part ownership of property, acquired by one's own labor in construction or renovation, as of a home in a run-down neighborhood.
   —sweat-equity, adjective: *Sweat-equity tenants were meeting with the Mayor to discuss their grievances.*

sweeten   Informal for "make more valuable" in the sense of adding an inducement to, say, a stock offering, a labor contract, or other transaction: *We'll even sweeten the deal by throwing in a rear-window defroster without charge.*

—sweetener, noun. An incentive: *The option bonds have built-in sweeteners that enable the buyer to redeem his investment for cash at a specified date before maturity/Even with corporate sweeteners, some executives cannot afford to accept promotions if it means they have to move to another city.*

sweetheart contract   A labor contract negotiated with the connivance of a union official to give the employer an advantage he would not otherwise have. Also any favored treatment for someone doing contractual work: *Some consultants obtain sweetheart contracts with state or local governments, not only getting paid, but getting payoffs as well.*

swindle sheet   Slang for an expense account voucher: *put it on the swindle sheet.*

syllabication   See **WORD DIVISION** 2.

syllabus   An outline or summary of a course of study. The plural is *syllabuses* (preferred) or *syllabi* (pronounced -bye): *the syllabus for the foreman's course/experience in preparing syllabuses.*

syndrome   A collection of signs or symptoms that, together, create an abnormal condition: *seeking new ways to beat the syndrome of simultaneous inflation and economic stagnation/waiting for car owners to go back to the buy-trade-buy syndrome/tactics that prove that the red herring syndrome is alive and well.*

synergy   Less frequently, *synergism.* The combined action of two or more forces, resulting in a total effect greater than if the forces were operating independently: *When Coca-Cola took over the Coca-Cola Bottling Company of New York, Wall Street cheered the synergy of the acquisition/The Consumer Service Division produced its own brand of synergy when it joined the Mortgage Division in a cooperative advertising campaign/A world leader in health care and a world leader in technology for health and other sophisticated applications have combined their strengths. Now the synergy begins.* [SmithKline Beckman] **—synergistic,** adjective: *The studios parcel out the work to more than one agency simultaneously. The result, as you might expect, is rarely synergistic.*

system   An increasingly popular designation for a product or service characterized by a number of interacting elements: *Mary Kay scientifically formulated skin care system/Sealy Posturepedic Hotel Sleep Sys-*

tem/The "Hands-Off" copier system that lets a secretary do what she does best. [Delsun Business Systems Inc.]

systematize A **LONG VARIANT** of *systemize: Science means systemized* (also *systematized*) *knowledge in any field.*

T

tablespoonfuls The plural is so spelled (not *tablespoonsful*). See **-FUL**.

tabular summaries Tables are used not only for statistical data, but for verbal data as well. Properly arranged, verbal tables supply relatively large amounts of information in a small space. They are interesting to examine, easy to grasp, and valuable as a reference. See illustration.

Table 1
VISUAL AIDS

Equipment	Audience Size	Advantages	Disadvantages
Flip Charts	Depending on size of chart, up to 30.	Inexpensive, easy to use, no projection required.	Limited audience size, difficult to carry around.
Desk Charts	Approximately 5.	Like flip chart, but may be placed on desk. Allows you to remain at desk. Easy to handle.	Limited audience size.
Blackboard	Up to 30.	Convenient, no planning required.	Unprofessional appearance, can't take advantage of colors or detailed diagrams.
Overhead Projector	Up to 45.	Best for materials requiring extensive discussion. Inexpensive. Allows you to face the group.	A projector and screen are required. Room needs to be shaped for ease in viewing the screen. Reduced light is encouraged.
35 mm Slides	Limited only by size of room and screen size.	Give image of professionalism and preparation.	Costly and time-consuming to produce. Room must be darkened. Screen and projector must be available.

Tabular summary

tabulated figures   See NUMERALS 6.

tack, track   A *tack* is a particular course of action, one of several available in the pursuit of a goal. *Track,* meaning "road" or "course," has a more general application: *Washington took the wrong tack in opposing new technologies/They take the tack of pretending that shortages do not exist.* But: *We believe we are on the right track* (not *tack*)/*If a senior management position is your goal, look into the career track we offer.* See also TRACK.

tacky   Informal for "dowdy," "shabby," "lacking in style or taste": *a tacky commercial/tacky furniture.*

tact   See COURTESY AND TACT.

take-home pay   A worker's net salary after deductions are made for WITHHOLDING TAX, contributions to pension, medical insurance, etc.

takeover   In finance, the acquisition of a controlling interest in one company by another: *succeeded in their takeover of Conoco.* Also, descriptive of such an acquisition: *declared that the company was not a takeover candidate/the game of valuing assets for takeover purposes.*

talent   Used collectively for "gifted people": *The company employs a host of talent.* Also informal for a person of talent: *When we spot a talent, we sign him up.*

talking head   A contemptuous term for a television performer whose role is confined to talking, as in an interview or panel show: *It's easy enough to understand why producers despair of the talking head. Why put a radio show on television? Where is the visual impact? Does anybody really expect many viewers to sit and watch mere talkers for an hour or more without a car chase to wake them up?*

talk turkey   A CLICHÉ for "discuss business bluntly": *Let's talk turkey.*

T & E   *Travel and entertainment.* See CHARGE CARD, CREDIT CARD.

tap into   To gain access to: *Subscribers to the newsletter use an office terminal or a personal computer to tap into the supplier's computer, which has stored the newsletter as it was received from the publisher.*

target   JARGON for some goal or object of effort or concentration: *meet the federal target for fuel reduction/the target date of July 1/using*

Scarsdale as our target area. Also a verb: *We'll target May 15 for the completion of the project.*

task force Borrowed from the military, the term is used in business to denote a temporary committee formed to carry out a particular objective: *a site selection task force/a task force of businessmen to advise the city on the financing of public transportation.*

tax-advantaged Descriptive of income sheltered to some degree from taxation: *The amount of the company's tax-advantaged income varied from 6 percent to 100 percent.* See also TAX SHELTER.

tax deductible Said of a business expense or CAPITAL LOSS that can be charged against income and so reduce the tax liability: *The cost of the subscription is tax deductible.*
—**tax-deductible,** adjective: *a tax-deductible expense.* See HYPHEN 1.

tax expenditure See TAX LOOPHOLE.

tax free Income that is not subject to taxation: *The dividends on municipal bonds are tax free.*
—**tax-free,** adjective: *Enjoy tax-free income.* See HYPHEN 1.

tax indexing See at INDEXING.

tax loophole A provision in the tax laws which, intentionally or not, makes it possible for certain individuals or groups to reduce their tax liability. A provision openly legislated to bestow such a tax benefit is euphemistically called a *tax expenditure.* Not taxed, for example, are property taxes on homes, mortgage interest, and employer contributions to employee pension funds.

taxpayer In real estate, a property put to use as, say, a parking lot or store to earn enough to pay the taxes on the land it occupies.

tax shelter An investment device aimed at avoiding or deferring income taxes; for instance, a pension plan through which a portion of earnings is set aside tax-free until retirement, or a life insurance policy on which interest is allowed to accrue as nontaxable income.

T-bill For "Treasury bill," a short-term obligation of the United States Government maturing in three months to a year.

teaspoonfuls The plural is so spelled. See -FUL.

technocrat One who believes in a social system controlled by technicians and engineers.

technologist A person engaged in a sophisticated order of applied science, engineering, or similar field. The term is used especially to distinguish such a professional from a mere technician or mechanic.

teen- Hyphened or not, as in *teen-age* (or *teenage*), *teen-aged* (or *teenaged*), *teen-ager* (or *teenager*). See also AGE, AGED.

telecommunication Also *-tions* (plural). A name encompassing all the methods by which messages are sent and received by electronic means; includes satellites, telephony, telegraphy, television, radio, the computer, and other systems employing sound, graphics, and printed words: *a telecommunication* (or *telecommunications*) *network.*

teleconference A conference in which participants at a distance from each other or from the point at which a message originates are brought together by telephone or closed-circuit television, when it then becomes a *videoconference.* Various types of hookups make it possible for each participant to play an active role in the discussion: *We use the teleconference to cut down the need for travel and make our executives more productive/The company offers temporary videoconference networks for firms not interested in building permanent facilities.* See also TELELECTURE.

telegraphic style A characterization of writing marked by the omission of articles, subjects, auxiliary verbs, or the like, as in a telegram. In correspondence, this style is at best stereotyped; at worst, it is discourteous because it gives the impression of haste: *Received yours of the tenth/Have sent bill and goods as requested/Hope to do more business with you in the future.*

telelecture A lecture conducted over closed-circuit television. The audience may be gathered at one point or scattered. See also TELECONFERENCE.

teletext A predominantly one-way system for the transmission of pages of graphic material and text—stock tables, for instance—onto television screens in homes and offices. The material is transmitted over the air and by cable. Compare VIDEOTEX.

televise So spelled (not *televize*). To broadcast by television: *a televised ceremony.*

telex ACRONYM for *tel*etypewriter *ex*change, a system for sending typewritten messages by wire. It is like a telephone service except that there are teletypewriters at both ends of the line. The sender types a message, dials the receiver's number and transmits the message, which is then printed at the receiving point. The word *telex* is used in several different ways: *installed a telex* (the machine)/*sent a telex* (the message)/*operates a telex service* (adjective)/*will telex the message* (verb; past tense, *telexed*).

temp A CLIPPED FORM of *temporary*, referring particularly to a temporary employee; part of the JARGON of help wanted advertisements: *temps wanted: typists, secretaries/fill the gap with several temps.*

10-K The report that U.S. corporations are required to file with the Securities and Exchange Commission each year. It often contains more information than the annual report sent to shareholders, though shareholders may obtain a copy from the company on request.

terminate 1. In one syllable, *end: performances terminate (end) on Saturday/terminated (ended) her association.* See LONG WORDS AND SHORT.

2. Harshly used in the sense of dismissing an employee: *They terminated Gardner after two weeks/There is nervous talk in the elevators. . . . A secretary wonders if her typewriter will be repaired before she, in the rather inelegant phrase that has become fashionable in Washington these days, is terminated [The New York Times].*

—**termination,** noun: *seeking voluntary alternatives to forced termination.*

terms See IN TERMS OF.

testate, intestate Lawyers' terms for dying with a legally valid will, and dying without one; better avoided in writing and talking to nonsophisticates: *since your father died intestate (died without leaving a will).*

testimonial In advertising, an endorsement by a presumed user of a product or service, who is usually compensated in money or other value: *testimonial advertising/an unsolicited testimonial.* See also PRESENTER.

TGIF For "Thank God it's Friday," a worker's farewell to a long week of toil.

than For case of pronoun following, see PRONOUNS 2(a). For omission of word following, see COMPARISONS 1.

than, then The two words are sometimes confused. *Than* is used to complete a comparison; *then* is an expression of time: *The price was higher than we anticipated.* But: *Raymond laid out the plan; then we debated some of its provisions.*

thanks much An affectation for "thank you very much," "many thanks," or "thanks a lot." A variation, "much thanks," is an archaic form, now also an affectation: *Much thanks (Many thanks, Thank you) for your note.*

thanks to An idiomatic phrase standing for "thanks be to" or "because of," used in expressions of gratitude: *Thanks to Lillian Hammer for her help with the charts/Thanks to the foundation's generosity, the recreation center can now be built.* Also used in a contrary sense: *Thanks to your intervention, we lost the account.*

thank you 1. The use of *thank you* is unexceptionable when it acknowledges a favor received: *Thank you for telling us how much you like our new billing procedure.* However, the phrase is not apt when no favor has been received. To say, for instance, "Thank you for your letter," regardless of the contents, quickly turns the "thank you" into a cliché. See **STEREOTYPED LETTER PHRASES.**

2. "I thank you" and "we thank you" are somewhat more formal than "thank you" alone.

—thanking you. Objectionable as a **PARTICIPIAL CLOSE** in such letter expressions as "Thanking you in advance," "Thanking you, we are," and "Thanking you, we remain."

thank you in advance Both stereotyped and presumptuous. The first objection vanishes, however, and the second is overlooked when a request is followed by "thank you" alone: *Won't you put your check in the mail today. Thank you.*

thank you kindly Is there any other way to be thankful? *Kindly* does not improve the sense. See also **KINDLY.**

that 1. *That* is not necessary to introduce a clause so long as there is no confusion of meaning: *They said [that] they would reserve judgment.* [The bracketed *that* is not necessary.] But: *They wrote on January 10 the robot welder was out of action.* [A *that* before *on* or after *January 10* would clear up the ambiguity.]/*We know the reason for their hesitancy is fear of reprisal.* [A *that* after *know* would prevent misreading of the sentence.]

2. *That* should not be inadvertently repeated: *We wanted them to know that if for any reason the settlement of the claim was delayed, that we were ready to advance them enough to cover current liabilities.* [The second *that* is redundant.] But (no redundancy): *One can only hope that, now that the threat of the strike is over, both sides will sit down and work out a lasting settlement.*

3. For clarity and force, *that* is better repeated before each of a series of parallel subordinate clauses: *They hoped that the statements would be brief, that both parties would get back to the bargaining table, and that there would be a fair resolution of the dispute.*

4. *That of* or its equivalent is often necessary for the logical completion of a comparison: *Their reputation for quality rivals that of J. C. Penney* (or *rivals J. C. Penney's*). See also COMPARISONS 1.

5. As a relative pronoun, *that* is used in reference to either people or things in restrictive clauses [see COMMAS 4(b)]. *The workers that* (or *who*) *left were not rehired/The furniture that* (or, less desirably, *which*) *looked so good in the old office seems a bit seedy here.* See also WHO, WHICH.

6. *That*, like *it*, *this*, and *which*, is not to be used to refer to an immediately preceding idea when the reference is ambiguous or nonexistent: *The company's announcement said it would discontinue the R-36 model. That was a disappointment.* [What was a disappointment? The announcement or the model?] See also PRONOUNS 1(c).

For the use of *that* in expressions of doubt, see BUT THAT.

that is 1. Not always necessary in introducing a short appositive: *The furnaces employ graphite, that is, a highly refined form of carbon* [omit *that is*]. But: *The mortgage commitment is made by an institutional lender, that is, a bank or insurance company* [the omission of *that is* would cause confusion].

2. *That is* is set off by commas when followed by a short appositive (as in Par. 1 above), but it preferably takes a semicolon before and a comma after when it is followed by a fuller statement: *The company pleaded nolo contendere; that is, they would not fight the charge brought against them, but would leave open the opportunity to deny the alleged facts in other proceedings.*

that which A formal, sometimes awkward, expression that is usually better avoided: *That which they favor is* (*What they favor is* or *They favor*) *a complete dissociation from the advertisement/We will have no part of that which suggests collusion* (*We will have no part of anything*

*that suggests collusion)/When that day which we all hope for arrives
. . . (When the day we all hope for arrives . . .).*

theater The preferred American spelling (but also, especially British,
-re); accented on the first syllable. In merchandising, a place, event, or
promotional concept employing theatrical effects. The idea is to provide not merely a setting for goods and services, but a participatory
experience: *The theater of a Burlington fashion presentation is not to
be missed/Bloomingdale's B'Way* [part of the New York store's main
floor] *is pure theater.*

theft The larcenous taking of property; the crime of stealing without
forcible entry (**BURGLARY**) or threat of violence (**ROBBERY**).

their, they're, there Often confused. *Their* shows ownership: *Their
products are well known in Germany/Their proposal deserves our consideration.*

They're is the contraction of *they are: They're a good company to
deal with.*

There is an adverb meaning "in that place": *We built our factory
there ten years ago.*

theirs, there's *Theirs* is a possessive form of *they: The decision is theirs*
(also, *It is their decision*). *There's* is the contraction of *there* and *is:
There's something else we want to do.*

themself Nonstandard for *themselves.* In a questionnaire distributed at
Howard Johnson's restaurants, patrons are asked, "Did the server introduce *themself* by name?" Since *server* is, in word and fact, singular
and either masculine or feminine, the required but awkward alternative
to *themself* is *herself or himself.* See also **SEXUAL BIAS**.

thereafter, thereby, etc. To the list may be added *therein, thereon,
therefrom, thereto,* and *therewith;* also *hereto, wherefrom,* and other
adverb-preposition compounds. Some are superfluous, and some are
better replaced by less stilted locutions.

The first shipment will be made on September 10. *Thereafter* we will send
you . . . (*After that,* we will send you . . .)

If the advertiser cancels the contract, he *thereby* forfeits (omit *thereby*).

You can open the box and remove the contents *therefrom* (omit *therefrom*).

We have your letter and the check enclosed *therein* (. . . and the accompanying check).

We have carefully examined the document, including the appendices *thereto* (omit *thereto*).

A table is located in each reception room, and flowers are placed *thereon* regularly (A table in each reception room is regularly supplied with fresh flowers).

therefor, therefore   *Therefor*, pronounced with the accent on the second syllable, is archaic for *for it, for that*, and similar expressions; it is often superfluous: *We have received the goods, but when we examined the invoice therefor . . .* (Omit *therefor*; or, if the sense requires, substitute *for them*.).

Therefore is a connective meaning "for that reason": *We knew we could meet the delivery date; therefore we accepted the order.* See also SEMICOLON 1.

there is, there are   The "preparatory" *there* in these constructions stands for a subject expressed later in the sentence: *There is a profit to be gained.* [That is, "A profit is to be gained."] *There*, in the original sentence, is a temporary substitute for *profit*, the real subject.

1. *There is* is used when a singular subject follows: *There is a copy of the letter in the file. There are* is used when a plural subject follows: *There are many ways in which we can help you lower your telephone costs.* In informal usage, however, a plural subject sometimes follows *there is: There's two ways to look at the proposition.*

2. When the preparatory *there* is followed by a compound subject of which the first element is singular, the verb is either singular or plural: *There was* (or *were*) *a round model and several rectangular ones to choose from.*

3. *There is* and *there are* help to form sentences and sometimes to avoid awkwardness, but they also have a tendency to create weak sentences: *There's a secret compartment in all E & W wallets for large bills* (Better: *All E & W wallets have a secret compartment for large bills*)/*There are five advantages to the plan* (Better: *The plan has five advantages*).

these kind   See KIND OF, SORT OF.

think tank   Informal for an organization of scholars dedicated to the analysis and solution of complex social, political, economic, or scientific problems. EXAMPLES: *The Hudson Institute, the Brookings Institution, the Institute for Policy Studies, the American Enterprise Insti-*

tute. The name is also given to any group applying expert knowledge to a common effort: *organize our own think tank.*

—think tankster. A member of a think tank: *When an Administration falls, it takes with it the think tanksters, the band of specialists with academic credentials dedicated to formulating arguments for previously determined positions.*

third-class mail Suitable for books, catalogs, and other printed matter, as well as seeds, bulbs, plant cuttings, etc. Weight limit is under sixteen ounces. Heavier packages may be sent by **PRIORITY MAIL** or **FOURTH-CLASS MAIL.** Bulk mailing permits are obtainable from the U.S. Postal Service.

this To be used with caution in referring to a general idea; see **PRO-NOUNS** l(c).

this date, this day Stilted for "today": *as of this date (as of today)/I have this day (today) written to Mr. Baker.*

this here, these here Nonstandard; *here* is superfluous: *This here model (This model) has several excellent features/We want these here people (these people) to be our customers.*

This is to, This will Stilted ways to begin a letter: *This is to acknowledge receipt of (We have received)/This will confirm our recent agreement (We are pleased to confirm, or This letter will confirm)/This is to inform you that the 1995 Keystone Bonds Series A are now quoted at 87½ (omit This is to inform you that).* Compare **WISH TO.**

this writer See **WRITER.**

tho A **SIMPLIFIED SPELLING** of **THOUGH.**

though Synonymous with, but somewhat less formal than, *although* or *however. Though (for Although) the competition will be close, we expect to obtain the contract/He said, though (for however), that he wouldn't mind a switch in dates/I'd like to take the offer; there's just one hitch, though (for however).*

throwaway 1. A handbill distributed on the streets or left on doorsteps. [Postal rules forbid putting unmailed matter in private mailboxes.]

2. Descriptive of a disposable (nonreturnable) container: *throwaway bottles.*

thru   SIMPLIFIED SPELLING of *through*. Nonstandard, but useful in signs, slogans, and headlines: *Last pickup, Mon. thru Fri., 5 p.m.* [sign on public mailboxes].

thrust   Supportable but overused in the sense of direction or tendency: *The thrust of the argument was that the capital gains tax was an abomination/The book's main thrust is an interpretation of listening theory/It's time to take our marketing thrust away from high fashion.*

thusly, thus, so   *Thusly* is nonstandard for *thus*, but *thus* itself is rather stiff and can often be replaced with good effect by *so, in this way,* or a similar expression.

> When the company decided to increase their capacity to take care of the rising demand, they went about it *thus* (or, better, *in this way;* not *thusly*).

> The Chinese are lacking in marketing savvy; *thus (so)* they tend to overproduce when they hear an article is in short supply.

> The "smart" robots are equipped with various sensors to do specific jobs. *Thus (For instance),* they can distinguish between different car models and lift, weld, and paint-spray without disturbing the assembly-line movement.

> *Thus far (So far)* all has gone well.

tick   1. A mark, like a check, placed next to an item on a list to draw attention to it or to show that it has already been given attention. Also a verb: *ticked his name on the roster* [marked the name with a tick]/*ticked off* [counted] *at least a half dozen competing products.*

2. On a graph, ticks are used to show intermediate values along the vertical or horizontal axis, e.g., 0 , , , , 10.

—tick off. To check off, as by a tick; to count or enumerate: *Lewis ticked off the names of some of the appliance discounters.*

—ticked off. Slang. Peeved, angry: *He was ticked off because, as a pioneer of the consumer movement, he was virtually ignored.*

tickler   A daybook, card file, or similar device with reminders, chronologically arranged, of tasks to be done.

tie-in   1. An offer permitting the purchaser to buy one or more items at the regular price and obtain an item of the same or a different kind at a special price: *buy the full-size can of shaving cream and get the after-shave lotion at half price.*

2. A promotional effort requiring the cooperation of two or more entrepreneurs, each of whom receives a benefit from it. Such a tie-in is effected, for example, when a publisher reissues a novel in paper-

back to coincide with the release of a motion picture based on the same book.

till A money box or drawer, as in a small retail store; also used FIG-URATIVELY: *spent $5 million on renovations and they've got much more in the till.*

till, until *Until* is more formal and better suited to the beginning of a sentence: *Until* (rather than *Till*) *we know the price, we are unable to make a decision/They will hold up the order till* (or *until*) *they hear from the supplier. 'Til* is an affectation; *'till* has no standing at all.

time The key word in several redundant phrases: *We have no plans for expansion at the present time* (Better: *at present, now,* or *at this time)/At this point in time (For the present, At this point) we can expect the market to be highly volatile/I cannot remember what action was taken at that period in time (at that time).* For times of day, see CLOCK TIME.

time deposit See CD.

time factor JARGON: *The time factor (Time) is always an important consideration/The FPC has undertaken to hasten the time factor in important rate cases (to speed up the disposition of rate cases) affecting the pipelines.*

time frame JARGON. With its companion *time horizon,* often vague or superfluous: *We're thinking of a time frame of six to eight weeks* (Possibly: *We're thinking of a delay of six to eight weeks)/What kind of time frame should be put on such investments? (time limitation?* Or, recasting the sentence: *For how long should we continue to make such investments?)/The time frame (construction schedule?) calls for completion of the building by October 1/We're thinking of planning expenditures within a longer time horizon (over a longer time).*

times In multiplication. 1. When words are used in multiplying one figure by another, the verb is singular: *The logic is as simple as two times two makes* (not *make) four.*

  2. Expressions like "times more" and "times less" must be used with care for their clarity: *They'll make four times more by switching to our line.* [What is four times more than, say, 20? Is it 80 or 100?] Better: *They'll make four times as much . . . /The job is ten times less difficult.* Better: *The job takes one tenth the effort.*

time-sharing From its application to the cooperative use of a computer facility by several companies, the concept of time-sharing has been extended to other uses, as leasing or buying the exclusive right to occupy a resort apartment for the same period every year.

—time-sharer. A member of a time-sharing group.

titles of courtesy Also *courtesy titles*. Titles preceding personal names, as in an address or introduction: *Mr., Miss, Dr.,* etc. See also **FORMS OF ADDRESS**.

titles of office For their use in letter makeup, see **INSIDE ADDRESS, SIGNATURE BLOCK**, and **ENVELOPE ADDRESS**. For capitalization in a running text, see **CAPITALS** 22.

titles of written material These are the names given to books, chapters, reports, and the like (see also **HEADINGS**).

1. If not set in solid capitals, the principal words are given an initial capital (see **CAPITALS** 21).

2. A title is best kept short. A long title will look better on the title page, however, if it is divided into several lines. The division should be made at a natural break in reading.

(a)   Operational Audit
of the Assembly Unit
Harmon Branch

(b)   Proposed Use of Regional Bank Depositories
by the Natco Chemical Company

3. A title occupying the principal position on a title page is usually placed in the optical center, which is a little above the actual center. A title on the first text page is best dropped one or two inches below the upper type margin, and separated from the first line of text by at least three or four line spaces.

to, too One is not to be carelessly substituted for the other. *To* is a preposition used generally in the sense of direction; *too* is an adverb used most often in the sense of degree: *walk to the office, go to waste, write to the customer.* But: *does too little, pays too high a price, acts too timid.* See also **NOT TOO MUCH**.

to all intents and purposes Trite as well as wordy: *By refusing to bid, the company was to all intents and purposes (in effect, practically) turning down a million dollars' worth of business.* See also **CLICHÉS**.

together See at **ALL TOGETHER, ALTOGETHER**.

token   A shaped piece of metal or other material designed to be used as a substitute for currency, as in subway turnstiles and wherever else the use of change or bills would be inconvenient.

tokenism   A policy of selective discrimination, as when a member of a minority group is placed in a highly visible position to denote that a policy of equal employment opportunity is followed, even when it is not.

tombstone ad   Also *tombstone*. A terse all-type advertisement conveying a formal announcement and set symmetrically like a tombstone inscription. Such advertisements are very likely to be found in the financial pages of a newspaper, and their succinct style is often the result of SEC rules governing financial advertising. See illustration.

This announcement appears as a matter of record only.

$50,000,000

Irrevocable Letter of Credit Facility for

Rogar Commercial Paper Corp.

We are pleased to have been selected as dealer
for this commercial paper program.

Larsen Capital Markets Inc.

Tombstone ad

too   See TO, TOO.

top dollar   As high as, or higher than, the prevailing price: *We pay top dollar for your used office furniture.*

totaled, totaling   Preferred to the variant spellings *totalled* and *totalling: an order totaling* (amounting to) *$2 million.*

totally, completely, entirely   These words are superfluous when the word modified is already absolute in meaning: *totally destroyed; completely eradicated; entirely wiped out.* But (no objection): *partially destroyed; nearly eradicated; almost wiped out.* Compare ABSOLUTE ADJECTIVES. See also WORDINESS 3.

touch, punch in, punch up   *Touch* or *press* (but not *push*) is used in a specific reference to the operation of a push-button telephone: *For room service, touch 22* [notice on a hotel-room telephone]. See also DIAL.

   Punch in is preferred in directions requiring more force and clarity than either *touch* or *press: To make a Sprint call, simply punch in your local "access" number, your personal Sprint authorization code, and the telephone number you wish to reach. . . . All you need is an ordinary push-button phone* [SP Communications].

   Punch up is the correct idiom to denote the accessing of services through a push-button phone or other keyboard device: *With this new kind of TV, it will be easy to shop at home. You'll just punch up your purchase on a keyboard, selecting from a catalog on the TV screen* [ITT].

tourism   The practice of traveling for pleasure; also, the business of providing packaged forms of recreation with set itineraries and selected accommodations and amenities. Tourism is sometimes unfavorably compared with travel, which is less regimented and presumably more instructive. A similar distinction might be made between a tourist and a traveler.

To Whom It May Concern   A SALUTATION used in some types of letters, including a letter of reference, when it is not known at the time of writing who the reader or readers will be. In the circumstances, the complimentary close (*Very truly yours,* for instance) has no significance and is better omitted.

track   1. Intransitive verb, meaning "follow a parallel path": *Our sales track remarkably with the participation of women in the work force.* See also FAST TRACK and TACK, TRACK.

2. Transitive verb, "to observe or monitor": *a security analyst that specializes in tracking IBM.*

track record   In financial parlance, the historical performance of a firm in such matters as sales, profits, and net worth. Also, a history of performance of any kind. In both uses, the word *track* adds atmosphere but not meaning: *The successful candidate must have a proven track record (a proven record) in developing procedure manuals in a service-oriented organization.*

trade   An occupation usually requiring skill with one's hands; a craft: *wanted to learn a trade/a carpenter by trade.* See also VOCATION and COMMERCE, TRADE.

trademark   Abbreviated TM. An officially registered word, picture, or symbol, or combination of these that identifies a product. Use of the trademark is legally restricted to its owner. Compare SERVICE MARK.

trade name   The distinctive name given to a product, service, or other article of commerce and qualifying for registration as a TRADEMARK. Also a BRAND NAME or the name under which a company does business.

trade-off   Also *tradeoff.* A strategic exchange of one advantage for another when both cannot be accommodated: *Nuclear power requires a trade-off between environmental purity and energy to light our homes and run our factories/The standards for new tires put consumers in the position of making trade-offs between tread wear on the one hand and traction and temperature on the other/There's always a trade-off when you use synthetic fabrics. You have to decide whether durability or comfort is more important.*

trade paper   Also trade publication or trade magazine. A periodical devoted to news and technical developments relating to some type of business or trade, as *Advertising Age, Iron Age, Aviation Monthly.*

tradesman   A shopkeeper or merchant: *a tradesman, like his father.* Not usually used in the sense of a worker skilled in some TRADE.

trade union   Also *craft union.* A labor union whose membership consists of persons engaged in the same kind of work, as the International Brotherhood of Electrical Workers, Stone Masons Union, United Brotherhood of Carpenters and Joiners, Airline Pilots Association, United Federation of Teachers. Compare INDUSTRIAL UNION.

trainee An employee being trained for proficiency in a particular job, as a credit trainee. The training may take place on the job or in a company course or courses. *Student* is not a satisfactory synonym, though it may be applied to anyone who takes training courses in a school or college.

transcriber A person who types from written or printed copy, shorthand notes, or voice recording. See also **CORRESPONDENCE SECRETARY.**

translucent Permitting light to pass through, but causing the blurring or obliteration of images: *translucent glass panels.* Compare **OPAQUE.**

transnational Extending across national boundaries: *The core of* The Economist's *[the British magazine] credibility is its ability to speak with a transnational voice.*

transnational company Also **MULTINATIONAL COMPANY:** *China is no longer immune to the pervasive influences of the transnational corporations in communication and other areas.*

transpire Best used in the sense of "leak out" or "become known indirectly": *The news of the appointment soon transpired/It transpired that the philanthropist was no other than the president of the institution.* The word is also used, but with some reservations, in the sense of "occur" or "happen": *What transpired (happened) is best told by the participants/She finds it hard to forget the events that transpired (occurred) afterward.*

treble *Triple* or another locution is usually preferred. Adjective: *a treble (triple) offer.* Verb: *profits trebled (tripled)/a trebling of (tripling of,* or *three-fold increase in) consumer demand.*

trendy Informal for "trend-setting," "advanced": *trendy Bloomingdale's/a trendy three-piece suit with pleated trousers.*

trigger Financial writers are attracted to the word as a colorful metaphor and tend to overuse it: *Today's decline was triggered (set off, precipitated) by the Fed's announcement of a sharp rise in the money supply/The rebates offered by Chrysler are expected to trigger responses by GM and Ford.*

triplification Nonstandard for *tripling* or *triplication: Let's have no more tripling (not triplification) of costs/The study showed not just duplication, but triplication (not triplification) of effort.* See also **TREBLE.**

trite   A phrase or statement is said to be trite when it is overworked and therefore stale and lacking in force: *last but not least, like a bolt from the blue, at the crack of dawn.* See also **CLICHÉS.**
   —triteness, noun: *The triteness of the eulogy would have evoked laughter if the occasion had not been so solemn.*

troops   Along with **SOLDIERS,** an overdramatic synonym for a well-disciplined staff: *The most important ingredient in any agency is the ability of the top man to lead his troops.* [David Ogilvy] Compare **LIEUTENANT.**

true fact   Redundant. See **FACT.**

truly   So spelled (not *truely*); part of the **COMPLIMENTARY CLOSE** of a letter in expressions like "Yours truly" and "Very truly yours."

try   As a noun, informal for "attempt" or "trial": *Haberman made a good try at it/We'll give the idea a try.*
   —try and. Common in informal usage, but *try to* is preferred in general English: *We will try and help (try to help).*

tube   Informal for "television": *Did you watch the tube last night?* Also, disparagingly, the *boob tube.*
   —go down the tube. Slang for "fail" or "become impracticable": *When our competition beat us to the punch, our plan for the new product went down the tube.*

turnkey   Descriptive of a place of business offered to a new owner furnished and equipped, and ostensibly ready for operation at the turn of a key: *South Koreans have paved roads and built turnkey plants throughout the Middle East/Doughnut shop, newsstand, and ice cream store offered in new mini-mart; downtown location, turnkey operations.*

twofer   Also *2-fer.* A blend of "two for"; informal for an offer of two tickets for a play or other event for the price of one: *With twofers, the show was kept alive for months.* Also two of anything for the same price: *2-fer sale. Men's suits 2-fer $150.*

two-track system   Any system permitting either alternative or dual routes to accomplishment: *Our two-track system permits engineers to advance in engineering or management/On-the-job supervision combined with classroom instruction provides a two-track system for training bank tellers.*

two-way communication Any form of COMMUNICATION in which receivers of messages are also senders. In the workplace, communication becomes two-way when workers are given the opportunity to express ideas to superiors. In-person and telephone conversations are inherently two-way systems. Written and mass media are likely to be one-way systems unless response in some form is sought and received. The response may come from coupon returns, opinion surveys, letters, sales, and the like. See also FEEDBACK.

tycoon Pronounced tie-*koon*. Informal for a rich and powerful person in business or industry. Analogous to MAGNATE and MOGUL.

type Often preferred to *typewrite* in general usage.

type of a The *a* is dropped in general usage: *What type of motor do you need?* (Informal: *What type of a motor . . .*). See also KIND OF A, SORT OF A.

typist's initials See IDENTIFICATION INITIALS.

typo Informal for a typographical error: *an unfortunate typo/look for the typos.*

U

uh, er See VOCALIZED PAUSE.

ultimo Abbreviated *ult*. Of the month before the present one. Now archaic. *Your letter of the 30th ultimo.* Compare INSTANT and PROXIMO.

umbrella policy Provides liability insurance for losses in excess of those covered by standard policies; available to businesses and individuals. Informally, *umbrella: Professional people often overlook the importance of personal umbrellas.*

unacceptable A EUPHEMISM used to conceal one's true feelings over a proposal, explanation, or excuse that ranges from the outrageous to downright lying: *The suggestion that we had anything to do with his resignation is unacceptable.*

unbundling The practice of dispensing with a single price that includes all services and substituting charges for each service performed. For a bank, unbundling may mean imposing charges, not previously made, for personalized checks, cashier's checks, certified checks, excess activity in an account, etc. See also BUNDLE 2.

under date of A STEREOTYPED LETTER PHRASE for "on" or "of"; a literal reference to the traditional position of the letter *under* the date line: *Under date of (On) March 14, we wrote you about/We have your letter under date of (of) October 2.* See also DATED.

underground Denoting participants in the UNDERGROUND ECONOMY: *The members of this underground don't even feel guilty anymore.*

underground economy A reference to cash transactions kept OFF THE BOOKS and out of the tax collector's grasp; an illegal practice.

underlining See ITALICS.

under separate cover See SEPARATE COVER.

underpriced A EUPHEMISM descriptive of discounted merchandise:

Magnificently designed modulars by Dorothy Blowers. Underpriced.
[Design Furniture Warehouse]

(the) undersigned 1. A stilted reference to the signer of a letter or memorandum; a term probably originating in the practice of having one person write for the signature of another: *When the quotation is received by the undersigned (When I receive the quotation)/Please address your letter to the attention of the undersigned (to my attention).* See also **(THE) WRITER**.

2. Aptly used in the preamble to a formal petition or similar document when a number of signatures follow: *We the undersigned . . .*

under the circumstances See **CIRCUMSTANCES**.

under way Two words: *Construction is under way for the company's new headquarters building.* The adjective *underway* (one word) is rare: *an underway experiment.*

unemployment Used informally in the sense of unemployment compensation: *receiving unemployment/has been on unemployment for eight weeks/eligible for unemployment.*

Uniform Product Code Abbreviated UPC. The ''bar code'' printed on packaged goods, permitting computer checkouts at markets equipped with ''scanners'' to read them. The bars provide a key to the product and price, which are printed on the cashier's tape. Used also by some companies as a **PROOF OF PURCHASE**. See illustration.

uninterested See **DISINTERESTED, UNINTERESTED**.

unionist Newspaper **JARGON** for a union leader: *Unionists Meeting at Bal Harbour.*

Uniform Product Code

unique Except informally, *unique*—meaning "the only one of its kind"—is not modified by words like *more, most,* or *very* since its meaning does not permit comparison: *The product is unique.* But (informal): *This product is very unique* (very distinctive). See **ABSOLUTE ADJECTIVES.**

unisex Used at first to denote clothing (shirts and jeans) or facilities (haircutting shops), unisex—the absence of sexual distinction—has become an issue in matters of insurance and annuities. The question is whether the cost of insurance and the benefits paid should be differentiated on the basis of the mortality tables for male and female participants, as they traditionally have been. The unisex insurance plans are also called "merged-gender" plans. These are the antithesis of the "sex-distinct" plans. See also **GENDER, SEX.**

unit Journalese for a business entity: *Servico unit* (subsidiary) *buys 2 Florida hotels.* The **AMBIGUITY** of *unit* can also be troublesome in any context: *The company is expected to open a new unit in Schenectady* (store? factory? warehouse?). See also **ABSTRACT AND CONCRETE WORDS.**

unsolvable, insolvable, insoluble The three words are interchangeable in the sense of "incapable of being solved." *Insoluble,* however, also means "incapable of being dissolved." Although there is little chance that *insolvable* and *insoluble* will be confused in any specific context, one can avoid trouble by using *unsolvable* rather than *insolvable* for the first sense, and *insoluble* for the second sense only.

unstructured Not planned or regimented; permitting the free interchange of human and natural forces: *an unstructured meeting/an unstructured working environment* [for creative people]/*A fair bet would be that Joo Seng, like most Chinese companies in these latitudes, is as unstructured as a plate of fried noodles [The Wall Street Journal].* Like its antonym **STRUCTURED,** *unstructured* is perhaps **JARGON,** but it is a useful word.

until See **TILL, UNTIL.**

unwired networks See at **WIRED NETWORKS.**

up Informal as a verb: *will up the price of their compact cars/have upped our estimate of his managerial skill.*

up-and-coming Promising; likely to succeed; eager and hardworking: *an up-and-coming young executive.*

upbeat Optimistic: *The mood is decidedly upbeat/The ad uses a lot of upbeat words.* Antonym, *downbeat.*

upcoming Informal for "coming" or "approaching": *the upcoming conference/The upcoming months mark the perfect season for these handsome wool coats* [Brooks Brothers].

update Acceptable as a verb or noun: *update our files; update our thinking/Let me give you an update on my plant visit.*

upfront Also *up-front.* Informal for "open," "candid": *Now you can be upfront about your drive for success.* [*Fortune*]

up front Informal for "in advance": *The seller requires $10,000 up front.* Also an adjective: *The up front money was not available.*

upon, on The two are synonymous, but *on* is simpler: *a drain upon (on) the property owner/commented upon (on) the figures for May/ upon (on) hearing the news/said that $10 million would be spent upon (on)/quoted prices ranging from $413,000 to $465,000, depending upon (on) options.*

uppercase See CAPITALS.

UPC See UNIFORM PRODUCT CODE.

UPS For United Parcel Service, a privately owned parcel delivery service much used especially for deliveries to retail stores by their suppliers and to retail customers by department and specialty stores.

upscale Marketing JARGON; indicative of, or appealing to, people with above-average personal income and liberal spending habits: *You can make a case that upscale magazines have been less affected than those serving the middle market/We looked hard at Visa and concluded that American Express had more in the way of upscale positioning/The "Tonight" edition was supposed to halt the* News's *circulation losses by adding upscale readers and advertisers to the morning tabloid's traditional blue-collar audience.*

up side Noun, two words. Higher in relation to the previous position; especially descriptive of market prices: *ITT closed on the up side/The day found the market aiming for the up side amid all the vagaries of interest rates.*

uptick An upward movement: *the recent uptick in interest rates.* Also, in stock exchange parlance, *plus tick;* descriptive of a stock sale at a higher price than that of the last previous sale of the stock on the same exchange. *Downtick* and *minus tick* are antonyms describing a stock sale at a lower price.

uptime   Time in service; not in need of repair: *This optional new service guarantees 99 percent uptime over any three-month period or your maintenance service on these critical components is free for the next month* [Hewlett Packard]. Antonym, **DOWNTIME**.

up to ——% off   An advertising **CLICHÉ**; also a vague and usually misleading indication of savings since the reader does not know what portion of the sale merchandise carries the higher reductions and on what price the reductions are based: *up to 60% off;* similarly, *25% to 80% reductions.* Legal or ethical codes usually require the addition of such phrases as "off original prices" and "selected items only."

up to the present writing   Also *up to this writing* and *at this writing.* **STEREOTYPED LETTER PHRASES** and wordy as well: *Up to the present writing (Until now) we have received 39 orders/Up to this writing (So far) we have not heard from the manufacturer/The survey has not been completed at the present writing (has not yet been completed).*

upward, upwards   *Upward* is favored over *upwards* as an adverb: *Prices moved upward* (rather than *upwards*) *in the afternoon.* Only *upward* may be used as an adjective: *There was an upward movement in the afternoon* (not *upwards movement*).

   —upward of, upwards of. Both are acceptable in the sense of "more than": *The machine costs upward of* (or *upwards of*) *$25,000.*

upward communication   See at **COMMUNICATION FLOW**.

upward mobility   The movement of an individual with some frequency to ever higher levels of responsibility and remuneration: *The upward movement of the M.B.A. recruits is not always appreciated by an employer who provides on-the-job training only to see them deliver their newfound skills to a rival company.* See also **MOBILITY**.

usage, use   Usage relates to customary practice, as in social behavior or language: *English usage, legal usage, social usage* (etiquette).

   Use, the more common word, relates to employment or utilization: *will find a profitable use for the by-products/encouraged the use of protective glasses/made more readable by the use of short words.*

usages   The language of business, like English itself, has no single criterion of acceptability. It is usually convenient, however, to recognize the several varieties or "levels" of usage. These can be roughly classified, in order of their utility, as *general, informal, formal,* and *nonstandard.*

1. GENERAL. Only general English has unlimited acceptability in speech and writing. The others are hedged by various restrictions ranging from the relatively inconsequential in informal English to the unquestionably serious in nonstandard English.

General English is the English used by literate persons in speech and writing. It is the prevailing language of business letters and reports; advertising; newspapers and magazines; fiction and nonfiction; radio and television. Words in the general vocabulary are not so identified in this volume except to emphasize some distinction in usage.

2. INFORMAL. Informal English is the spoken language of cultured people and the language used in writing when casual or familiar expression is desired. It may include shoptalk and some slang. Also characteristic of informal English are the first-person pronouns *I* and *we,* and common contractions: *I'll, can't, you're,* etc.

A great deal of business writing, including letters, memorandums, and advertising in the popular media, leans to informal expression. The line between general and informal English is not always sharply drawn, but when the consensus appears to favor such a classification, the word is labeled *informal* in the vocabulary entry. Informal words more suited to speech than to writing are labeled *colloquial.*

3. FORMAL. Formal English is restricted to special audiences and situations: in correspondence to high government officials, in technical reports and journal articles, in formal notifications and announcements, in legal documents, and in letters and other documents having legal implications. Formal language is restrained, sometimes ceremonious or stiff. Words exhibiting these characteristics are labeled *formal* in the vocabulary entry.

Many formal terms are flawed in one way or another. These may be described in the vocabulary entry as *stilted* (stiffly formal), *hackneyed* (overused and trite), *pretentious,* or *pompous.* See also JARGON and OFFICIALESE.

4. NONSTANDARD. Nonstandard (also called "substandard") English is the language of the streets, shops, and close conversation among friends and enemies. It includes the obscene and profane, misuses of standard words *(ain't, irregardless, confliction),* and noticeably unconventional grammar *(don't got, they was, should of).*

Nonstandard English is sometimes used facetiously or for emphasis in general speech and writing.

5. OTHER USAGES. In addition to the usages already named, the reader will find some vocabulary entries labeled archaic (antiquated, as *anent* and *amanuensis*) and dialect (local terms, as *reckon* and *you all*). These usages are sometimes classified as nonstandard.

used to   Although the phrase sounds like "use to," the correct spelling is usually *used to: It used to be fun/They used to cooperate with us/I am not used to this way of doing things.* However, *use to* can be correctly though awkwardly used after a past-tense auxiliary verb in a negative statement or a question: *We did not use to rely so much on part-time help/Didn't customers use to pay for alterations?*

user fee   A politically favored EUPHEMISM for a tax affecting those who buy the product or service on which the tax is levied or benefit from the use to which the tax is put. Favorite types of user fees are those on cars and trucks, gasoline, liquor, cigarettes, and licenses of various sorts.

USP   Not just the *U.S. Pharmacopoeia*, but also the *Unique Selling Proposition*, a name originated by Ted Bates & Company, the advertising agency, for the "extra ingredient" in the advertising they prepare. The advertisements are intended to be original, dramatic, and hard-hitting. Examples: urging prospective buyers of Prudential insurance to "get a piece of the Rock," a reference to Gilbraltar in the Prudential trademark; using a dye to penetrate white chalk as a way of showing how the fluoride in Colgate toothpaste works; claiming with "laboratory evidence" that Rolaids ("some people say it spells r-e-l-i-e-f") consume 47 times their weight in stomach acid; coating ping-pong balls with Maybelline nail polish and putting them in play, to demonstrate Maybelline's chip resistance.

USPS   United States Postal Service.

usury   Pronounced *you*-zhuh-ree. The practice of lending money at exorbitant rates: *Usury affects the small lender most/Legislation controls usury ceilings.*
   —usurious, adjective: *usurious rates.*

utilize   The shorter word *use*, meaning to employ or put to use, is appropriate in most instances; *utilize*, however, is well used in the restricted sense of making useful in a new or unaccustomed way: *The* *company utilizes its beef byproducts to make industrial oils.* But: *We will use* (rather than *utilize*) *the product if the cost is within reason/They say they can use her talents in the art department.*

—utilization, noun: *Century Builders is a leader in the utilization of solar technology.* But: *The use* (rather than *utilization*) *of fluoride in drinking water is now well established.*

V

V Veteran. See at EQUAL OPPORTUNITY EMPLOYER.

v., vs. Abbreviations of *versus*, but the first is preferred in legal citations: *Marcy v. Union Oil Co.*

vagary Pronounced *vay*-guh-ree or vay-*gair*-ee. Erratic action; usually found in the plural: *the vagaries of the stock market.*

validated parking Limited free parking provided at a nearby facility for customers who are given some official verification that they have spent time or transacted business with the host company: *Validated parking—2-hour limit.*

valuation, evaluation The words are synonymous for the assessment of merit or value, but *valuation* may be preferred when the assessment involves an appreciation of intangibles, and *evaluation* when it means finding a numerical expression for: *The large retrospective show makes possible a fair valuation of Matisse's artistry.* But: *The auctioneers' evaluation* [in dollars] *took into account both the rarity and condition of the articles.*

value, evaluate The words are synonymous in the sense of making an appraisal, as in monetary terms; *evaluate*, however, is more formal than *value* and is the older and more established term: *evaluated the vase at $12,000* (also *valued*). Only *value* is appropriately used in the sense of esteem or having a high opinion of: *valued the vase enough to bid $12,000 for it.*

value-added tax See VAT.

valued Stereotyped in such phrases as ''appreciate your valued patronage'' and ''have been reviewing your valued account,'' but still well used in other contexts: *Theirs is a much valued account/Mrs. Ditmars has been a valued customer for ten years/He will make a valued addition to our staff of analysts.* See also STEREOTYPED LETTER PHRASES.

vanity press Also *vanity publisher(s)*. A PEJORATIVE for a company that publishes books at the author's expense, unlike the traditional book publisher, which normally assumes the financial risks and pays royalties to its authors out of the proceeds.

variety, in sentences   See SENTENCES 3.

VAT   Also *V.A.T.* ACRONYM for *value-added tax*, a national tax on each step in the chain of production from raw materials to retail sales. The tax, widely applied in Western Europe, has only been talked about in the United States.

vault   The term is sometimes misused for "safe-deposit box." A vault is a room or compartment, often made of steel, for the safekeeping of valuables: *a bank vault/a hotel vault*. A safe-deposit box is usually one of many strongboxes built into a vault: *rent safe-deposit boxes from $10 a year*.

VCR   Video cassette recorder.

veep   A slang version of V.P. for "vice president": *looking for a new veep to take charge of public relations*.

vehicle   A handy term used by communicators to distinguish a particular newspaper, magazine, or broadcasting station from the class of MEDIUM to which it belongs. Thus *Business Week* is a *vehicle*, and magazine or print, the *medium*.

vent   See VENTILATE 2 below.

ventilate   1. To expose to examination or discussion feelings that might otherwise be repressed: *The meeting was called to permit union representatives to ventilate their grievances*.

2. With *vent*, personnel JARGON when used in the sense of giving a dismissed employee an EXIT INTERVIEW: *After his termination, the employee is ventilated and then encouraged to start thinking about his future/Three days of venting is a good target to aim for*. Also jargon when used reflexively: *After you've vented yourself* (submitted to an exit interview), *you can start organizing your campaign for a new job*.

verbal   A word to be used with care. *Verbal* pertains literally to words, spoken or written: *Almost any verbal message on economics is made more effective by the addition of charts*. However, *verbal* is also a common synonym for "spoken" or "oral": *made a verbal agreement/took a verbal beating from the supervisor*. A writer who senses the possibility of misunderstanding will put aside *verbal* and use *oral* or *written,* as the sense requires.

verbatim   So spelled (not *-um*) and pronounced vur-*bay*-tim. In exactly the same words: *took down the conversation verbatim/a verbatim copy of the interview.*

version   Verb; to adapt a movie or television show to a particular market. As an example, the BBC's *Life on Earth* was *versioned* for American television in order to give it a livelier pace. This was done by cutting 8 minutes from the 59-minute running time.

versus   See V., VS.

very   1. Much overused. "I am enthusiastic" can be just as emphatic as "I am very enthusiastic," if not more so.

   2. *Very much* is more formal than *very* before a past participle, and some consider it the only "correct" form; but its use is waning: *am very much impressed* (for *am very impressed*)/*was very much inconvenienced* (for *was very inconvenienced*). It is especially doubtful that anyone would quarrel with such locutions as "very pleased," "very disappointed," and "very delighted," where the past participle has the character of a simple adjective.

via   Pronounced *vie*-uh or *vee*-uh. Generally accepted in the sense of "by way of" or "by means of": *The shipment was routed to Des Plaines via* (by way of) *Chicago/The best pineapples are shipped via* (by means of) *air to the mainland. Via* is used only informally, however, in the sense of "as a result of": *Her success came via brains and hard work.*

viable   Capable of living or developing; PRACTICABLE. There is a tendency to overuse the word: *a viable (growing, healthy) industry/a viable (workable) solution.*

vice president   Abbreviated V.P. Preferred to *vice-president.* But (correct): *vice-presidency: appointed vice president/assumed the vice-presidency.*

vicinity   "In the vicinity of" is nonstandard when used for "about" with numbers or amounts: *owes in the vicinity of (about) $50,000/an orchard covering in the vicinity of (about) 150 acres.* Compare with AREA and NEIGHBORHOOD.

videoconference   A TELECONFERENCE employing television transmission.

videotex A two-way communications service using the telephone network to connect a television-like terminal in the home with a central computer. By typing instructions onto the keyboard, the user can summon desired information from the computer "bank." The system also has the potential for taking orders, transferring bank funds, and performing other utilitarian functions. Compare TELETEXT.

viewpoint The objection to *viewpoint* appears to have subsided, possibly because it helps to avoid the awkwardness of *point of view*. However, a substitute for either can often be found: *From the viewpoint of economy (For economy) the four-cylinder model has the edge over all its competitors/From the point of view of (In the view of) the participants, the meeting was outstanding.* See also the "YOU" VIEWPOINT and, for consistency of viewpoint, SENTENCES 4.

view to "With a view to," when not unnecessarily wordy, is better followed by an *-ing* form of the verb than by an infinitive: *took the cash with a view to investing it* (rather than *with a view to invest it*) *in a new venture.* But (more definite): *took the cash to invest in a new venture.*

VIP Pronounced as three words, *vee eye pee.* Informal for "very important person": *The VIPs have not yet arrived/acts like a VIP/the VIP lounge.*

virgule Also SLANT, slash, or diagonal; the symbol /. Pronounced *vurjyool.* See ABBREVIATIONS 5 and AND/OR, ETC.

virtually Essentially: *Use Cascade for virtually spotless dishes.* See also at PRACTICALLY 3.

vis-à-vis French; pronounced vee-zuh-*vee.* Literally, "face-to-face," but more commonly used in the sense of "as compared with" or "in relation to": *Many corporations feel the legislation puts them at a disadvantage vis-à-vis their foreign competitors.* See also FOREIGN WORDS.

visceral EUPHEMISM for "gut." Expressive of deep feeling, and relating to an instinctive or emotional, rather than a rational, response: *a visceral hostility/a visceral reaction.*
    —viscerally, adverb: *was viscerally unprepared for the transfer to Des Moines.*

visible Attention-getting; often suggestive of exposure to risk: *As com-*

pany spokesperson, she is highly visible. Analogous to having a **HIGH PROFILE.**

—visibility, noun: *His visibility makes him a target for the complaints against the entire industry/Markey attributes her success to her low visibility.*

visitation   When visitation is not used negatively, as in "a visitation of the plague," it denotes a formal visit for an inspection or similar purpose: *a visitation of the Board of Supervisors.* It is not otherwise a good synonym for "visit": *a visit to the Exchange; a visit by their salesman* (not *visitation*).

visit with   "To visit with" is not necessarily "to call on"; rather, the term is used informally in the sense of "talk with," whether in person or by telephone: *Come and visit with us for a while/It was good to visit with you; please phone again when it's convenient.*

vita   See **CURRICULUM VITAE.**

viz.   Abbreviation of the Latin *videlicet,* meaning "namely." Used to introduce an example or a list of some sort. Better avoided, but if it has to be read aloud, the speaker says "namely," not "viz."

vocalized pause   A momentary pause in speaking, characterized by involuntary sounds like *uh* and *er;* a fault avoided by practiced speakers.

vocation   An occupation for which a person is assumed to have some special aptitude or training: *A diplomat by vocation, Stearns is also an amateur painter.* Compare **CAREER, JOB.**

—vocational, adjective: vocational training.

voice-over   Also *voice-under.* In television, the commentary by an unseen speaker: *Pete Daniels provided the voice-over/Texan's voice-under: Garkone, avez vous any more of that Pere Pat?* [From the script for a television commercial]

V.P.   Abbreviation of **VICE PRESIDENT.** Pronounced *vee pee;* also, familiarly, **VEEP.**

W

wage See SALARY, WAGES.

waive To give up voluntarily a claim or privilege; not to be confused with *wave* (to signal by a back-and-forth movement): *They agreed to waive the commission.*
—**waiver**, noun: *A waiver* (relinquishment) *of the fee was denied.*

walkup Also *walk-up*. 1. A business place open to public access without the constraint of a wall or door, as a retail sales space or banking facility in a building lobby or subway concourse.
  2. A building without an elevator; also an apartment or place of business in such a building: *a six-story walkup/occupied a walkup office above the pawnshop.*

want in, want out Informal for wanting to join (or quit) some business undertaking: *If the scheme is going to make a profit, we want in/We think it's a fair deal, but if you want out, speak up.*

ware In the singular—as the latter part of a compound—*ware* denotes articles of the same class: *glassware, hardware, ovenware.* The plural *wares*, used independently, stands for goods or anything else bought and sold, including services: *They will sell their wares to anyone who'll pay for them/Now that the ad agency has lost its beer account, it's peddling its wares to a competing brewer.*

warranty A seller's assumption of responsibility for the quality or performance of the goods sold. In law a *warranty* is more binding than a GUARANTEE: *Motorists should shop around for extended warranties as carefully as they do for insurance.* [Automobile Club of New York]
—**warrant**, verb: *The tires are warranted* (not *warrantied*) *for 40,000 miles.*

Washington, D.C. Washington, referring to the nation's capital, is not to be abbreviated in an address or otherwise. The postal abbreviation of the District of Columbia is DC (no periods). See also STATE POSTAL ABBREVIATIONS.

watchdog A person or agency whose official or self-appointed task is to check on compliance with laws and regulations: *the government's environmental watchdogs/tracked by Nader-inspired watchdogs*. Also an adjective: *a watchdog agency*.

WATS ACRONYM for AT&T's *W*ide *A*rea *T*elephone *S*ervice. WATS numbers, prefixed 800, permit calls to be made toll-free. Companies pay an installation fee, service charge, and a usage fee based on the number of calls. Many companies use the 800 number as a HOT LINE for customers' inquiries, complaints, and calls for service.

ways and means A CLICHÉ. *Ways* suggests methods, and *means*, money; but the distinction is usually lost or nonexistent: *A good office manager will find the ways and means (will find a way) to get the work done.*

we For the use of the corporate *we*, see I, WE.

well Usually hyphened to a past participle preceding a noun: *a well-known rug importer/a well-deserved compliment*. However, the hyphen is omitted when the expression follows the noun or predicate verb: *a merchant well known in discounting circles/was well prepared for the occasion*. See also HYPHEN 1(a).

well, good See GOOD 2 and 3.

well and favorably known Not necessarily a CLICHÉ or a REDUNDANCY. In a credit recommendation, especially, *well known* and *favorably known* do not mean the same thing; rather, they complement each other in providing a positive recommendation of a prospective debtor: *The company is well and favorably known to us as licensees of a number of patents they hold for zippers and other types of closures.*

"we" viewpoint See "YOU" VIEWPOINT.

wheel and deal To engage in intensive negotiation. Informal, often used prejudicially: *wheeled and dealed their way into a fat government contract.*
—**wheeler and dealer,** noun: *has a reputation as a wheeler and dealer.*

when, where Used awkwardly in definitions; see IS WHEN, IS WHERE.

whence Since *whence* means "from where," the *from* in "from whence" is superfluous. *Whence* itself is overformal, if not archaic, and many writers and speakers avoid it: *We do not know whence they came*. Better: *We do not know where they came from.*

when issued Abbreviated w.i. A term denoting that a listed issue of a stock or bond has been authorized, but is not yet available for distribution. The securities may be bought or sold on the when-issued basis, but the actual settlement of the transaction does not take place until the formal date of issuance.

where 1. Used only informally for "that": *I see where (that) Darnell has been made treasurer.*

2. Nonstandard with "at": *Where is your office at?* (Omit *at*.)

3. Better not used for "when" or "if": *The discount applies only if* (rather than *where*) *the customer buys a dozen or more/When* (rather than *Where*) *a seminar is booked to capacity, provision should be made to accommodate the overflow.*

For "is where," see IS WHEN, IS WHERE.

whereas Suitable in a formal RESOLUTION, but otherwise stuffy: *Whereas (While) we were prepared for the increase in demand, our competitors were not/Myers thought he had the order in his pocket whereas (but) he was wrong.*

whereby Overformal for "by which," but that expression makes an awkward sentence and is also better avoided: *the method whereby (by which) the merger was accomplished* (but better: *the way the merger was accomplished*)/*will take several steps whereby the debt will be paid off (will take several steps to repay the debt).*

wherein Archaic and better retired: *the office wherein (where) the work was done/can't see wherein (how) he failed.*

wherewithal Archaic: *must find the wherewithal (the means, the money) to replace the obsolete equipment.*

whether or not 1. Except in formal usage, the *or not* is usually dropped; it is especially not needed when the statement preceding is already negative: *I'll wait to see whether or not they keep their promise (I'll wait to see whether they keep their promise)/They do not know whether or not the offer was accepted (They do not know whether the offer was accepted).* See also IF, WHETHER.

2. The *or not* can be useful for emphasis, but it should not be separated from *whether* if the result is clumsy: *I'd like to know whether to run the promotion next week or not* (Better: *I'd like to know whether or not to run the promotion next week*). But (separation satisfactory): *We'll decide tomorrow whether we'll buy or not.*

which 1. *Which* is awkward, sometimes vague, when it stands within a sentence for the whole idea expressed in a preceding clause: *The practice of accounting becomes more and more complex, which tends to increase the level of specialization within the profession and adds to the demand for accountants.*

If the context permits, the whole sentence can be recast to avoid the *which: The increasing complexity of accounting tends to increase the level of specialization within the profession and adds to the demand for accountants.* Another alternative is to retain the initial clause and start a new sentence, substituting some other connective for *which,* as: *This complexity tends to increase the level of specialization . . . ;* or: *As a result, the level of specialization within the profession tends to increase and, with it, the demand for accountants.* See also **PRONOUNS** 1(c).

2. An initial *which,* referring to an idea expressed in the preceding sentence, is used only informally. It is common in advertising: *The G-K car rental people offer a 20 percent company discount. Which is more than we can say for our competitors/Last year, some two million trees were harvested to produce the 112 billion envelopes you and we used to package our communications. Which means our essential need for envelopes could conflict with our emotional attachment to trees* [Boise Cascade].

3. *Whose* is often a desirable substitute for the possessive *of which.* Awkward: *They have built a number of houses, of which the foundations are now sinking.* Better: *They have built a number of houses whose foundations are now sinking.*

See also **WHO, WHICH**.

which is, who is These clumsy locutions can often be beneficially omitted: *The report addresses the long-term prospects of Montgomery Ward, which is the No. 6 retailer of general merchandise in the United States* (omit *which is)/Grimes, who is their vice president, answered the call* (omit *who is).*

while Well used in the sense of "during the time that": *Grayson will be in Los Angeles while the negotiations go on here.* In other uses, however, *while* is often ambiguous and less accurate than *though, although, but,* or *whereas: While (Though or Although) leather is ideal, we could make do with a good synthetic/The last year was relatively good for all-cotton shirts, while (but) the year before was a positive disaster/Bailey was not available for comment while (whereas) Simmons was available and noncommittal.*

whistleblower   A person who reports improper or unlawful acts, particularly those committed by an employer in business or government: *asked for a bill of rights protecting whistleblowers/was known in the company as a whistleblower and worse.*

white-collar crime   A crime, like embezzlement or forgery, committed by a **WHITE-COLLAR WORKER.**

white-collar worker   A person engaged in clerical, professional, or executive duties requiring dress suitable to office work. Compare with **BLUE-COLLAR WORKER** and **GRAY-COLLAR WORKER.**

white pages   Also *White Pages.* The Bell System's publicly distributed listing of telephone subscribers; in some communities, sharing the directory with the **YELLOW PAGES.**

who, which   1. *Who* refers to persons, *which* to things: *The salesperson who sold us the machine is no longer with the company/The floor, which is in poor condition, must be replaced.*

2. *Which* is used almost exclusively to introduce nonrestrictive clauses. These are word groups not essential to the sense of the sentence and set off by commas. See **COMMA** 4.

See also **WHICH** and **THAT** 5.

who, whom   1. *Who* is the nominative case form of the pronoun; *whom,* the objective case form. *Who* is often used for *whom,* however, in both informal and general usage. This substitution is especially likely whenever the pronoun precedes the verb, probably because—especially in dictation and conversation—it takes too long to determine which pronoun the grammar of the sentence calls for. *Whom,* though, is used fairly consistently as the object of an immediately preceding preposition.

OBJECT OF VERB: *Who* do you think he will appoint? [Object of *will appoint.* More formal: *Whom* do you think he will appoint?]

OBJECT OF VERB: I wish I knew *who* top management considers eligible for the job. [Object of *considers.* More formal: . . . *whom* top management considers eligible for the job.]

SUBJECT OF INFINITIVE (normally in the objective case): Grady did not know *who* to blame. [More formal: Grady did not know *whom* to blame.]

OBJECT OF PREPOSITION FOLLOWING: *Who* shall I address the memorandum to? [More formal: *Whom* shall I address the memorandum to?]

OBJECT OF IMMEDIATELY PRECEDING PREPOSITION (all usages): To *whom* shall I address the memorandum?

2. When the pronoun is the subject of a verb from which it is separated by other words, the nominative form *who* is required: I wanted to hear *who* (not *whom*) he thought was responsible. [Subject of *was*]

3. When there is doubt about the use of *who* or *whom*, the better choice is usually *who*.

who is A wordy locution. See **WHICH IS, WHO IS**.

who's, whose *Who's* is the contraction of *who is* or *who has*: *Who's going to do the work?/Who's* (Who has) *got the overhead projector?*

Whose stands for the possessive "of whom" or "of which": *We don't know whose proposal we will eventually accept/We found several cartons whose contents were not marked*. See also **WHICH** 3.

w.i. Abbreviation of **WHEN ISSUED**.

width Abbreviated w.; pronounced *width* or *with* (rhymes with *pith*). See also **IN LENGTH, IN NUMBER, IN SIZE**.

will A testamentary document; often capitalized to prevent confusion with other uses: *The Will will be presented for probate on May 10*. For *will* as an auxiliary verb, see **SHALL, WILL; SHOULD, WOULD**.

windfall A sudden and unexpected stroke of good fortune: *The sale of the old factory was a windfall for the company*. Also used descriptively as a **PEJORATIVE**, as by those who wish to penalize "*windfall* profits" with a "*windfall* tax."

window An opening, as in a wall; figuratively used in the military's phrase "window of vulnerability," but also useful in positive business expressions: *The ten-year contract gives the company a window on the booming field of genetic engineering*.

window dressing Also, *window-dressing*. In a statement or report, any information intended to create a good impression by distracting attention from the unfavorable information in the same document. For example, a mutual fund may make much of an increase in asset value (the *window dressing*) while it glosses over a drop in the rate of return.

window envelopes Window envelopes save time in addressing, but they give an impersonal or official look to letters and are better used for bills, receipts, routine notifications, and the like.

Letterheads and other forms designed for use with window envelopes are preferably printed to show by dots or corner markings the extremities of the space reserved for the **MAILING ADDRESS**, and by ticks on the sides of the sheet at the points at which the folds are to be made. The position of the address within the "window" should allow for at least a quarter of an inch of white space on all sides. If the enclosure is too small or improperly folded, movement within the envelope may obscure the address.

wire General English for a telegram: *received a wire from Drew*. Also a verb: *wired Brown this morning*.

—**pull wires.** To use one's influence to gain an advantage: *thought they could get the contract if they pulled some wires*.

wired network A formally established radio network, as ABC, CBS, NBC, or Mutual. The antithesis is the "unwired network," consisting of a group of stations independently joining forces for one or more special programs.

-wise 1. A suffix in general usage, forming adverbs denoting manner, position, or direction: *likewise, contrariwise, clockwise, sidewise*.

2. JARGON when used as a suffix to nouns in the sense of "with reference to": *Saleswise we are doing remarkably well (Our sales are remarkably good)/The lot is small areawise; but locationwise it can't be beat (The lot is small, but the location can't be beat)*.

wish Formal, sometimes affected, for "want": *He wished (wanted) to see Mr. Delmar/Do you wish (want) to invest the entire proceeds?*

wish to Superfluous and stilted in such phrases as "wish to advise you," "wish to acknowledge," and "wish to announce"; better not used in ordinary correspondence. However, such expressions are characteristic of formal or official announcements, where dignity is considered more important than naturalness. See also STEREOTYPED LETTER PHRASES and WORDINESS 2.

with Sometimes misused for another preposition or used in a construction that would be more felicitous if it were recast: *Day and evening shifts with 60 and 72 workers were employed (Day and evening shifts of 60 and 72 workers were employed)/The economy is undoubtedly improving, but with our business, it is still sluggish (but our business is still sluggish)*.

with a view to See VIEW TO.

with further reference to See FURTHER.

withholding tax A misnomer because "withholding" is not a tax, but a portion of salary or other income withheld by the payer and submitted periodically to the IRS or corresponding state agency for credit toward the payee's income taxes: *withholding on gambling income/exemption from withholding/a weekly salary of $465.20 after withholding*. See also **W-2 FORM**.

within *Within* occasionally expresses an idea more precisely than *in*, but the shorter word does as well or better in other instances: *arrived within minutes/comes within the jurisdiction of the Civil Court*. But: *accomplished the task in* (or *within*) *the allotted time/inserted the letter in* (rather than *within*) *the envelope*.

with reference to See **REFERENCE**.

with regard to See **REGARDING, AS REGARDS, ETC.**

with respect to See **IN RESPECT TO, WITH RESPECT TO**.

with the result that Wordy for "so": *We buy in large quantities, with the result that (so) we save our customers money*. See also **WORDINESS** 4.

woman, lady See **LADY**.

word division A word is divided at the end of a line to prevent a ragged margin. As a rule, such divisions should not occur in more than two successive lines, nor in the last word of a paragraph, nor in the last line of a page. Only in legal work is the last word sometimes divided to show that the text is carried over.

1. UNDIVIDED WORDS. 2. SYLLABIC DIVISION. 3. PROPER NAMES AND TITLES. 4 FIGURES. 5. DATES.

1. UNDIVIDED WORDS. Not to be divided:

(a) A word pronounced as one syllable

   bought   stock   earned   passed

(b) A word of four letters or less

   undo   item   even   also

(c) A contraction

   can't   hasn't   wouldn't   o'clock

(d) An abbreviation

   ASME   diam.   Ph.D.   AT&T.

2. SYLLABIC DIVISION. If words are divided at all, they are divided phonetically between syllables.

(a) A word is preferably divided after a prefix of at least two letters or before a suffix of at least three letters. However, a prefix or suffix itself should not be divided, nor should any division be made before a suffix that does not form an extra syllable.

un-able	invest-ment
mis-place	dial-ing
post-date	renew-able
retro-spect	prestig-ious

not: a-round/element-al/un-derstand/renewa-ble/allow-ed

(b) A word should not be divided before a final syllable with a silent vowel.

gentle (*not* gen-tle)
poss-ible (*not* possi-ble)
prin-ciple (*not* princi-ple)

(c) A word may be divided after a single consonant or between two consonants, except when a double consonant occurs in the root word.

rel-evant (*not* re-levant)		invok-ing (*not* invo-king)	
con-cert	foun-dation	abut-ting	process-ing
call-ing	sell-ing	pass-able	poul-try

(d) A word may be divided after a vowel forming a syllable within a word, or between two vowels pronounced separately.

ele-vate	ori-gin	perme-ate	flu-ency

(e) A solid compound should be divided only between the words that compose the compound. A hyphened compound should be divided only at the hyphen.

back-slider, carry-all (*division of the solid compounds* backslider *and* carryall)

self-winding; secretary-treasurer (*division of hyphened compounds*)

(f) A word should never be divided so that it causes misreading.

ready-ing (*not* rea-dying)	oasis (*not* oa-sis)
often (*not* of-ten)	paltry (*not* pal-try)

3. PROPER NAMES AND TITLES. Proper names are better not divided, but a last name preceded by a given name (not initials alone) may be carried over to the next line. However, titles of courtesy (Mr.,

Dr., Rev., etc.); endings like Jr., Sr., and Esq.; and letters standing for degrees (M.D., LL.D., etc.) should never be separated from the name. The slant (/) in the following examples shows where line divisions can and cannot be made:

ACCEPTABLE: Dr. James W. Marshall Jr.; Dr. James W./Marshall Jr.

UNACCEPTABLE: Dr./James W. Marshall Jr.; Dr. James W. Marshall/Jr.

4. FIGURES. A figure should not be divided, nor should an abbreviation be separated from the figure to which it belongs.

ACCEPTABLE: $1,235,000; 400 sq. ft.

UNACCEPTABLE: *(slant shows line division):* $1,235/000; 400/sq. ft.

5. DATES. A date is divided, if it is divided at all, between the day and the year, not between the month and the day.

ACCEPTABLE *(slant shows line division):* October 22,/19xx.

UNACCEPTABLE: October/22, 19xx.

wordiness Since business makes a virtue of efficiency, one might wonder why business writing is so often verbose. The reasons go beyond mere thoughtlessness or lack of discipline. Sometimes words are multiplied to compensate for thin substance and to cloak the most ordinary ideas in a formality that verges on pomposity. Fear of error encourages the use of stereotypes that have already been sanctioned by the organization and discourages any innovation in phrasing that might result in conciseness. It takes boldness to write a letter of a couple of lines when the standard letter sheet offers a hundred square inches to be filled. Like most speech, dictation itself is verbose and cannot conveniently be edited. The pressures of time are also to be blamed. "I have made this letter longer than usual," wrote Pascal, "because I lack the time to make it short."

It is not easy to control wordiness, but a sensitivity to some of the obvious symptoms can help.

1. NONESSENTIAL DETAILS.   2. DEADWOOD.   3. REDUNDANCY.
4. WORDY CONNECTIVES.   5. FLABBY VERB PHRASES.
6. WORDY MODIFIERS.   7. INDIRECTNESS.   8. RECASTING FOR CONCISENESS.

See also TELEGRAPHIC STYLE.

1. NONESSENTIAL DETAILS. A basic cause of wordiness, the inclusion of unnecessary details is often the result of formula writing. For instance: Is reference to an incoming letter always necessary in the reply? Must the contents of the incoming letter be repeated? Must

a negative idea be introduced when a positive statement is going to reverse it anyway? Straight thinking can cut the message to its essentials.

WORDY: Replying to your inquiry regarding the name of our sales representative in Chicago, we are represented there by R. F. Dorman, 1310 North State Street.

CONCISE: Our sales representative in Chicago is R. F. Dorman, 1310 North State Street.

WORDY: On September 18 we wrote you for a duplicate of your invoice of August 12 for $265.53, but to date we have not yet received an answer. Will you please send us the duplicate copy we requested.

CONCISE: May we have the duplicate copy of your invoice of August 12 for $265.53, as we requested in our letter of September 18.

2. DEADWOOD.   Some words and phrases can be omitted without damage to the sense: *For your information,* the annuitant's address is/*we wish to take this opportunity to* thank you for/We appreciate your cooperation *in this matter*/They are now *in the process of* tabulating.

3. REDUNDANCY.   (a) Although the term is used for superfluity in any form, redundancy is more particularly the use of a word or phrase that unnecessarily repeats the idea expressed in another word or phrase. The words in parentheses below repeat the sense of the words to which they are linked.

enclosed (herewith)	the (alleged) suspect
in (close) proximity	cooperate (together)
as a (general) rule	the (true) facts
the (remaining) balance	continue (on)
the (basic) fundamentals	consensus (of opinion)
depreciate (in value)	repeat (again)
revert (back) to	the (exact) same
a (free) gift	letter (under date) of
(young) juveniles	the (end) result

See also IN LENGTH, IN NUMBER, IN SIZE.

(b) Some word pairings that seem redundant are actually throwbacks to established single words whose meaning has in some way been put in doubt. *Natural grass, genuine leather,* and *solid walnut,* for example, are intended to differentiate the real from the synthetic. A *new initiative* follows a prior attempt at innovation. A *movie movie* is one made originally for presentation on a theater screen and only later shown on television.

4. WORDY CONNECTIVES.   A simple preposition or conjunction may effectively take the place of a connecting phrase.

prior to the meeting *(before)*
subsequent to your call *(after)*
with respect to this inquiry *(about)*
under date of May 8 *(on)*
in the event that it succeeds *(if)*
in the amount of $20 *(for)*
in accordance with your request *(at)*
in connection with the feasibility of *(on)*
in the nature of a bonus *(like)*
on the ground that (because)
with the result that (so)
in view of the fact that (since)

5. FLABBY VERB PHRASES.   In some circuitous verb-noun expressions, the principal meaning is carried by the noun. Changing the expression so that the verb carries the meaning of the noun saves words and adds emphasis.

[when you] come to a decision (decide)
gave her endorsement to (endorsed)
is engaged in the importation of (imports)
came to the conclusion (concluded)
place your signature on (sign)
are sending the enclosed (are enclosing)
made a tunnel [through the mountain] (tunneled)
acted as a witness to (witnessed)
are in receipt of (received)
are of the belief that (believe)

6. WORDY MODIFIERS.   Some phrases can be reduced to a simple adjective or adverb, and some clauses (especially those beginning with *who, which,* or *that*) can be reduced to a word or phrase.

the success *of the company (the company's* success)
the system *presently in use* (the *present* system)
experience has been *of a favorable nature (favorable)*
the requirements *relative to safety* (the *safety* requirements)
has the potentiality of being an excellent customer *(is potentially)*
and thank you *for giving me the opportunity of explaining (for letting me explain)*
to Mr. Gordon, *who is the sales manager (the sales manager)*

a feature which this machine possesses and makes it very desirable (a desirable feature of this machine)

feel that the system *which is presently in use* is basically *sound as to the efficiency it provides* (the *present* system is basically *efficient*)

introduced a factor *which will have an effect that we have as yet been unable to assess* (introduced a *new and uncertain* factor)

a windshield wiper *that is in good condition* (a windshield wiper *in good condition*)

7. INDIRECTNESS. Wordy or unnecessary qualifying phrases sap the vitality of sentences.

I think I may say without fear of rebuttal that I was right all along.

It so happens that the machine shop had to stop operations because of flooding.

Loyalty *can be shown to be* one of his many virtues. *(is)*

They had *what might be called* a disagreement.

Palmer is *inclined to be* somewhat shy about asking for credit.

Permit me to say how expertly you handled the situation.

8. RECASTING FOR CONCISENESS. Sometimes the only satisfactory remedy for a wordy passage is complete revision.

WORDY: Our reply to the manufacturer will incorporate a request that they inform us of any product improvements they have made relevant to the several serious shortcomings in their central dictation system.

RECAST: We will ask the manufacturer what they have done to correct the serious shortcomings in their central dictation system.

word of mouth   One person speaking to another: *Our merchandise sells by word of mouth.* Also used informally in the sense of having a reputation built on word of mouth: *Executives at the studio speak of the picture as a dynamite word of mouth.*

—word-of-mouth, adjective: *word-of-mouth advertising.*

word processing   Abbreviated WP. The conversion of a message into a finished typescript with the aid of a computerized typewriter. Messages and message parts, electronically recorded and stored, can be recalled at will for editing, assembly, and final typing directly on the machine.

word processor   A computer-assisted typewriter used in WORD PROCESSING. Also, the operator of such a machine.

work-   No HYPHEN in the compounds *workbench, workbook, workbox, workday, workhorse, workplace,* and *workweek.*

workaholic A blend of *work* and *alcoholic;* a person who, by choice, is given to long hours of work with little time off for recreation. The term is often used approvingly: *Actually, there is no way to transform a workaholic, but there's a lot to say about what's right with being one.* [Marylin M. Macklowitz]
—**workaholism.** The condition of being a workaholic: *Workaholism in a manager is not a guarantee of good performance.*

work ethic The concept of work, not as a drag on men and women, but as a spur to their spiritual development; also an expression of Americans' traditional reverence of work for its own sake: *The work ethic is not dead, but it is weaker now.* [Lance Morrow, *Time*]/*The GAO report found that requiring work of welfare clients is administratively effective and can result in creating a work ethic among food stamp recipients.*

workfare The practice, usually only talked about, of requiring recipients of public aid to reciprocate by performing chores like cleaning up parks and staffing day-care centers.

work force Two words: *a work force of 2,600.*

working Employed, as a "working husband and wife"; and operating, as a "working elevator." But the word is also used in a variety of other ways: *working capital* (a company's current assets less its current liabilities)/*working control* (ownership of sufficient voting stock in a corporation to control its management)/*a working costume* (for use at work)/*a working drawing* (for use as a guide)/*a working majority* (a sufficient number of persons to ensure action)/*a working model* (functioning).

(the) working poor Workers who do not earn enough to maintain a standard of living above the poverty level: *Unfortunately, the burdens of the proposed budget would be concentrated on the poor and working poor.*

workshop A training session at which the participants are given cases or problems requiring solution by team or individual effort. See also ROLE PLAYING.

work sharing The temporary reduction of the working hours of a homogeneous group of employees, so that layoffs are avoided. Compare TIME SHARING.

work station An assigned position for work in a shop or office, especially a place where the worker has command of a machine or works as part of a production team: *concerned about hazards caused by the accumulation of waste around work stations/a prediction that work stations will eventually do away with most private offices/designed a smaller executive work station with its own computer and telecommunications facilities.*

workup   A professional study and analysis of a problem: *Before making a recommendation, I want to do a complete financial workup of the client's needs.*

world   In the sense of a sphere of activity, often superfluous: *decided on a career in the world of business (decided on a business career)/made his success in the world of finance (in finance).*

world-class   A term common in competitive sports, now used descriptively of anything worthy of competing internationally with others of the same kind: *Escort—Ford's world-class car/a world-class art exhibit with works from the collections of leading business corporations.*

worst of any   See BEST OF ANY, WORST OF ANY.

worth   In expressions like "your money's worth," "two cents' worth," and "a dollar's worth," the word preceding worth requires an APOSTROPHE.

would   Usually a hindrance to direct expression when followed by *appear, seem, think,* and the like: *It would appear that the fan belt slipped (It appears that the fan belt slipped;* or, if the facts warrant, *The fan belt slipped.)*

For *would* used instead of *will,* see SHOULD, WOULD.

would, should   See SHOULD, WOULD.

would like to   See at LIKE.

would rather   See HAD RATHER, WOULD RATHER.

WP   Abbreviation for WORD PROCESSING.

write down   A verb phrase with a number of acceptable meanings: *Don't write down to the audience* (condescend)/*Write this down* (put it on paper)/*decided to write down the inventory* (put a lower value on it; take a paper loss).

—write-down, noun. A reduction in the recorded value of an asset: *a write-down of their inventory.*

write off Verb: *write off the debt* (cancel it in the account books)/*wrote him off as a failure* (gave up on; washed one's hands of).

—**write-off,** noun: *take a write-off* (a depreciation or cancellation of an amount recorded as an asset).

(the) writer 1. Akin to the UNDERSIGNED. At least in letters, such a reference to himself by the writer is stilted and self-consciously impersonal: *Please address your reply to the writer (to me).* See also LETTER WRITING 3.

2. Writers of MEMORANDUMS and REPORTS who feel shy about injecting themselves into the narrative, or who wish for other reasons to keep the tone objective, may wish to refer to themselves as "the writer," "this investigator," "the analyst," and so forth. This practice appears justified when the writer must be clearly identified without use of the more personal "I" or "we." When, however, such identification is not important, phrasing can be found that avoids reference to the writer altogether: *A visit to the premises showed/It was learned that/A count of the number of complaints revealed.* See also ACTIVE VOICE, PASSIVE VOICE 6.

—**the present writer.** The word *present* adds nothing to the sense.

write to Expressions like "write to the customer" are somewhat more formal than "write the customer," but there is no other distinction.

write up Verb: *Have the public relations department write up the story for immediate release* (write for publication).

—**write-up,** noun: *take a write-up* (an upward evaluation of an asset)/*carried a write-up of the annual meeting* (a published report).

W-2 form Also, for short, *W-2.* The annual statement employers issue to all employees, indicating wages paid and federal and state taxes withheld. Employees must attach a copy of the statement to their federal and state income tax returns. If a worker is also subject to a city withholding tax, the W-2 shows the amount of tax withheld, and the employee must enclose a copy with the city income tax return.

X

xenomarkets Pronounced *zen*-uh-. The Greek prefix means "foreign." A successor to "Eurocurrency markets"—markets in the U.S. dollar outside the United States—the newer term acknowledges the spread of those markets around the world.

xerography A dry photocopy process, such as that used in the Xerox copier, by which an image formed by a resinous powder on an electrically charged plate is transferred to plain paper.

Xerox 1. The trademark for the Xerox copier, a machine that employs **XEROGRAPHY.**

2. Noun and verb: *Make me a Xerox/Please Xerox this contract.*

3. Although the practice is justly decried by the Xerox Corporation, Xerox is sometimes lowercased and used to denote any dry-copy machine or a copy made from it.

Y

yardstick Figuratively, a synonym of CRITERION: *By what yardstick shall we measure their performance?*

ye 1. Pronounced *thee*. An archaic form of *the;* occasionally found in such simulated antique names as *Ye Olde Sweet Shoppe.*
2. Pronounced *yee*. An archaic form of *you.*

year-end Hyphened both as an adjective and a noun: *a year-end dividend* (an extra dividend paid at the end of the fiscal year)/*expected to make the change by year-end* (also *by the year's end* or *by the end of the year*).

year round Preferred over "year around": *The resort is open the year round.* Only the adjective is hyphened: *It's a year-round resort.*

yellow-pad job The composition of a speech, report, or other document or part of one, by writing a draft in one's own hand: *Nothing quite excites the awe of his secretary as a yellow-pad job by the chief himself.*

yellow pages Also *Yellow Pages.* The classified telephone directory, sometimes called "the Red Book." It is either bound into the regular telephone directory (the WHITE PAGES) or, in larger cities, published in a separate volume. In the largest cities, two classified directories are issued, one for business users and the other for consumers.

you 1. Sometimes overdirect and tactless. See ACTIVE VOICE, PASSIVE VOICE 3.
2. Informal when used as an indefinite reference. See PRONOUNS 1(d).

you all Also *you-all.* American dialect, pronounced yoo-*awl;* used especially in the South in referring to two or more persons, of whom at least one is being addressed: *You all come to visit us now.*

your, yours Possessive forms of *you.* Neither takes an apostrophe: *Please let us know your* (not *you're*) *requirements*/*The book is yours* (not *your's*) *to keep.*

you're The contraction of *you are;* not to be carelessly used for *your: Please return the brochure when you're through with it.* See also **YOUR, YOURS.**

yours 1. Stilted when used for "your letter": *We have yours (your letter) of September 10.*
2. A conventional part of the **COMPLIMENTARY CLOSE** of most letters: *Very truly yours, Yours sincerely,* etc.

yourself, -selves Not to be used for "you" when part of a compound subject or object: *Fred and you* (not *yourself*) *will take over the responsibility/We would like to divide the territory between Fielding and you* (not *yourself*). But (correct): *You yourself must have known the outcome* [intensifier]/*You worked yourself into a corner* [reflexive object]. See also **MYSELF.**

"you" viewpoint As instruments of persuasion, business messages center on the receiver's interests; and their language and content seek to bring about the desired response. The sender's interests are subordinated only in the sense that the interests of the receiver—the *you* of the "you" viewpoint—are served first. To put the point less elegantly, the taste of the fish determines the bait.
1. In letters, especially, the "you" viewpoint gives prominence to the pronoun *you,* but it by no means excludes *I* and *we.* The important consideration is the attitude expressed. *I,* as in "I appreciate," can be ingratiating; and *you,* as in "You must understand" can be offensive (see also **I, WE**). Still, there is a better chance of getting the "you" viewpoint with the *you* than without it.

WE: The new deposit slips will make our operation more efficient.

YOU: The new deposit slips are designed to prevent error and save you time.

WE: Our pamphlet spells out federal and state taxes affecting estates and gifts.

YOU: As an attorney, you will find this pamphlet helpful in discussing federal and estate taxes with your clients.

WE: We need your new address to correct our records.

YOU: Please let us have your new address promptly so we'll know where to send your dividend checks.

WE: Our policy is to charge a nominal fee for picking up returned merchandise.

YOU: We offer the convenience of picking up returned merchandise for a nominal charge. [Here, consideration of the reader is evident without the use of *you*.]

2. In more formal messages, the pronoun *you* is usually absent, even while the "you" viewpoint is preserved. Here, for instance, AT&T talks about itself, but the message is not lost on the shareholders to whom it is addressed.

The fact of competition imposes some nev economic requirements on the Bell System, and, in some cases, the general public as well. It requires repricing of products and services—pricing them according to cost and market conditions rather than on "value of service" considerations. And it requires recovering capital more quickly through depreciation rates that reflect the shorter service lives of plant due to rapid changes in technology and market conditions.

See also **APPEALS**.

Z

zero-based Starting at zero; not layered on existing figures or conditions: *zero-based budgeting/a zero-based review of the agency's functions and performance.*

zero in With "on," to concentrate; close in: *The company now intends to zero in on the industrial market.*

zilch Slang for "nothing"; zero: *adds up to zilch.*

zip Informal for "nothing"; zero: *an 8-zip decision.*

ZIP Code Also *Zip code* or *ZIP* (for Zone *I*mprovement *P*lan). A numeric symbol required on postal addresses to speed mail processing. Until 1981, the Code consisted of five digits uniformly. The U.S. Postal Service has since devised a nine-letter code to be used initially by mass mailers. The longer code is made up of the old code followed by a dash and four new numbers—the last giving blocks, buildings, and businesses their own *ZIPs*, as *20004–6789*. See also ENVELOPE ADDRESS.

ZIP Code marketing The use of selected ZIP CODE areas to direct selling effort to markets exhibiting the most wanted DEMOGRAPHIC characteristics.

Bibliography

I. DICTIONARIES OF THE ENGLISH LANGUAGE

American Heritage Dictionary of the English Language. 2d college ed. Boston: Houghton Mifflin.

Random House Dictionary of the English Language. Rev. ed. New York: Random House.

Webster's Ninth New Collegiate Dictionary. Springfield, Mass.: Merriam-Webster.

Webster's New International Dictionary. 3d ed. [Unabridged]. Springfield, Mass.: G. & C. Merriam.

Webster's New World Dictionary of the American Language. 2d college ed. New York: Simon and Schuster.

II. SPECIALIZED DICTIONARIES

Acronyms, Initialisms & Abbreviations Dictionary. Vol. 1, 7th ed. Detroit: Gale Research Co., 1980. Vol. 2 [additions to vol. 1], 1981.

AMMER, CHRISTINE, and DEAN S. AMMER. *Dictionary of Business and Economics.* New York: Free Press, 1977.

BARNHART, CLARENCE L., SOL STEINMETZ, and ROBERT K. BARNHART. *The Second Barnhart Dictionary of New English.* Bronxville, N.Y.: Barnhart Books, 1980.

BERENYI, JOHN. *The Modern American Business Dictionary.* New York: William Morrow, 1982.

BROWNSTONE, DAVID M., IRENE M. FRANCK, and GORTON CARRUTH. *The VNR Dictionary of Business and Finance.* New York: Van Nostrand Reinhold, 1980.

DAVIDS, LEWIS E. *The Instant Business Dictionary.* Little Falls, N.J.: Career Publishing Co., 1981.

DE SOLA, RALPH. *New International Abbreviations Dictionary.* 5th ed. New York: Elsevier, 1978.

DOWNING, DOUGLAS. *Encyclopedia of Computer Terms.* Woodbury, N.Y.: Barron's Educational Series, 1983.

ESTES, RALPH W. *Dictionary of Accounting.* Cambridge: MIT Press, 1981.

GIORDANO, ALBERT G. *Concise Dictionary of Business Terminology.* Englewood Cliffs, N.J.: Prentice-Hall, 1981.

GREENWALD, DOUGLAS, and associates. *Dictionary of Modern Economics.* 3d ed. New York: McGraw-Hill, 1983.

MAGER, N. H. and S. K. MAGER. *The Morrow Book of New Words.* New York: William Morrow, 1982.

MEADOWS, A. J. *Dictionary of New Information Technology.* New York: Random House, 1982.

NEMMERS, ERWIN E. *Dictionary of Economics and Business.* 4th enl. ed. Totowa, N.J.: Littlefield, Adams, 1979.

PESSIN, ALLAN H., and JOSEPH A. ROSS. *Words of Wall Street: Two Thousand Investment Words Defined.* Homewood, Ill.: Dow Jones–Irwin, 1983.

ROSENBERG, JERRY M. *Dictionary of Banking and Finance.* New York: Wiley, 1982.

————. *Dictionary of Business and Management.* New York: Wiley, 1978.

ROTHENBERG, ROBERT. *The Plain-Language Law Dictionary.* New York: Penguin, 1981.

SHAPIRO, IRVING J. *Dictionary of Marketing Terms.* 4th ed. Totowa, N.J.: Littlefield, Adams, 1981.

URDANG, LAURENCE. *Dictionary of Advertising Terms.* Chicago: Crain Books, 1979.

III. GUIDES TO ENGLISH USAGE

BERNSTEIN, THEODORE M. *The Careful Writer: A Modern Guide to English Usage.* New York: Atheneum, 1965.

BOATNER, MAXINE T., JOHN E. GATES, and ADAM MAKKAI. *A Dictionary of American Idioms.* Rev. ed. Woodbury, N.Y.: Barron's Educational Series, 1975.

COPPERUD, ROY H. *American Usage and Style: The Consensus.* New York: Van Nostrand Reinhold, 1980.

EVANS, BERGEN, and CORNELIA EVANS. *A Dictionary of Contemporary Usage.* New York: Harper & Row, 1957.

FOLLETT, WILSON, and others. *Modern American Usage.* New York: Hill and Wang, 1966.

FOWLER, H. W. *A Dictionary of Modern English Usage.* 2d ed., rev. by Sir Ernest Gowers. New York: Oxford University Press, 1965.

MENCKEN, H. L. *The American Language.* 4th ed. and the supplements, abridged and with new annotations by Raven I. David, Jr. New York: Knopf, 1977.

MILLER, DON. *The Book of Jargon.* New York: Macmillan, 1980.

MORRIS, WILLIAM, and MARY MORRIS. *Harper Dictionary of Contemporary Usage.* New York: Harper & Row, 1975.

MUELLER, ROBERT KIRK. *Buzzwords: A Guide to the Language of Leadership.* New York: Van Nostrand Reinhold, 1974.

NICHOLSON, MARGARET. *A Dictionary of Modern American-English Usage* [based on Fowler's *Modern English Usage*]. New York: Oxford University Press, 1957.

PARTRIDGE, ERIC. *A Dictionary of Clichés.* 5th ed. Boston: Routledge and Kegan, 1978.

QUINN, JIM. *American Tongue and Cheek: A Populist Guide to Our Language.* New York: Pantheon, 1981.

RAWSON, HUGH. *A Dictionary of Euphemisms and Other Double Talk.* New York: Crown, 1981.

SAFIRE, WILLIAM. *On Language.* New York: Times Books, 1980.

WENTWORTH, HAROLD, and STUART B. FLEXNER. *Dictionary of American Slang.* 2d ed. New York: Thomas Y. Crowell, 1967.

IV. HANDBOOKS OF ENGLISH AND STYLE MANUALS

The Chicago Manual of Style. 13th ed. Chicago: University of Chicago Press, 1982.

EBBITT, WILA R., and DAVID R. EBBITT. *Writer's Guide and Index to English.* 7th ed. Chicago: Scott, Foresman, 1981.

GORRELL, ROBERT M., and CHARLTON LAIRD. *Modern English Handbook.* 6th ed. Englewood Cliffs, N.J.: Prentice-Hall, 1976.

MILLER, CASEY, and KATE SWIFT. *The Handbook of Nonsexist Writing.* New York: Lippincott & Crowell, 1980.

MLA Handbook for Writers of Research Papers, Theses, and Dissertations. New York: Modern Language Association, 1977.

The Oxford Dictionary for Writers and Editors. New York: Oxford University Press, 1981.

SABIN, WILLIAM A. *The Gregg Reference Manual.* 5th ed. New York: McGraw-Hill, 1977.

STRUNK, WILLIAM, JR., and E. B. WHITE. *The Elements of Style.* 3d ed. New York: Macmillan, 1978.

SWANSON, MARY STEWART, ed. *FLS Financial Writing Guide: A Manual of Style for the Securities Industry.* Minnetonka, Minn.: Financial Learning Systems, 1982.

THOMPSON, MARGARET H., and J. HAROLD JANIS. *Revised Standard Reference for Secretaries and Administrators.* New York: Macmillan, 1980.

U.S. Government Printing Office. *Style Manual.* Rev. ed. Washington, D.C., 1973.

V. NEWSPAPERS AND PERIODICALS

Advertising Age
Barron's
Business Week
College English [National Council of Teachers of English]
Dun's Business Month
Forbes

Fortune
Harvard Business Review
Journal of Business Communication [American Business Communication Association]
Journal of Communication [Annenberg School of Communications, University of Pennsylvania]
Money
Nation's Business
Newsday [Long Island, N.Y.]
Newsweek
The New York Times
PMLA [Modern Language Association]
Time
U.S. News & World Report
The Wall Street Journal
Vital Speeches

VI. BOOKS ON COMMUNICATION AND COMPOSITION

AMERICAN MANAGEMENT ASSOCIATION. *Communicating Effectively*. AMA Reprint Collection Series. New York, 1975.

ANDERSEN, KENNETH. *Persuasion: Theory and Practice*. 2d ed. Boston: Allyn and Bacon, 1978.

ATWATER, EASTWOOD. *I Hear You: Listening Skills to Make You a Better Manager*. Englewood Cliffs, N.J.: Prentice-Hall, 1981.

BOULDING, KENNETH E. *The Image: Knowledge in Life and Society*. Ann Arbor: University of Michigan Press, 1956.

BROWN, LELAND. *Communicating Facts and Ideas in Business*. 3d ed. Glenview, Ill.: Scott, Foresman, 1982.

CHASE, STUART. *The Tyranny of Words*. New York: Harcourt Brace Jovanovich, 1983.

DE MARE, GEORGE. *Communicating at the Top*. New York: Wiley, 1979.

DIZARD, WILSON. *The Coming Information Age*. New York: Longman, 1982.

EWING, DAVID W. *Writing for Results: In Business, Government, the Sciences, and the Professions*. 2d ed. New York: Wiley, 1979.

FAST, JULIUS. *Body Language*. New York: M. Evans, 1970.

FESTINGER, LEON. *A Theory of Cognitive Dissonance*. New York: Harper & Row, 1957.

FLESCH, RUDOLF. *The Art of Readable Writing*. Rev. ed. New York: Harper & Row, 1974.

GOLDHABER, GERALD M. *Organizational Communication*. 2d ed. Dubuque, Ia.: Wm. C. Brown, 1979.

GOOTNICK, DAVID. *Getting a Better Job*. New York: McGraw-Hill, 1978.

HALL, EDWARD T. *The Silent Language*. Garden City, N.Y.: Doubleday, 1959.

HAYAKAWA, S. I., and others. *Language in Thought and Action*. 4th ed. New York: Harcourt Brace Jovanovich, 1978.

HOLCOMBE, MARYA, and JUDITH K. STEIN. *Writing for Decision Makers: Memos and Reports with a Competitive Edge*. Belmont, Calif.: Lifetime Learning Publications, 1981.

HOVLAND, CARL I., IRVING L. JANIS, and HAROLD B. KELLEY. *Communication and Persuasion*. New Haven, Conn.: Yale University Press, 1953. Reprinted 1982 by Greenwood Press, Westport, Conn.

JANIS, J. HAROLD. *Writing and Communicating in Business*. 3d ed. New York: Macmillan, 1978.

KARLINS, MARVIN, and HERBERT I. ABELSON. *Persuasion: How Opinions and Attitudes are Changed*. New York: Springer, 1970.

KATZ, DANIEL, and ROBERT L. KAHN. *The Social Psychology of Organizations*. 2d ed. New York: Wiley, 1978.

KNAPP, MARK L. *Essentials of Nonverbal Communication*. New York: Holt, Rinehart, and Winston, 1980.

KOHLMEIER, LOUIS M., JR., JOHN G. UDELL, and LAIRD B. ANDERSON, eds. *Reporting on Business and the Economy*. Englewood Cliffs, N.J.: Prentice-Hall, 1981.

LEAVITT, HAROLD J. *Managerial Psychology*. 4th ed. Chicago: University of Chicago Press, 1978.

LESIKAR, RAYMOND V. *Report Writing for Business*. 6th ed. Homewood, Ill.: Irwin, 1981.

McGREGOR, GEORGETTE F., and JOSEPH A. ROBINSON. *The Communication Matrix: Ways of Winning with Words*. New York: American Management Association, 1981.

McLUHAN, MARSHALL. *Understanding Media: The Extensions of Man*. New York: McGraw-Hill, 1964.

MEUSE, LEONARD F., JR. *Mastering the Business and Technical Presentation*. Belmont, Calif.: Lifetime Learning Publications, 1980.

MOYER, RUTH, ELEANOR STEVENS, and GEORGE SWITZER. *The Research and Report Handbook for Managers and Executives in Business, Industry, and Government*. New York: Wiley, 1981.

RIVERS, WILLIAM E. *Business Reports: Samples from the Real World*. Englewood Cliffs, N.J.: Prentice-Hall, 1981.

ROGERS, EVERETT M., and REKHA AGARWALA ROGERS. *Communication in Organizations*. New York: Free Press, 1976.

SIGBAND, NORMAN B. *Communication for Management and Business*. 3d ed. Glenview, Ill.: Scott, Foresman, 1982.

SIMON, JERROLD G., and DANIEL A. HAMEL. *A Guide to Résumé Writing*. Rev. ed. Boston: Office of Career Development, Harvard Business School, 1980.

STEINBERG, CHARLES. *The Creation of Consent: Public Relations in Practice*. New York: Hastings House, 1975.

STURGIS, ALICE F. *Sturgis' Standard Code of Parliamentary Procedure.* 2d ed. New York: McGraw-Hill, 1966.

TACEY, WILLIAM F. *Business and Professional Speaking.* 3d ed. Dubuque, Ia.: William C. Brown, 1980.

VARDAMAN, GEORGE T. *Making Successful Presentations.* New York: American Management Association, 1981.

ZAND, DALE. *Information, Organization, and Power: Effective Management in the Knowledge Society.* New York: McGraw-Hill, 1981.

ZELKO, HAROLD P. *The Business Conference: Leadership and Participation.* New York: McGraw-Hill, 1969.

ZINSSER, WILLIAM. *Writing with a Word Processor.* New York: Harper & Row, 1983.